T0314305

HEALTH IN THE ANTHROPOCENE

Living Well on a Finite Planet

Edited by Katharine Zywert and Stephen Quilley

Adding to a growing body of knowledge about how the social-ecological dynamics of the Anthropocene affect human health, this collection presents strategies that both address core challenges, including climate change, stagnating economic growth, and rising socio-political instability, and offers novel frameworks for living well on a finite planet.

Rather than directing readers to more sustainable ways to structure health systems, *Health in the Anthropocene* navigates the transition toward social-ecological systems that can support long-term human and environmental health, which requires broad shifts in thought and action, not only in formal health-related fields but in our economic models, agriculture and food systems, ontologies, and ethics.

Arguing that population health will largely be decided at the intersection of experimental social innovations and appropriate technologies, this volume calls readers to turn their attention toward social movements, practices, and ways of living that build resilience for an era of systemic change. Drawing on diverse disciplines and methodologies from fields including anthropology, ecological economics, sociology, and public health, *Health in the Anthropocene* maps out alternative pathways that have the potential to sustain human well-being and ecological integrity over the long term.

KATHARINE ZYWERT is a PhD candidate in the School of Environment, Resources and Sustainability at the University of Waterloo.

STEPHEN QUILLEY is an associate professor of Social and Environmental Innovation in the School of Environment, Resources and Sustainability at the University of Waterloo.

HEALTH
IN THE
ANTHROPOCENE

EDITED BY
KATHARINE ZYWERT AND STEPHEN QUILLEY

LIVING WELL ON
A FINITE PLANET

UNIVERSITY OF TORONTO PRESS
Toronto Buffalo London

© University of Toronto Press 2020
Toronto Buffalo London
utorontopress.com
Printed in Canada

ISBN 978-1-4875-0616-2 (cloth)   ISBN 978-1-4875-3342-7 (EPUB)
ISBN 978-1-4875-2414-2 (paper)   ISBN 978-1-4875-3341-0 (PDF)

Library and Archives Canada Cataloguing in Publication

Title: Health in the Anthropocene: Living well on a finite planet / edited by
Katharine Zywert and Stephen Quilley.
Names: Zywert, Katharine, 1986– editor. | Quilley, Stephen, editor.
Description: Includes bibliographical references.
Identifiers: Canadiana 20190205156 | ISBN 9781487506162 (cloth) |
ISBN 9781487524142 (paper)
Subjects: LCSH: World health. | LCSH: Health – Social aspects. | LCSH:
Environmental health. | LCSH: Global environmental change – Health aspects. |
LCSH: Human ecology – Health aspects.
Classification: LCC RA441.H43 2019 | DDC 362.1–dc23

This book has been published with the help of a grant from the Federation for the
Humanities and Social Sciences, through the Awards to Scholarly Publications
Program, using funds provided by the Social Sciences and Humanities Research
Council of Canada.

University of Toronto Press acknowledges the financial assistance to its publishing
program of the Canada Council for the Arts and the Ontario Arts Council, an agency
of the Government of Ontario.

Canada Council   Conseil des Arts
for the Arts   du Canada

Funded by the   Financé par le
Government   gouvernement
of Canada   du Canada

Canada

Contents

Illustrations

Tables

Acknowledgments

We would like to thank CIHR's Institute of Population and Public Health for the planning and dissemination grant that made our work on this collection possible by supporting contributors to come together for the Health in the Anthropocene workshop held at the University of Waterloo in April 2018. We are also grateful for contributions from the Waterloo Institute for Social Innovation and Resilience (WISIR) and the Faculty of Environment, University of Waterloo.

HEALTH IN THE ANTHROPOCENE

Living Well on a Finite Planet

Introduction

KATHARINE ZYWERT AND STEPHEN QUILLEY

Human health depends fundamentally on the integrity of local ecosystems and on the ability of planetary biophysical systems to operate within the narrow parameters that can support the flourishing of our species. The environmental conditions of the Holocene epoch, which began approximately 11,700 years ago around the end of the last ice age, have been particularly conducive to human health. This is primarily due to its stable climate, which for thousands of years maintained temperatures well-suited to human life across most of the globe, and created predictable growing seasons that enabled the development of increasingly complex agricultural civilizations (see Rockström, 2009; Whitmee et al., 2015; Steffen et al., 2015). Evidence that the accumulation of greenhouse gases in the atmosphere is moving the biosphere out of this stable climatic equilibrium has been growing since the 1970s. In the early 2000s, Earth-systems scientists proposed that humanity's impact on the planet has been extensive enough to warrant the designation of a new geological time scale, the Anthropocene epoch (Crutzen, 2002; Zalasiewicz et al., 2010). The Anthropocene is named for its defining characteristic: the unprecedented effects of human activities on the planet's biophysical systems. In the Anthropocene, the Earth's climate is destabilizing, temperatures are warming overall and are becoming more extreme at local scales, and drought and flooding are exacerbated. Sea levels are rising, the atmosphere is being overloaded with greenhouse gas emissions, the oceans are becoming more acidic, biodiversity is plummeting, and biogeochemical cycles are shifting (Steffen et al., 2015). These ecological changes are becoming increasingly strong determinants of health, affecting the habitability of vast regions of the world, the virulence of infectious diseases, and the security of our food systems (CPHA, 2015). Despite the existence of multilateral agreements to limit global temperature rise to under two degrees Celsius, we are currently on a trajectory towards a planet that is four degrees warmer than preindustrial levels. To understand what this might mean for humanity, we need only consider that the last ice age, which saw a near collapse of the human population, was on average four degrees colder (Matthews, 2017).

This alarming finding illustrates the fragility of human health and well-being on a planet in ecological crisis. However, there is no single concept or event that can fully capture the profound implications of the Anthropocene for human health. In the second decade of the twenty-first century, the story is only beginning to be pieced together. The rubble of bombed hospitals and makeshift medical centres in Syria are part of the story (Fouad et al., 2017), as are the deaths of elderly people living alone as heatwaves sweep across Europe (D'Ippoliti et al., 2010). Technology, and the mark it will leave on the Earth long after our bodies are gone, is also part of the story; pacemakers, bone screws and plates, prosthetic limbs, and silicone implants will one day reside in Anthropocene strata. The story is about the ways in which infectious diseases interact with ecological destruction to deepen the vulnerability of some of the poorest populations in the world (Singer, 2009). It is a story about the health effects of rising global economic inequality, and of the political economic arrangements and ideologies that perpetuate poverty and ill health (Benatar, 2016; Butler, this volume). It is also about desertification, food insecurity, and the declining nutrient content of our food (Myers et al., 2017).

The term Anthropocene draws attention to human-induced planetary change, and yet the story of the epoch's effects on health is one of countless species connected through complex adaptive systems to the biophysical dynamics of our world. In the heat, mosquitoes breed faster and find new homes in mountainous areas where previously they could not have survived the cold (McElroy and Townsend, 2014; Baer, Singer, and Susser, 2013). Bacteria and microbes, in the soil and in our guts, all have a role in the story, as do grain and vegetable crops, medicinal plants, and the animal species that we consume for sustenance. Our cultural beliefs about the world, our regard (or disregard) for nature and for one another, and the subconscious drivers that motivate our actions also affect health in an era of growing social-ecological instability (Butler, 2017; Zywert, 2017; CPHA, 2015; Benatar and Poland, 2015). The worldviews and economic systems that rose to dominance during the industrial revolution are increasingly failing to improve general well-being (see Butler, 2017). Capitalist modernity has enabled and repeatedly justified the wealthiest 20 per cent of the world's population to consume 80 per cent of global resources (Benatar, 2016). In the current political economy, technology and philanthropy are upheld as the most reasonable and righteous solutions to global health problems, yet they do little to shift the underlying beliefs and structures that damage the health of the planetary systems on which all life depends. These neoliberal belief systems uphold individualism, short-sightedness, and economic rationality, entrenching ill health for all but a privileged few, with the worst outcomes concentrated among the billions of people who live on less than USD$3 per day (Benatar, 2016).

Yet whilst global capitalism is synonymous with enormous structured inequality at every scale, beginning with the enclosure movement in early modern England (Polanyi, 1944) to the headlong urbanization of contemporary China, the process of capitalist modernization (i.e. the disruption of traditional agrarian social order and associated processes of individualization and urbanization) has made now taken-for-granted notions of individual freedom, human rights, citizenship, and democracy even thinkable (Quilley, 2012). Capital accumulation and the disembedding of markets was also a necessary concomitant of technical progress and a pattern of economic activity that lifted millions of people in the Western countries out of poverty and generated the fiscal transfers that make possible all manner of public infrastructure, including welfare safety nets and public health systems. And contrary to critical commentaries in the 1970s, the same dynamics have, albeit at staggering social and ecological cost, continued to lift hundreds of millions of people out of poverty in middle- and lower-income countries (not least China and India). For instance, the shift of manufacturing activity from the north to the Global South consequent upon globalization has created millions of more highly paid working-class jobs in urban manufacturing (relative, that is, to subsistence agriculture). At the same time in India and China (not to mention the capital cities of countries such as Nigeria, Kenya, Vietnam, and Indonesia) a burgeoning middle class of hundreds of millions of people enjoy Western levels of consumption and benefit from sophisticated and extensive education and health systems (whilst of course often suffering along with the rest of the population from the externalities of unregulated capitalist modernization – not least pollution, smog and violent crime) (Pinker, 2018; Jaffrelot and Veer, 2008; Malviya and Thakkar, 2016; Di, 2012; Pascal Zachary, 2008; Houlihan, 2018). It is not at all clear that a radically different form of noncapitalist political economy could have delivered an alternative and more equitable modernity (the "primitive accumulation" associated with socialist and communist modernization paths was every bit as murderous and much less successful in delivering welfare and technical progress). And although a more Keynesian approach to economic modernization throughout the past five decades of rapid globalization would likely have generated more gains for human health and well-being than neoliberal economics, welfare states would not have avoided the looming challenges of ecological overshoot (see Quilley, 2012). The wicked dilemma or paradox we now face is the problem of biophysical limits. The hockey stick growth curves will not continue indefinitely, and it seems very likely that the historical progress enjoyed by the most affluent 20 per cent as well as the real material gains experienced by billions of other people in the bottom 80 per cent may be reversed or even wiped out as capital accumulation runs into a concatenation of resource, ecological and geopolitical constraints. So even if a noncapitalist political economy may never have been able to light the touch paper of modernization and to generate the kind of complexity that we now take for granted, it does seem that safeguarding and future-proofing progress (such as it is) now depends on developing an alternative modernity. The story of health in the Anthropocene must therefore also be one of emerging meaning frameworks and ways of living that offer new ontologies, relationships, and practices for thriving together on an altered Earth (see Zywert, 2017; Zywert and Quilley, 2017).

The collection of papers in this volume aim to contribute to this unfolding story. Above all, we are concerned with how humanity can learn to live well within the ecological constraints of a finite planet. We propose that this will not occur without fundamentally disrupting dominant feedback loops within our social-ecological systems; it is a process that can only be accomplished by radically reorienting our political economies, our cultures, and our communities. Existing systems are caught in feedback patterns that maintain society's dependence on ever-increasing economic growth and rising complexity, coupled with a constantly expanding throughput of materials and energy that together drive ecological change (Odum, 2007; Quilley, 2013). With the technological advancements of the industrial revolution, a growing capacity to unearth fossil energy, and the expansion of the market economy, the nineteenth and early twentieth centuries lay the foundation for what has been called the Great Acceleration (Steffen et al., 2015). Beginning around 1950, the metrics of human impact on the Earth's biophysical systems surged dramatically upward. It was at this time that we began to see an exponential rise in carbon dioxide emissions, surface temperature, ocean acidification, and biosphere degradation. Over the same time period, we can track rapid increases in human population, primary energy use, urbanization, real GDP, and metrics of global connectivity such as telecommunications, international travel, and transportation networks (Steffen et al., 2015). The gains of the Great Acceleration for human well-being have disproportionately accrued to the wealthiest nations, which are also responsible for consuming the greatest share of the world's resources and thus for driving planetary biophysical change (Steffen et al., 2015). Low-income countries have not only been to a significant extent excluded from the benefits of the Great Acceleration, they have become increasingly vulnerable to emerging health threats attributable to rising levels of local pollution, extreme heat, new infectious diseases, and geopolitical conflict (see Butler, this volume; Cole, this volume).

Now, nearly seventy years after the Great Acceleration began to gather momentum, human activities (particularly those of the most economically privileged humans) exert a stronger influence on the planet's ecology than those of any other single species since the beginning of life on Earth. The nature of our influence and what can be done to mitigate or adapt to emerging social-ecological challenges is, however, psychologically difficult to conceptualize. Human beings have an evolutionary predisposition to focus on immediate threats, remaining blind to or ignoring long-term vulnerabilities (Wright, 2004). The Earth's biophysical systems, in contrast, operate on timescales that make the duration of a human generation insignificant. Complex systems like the Earth's climate are slow to change. The warming and instabilities that we experience today are the delayed effects of increased GHG emissions that began in the industrial revolution. Similarly, the biophysical effects of any drastic reductions in emissions that we make over the next half century will not be experienced by those alive to witness the transition (Inman, 2008). In a cultural landscape of growing individualism, a societal propensity for narcissism, and sustained materialism, it is not surprising that there remain strong movements to deny that planetary systems are changing at all, or to insist that humanity is not responsible.

It is not only the long time horizons that pose a challenge for those seeking to effect change. The complexity of cause-and-effect relationships in linked social-ecological systems is also a barrier to comprehension and action. The feedback loops that define social-ecological dynamics cross geographic, temporal, disciplinary, and sectoral boundaries. They involve complex and often nonlinear interactions between human systems relating to political economy and culture and ecological systems, with variables relating to the earth's atmosphere, biochemical flows, or water systems. Recent research from Dan O'Neill and colleagues found that no countries in the world meet human needs like nutrition, education, access to energy, and life satisfaction without significantly exceeding the per capita ecological footprints compatible with planetary boundaries (2018). Human flourishing is currently coupled with ecological devastation at a scale that threatens not only the health, but the survival of our species. Escaping these destructive path dependencies will require us to meet our basic needs and achieve quality of life by using resources and energy in dramatically different ways (O'Neill et al., 2018).

This collection does not put forward solutions that rely on the mechanisms of technological innovation, global governance, or sustainable development practice. These strategies are the mainstays of many public health researchers, philanthrocapitalists, and multilateral organizations, and have been effectively elaborated elsewhere (Whitmee et al., 2015; Watts et al., 2017; UNEP, 2016). Instead, the chapters in this collection explore the possibility that we might arrive at a healthy future by an alternate route. The authors present unconventional views of diverse potential pathways forward. The first point of departure for contributors is that the Anthropocene is likely to be a time of social-ecological transformation in which human societies will need to navigate unprecedented transitions at the scale of the political economy, culture, social arrangements, ecology, and health. To make our way through these transitions – to live well in the Anthropocene – we must turn our attention towards social movements, practices, meaning frameworks, and ways of living that build resilience for an era of systemic change. Strategies that aim to reform existing systems by achieving incremental improvements are often perceived as the most expedient way to enhance the environmental sustainability of human activities. We suggest, however, that these managerial solutions will not be enough to address the core challenges of a new geological epoch, but may instead unintentionally preserve the status quo, upholding patterns of belief and behaviour that undermine the ecological foundations of health. The chapters in this volume argue that population health will be decided at the intersection of experimental social innovations, appropriate technologies, and embedded worldviews that arise amid the creative destruction of capitalist modernity. Together, these approaches map out alternative pathways with the potential to generate human well-being and sustain ecological integrity over the long-term.

Still, learning to live well in the Anthropocene is unlikely to be a utopian exercise. None of the alternatives presented in this book will yield human societies that can exist in perfect harmony with one another and the natural world, at least not right away, or in every context, or for all time. The early stages of a global sustainability transition will inevitably involve some combination of intentionally dismantling or struggling to adapt to the collapse of environmentally corrosive energy systems, economic models, and social arrangements. Communities will encounter increasingly stringent ecological constraints on a local scale, and those who first enact alternative ways of living that are suited to the realities of a finite planet in ecological crisis will contend with a host of paradoxical problems with no obvious solution. Along the way, these communities will be forced to confront tensions and trade-offs that may involve relinquishing cherished beliefs and behaviours to cope with an altered world (see Kish and Quilley, 2017; Kish, this volume).

Many of the strategies we present offer potential alternative arrangements for the wealthiest 20 per cent of the world's population, whose beliefs and patterns of consumption are disproportionately responsible for the biophysical changes experienced in the Anthropocene, and who continue to wield significant economic and cultural power to resist systemic change. However, many of the practices from which these strategies draw inspiration originated in resource-poor settings. The Anthropocene raises the vexed question as to whether the seemingly innate process of social development set in train by the evolutionary innovations of fire, language, tool use, and farming engenders an unavoidable clash between any kind of modernity and the ecological integrity of the biosphere (or at least the kind of benign Holocene environment that made civilization possible). It has frequently been observed that sustainability discourse may become a thinly veiled vehicle for the advanced industrial nations to pull up the ladder, blocking development in the Global South. But, in fact, there has been a very long tradition of critique from within the industrial north, that looks to traditional social forms and "Third World" responses to neocolonial industrialism as the seeds for a possible alternative modernity. This tradition runs from Tolstoy's romantic defence of the Russian peasantry through Gandhi's vision of village development (Ishii, 2001) right through to Schumacher's *Small Is Beautiful* (1989).

In the 1970s critics such as Christopher Alexander (1987; 2005), Jane Jacobs (1978), John Turner (1976) and Colin Ward (1976) looked to the favelas and shanty towns of South America, identifying a generative process of self-organization that produced more organic, functionally coherent and cheaper forms of community design and architecture than top-down development. Their insights chimed with the wider movement for "appropriate technology" (CHF-BRI, 1983; Hazeltine and Bull, 2003) that drew explicitly on Gandhi and Schumacher as well as the highly influential work of Ivan Illich (1973) and radical innovations such as China's "barefoot doctor" program (Zhang et al., 2011). The common thread running through this cluster of ideas is the commitment to finding forms of technology and linked social institutions that can deliver "development" and some vision of modernity at a much lower "price point" in terms of the energy and material flows as well as the prerequisite fiscal transfers drawn (ultimately) from the market sector. All of these authors and theorists understood implicitly that the Western model of consumer society, extreme forms of individualization, and a top-heavy state/market complex probably could not be sustained in the West, let alone transferred to the Global South. They sought to reconcile an indictment of aggressive consumer capitalism with a commitment to a different kind of modernity.

It seems likely that any vision of an alternative modernity for the Anthropocene based on a rebalancing of the state/market with the domain of "livelihood" must inevitably engage once again with solutions and social, technical, architectural and institutional forms of traditional society, as well as the now well-established pattern of "appropriate" from grass roots practitioners in developing societies. Having said this, critical questions remain unresolved. It is unclear to what level technology and the trajectory of innovation are compatible with an "appropriate scale" of economy vis-à-vis the ecology of the biosphere. Nor is it clear whether the corresponding "appropriate scale for society" (i.e. for institutions, the division of labour, and social complexity, etc.) is compatible with the kind of society of individuals that is the necessary underlay for any liberal or democratic society (Quilley, 2013). For example, the recent furores and scandals in India over egregious instances of rape and ill treatment of women have: come from the educated and cosmopolitan constituencies in cities, been facilitated by the low entropy technical infrastructure of social media and the internet, and have often been directed at the traditional least-developed rural villages. It was not without reason that Marx, anticipating and scoffing at Tolstoy, once rather rudely referred to the idiocy of peasant life. It is this dependence of progressive forms of society on social complexity as much as the intrinsic ecological cost of technology and innovation that make any realistic vision of an alternative modernity so elusive. And yet, in the Anthropocene, the choice is not, as Rosa Luxembourg argued in 1916, between barbarism and a shiny and clear-cut socialism. Rather, the problem of reconciling planetary health with healthy societies and individuals seems to be a messy, multidimensional imperative to construct ad hoc local societal configurations that: reduce the scale of the state and its dependence on the market; re-embed market relations in wider societal frameworks of culture, social pressure, and reciprocity; generate widely shared mythologies and vehicles for enacting such stories and values through rituals of family, community, work, and religious or spiritual life; and reduce the salience of materialism and consumption in defining a good or successful life. On the other hand, revisiting the work of Alexander and Turner, Robert Neuwirth lived for long periods in the extralegal pockets and "squatopolises" of Istanbul, Mumbai, Nairobi, and Rio. To his surprise, at the interstices of state, market, and the informal domain of livelihood, he did indeed discover a generative process delivering impeccable civility, sophisticated forms of self-organized local government, bustling markets embedded in strong community structures, low crime rates, and even squatter millionaires. As one reviewer noted, Neuwirth's (2006) account provided a glimpse into our urban future and showed new visions of what constitutes property and community. It is perhaps with such visions that the concept of "planetary health" for the Anthropocene may gain traction.

As editors and authors of this collection, our primary goal is to contribute to a growing interdisciplinary field investigating strategies that both address the core challenges facing health in the Anthropocene and offer novel frameworks for living well on a finite planet. Our emphasis is not strictly on finding more sustainable ways to provision health care services or even to structure health systems. Rather, it is on navigating the transition towards social-ecological systems that can support long-term human and environmental health. This will undoubtedly require transformation of existing health systems, but only in the context of broader shifts in our economic models, agriculture and food systems, ontologies, and ethics. By taking a systemic perspective, the papers in this collection also add to a growing body of knowledge about the effects of the social-ecological dynamics of the Anthropocene on human health, including the interacting and cumulative impacts of climate change, demographic shifts, stagnating economic growth, rising sociopolitical instability, and changing ecological determinants of health.

Part 1 of this book considers the state of human health now and what is at stake in the transition to an alternative social-ecological system defined by ecological constraints. Chapters discuss complex problems such as whether individualism will continue to be a relevant frame of reference for health and how health economics can adapt to limits to growth. Part 2 introduces diverse social innovations that together prefigure viable health systems for the Anthropocene. The innovations profiled are drawn from a range of disciplines and experiences, and include grassroots social movements, care farming, improving the soil sponge, nature's role in palliative care, and complexity medicine. Part 3 brings together a series of alternative ontological approaches that could lay the groundwork for living well within the Earth's biophysical limits. Chapters present unconventional ways of thinking about health, well-being, and even death, exploring the health benefits of degrowth, ecological consciousness formation, alternative embodiments, socioecological approaches, and insights from terror management theory.

The papers assembled in this collection do not represent a unified new paradigm for researching or acting on issues surrounding health in the Anthropocene. Rather, it was our intention as editors to gather together work that:

1. Acknowledges and deeply considers the potential for and/or implications of systems-level change in the Anthropocene at the scale of the political economy, culture, social arrangements, and health systems. We are convinced that what is called for now is work that seeks to build resilience in a context of change rather than that attempts to shore up the current system against disruption.
2. Explicitly discusses or exposes the insidiousness of wicked dilemmas, paradoxes, tensions, and/or trade-offs posed by alternative approaches to health in the Anthropocene. In choosing papers to include in this collection, we take as a foundational premise that living well within ecological constraints may involve letting go of long-held beliefs and ways of living and adopting new ones that align with emerging social-ecological realities.
3. Proposes transformational instead of managerial solutions in the form of, for instance, experimental social innovations, appropriate technologies, and new ways of thinking for an alternative modernity as opposed to more conventional sustainable development approaches.

This volume presents an eclectic collection of strategies that originate in multiple disciplinary, interdisciplinary, and practitioner perspectives, many of them unexpected and too often overlooked. The changes we are considering are paradigmatic; we are taking seriously the potential for a complete transformation of human society in response to equally drastic transitions in ecological systems. When moving out into the unknown, incorporating a diversity of perspectives is the only guarantee of covering any meaningful terrain. That being said, there is no guarantee that these perspectives always hang together. One of the problems we encounter when dealing with change at this paradigmatic scale is that absolutely nothing in the landscape is stable. Not even the units of analysis are stable. In modern health systems, for instance, the rights of individuals overshadow other facets of population or planetary health. This was a progressive and functional approach in the Holocene, but it is conceivable that other units of analysis (populations of humans, microbes, animals, plants, and/or their interactions, for instance) could rise to prominence within health systems developing in a very different kind of modernity. It is equally possible that the range of progressive positions for health in the Anthropocene is as yet unknown, and that holding one position could make other currently progressive positions untenable (imagine, for instance, how individual rights could be affected if the health of ecosystems was valued above the health of individual humans). When thinking about change at the level of social-ecological systems, the end goals of any current initiative or approach are no longer clear or uncontested. The Anthropocene implies an entirely new landscape. The point of putting together a collection like this at this juncture in the transition is to encourage people to walk out into a series of thought experiments that begin to traverse the unknown. The authors and readers of this book are not all going to agree. In some ways, the more they disagree, the more likely we are to be exploring different facets of the landscape. This collection is by no means presenting a unified call to action or trying to have the last word. The chapters that follow will instead evoke an emerging, unconventional solution space for living well on a finite planet. This space may at times be uncomfortable and at times vividly hopeful, much like the broader unfolding story of health in the Anthropocene.

REFERENCES

Alexander, C. (1987). *A new theory of urban design*. New York: Oxford University Press.

Alexander, C. (2005). *The nature of order: Books one to four*. Berkeley, CA: Center for Environmental Structure.

Canadian Hunger Foundation & Brace Research Institute. (1983). *A handbook on appropriate technology* (3rd ed.). Ottawa: Canadian Hunger Foundation.

Baer, H. A., Singer, M., Susser, I. (2013). *Medical anthropology and the world system: Second edition*. Westport, CT: Praeger.

Benatar, S., & Poland, B. (2016). Lessons for health from insights into environmental crises. *International Journal of Health Services, 46*(4): 1–18. https://doi.org/10.1177/0020731415596296

Benatar, S. (2016). Politics, power, poverty and global health: Systems and frames. *International Journal of Health Policy Management, 5*(10): 599–604. https://doi.org/10.15171/ijhpm.2016.101

Butler, C. (2017). Limits to growth, planetary boundaries, and planetary health. *Current Opinion in Environmental Sustainability, 25*: 59–65. https://doi.org/10.1016/j.cosust.2017.08.002

Canadian Public Health Association. (2015). *Global change and public health: Addressing the ecological determinants of health*. Ottawa: Canadian Public Health Association.

Crutzen, P. J. (2002). Geology of mankind. *Nature, 415*, 23. https://doi.org/10.1038/415023a

Di, Z. (2012). The Chinese middle class and their consumption patterns. *Sociologia & Antropologia, 2*(3), 203–35. http://dx.doi.org/10.1590/2238-38752012v239

D'Ippoliti, D. et al. (2010). The impact of heat waves on mortality in 9 European cities: Results from the EuroHEAT project. *Environmental Health, 9*(37). https://doi.org/10.1186/1476-069X-9-37

Fouad, F. M. et al. (2017). Health workers and the weaponisation of health care in Syria: A preliminary inquiry for The Lancet American University of Beirut Commission on Syria. *The Lancet, 390*(10111): 2516–26. https://doi.org/10.1016/S0140-6736(17)30741-9

Hazeltine, B., & Bull, C. (2003). *Field guide to appropriate technology*. Boston: Amsterdam: Academic.

Houlihan, E. (2018). China's new world order. *The International Economy, 32*(3), 6–7.

Illich, I. (1973). *Tools for conviviality*. (1st ed.). New York: Harper & Row.

Inman, M. (2008). Carbon is forever. *Nature reports: Climate change, 812*: 156–8. https://doi.org/10.1038/climate.2008.122

Ishii, K. (2001). The socioeconomic thoughts of Mahatma Gandhi: As an origin of alternative development. *Review of Social Economy, 59*(3), 297–312. https://doi.org/10.1080/00346760122324

Jacobs, J. (2011). *The death and life of great American cities* (50th anniversary ed.). New York: Modern Library.

Jaffrelot, C., & Veer, P. (2008). *Patterns of middle class consumption in India and China*. New Delhi, IN: Sage.

Kish, K., & Quilley, S. (2017). Wicked dilemmas of scale and complexity in the politics of degrowth. *Ecological Economics, 142*: 306–17. https://doi.org/10.1016/j.ecolecon.2017.08.008

Matthews, D. "Keynote presentations theme 1: Biophysical limits." Paper presented at the Canadian Society for Ecological Economics & Economics for the Anthropocene Conference, Montreal, QC, October 2017.

McElroy, A., & Townsend, P. K. (2014). *Medical anthropology in ecological perspective.* Boulder: Westview Press.

Myers, S. S. (2017). Climate change and global food systems: Potential impacts on food security and undernutrition. *Annual Review of Public Health, 38*: 259–77. https://doi.org/10.1146/annurev-publhealth-031816-044356

Neuwirth, R. (2006). *Shadow cities: A billion squatters, a new urban world.* London: Routledge.

Odum, H. (2007). *Environment, power, and society for the twenty-first century: The hierarchy of energy.* New York: Columbia University Press.

O'Neill, D. et al. (2018). A good life for all within planetary boundaries. *Nature Sustainability, 1*: 88–95. https://doi.org/10.1038/s41893-018-0021-4

Pascal Zachary, G. (2008). "The coming revolution in Africa." *The Wilson Quarterly, 32*(1): 50.

Pinker, S. (2018). *Enlightenment now: The case for reason, science, humanism, and progress.* London, UK: Allen Lane.

Polanyi, K. (1944). *The great transformation.* Boston, MA: Beacon Press.

Quilley, S. (2012). System innovation and a new 'great transformation': Re-embedding economic life in the context of 'de-growth.' *Journal of Social Entrepreneurship, 3*(2): 206–29. https://doi.org/10.1080/19420676.2012.725823

Quilley, S. (2013). De-growth is not a liberal agenda: Relocalisation and the limits to low energy cosmopolitanism. *Environmental Values, 22*(2): 261–85. https://doi.org/10.3197/096327113X13581561725310

Rockström, J. et al. (2009). A safe operating space for humanity. *Nature 461*: 472–5. https://doi.org/10.1038/461472a

Sagar, M., & Thakkar, K. (2016). 25 years of reforms: Middle-class in centre stage – Effects of the Great Indian consumption boom. *The Economic Times*, July 22.

Schumacher, E. (1989). *Small is beautiful: Economics as if people mattered.* San Bernardino, CA: Borgo Press.

Singer, M. (2009). Ecosyndemics: Global warming and the coming plagues of the 21st century. In A. Swedlund and A. Herring (Eds), *Plagues and epidemics: Infected spaces past and present* (pp. 21–38). London: Berg.

Steffen, W. et al. (2015). The trajectory of the Anthropocene: The Great Acceleration. *The Anthropocene Review, 2*(1): 81–98. https://doi.org/10.1177/2053019614564785

Turner, J. F. C. (1976). *Housing by people.* London, UK: Marion Boyars.

United Nations Environment Programme. (2016). *Healthy environment, healthy people.* Nairobi: United Nations Environment Programme.

Ward, C. (1976). The do-it-yourself new town. *Ekistics, 42*(251): 205–7.

Watts, N. et al. (2017). The Lancet countdown: Tracking progress on health and climate change. *The Lancet, 389*: 1151–64. https://doi.org/10.1016/S0140-6736(16)32124-9

Whitmee, S. et al. (2015). Safeguarding human health in the Anthropocene epoch: Report of The Rockefeller Foundation – Lancet Commission on planetary health. *The Lancet, 386*: 1973–2028. https://doi.org/10.1016/S0140-6736(15)60901-1

Wright, R. (2004). *A short history of progress*. Toronto: House of Anansi Press.

Zalasiewicz, J. et al. (2010). The new world of the Anthropocene. *Environmental Science & Technology, 44*(7): 2228–31. https://doi.org/10.1021/es903118j

Zhang, E., Kleinman, A., & Tu, W. (2011). *Governance of life in Chinese moral experience: The quest for an adequate life*. Abingdon, Oxon; New York, NY: Routledge.

Zywert, K. (2017). Human health and social-ecological systems change: Rethinking health in the Anthropocene. *The Anthropocene Review, 4*(3): 216–38. https://doi.org/10.1177/2053019617739640

Zywert, K. & Quilley, S. (2017). Health systems in an era of biophysical limits: The wicked dilemmas of modernity. *Social Theory & Health, 16*(2): 188–207. https://doi.org/10.1057/s41285-017-0051-4

PART I

Population Health in the Anthropocene: Addressing Wicked Problems in the Transition to an Alternative Social-Ecological System Guided by Ecological Constraints

From prehistory to the present, ecological conditions have significantly affected human health and well-being (McMichael, 2014; CPHA, 2015; McElroy and Townshend, 2014). Both anatomically and as a species with an evolved psychology, symbol-mediated culture, and an individual self-awareness, modern humans evolved during the Pleistocene. This period was characterized by repeated cycles of glaciation in which early humans were vulnerable to the dangers of extreme weather, predation, infectious disease, accidents, and (in an evolutionary sense) rapid changes in the environment. Looking back, one might define health in the Pleistocene as the capacity to enjoy plentiful foraged and hunted foods, to grow physically strong, to reproduce young, and to live (on average) into the mid-thirties. With the transition to the Holocene 11,700 years ago, the warmer, more stable climate favoured the development of agricultural practices and the formation of settled communities, beginning a period of rapid social complexification. Populations grew, role differentiation became more pronounced, and communities developed trade networks and new hierarchies of power that, for the first time, created an unequal distribution of health outcomes within societies. Compared to the hunting and gathering mode of subsistence, the early days of agriculture saw declining nutrition, with resulting bone weaknesses, deformities, and growth restrictions evident in the skeletal record (McMichael, 2014). Denser living arrangements, close proximity with animals, and fecal contamination created ideal conditions for the transmission of infectious disease (Armelagos, Turner, and Brown, 2005; Barrett et al., 1998). Although culture was becoming an increasingly strong determinant of health for humans throughout the Holocene, environmental conditions continued to exert a strong influence, with droughts and other disruptions causing serious famines in populations that had become reliant on seasonal crops (McMichael, 2014).

The industrial revolution marked another significant transition for human health. With intensifying urbanization, poverty, and air pollution, early industrial cities incubated infectious diseases and exposed their populations to industrial toxins (McMichael, 2014). Shortly after industrialization, however, the development of germ theory, increased attention to hygiene, and the emergence of the public health movement led to greater control over infectious disease. The discovery of antibiotics further reduced the prevalence of infectious diseases and enabled more complex surgical procedures, dramatically expanding modern medical capacities (Harrison, 2004). Affluent countries began to see a rise in chronic and degenerative conditions due to longer lifespans and more frequent exposure to the environmental pollutants of industrialization (Barret et al., 1998; Harrison, 2004). Many of these conditions, such as heart disease, diabetes, and cancer, are exacerbated by the growing divide between the evolutionary context in which the human species evolved and modern lifestyles, including the increase in sedentary behaviours and higher consumption of processed, fatty, and sugary foods (Hidaka, 2012). Despite the rise of chronic conditions, improvements in food yields and declining prevalence of infectious disease led to stronger maternal health, lower child mortality rates, and longer lifespans as modernity unfolded (McMichael, 2014). Modernization therefore brought both gains and losses for population health:

> The experience of the past two industrialising and urbanising centuries has shown that literacy, emancipation of women, food security, safe drinking water, good housing, modern preventive medicine and public health are all essential for health. In contrast, industrial food processing, commercially inculcated consumerism, industrial and agrochemical pollution of local environments (air, water, soil), loss of sense of community, mass-marketed tobacco products, road trauma and many industrial workplace exposures are all bad for health. (McMichael, 2014, p. 48)

When the Great Acceleration began gathering momentum in the mid-twentieth century (Steffen et al., 2015), human impacts on the biosphere started to undermine the ecological bases of health on a global scale (McMichael, 2014; Whitmee et al., 2015; CPHA, 2015). Climate change, biodiversity loss, and changes to the nitrogen cycle and to the acidity of our oceans are and will continue to affect human health as we move deeper into the Anthropocene, generating both immediate and long-term consequences for human well-being (Rockström, 2009; Lovelock, 2014; CPHA, 2015). Health effects that can be attributed to human-induced ecological change include:

- Rising likelihood of global pandemics due to the emergence of new infectious diseases and antibiotic-resistant pathogens, as well as high global interconnectivity and social mobility (Armelagos et al., 2005; Barrett et al., 1998)
- Exacerbated malnutrition and food insecurity caused by ecological destruction and climate change (Friel, 2010; Whitmee et al., 2015)
- Expanded range and increased virulence of infectious diseases due to warming temperatures that enable disease vectors to propagate more quickly and expand into new territories (Alley and Sommerfeld, 2014)
- Increasing vulnerability to illnesses, injuries, and death as a result of fires and heat waves (IPCC, 2014 as cited in CPHA, 2015)
- Higher rates of anxiety and stress-related mental illnesses caused by climate change and environmental damage (Doherty and Clayton, 2011; Hidaka, 2012)
- Growth in the prevalence of diarrhoeal diseases, lower respiratory infections, and malaria as a result of rising pollution and ecotoxicity (WHO as cited in CPHA, 2015)
- Synergistic effects of ecological change, inequality, and ecologies of disease, rendering socioeconomically vulnerable people more likely to contract a range of diseases (Singer, 2009)
- The extinction of medicinal plant species alongside the destruction of tropical forests (Blakemore, 2016)

In the Anthropocene, the way we think about the health of people and the environment, and the way we fund and structure health systems, must shift to accommodate the social-ecological dynamics of a planet in ecological crisis (CPHA, 2015; Benatar and Poland, 2015; Zywert, 2017). Over the past decade, the public health community has begun to embrace ecological conditions as increasingly important determinants of human health, and has recognized the need to remain within planetary boundaries to secure health and well-being into the future (Hancock, 2017; CPHA, 2015; Whitmee et al., 2015). There is also growing awareness of the need to not only avoid crossing ecological thresholds, but to do so in a way that creates a more socially just world. Kate Raworth's doughnut economics, for instance, seeks to define an "ecologically safe and socially just space in which all of humanity has the chance to thrive" (2017, p. e48). In Raworth's model, this space is represented as a narrow tier signifying the amount of resource consumption and economic activity that lies between the "ecological ceiling" (planetary boundaries) and "social foundation" (the minimum requirements for well-being, such as access to water, food, energy, education, social equity, etc.) (Raworth, 2017). Achieving this balance on a global scale, however, will be no easy feat.

Although the field of public health, joined by diverse health practitioners and researchers concerned with environmental issues, has taken important steps towards reconceptualizing health (see Del Bianco et al., this volume) and redesigning health systems to promote social-ecological well-being, much of this literature and its resulting recommendations for policy and practice do not take into account the broader wicked tensions involved in protecting human health while preserving the Earth's biophysical systems. One of these tensions, for instance, is the extent to which human well-being is currently premised on overexploitation of material resources and energy. As O'Neill and colleagues (2018) have discovered, no country in the world currently meets the basic human needs enumerated in Raworth's "social foundation" without pushing past the "ecological ceiling." For health, it is clear that the long life expectancies, low levels of infant and maternal mortality, and low infection rates of the past century have up to this point had a high ecological cost (Zywert and Quilley, 2017). At the very least, decoupling the environmental impact of health care systems from their positive outcomes for human health will require us to confront a series of wicked problems.

Wicked problems are inherently complex and paradoxical. They are difficult to define and appear quite different when considered from different perspectives. Potential solutions to wicked problems involve negotiating trade-offs, engaging with murky and at times conflicting social values, and finding unusual arrangements that deliver mutual benefits in unexpected ways. Because wicked problems are often nested within broader complex tensions at higher and lower scales, the long-term implications of any solution are difficult to predict, and all potential courses of action carry unintended consequences (Rittel and Webber, 1973; Meadows, 2008). Part 1 of this collection aims to dive in to these tensions by considering what is at stake in the transition to an alternative social-ecological system defined by ecological constraints. The papers are drawn from a variety of disciplines, from ecological economics to anthropology, sociology, environmental politics, and public health.

The section opens with a chapter by Stephen Quilley that considers the wicked tensions of ontological individualism in liberal societies and its implications for long-term individual and group health. Quilley argues that while the lens of complexity reveals health to be an emergent function of social-ecological systems, the fixation of mainstream biomedicine on individual health discounts the ecological, economic, and social costs of modern health systems. The chapter presents a theoretical background on the emergence of individualism within modern society, as well as the implications of rising individualization for broader social relations, the political economy, and the transition to a postgrowth society. Next, Colin Butler argues that limits to growth are already causing "regional overload" at a local scale, a precursor to the broader "planetary overload" proposed by public health researcher Anthony McMichael (1993). Conflicts and health crises in Syria, Yemen, Sub-Saharan Africa, and Venezuela are shown to be affected by impending limits including water scarcity, falling fossil fuel income, climate change, famine, and high fertility rates. Despite these indicators of regional overload, however, the public health community remains largely complacent due to neoliberal agendas and other systemic biases. Butler's contribution aims to reawaken the public health community to the risk of planetary overload as we edge ever closer to the limits to growth.

Three chapters then discuss the economic implications of the Anthropocene for the way we finance and structure health systems. In "Medicine and Health Care in the Anthropocene," Jennifer Cole asks what we mean by "medicine" and how it will be shaped by the social-ecological characteristics of the age of human impact. Focusing on wicked dilemmas at the intersection of increased lifespan, declining fertility rates, and rising health care costs, Cole draws on insights from the history of medicine and evolutionary anthropology to argue for a new model of medical provision founded on humanity's innate capacity for altruism and cooperation. Martin Hensher then considers how a range of macroeconomic models that are consistent with planetary boundaries could transform health care systems from green growth, the steady state economy, and voluntary degrowth to the possibility of involuntary degrowth (socioeconomic collapse). Hensher argues that to remain within planetary boundaries, health care systems will need to lower their material consumption and resource use while avoiding rebound effects, eliminate wasteful overconsumption that delivers minimal health benefits, and reconsider the scope of "needs" and "wants" in a context of more limited resources. Also bringing insights from the field of ecological economics to bear on the wicked problems of health in the Anthropocene, Kaitlin Kish's "What about My Pineapples?" considers the trade-offs we may need to make to live in more sustainable ways. She argues that growth and social progress in the form of access to individual rights, child care, and health care are fundamentally intertwined. Because they evolved together, picking apart the growth economy and its underlying worldviews is difficult and potentially impossible. To illustrate the kinds of trade-offs that may be necessary, Kish considers the case of women's emancipation.

Two papers exploring the future of health in the Anthropocene conclude part 1. Katharine Zywert first presents findings from interviews that asked health researchers and practitioners to imagine their best- and worst-case scenarios for health systems 150 years in the future. Zywert identified core themes such as adaptation to civilizational collapse, connectedness to nature and to each other, and reinventing past modes of social organization to inform emerging practices. Together, these ideas begin to piece together potential alternative futures for health systems and contribute to a growing dialogue about the health effects of long-term social-ecological change. To close part 1, Blake Poland and colleagues consider how scenario thinking can help to realign public health with the demands of emerging energy and resource constraints. Based on a report written for the Canadian Public Health Association, the chapter explores the implications of three possible scenarios: "doing the same things," "doing the same things better," and "doing better things." In exploring these three scenarios, the chapter offers insight into how divergent cultural narratives and values could play out in health-related fields over the coming decades.

REFERENCES

Alley, C., & Sommerfeld, J. (2014). Infectious disease in times of social and ecological change. *Medical Anthropology, 33*(2), 85–91. https://doi.org/10.1080/01459740.2013.850590

Armelagos, G. J., Brown, P. J., & Turner, B. (2005). Evolutionary, historical and political economic perspectives on health and disease. *Social Science & Medicine, 61*(4), 755–65. https://doi.org/10.1016/j.socscimed.2004.08.066

Barrett, R., Kuzawa, C. W., McDade, T., & Armelagos, G. J. (1998). Emerging and re-emerging infectious diseases: The third epidemiological transition. *Annual Review of Anthropology, 27*, 247–71. https://doi.org/10.1146/annurev.anthro.27.1.247

Benatar, S., & Poland, B. (2015). Lessons for health from insights into environmental crises. *International Journal of Health Services, 46*(6), 1–18. https://doi.org/10.1177/0020731415596296

Blakemore, E. (2016). Will medicine survive the Anthropocene? *Smithsonian Magazine Online.* http://www.smithsonianmag.com/science-nature/will-medicine-survive-anthropocene-180959473/?no-ist

Canadian Public Health Association. (2015). *Global change and public health: Addressing the ecological determinants of health.* Ottawa: Canadian Public Health Association.

Doherty, T. J. & Clayton, S. (2011). The psychological impacts of global climate change. *American Psychologist, 66*(4), 265–76. https://doi.org/10.1037/a0023141

Friel, S. (2010). Climate change, food insecurity and chronic diseases: Sustainable and healthy policy opportunities for Australia. *New South Wales Public Health Bulletin, 21*(6), 129–33. https://doi.org/10.1071/NB10019

Hancock, T. (2017). Beyond health care: The other determinants of health. *CMAJ, 189*, E1571. https://doi.org/10.1503/cmaj.171419

Harrison, M. (2004). *Disease and the modern world: 1500 to the present day.* Cambridge: Polity Press.

Hidaka, B. H. (2012). Depression as a disease of modernity: Explanations for increasing prevalence. *Journal of Affective Disorders, 140,* 205–14. https://doi.org/10.1016/j.jad.2011.12.036

Intergovernmental Panel on Climate Change. (2014). Climate change 2014: Impacts, adaptation, and vulnerability. Cambridge: Cambridge University Press.

Kish, K. & Quilley, S. (2017). Wicked dilemmas of scale and complexity in the politics of degrowth. *Ecological Economics, 142,* 306–17. https://doi.org/10.1016/j.ecolecon.2017.08.008

Lovelock, J. (2014). *A rough ride to the future.* New York: The Overlook Press.

McElroy, A., & Townsend, P. K. (2014). *Medical anthropology in ecological perspective.* Boulder: Westview Press.

McMichael, A. J. (1993). *Planetary overload. Global environmental change and the health of the human species.* Cambridge: Cambridge University Press.

McMichael, A. J. (2014). Population health in the Anthropocene: Gains, losses and emerging trends. *The Anthropocene Review, 1*(1), 44–56. https://doi.org/10.1177/2053019613514035

Meadows, D. (2008). *Thinking in systems: A primer.* Vermont: Chelsea Green Publishing.

O'Neill, D. et al. (2018). A good life for all within planetary boundaries. *Nature Sustainability, 1,* 88–95. https://doi.org/10.1038/s41893-018-0021-4

Prüss-Üstün A., & Corvalán C. (2006). *Preventing disease through healthy environments: Towards an estimate of the environmental burden of disease.* Geneva: World Health Organization (WHO).

Raworth, K. (2017). A doughnut for the Anthropocene: Humanity's compass in the 21st century. *Lancet Planetary Health, 1*(1), e48–e49. https://doi.org/10.1016/S2542-5196(17)30028-1

Rittel, H. & Webber, M. (1973). Dilemmas in a general theory of planning. *Policy Sciences, 4*(2), 155–69. https://doi.org/10.1007/BF01405730

Rockström, J. et al. (2009). A safe operating space for humanity. *Nature, 461,* 472–5. https://doi.org/10.1038/461472a

Singer, M. (2009). Ecosyndemics: Global warming and the coming plagues of the 21st century. In A. Swedlund and A. Herring (Eds). *Plagues and epidemics: Infected spaces past and present* (pp. 21–38). London: Berg.

Steffen, W. et al. (2015). The trajectory of the Anthropocene: The Great Acceleration. *The Anthropocene Review, 2*(1), 81–98. https://doi.org/10.1177/2053019614564785

Trinkaus, E. (2011). Late Pleistocene adult mortality patterns and modern human establishment. *Proceedings of the National Academy of Sciences of the United States of America, 108*(4), 1267–71. http://doi.org/10.1073/pnas.1018700108

Whitmee, S. et al. (2015). Safeguarding human health in the Anthropocene epoch: Report of The Rockefeller Foundation – Lancet Commission on planetary health. *The Lancet, 386*(10007), 1973–2028. https://doi.org/10.1016/S0140-6736(15)60901-1

Zywert, K. (2017). Human health and social-ecological systems change: Rethinking health in the Anthropocene. *The Anthropocene Review, 4*(3), 216–38. https://doi .org/10.1177/2053019617739640

Zywert, K. & Quilley, S. (2017). Health systems in an era of biophysical limits: The wicked dilemmas of modernity. *Social Theory & Health, 16*(2), 188–207. https://doi .org/10.1057/s41285-017-0051-4

1 Individual or Community as a Frame of Reference for Health in Modernity and in the Anthropocene

STEPHEN QUILLEY

Introduction

Above all modern societies are predicated on the spatial, social, and occupational mobility of citizens – individuals who are construed as rational, sovereign agents. This is what Elias had in mind when he characterized complex, capitalist democracies, with an extended social division of labour, in terms of the "society of individuals" (2010). In conditions of modernity, ordinary people are able, for the first time in history, to ask questions like "who am I?" and "what might I become?" One of the earliest and repeated conversations that a (grand)parent or kindergarten teacher might have with a young child starts with "what would you like to do when you grow up?" And of course, it is no longer possible to ask such questions without attending to the possibility of "gender conditioning" – that otherwise unremarkable choices may be tainted by the strictures and values of traditional gender roles. This anxiety intimates a second assumption relating to the plasticity of human nature. Reflecting the unprecedented fluidity of both social role and psychological personality in the fast-growing Protestant metropolises of early modern England, John Locke (1689) speculated that the mind of a newborn baby was a "tabula rasa." For all that this notion has been debunked thoroughly in both scientific and popular arenas (Pinker, 2002), the concept has proved highly resilient and remains central to the legitimating discourses of modern society across very different domains such as law, education, and moral philosophy. It provides a foundational architecture for the more general ontological commitment to the individual as separate, sovereign, and potentially rational and accountable. Thus, our school systems are predicated on the twin ideas that (a), inequalities of outcome must result from failures in the pedagogical environment rather than innate capacities, and that (b), people should engage with the social stock of knowledge (our societally specific "means of orientation") as individual vessels to be filled.

Students are construed as consumers or clients in a transactional exchange of knowledge understood as abstract, context-free information – rather than interdependent participants in a lattice of ongoing relationships linking not only people and groups but also a landscape and wider ecological community (see Gellner, 2008; Ong, 2002). And likewise, it is taken for granted that the raison d'être of medicine and health systems should be the stable persistence of individual person-organisms over the longest period. Such somatic equilibrium is consistently privileged over any ineffable and incommensurable experience of quality. This somatically stable and circumscribed individual is understood as hermetically bounded, undifferentiated, and fundamentally material and mechanistic in nature.

In what follows, I will explore the wicked dilemmas of this ontological individualism in liberal societies and their implications for individual and group health and well-being over (possibly conflicting) medium and long time frames.

Part I: Me, Myself, and I in the Anthropocene – The "Society of Individuals" and the Post-Growth Society

The Creation of Individuals: Modernity as Disembedding

The process of modernization has been inextricably linked with increasing social and economic complexity and individualization – the "disembedding" of individuals from the lattice of reciprocal obligation and constraint associated with traditional patterns of community and land-based livelihood, and the loosening of ascriptive occupational and social roles and much greater social and spatial mobility (Polanyi, 1957). But the "freedom" to move, work, trade, marry, and generally make a life came at the cost of the weakening or loss of traditional "survival units" and much greater insecurity for individuals. Though hierarchical, traditional agrarian society locked individuals into nested familial, clan, and community units that culminated in the organization of the rural estate and feudal landownership. Starting with the enclosure movement and the highland clearances, for the subaltern classes rural emancipation was synonymous with insecurity. From the early modern period, emerging patterns of class politics can be understood in terms of an imperative to create new survival units. Bottom-up strategies by working people included of course unions and syndicates but also friendly societies, cooperatives, guilds, religious care communities, and even (in the Basque country) cooking clubs (Quilley, 2012; Goldstein and Godemont, 2003; Hess, 2007). Top-down strategies by the state centred on the regulation of labour markets, social housing, health systems, and social insurance. In the end, it was the latter processes that came to dominate; now the archetypical "survival unit" for modern societies is the nation-state. Individuals who suffer unemployment or ill health look much less to family, not at all to tribe or face-to-face community, nor any longer, to creative, quasi-familial innovations such as the early-modern guild or the Basque gastronomic society. Modern individuals look rather to abstract citizen-based systems (i.e. social or private insurance and contracts) constructed and/or regulated by the state, even if sometimes provided through monopolistic market systems. This goes a long way to explaining the dyadic, mutual dependency of the nation-state and the sovereign individual agent who has appeared as a foundational postulate in the great works of moral philosophy, law, political polemic, and economic theory since the eighteenth century. The liberal state needs individuals unencumbered by conflicting affective and political affiliations, just as much as the individual depends utterly on the abstract systems of state and market. It is for this reason that nation-states function as an indivisible national family, or in Anderson's (1991) memorable phrase, an "imagined community." It is also why the process of state formation involves the systematic destruction of competing imaginaries, languages, and cultures with the potential to form alternative poles of identity. For Gellner (2008), a defining characteristic of the nation-state is the monopoly that it exerts over professionalized "exo-education." Such systems are charged specifically with equipping individuals with the generic technical skills (literacy and numeracy) and the necessary ontological commitments to the national imaginary and "we-identity." But such commitments are neither a "false consciousness" nor simply an imposition, but rather attend to an existential reality for these newly emancipated citizens: that their biophysical security depends very directly on the cohesiveness of the new national imaginary. This is because it is the abstract, symbolic kinship linking millions of strangers, that legitimates and makes possible the fiscal transfers necessary for the health, education, and policing systems, and so allows the nation-state to function as a survival unit at all. Thus, Ontario taxpayers are happy to subsidize the health care of Nova Scotians because "after all ... [and self-evidently], we are all Canadian."

Figures 1.1 and 1.2 capture this transition. In the embedded society (figure 1.1), there is no distinct sphere of the "economy" as such. Processes of subsistence are cognitively and substantively entwined with the reproduction of families, political hierarchies, gender relations and the (re)articulation of a cosmology. Malinowski's (1922) description of the pattern of livelihood of people spread out across the Pacific Trobriand Islands provided an archetype for production and exchange embedded in wider processes of social reproduction and meaning creation. The situation he described was not dissimilar in the social systems of traditional agrarian society (figure 1.1). Thus, prior to the enclosure of the commons described by Polanyi (1964), the great majority of the population subsisted in circular, place-bound economies organized around more or less self-sufficient agricultural estates. In such a situation, the "economic" role of any individual coincided with their social role. Their (spatial, occupational, social) position in a highly stable figuration of interdependent individuals was ascribed more or less by birth and is defined by taken for granted and regular, albeit often asymmetric patterns of reciprocity. Markets were very local and prices mediated by convention as much as by supply and demand. The survival unit that guaranteed individual safety and security was familial, place-bound and community or clan based.

In contrast, with the process of modernization, individuals were uprooted from such local contexts. With the spatial and social mobility associated with urbanization, identity becomes much more open, meritocratic, and achievement-oriented. With the undermining of the survival units associated with extended family and place-bound communities, early modern society sees the balance between the "I" and the "we" begin to tilt towards the former (Elias, 2010). As intimated in Marx's bitter epithet "wage slavery," the kind of social emancipation represented by these processes was both real and pyric, forcing millions of individuals into insecurity and dependence on the vagaries of the market – a process ongoing with the great urban transition that continues to empty rural landscapes across the Global South. What follows this unleashing of market forces was and is quite predictable. Left to its own devices, the market would destroy both people and landscapes and engender existential class conflicts and patterns of social polarization. In the end, in what Polanyi described as "the double movement," it is the state that comes to the rescue of capitalism in the form of "countervailing movements for societal protection." The end result of this process is summarized in figure 1.2. Taking over as the survival unit of first resort, the nation-state coevolves an intimate and mutually dependent relation with both individuals and markets (Loyal and Quilley, 2018; Scott, 1998). Individual security is guaranteed first of all by engagement with dynamic labour markets on the back of a growing economy, and secondly by access to forms of social insurance provided directly or underwritten by the state – in the form of education and health services, military and police protection, regulatory interventions, and the provision of infrastructure, etc. Thus, both the state and the market require individual actors to be unencumbered by commitments to family, clan, ethnic group, or other intermediate forms of association. The more a society approximates to this vision of a sovereign citizenry, the better will function both liberal democratic and legal systems and economic markets. It is for this reason that in a well-functioning capitalist liberal-democracy, the domain of livelihood must remain residual and weak. Thus, even in the case of youth unemployment, advocates of social democracy would see family responsibility as a failure, the ideal being housing benefit, social insurance, and Keynesian interventions to stimulate the economy.

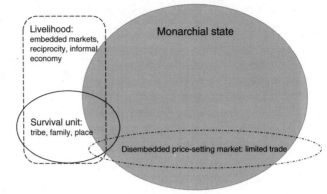

- "Gemeinschaft"
- The "I" embedded in the "We"
- The survival unit is local, familial, tribal, and place-bound
- Markets are largely embedded
- Widespread use and dependence on the "commons"
- Ubiquitous reciprocity and gifting
- The central state distant and minimally intrusive in day-to-day life and economy

Figure 1.1 Traditional society

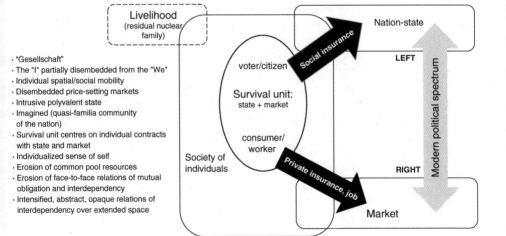

- "Gesellschaft"
- The "I" partially disembedded from the "We"
- Individual spatial/social mobility
- Disembedded price-setting markets
- Intrusive polyvalent state
- Imagined (quasi-familia community of the nation)
- Survival unit centres on individual contracts with state and market
- Individualized sense of self
- Erosion of common pool resources
- Erosion of face-to-face relations of mutual obligation and interdependency
- Intensified, abstract, opaque relations of interdependency over extended space

Figure 1.2 Modern society

The Emergence of Individualist Ontologies in Language, Psychology, and the Operating Procedures of Institutions

Drawing on the social psychology of G.H. Mead (1934), Elias refers to this image of the closed-off individual as *Homo clausus*. The image is misleading and causes people to underestimate the extent to which the self is relational – a more or less stable configuration that emerges from (i), the ongoing pattern of interdependence between figurations of interdependent individuals (*Homines aperti*) and (ii), the contingencies of particular social situation (Ross and Nisbett, 1991) – albeit to a degree of social-situational plasticity conditioned by (iii) the parameters of those heritable dimensions of personality.

Nevertheless, however misleading in a technical sense, the image of the closed-off, Crusoe-esque, "thinking statue" (Descartes's "cogito ergo sum") that has dominated Western philosophical imaginary for centuries, does to some extent mirror the social reality of modern societies. Despite the underlying relational architecture of self-formation, the image of a "society of individuals" has become progressively more congruent with reality over the course of the nineteenth and twentieth centuries. People *have* become less attached to place, to family, to ascriptive occupational and social identities. Narratives of progress *have* come unconsciously to reflect the ideal of sovereign and rational selfhood.

Certainly, the chaotic unravelling of the social and communitarian structures of traditional society created chronic social and political instability. But the corrective "counter-movement," when it came, did nothing to rebuild the lattice of social capital and reciprocity but rather matched the individualism in the economy and civil society with the overarching collective institutions of state (Quilley, 2012). As a result, in Western-type societies the idea of the sovereign and rational individual has become a ubiquitous grounding assumption of both institutions and ideational discourses (see table 1.1).

Underlying all of these ideational and institutional forms, there is a very specific sociological pattern of individualization (Beck, 1992; Giddens, 1991; Elias, 2010). The "social emancipation" of the peasants (Russia in 1861), of women after the First World War, of gay people, and the process of "disembedding" more generally all refer to a very specific loosening of the ascriptive parameters that previously circumscribed the lives and destinies of individuals: in other words, the peasants who have moved to the city to take up jobs in factories; young people now immersed in "youth culture" and who are able and perhaps forced to make endless choices about place, occupation, faith, and politics; young women who are now able to exercise more choice over sex, marriage, work, and motherhood; gay people who are now able to express their sexuality in public.

Table 1.1 Rational individualism in the architecture of modern institutions and associated ideational discourses

Domain (Source)	Traditional society	Late-modern societies
Economics (Polanyi, 1964; Polanyi, 1968)	Subsistence embedded in culture	Rational individual expressing preferences in the market.
Law	Restorative justice; familial/ clan/place as unit of justice	Citizenship as individual membership and the principle of equality of individuals under the law.
Politics (Weiner, 2013, Elias, 2010; Gellner, 2008; Anderson, 1991)	Tribal, clan, or community-based units of analysis and hierarches	The primacy of the individual relation to the state. Voting as individuals rather than families or clients of local "big man." Citizenship as individual membership of a nation state; gives rise eventually to human-rights concepts that uncouple the idea of rights from "membership."
Philosophy (MacIntyre, 1966)	Aristotelian/Thomist virtue ethics	Ontological, epistemological, methodological, and moral individualism (across diverse utilitarian, natural rights, Kantian, Rawlsian traditions).
Social science (Watkins, 1968)	No real equivalent (theology)	Methodological individualism, rational choice – but also the individualism implicit in otherwise radical feminist, human rights, and other activist strands.
Literature (Ong, 2002)	"Functionally clichéd," universal, archetypal tropes of oral poetic traditions	Increasing concern with the interior psycho-affective drama of feelings, self-realization; highly individuated and differentiated understanding of the (anti)hero.
Sexuality, marriage, and family	Sex and (arranged) marriage linked to reproduction and construed as family/ community concern	Sex decoupled from reproduction and from marriage; marriage and reproduction decoupled from wider family/community concerns; reproduction decoupled from marital partnership and even sex.

(*continued*)

Table 1.1   Rational individualism in the architecture of modern institutions and associated ideational discourses (continued)

Domain (Source)	Traditional society	Late-modern societies
Religion (Seligman, 2010)	Pagan and indigenous hearth religions construed religious experience and practise as a function of a lattice of relations to people (the hearth), gods/spirits (the sacred), and the land (other kinds of people)	The Judeo-Christian insistence on the unique and sacred quality of individuals created in the likeness of God; moderated to some extent by ritual modes that prioritize group cohesion and conformity. With Protestantism, the unmediated relation between individual and God as a proxy for subsequent relation between citizen and state (Loyal and Quilley 2018); the balance between modes of *sincerity* and *ritual* shifts sharply towards the former (Seligman 2010).
Psychiatry (R.D. Laing, 1962)	Muted patterns of individuation with less room for the expression of social-psychologically driven forms of depression and mental disorder	Individuation combined with patterns of alienation, anomie, and disenchantment (crises of meaning) create more room for expression of mental instability and depression. Consistent privileging of pathological individual over the pathological society.
The politics of emancipation and freedom	No real equivalent	Liberal and radical social movements alike prioritize almost unconsciously a highly individuated sovereign self as the incumbent of inalienable human rights. Animal rights discourses extend individual personhood to animals. Peter Singer's (1990) criterion "can they suffer" relates to the embodied pain of individual subjects.

Enlightenment Progress and the Society of Individuals

Across several hundred years and a great variety of societies, the hard edge of modernization has been experienced by ordinary people as a combination of opportunity and insecurity. Whether Irish peasants working in Manchester textile mills, Europeans crossing the Atlantic in their millions, or peasant workers crowding into the cities of southeast China today, modernity involves an endless set of trade-offs. As Berman put it:

> To be modern is to find ourselves in an environment that promises us adventure, power, joy, growth, transformations of ourselves and the world – and at the same time, that threatens to destroy everything that we have, everything that we know, everything that we are. Modern environments cut across all boundaries of geography, ethnicity, or class and nationality, of religion and ideology: in this sense, modernity can be said to unite all of mankind. But it is a paradoxical unity, a unity of disunity: it pours us all into a maelstrom of perpetual disintegration and renewal, of struggle and contradiction, of ambiguity and anguish. To be modern is to be part of a universe in which, as Marx said "all that is solid melts to air." (1983)

Typically, the exposure of societies to rampant market forces creates crises of social cohesion and political stability – which has resulted in a variety of nationalist, populist, and socialist revolutions. Stepping back from the historical detail of specific cases, one thing becomes absolutely clear. The process of stabilization of any new proto-modern, industrial configuration always centres on the moderating function of the nation-state, which in turn depends on the consolidation of a national "imagined community" (Weber, 1976; Anderson, 1991; Gellner, 2008; Quilley and Loyal, 2018).

What this has meant is that almost invariably, the response on the part of both newly emancipated/disembedded individuals, a wide variety of otherwise diverse social movements, left- and right-wing political parties and elite policymakers charged with formulating coherent responses has been in many ways remarkably uniform. Not only consensus politics, but to a great extent even the extremities of right and left have accepted the society of individuals. They have accepted that the landscape of modern politics relates primarily to the relationship between mobile individuals, the state, and the market. On this basis, the left-right spectrum hinges almost entirely on the extent and structure of the social safety net (social insurance), forms of private insurance, the labour market, the business cycle, and the coercive powers of the military and police. In all cases the primary and overlapping survival units are (i), the imagined community and coercive/protective power of the state and (ii), the national economy. The latter delivers not only jobs and a means for citizens to fund themselves and their families, but also fiscal resources, which in turn fund (a), the protective (educational, health and welfare) institutions of the state and (b), the coercive institutions of police and military, which guarantee territorial integrity, physical security, and political stability. And clearly there is a delicate balance between the state and the market. A dynamic and growing market economy provides fiscal resources for the welfare state. The welfare state underpins social cohesion. And cultural imaginaries that promote high levels of mutual identification legitimate the flow of fiscal resources from the private to the public sector. This is essentially a description of the much-lauded Scandinavian model in the post-war period. Market crisis and/or overextension of the welfare state along with systemically lower levels of mutual identification (imagined communities with less affective traction) have not changed the essentials of this system. Rather they engender a more violent left/right swinging pattern in party politics and a greater dependence on the coercive powers of the state to secure social and political stability.

This pattern of left/right politics and the ebb and flow of market and state all takes place on the right-hand side of figure 1.2. What has never happened in a modern state has been any concerted move towards the modality of livelihood, or a change in the nature of the survival unit (i.e. a shift towards the left-hand side of figure 1.2). The narrative of social progress that emerged during the Enlightenment and gathered pace from the end of the nineteenth century conjoined advances in individual well-being with wider social progress whilst prioritizing the ontological and epistemological basis of the former. In modern societies individuals are paramount, and the fundamentals of their safety, security, and well-being are secured by the oscillating matrix of state and market institutions. Where market and political-cultural factors allow, this survival unit will be dominated by what Bourdieu called the "left hand of the state," in other words functions of welfare and the discourse of social and political rights (Loyal and Quilley, 2018). In less propitious circumstances and where fiscal crisis engenders what Habermas (1975) referred to as a "legitimation crisis," the military/policing functions of the state will come to the fore.

In this context, pretty well everything that has been constituted the trajectory of social and political progress is both framed exclusively as a function of the society of individuals and depends on the fiscal resources generated by the growing economy. Thus, for instance, since Tom Paine's *Rights of Man* and Wolstonecraft's feminist addendum, political rights have been understood exclusively as a natural concomitant of ontologically a priori individuals. The Enlightenment codified a natural basis for individual political citizenship. Likewise, progressive law is framed in terms of the rights (and, much more rarely, duties) of individuals. Social welfare and safety nets operate in relation to the social rights of individuals, theorized as "social citizenship" and the extension of political franchise (Titmuss, 1958; Marshall, 1950). More prosaically, the lifestyle freedoms associated with occupational and social mobility, the extension of higher education, and the spatial (auto)mobility and freedom to travel in unprecedented safety were all construed and understood in terms of the freedom of young people, on reaching the age of majority, to make a proliferating array of life choices (Beck, 1992: chapter 5). The scope of such choices is now expanding into domains that Titmuss and Marshall could not even have dreamed, most notably with the increasing involvement of the state in underwriting the medical and social costs of gender transition.

The stark reality, however, is that these rights and choices and indeed, the existence of the rights bearing and choosing individuals, all depend upon economic growth:

- to sustain the complex and extending division of labour that engenders the necessary proliferation of fluid role identities and socio-spatial mobility.
- to generate the fiscal resources necessary to fund public services, welfare, and infrastructure – all of which combine to provide a surrogate survival unit allowing individuals to become partially or completely independent of family and place-based communities of fate.
- to provide the extensive material and institutional resources for the meaningful elaboration of individual political and social rights rooted initially in membership-based legal concepts of citizenship and more recently the supranational idea of universal human rights.

Individualism and the End of Growth

As humanity contemplates emerging from the benign and stable parameters of the Holocene, this unmediated marriage of individual and society is becoming problematic in a number of ways. Primarily, the globalizing consumer economy is rapidly approaching biophysical limits to growth (Quilley, 2017; Spash, 2012; Trainer, 2013; Turner, 2012; Ophuls, 2011; Rees, 2005). The unpalatable truth is that there is a zero-sum tension between capitalist modernization and the consumer society and the long-term ecological integrity of the biosphere – at least in so far as it can support a global civilization.

Whether as a result of involuntary economic contraction (the impact of concatenating economic crisis, climate change and geo-political tension) or voluntary degrowth (Cosme and O'Neill, 2017; Sekulova et al, 2013), any failure of the logic of capitalist accumulation would almost immediately engender a series of legitimation crises (Habermas, 1975; Quilley, 2013; Kish and Quilley, 2017). Any significant unemployment combined with a serious failure in the state's ability to provide a health and income safety net would undermine the historical compromise between capital and labour and eventually the entire edifice of consensus politics. In the first instance, this might lead to both leftist and fascist political reactions, both focusing on an expanded role for the state and some kind of renewal of the compact between states and citizens. However, unlike in the twentieth century, ecological limits to growth are a threat to industrial-consumer society per se. State monopoly and authoritarian forms of capitalism are just as vulnerable as liberal consumer societies. In the medium term (decades), systemic contraction and relocalization would change the fundamental nature of the individual's survival unit. Unable to rely on the impersonal dynamics of abstract national and international labour markets, people would come to depend more upon more locally embedded economic systems. Relocalization along these lines would see the delivery of goods and services responsive not only to price-setting markets but to an array of political and cultural conventions or expectations, to informal barter, and to re-emerging patterns of reciprocity, in other words the kind of relationships that dominated traditional rural economies and can still be observed in Amish and Mennonite communities (Jellison, 2014; Paul, 2007).

At the same time, unable to rely on state services and safety nets, people would necessarily become once again mutually dependent on extended family and kin networks and on place-bound forms of community. And in this context, sub-state forms of ethnic and religious association that function to extend and consolidate the boundaries of symbolic family would find a new function and utility in the stitching together of viable "communities of fate." In such survival units, the abstract, fungible, and transactional currency of state and market structures would be replaced by the highly personal and non-fungible dynamics of social groups.

Part II: The Double-Edged Discourse of Individualism in Medicine – How Ontological Commitments to the Rational Individual Impede Efforts to Achieve Population Health

Complexity, Health, Ecology, and Homines aperti

That the individual as a unit of analysis has become so natural and "self-evident" in highly mobile and individuated modern societies predisposes science and policy to underestimate the deeply relational dimensions of human health. It is very difficult for modern people to unthink the "I" or experience the unconscious, embodied, distributed "we-cognition" (Green, 2014; Cárdenas-García and Ireland, 2017) associated with what Berman (2000) calls our ancestral "participating consciousness." This becomes very clear if one compares the forty-thousand-year unbroken tradition of ritualized, tactile, communal responses (including the "all hands on" "trance dance") to both ill-health and social-spiritual malaise practised by Indigenous groups such as the !Kung (San) to the individual focus of both modern psychiatry and psychology. San bushmen conceptualize individual ill health as a disorder in an invisible web of relationships. Western medicine has historically focused on the body as a separate vessel (Low, 2008; Isaacson, 2001; Marshall, 1969; Marshall-Thomas, 2006; Katz, 1982).

However, greater understanding of health and medicine through the lens of complexity is now revealing (or rather recovering older insights as to) important ways in which the health and physiology of individuals is very much an emergent function of social-ecological systems. Examples include the following:

i. *The gut, the field, and the mind: Nested systems and units of analysis.* Research is revealing a complex web of interactions between the diversity and profile of gut bacterial ecosystems, agro-ecological systems, and emergent patterns of mental health and well-being. Initially this contrast relates to the diversity of hunter-gatherer diets and the transition to agriculture. Although modern populations have reversed many of the deleterious health impacts of early farmers, the further narrowing of crop diversity and the over-reliance on processed carbohydrates is now linked increasingly to a wide range of chronic diseases of affluence from gut and digestive disorders, dietary intolerances, autoimmune problems, and psychological depression. These relationships point to problems relating to the appropriate unit of analysis for health research (Quigley, 2013). The self-evident human organism turns out to be indivisibly interdependent with an ecosystem of species and trillions of individual bacteria, fungi, archaea, and viruses (e.g. Sender et al., 2016).

ii. *Agriculture and disease.* A great number of human diseases, vectors and pathogens have been shown to be a direct consequence of agriculture, either directly as with viruses jumping from domesticates such as pigs, and other fellow travellers, or indirectly as with the link between mosquito vectors, deforestation, and human impacts on water courses (Wolfe et al., 2012).

iii. *Social hierarchy, stress, and health.* There is now strong evidence relating to humans but also other primates and social mammals that position in social hierarchies has a profound influence on individual stress levels and physiological resilience (Marmot and Sapolsky, 2014). Since human culture is so variable, it seems very likely that the size, scale, and complexity of any particular human society is likely to be linked to specific patterns of stress and (ill) health.

iv. *Privileging the individual and antibiotic resistance.* Growing antibiotic resistance is in part a function of the individual rights or client-based approach to (over)prescription and overuse of pharmaceuticals in agribusiness. Rational individualism at the level of both doctors and patients sets up a tension between the immediate interests of individuals and the emergent dynamics of the system as a whole – a tension that is often characterized as a "tragedy of the global health commons" (Conly, 2010; Song, 2017). That "herd health" doesn't sit easily with the individualist ontologies of modern societies is perhaps most evident in the antivaccination movement in the US (Laskowski, 2016; Parmet, 2011).

v. *Social capital and mental health.* There is an enormous body of evidence linking depression and mental health/disease to systemic patterns of social interaction and interdependence – in the first instance the shift from face-to-face cultures to complex, mobile urban systems fostering endless interactions between relative strangers, and more latterly the declining stocks of social capital associated with highly individuated and independent patterns of modern life (e.g. Putnam, 2000).

vi. *Sedentary urban lifestyle.* Somatic and psychological impacts of sedentary lifestyles, a consistent pattern of chronic (rather than episodic/acute) stress, technology, and urban systems that undermine walking and face-to-face interactions.

vii. *Rights, duties, and social and culturally sanctioned relationships.* The impacts of declining marriage rates, rising divorce rates, single parent households, loneliness, and isolation in old-age on health, happiness, and poverty are now well established. Repeated studies have shown that children born out of wedlock are considerably more likely to fall into poverty and suffer ill health and depression, that divorced or unmarried men suffer greater ill health and depressive illness, and that marriage and a strong family network provides the best insulation against unhappiness and ill health (e.g. Brooks, 2015; Sommerlad et al., 2017).

viii. *Disenchantment and secularism.* Going back to Max Weber (1964) the impact of scientific rationality and "disenchanted humanism" on happiness and mental health has been a staple of sociological commentaries on modernity. There is a great deal of evidence that religious faith is associated with happiness and lower levels of mental ill health (e.g. Brooks, 2015; Croezen et al., 2015; Berman, 2000).

These kinds of insights as to the interweaving connectivity of nested systems, the more differentiated and less rigid understanding of appropriate units of analysis are now percolating into the vernacular epistemology of alternative health (e.g. local honey as an antidote to hay fever from local pollen) and popular culture, most notably with the sensuous phantasmagoria of the film *Avatar*.

Homo clausus *and the Long Now*

At the same time, the predominant focus on the health (at all, or any, cost) of individuals discounts the wider and long-term economic and ecological costs borne by future generations and the wider ecosystem. This is significant because perhaps the greatest achievement of the West has been to create an economic and political system that entrenches and valourizes the Judeo-Christian understanding of the sanctity of the individual (with each person carrying a divine spark – qua humanity; see Joas, 2013). This principle has underpinned the unfolding institutional and cultural web of democratic franchise; individual freedoms of association, belief, and conscience; constitutional authority; a free press; the curtailment and banning of torture, genocide, and slavery, etc. And most of all it is incarnated in the legal and cultural halo of "universal human rights."

It is now impossible for even the most cynical dictator to eschew nominal affiliation to the idea of human rights as a taken-for-granted principle of jurisprudence. And yet it is obvious, after only a moment's thought, that making sacrosanct the life and interests of each individual in the present must have consequences. Divorcing the trajectory of each individual life from the reciprocal obligations and entanglements of the wider community, the flow of generations over time, and even the ecological landscape that we render so obliquely as the "environment" must accumulate a growing burden of thermodynamic and ecological debt. A few examples should suffice to show why.

Consider first of all the systemic costs of an aging society. For most of human development, life expectancy was about half that of modern societies or less. This is not to say that people didn't *experience* long lives – because perception of age and longevity is difficult to pin down and compare in phenomenological terms. What is certainly true is that hunter-gatherer and simple agrarian societies for the most part did not have the wherewithal to sustain incapacitated, senile, or unproductive members of the community for any length of time. This is not to say it did not happen, but both direct and indirect senicide (and indeed infanticide) and abandonment were recurring features of most human societies. Since the 1960s women's control over fertility, greater choice in relation to marriage, access to education, and entry into the labour market has seen a sharp decline in birth rates in most Western societies. Women have fewer children (below replacement rates) and they have them later. The result is a demographic crisis that is beginning to overtake population growth in the existential nightmares of long-range planners. Just as the proportion of seniors with escalating medical, health, and social needs is ballooning, numbers in the workforce are falling off a cliff. In countries such as Germany, Japan, and Russia this phenomenon is creating enormous questions not only about economic growth but societal reproduction. Partial solutions are conceivable. Japan is attempting to solve the problem by focusing on automation and the application of more technology. Germany recently admitted a million Middle Eastern and African migrants in a single year – albeit paying a heavy cost in social cohesion and political stability. But these contingent symptoms bear witness to a much more long-term problem. The laudable Enlightenment commitment to the individual has ensured that elderly care and the goal of a happy active retirement have, since the Second World War, become central, legitimating tenets of the liberal democratic society. Medical technology has effectively prolonged life to such an extent that society is unable to keep up. The result has been a growing population of seniors, often with little or no contact with immediate family and dependent on ever more complex social care arrangements. Because of an entrenched commitment against discrimination of any kind, the flows of technological, surgical, and pharmaceutical interventions are made routinely available to older and older patients. For instance, in the UK in 2018, women in their seventies are being offered compensation in relation to failures in routine breast cancer screening. And so, it goes on.

The point of this example is not that elder care is "wrong" (clearly). Rather it shows (i), how in less than two generations, a modest commitment to retired citizens who were expected, on average, to die only a few years after retiring, has become a juggernaut budget line that seems impossible to slow down or scale back, and (ii), how the expectation that social care should be a function of the state's relation to the individual citizen (as opposed to care within family/ clan survival unit) has further created an enormous welfare ratchet that depends on continuing economic growth. The state/individual model functions as a cost escalator for a whole raft of reasons not least that as individuals, elderly people expect and are expected to have either an independent household or separate state- or private-run shelter or institutional accommodation. This is clearly much more expensive in both financial but also energetic/material terms than sharing a house with children. And of course, a separate household involves doubling up on transport arrangements and all the accoutrements and "mod cons." And finally, the state-individual relation must be part of the formal economy with all that means in terms of wages, insurance contributions for workers, health and safety regimes, insurance and liabilities, etc. These all directly or indirectly draw on state budget lines. Care in the formal economy is expensive, period.

Now this ratio of the active workforce to an inactive and more health-dependent non-working population would be difficult to reconcile with economic policy at any time. Fiscal transfers are insufficient to match demands on public services, but any retrenchment serious enough to match the problem would cause unprecedented political conflict. Thus, for instance, for all her championing of monetarism and fiscal austerity, under Mrs Thatcher UK public spending in the early 1980s rose on average by 1.1 per cent a year. In societies that have seen real sharp cuts, such as Greece in 2008–11, the result has been unsustainable levels of social conflict. Nevertheless, if there is a biophysical limit to economic growth, then it seems likely that those era-defining post-war commitments to elder health and social care independent of the family may eventually be reneged upon.

Medical technology and health innovations necessarily involve a more general commitment to future spending to the extent that they allow humanity to temporarily dodge the winnowing effect of natural selection. The overwhelming focus on the sacred value of individuals combined with technical knowhow and a political-institutional commitment to divert the necessary funds has the consequence of keeping people both alive and fertile – people who otherwise would often have died very young and without children. Aside from anything else this must result in a rising cost of continuing care and medical interventions. At the population level, higher levels of congenital/genetic disorders are manageable but only on the basis of an elaborate and expanding industrial health system. More generally, the extension of disability rights since the 1960s has been advanced almost exclusively in relation to the ontological insistence of individual rights initially qua citizenship and more recently in relation to human rights – in both cases, rights that are inextricable from the legislative, institutional, and welfare commitments advanced through the state and often framed in terms of lifting the responsibility (and sometimes the opportunity) for care from families.

The same kind of considerations apply to the agenda and programmatic success of feminism. Although academics tend to play up the role of intellectual activism, the great social advances for women in the latter half of the twentieth century can be attributed to two factors – namely the technology of birth control and access to a rapidly expanding labour market on a (more and more) equal basis with men. And all things considered, it has been profoundly successful. But tying the meaning of gender emancipation to the labour market has some paradoxical consequences. Most significantly, the advancement of women has depended on the enormous expansion in state services for the care of children, people with disabilities, and seniors. (This is obvious and has been dealt with in previous paragraphs.) Fault-free divorce has transformed the lives of many women, freeing them from unhappy and sometimes abusive marriages. But of course, this change in the law also required a corollary expansion in the benefits and services available to single parents – not least in terms of housing and childcare. And with the normalization of non-traditional families and the active destigmatization of youthful sexual activity outside of marriage, there has also been an enormous surge in single parenting as a life choice – most often both young teenage girls and now increasingly older professional women. Finally, with the centre of gravity in exhortation and role-modelling shifting to labour market success, the ever-extending remit of youth culture, and the more general individualistic focus on self-knowledge and self-realization, women have been having babies much later. This is partly a result of personal choices. But as Camilia Paglia often points out, the permissive society had the unintended consequence of liberating both men and women from responsibility. "Sex without responsibility" was the unifying meta-narrative underlying the narcissistic youth countercultures that grew up from the 1960s (Twenge, 2010). But whilst men are able, should they choose, to carry on enjoying such a care-free, live-fast-die-not-so-young lifestyle without much restraint (facilitated by moguls such as Hugh Hefner), for women the situation often becomes more complex and less fun over time. When the biological clock does begin to tick more audibly, they often find it hard to find a willing and responsible partner because the marriage pool of such eligible men has been shrinking rapidly. With would-be mothers getting older and sometimes attempting to have children without a man, there has been an enormous rise in the routine use of fertility interventions such as IVF and obstetric interventions such as birth by caesarean section. And of course, this whole raft of institutions, technologies, and innovations depends on a combination of fiscal subsidy and private investment – funds derived from a growing economy. In these ways, extant and now largely unquestioned feminist priorities with regard to financial-legal autonomy, career advancement, and motherhood have come to depend to a very great extent on a naturalized vision of mobile individuals supported by the state and a dynamic market.

This is not to say that any of these developments should be judged categorically as either progressive or regressive. Rather, it is simply to point out that as a social and political programme, the way in which gender emancipation has unrolled has had unintended consequences, and that it comes with a fiscal and ecological price tag. To sustain the kind of world that has been normalized by freeing women from the home requires a continuing flow of fiscal resources to fund investment in state services and expansion of the formal economy (public and private). In this way, the fate of the social project of feminism has become absolutely intertwined with the society of individuals and depends completely on growth. Of course, this doesn't exhaust the conceptual range of feminist politics or women's emancipation. Kaitlin Kish (2018) has intimated a radical feminist politics of the hearth that is rooted in an expansion of the informal economy and the domain of livelihood (to the left of figure 1.2). But what she refers to as "polioikos" (the feminist political economy of the home) would represent a sharp break with the feminist narrative that has dominated left and green thinking since the 1960s.

The same considerations apply to other interlocking domains of social emancipation and progess. Thus, legitimating a relaxed stance towards immigration, a proactive movement against racism, and an, often vague, commitment to an ill-defined "decolonization," the politics of multiculturalism and diversity combine a seemingly self-evident natural justice with an unexpected ecological price tag and institutional prerequisites. However, its "self-evident" quality is predicated upon the prior construction of the society of individuals, nation-state formation and the institution of citizenship. Ironically, although multiculturalism has sometimes engendered conflictual forms of identity and ethno-politics, it is only conceivable as a development of a national society in which traditional tribal allegiances have been dissolved and individuals mutually identify through the imagined community of the nation (Anderson, 1991; Gellner, 2008). On the upswing, inward migration and social and economic diversity more generally promote growth and enhance innovation. But this said, diversity also presents a challenge to social cohesion and undermines the mythology of "naturalness" and "historical destiny" that is so central to the national imaginary. In a growing consumer economy, these tensions can be lessened by rising standards of living, high levels of spending on health, education, and public services, and by the availability of fiscal resources to deal with costs arising directly from the coexistence of multiple language, religious, and ethno-cultural groups. Thus, for example, in cities like London, the principle of equity in access to the law, health services, local government, etc., requires an enormous infrastructure of simultaneous and document translation to accommodate hundreds of language-culture groups. This language superstructure is a form of complexity that was absent fifty years ago but is now central to the processes of legitimation and social cohesion in multicultural societies.

Perhaps the most telling example relates to the UN Sustainable Development Goals (SDGs) (Kish, 2018). The UN definition of sustainable development in the Anthropocene is "development that meets the needs of the present whilst safeguarding Earth's life-support system, on which the welfare of current and future generations depends" (Griggs et al., 2013). The updated development goals, which include ending poverty, universal education, gender equality, health, environmental sustainability, and global partnerships, all depend to a significant degree upon high energy systems. The associated policy vehicles rely on fiscal transfers from a growing economy. Thus, for example, institutional education; the innovation, manufacture, and delivery of vaccines; governance systems to advance women; the delivery of multiple systems of cheap contraception; market and state pension systems that relieve aging citizens of dependence on uncertain family arrangements – all in different ways replace less complex systems in the informal/livelihood sector with more complex systems in the domain of the formal economy, the state, and the market. Alongside such implicit dependence, one of the SDGs is explicitly to promote economic growth as measured by GDP, labour productivity, and access to financial services. From any ecological-economic perspective, this dependence of development on growth is problematic. In a recent paper, Dan O'Neill et al. (2018) quantified the resource use associated with meeting basic human needs for over 150 countries. Comparing this to what is deemed to be globally sustainable, they found that there is currently no country that achieves a good life for its citizens at a level of resource use that could be extended to all people on the planet. This suggests a prima facie case for the oxymoronic incoherence of the SDGs.

Liberal Democratic Societies Are Always Likely to Discount the Future and to
Undervalue Supra-individual Units of Analysis

Once the process of nation-state formation has dissolved intermediate forms of association and individuals relate more or less directly to the state, the dynamics of political behaviour change rather dramatically. Human beings have evolved to respond to the interests of the group (Sloan-Wilson, 2002), and as Hume pointed out, culture functions to determine the boundaries of the relevant community (Quilley, 2009).

The political sociology of individualist liberal polities certainly centres on identity and group enfranchisement. But in a nation-state the relevant community becomes increasingly abstract and "imagined." The nation can't be experienced directly. Given the legitimating discourse of individual rights, liberal democracy actively, although perhaps also inadvertently, promotes movements to equalize the material and cultural experience of individuals. But, somewhat ironically, given the antecedent process of detribalization, the logic of the democratic process requires individuals to "combine" in order to press such claims "in aggregate." This begins with the process of working-class franchise, the abolition of slavery, and in time the political emancipation of women. However, without any natural brake, liberal societies tend to proliferate intermediate groupings and identities that press claims for material redress and symbolic recognition through political, legal, and cultural systems.

However, it is important to recognize that the kind of "association" represented by disability activism or sexual minorities or any other kind of visible minority never constitute "survival groups" in Elias's sense. That is to say, they do not represent the re-emergence of a truly tribal or clannish form of organization involving integrated or total identities. Rather they become vehicles for otherwise disaggregated individuals to press for a very one-dimensional group advantage – one-dimensional in the sense that the perceived or claimed benefit relates to one aspect of "intersectional" disadvantage (see Hankivsky, 2014), the redress of which is designed to allow individuals to participate fully in the broader society of individuals. Examples include affirmative action for women, black people, or other minorities. The vaunted goal is not that women or black people or people with disability should aspire to function as mutually self-sufficient communities. Rather it is to democratize the "imagined community" of the nation-state; to realize fully the liberal vision of what Habermas (1990) referred to as the "ideal speech situation" in which all individuals had a seat at the table and were able to take a full part in societal deliberations and decision-making. Of course, if pushed too far, identity politics becomes incipiently separatist in tone and direction. Hence the usually unspoken possibility associated with 1960s Black Power movements and now at the fringes of "Black

Lives Matter" is precisely that (remote) prospect of a genuinely autonomous survival unit. Independence is a slightly less remote prospect for First Nations and Native American activists.

Ironically, at the same time, once the discourse of (universal) "human rights" begins to supplant (membership-based) citizenship as the focus for radical liberal politics, this begins to undermine the very "imagined community" of the nation, which for two centuries provided the legitimating glue for advances in welfare. This accounts for a great deal of the current tension between cultural globalists pushing cosmopolitan human rights agendas and populist movements defending the territorial integrity and exclusive solidarity associated with national citizenship.

In this way liberal-democratic politics tends to proliferate coalitional group identities that press for allocational advantage whilst being separate from the responsibility for generating wealth, stewarding social and ecological capital, and providing physical security. These examples are listed not to invalidate the goals or values associated with liberal society. Rather, they draw attention to a fundamental tension between liberal politics and any green politics predicated on limits.

Because of the kind of sectional/coalitional politics described above, radical politics in liberal societies will always tend to the acceleration and maximization of the allocative principles of liberal capitalism. Specifically, groups will invariably tend to seek solutions that expand the range of compensatory state activity by redistributing more from the private sector. With regard to figure 1.2, they operate purely in the classical tug-of-war domain of left/right politics that pits the state against the market. To the extent that they are successful, the strategy depends on sustained growth. To the extent that growth fails, they cannot be successful.

Relational Health for Pluralities of Interdependent Individuals

Drawing upon the previous discussion, this concluding section will address the parameters of health in the Anthropocene, with the latter construed as a period of sustained ecological crisis and the emergence of novel global ecosystems that are less benign and that are providing a less stable backdrop for the development of culture. Biophysical limits to growth will curtail the continuing expansion of population, GDP, and social-economic integration and complexity whilst making more likely regional conflict, failing states, non-linear civilizational shocks, and possible collapse (i.e. a sustained and cascading loss of complexity). In such a context, a viable new paradigm for human health might conceivably depart substantially from the axiomatic frames of early twenty-first century health systems; in other words ontological individualism, hodiecentrism ("today-centred thinking"), disenchantment and mortality avoidance, physiological rather than ecological units of analysis, and health as a disembedded domain distinct from culture.

i. *The political economy of livelihood*. Polanyi (1964) observed that left to its own devices the market society would rather rapidly undermine both nature and the reproduction of labour power (the "fictitious commodities" of land and labour). The process of re-regulation of capital that started with modest housing and factory legislation in the 1860s and ended, after the Second World War, with the establishment of Keynesian welfare states were understood as a "counter-movement for societal protection." But as argued above, this counter-movement played out entirely in the tug of war between the state and the market (figure 1.2). In many ways protective interventions by the state re-enforced the society of individuals and the "imagined community" of the nation-state as the principle survival unit. In the end, the dependence of such state interventions on the flow of fiscal resources from a growing economy and an ever-expanding labour market have accelerated environmental and resource problems – driving what has become known as the Great Acceleration (Steffen et al, 2007). By definition, any significant process of degrowth and the contraction in the metabolic scale of the global economy vis-à-vis energy and resource flows in the biosphere will see some move away from the political economy, politics of the state-market, and the dominance of the formal economy. Such a scenario would seem to require the re-emergence of a more three-dimensional political-economy involving not only the state and the market, but also the domain of livelihood. This scenario is summarized in figure 1.3. From an economic perspective what is most notable is the re-emergence of circular and invisible (to the state) flows of energy, materials, and value in the informal economy. From a political perspective, the scenario points to the partial re-embedding of individuals in place-bound, familial, and community forms of interdependence that provide security (welfare, physical safety, care) but also increase the social pressures of reciprocity and mutual obligation. Greater social viscosity would imply less individual freedom and less social-spatial-occupational mobility – not least because of a marked diminution in the transactional, commodified and citizenship-based forms of public infrastructure that have underpinned such individual choices. A good example would be any shift away from corporate and state childcare back towards informal/familial arrangements, or reductions in welfare supports for single parents, retirees, or the unemployed, and maintenance grants for students.

From a political point of view, the political economy of livelihood implies a radically new configuration of state and society combining aspects of the society of individuals and corresponding state and market provisions with familial and community survival units that are more tribal and ascriptive in nature. It is not at all clear that these two different principles of social cohesion – tribal versus individual/state/market – can be reconciled and made to work together. And yet this would seem to be what is implied by any kind of "alternative modernity." Interestingly, it is also what seems to be implied by the wicked dilemma facing Indigenous communities attempting to find their way within the imagined community of nation-states. How is it possible to be both Canadian and Ojibwe? Or to access and benefit from a modern nation-state and dynamic market economy and the forms of livelihood associated with the reservation, the commons, and traditional relations with both kin and the land?

Finally, it is important to note that, just as market liberals, neo-conservatives, and social democrats (and many greens) alike are committed to the two-dimensional model of state/market described in figure 1.2, there are socialist, liberal, and conservative/traditionalist routes back to the political economy of livelihood (the Catholic tradition of Distributism as a "third way" for instance. See Lottieri, 2011). The project of alternative modernity will necessitate strange political alliances and bed fellows.

Implications: If the Anthropocene turns out to be an era of chaotic climatic and ecological turbulence, geo-political instability and systemic energy/resource constraints, then viable health systems in those societies and regions that manage to develop resilient forms of economy and culture are likely to be characterized by the re-emergence of a political economy of livelihood alongside the systems of state and market. In such a three-legged system, health policies and systems will focus to a greater degree on prevention and community/place-based management, whilst care will depend to a much greater extent on the gig economy, on family and clan, and on neighbourly systems of reciprocity.

ii. *Time.* The abstract conceptualization of time has become part of the deep structure of modern social relations. As Elias (2007) points out, the process of abstract codification has advanced in the course of development as a means of coordinating ever more complex social activities. Thus, an important aspect of early industrialization was the forcible shift from the looser, cyclical, and flexible, task-based forms of temporal coordination associated with rural life, to the highly regulated rhythms of the factory – a form of social regulation incarnated in the factory and town hall clocks that dominate the textile towns of Lancashire as surely as the church bells signalled the circadian rhythm of medieval worship (Thompson, 1967). Significant shifts in the development of national and global markets were associated with the synchronization activities across space associated with "railway time" and later time zones and the Greenwich meridian. This progressive synchronicity has perhaps reached its zenith with the ubiquity

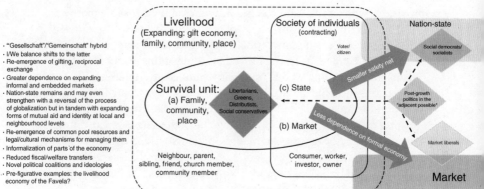

Figure 1.3 Low, no-growth society

of smart phones and real-time global communications systems for both individuals and economic systems (such as stock exchanges): the individual with the group, the group with other groups, figurations of interweaving economic decision-making in one location with similar figurations at every other location. This is in part what Harvey (1989) refers to as space-time compression.

It is notable that as time becomes more fragmented, more costed, and self-consciously accounted for, people in advanced societies have been living longer and longer. It is also notable that modern societies have seen the unprecedented invention of "free time," the "weekend," and "leisure" (Burke, 1995). We now live in a consumer society in which considerable effort and a large slice of the national product is both produced by and devoted to commodified fun. It would seem that in many ways, modern people have never had it so good. On the other hand, it is equally the case that since the onset of capitalism, commentators have been struck by the persistent intuition that modernity is bad for mental health and that city living makes people unhappy. In the early 1970s Marshall Sahlins captured the zeitgeist with his assessment of the Palaeolithic hunter-gathers as the "original affluent society" (1974).

Sahlins's thesis has been the subject of a great deal of critique and counter-critique. One real problem relates to the phenomenology of time. Quite clearly people now live longer – more than twice as long as their distant ancestors. At the same time, it seems clear also that people in modern societies suffer more depression and chronic unhappiness than hunter-gathers. They more frequently experience boredom and neurotic behaviour, and even normal and well-adjusted individuals spend a great deal of time zoning out with the help of screens, fantasy, drugs, and alcohol.

Thus, it could be generalized that whilst much more sensitive to the quantity and allocation of time, modern societies are perhaps less sensitive to the quality of time. It is a ubiquitous sensation among human beings that time speeds up or slows down depending on things such as attention and engagement. It is also true that highly individuated modern personalities that are more hermetically self-contained and one-step removed from the sensual, collective, and immersive warp and weft of traditional group identity and work/play rhythms seem to have a more self-aware and detached view of time as a finite resource, "passing," and to be used or lost. So although it is indisputable that modern people live somewhat longer, it is not possible to be sure that their *subjective experience* of longevity corresponds to a cornucopian feeling of temporal abundance. A small-scale traditional society might well refer to a forty-year-old as "an elder"—and for such an individual death is likely to be closer at hand than for a youthful fifty-year-old in a modern society. But in phenomenological terms, the comparison just doesn't make sense. In subjective terms, the experience of the elder of a long life, of the birthing and nurturing of multiple generations and of an appropriate time for death may all engender greater life satisfaction and much less anxiety about "time passing."

Implications: In a "three-legged" political economy and culture rooted in livelihood, some household/community productive and subsistence activity will be re-embedded in encompassing forms of religion, spirituality, culture, and ritual, in other words the symbolic reproduction of society and the cosmos in the warp and weft of everyday life. In this context, affective and psychological drivers of behaviour may become more focused on the quality and meaning of relationships in the present, rather than, for instance, escapist forms of consumption bought on the back of a heavily discounted ecological future. Any informalization and decommodification of productive activity would likely have the effect of loosening the temporal connectivity that ties together myriad activities across all areas of life and between different communities spread out across the globe (for instance with "just in time" production and distribution schedules). Looser and more autonomous temporalities relating to different activities might allow a shift away from the tyrannical fungibility of the clock and hourglass expressed in the epithets "time is money" and the "sands of time." In the field of health, this includes less anxiety about time wasted and greater attention to the quality of life and relationship

iii. *Generations, places, and relationships.* A more circular concept of time in premodern societies usually meant that the sequence of generations – ancestors and descendants – was conceived as a flow that was either disconnected from any notion of directional change (let alone progress) in society, or as a non-linear alternation between skipping generations, where daughter was in some way equivalent to grandmother (Fox, 2011). Certainly, the linear Judeo-Christian conception of time linked to the Enlightenment understanding of progress has provided the ontological framework for a process of individualization that makes conceivable the idea of human rights precisely because it valourizes the value of each and every person irrespective of genealogy. But this same conception has undermined and almost eliminated the relational matrix linking not only passing generations but also, by a process of metonymic extension, human communities with non-human persons and entities.

Implications: Precisely this shift was both driven by and a product of the disorganization of place/kin-bound survival units and their replacement by the triad of state/market/individual citizen. To the extent that a re-emerging political economy of livelihood is associated with retrenchment in the scale and scope of market relations in the formal economy and a reduction in the sphere and capacity of state interventions, individuals will once again become dependent on local survival units rooted in neighbour and kin networks woven together by patterns of economic interdependence, reciprocation, a shared ontology reinforced by more/or less intentional ritual practices, and shared common pool resources in a cherished ecological landscape that increasingly takes on the character of a "taskscape" (Ingold, 2000), which is to say a relational matrix in which human (and perhaps non-human) persons, ecological processes, land forms, and aspects of culture are tied together by the web of activities unfolding over time.

iv. *Mortality and death.* A concomitant of a rationalized, individually focused, and scientific/industrial health system is a pattern of disenchantment and ontological insecurity that makes the death-defying emphasis on longevity and cures ever more necessary (whatever the ecological and economic cost), whilst undermining a more relational and perhaps graceful accommodation of death and mortality. Building on the work of Ernest Becker (1973), the field of "terror management theory" (Solomon, this volume) explores the ways in which mortality awareness and anxiety is a driver of human behaviour and culture. There is now good evidence that precisely because modern consumer societies are both disenchanted and highly individualized, traditional cosmologies function much less effectively as both sources of meaning and self-esteem ("hero projects") and a psychological to assuage fear of death ("immortality projects"). In this sense, for Dickinson (2009) narcissistic consumerism has become the default hero-immortality project – the vehicle through which people seek to make life meaningful and death less threatening. The details of this thesis are explored elsewhere (Solomon, this volume; Davy, this volume). However, it is perhaps significant that any re-emergence of kin/place-based survival units in a context of a more livelihood-oriented economy would re-establish very direct ties of reciprocation and meaning both between individuals and between successive generations. Locating the "meaning" of individual lives in the context of this web of relationships extending over time, between people and even with other living entities and ecological processes, would perhaps be conducive to the re-emergence of the kind of meaning frameworks and forms of social integration or hero-immortality projects, much more characteristic of traditional, pre-modern societies.

Implications: A low energy, zero-growth, livelihood-based health system will never be able to deliver the constant improvements and death-defying technical innovations that Western societies have begun to take for granted. On the other hand, to some degree enforced constraint, if channelled the right way, could deliver great improvements in public health – particularly in relation to nutrition and diet, exercise and transport systems, activity and lifestyle. And there is no need to suppose that a zero-growth society would automatically lose all the advances that have come on the back of basic scientific knowledge (germ theory, epidemiology etc.). However, for some classes of disease and accident it seems likely that any significant loss of complexity in the medical health system will be accompanied by greater mortality rates. It may be that death and dying becomes, once again, a more regular feature of human experience in the West. In this context, the possibility of meaning frameworks that allow people to escape the terrifying existential nihilism that seems to be a logical concomitant of the Cartesian "thinking statues" conception of the individual, in other words that the self is a closed entity rattling round the body as a vessel, disconnected from other selves and the cosmos and doomed to oblivion along with the vessel (Elias, 2010, Elias 2011). Similarly, the re-integration of individuals into patterns of living much more regulated by processes of ritual construction of meaning, mutual obligation and perceived commonality of interest/fate would certainly involve a reduction of freedom and a greater experience of constraint, by modern standards. And it is at least a possibility, if not an inevitability, that such a burden would not be borne equally (not least by women, or people with disability, or intellectual non-conformists, etc.). At the same time, it seems also likely that more integration, obligation, and reciprocation would reduce the prevalence of modern mental diseases of affluence – the expression of personality disorders, depression, narcissism, eating disorders, etc. It is possible and even likely that more coherent and consensual (albeit local) vehicles for the garnering of social esteem (recognized social roles; "heroism") and cosmologies focusing at minimum on connection and inter-generational continuity and at most on compelling narratives and rituals of afterlife ("immortality") might in the end make people happier, even in the context of greater prevalence of death and perhaps even physical suffering.

Conclusion: Population Health as *Orlaeg* – The Simultaneous Layering of Healthy Mind and Tissue for the Intergenerational Flow of Individuals

Any significant loss of complexity and reduction in the scale of the global and national economy will certainly have the long-term benefit of reducing the flows of materials and energy in the human economy relative to those of the biosphere as a whole. Possibly in the very long term, this may bring human civilization into some kind of balance with the Earth upon which it depends. But much more immediately, such a transition will destabilize all of the systems of economic, political, social, and health security upon which modern people have come to depend. In this paper, I have attempted to delineate the complex relationship between: the economy and processes of subsistence; the institutions of state and market; the social-psychological construction of individuals; and ontological meaning frameworks through which people make sense of the world and which connect the web of human activities to ecological systems and landscapes. There is no hiding the fact that for the advanced and developing economies alike, the loss of complexity will damage health systems and cause death and suffering from both accident and disease to escalate rapidly, with increasing child mortality and the resurgence of epidemic disease. At the same time, it will curtail the arc of medical-technological progress and our capacity to cheat death and continually to extend life, seemingly beyond any biological limit. Left unchecked, this capacity would surely mean that humanity would have, at some point, to take responsibility for its own demography – a process that has already begun with the increasing acceptability of voluntary euthanasia. The nightmare extensions of this principle are a frequent trope of science fiction (e.g. Anthony Trollope's *The Fixed Period*) – the industrialized homologue of the senicide and infanticide practised by Palaeolithic hunter-gather societies. The spectre of collapse and simplification may spare humanity at least from this political-ethical quagmire.

Imagining a significant re-emergence of livelihood as the embedded "third pole" of political economy, balancing the dyadic tension between market and state, provides at least some indicators as to the possible parameters of an alternative modernity ("the third basin of attraction" intimated in figure P2.1, this volume). Recovering at least some of the warp and weft in the weave of mutual obligation and reciprocation would have the effect of decentring the individual as the exclusive unit of analysis in relation to both epistemology, default scientific methodology, public policy, and ontology. Such a scenario could be associated with a range of significant preventative/public health benefits in relation to the so-called diseases of affluence – particularly the psychological pathologies associated with individualization, rationalization, and the disenchantment of human life, but also the somatic and physiological problems associated with passive and sedentary consumerism, unconstrained dietary choices, etc.

Perhaps the most significant silver lining would relate to the recovery of meaningful work (tied to relationships), meaningful belief systems (tied to shared rituals and mythological narratives, and perhaps organized religion), and integrated households based on traditional nuclear and extended families. This could be summarized as the re-emergence of a matrix of faith, community, family, and meaningful work. This "silver lining" might of course involve also significant losses with regard to freedoms of action, expression, and sexuality that have become normalized and, with good reason, valourized in modern liberal societies. The extent of safeguards and the balance between individual mobility and freedom, the state and the market and constraining institutions of livelihood would depend very much on the extent of any loss of complexity. Intuitively, the sooner Western societies begin to move in this direction, the gentler and the less catastrophic will be the subsequent swing.

Pre-Christian Anglo-Saxon orthopraxy centred on the concept of *orlaeg* (Old Norse *örlög*) that is sometimes translated rather inaccurately as "fate" and is better understood as analogous to karma (Wodening, 2010). Log/laeg relates to the Old Norse *leggja*, to lay down or layer and the prefix *or* relates to something primal. In this way, orlaeg refers to the continual laying down of strata and speaks to the complex ways that, for both individuals and whole communities, the unfolding present builds on the accumulation of deeds and actions in the past (this principle is still reflected in English common law in the form of "precedent"). An individual and a community are associated with a particular accretion or layering of spiritual and relational strength (*maegen* – Wodening, 2011). The closer people or communities are to each other, the more their own accretions will affect each other. At the same time, orlaeg is passed down and inherited by individuals and communities, such that personally and as members of groups, people inherit spiritual strengths but also social-relational and spiritual obligations, not least the imperative to improve the orlaeg that will be passed on.

Moving back into a more relational, reciprocal, and consciously/ritually interwoven form of communal life, underpinned by much stronger processes of mutual identification ("we-identity" – Elias, 2010) and common membership of a very literally understood "survival unit" is likely to significantly change the meaning of (ill) health, medicine, and what counts as success. Population health in an era of degrowth and a political economy tilted towards livelihood might best be conceived as the re-emergence of a conception of orlaeg. The shift from a narrow focus on the individual as separate organism to the relational focus on the flow of generations and community relationships with other species and the landscape writ large will essentially change the rationale for intervention and the benchmarks for success. There will be a greater emphasis on the integrity of local ecological relationships, immediate social relationships and the flow of ecological and spiritual health or maegen over time. It is hard for those on the cusp of change to experience much of this positively. But over the longer term, it may be that an alternative modernity trades reduced longevity for more intense and meaningful lives, greater happiness, more opportunities for effective hero-immortality projects, and less ontological insecurity.

REFERENCES

Anderson, B. R. O'G. (1991). *Imagined communities: Reflections on the origin and spread of nationalism* (Revised and extended ed.). London: Verso.

Beck, U. (1992). *Risk society towards a new modernity*. London; Newbury Park, CA: Sage Publications.

Becker, E. (1973). *The denial of death*. New York: Simon & Schuster.

Berman, M., & Project Muse. (2000). *Wandering God: A study in nomadic spirituality*. Albany: State University of New York Press.

Brooks, S. (2015). Does personal social media usage affect efficiency and well-being? *Computers in Human Behavior, 46*, 26–37. https://doi.org/10.1016/j.chb.2014.12.053

Burke, P. (1995). Viewpoint: The invention of leisure in early modern Europe. *Past & Present, 146*(1), 136. https://doi.org/10.1093/past/146.1.136

Cárdenas-García, J., & Ireland, F. (2017). Human distributed cognition from an organism-in-its-environment perspective. *Biosemiotics, 10*(2), 265–78. https://doi.org/10.1007/s12304-017-9293-8

Conly, J. (2010). Antimicrobial resistance: Revisiting the 'tragedy of the commons.' *Bulletin of the World Health Organization, 88*(11), 805–6. https://doi.org/10.2471/BLT.10.031110

Croezen, S., Avendano, M., Burdorf, A., & van Lenthe, F. (2015). Social participation and depression in old age: A fixed-effects analysis in 10 European countries. *American Journal of Epidemiology, 182*(2), 168–76. https://doi.org/10.1093/aje/kwv015

Dana, L. P., (2007). A humility-based enterprising community: The Amish people in Lancaster County. *Journal of Enterprising Communities: People and*

Places in the Global Economy, 1(2), 142–54. https://doi.org/10.1108
/17506200710752566

Dickinson, J. L., (2009). The people paradox: Self-esteem striving, immortality ideologies, and human response to climate change. *Ecology and Society, 14*(4), 34. https://
doi.org/10.5751/ES-02849-1401346

Elias, N. (2011). *On the process of civilization.* (Revised ed.). Belfield, Dublin:
University College Dublin Press.

Elias, N. (2010). *The society of individuals.* (Revised ed.). Belfield, Dublin: University
College Dublin Press.

Elias, N. (2007). *An essay on time.* (Revised ed.). Belfield, Dublin: University College
Dublin Press.

Elias, N. (2010). *The loneliness of the dying and* Humana conditio. (Revised ed.).
Belfield, Dublin: University College Dublin Press.

Fox, R. (2011). *The tribal imagination.* Boston, MA: Harvard University Press.

Gellner, E. (2008). *Nations and nationalism.* (2nd ed.). Ithaca, NY: Cornell University Press.

Giddens, A. (1991). *Modernity and self-identity: Self and society in the late modern age.*
Cambridge: Polity Press.

Goldstein, J., & Godemont, M. (2003). The legend and lessons of Geel, Belgium: A
1500 year-old legend, a 21st-century model. *Community Mental Health Journal, 39,*
441–58. http://dx.doi.org/10.1023/A:1025813003347

Green, A. (2014). Evaluating distributed cognition. *Synthese, 191*(1), 79–95. https://doi
.org/10.1007/s11229-013-0305-1

Griggs, D., Stafford-Smith, M., Gaffney, O., Rockström, J., Ohman, M. C.,
Shyamsundar, P., Steffen, W., Glaser, G., Kanie, N., & Noble, I. (2013). Policy:
Sustainable development goals for people and planet. *Nature, 495*(7441), 305–7.
https://doi.org/10.1038/495305a

Habermas, J. (1975). *Legitimation Crisis.* Boston, MA: Beacon Press.

Habermas, J. (1990). Discourse ethics: Notes on a program of philosophical justification. In Lenhart, C. (Trans.) and Nicholson, S.W. (Ed.). *Moral consciousness and
communicative action.* (pp. 43–115). Cambridge: MIT Press.

Hankivsky, E. (2014). Intersectionality 101. Retrieved from http://vawforum-cwr.ca
/sites/default/files/attachments/intersectionallity_101.pdf

Harvey, D. (1989). *The condition of postmodernity: An enquiry into the origins of cultural change.* Cambridge, MA: Blackwell

Hess, A. (2007). The social bonds of cooking: Gastronomic societies in the Basque
Country. *Cultural Sociology, 1,* 383–407. https://doi.org/10.1177/1749975507082056

Inês Cosme, R. S., & O'Neill, D.W. (2017). Assessing the degrowth discourse: A review
and analysis of academic degrowth policy proposals. *Journal of Cleaner Production,
149,* 321–34. https://doi.org/10.1016/j.jclepro.2017.02.016

Ingold, T. (2000). *The perception of the environment.* London, UK: Routledge.

Isaacson, R. (2004). *The healing land: The bushmen and the Kalahari desert.* New York:
Grove Press.

Jellison, K. (2014). Research note: Amish women and the household economy during the great depression. *Mennonite Quarterly Review, 88*(1), 97.

Joas, H. (2013). *The sacredness of the person. New genealogy of human rights.* Washington, DC: Georgetown University Press.

Katz, R. (1982). Accepting 'boiling energy.' *Ethos, 10*(4), 344–68. https://doi .org/10.1525/eth.1982.10.4.02a00050

Kish, K. (2018). Ecological economic development goals: Reincorporating the social sphere in ecological economic theory and practice. (Doctoral dissertation). Retrieved from https://uwspace.uwaterloo.ca/handle/10012/13199

Kish, K., & Quilley, S. (2017). Wicked dilemmas of scale and complexity in the politics of degrowth. *Ecological Economics, 142*, 306–17. https://doi.org/10.1016/j .ecolecon.2017.08.008

Laing, R. D. (1962). *The divided self.* London, UK: Penguin Books, Ltd.

Laskowski, M. (2016). Nudging towards vaccination: A behavioral law and economics .approach to childhood immunization policy. *Texas Law Review, 94*(3), 601–28.

Locke, J. (1996). *An Essay Concerning Human Understanding.* Winkler, K.P. (Ed.). Indianapolis, IN: Hackett Publishing Company. (Original work published 1689).

Lottieri, C. (2011). Toward a truly free market: A distributist perspective on the role of government, taxes, health care, deficits, and more. *Journal of Markets & Morality, 14*(1), 221.

Loyal, S., & Quilley, S., (2018). *State power and asylum seekers in Ireland.* New York, NY: Springer.

Low, C. (2008). *Khoisan medicine in history and practice.* Köln: Rüdiger Köppe Verlag.

MacIntyre, A. (1998). *A short history of ethics.* (2nd ed.). London and New York: Routledge & Kegan Paul.

Malinowski, B. (2013). *Argonauts of the Western Pacific: An account of native enterprise and adventure in the Archipelagoes of Melanesian New Guinea.* Long Grove, IL: Waveland Press. (Original work published 1922)

Marmot, M.G., Sapolsky, R. (2014). Of baboons and men: Social circumstances, biology, and the social gradient in health. In M. Weinstein & M. A. Lane (Eds), *Sociality, hierarchy, health: Comparative biodemography.* Washington, DC: The National Academies Press.

Marshall, L. (1969). The medicine dance of the !Kung bushmen. *Journal of the International African Institute, 39*(4): 347–81. https://doi.org/10.2307/1157382

Marshall, T. H. (1950). *Citizenship and social class: And other essays.* Cambridge, UK: Cambridge University Press.

Mead, G. H. (1934). *Mind, self, and society.* Morris, Charles W. (Ed.). Chicago, IL: University of Chicago Press.

O'Neill, D., Fanning, A. L., Lamb, F., & Steinberger, J. K. (2018). A good life for all within planetary boundaries. *Nature Sustainability, 1*, 88–95. https://doi.org /10.1038/s41893-018-0021-4

Ong, W. (2002). *Orality and literacy: The technologizing of the word.* (2nd ed.) New York: Routledge.

Ophuls, W. (2011). *Plato's revenge: Politics in the age of ecology.* Cambridge, MA: MIT Press.

Parmet, W. (2011). The individual mandate: Implications for public health law. *The Journal of Law, Medicine & Ethics, 39*(3), 401–13. https://doi.org /10.1111/j.1748-720X.2011.00610.x

Pinker, S. (2002). *The blank slate: The modern denial of human nature.* New York, NY: Viking Penguin.

Polanyi, K. (1957). *Trade and market in the early empires; Economies in history and theory.* Polanyi, K., Arensberg, C.M., & Pearson, H.W. (Eds). Glencoe, IL: Free Press.

Polanyi, K. (1964). *The Great Transformation.* Boston: Beacon Press.

Polanyi, K. (1968). *Primitive, archaic, and modern economies; Essays of Karl Polanyi.* Dalton, George (Ed.). Garden City, NY: Anchor Books.

Putnam, R. D. (2000). *Bowling alone: The collapse and revival of American community.* New York: Simon & Schuster. https://doi.org/10.1145/358916.361990

Quigley, E. M. (2013). Gut bacteria in health and disease. *Gastroenterol Hepatol (NY), 9*(9): 560–9.

Quilley, S. (2009). The land ethic as an ecological civilizing process: Aldo Leopold, Norbert Elias, and environmental philosophy. *Environmental Ethics, 31*(2), 115–34. https://doi.org/10.5840/enviroethics200931215

Quilley, S. (2012). System innovation and a new 'Great Transformation': Re-embedding economic life in the context of de-growth. *Journal of Social Entrepreneurship, 3,* 206–29. http://dx.doi.org/10.1080/19420676.2012.725823

Quilley, S. (2013). De-growth is not a liberal agenda: Relocalisation and the limits to low energy cosmopolitanism. *Environmental Values, 22*(2), 261–85. https://doi.org /10.3197/096327113X13581561725310

Quilley, S. (2014). Navigating the Anthropocene: Environmental politics and complexity in an era of limits. In P.A. Victor & B. Dolter (Eds), *Handbook on Growth and Sustainability* (pp. 439–70). Cheltenham, UK: Edward Elgar.

Rees, W. (2005). Contemplating the abyss. *Nature, 433*(7021), 15–16. https://doi.org /10.1038/433015a

Ross, L. & Nisbett, R. E. (1991). *The person and the situation: Perspectives of social psychology.* Philadelphia: Temple University Press.

Sahlins, M. (1974). The original affluent society. *Ecologist, 4*(5), 181.

Sender, R., Fuchs, S., & Milo, R. (2016). Are we really vastly outnumbered? Revisiting the ratio of bacterial to host cells in humans. *Cell, 164*(3): 337–40. https://doi.org /10.1016/j.cell.2016.01.013

Scott, J. C. (1998). *Seeing like a state: How certain schemes to improve the human condition have failed.* New Haven, CT; London: Yale University Press.

Sekulova, F., Kallis, G., Rodriguez-Labajos, B., & Schneider, F. (2013). Degrowth: From theory to practice. *Journal of Cleaner Production, 38*(1), 1–6. https://doi.org /10.1016/j.jclepro.2012.06.022

Seligman, A. B. (2010). Ritual and sincerity: Certitude and the other. *Philosophy and Social Criticism, 36*(1), 9–39. https://doi.org/10.1177/0191453709348416

Singer, P. (1990). *Animal liberation* (2nd ed.). New York, NY: New York Review of Books.

Sloan-Wilson, D. (2002). *Darwin's cathedral: Evolution, religion, and the nature of society*. Chicago, IL: University of Chicago Press.

Sommerlad A., Ruegger, J., Singh-Manoux, A., Lewis, G., Livingston, G. (2018). Marriage and risk of dementia: Systematic review and meta-analysis of observational studies. *Journal of Neurol Neurosurg Psychiatry, 89*, 231–8. https://doi .org/10.1136/jnnp-2017-316274

Song, J. (2017). Global and regional impact of antimicrobial resistance: A tragedy of the commons. *International Journal of Antimicrobial Agents, 50*(S1), S4–S5. https:// doi.org/10.1016/S0924-8579(17)30340-0

Spash, C. (2012). New foundations for ecological economics. *Ecological Economics, 77*(C), 36–47. https://doi.org/10.1016/j.ecolecon.2012.02.004

Steffen, W., Crutzen, P., & McNeill, J. (2007). The Anthropocene: Are humans now overwhelming the great forces of nature? *Ambio, 36*(8), 614–21. https://doi.org /10.1579/0044-7447(2007)36[614:TAAHNO]2.0.CO;2

Titmuss, R. M. (1958). *Essays on the Welfare State.*

Thomas, E. M. (2006). *The old way.* New York: Sarah Crichton Books.

Thompson, E. (1967). Time, work-discipline, and industrial capitalism, *Past & Present, 38*(1), 56–97. https://doi.org/10.1093/past/38.1.56

Trainer, T. (2013, November 4). *Why a consumer society can't fix the climate.* Bulletin of the Atomic Scientists.

Turner, G. (2012). On the cusp of global collapse? Updated comparison of the limits to growth with historical data. *Gaia, 21*(2), 116–24. https://doi.org/10.14512 /gaia.21.2.10

Twenge, J. (2010). *The narcissism epidemic: Living in the age of entitlement.* New York: Atria.

Watkins, J. W. N. (1968). Methodological individualism and social tendencies in Brodbeck, May, *Readings in the philosophy of the social sciences.* London, UK: Macmillan.

Weber, E. (1976). *Peasants into Frenchmen: The modernization of rural France, 1870–1914.* Stanford, Calif.: Stanford University Press.

Weber, M. (1964). *The sociology of religion.* Fischoff, E. (Trans.) and Winckelmann, J. (Ed.). (4th ed.). Boston, MA: Beacon Press.

Weiner, M. S. (2013). *The rule of the clan: What an ancient form of social organization reveals about the future of individual freedom.* New York: Farrar, Straus and Giroux.

Wōdening, E. (2011). *We are our deeds: The elder heathenry.* (2nd ed.). Baltimore, MD: White Marsh Press.

Wodening, S. (2010). *Hammer of the gods. Anglo Saxon paganism in modern times.* California: CreateSpace.

Wolfe, N. D., Dunavan, C. P., & Diamond, J. (2012). Origins of major human infectious diseases. In *Improving food safety through a one health approach: Workshop summary.* Washington, DC: National Academies Press. Available from https://www.ncbi.nlm .nih.gov/books/NBK114494

2 "Regional Overload" as an Indicator of Profound Risk: A Plea for the Public Health Community to Awaken

COLIN DAVID BUTLER

The History and Courage of Public Health

In medicine, public health is the sub-discipline charged with protecting human well-being on a large-scale population level by identifying health risks and then developing and implementing effective strategies to lower such dangers. Public health roots can be traced for millennia to practices and principles identified in Mesopotamia, Greece, India, and China (Porter, 1999). Indigenous public health practices and insights, though less well documented, are also likely to be ancient (Colomeda and Wenzel, 2000, McNeill, 1976).

Public health challenges that have long been recognized and grappled with, though not universally, include contaminated water, vermin such as rats, and contagious diseases, including leprosy and plague. The fact that visitors from afar can introduce novel diseases was recognized over six centuries ago by authorities in trading ports such as Venice, leading to the practice of quarantine (Gensini, Yacoub, and Conti, 2012).

Public health workers have a long history of promoting new paradigms and tackling vested interests, often with great difficulty and against strong opposition. Their theories and campaigns can take decades to be successful, even at a regional scale. One such paradigm is infectious diseases. According to Burns (2007), the existence of particles as the cause of disease had been suspected in Roman times. In 1546, Fracastoro (1478–1553), born in Verona, published *De Contagion*, which proposed that infection resulted from tiny particles or "spores" that could be spread by direct or indirect contact, through infected objects, or even by air (Konteh, 2009). It may thus be regarded as the first treatise on the germ theory (Howard-Jones, 1977). But this idea took centuries to displace the miasma theory, an alternative hypothesis that proposed indiscriminate contagion from vapours, with a burden of disease that could thus not be alleviated by hand washing, boiling drinking water, or lowering the groundwater level by drainage (although the later technique was tried).

The success of ideas in public health also often depends on co-mingled, co-evolving economic and technological determinants, waves of ideas and fashions in which public health ideas sometimes successfully surf, but sometimes vanish or even drown. One such idea that eventually succeeded in nineteenth-century Britain, then the most technologically advanced nation on Earth, and also the richest, was of widespread urban sanitation (Konteh, 2009). But this too was initially resisted (Szreter, 1997).

The challenge that global resource scarcity poses to public health can be likened to the germ theory in the age of miasmas, or of smoking in the 1950s. Enthusiasts recognize it, but the majority of researchers have other preoccupations. Technology and socioeconomic circumstances are evolving in ways that both threaten and provide hope that a new, sustainable paradigm can take firm root, but to date public health workers do not sufficiently recognize either the urgency or the opportunity.

Inequality, Neoliberalism, Globalization, and the Ecological Rift

Another deep problem, related and tenacious, is of economic and other forms of inequality, now on a planetary scale. Until the nineteenth-century poverty was almost universal, other than for aristocrats (including in ancient empires) and some Indigenous peoples (Sahlins, 1972). Inequality, therefore, was comparatively low, globally. But today, perhaps 20 per cent of the population experiences a level of material affluence that would once have caused royalty to be envious. As few as eight people own the same wealth as half of the world's population (OxFam, 2017). These eight people (and, of course, other ultrawealthy) exert vastly disproportionate influence over economic and political policy in many countries. While some appear socially liberal, and while two (Bill Gates and Warren Buffett) make a substantial effort to improve global health, only one (Buffett) is known for any attempt to promote a fairer tax system (Buffett, 2011; Urry, 2013). Most of the world's wealthiest people seem to favour the reverse: ongoing reductions in personal and company taxes, further erosion of public goods, and minimum wages in exchange for private wealth used for gated communities and other systems of security for a diminishing proportion.

Few of the world's richest eight (and far too few of the world's wealthiest 20 per cent) seem to have a deep understanding of the ecological and climatic peril that civilization faces. They are instead either openly opposed (often funding overt and covert programs to undermine environmental protection), indifferent, or prefer technological, rather than more fundamental solutions. Bill Gates, though claiming to be "passionate about fighting global warming" has been criticized for his support of "energy moonshots" (Voss, 2016) such as advanced nuclear technologies (Friedman, 2018) rather than mitigation or fossil fuel divestment (Howard, 2015).

Entrepreneurs, governments, and other wealthy actors in developing countries and emerging markets (including Russia and China) are claimed to illicitly transfer about a trillion US dollars each year to clandestine tax havens (Spanjers and Foss, 2015). Although this amount is contested, it is undoubtedly high (Nitsch, 2016). A high-level panel chaired by former South African prime minister Thabo Mbeki reported a lower (proportionate) illicit figure for transfers from Africa, though still at least US$50 billion per annum (Joint African Union Commission/United Nations Economic Commission for Africa, 2015). Even this is considerable, given the poverty of Africa. Such funds are diverted from development and poverty alleviation (Abayomi 2018).

An estimated 8 per cent of the world's financial wealth is hidden from tax (Alstadsæter, Johannesen, and Zucman, 2018). However, while many denounce, with justification, the economic doctrine of neoliberalism (hyper-capitalism) (George, 1999) as a deep underlying cause for inequality and unsustainability (Benatar, Upshur, and Gill, 2018; Rose and Cachelin, 2018), it is important to realize that autocratic societies such as Russia and Saudi Arabia also contribute extensively to ecological and climatic disruption. Are such countries neoliberal? Even if they are defined as such, communist countries in Eastern Europe also had poor environmental records.

Attributing either neoliberalism or capitalism (Foster, Clark, and York, 2010) as the sole, or even the dominant cause of our peril may be simplistic. Other contributing factors are evolutionary. For example, humans appear (with good reason) to have evolved to better confront immediate and tangible threats rather than those that are conceptual and far away (Ornstein and Ehrlich, 1989). While the threat of climate change is increasingly proximate to those who closely follow the issue, for others it seems likely to be only an occasional thought, such as during a heatwave or the wildfire season. Limits to growth, more broadly, was probably better understood in high-income populations during the first oil crisis of the 1970s than it has been since. Another evolutionary factor persists in modern forms of tribalism (or "groupism"). Many groups with which people closely identify today are orders of magnitude greater than for hunter-gatherers. But these groups are not yet global. Insights from game theory, such as those involving the iterated prisoner's dilemma (Press and Dyson, 2012) and theory of mind (Johnson and Berring, 2006), suggest that cooperation can continue to evolve, but there is still far to go.

But, perhaps as an outcome of these evolutionary (as well as cyclic) factors, in recent decades, the dominance of neoliberalism in the world's richest nations has captured many academics, universities, and journals, inhibiting the voices of theorists who have tried to stress the importance of natural capital to human well-being and enduring economic wealth (Daly, 2013; Butler and Higgs, 2018). The roots of neoliberalism ("liberalism") can be traced to the eighteenth century, rearising in the 1940s, in reaction to the more collective, higher-taxing environment in the US under President Roosevelt's New Deal, and in much of Western Europe (Butler, 2000; Labonté and Stuckler, 2016). However, neoliberalism (of which an earlier form of comparatively unregulated capitalism existed in parts of the nineteenth century) needed a milieu in which to (again) take root. This was first provided by the economic crisis known as "stagflation" in the 1970s, triggered in large part by the rise in the oil price, led by the Organization of Petroleum Exporting Countries (OPEC).

The oil price hike can be interpreted as an attempt to create a fairer world, as most OPEC countries were poor, selling an irreplaceable natural resource far too cheaply, mainly to far wealthier populations. Indeed, the global income distribution may have recently stabilized (rather than becoming even more unequal) but if so, at a level of inequality that is far more unequal than in any country (Butler, 2000; Milanovic, 2013). However, although the rising oil price led to large monetary inflow to countries such as Saudi Arabia, few oil-rich nations in the Global South have been able to generate enduring, distributed prosperity.

The British sociologist Simon Szreter has likened the receptivity of the expanding middle class in high-income countries to neoliberal doctrines to a naive prospector's deception by fool's gold (1997). As neoliberalism strengthened, it provided increasing opportunities for its beneficiaries to cement and to magnify their advantage, a process called the "Matthew effect," by which gains accrued to those who already have (Wade, 2004). An example is the Glass-Steagall Act (1993), lobbied for for years by Citigroup and other players in the financial services industry (Merino et al., 2010). In so doing, US president Clinton reversed legislation introduced during the Depression that had restricted the capacity of US banks to speculate. This reversal was a key step in incubating the 2008 global financial crisis (Merino et al., 2010). The global dominance of neoliberalism was also reinforced by the collapse of the Soviet Union and its vassals in Eastern Europe, which eroded the countering power of an alternative ideology to capitalism.

Neoliberalism has long been forecast, by its critics, to erode social harmony (Polanyi, 1944). An increasing number of critics are pointing to approximately forty years of neoliberal dominance and growing inequality in the US and elsewhere as a contributor to the demise of neoliberalism to be followed by either neo-fascism or – perhaps – a fairer form of capitalism. For example, the African American philosopher and social critic Cornel West called the presidency of Barack Obama the last gasp of neoliberalism, replaced by a "neofascist bang" (West, 2016). A former US secretary of state, Madeline Albright, has also warned of the re-emergence of fascism in countries from the US to Turkey and Venezuela (Albright and Woodward, 2018). With a few exceptions, such as in California, the US under President Trump shifted American policies even further from an ecological perspective and towards deepening inequality and worsening social tension, both domestically and globally (Agence France-Presse, 2018).

Global Environmental Resource Scarcity, Planetary Overload, and Malthus

Although the threat to global public health from resource scarcity and the social reaction to it is barely visible within public health circles, some of its many manifestations have been recognized. Like the fable about the four blind men who feel different parts of an elephant, these identified protuberances include ecological public health (Lang and Rayner, 2012), ecosystem health (Rapport, 1989), ecohealth (Wilcox et al., 2004), climate change and health (Butler, 2014), one health (Zinsstag et al., 2011), and planetary health (Whitmee et al., 2015; Butler, 2017; Prescott and Logan, 2018). Tropical medicine has evolved to be called international health and, more recently, global health, a term interpreted by some as distinct through its stress on the impact of global phenomena (such as trade or climate change) on the health of vulnerable populations, even though some live in high-income enclaves in the Global North (McMichael, 2014). There is also widespread awareness, within public health, of the threat arising from nuclear war, which has seen the awarding of two Nobel Peace prizes to health-related lobby groups.[1]

In this chapter I argue that none of these emerging sub-disciplines fully integrate the risk to global health from the coalition of factors that public health worker Tony McMichael identified in 1993 in his book *Planetary Overload* (1993). McMichael, in turn, was influenced by ideas long known but brilliantly popularized by Thomas Robert Malthus initially in "The Principle of Population" (1798), with five following editions. This work, partly written to refute the optimism in a then-recent publication of the Marquis de Condorcet, underpinned the theory of evolution, jointly proposed sixty years later by Darwin and Wallace (1858).

Central to the evolutionary conceptualization of competition and limits is the idea that all species, often in cooperating groups, struggle to survive and to increase in number and size at the expense of other species and groups (Nekola et al., 2013). Furthermore, such struggle, cooperation, and competition are often among the same species, and is particularly clear in the case of our own.

Earth is limited, not only in size, but in resources. Human population exceeds 7.5 billion, and the rapidity of this rise is as relevant as the total number. If global population had been over seven billion for centuries (as it might conceivably be on a habitable planet the size of Jupiter), then it could more reasonably be considered sustainable, although resource crises could still occur.

But human population has more than doubled in the last 50 years, and still rises by at least 80 million people per annum (Population Reference Bureau, 2016).

The pressure of human numbers and the resulting "consumption bomb" (Butler, 1997) has not only depleted Earth's resources, but has done so with a speed that might be even more alarming if the average human lifespan were not so brief. The speed of population growth has also reduced or made impossible the poverty-alleviating benefit of the "demographic dividend," the acceleration of per capita economic growth that can result from a population structure with fewer dependents, especially of children (Campbell et al., 2007).[2] At the same time, rapid population growth has enhanced the risk of "demographic entrapment" (King, 1990).[3] We are in novel territory, relying on old maps and outdated civilizational paradigms.

Biodiversity and forests have been sacrificed and converted for the human enterprise, but so too have enormous quantities of non-living materials, not only fossil fuels (oil, coal, gas) but others, including phosphorus, rare earths, and, in many places, groundwater and river flows (Butler, 2009). This transformation has profound and ominous consequences to human health, as yet barely realized (Butler, 2016a).

Key Concepts and Caveats

The chapter next briefly reviews the debate between pessimists and optimists and the concept of risk multiplication, contrasted with the "strawman" of environmental determinism. It then discusses regional overload in the context of emerging planetary overload. Here, detail is provided for the case that many recent global conflicts and famines can and should be conceptualized as having common roots, with disturbing implications. Figure 2.1 presents the key arguments in this chapter.

There are several caveats. One is to acknowledge that these arguments will dissatisfy critics whose a priori position is to reject Malthusian arguments and to argue that limits to growth are far away, that human progress is more or less unstoppable. The chief concept introduced (regional overload) is poorly understood in the literature, except, perhaps in military studies. Regional overload could benefit from neologisms, but instead are here divided into two main forms.

The chapter relies on a selective literature review to support a series of arguments. The topics are from too many disciplines for a systematic literature review. The chapter scarcely mentions empirical studies, partly because of their scarcity (in addressing the issues discussed), and also because I have come to distrust them as suitable tools to examine the questions considered.[4]

The views in this chapter are rare within public health, and even the broader literature. That is remarkable, given the gravity of the issues in question. This scarcity in part reflects the inherent bias to hope and optimism in the human mind (Sharot, 2011),[5] and particularly to those in power.

Table 2.1   Historical examples of "Malthusian checks." History is replete with crises, many of which lead to reductions in population and can be called malignant Malthusian checks.[6] Some examples listed here are discussed in the text.

	Past	Current, very recent	Future
War, famine, disease, flight (sometimes panics)	Black Death (fourteenth century), First World War & influenza pandemic	Violent civil wars in South Sudan, Yemen, Somalia (all ongoing), Rwandan genocide (1994)	South Asian famine and conflict
	Irish famine, emigration (c. 1848–52)	Syrian civil war, mass migration to Europe from Syria and many parts of the Sahel and Sub-Saharan Africa	Gulf states heat crisis and emigration, island emigration, coastal retreat
Non-integration	Expulsion of Jews from Iberia (late fourteenth century)	Rohingya (Myanmar), Israeli expulsion of 20,000 Africans, Australia's off-shore detention of asylum seekers (contrary to the refugee convention, which it has ratified), US ban on entry to some Muslims	US expulsion of Hispanics/Muslims; forced "repatriation" of many Africans from Europe; expulsion of Muslims from Assam, India (already threatened)
Gradual decline	Greenland Norse at start of Little Ice Age (fourteenth century)	Russian fall in life expectancy 1990s, Venezuelan crisis (contemporary)	Decline in culturally homogenous, egalitarian populations, avoiding civil war
Multi-system	Bronze Age collapse (twelfth century BCE)	Sahel crisis, terrorism in Europe, many reactions to it	Reduced trade, multi-civilizational retreat, heralding new Dark Age

Optimists Debate Pessimists

A recent book (Mann, 2018a) contrasts the ecologist William Vogt, author of *Road to Survival* (1948) with the agricultural scientist Norman Borlaug, though without noting that Borlaug, like Vogt, was deeply concerned about human population size. In turn, Paul Ehrlich, author of *The Population Bomb*, has credited Vogt with his own interest in environmentalism, after reading his book while attending high school (Lewis, 1995).[7]

Mann credits Vogt with founding what Betsy Hartmann, a fierce critic of population "control" (Hartmann, 1987) called "apocalyptic environmentalism." Mann defines this as the belief "that unless humankind drastically reduces consumption and limits population, it will ravage global ecosystems" (2018b). But this definition is mild. It might be better phrased as the view that the long-term "human carrying capacity" (Butler, 2004) of the global ecosystem is lower than 7.5 billion, hence, sooner if not later, global population will decline through catastrophic

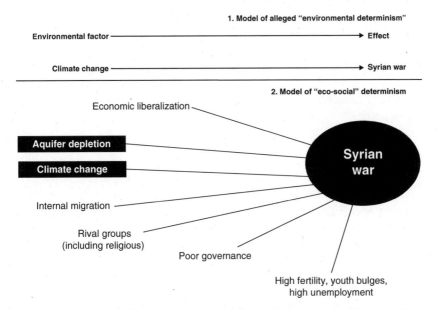

Figure 2.1 "Eco-social" determinism as it applies to the Syrian war, as one of many potential case studies, contrasted with models of alleged "environmental determinism." Several competing models are used to explain the arising of complex social phenomena, such as conflict. According to the "environmental determinist" caricature, an environmental factor such as climate change completely causes or "determines" an event, even one as complex as war. The preferred "eco-social" explanation is one in which multiple ecological, environmental, and social factors interact. The seven factors listed above as contributing to the Syrian war are themselves simplified because they all continually interact with each other. Finally, note that economic liberalization is a synonym for neoliberalism.

increases in mortality, with widespread chaos and suffering. Minimizing this possibility should be central to the agenda of the public health profession.

Other articles and books in this genre (Desrochers and Hoffbauer, 2009) have compared the highly optimistic "cornucopian" Julian Simon against both Ehrlich, the best-known living exponent of apocalyptic environmentalism (Ehrlich and Ehrlich, 2013) and Norman Myers (Myers and Simon, 1994).

The debate that Mann and others describes extends far beyond these scholars, and can be heated. Optimists sometimes seek to discredit forecasts of future collapse by quoting ancient warnings as evidence of false prophecy or "crying wolf." However, numerous counter-examples for the cornucopian argument can be found (Taylor and Tainter, 2016). Irrespective of whether the *Epic of Gilgamesh* warned against deforestation in Mesopotamia, it is now known that salinity (likely contributed to by deforestation and irrigation) contributed to the reduction in wheat yields, its replacement with barley (Jacobsen and Adams, 1958) and the eventual dissolution of the Sumerian civilization. China too has experienced many famines and periods of population decline over its long-documented history (Zhang et al., 2007). These examples are a tiny sample from an enormous pool.

Climate Change, Conflict, and Risk Multiplication

In 2018, the impact of anthropogenic global warming upon the Earth system, though substantial, is still minor compared to the predictions for later this century. The manifestations resulting from increased concentrations of heat-trapping atmospheric molecules are numerous, from extreme weather events such as increased flooding in some regions, drought in others (at the time of writing, the people in the South African city of Cape Town have been placed on a daily quota of 50 litres of water, barely sufficient for drinking, cooking, washing, and sanitation) (Gleick, 1996), and, in a growing number of locations, intensifying inundation from the rising ocean. Heatwaves are also already causing substantial harm to health, and in some regions to crops and livestock (Butler and McFarlane, 2018). In future, heatwaves could make substantial parts of South and Southwest Asia uninhabitable (Im, Pal, and Eltahir, 2017; Pal and Eltahir, 2016).

There is also growing acceptance that climate change can be conceptualized as influencing all extreme weather events, rather than them being "all or none" phenomena (Rahmstorf and Coumou, 2011). For example, while it cannot be said that climate change, acting alone, "caused" the 2017 Houston flood associated with Hurricane Harvey, it can be said that climate change increased its likelihood and severity, including through sea-level rise (Rahmstorf, 2017). Other anthropogenic factors also worsened the flooding, including the paving of grasslands, which increased run-off.

Finally, there is growing acceptance that environmental factors, sometimes including climate change, act as "risk multipliers," influencing complex "eco-social" phenomena, such as conflict, migration, and famine. Among numerous examples of these phenomena are conflicts in Syria (Kelley et al., 2017; Gleick, 2014), parts of the Sahel (Potts, Henderson, and Campbell, 2013) and Afghanistan (Schleussner et al., 2016).

In this conceptualization, environmental and ecological factors interact with social determinants, including those that are economic, demographic, and political, to produce these complex phenomena (Bowles, Butler, and Morisetti, 2015). This contrasts with the assertions by some authors that to link climate change and other environmental factors with social endpoints such as conflict is "environmental determinism" (Buhaug et al., 2014; Butler, 2017; Butler and Kefford, 2018). To exclude environmental factors from the explanatory model could be called "social determinism," a simplification as flawed as environmental determinism is alleged to be (see figure 2.1).[8]

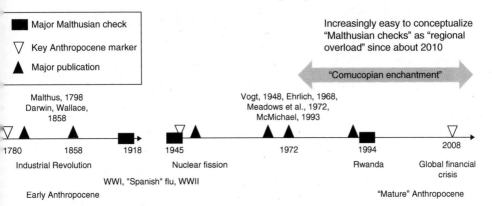

Figure 2.2 Malthusian checks timeline. This chapter proposes that many recent malignant Malthusian checks can be conceptualized as early warnings of "planetary overload," which, should it occur, may trigger a new global dark age.

Regional Overload

In 2016 I coined and published the term "regional overload" (Butler, 2016b), developing the idea that "sentinel" cases may foreshadow global civilization retreat or even collapse (Butler, 2016a). The phrase is derived from the title of "Planetary Overload" (McMichael, 1993). Although I, together with many pessimists, argue that the overload of Earth with an ingenious but rapacious human species is now well advanced, it has not yet reached a stage where the collapse of civilization is either inevitable or extremely close (though it could happen this century).

If planetary overload is to occur, then it is most unlikely to emerge evenly in space and time. It is more likely early signals will be detected. There are an increasing number of potential examples; in addition to Syria and Afghanistan (mentioned above) they include conflicts (sometimes with famine) in Myanmar, Yemen, and many parts of Africa (see tables 2.1 and 2.2).

I propose that regional overload can be classed into either of two groups: past (type A) and emergent (type B). If the idea of regional overload, *as a near precursor of planetary overload*, (type B) is to be accepted then it may also be useful to establish criteria to distinguish it from previous malignant Malthusian checks; the myriad other conflicts, famines, genocides, and pestilences of the past that have resulted in significant loss of population.[9] Some preliminary principles are listed in table 2.3.

Table 2.2 Contemporary and recent examples of regional overload. Not all necessarily presage global collapse. The burden of disease of HIV/AIDS in Sub-Saharan Africa (SSA) has now reduced, though it could be re-inflamed by regional economic collapse and deepen any future crisis.[10] The 1994 genocide in Rwanda, even if repeated there, need not have global significance. However, its brutality could be echoed in other parts of the world.

Example	Water scarcity	Falling fossil fuel income	Anthropogenic climate change (strong signal)	Famine	High fertility rate
Dem. Rep. Congo	no	no	no	yes	yes
Myanmar	no	no	no	no	yes
Nigeria (NE)	yes	no	possible	yes	yes
Rwanda	no	no	no	no	yes
South Sudan	no	yes	no	yes	yes
Sub-Saharan Africa HIV/AIDs	no	no	no	"new variant"	yes
Syria	yes	yes	probable	no	yes
Venezuela	no	yes	no	no	?
Yemen	yes	yes	no	yes	yes

In this chapter, regional overload is mainly discussed in the context of tightening global limits to growth (see figure 2.3). But it is clear that there are many earlier cases that could potentially illustrate regional overload (see figure 2.1 and table 2.2). Cases of regional overload may also be classed as malignant Malthusian checks.[11] Of these older cases, the well-documented degeneration of the Easter Island civilization is one of the best known (Diamond, 1994; Diamond 2007), irrespective of the role of rats (a species introduced by Polynesians) in deforestation, the time of human arrival, or the undoubted additional harm arising through European contact and colonisation (Hunt, 2006; Stephenson et al., 2015).

Strictly, a "malignant" Malthusian check refers to reduction in population, arising through war, famine, epidemic, or emigration. But Malthus also recognized the possibility of preventive ("benign") checks, such as through delayed marriage or family planning. Some putative cases of regional overload result in comparatively few deaths, at least to date. Perhaps the clearest contemporary example is in Venezuela, which is, at the time of writing, experiencing riots, failing health care, data gaps, and increased rates of infant and maternal mortality (Fraser, 2018; Bello et al., 2018). In part this is from its recent political strategies, including corruption (Warf and Stewart, 2016). Even though the country has vast oil reserves, at current world prices they are not very profitable, as they take the form of tar sands, with low net energy (Hall and Klitgaard, 2011). Cuba has also experienced a decline in living standards, following its loss of support from the Soviet bloc.

Table 2.3   Potential causes of past and contemporary regional overload, classed as type A and B. The causal factors listed are incomplete.

Regional overload			
Type A: pre-1945		Type B: post-1945 (mature Anthropocene)	
Risk multiplier			
Resource scarcity, including of fossil fuel, but only since c. 1900		Proximity to planetary boundary (e.g. anthropogenic climate change, fresh-water scarcity), fossil fuel scarcity, high population growth, ecological loss	
Black Death	climate change, crop failure	**Ebola in West Africa**	high fertility, poverty, deforestation
Invasion of New World	new technologies, opportunities, in part motivated by fewer opportunities in the Old World	**Syrian civil war**	climate change, aquifer depletion, complex (see figure 2.1)
Irish potato famine and emigration	crop failure, inadequate relief	**South Sudanese war, famine**	high fertility, limited oil revenue, tribalism, kleptocracy, inadequate relief
Bronze Age collapse (twelfth century BCE)	linked disappearance of several Eastern Mediterranean civilizations; loss of tin a factor	**Global civilizational decline under "business as usual?"**	severe or even runaway climate change, multi-factorial limits to growth crisis, low net energy, soil depletion, pollinator loss

However, it has avoided the chaos and trauma seen in Venezuela, in part through its culture of sharing, sacrifice, and resilience, albeit imperfect (Morris, 2014).

I propose that the confluence, pattern, and common causes of recent, current, and future cases of regional overload (even if some examples are rejected as too speculative) should signify to public health workers, and to wider society, that we may already be in a declining phase of civilization. A parallel, explicitly recognized as relevant to contemporary times, is the linked events in antiquity that heralded the end of the Bronze Age, for example described in the book *1177 B.C.: The Year Civilization Collapsed* (Cline, 2014). Cline points out that in that time a cascade of linked events occurred in the Eastern Mediterranean, Egypt, and the Middle East. He regards "systems failure" as the most plausible explanation, analogous to how I would describe the Syrian conflict; that is, far more than climate change, though climate change may be a contributor.

Today, several cases of regional overload are coalescing, such as migration from Sub-Saharan Africa via Libya to Europe, and the political and other changes in response, including rising xenophobia in Italy, Hungary, and elsewhere in Europe. Other shared causes related to the scarcity of physical resources and lost revenue, such as diminishing oil revenues in Yemen (Breisinger et al., 2011), South Sudan (de Waal, 2014), and Venezuela (Wang and Li, 2016). These events are not yet overwhelming in scale, but the risk to global security is perceived by some military theorists[12] and sociologists (Centeno et al., 2015).

I have developed this theory after decades of observation and participation in the optimist-pessimist debate (Butler, 1994), and through growing concern that the escape from scarcity, long forecast by optimists during the "cornucopian enchantment" (Butler, 2007) may be elusive. I reason that if the optimists are broadly correct, then Earth should not, at the time of writing, be home to five major famines.[13] On the road to progress and sustainability, one or even two contemporary famines might be considered regrettable but acceptable, but surely not five. In addition, civil wars and other forms of insecurity have generated a steep increase in the number of displaced people, especially since 2012, another suggested indicator of contemporary regional overload (United Nations High Commissioner for Refugees, 2017).

Malthusian Checks and Tolerance

I have argued that the central concept of both kinds of regional overload can reasonably be termed as Malthusian, even though the ideas did not originate with him. One consequence of the work of Malthus that informs evolutionary theory is especially controversial. This is the interaction between environmental and social limits. For example, European "colonizers" of Tasmania (then called Van Diemen's Land) in the early nineteenth century tried to corral every Indigenous person then alive on the island (Taylor, 2013).[14] This occurred even though the Indigenous population was tiny (as few as eight thousand) and even though, by introducing new animals and crops, Europeans had enormously expanded the number of human beings who could be fed from the island's resources. In nineteenth-century Tasmania, ample physical ("natural") resources existed to support the combined population of Europeans and Tasmanians. What was lacking was sufficient tolerance.[15]

There are many other comparatively recent examples of conflict, sometimes genocide, between European farmers and Indigenous gatherer-hunters (Adhikari, 2017). In the US, buffalo herds were deliberately hunted to demoralize Indigenous people and to usurp their resources, especially fertile land (Hixson, 2013). In 1851, the governor of California stated: "A war of extermination will continue to be waged ... until the Indian race becomes extinct ... the inevitable destiny of the race is beyond the power or wisdom of men to avert" (Madley, 2004).

Coexistence between disparate groups sharing almost the same location occurs, but is not invariable. Where different groups do coexist it is usually because of strict control, such as in China (Ringen, 2016) or modern Rwanda (Reyntjens, 2015), or in democracies that offer shared vision and tolerable distribution of physical resources, freedom, and political power.

If natural resources are abundant, populations can grow rapidly, with considerable individual freedom and tolerance for some outsiders, such as for non-English speaking European migrants to America. However, even in the nineteenth century tolerance of some groups in the US (African Americans, Chinese, as well as Indigenous Amerindians) was limited. As with Tasmania, ample resources existed in the US to feed all these peoples. But while some in these other groups endured, they did so in straightened circumstances and (for the Indigenous and initially the Chinese) in small numbers.

In a less "full" world (Daly, 2013) some victors can tolerate vanquished peoples to be banished, or escaping to endure harsher conditions, such as the Indigenous Jhummas of the hilly district in southern Bangladesh (Shapan, 2007), or even as landless sea nomads in the Indonesian seas (Kusuma et al., 2017). In today's fuller world, the Chittagong Hill Tracts are being increasingly peopled by Bengali lowlanders,[16] while in China, the Han Chinese are colonizing Tibet, even though they lack the Tibetan genetic adaptations for high altitude (Beall et al., 2001). And, in an increasing number of countries with common land borders, walls are being planned or constructed to obstruct migration.[17]

It has been hypothesized that conformity and self-defence within groups, bonded emotionally or by other means such as shared history, language, religion, and belief has evolved, promoted and regulated by neurotransmitters such as oxytocin (De Dreu and Kret, 2016). In some cases, this shared behaviour may extend to extreme intolerance and even attempted or completed genocide against the other, perceived accurately or not, as a threat.

Self-sustaining mass violence is common, once conflict is well underway. Consider the tragedy and brutality of the US Civil War and the two World Wars, which, once started, led to temporarily unstoppable waves of revenge. However, extreme group violence and even genocide can sometimes erupt from the kindling of small events that in other cases may fizzle out. An example of such an inferno is the 1994 Rwandan genocide, where population pressure in the context of two major, mutually distrustful groups (Hutu and Tutsi) led, within weeks, to the death of at least 10 per cent of the population (André and Plateau, 1998). A contemporary example is the civil war in South Sudan, waged with brutal terror largely between two Christian tribes (Dinka and Nuer) (de Waal, 2014). Another is the expulsion of almost a million Rohingya from Myanmar in late 2017 (Beyrer and Kamarulzaman, 2017).

In all of these cases, and countless others, sufficient physical resources exist at the start of the conflict to feed, house, and clothe all parties, were they shared. But the social glue to share these resources between competing groups is lacking.[18] However, once war starts, physical and other resources to avert famine and epidemic can easily be damaged, such as by the burning of villages and crops, the bombing of concrete dwellings and the mining of fields. Hospitals and health workers are sometimes targeted, ports bombed or blockaded and aid convoys hijacked. These actions increase suffering, and may reach sufficient scale to substantially reduce populations – Malthusian checks, arising via regional overload.

Tolerance, Thresholds, and the Fallacy of Garret Hardin

Tolerance can thus be considered as a limited resource, just as fossil fuels, fresh water, and fertile soil are. But this statement should not be interpreted as support for ethnic cleansing, although some writers, influenced by their interpretation of Malthus (and social Darwinism) have written articles that can be interpreted in this way, such as by Garret Hardin (Hardin, 1974). One problem with the "lifeboat" strategy Hardin advocates is that it assumes the fortress strategy is indefinitely sustainable. It may, instead, be a recipe for endless resentment and tension.[19]

A recent example of the exhaustion of local tolerance is the decision, taken in Israel, to expel approximately twenty thousand African migrants, currently living precarious lives in Tel Aviv. In a radio interview in February 2018, Professor Sabel commented how, initially, such migrants were welcomed with compassion and understanding (Radio National, 2018). But, lacking education, language, and other skills, most could neither integrate nor contribute meaningfully to the economy. While a few may have been welcomed as cheap, undocumented labour, the social tolerance for them was limited. This follows many previous examples in Israel, Ireland, and elsewhere (Lentin and Moreo, 2015), though this may be the largest expulsion as yet from Israel. But even if populations are closely related, sharing similar beliefs, conflict can still erupt, although before then, during subsistence crises, desperate methods may be preferred to increase food production with violence as a last resort, such as what appears to have been the case at Easter Island (Diamond, 2007).

Regional Overload and Limits to Growth

Above, I have suggested that there are two forms of regional overload, of which one (type B) is a possible precursor to planetary overload. Although McMichael was influenced by Malthus, another important influence on his work was "The Limits to Growth" (LTG) (Meadows et al., 1972). This report, dense with charts and ridiculed by conservative economists, struck a surprising chord with its

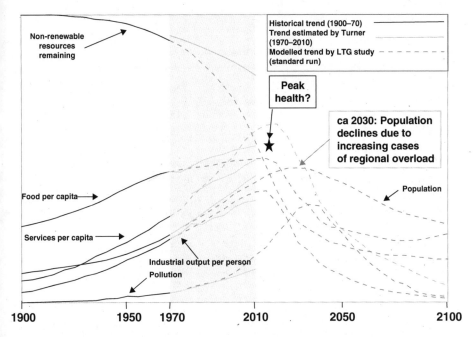

Figure 2.3 Standard run of the limits to growth. Adapted from Turner, this figure suggests population may decline this century.

audience, and is still the best-selling environmental book of all time (Parenti, 2012). It explored the complex interactions between human civilization and the physical world under a range of assumptions. These assumptions ranged from a "business as usual" scenario to one in which population stabilized, production was halted and advanced technologies were extensively applied to reduce pollution. In this model only, the human project continued without global crisis, that is without significant planetary overload, and (using the theory in this chapter) with little more than the background rate of regional overload.

But the LTG found that "business as usual" would collide with limits in the second half of the current century, triggering a reduction in population. In 2008 and 2014 Turner published reports that compared the LTG projections with data that had accrued since 1972, finding a close consistency between the standard run (business as usual) and data until 2010 (see figure 2.3) (Turner, 2014). The LTG did not speculate how global population would decline this century, but an increasing frequency and severity of regional overload, including, perhaps, limited nuclear war (Xia et al., 2015) is one mechanism. If these predictions are broadly correct, then planetary overload is already unfolding, though scarcely recognized as such.

Conclusion

This chapter has proposed the theory that many indicators of regional overload, such as the growing number of wars, famines and displaced people, signify an emerging crisis, planetary in scale. There are many reasons for the scarcity of analysis of these issues. One is the bias within most public health fields towards problems in high-income settings (a consequence amplified by neoliberalism). Publications on (for example) public health in non-urban South Sudan are rare, and data-rich papers almost non-existent, due in part to the difficulties of safely obtaining these data. This leads to a reinforcing cycle where there is little market or appetite for such analysis, and where any such papers, if submitted, may be rejected.

A related impediment is of disciplinary boundaries (or lenses) and wariness of the "academic other," generating disrespect and difficulty in publishing and winning grants. There is also a failure of academic institutions and health funders, overwhelmingly embedded in a milieu of neoliberal signals and incentives, to recognize the need for a new paradigm to emerge, if humanity is to thrive in this and coming centuries.

The conceptualization of regional overload is an attempt to awaken an increasingly exhausted, hostile, patrolled and indifferent world, including within public health, to the reality and risk of planetary overload and nearing limits to growth. Managerial solutions to these risks are inadequate. Although a daunting task, transformation is necessary, at many levels. Of these levels, conceptual transformation is perhaps the most important. Global civilization is in peril and its current trajectory must be changed.

ACKNOWLEDGMENTS

I thank Drs Carol Colfer and Jane O'Sullivan for their extremely helpful comments.

NOTES

1 In 1985 and 2017.
2 This term has been criticized; it is difficult to disentangle the elements that contribute to the demographic transition, such as education, confidence children will survive, and improved human rights, from the benefits that accumulate to health and infrastructure, such as from smaller families and less crowded, better equipped schools and a more favourable dependency ratio.
3 These concepts argue that high population growth rates impede economic take-off, except in unusual and short-lived settings that have a large spare human "carrying capacity" (Butler, 2004). Examples of the latter are the rapidly expanding territory

of the US in the late 1800s, and in Australia in the decades following the Second World War.

4   Such as regression studies examining climate change and conflict, or population growth rates and development. In my opinion, the methods are too crude and the data often dubious.

5   Sharot states: "the optimism bias ... is one of the most consistent, prevalent, and robust biases documented in psychology and behavioral economics" (2011, p. R491).

6   Darwin and Wallace (1858) repeatedly used the term "check," as well as referring to Malthus.

7   Mann lists several authors preceding Vogt, who, writing soon after the First World War also warned of overpopulation.

8   A recent editorial in *Nature* (Anonymous, 2018) about climate change and conflict was subtitled "Many studies that link global warming to civil unrest are biased and exacerbate stigma about the developing world." The same editorial stated that: "Climate change is never the sole cause of war, violence, unrest or migration" without making it clear that there are no such papers, this is the "straw man," easy to knock over.

9   Older malignant checks are not here considered as precursors. Although they may indicate regional overload, they are too distant in time. The possibility of regional overload at the *planetary* scale is recent.

10 Some may struggle to conceptualise HIV/AIDS in Sub-Saharan Africa (SSA) as regional overload. However, the low standard of public health and education there contributed to the very high burden of disease from HIV/AIDS and the delayed response to it, both of which lowered life expectancy. Compare, for example, the social response to HIV/AIDS in the gay community in the US, which was much more rapid among an educated, affluent, and motivated population. Other social factors also magnified the scale of the epidemic in SSA. "New variant famine" was coined to describe the phenomenon of food insecurity due to so many ill and dead farmers lost from HIV/AIDS.

11 Although the work of Malthus has been unpopular, in some circles, since its publication, its most central idea that all species compete for resources (the idea that underpins evolution) is as accepted as other key scientific principles, such as gravity.

12 I have participated in military meetings in three countries, under Chatham and Lancaster House rules. I cannot reveal identities, but my themes have credence in these circles.

13 Democratic Republic of Congo, northeastern Nigeria, Somalia, South Sudan, and Yemen.

14 They were unsuccessful. However, disease and demoralization saw the demise of all genetically "pure" Tasmanians by the 1890s. Today, however, thousands identify as Indigenous Tasmanians, descendants of intermarriage.

15 Diseases such as smallpox and measles contributed to the Tasmanian demise, but so too did collective despair, from loss of land and lifestyle.

16 And perhaps Rohingya.

17 Such as the US, India, Myanmar (both with Bangladesh), Israel and Gaza and the West Bank (with plans to extend this underground), and in parts of Europe, such as Austria with Italy and Hungary with Serbia.

18 Claims are made, perhaps valid, that one group is more aggressive, refusing to accept the status quo. This then may lead to retaliation. Truth is the first casualty of war and independent verification is rare. What is clear, however, is the reality of insufficient tolerance.

19 The walls (physical and virtual) need maintenance; the guardians need funding and motivating. There is a risk of militarization and "coarsening" of the entire community within the fortress who share a common fear and hatred of the "other."

REFERENCES

Abayomi, O. (2018). Comparing the illicit financial flows in some African countries: Implications for policy. *African Journal of Economic Review, 6*(2), 72–195.

Adhikari, M. (2017). Invariably genocide? When hunter-gatherers and commercial stock farmers clash. *Settler Colonial Studies, 7*(2), 192–207. https://doi.org/10.1080/2201473X.2015.1096864

Agence France-Presse. (2018). Trump 'almost sent tweet that North Korea would have seen as warning of attack.' *The Guardian*. Retrieved from https://www.theguardian.com/us-news/2018/sep/10/trump-almost-sent-tweet-north-korea-imminent-attack

Albright, M., & Woodward, B. (2018). *Fascism: A warning*. New York: HarperCollins.

Alstadsæter, A., Johannesen, N., & Zucman, G. (2018). Who owns the wealth in tax havens? Macro evidence and implications for global inequality. *Journal of Public Economics, 162*, 89–100. https://doi.org/10.1016/j.jpubeco.2018.01.008

André, C., & Platteau, J.-P. (1998). Land relations under unbearable stress: Rwanda caught in the Malthusian trap. *Journal of Economic Behavior and Organization, 34*(1), 1–47. https://doi.org/10.1016/S0167-2681(97)00045-0

Anonymous. (2018). Don't jump to conclusions about climate change and civil conflict. *Nature, 554*, 275–6. https://doi.org/10.1080/00263206.2013.850076

Beall, C. M., Laskowski, D., Strohl, K. P., Soria, R., Villena, M., Vargas, E., Maria Alarcon, A., Gonzales, C., & Erzurum, S. C. (2001). Pulmonary nitric oxide in mountain dwellers. *Nature, 414*, 411–12. https://doi.org/10.1038/35106641

Bello, R. J., Damas, J. J., Marco, F. J., & Castro, J. S. (2018). Venezuela's health-care crisis. *The Lancet, 390*(10094), 551. https://doi.org/10.1016/S0140-6736(17)31831-7

Benatar, S., Upshur, R., & Gill, S. (2018). Understanding the relationship between ethics, neoliberalism and power as a step towards improving the health of people and our planet. *The Anthropocene Review, 5*(2), 155–76. https://doi.org/10.1177/2053019618760934

Beyrer, C., & Kamarulzaman, A. (2017). Ethnic cleansing in Myanmar: The Rohingya crisis and human rights. *The Lancet, 390*(10102), 1570–3. https://doi.org/10.1016/S0140-6736(17)32519-9

Bowles, D. C., Butler, C. D., & Morisetti, N. (2015). Climate change, conflict, and health. *Journal of the Royal Society of Medicine, 108*(10), 390–5. https://doi.org /10.1177/0141076815603234

Breisinger, C., Diao, X., Collion, M.-H., & Rondot, P. (2011). Impacts of the triple global crisis on growth and poverty: The case of Yemen. *Development Policy Review, 29*(2), 155–84. https://doi.org/10.1111/j.1467-7679.2011.00530.x

Buhaug, H., Nordkvelle, J., Bernauer, T., Böhmelt, T., Brzoska, M., Busby, J. W., Ciccone, A., Fjelde, H., Gartzke, E., Gleditsch, N. P., Goldstone, J. A., Hegre, H., Holtermann, H., Koubi, V., Link, J. S. A., Link, P. M., Lujala, P., O'Loughlin, J., Scheffran, C., Schilling, J., Smith, T. G., Theisen, O. M., Tol, R. S. J., Urdal, H., & von Uexkull, N. (2014). One effect to rule them all? A comment on climate and conflict. *Climatic Change, 127*(3–4), 391–7. https://doi.org/10.1007/s10584-014-1266-1

Buffett, W. E. (2011). Stop coddling the super-rich. *The New York Times.* Retrieved from http://www.teamsters952.org/NYT_Stop_Coddling_the_Super-Rich.pdf

Burns, H. (2007). Germ theory: Invisible killers revealed. *BMJ, 334*(suppl 1), s11. https://doi.org/10.1136/bmj.39044.597292.94

Butler, C. D. (1994). Overpopulation, overconsumption, and economics. *The Lancet, 343*, 582–4. https://doi.org/10.1016/S0140-6736(94)91526-1

Butler, C. D. (1997). The consumption bomb. *Medicine Conflict and Survival, 13*(3), 209–18. https://doi.org/10.1080/13623699708409341

Butler, C. D. (2000). Inequality, global change and the sustainability of civilisation. *Global Change and Human Health, 1*(2), 156–72. https://doi.org /10.1023/A:1010029222095

Butler, C. D. (2004). Human carrying capacity and human health. *Public Library of Science Medicine, 1*(3), 192–4. https://doi.org/10.1371/journal.pmed.0010055

Butler, C. D. (2007). Globalisation, population, ecology and conflict. *Health Promotion Journal of Australia, 18*(2), 87–91.

Butler, C. D. (2009). Food security in the Asia-Pacific: Climate change, phosphorus, ozone and other environmental challenges. *Asia Pacific Journal of Clinical Nutrition, 18*(4), 590–7.

Butler, C. D., ed. (2014). *Climate change and global health.* Wallingford, UK; Boston, US: CABI.

Butler, C. D. (2016a). Sounding the alarm: Health in the Anthropocene. *International Journal of Environmental Research and Public Health, 13*, 665. https://doi.org /10.3390/ijerph13070665

Butler, C. D. (2016b). Planetary overload, limits to growth and health. *Current Environmental Health Reports, 3*(4), 360–9. https://doi.org/10.1007 /s40572-016-0110-3

Butler, C. D. (2017). Limits to growth, planetary boundaries, and planetary health. *Current Opinion in Environmental Sustainability, 25*, 59–65. https://doi .org/10.1016/j.cosust.2017.08.002

Butler, C. D., & Higgs, K. (2018). Health, population, limits and the decline of nature. In Marsden, Terry (Ed.), *The Sage Handbook of Nature*, pp. 1122–49. London: Sage.

Butler, C. D., & Kefford, B. J. (2018). Climate and conflict: Magnifying risks. *Nature,* 555, 587. https://doi.org/10.1038/d41586-018-03795-0

Butler, C. D., & McFarlane, R. A. (2018). Climate change, food security and population health in the Anthropocene. In DellaSala, D. A. (Ed.), *Encyclopaedia of the Anthropocene,* pp. 453–9. Amsterdam: Elsevier.

Campbell, M., Cleland, J., Ezeh, A., & Ndola, P. (2007). Return of the population growth factor. *Science, 315,* 1501–2. https://doi.org/10.1126/science.1140057

Centeno, M. A., Nag, M., Patterson, T. S., Shaver, A., &, Windawi, J. A. (2015). The emergence of global systemic risk. *Annual Review of Sociology, 41*(1), 65–85. https://doi.org/10.1146/annurev-soc-073014-112317

Cline, E. H. (2014). *1177 B.C. The year civilization collapsed.* Princeton: Princeton University Press.

Colomeda, L. A., & Wenzel, E. R. (2000). Medicine keepers: Issues in Indigenous health. *Critical Public Health, 10*(2), 243–56. https://doi.org/10.1080/713658247

Daly, H. (2013). A further critique of growth economics. *Ecological Economics, 88,* 20–4. https://doi.org/10.1016/j.ecolecon.2013.01.007

Darwin, C., & Wallace, A. (1858). On the tendency of species to form varieties; and on the perpetuation of varieties and species by natural means of selection. *Journal of the Proceedings of the Linnean Society of London. Zoology, 3*(9), 45–62. https://doi.org/10.1111/j.1096-3642.1858.tb02500.x

De Dreu, C. K.W., & Kret, M. E. (2016). Oxytocin conditions intergroup relations through upregulated in-group empathy, cooperation, conformity, and defense. *Biological Psychiatry, 79*(3), 165–73. https://doi.org/10.1016/j.biopsych.2015.03.020

de Waal, A. (2014). When kleptocracy becomes insolvent: Brute causes of the civil war in South Sudan. *African Affairs, 113*(452), 347–69. https://doi.org/10.1093/afraf/adu028

Desrochers, P., & Hoffbauer, C. (2009). The post war intellectual roots of the population bomb. *The Electronic Journal of Sustainable Development, 3*(1).

Diamond, J. M. (1994). Ecological collapses of ancient civilizations: The golden age that never was. *Bulletin of the American Academy of Arts and Sciences, XVLII*(5), 37–59. https://doi.org/10.2307/3824451

Diamond, J. M. (2007). Easter Island revisited. *Science, 317,* 1692–4. https://doi.org/10.1126/science.1138442

Ehrlich, P. R., & Ehrlich, A. H. (2013). Can a collapse of global civilization be avoided? *Proceedings of the Royal Society B: Biological Sciences, 280*(1754). https://doi.org/10.1098/rspb.2012.2845

Foster, J. B., Clark, B., & York, R. (2010). *The ecological rift: Capitalism's war on the earth.* New York, NY: NYU Press.

Fraser, B. (2018). Data reveal state of Venezuelan health system. *The Lancet, 389*(10084), 2095. https://doi.org/10.1016/S0140-6736(17)31435-6

Friedman, E. A. (2018). Bill Gates in search of nuclear nirvana. *Scientific American.* Retrieved from https://blogs.scientificamerican.com/observations/bill-gates-in-search-of-nuclear-nirvana/

Gensini, G. F., Yacoub, M. H., & Conti, A. A. (2012). The concept of quarantine in history: From plague to SARS. *Journal of Infection, 49*(4), 257–61. https://doi .org/10.1016/j.jinf.2004.03.002

George, S. (1999). *The Lugano report: On preserving capitalism in the twenty-first century.* London: Pluto Press.

Gleick, P. H. (1996). Basic water requirements for human activities: Meeting basic needs. *Water International, 21,* 83–92. https://doi.org/10.1080/02508069608686494

Gleick, P. H. (2014). Water, drought, climate change, and conflict in Syria. *Weather, Climate, and Society, 6*(3), 331–40. https://doi.org/10.1175/wcas-d-13-00059.1

Hall, C. A. S., & Klitgaard, A. (2011). *Energy and the wealth of nations.* New York: Springer.

Hardin, G. (1974). Lifeboat ethics: The case against helping the poor. *Psychology Today.* Retrieved from http://www.garretthardinsociety.org/articles/art_lifeboat_ethics _case_against_helping_poor.html

Hartmann, B. (1987). *Reproductive rights and wrongs; the global politics of population control.* Boston, MA: South End Press.

Hixson, W. L. (2013). 'They promised to take our land and they took it': Settler colonialism in the American West. In Hixson, Walter L. (Ed.) *American Settler Colonialism: A History,* pp. 113–44. New York: Palgrave Macmillan US.

Howard, E. (2015). Bill Gates calls fossil fuel divestment a 'false solution.' *The Guardian.* Retrieved from: https://www.theguardian.com/environment/2015/oct /14/bill-gates-calls-fossil-fuel-divestment-a-false-solution.

Howard-Jones, N. (1977). Fracastoro and Henle: A re-appraisal of their contribution to the concept of communicable diseases. *Medical History, 21*(1), 61–8.

Hunt, T. L. (2006). Rethinking the fall of Easter Island. *American Scientist, 94* (Sept.–Oct.), 412–19. https://doi.org/10.1017/S0025727300037170

Im, E.-S., Pal, J. S., & Eltahir, E. A. B. (2017). Deadly heat waves projected in the densely populated agricultural regions of South Asia. *Science Advances, 3*(8). https:// doi.org/10.1126/sciadv.1603322

Jacobsen, T., & Adams, R. M. (1958). Salt and silt in ancient Mesopotamian agriculture. *Science, 128,* 1251–8. https://doi.org/10.1126/science.128.3334.1251

Johnson, D., & Bering, J. (2006). Hand of God, mind of man: Punishment and cognition in the evolution of cooperation. *Evolutionary Psychology, 4,* 219–33. https://doi.org/10.1177/147470490600400119

Joint African Union Commission/United Nations Economic Commission for Africa (AU/ECA). (2015). Report of the high level panel on illicit financial flows from Africa. Retrieved from: https://www.uneca.org/sites/default/files/PublicationFiles /iff_main_report_26feb_en.pdf

Kelley, C., Mohtadi, S., Cane, M., Seager, R., & Kushnir, Y. (2017). Commentary on the Syria case: Climate as a contributing factor. *Political Geography, 60,* 245–7. http:// dx.doi.org/10.1016/j.polgeo.2017.06.013

King, M. (1990). Health is a sustainable state. *The Lancet, 336,* 664–7. https://doi.org /10.1016/0140-6736(90)92156-C

Konteh, F. H. 2009. Urban sanitation and health in the developing world: Reminiscing the nineteenth century industrial nations. *Health & Place, 15*(1), 69–78. https://doi.org/10.1016/j.healthplace.2008.02.003

Kusuma, P., Brucato, N., Cox, M. P., Letellier, T., Manan, A., Nuraini, C., Grangé, P., Sudoyo, H., & Ricaut, F.-X. (2017). The last sea nomads of the Indonesian archipelago: Genomic origins and dispersal. *European Journal of Human Genetics, 25*, 1004. https://doi.org/10.1038/ejhg.2017.88/jrn

Labonté, R., & Stuckler, D. (2016). The rise of neoliberalism: How bad economics imperils health and what to do about it. *Journal of Epidemiology and Community Health, 70*, 312–18. https://doi.org/10.1136/jech-2015-206295

Lang, T., & Rayner, G. (2012). Ecological public health: The 21st century's big idea? *BMJ, 345*, e5466. https://doi.org/10.1136/bmj.e5466

Lentin, R., & Moreo, E. (2015). Migrant deportability: Israel and Ireland as case studies. *Ethnic and Racial Studies, 38*(6), 894–910. https://doi.org/10.1080/01419870.2014.948477

Lewis, C. H. (1995). Ehrlich, Paul. In Paehlke, R. C. (Ed), *Conservation and environmentalism: An encyclopedia*. London: Fitzroy Dearborn Publishers.

Madley, B. (2004). Patterns of frontier genocide 1803–1910: The Aboriginal Tasmanians, the Yuki of California, and the Herero of Namibia. *Journal of Genocide Research, 6*(2), 167–92. https://doi.org/10.1080/1462352042000225930

Malthus, T. R. (1798). *An essay on the principle of population.* London: J. Johnson.

Mann, C. C. (2018a). *The wizard and the prophet: Two remarkable scientists and their dueling visions to shape tomorrow's world.* New York: Alfred A. Knopf.

Mann, C. C. (2018b). Can planet earth feed 10 billion people? *The Atlantic.* Retrieved from https://www.theatlantic.com/magazine/archive/2018/03/charles-mann-can-planet-earth-feed-10-billion-people/550928

McMichael, A. J. (1993). *Planetary overload. Global environmental change and the health of the human species.* Cambridge: Cambridge University Press.

McMichael, A. J. (2014). Climate change and global health. In Butler, C. D. (Ed.), *Climate Change and Global Health*, pp. 11–20. Wallingford, UK: CABI.

McNeill, W. H. (1976). *Plagues and peoples.* (1st ed.) Garden City, NY: Anchor Press.

Meadows, D., Meadows, D., Randers, J., & Behrens III, W. W. (1972). *The limits to growth.* New York: Universe Books.

Merino, B. D., Mayper, A. G., & Tolleson, T. D. (2010). Neoliberalism, deregulation and Sarbanes-Oxley: The legitimation of a failed corporate governance model. *Accounting, Auditing & Accountability Journal, 23*(6), 774–92. https://doi.org/10.1108/09513571011065871

Milanovic, B. (2013). Global income inequality in numbers: In history and now. *Global Policy, 4*(2), 198–208. https://doi.org/10.1111/1758-5899.12032

Morris, E. (2014). Unexpected Cuba. *New Left Weekly, 88*, 4–45.

Myers, N., & Simon, J. L. (1994). *Scarcity or abundance? A debate on the environment.* New York: W.H. Norton.

Nekola, J. C., Allen, C. D., Brown, J. H., Burger, J. R., Davidson, A. D., Fristoe, T. S., Hamilton, M. J., Hammond, S. T., Kodric-Brown, A., Mercado-Silva, N., & Okie, J. G. (2013). The Malthusian-Darwinian dynamic and the trajectory of civilization. *Trends in Ecology & Evolution, 28*(3), 127–30. https://doi.org/10.1016/j.tree.2012.12.001

Nitsch, V. (2016). Trillion dollar estimate: Illicit financial flows from developing countries. *Darmstadt Discussion Papers in Economics, 227.* Retrieved from: https://www.econstor.eu/handle/10419/141281.

Ornstein, R., and E., Paul. (1989). *New world, new mind.* London: Methuen.

OxFam. (2017). Just 8 men own same wealth as half the world. Retrieved from https://www.oxfam.org/en/pressroom/pressreleases/2017-01-16/just-8-men-own-same-wealth-half-world.

Pal, J. S., and Eltahir, E. A. B. (2016). Future temperature in Southwest Asia projected to exceed a threshold for human adaptability. *Nature Climate Change, 6,* 197–200. https://doi.org/10.1038/nclimate2833

Parenti, C. (2012). 'The limits to growth': A book that launched a movement. *The Nation.* Retrieved from https://www.thenation.com/article/limits-growth-book-launched-movement/

Polanyi, K. (1944). *The Great Transformation.* Boston, MA: Beacon Hill.

Population Reference Bureau. (2016). The world population will reach 9.9 billion in 2050, up 33 percent from an estimated 7.4 billion now. Retrieved from: http://www.worldpopdata.org/

Porter, D. (1999). *Health, civilization, and the state: A history of public health from ancient to modern times.* London, UK: Routledge.

Potts, M., Henderson, C., & Campbell, M. (2013). The Sahel: A Malthusian challenge? *Environmental and Resource Economics, 55*(4), 501–12. https://doi.org/10.1007/s10640-013-9679-2

Prescott, S. L., & Logan, A. C. (2018). Larger than life: Injecting hope into the planetary health paradigm. *Challenges, 9*(1), 13. https://doi.org/10.3390/challe9010013

Press, W. H., & Dyson, F. J. (2012). Iterated prisoner's dilemma contains strategies that dominate any evolutionary opponent. *Proceedings of the National Academy of Sciences* (USA), *109*(26), 10409–13. https://doi.org/10.1073/pnas.1206569109

Radio National. (2018). Israel issues deportation notices to African migrants. Retrieved from http://www.abc.net.au/radionational/programs/breakfast/israel-issues-deportation-notices-to-african-migrants/9403492

Rahmstorf, S. (2017). Rising hazard of storm-surge flooding. *Proceedings of the National Academy of Sciences (USA), 114*(45), 11806–8. https://doi.org/10.1073/pnas.1715895114

Rahmstorf, S., & Coumou, D. (2011). Increase of extreme events in a warming world. *Proceedings of the National Academy of Sciences (USA), 108*(44), 17905–9. https://doi.org/10.1073/pnas.1101766108

Rapport, D. J. (1989). What constitutes ecosystem health? *Perspectives in Biology and Medicine, 33*(1), 120–32. https://doi.org/10.1353/pbm.1990.0004

Reyntjens, F. (2015). *Political governance in post-genocide Rwanda.* Cambridge and New York: Cambridge University Press.

Ringen, S. (2016). *The perfect dictatorship: China in the 21st century.* Hong Kong: Hong Kong University Press.

Rose, J., & Cachelin, A. (2018). Critical sustainability: Incorporating critical theories into contested sustainabilities. *Journal of Environmental Studies and Sciences, 8*(4), 518–25. https://doi.org/10.1007/s13412-018-0502-9

Sahlins, M. D. (1972). *Stone age economics.* Chicago: University of Chicago Press, Walter De Gruyter.

Schleussner, C.-F., Donges, J. F., Donner, R. V., & Schellnhuber, H. J. (2016). Armed-conflict risks enhanced by climate-related disasters in ethnically fractionalized countries. *Proceedings of the National Academy of Sciences, 113*(33), 9216–21. https://doi.org/10.1073/pnas.1601611113

Shapan, A. (2007). Migration, discrimination and land alienation: Social and historical perspectives on the ethnic conflict in the Chittagong Hill Tracts of Bangladesh. *Contemporary Perspectives, 1*(2), 1–28. https://doi.org/10.1177/223080750700100201

Sharot, T. (2011). The optimism bias. *Current Biology, 21*(23), R941–5. https://doi.org/10.1016/j.cub.2011.10.030

Spanjers, J., & Håkon Frede, F. (2015). Illicit financial flows and development indices: 2008–2012. *Global Financial Integrity.* Retrieved from https://www.gfintegrity.org/wp-content/uploads/2015/05/Illicit-Financial-Flows-and-Development-Indices-2008-2012.pdf

Stevenson, C. M., Puleston, C. O., Vitousek, P. M., Chadwick, O. A., Haoa, S., & Ladefoged, T. N. (2015). Variation in Rapa Nui (Easter Island) land use indicates production and population peaks prior to European contact. *Proceedings of the National Academy of Science* (USA), *112*(4), 1025–30. https://doi/10.1073/pnas.142071211

Szreter, S. (1997). Economic growth, disruption, deprivation, disease and death: On the importance of the politics of public health. *Population and Development Review, 23*(4), 693–728. https://doi.org/10.2307/2137377

Taylor, R. (2013). Genocide, extinction and Aboriginal self-determination in Tasmanian historiography. *History Compass, 11*(6), 405–18. https://doi.org/10.1111/hic3.12062

Taylor, T. G., & Tainter, J. A. (2016). The nexus of population, energy, innovation, and complexity. *American Journal of Economics and Sociology, 75*(4), 1005–43. https://doi.org/10.1111/ajes.12162

Turner, G. M. (2014). *Is global collapse imminent? An updated comparison of the limits to growth with historical data.* Melbourne: Melbourne Sustainable Society Institute, The University of Melbourne.

United Nations High Commissioner for Refugees (UNHRC). (2017). Global Trends Report. Forced Displacement in 2016.

Urry, J. (2013). The rich class and offshore worlds. *Discover Society 3*. Retrieved from https://discoversociety.org/2013/12/03/the-rich-class-and-offshore-worlds/.

Vogt, W. (1948). *Road to survival*. New York: William Sloan.

Voss, S. (2016). We need an energy miracle. *The Atlantic*. Retrieved from http://www.theatlantic.com/magazine/archive/2015/11/we-need-an-energy-miracle/407881/.

Wade, R. H. (2004). On the causes of increasing world poverty and inequality, or why the Matthew effect prevails. *New Political Economy, 9*(1), 163–88. https://doi.org/10.2190/5YLF-X5K4-TGFH-EM56

Wang, Q., & Rongrong, L. (2016). Sino-Venezuelan oil-for-loan deal – The Chinese strategic gamble? *Renewable and Sustainable Energy Reviews, 64*, 817–22. https://doi.org/10.1016/j.rser.2016.06.042

Warf, B., & Sheridan, S. (2016). Latin American corruption in geographic perspective. *Journal of Latin American Geography, 15*(1), 133–55. https://doi.org/10.1353/lag.2016.0006

West, C. (2016). Goodbye, American neoliberalism. A new era is here. *The Guardian*. Retrieved from https://www.theguardian.com/commentisfree/2016/nov/17/american-neoliberalism-cornel-west-2016-election.

Whitmee, S., Haines, A., Beyrer, C., Boltz, F., Capon, A. G., de Souza Dias, B. F., Ezeh, A., Frumkin, H., Gong, P., Head, P., Horton, R., Mace, G. M., Marten, R., Myers, S. S., Nishtar, S., Osofsky, S. A., Pattanayak, S. K., Pongsiri, M. J., Romanelli, C., Soucat, A., Vega, J., & Yach, D. (2015). Safeguarding human health in the Anthropocene epoch: Report of The Rockefeller Foundation – Lancet Commission on planetary health. *The Lancet, 386*, 1973–2028. https://doi.org/10.1016/S0140-6736(15)60901-1

Wilcox, B. A., Aguirre, A. A., Daszak, P., Horwitz, P., Martens, P., Parkes, M., Patz, J. A., & Waltner-Toews, D. (2004). EcoHealth: A transdisciplinary imperative for a sustainable future. *EcoHealth, 1*, 3–5. https://doi.org/10.1007/s10393-004-0014-9

Xia, L., Robock, A., Mills, M., Stenke, A., & Helfand, I. (2015). Decadal reduction of Chinese agriculture after a regional nuclear war. *Earth's Future, 3*(2), 37–48. https://doi.org/10.1002/2014EF000283

Zhang, D. D., Brecke, P., Lee, H. F., He, Y.-Q., & Zhang, J.. (2007). Global climate change, war, and population decline in recent human history. *Proceedings of the National Academy of Sciences, 104*(49), 19214–19. https://doi.org/10.1073/pnas.0703073104

Zinsstag, J., Schelling, E., Waltner-Toews, D., & Tanner, M. 2011. From 'one medicine' to 'one health' and systemic approaches to health and well-being. *Preventive Veterinary Medicine, 101*, 148–56. https://doi.org/10.1016/j.prevetmed.2010.07.003

3 Medicine and Health Care in the Anthropocene: Who Pays and Why?

JENNIFER COLE

Introduction

The aim of this paper is to examine the nature of medicine and health care in the Anthropocene, in particular what exactly we mean by, and should aim to include in, the term "medicine," how this is shaped by the characteristics of the Anthropocene, and what implications this has for "medicine" as we move forward. It will consider how the provision of medicine may need to adapt to specific challenges such as the doubling of the average human lifespan since the Pleistocene, resulting in larger numbers of elderly, less economically active members of society against a socioeconomic context in which financial wealth is the main determinant of health across the life course. As these less contributory members need to be supported from within the existing resources and capital of their society, the paper will explore motivations for providing this support, both within populations and at an international level. The latter is particularly important as geopolitical tensions and conflict threaten to disrupt access to medicine and medical systems at a local level, leaving affected populations dependent on the international community for medical support. Last, by drawing on historical and archaeological evidence along with theories from evolutionary anthropology on the development of compassion, altruism, and cooperation, it will make a case for considering cross-disciplinary approaches to human behaviour in the Anthropocene.

Why Do We Need Medicine?

Before considering how medicine is delivered, it is worth taking a moment to reflect on what requires us to need medicine and health care and how this has changed over the course of Anthropocene history. In pre history, ill health was largely caused by a breakdown or failure of human biological processes in the face of equally biological challenges. From complications during birth, a reflection of the relatively large heads of human infants resulting in a difficult passage through a relatively narrow birth canal (Macfarlane, 2018), through challenges in procuring sufficient nutrition for energy, growth, and maintenance of metabolic functions (Speth and Speilmann, 1983), to countering pathogens that overwhelm our immune system (Rifkin, 2017), our bodies fight a constant battle with nature from conception to death. While current thinking suggests that the upper limit of a natural human lifespan is approximately 120 years (Dong, 2016), in practice only one person in history is known to have lived until their thirteenth decade: the Frenchwoman Jeanne Calment, who died in 1997 at the age of 122. The rest of the human race is constantly picked off by the world around us throughout our lives.

Picture a theoretical cohort of one thousand babies. From the moment they are conceived, nature throws stones of ill health at the cohort. Some do not survive gestation; others die in childbirth; many fall in infancy and early childhood from infectious disease before their immune systems are fully developed, or in older age when it is failing. Others starve when harvests fail, or fall foul of severe cold, heat, or floods. Yet others – though in relatively small numbers – develop cancers, diabetes, and heart disease. The older they get, the more of them simply wear out. Eventually, none are left – long before any come close to 120 years of age.

But, over time, we have developed new tools to fight back against nature. Prehistorical burials with herbs known to have healing qualities, and which may represent early attempts at medicine, date back to the Neolithic (Lietava, 1992) as do early surgical procedures (Ackerknecht, 2016). As farmers and agriculturalists replaced hunter-gatherers to provide a more secure food supply and protection from starvation (Bar-Yosef, 2017), healers also emerged within stratifying human societies to provide protection from disease and sickness (Jùnior, 2018). Over the centuries, we have gradually developed more and more tools with which to ward off illness, just as fire allowed us to ward off cold and spears to ward off predators. The toolbox of the modern physician is vast: ultrasound scanners monitor the health of the unborn child, caesarean section sidetracks labour complications, and antibiotics protect the mother and infant from infection; vaccination protects against many diseases while others have been eradicated entirely (Hervé, 2000); cancer can be diagnosed, treated, and survived (Allemani, 2018), as can diabetes, HIV, and many other forms of ill health. When nature throws stones, we can reach for shields. There is an increasing number of researchers who believe that not only will more people survive until well past 100 years of age, but that artificial genetic modification will soon enable the natural ceiling of a 120-year lifespan to be extended (Ben-Haim et al., 2017).

Against this, however, the environmental damage we are inflicting on the Earth means that nature's arsenal is also growing (Cole, 2018). Crowded urban environments enable new diseases to emerge and old ones to spread more quickly (McMichael, 2001; Weiss, 2004), and air pollution causes millions of deaths each year (Cohen, 2017), as does the modern preference for high-sugar, high-salt, and high-fat diets (Whalen, 2017). Nature is no longer the only stone-thrower: we throw stones at one another, too.

This is particularly tragic when we consider that the tools to ward off ill health cost money. Not everyone can afford an equal array and some cannot afford any at all. Health is strongly correlated with the individual's ability to pay (Deaton, 2003). This in turn is correlated with the social environment in which they live (Marmot, 2005); pollution is worse in poorer environments (Landrigan, 2017) from anthropogenic chemicals and dirt and natural pathogens. The ill health we inflict on the Earth is batted towards those least able to deflect it. Wealth enables the rich to protect themselves from nature's stones and deflect humanity's onto others, creating gulfs of health between populations. Life expectancy at birth is more than eighty years in the world's richest economies, less than fifty in its poorest (Cole, 2018).

We need to keep this inequality in mind as we consider how the medical and health care systems of the Anthropocene are arranged and maintained, and for whom this arrangement is made. The history of human care and compassion that will be explored across this chapter is intertwined with the history of economic development, charity, state provision, and private enterprise. The human endeavour to bargain with nature over our health must acknowledge and accept that nature is no longer our only challenger: for many aspects of our ill health, we have only ourselves to blame. The future of our health will depend on our ability to maintain the health of the environments in which we live. While this chapter focuses on medicine and health care for our bodies, a better health care system for the planet is urgently needed.

How Do We Define "Medicine"?

The Oxford English Dictionary (OLD, 2018) defines medicine as: "The science or practice of the diagnosis, treatment, and prevention of disease (in technical use, often taken to exclude surgery)." Positioning medicine as a science or a practice embeds it firmly as a product of civilization, of the stratification of humanity within complex societies that is synonymous with the early Anthropocene model (Ruddiman, 2013). Practitioners of medicine are specialists of the kind that, like scholars, engineers, and lawyers, can only emerge within complex social systems.

In the *Etymology of Medicine* (Charen, 1951), Thelma Charen traces the word to a Latin root – medicina – meaning the healing art, a remedy. This has an implication of righting a wrong, of making something better. Further back is the ancient Indo-European root ma/mad/med, to think, to reflect or to consider. From this also comes meditate, an integral part of healing practice in many cultures, such as the Indian tradition of Ayurveda (Kraft, 2009). The

Indo-European root extends to diagnostic appraisal and clinical evaluation: the medical practitioner meditates on and weighs the illness, judges, and counsels, in addition to attending and treating the patient. This dual role of medicine – to contemplate the illness and its causes, as well as to treat – is more important to shaping our understanding of what the future of medicine should look like.

Humans today are living longer on average than at any other time in history. Average life expectancy remained reasonably constant, at around 30–40 years, from the Pleistocene (Hoggan, 2010) to the late nineteenth century but stands at more than 80 years in some parts of the world today (WHO, 2015). An average life expectancy of 40 does not mean that most people will die at around 40 years of age, however: the figure is reached by a large number of deaths in infancy, while other members of the population may reach old age. The average age increases as more infants and children survive to (late) adulthood: mortality of children under five has dropped from 50 per cent before the nineteenth century to a fraction of 1 per cent in most developed countries today.

Deaths across the Life Course: Low-, Middle-, and High-Income Economies

Some of this increase is down to advances in medical science – including vaccination, antibiotics, and treatments for cancer, diabetes, and other non-communicable diseases – though medical science alone cannot take all the credit. Sanitation has also had an enormous impact on health and life expectancy, from the ancient cities of Mesopotamia (Mitchell, 2015) to the widespread introduction of piped, clean water and waste management systems in late nineteenth-century Europe (Geels, 2006). The developing world is yet to catch up, however: 18 per cent of childhood deaths in Africa are due to diarrhoea, which is linked to poor sanitation (Black et al., 2003; Kinney et al., 2010) and (excluding North Africa) the continent is estimated to be losing approximately 5 per cent of its annual GDP because of health problems linked to water and sanitation deficits (UN, 2008). Infrastructure can, clearly, be as important to health as cures and treatments.

In its 2008 report on the social determinants of health (WHO, 2008a), WHO set out five factors necessary for health care systems to function: a supply chain, simple management measures, training of staff, availability of frontline health workers, and financing. This emphasizes the importance of health as a collective endeavour. Humanity needs to make collective decisions on how to organize and provide the complex health care systems and infrastructure on which medical science depends.

The cost of this can be borne by individuals or society collectively, with figures suggesting that it is much more efficient and effective when borne collectively. At the national and international level, population-level approaches to health

High-income countries

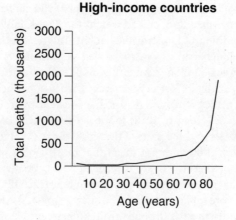

Middle-income countries

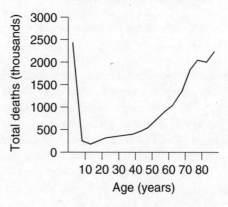

Low-income countries

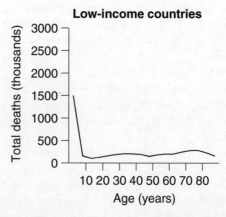

Figure 3.1 The number of female deaths across the life course in thousands for low-, middle-, and high-income countries. While numbers differ slightly for males, the distribution pattern is similar for both genders (adapted from Harper, 2016).

cost on average five times less than individual interventions (Nurse et al., 2014). Interventions for specific diseases, such as measles and rubella, work best when combined with strengthening health care systems overall (Andrus et al., 2016). A country's average health outcomes show a linear relationship with increasing GDP per capita, but improve even more quickly with an increase in average health spending per capita (OECD, 2011), and countries with better-funded health provision tend to have healthier populations; however, these advances often come at the cost of increased pollution and greenhouse gas emissions and depletion of natural and mineral resources (Landrigan et al., 2017), creating a wicked dilemma. Furthermore, this damage is often displaced onto future generations (Guerry et al., 2015) and onto countries at an earlier stage of development. Governments of low-income, resource-poor countries may see themselves dependent on accepting polluting industries to grow their own economies (Atapattu, 2002), further complicating the issue. At an international level, some of the medical achievements we have already seen, such as smallpox eradication, and those we hope for in the future, such as polio eradication, can only be achieved through international cooperation (Cole, 2015). Scott Barrett (2007) in particular has put forward many arguments for (as well as identifying persistent barriers to) international cooperation on health as a global public good.

Challenges of Medical Advancement

Increased life expectancy presents a wicked problem, however, particularly when using pure accounting models of financing. Older members of society tend to be economically unproductive (or at least less productive), consuming more of the resources of the society in which they live than they generate: an 85-year-old male costs the United Kingdom's National Health Service (NHS) about seven times more on average than a male in his 30s, for example. Health spending per person in the UK is less than £2,000 per person on average – even for children under 5 – until around the age of 50 but rises steeply from the 60–4 age group onwards to an average of £7,000 a year for those over 85 (ONS, 2015). The survival of large numbers of people into old age may be an inevitable consequence of providing good health services through infancy, childhood, and adulthood, but it incurs a high financial cost to society. How to pay for it in the most cost-effective manner is a key consideration for the Anthropocene. So too is whether the "cost," and its attendant benefits, should only be considered in financial terms, or if there are other benefits that drive society's investment, such as the sense of well-being, and superiority to animals, we gain from engaging in acts of compassion (Spikins et al., 2010).

As the global population over 65 has grown from 5 per cent in 1960 to 8.5 per cent in 2015, with the percentage of children (aged 0–14) dropping from 37 per cent in 1960 to 26 per cent in 2015, the economically active percentage of the population has shrunk. It is likely to shrink further as those moving from the 15–64 age group into the 65 and over demographic are not replaced at the same rate, which may strain economies in future. A pure accounting model of health might advocate withholding state financing for medical care after retirement age, leaving health in old age dependent on the individual's ability to afford treatment (Lubitz et al., 2003), but welfare economics considers wider benefits and values that are harder to cost, such as the emotional value we place on family members (Daatland and Lowenstein, 2005) and the experience and advice older members of a society can contribute (Warburton and MacLoughlin, 2007). It is therefore important to reflect on how society's approach to health care and medical provision has developed over time, and what incentives, financial and otherwise, have been identified for a collective approach. This may help us to determine how health systems can adapt.

Health Care: A Collective Endeavour

One approach to reflecting on the provision of complex health care systems is to examine them through the lens of Collective Intelligence, a sociopolitical theory in which collaboration and collective decision-making create something greater than the sum of its parts. Collective Intelligence both influences and is influenced by society. In 1906, sociologist Lester F. Ward (Ward, 1906, p. 39) wrote, "The extent to which [society will benefit] will be based upon collective intelligence. This is to society what brainpower is to the individual." Ward believed that individual geniuses could do nothing without a social structure that enables them to emerge, supports them, and allows them to thrive. Only by working together through an enabling mechanism can individual members of a society help to improve that society. Collective Intelligence also enables the development of intelligently networked groups who share and pool knowledge so that others can draw from it (Lévy, 1997). Schools and professional societies that train and accredit doctors, as well as the pharmaceutical companies that develop new drugs and distribute them around the world, can be seen as manifestations of collectively intelligent systems.

A second approach is to consider the origins of cooperation and collaboration identified by the field of evolutionary biology: early humans began to pool their mental attitudes and skills once they realized they could not respond to increasing environmental pressure alone, overcoming individual limitations to construct artefacts that enabled knowledge to be shared across people, time, and space (Tomasello, 2009).

The Prehistory of Health Care

How a society approaches health care is one of the clearest and most visible expressions of its attitude to the value of life, particularly where saving a life incurs a cost to others. In such cases, a value has to be placed on the benefits to the community – as well as to the individual – of the individual's life. Humans appear to have valued life for many thousands of years. Care for the ill and infirm is evidenced in the archaeological record through skeletons such as the Old Man of Shanidar (Solecki, 1957), a Neanderthal male who died aged approximately 40 years, circa 35–45,000 BCE. Injuries he had suffered early in his life had left him with a withered arm, a crippled leg, and a possibly sightless left eye (Trinkaus and Zimmerman, 1982) and it is unlikely he would have been able to survive without the support of his wider social group (though unusually worn teeth suggest he may not have been inactive, but simply given other work to do if he was unable to hunt or gather, such as chewing skins to soften them). This and other evidence of debilitating conditions in the Palaeolithic record – from dwarfism to palsy, toothlessness to arthritis – show that assistance to those with impairments, who would constitute an economic hazard to their social group (Winzer, 1993) has a very long history.

The Shanidar graves also contain remains of herbs that appear to have been intentionally buried. Some, such as *Ephedra altissima* (used to relieve wheezing and congestion) and *Senecio-types* (used to relieve pain and inflammation) have therapeutic qualities, leading to theories that this may be the reason they were chosen as grave offerings (Lietava, 1992). Seeds possibly used in herbalism have also been found in Bronze Age China (Mousume, 2017). As archaeology moves into history, written records of herbalism confirm the existence of early medical systems.

The History of Health Care Systems

The development of writing makes clear not only that herbs and plants were used as primitive medicines, but also that knowledge of which plants could be used, and how, had developed as part of a system that included the recording and sharing of knowledge and the specialization of some members of society into healing roles.

The earliest written evidence of herbal remedies dates back more than five thousand years. The Sumerians compiled lists of plants with therapeutic qualities (Borchardt, 2002), and the Egyptians recorded their use of medicinal plants including cumin and aloe vera in the Ebers Papyrus, circa 1550 BCE (Aboelsoud, 2010). The fourth century BCE Greek *Historia Plantarum* (Preus, 1988) includes both beneficial and harmful properties of herbs along with information on how and when to harvest them. The Egyptian Imhotep, 2650–2600 BCE, often described as the first physician in history, is thought to be the original author of the medical text recorded on the Edwyn Smith papyrus (Brandt-Rauf and Brandt-Rauf, 1987), which details the diagnosis, prognosis, and treatment of forty-eight traumatic and accidental injuries, and the Indian surgeon Suśruta, circa 600 BCE, authored the *Suśruta-samhitā* (Veith, 1961), a book describing over 300 surgical procedures and 120 surgical instruments. Hippocrates (circa 470–360 BCE) is credited with having made a systematic review of the medical knowledge available during his lifetime.

The fact that such detailed information was being written down reveals two key points about medical knowledge in the ancient world: first, that it was highly valued, as literacy was rare outside the very highest social strata, and second that there was already a system into which these authors fit. They were recording knowledge in order to contribute to a pool of knowledge from which others could draw, pointing to a collective body of medics who were doing more than simply practising healing: they were laying the foundations of complex medical systems.

Alongside this early codification of medical knowledge the institutionalization of medicine also appears. Hippocrates founded a medical school on the Greek island of Kos, and there is at least one known older Greek medical school, the Cnidian (Lonie, 1978). Suśruta also taught in a medical school, indicating that such institutions existed in India too, during his lifetime. Further evidence of the institutionalization of medicine is the establishment of hospitals. Romans built valetudinarii for the care of sick slaves, gladiators, and soldiers from around 100 BCE.

Following the adoption of Christianity, every cathedral town had a hospital, and some also maintained libraries and training programmes. Houses that dispensed medicines to the poor and sick existed in fifth century CE India (Liu, 2016), and an early hospital was established on Sri Lanka, as part of the Buddhist complex at Mihintale (Mueller-Dietz, 1996) in either the ninth or tenth century CE. Medieval Islamic hospitals or bīmāristāns ("asylum of the sick") such as the one established in Baghdad as early as 805 CE (Cope, 2016, p. 1286), were elaborate institutions that combined care homes for the aged and infirm with hospitals divided into separate areas for treating disease, ophthalmology, orthopaedics, and mental disease (Tschanz, 2017). They also tended to have lecture theatres and libraries, serving a dual purpose as hospital and medical school, set examinations for students, and issued diplomas.

Who Finances Health Care and Why?

Bīmāristāns were forbidden by law to turn away patients who couldn't pay, a reflection of the Islamic moral imperative to treat the ill regardless of financial status: their establishment also led to the emergence of charitable foundations called waqfs (Al Ansari, 2013), as well as contributions from state budgets – an early model for health care delivery. While it has been offered that "anyone who wishes to be considered humane has ample cause to consider what it means to be poor and sick in the era of globalization and scientific advancement" (Farmer, 2003), and also acknowledged that early public health systems were often public health policing to keep the infected poor away from the more sanitary rich (Slack, 2012), the issue of who pays for health care, and the systems that deliver it, is a key Anthropocene challenge, particularly as the cost of medicines and health care individuals need (and expect) throughout their life increases with increasing life expectancy.

These costs can be borne by civil society, through philanthropic organizations, charitable donations, or private enterprise, or the state, mostly financed through taxation or private enterprise, with patients paying through health care insurance schemes or at the point of health care delivery. The favoured early model appears to be either funding by the ruling elite as a service to their citizens, by religions orders as part of their moral duty, or by charitable organizations for the same reason. Early Ayurvedic establishments in Sri Lanka – Sivikasotthisala – were funded by the king from the fourth century BCE onwards (Gunawardana, 2010), and India, which had houses for dispensing charity and medicine as early as 400 CE (Legge, 1965) may have been one of the earliest civilizations to provide civic care to the ill (Wujastyk, 2003), but most early health care systems were provided and paid for by religious institutions.

In early history medicine and mysticism were closely linked. Priests often had a dual role as healers: in ancient Greece, temples dedicated to the healer god Asclepius, known as Asclepieia, functioned as centres of medical advice, prognosis, and healing. In medieval Europe, hospitals were largely run by monks and nuns as part of religious communities, particularly following the fall of the Roman Empire, though funding also came from "pious laypeople," professional and municipal associations (Brodman, 2009).

The church remained the main supporter of hospitals across Europe for the next millennium, ending in the UK only with the dissolution of the monasteries in 1540 by Henry VIII. Afterwards, the crown directly endowed some hospitals, such as St Bartholomews (Bart's), St Thomas's and St Mary's of Bethlehem (Bedlam) in London following a petition from the populous, who by now expected hospitals and medical care to be provided. In Catholic countries such as France, hospitals remained linked to religious institutions until the Enlightenment. Later, in the eighteenth and nineteenth centuries, hospitals were often funded by civil philanthropists – such as Guy's by wealthy merchant Thomas Guy in the UK. US charitable hospitals such as Pennsylvania, New York, and Massachusetts General also worked to this model. Protestant churches and Methodist churches re-entered the health field in the mid nineteenth century as part of a growing interest in social work (Washburn, 1931). An important part of European colonial expansion, particularly during the nineteenth century, was the provision of health care services by missionaries, though whether the main purpose of this was to improve the health of local populations or to prevent the spread of tropical diseases to the colonisers is debatable (Manji and O'Coill, 2002). More than a century later, 25–50 per cent of African health care was still provided by voluntary faith-based organizations (Good, 1991).

As nations have developed, the funding of medical systems has increasingly come to be seen as a public service, at least organized, regulated, and overseen by the state and in most cases at least partly funded by it. Most OECD nations provide health care to their citizens through the state to some degree. In 2000, average EU spending on health care (public and private) was 8.5 per cent of GDP (The King's Fund, 2016) increasing to 9 per cent by 2014, due largely to aging populations (OECD, 2014). More recently, the difficulties in financing health care following the economic crisis of 2008 has been blamed on the slowing down (and in some cases reduction) of increases in life expectancy in Europe (Hiam, 2018).

Incentives to Fund Health Systems

The rewards for investment in health care systems may not be as straightforward for the state as they are for individuals, however, particularly as the benefits of investment in health may not be returned within the current generation, let alone within a single term of political office. For an individual, investment – through private insurance or tax and national insurance – ensures complex health care will be there when needed. But at state level, an increase in health care investment, which helps to increase average population life expectancy, may not lead to a corresponding increase in GDP, and certainly not an immediate one (Acemoglu and Johnson, 2006). GDP can initially drop and may not recover for 30–60 years, as the overall resources generated by economically active members of society need to be shared with an increasingly large economically inactive population. Income per person can be lower initially than if life expectancy had not improved (Ashraf et al., 2008). It may, however, be economically more beneficial for state medical systems to focus on treating diseases that do not necessarily kill, but affect productivity – for example, reducing hookworm and malaria can lead to a fitter and more productive workforce, with fewer days on which individuals could otherwise be economically active lost to sickness (Bleakley, 2010), while better health in earlier life may reduce the age at which the elderly begin to require extensive health spending (Lubitz et al., 2003). It may also be the case that slower growth in GDP avoids too fast a move towards a more polluting, natural-resource depleted society, however, which may have co-benefits for health. It is interesting to note that many of the countries that come closest to having achieved all the Sustainable Development Goals while living within Planetary Boundaries (O'Neill et al., 2018), are middle-income countries such as Vietnam and Costa Rica.

To understand what other incentives may drive collectively intelligent systems, we can turn to the Collective Intelligence Genome (GIC) (Malone et al., 2009), which conceptualizes the components of a system and the motivations behind its use. The GIC has four basic building blocks: what, who, why, and how. Each of these has variations that can be combined and recombined in

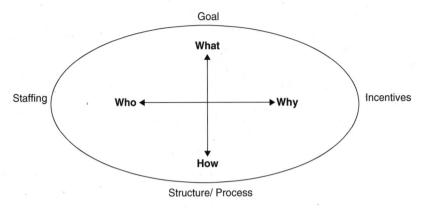

Figure 3.2 The collective intelligence genome (Malone et al., 2009)

different ways. The why – the incentives – has the variants money (reward), love (altruism), and glory (power).

If, as has been shown above, "money" or financial reward in terms of increased GDP is not necessarily an (immediate) outcome of state investment in medicine, what else might be?

Though there is at least some evidence of "glory," which high-status medical practitioners have enjoyed throughout history, "love" – in the form of altruism and compassion – is a stronger candidate. Compassion has very ancient evolutionary roots (De Waal, 2008), and compassion that requires planning and rational thought emerged around 1.8 million–300,000 years ago (Walker and Shipman, 1997).

Compassion is associated with love, commitment to others, willing self-sacrifice – characteristics that make us "human" and separate us from other animals (Spikins et al., 2010). In this sense, we could also see the payoff as "glory," a sense that we are better and more advanced than others who do not demonstrate similar compassion. Even apparently altruistic acts confer some rewards, however. Undertaking a compassionate act that is not an obligation and has no selfish gain releases the hormone oxytocin, creating a sense of well-being and happiness (Shen, 2015) that may motivate the actor to do the same thing again in similar circumstances.

Compassion is observed in several animals, including dolphins and elephants, but seems particularly important in higher primates with complex social structures; it may help to develop long-term relationships, and has been described as "the glue that holds society together" (Baron-Cohen and Wheelwright, 2004). This suggests a particularly valuable role in the Anthropocene's larger, more complex societies than in the Pleistocene's more immediate family group structure.

If the main motivation for providing state-level cooperation in health systems is compassion, the issue then becomes, how far is this compassion likely to extend? It has, so far throughout history, moved from being provided by the immediate family group, to the city state, to the state. In larger and more complex social units, it is activated by patterns of mutual identification (Elias, 1994), a sense of community now and in the future (Anderson, 2010), and/or a shared high culture (Gellner, 2008), all of which create a function of compassion for those who share membership of the group with which they identify. There is no global health provider, but there is a strong argument for the richer regions of the world subsidising the health of the poorer regions, and this may be possible to incentivize through stronger emphasis on human beings as a single race, in which all members have obligations to all others. Among other benefits, such global investment in ideas of citizenship as well as medical equipment and services would help to ensure that health challenges such as disease outbreaks like the 2014–15 Ebola epidemic are better controlled and regions like Africa do not suffer because of a sense of detachment in more developed countries that see such regions as distant and unrelated (Honigsbaum, 2014; Schuklenk, 2014).

Breakdown of Health Care Systems in Times of Conflict

From a selfish perspective, there is a strong incentive to shore up other states' failed systems in order to protect ourselves, as it is more efficient to treat health problems at source. Two recent Public Health Emergencies of International Concern (PHEICs) (WHO, 2008b) – the 2014–15 West Africa Ebola crisis and the polio outbreak that began in Syria in 2014 – illustrate this point.

In West Africa, Ebola emerged in a region where health care facilities were extremely basic (Cole, 2014). For example, prior to the outbreak in 2012, Sierra Leone spent just US$96 per capita on health care and had 0.02 doctors per 1,000 people: in the UK per capita spending stood at US$3,468 (WHO, 2012) and there were 2.7 doctors per 1,000 members of the population. Such a basic medical system hampered early detection, early infection control, and early containment of the outbreak, enabling it to spread rapidly. No vaccine existed because there had been insufficient incentive for pharmaceutical companies to meet the cost of developing treatments for a disease that affected only small numbers of people in the very poorest countries. Fast-tracking vaccine development in the wake of the outbreak meant that we will be better protected in future, but international cooperation to provide decent health care in poorer regions of the world beforehand might have proved a more efficient and effective way of producing the same end result (Rull et al., 2015).

It is also important to consider how the international community should respond to countries whose previously functioning health care systems are disrupted by conflict and disaster. While Ebola was spreading in West Africa,

crisis-torn Syria was experiencing a re-emergence of polio, a previously eradicated disease (Soghaier et al., 2015). At the time the crisis began, Syria was a
medically advanced country: there were 1.5 doctors per 1,000 people, near universal vaccination (an estimated 95 per cent of the population was vaccinated
against polio), and sound surveillance and monitoring systems. As the crisis
unravelled, however, the Syrian health care system was severely damaged.

By 2012, just a year after the crisis began, vaccination coverage had dropped
to barely 50 per cent of the children eligible that year, sparking fears that unvac-
cinated children were at risk of contracting polio from environmental reser-
voirs. These fears were realized in July 2013, and by the end of January 2014 36
cases had been recorded in Syria, putting seven neighbouring countries at risk.
Though the outbreak was quickly contained through a concerted effort by the
WHO and neighbouring countries, the episode highlighted the fragility of the
medical system.

The conditions that led to these PHEICs show that health needs to be
approached from directions other than purely medical science: economic
and cultural challenges can be just as great. The more cross-disciplinary the
approach, the more likely solutions are to succeed, particularly in societies and
situations where the barriers to the implementation of medical solutions are
high. Episodes of diphtheria were common after the break-up of the former
Soviet Union due to lack of vaccine supply (Vitek and Wharton, 1998) and outbreaks of malaria affected up to 100,000 people per year in Iraq in the period
following the First Gulf War (WHO, 2003). The increasing dynamic mobility of
people across the world, whether refugees fleeing war and civil unrest, victims
of disasters and climate change, or simply economic migrants following the
best opportunities, may require a more coordinated international approach to
health systems than we have seen in the past (Stein, 2015).

Conclusions

Medicine works best when it is a collective endeavour: a medical system that
is accessible to all. Knowledge needs to be recorded, pooled, shared, and distributed equitably. Centralization and institutionalization of medicine provide economies of scale and encourage specialization, enabling medicine as a
field to grow. Complex systems require financing, however. How we finance
medicine is partly influenced by the cost-benefit analysis to individuals and
to society as a whole and partly influenced by evolutionary drivers of human
behaviour. Compassion and care for the infirm has been part of humanity since
the Palaeolithic, but the challenge today is that due to demographic changes, a
higher percentage of the population are infirm, for longer, than has been the case
in the past. This is, at its heart, a difference between a purely accounting model
of financing health care, which looks only at the money spent, and a welfare

economics model that considers wider benefits, such as family ties, the experience and wisdom the elderly can offer the young, individuals' own desire to grow old, and adhering to moral norms (Theixos, 2013). The welfare economist would argue that not all rewards and incentives are financial, and evolutionary biology would appear to favour this approach. This does not mean that we cannot measure the benefits of health care through financial instruments, however, particularly in a world where resources are finite and competition for them may increase. In fact, the very act of doing so may help us to reconsider how, as we navigate the Anthropocene, we refinance medical systems to support good health throughout life and preventative care for everyone, so that longer life does not automatically place a financial burden on the very health systems that have enabled it and exclude those individuals and populations who are less able to pay. Authors such as Scott Barrett (2016) and Ramanan Laxminarayan (2016) have analysed economic incentives for the provision of public goods; others have considered the role of social norms as solutions (Nyborg et al., 2016) or commented on the value of international investment in the health care systems of low-income countries to protect against future health emergencies (Dzau, 2016). Looking to the history of medicine and the anthropological/evolutionary roots of cooperation and altruism for inspiration offers an additional approach. The best insights will no doubt be gained by combining and drawing on all these fields, enabling us to build a framework for medical provision and its incentives that will help us move through the Anthropocene's demographic changes and challenges towards a future where medicine might be provided by global systems that are less vulnerable to local disruptions, more equitably distributed, and more capable of acting at source.

REFERENCES

Aboelsoud, N. H. (2010). Herbal medicine in ancient Egypt. *Journal of Medicinal Plants Research, 4*(2), 82–6.

Acemoglu, D., & Johnson, S. (2006). Disease and development: The effect of life expectancy on economic growth. BREAD Working Paper No. 120.

Ackerknecht, E. H., & Haushofer, L. *A short history of medicine.* Baltimore, MD: JHU Press, 2016.

Al Ansari, M. (2013). *Bīmāristāns and the wafq in Islam.* (Doctoral dissertation). The University of Sydney.

Allemani, C., Matsuda, T., Di Carlo, V., Harewood, R., Matz, M., Nikšić, M., Bonaventure, A. et al. (2018). Global surveillance of trends in cancer survival 2000–14 (CONCORD-3): Analysis of individual records for 37,513,025 patients diagnosed with one of 18 cancers from 322 population-based registries in 71 countries. *The Lancet, 391*(10125), 1023–75. https://doi.org/10.1016/S0140-6736(17)33326-3

Anderson, B. (2010). Preemption, precaution, preparedness: Anticipatory action and future geographies. *Progress in Human Geography, 34*(6), 777–98. https://doi .org/10.1177/0309132510362600

Andrus, J. K., Cochi, S. L., Cooper, L. Z., & Klein, J. D. (2016). Combining global elimination of measles and rubella with strengthening of health systems in developing countries. *Health Affairs, 35*(2), 327–33. https://doi.org/10.1377 /hlthaff.2015.1005

Ashraf, Qa., Lester, A., & Weil, D. (2008). *When does improving health raise GDP?* In *National Bureau of Economic Research Macroeconomics Annual 2008* (Vol. 23). Chicago, IL: University of Chicago Press

Atapattu, S. (2002). The right to a healthy life or the right to die polluted? The emergence of a human right to a healthy environment under international law. *Tulane Environmental Law Journal, 16*(1), 65–126.

Bar-Yosef, O. (2017). Facing climatic hazards: Paleolithic foragers and Neolithic farmers. *Quaternary International, 428*, 64–72. https://doi.org/10.1016 /j.quaint.2015.11.037

Baron-Cohen, S., & Wheelwright, S. (2004). The empathy quotient: An investigation of adults with Asperger syndrome or high functioning autism, and normal sex differences. *Journal of Autism and Developmental Disorders, 34*(2), 163–75. https:// doi.org/10.1023/B:JADD.0000022607.19833.00

Barrett, S. (2007). *Why cooperate? The incentive to supply global public goods.* Oxford, UK: Oxford University Press.

Barrett, S. (2016). Coordination vs. voluntarism and enforcement in sustaining international environmental cooperation. *Proceedings of the National Academy of Sciences, 113*(51), 14515–22. https://doi.org/10.1073/pnas.1604989113

Bazin, H., & Jenner, E. (2000). *The eradication of smallpox.* London: Academic Press.

Ben-Haim, M. S., Kanfi, Y., Mitchel, S. J., Maoz, N., Vaughan, K., Amariglio, N., Lerrer, B., de Cabo, R., Rechavi, G., & Cohen, H. Y. (2017). Breaking the ceiling of human maximal lifespan. *The Journals of Gerontology: Series A, 73*(11), 1465–71. https://doi .org/10.1093/gerona/glx219

Black, R. E., Morris, S. S., & Bryce, J. (2003). Where and why are 10 million children dying every year? *The Lancet, 361*(9376), 2226–34. https://doi.org/10.1016 /S0140-6736(03)13779-8

Bleakley, H. (2010). Malaria eradication in the Americas: A retrospective analysis of childhood exposure. *American Journal of Applied Economics, 2*(2), 1–45. https://doi .org/10.1257/app.2.2.1

Borchardt, J. K. (2002). The beginnings of drug therapy: Ancient Mesopotamian medicine. *Drug News Perspect, 15*(3), 187–92. https://doi.org/10.1358 /dnp.2002.15.3.840015

Brandt-Rauf, P. W., & Brandt-Rauf, S. I. (1987). History of occupational medicine: Relevance of Imhotep and the Edwin Smith papyrus. *British Journal of Industrial Medicine, 44*(1), 68. https://doi.org/10.1136/oem.44.1.68

Brodman, J. (2009). *Charity and religion in medieval Europe*. Washington, DC: CUA Press.

Charen, T. (1951). The etymology of medicine. *Bulletin of the Medical Library Association, 39*(3), 216.

Cohen, A. J., Brauer, M., Burnett, R., Ross, A. H., Frostad, J., Estep, K., Balakrishnan, K. et al. (2017). Estimates and 25-year trends of the global burden of disease attributable to ambient air pollution: An analysis of data from the Global Burden of Diseases Study 2015. *The Lancet, 389*(10082), 1907–18. https://doi.org/10.1016/S0140-6736(17)30505-6

Cole, J. (2014). Conflict, post-conflict and failed states: Challenges to healthcare. *The RUSI Journal, 159*(5), 14–18. https://doi.org/10.1080/03071847.2014.969934

Cole, J. (2015). The failure of polio eradication: Blame geopolitics, not religion. *Georgetown Journal of International Affairs*. Retrieved from https://www.georgetownjournalofinternationalaffairs.org/online-edition/the-failure-of-polio-eradication-blame-geopolitics-not-religion.

Cole, J. (2018). Human health in an era of global environmental change. *Rockefeller Economic Council on Planetary Health*. Oxford Martin School.

Cope, Z. (2016). *The Palgrave encyclopedia of imperialism and anti-imperialism*. Ness, I. (Ed). Basingstoke, UK: Palgrave Macmillan.

Daatland, S. O., & Lowenstein, A. (2005). Intergenerational solidarity and the family- welfare state balance. *European Journal of Ageing, 2*(3), 174–82. https://doi.org/10.1007/s10433-005-0001-1

Deaton, A. (2003). Health, inequality, and economic development. *Journal of Economic Literature, 41*(1), 113–58. https://doi.org/10.1257/002205103321544710

De Waal, F. B.M. (2008). Putting the altruism back into altruism: The evolution of empathy. *Annual Review of Psychology, 59*, 279–300. https://doi.org/10.1146/annurev.psych.59.103006.093625

Dong, X., Milholland, B., & Vijg, J. (2016). Evidence for a limit to human lifespan. *Nature, 538*(7624), 257. https://doi.org/10.1038/nature19793

Dzau, V. J., & Sands, P. (2016). Beyond the Ebola battle – Winning the war against future epidemics. *New England Journal of Medicine, 375*(3), 203–4. https://doi.org/10.1056/NEJMp1605847

Elias, N., & Scotson, J. L. (1994). *The established and the outsiders* (Vol. 32). Thousand Oaks, CA: Sage.

Farmer, P. (2003). Pathologies of power: Health, human rights, and the new war on the poor. *North American Dialogue, 6*(1), 1–4. https://doi.org/10.1525/nad.2003.6.1.1

Geels, F. W. (2006). The hygienic transition from cesspools to sewer systems (1840–1930): The dynamics of regime transformation. *Research policy, 35*(7), 1069–82. https://doi.org/10.1016/j.respol.2006.06.001

Gellner, E. (2008). *Nations and nationalism*. Ithaca, NY: Cornell University Press.

Good, C. M. (1991). Pioneer medical missions in colonial Africa. *Social Science & Medicine, 32*(1), 1–10. https://doi.org/10.1016/0277-9536(91)90120-2

Guerry, A. D., Polasky, S., Lubchenco, J., Chaplin-Kramer, R., Daily, G. C., Griffin, R., Ruckelshaus, M. et al. (2015). Natural capital and ecosystem services informing decisions: From promise to practice. *Proceedings of the National Academy of Sciences, 112*(24), 7348–55. https://doi.org/10.1073/pnas.1503751112

Gunawardana, V. D. N. S. (2010). *The ancient hospital complex at Mihinthale in Sri Lanka.* Sri Lanka: 3rd International congress, Society of South Asian Archaeology (SOSAA), Centre for Asian Studies, University of Kelaniya.

Harper, S. (2016). *How population change will transform our world.* Oxford, UK: Oxford University Press.

Hiam, L., Harrison, D., McKee, M., & Dorling, D. (2018). Why is life expectancy in England and Wales 'stalling'? *J Epidemiol Community Health, 72*(5), 404–8. https://doi.org/10.1136/jech-2017-210401

Hoggan, R. (2015). Life expectancy in the paleolithic. http://paleodiet.com/life -expectancy.htm. Accessed 2 October 2019.

Honigsbaum, M. (2014). Ebola: Epidemic echoes and the chronicle of a tragedy foretold. *The Lancet, 384*(9956), 1740–1. https://doi.org/10.1016 /S0140-6736(14)62063-8

Júnior, W. S. F., & Ulysses, P. A. (2018). A theoretical review on the origin of medicinal practices in humans: Echoes from evolution. *Ethnobiology and Conservation, 7.* https://doi.org/10.15451/ec2018-02-7.03-1-7

Kinney, M. V., Kerber, K. J., Black, R. E., Cohen, B., Nkrumah, F., Coovadia, H., Michael Nampala, P., & Lawn, J. E. (2010). Sub-Saharan Africa's mothers, newborns, and children: Where and why do they die? *PLOS Medicine, 7*(6), e1000294. https:// doi.org/10.1371/journal.pmed.1000294

Kraft, K. (2009). Complementary/alternative medicine in the context of prevention of disease and maintenance of health. *Preventive Medicine, 49*(2), 88–92. https://doi .org/10.1016/j.ypmed.2009.05.003

Landrigan, P. J., Fuller, R., Acosta, N. J. R., Adeyi, O., Arnold, R., Bibi Baldé, A., Bertollini, R. et al. (2017). The Lancet Commission on pollution and health. *The Lancet.*

Laxminarayan, R. (2016), Trans-boundary commons in infectious diseases. *Oxford Review of Economic Policy, 32*(1), 88–101. https://doi.org/10.1093/oxrep/grv030

Legge, J. (1965). *A record of Buddhistic kingdoms: Being an account by the Chinese monk Fâ-Hien of his travels in India and Ceylon (399–414 CE) in search of the Buddhist books of discipline.* Oxford, UK: The Clarendon Press.

Lévy, P. (1997). *Collective intelligence.* New York: Plenum/HarperCollins.

Lietava, J. (1992). Medicinal plants in a Middle Paleolithic grave Shanidar IV? *Journal of Ethnopharmacology, 35*(3), 263–6. https://doi.org/10.1016/0378-8741(92)90023-K

Liu, Y. (2016). Stories written and rewritten: The story of Faxian's search for the dharma in its historical, anecdotal, and biographical contexts. *Early Medieval China, 2016*(22), 1–25. https://doi.org/10.1080/15299104.2016.1226420

Lonie, I. M. (1978). Cos versus Cnidus and the historians: Part I. *History of Science, 16*(1), 42–75. https://doi.org/10.1177/007327537801600103

Lubitz, J., Cai, L., Kramarow, E., & Lentzner, H. (2003). Health, life expectancy, and health care spending among the elderly. *New England Journal of Medicine, 349*(11), 1048–55. https://doi.org/10.1056/NEJMsa020614

Macfarlane, D. (2018). Controversy regarding the obstetric dilemma. *Aisthesis: Honors Student Journal, 9*(1), 27–30.

Malone, T. W., Laubacher, R., & Dellarocas, C. (2009). Harnessing crowds: Mapping the genome of collective intelligence. *MIT Sloan Research Paper No. 4732-09.*

Manji, F., & O'Coill, C. (2002). The missionary position: NGOs and development in Africa. *International Affairs, 78*(3), 567–84. https://doi.org/10.1111/1468-2346.00267

Marmot, M. (2005). Social determinants of health inequalities. *The Lancet, 365*(9464), 1099–104. https://doi.org/10.1016/S0140-6736(05)74234-3

McMichael, A. J. (2001). Human culture, ecological change, and infectious disease: Are we experiencing history's fourth great transition? *Ecosystem Health, 7*(2), 107–15. https://doi.org/10.1046/j.1526-0992.2001.007002107.x

"Medicine." Oxford Living Dictionaries. (2018). Retrieved from: https:// en.oxforddictionaries.com/definition/medicine

Mitchell, P., ed. (2015). *Sanitation, latrines and intestinal parasites in past populations.* Farnham, UK: Ashgate Publishing, Ltd.

Mousume, R. B. (2017). Antioxidant and antimicrobial investigations of dichloromethane (DCM) extract of Garcinia cowa bark. (Doctoral dissertation). East West University.

Mueller-Dietz, H. E. (1996). Stone 'sarcophagi' and ancient hospitals in Sri Lanka. *Medizinhistorisches Journal, 31*(1–2), 49–65.

Nurse, J., Dorey, S., Yao, L., Sigfrid, L., Yfantopolous, P., McDaid, D., Yfantopolous, J., & Martin, J. M. (2014). *The case for investing in public health: A public health summary report for EPHO 8.* Copenhagen, Denmark: World Health Organization Regional Office for Europe.

Nyborg, K., Anderies, J. M., Dannenberg, A., Lindahl, T., Schill, C., Schlüter, M., & Adger, N. W. et al. (2016). Social norms as solutions. *Science, 354*(6308), 42–3. https://doi.org/10.1126/science.aaf8317

OECD. (2011). Health at a glance 2011: OECD indicators – Health status – Life expectancy at birth. Retrieved from http://www.oecd-ilibrary.org/sites/health _glance-2011-en/01/01/index.html?/ns/Chapter&itemId=/content/chapter/health _glance-2011-4-en

OECD. (2014). Total expenditure on health per capita. At current prices and PPPs. Retrieved from http://www.oecd-ilibrary.org/social-issues-migration-health /total-expenditure-on-health-per-capita_20758480-table2

Office of National Statistics. (2015). Country and Regional Analysis: 2015.

O'Neill, D. W., Fanning, A. L., Lamb, W. F., & Steinberger, J. K. (2018). A good life for all within planetary boundaries. *Nature Sustainability, 1*(2), 88. https://doi.org /10.1038/s41893-018-0021-4

Preus, A. (1988). Drugs and psychic states in Theophrastus' *Historia plantarum* 9.8–20. In Fortenbruagh, William W., & Sharples, Robert W. (Eds), *Theophrastean studies. On natural science, physics and metaphysics, ethics, religion, and rhetoric* (pp. 76–99). New Brunswick, NJ: Transaction Books :

Rifkin, R. F., Potgieter, M., Ramond, J., & Cowan, D. A. (2017). Ancient oncogenesis, infection and human evolution. *Evolutionary Applications, 10*(10), 949–64. https://doi.org/10.1111/eva.12497

Ruddiman, W. F. (2013). The Anthropocene. *Annual Review of Earth and Planetary Sciences, 41*, 45–68. https://doi.org/10.1146/annurev-earth-050212-123944

Rull, M., Kickbusch, I., & L., Helen. (2015). Policy debate | International responses to global epidemics: Ebola and beyond. *International Development Policy | Revue internationale de politique de développement, 6*(2). https://doi.org/10.4000/poldev.2178

Schuklenk, U. (2014). Bioethics and the Ebola outbreak in West Africa. *Developing World Bioethics, 14*(3), ii–iii. https://doi.org/10.1111/dewb.12073

Shen, H. (2015). The hard science of oxytocin. *Nature, 522*(7557), 410. https://doi.org/10.1038/522410a

Slack, P. (2012). *Plague: A very short introduction* (Vol. 307). Oxford, UK: Oxford University Press.

Soghaier, M. A., Saeed, K. M. I., & Zaman, K. K. (2015). Public Health Emergency of International Concern (PHEIC) has been declared twice in 2014; Polio and Ebola at the top. *AIMS Public Health, 2*(2), 218–22. https://doi.org/10.3934/publichealth.2015.2.218

Solecki, R. S. (1957). Shanidar cave. *Scientific American, 197*(5), 58–65. https://doi.org/10.1038/scientificamerican1157-58

Speth, J. D., & Spielmann, K. A. (1983). Energy source, protein metabolism, and hunter-gatherer subsistence strategies. *Journal of Anthropological Archaeology, 2*(1), 1–31. https://doi.org/10.1016/0278-4165(83)90006-5

Spikins, P. A., Rutherford, H. E., & Needham, A. P. (2010). From homininity to humanity: Compassion from the earliest archaics to modern humans. *Time and Mind, 3*(3), 303–25 https://doi.org/10.2752/175169610X12754030955977

Stein, R. A. (2015). Political will and international collaborative frameworks in infectious diseases. *International Journal of Clinical Practice, 69*(1), 41–8. https://doi.org/10.1111/ijcp.12489

The King's Fund. (2009). How does NHS spending compare with health spending internationally? Retrieved from https://www.kingsfund.org.uk/blog/2016/01/how-does-nhs-spending-compare-health-spending-internationally#footnoteref1_mdlg5b2

Theixos, H. (2013). Adult children and eldercare: The moral considerations of filial obligations. *Michigan Family Review, 17*(1). https://doi.org/10.3998/mfr.4919087.0017.105

Tomasello, M. (2009). *Why we cooperate*. Cambridge, MA: MIT Press.

Trinkaus, E., & Zimmerman, M. R. (1982). Trauma among the Shanidar Neandertals. *American Journal of Physical Anthropology, 57*(1), 61–76. https://doi.org/10.1002 /ajpa.1330570108

Tschanz, D. W. (2017). The Islamic roots of the modern hospital. *Aramco World.*

UN Economic Commission for Africa/African Union. (2008). Economic report on Africa 2008. Africa and the Monterey consensus: Tracking performance and progress. Economic Commission for Africa.

Veith, I. (1961). The surgical achievements of ancient India: Sushruta. *Surgery, 49*(4), 564–8.

Vitek, C. R., & Wharton, M. (1998). Diphtheria in the former Soviet Union: Reemergence of a pandemic disease. *Emerging infectious diseases, 4*(4), 539. https:// doi.org/10.3201/eid0404.980404

Walker, A., & Shipman, P. (1997). *The wisdom of the bones: In search of human origins.* New York, NY: Vintage Press.

Warburton, J., & McLaughlin, D. (2007). Passing on our culture: How older Australians from diverse cultural backgrounds contribute to civil society. *Journal of Cross-Cultural Gerontology, 22*(1), 47–60. https://doi.org/10.1007/s10823-006-9012-4

Ward, L. F. (1906). *Applied sociology.* Boston: Ginn.

Washburn, H. B. (1931). *The religious motive in philanthropy: Studies in biography* (Vol. 14). Philadelphia, PA: University of Pennsylvania Press.

Weiss, R. A., & McMichael, A. J. (2004). Social and environmental risk factors in the emergence of infectious diseases. *Nature Medicine, 10*(12s), S70. https://doi .org/10.1038/nm1150

Whalen, K. A., Judd, S., McCullough, M. L., Flanders, D. W., Hartman, T. J., & Bostick, R. M. (2017). Paleolithic and mediterranean diet pattern scores are inversely associated with all-cause and cause-specific mortality in adults. *The Journal of Nutrition, 147*(4), 612–20. https://doi.org/10.3945/jn.116.241919

Winzer, M. A. (1993). *The history of special education: From isolation to integration.* Washington, DC: Gallaudet University Press.

World Health Organization. (2003). Potential impact of conflict on health in Iraq. https://www.who.int/features/2003/iraq/briefings/iraq_briefing_note/en/

World Health Organization. (2008a). Closing the gap in a generation: Health equity through action on the social determinants of health. Final report of the Commission on the social determinants of health. Geneva, Switzerland: World Health Organization.

World Health Organization. (2008b). *International health regulations* (2005). Geneva, Switzerland: World Health Organization

World Health Organization. (2012). Health financing: Per capita total expenditure on health at average exchange rate (US$): 2012. http://gamapserver.who.int/gho /interactive_charts/health_financing/atlas.html?indicator=i3

World Health Organization. (2015). Life expectancy. Global Health Observatory (GHO) data. Retrieved from http://www.who.int/gho/mortality_burden_disease /life_tables/situation_trends/en/

Wujastyk, D. (2003). *The roots of Ayurveda: Selections from Sanksrit medical writings.* London; New York: Penguin Books.

4 Anthropocene Health Economics: Preparing for the Journey or the Destination?

MARTIN HENSHER

Health Care, the Great Acceleration, and the Anthropocene

Modern health care is intimately linked with the period that Steffen, Broadgate, et al. (2015) have dubbed the "Great Acceleration." Before the Second World War health care appears to have constituted some 2 to 3 per cent of Gross Domestic Product (GDP) in countries such as the United States and United Kingdom, and this proportion appears to have been reasonably constant during the 1920s and 30s (Getzen, 2016; Gordon, 2016). Yet after the Second World War, in high-income countries health care began an inexorable expansion, not only in absolute terms but also by growing its share of GDP (Newhouse, 1977; OECD, 2006), so that today health spending is some 10 per cent of global GDP (see figure 4.1). While health care's share of GDP has also risen in low-income and middle-income countries, its rate of growth there has been slower and has started from a much lower baseline (see figure 4.1), so that the great majority of this increase has accrued to the high-income countries. Thus the evolution of modern health care systems has followed the Great Acceleration trajectory and displays the equity problem noted by Steffen, Broadgate, et al. (2015), namely that the Great Acceleration has been driven largely by (and its benefits largely consumed by) a minority of the human population.

At the time of writing, there appear to be no papers published by health economists explicitly concerning the economics of health care systems in the Anthropocene. A small number of papers from other disciplines raise questions concerning the economic consequences of planetary boundaries for health care systems (Borowy and Aillon, 2017; Zywert and Quilley, 2017), while the relationship between "planetary health" and wider economic systems is clearly acknowledged (Whitmee et al., 2015). Meanwhile, an extensive literature exists on ecological macroeconomics, examining alternative models of the wider economy that might allow the decoupling of human prosperity and well-being from ecological damage (Hardt and O'Neill, 2017; Bowen and Hepburn, 2014; Daly, 1977;

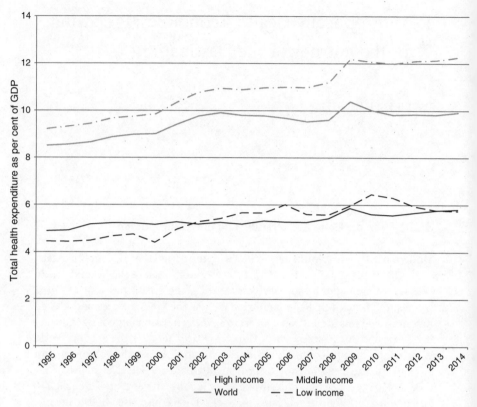

Figure 4.1 Global total health expenditure as per cent of GDP, 1995–2014.
Source: World Bank Open Data, Indicator SH.XPD.TOTL.ZS (accessed 15 October 2017).

Jackson, 2009; Kallis, Kerschner, and Martinez-Alier, 2012; Lawn, 2010). This chapter will therefore examine the likely economics of health care systems in the Anthropocene. It will focus on the economic problems to which health care systems will need to respond in the Anthropocene era, and will outline some of the economic tools and strategies that may be of value in mounting such a response.

Summarizing Alternative Ecological Macroeconomic Models

The health sector is an important segment of the economy in all developed and middle-income countries when its share of GDP is considered (WHO, 2017), and its small share of GDP in the poorest countries is almost certainly a problem for human welfare. The fate of the health care sector is therefore closely intertwined with that of the wider economy. There are essentially two sets of mechanisms by which the conditions of the Anthropocene era will impact upon the economy overall. The first mechanism is via those policy or market responses that occur in an attempt to mitigate further environmental harm – that is, active reform or transformation of economic models. The second is via the direct consequences of those environmental harms that have not been avoided – human and economic losses and costs incurred as a result of environmental damage, and the costs of adaptation to a changing environment. These two sets of mechanisms clearly interact with each other, creating two states for the economy. In one state, the economy remains broadly under control and at least partially responsive to policy interventions; in the other state, the economy is essentially out of control, with policy interventions unable to prevent a collapse spiral, resulting in loss of societal complexity, productive capacity, and human life. Avoiding an abrupt and involuntary state shift into such a collapse spiral (hence preventing avoidable and undesirable loss of complexity) is arguably one of the most crucial goals of all public policy in the Anthropocene. Yet we must always acknowledge the possibility that society may not prove able to prevent a relatively sudden loss of complexity. Rather than simply regarding this possibility as a counsel of despair, we might identify two possible goals for public policy in anticipation of any future collapse spiral. One goal involves identifying certain key institutions and functions and taking active measures to improve their resilience to significant reductions in societal and economic complexity, so that they might be best positioned to remain useful and functional. The other is to consider how to be ready to take advantage of opportunities for "catagenesis" or "creative renewal" following a phase of breakdown (Homer-Dixon, 2006; Zywert and Quilley, 2017) to encourage the mental and institutional habits that can wrest positive renewal from the jaws of apparent catastrophe.

A wide range of "ecological macroeconomic" models have been proposed as transformational alternatives to the "business as usual" of growth-driven, finance capitalism that has been the dominant economic model globally since the 1970s (Streeck, 2016). A brief overview of these models will facilitate a discussion of what each might mean for health care systems.

It would be tempting to suggest that our baseline macroeconomic model for comparison is a neoliberal, globalized finance capitalism of the kind sketched by Klein (2014). Yet – in a long series of decisions stretching back several decades – governments and international institutions have committed global policy strongly towards "sustainable development" (UN, 2015), to be achieved by a process of "green growth" (Bowen and Hepburn, 2014). The latter define green growth as a strategy of increasing human well-being through continued increases in economic activity, yet without reducing aggregate natural capital. The green growth model requires effective decoupling (or dematerialization) of material resource use from economic growth – and in the long term that this decoupling be absolute, not just relative. The real feasibility of decoupling remains heavily contested, with apparent progress often proving to be illusory

(Bithas and Kalimeris, 2018; Ward et al., 2016). Green growth's inherent risk is that the temptation to drive too hard for "growth" at the expense of "green" will always be too great in a world of stark inequalities, especially if the basis for decoupling is assumption rather than fact. Green growth for "sustainable development" is the default consensus aspiration of governments and institutions – yet, if it is a poor bet, what other macro models are on offer?

A well-established and well-developed alternative to business-as-usual "sustainable development" has been available for forty years in the form of Herman Daly's "steady state economy" model (Daly, 1977). The logic of the steady state economy is simple: the aim of economic policy should be to maximize human well-being at a stable level of material throughput (i.e. use of natural and non-renewable resources and pollution sinks) that can be sustained indefinitely. Whether the size of the economy (measured in monetary terms) grows or shrinks is entirely secondary to these two objectives. Daly's vision therefore centres on two areas of effort – defining and measuring human well-being more effectively while defining and enforcing quantitative limits on material throughput (both resource use and pollution). Daly and his followers (e.g. Lawn, 2011) generally view the steady state economy as compatible with a market society; however, government plays a critical role in setting goals for human well-being, and in controlling and rationing the supply of natural resources and pollution rights through ongoing auctions. Thus the state sets the goals for human flourishing and determines the quantity constraint on material throughput, while market ingenuity can then achieve those goals and use those resources to best effect within clearly constrained policy parameters. More recent calls for a stance of "agrowth" (van den Bergh, 2017), or "agnosticism about growth" (Raworth, 2017) can be seen as belonging firmly within the tradition of the original steady state economy model.

In the last decade, some have moved beyond the steady state model, suggesting that – at least in the richer countries of the world – a period of voluntary "degrowth" is required (e.g. Alexander, 2012; Kallis, 2011; Kallis, Kerschner, and Martinez-Alier, 2012). Proponents of degrowth argue that the negative ecological and social effects of economic growth have now become so severe that a period of deliberate, planned contraction in the scale of material throughput and economic activity is required as an essential prelude to stabilizing human economic activity at an ecologically and socially sustainable equilibrium in the future. Characterizing "degrowth" is complex, as it combines many features, actors, and policy proposals across many areas, coming together in a social movement described as seeking a "multi-scalar *transformation* beyond capitalism" (Asara et al., 2015). Degrowth scenarios typically involve substantial and relatively rapid reductions in GDP, energy, and material use in high-income countries while allowing for some continued growth in all these variables in the lower-income regions of the world (e.g. Capellán-Pérez et al., 2015). The tentative estimates that modelling of such scenarios have produced are challenging: for example, four-fold reductions in energy use and reversion to current global GDP per capita levels are required in high-income countries according to Capellán-Pérez et al. (2015), while O'Neill et al. (2018) suggest that universally meeting a basket of basic needs and social development thresholds from the safe and just space framework for the global population may require "provisioning systems" (i.e. the economic transformation of resources into social outcomes) to become two to six times more efficient than at present.

Voluntary degrowth (or socially sustainable degrowth) must, however, be distinguished from its less convivial cousins, unsustainable degrowth (Asara et al., 2015) and *involuntary* degrowth (Bonaiuti, 2014; Bonaiuti, 2018). Unsustainable degrowth refers to unplanned GDP contraction in an untransformed capitalist economy – an economic recession or depression. It recognizes that much loss of human welfare typically accompanies economic recession in modern economies. Unsustainable degrowth is clearly an inherent macroeconomic risk of any concerted efforts to achieve a voluntary degrowth transition: incorrectly calibrated degrowth policies could easily trip dramatic financial and economic crises, which would be highly likely to discredit, rather than support, the eventual goals of degrowth (Klitgaard and Krall, 2012; Tokic, 2012). By contrast, Bonaiuti (2014, 2018) uses the term involuntary degrowth to reflect the possibility that modern capitalist economies have entered a period of diminishing marginal returns to complexity, with a substantial risk that overlapping crises will tip societies into an abrupt and unpleasant reduction in social and economic complexity. At the extreme, this kind of involuntary degrowth reflects the overshoot and collapse outcomes of the limits to growth standard run model (Meadows et al., 1972). While not using these terms, Malmaeus and Andersson (2017) review a range of historical GDP contractions over the last fifty years. They note that, while short-term consequences of recession or depression may be substantial, the longer-term consequences of these GDP crises have typically been less dramatic. They thus emphasize the difference between the experiences of zero or low growth that have been encountered in the modern era and the kinds of negative feedback loops that might trigger the collapse dynamics that have thus far not been experienced in recent history (Malmaeus and Andersson, 2017). In the rest of this paper, the term involuntary degrowth will be used to describe the latter – unplanned and undesired collapse and loss of complexity.

Health Care under Different Ecological Macroeconomic Models

What then are the types and mechanisms of impact on health care systems that we might expect in an Anthropocene world? This section develops a typology of impacts that can be used to consider possible consequences and responses under the scenarios described above of i) a steady state/growth agnostic economy (SSE), ii) voluntary degrowth (VDG), and iii) involuntary degrowth (IDG).

Table 4.1 summarizes some critical economic consequences of these three scenarios, against a range of factors likely to have relevance to the functioning

Table 4.1 Potential Anthropocene-induced economic impacts on health care systems

Macroeconomic factors	Steady state economy	Voluntary degrowth	Involuntary degrowth
Real resource physical availability (scarcity or controls)	SSE operates through strict policy-driven quantity controls on material throughput.	Likely to use quantity controls but also potential scarcity driven by demand destruction.	Absolute scarcity and potential loss of ability to extract or distribute key resources.
Real resource prices	Fixed quantities mean that resource prices are set by policy auctions. Policy-induced scarcity will raise prices of many resource inputs.	As SSE – but demand destruction might lead to price falls for some resources.	Highly unpredictable. Absolute scarcity may drive high prices; demand destruction may lead to low prices and industry collapse.
Pollution controls – physical controls/bans	An increased number of polluting products/compounds likely to be banned or strictly controlled.	An increased number of polluting products/compounds likely to be banned or strictly controlled.	Enforcement capability undermined; collapse of modern manufacturing may lead to use of more harmful substitutes.
Pollution pricing/ taxation	May well be used alongside resource auctions, further raising effective prices.	As SSE.	Enforcement/collection capability undermined.
Relative prices	Relative price of labour likely to fall (notwithstanding other demographic effects), reducing capital intensity and saving automation for high value applications.	As SSE – although wages may fall significantly under GDP degrowth.	Highly unpredictable.
Macroeconomic and financing capacity	Successful SSE policies likely to create strong and stable financing for social sectors, but no longer able to support absolute and relative growth in health spending.	Voluntary GDP degrowth likely to be challenging for health system financing capacity; significant risks of overshoot and policy error causing periodic economic crises.	Depth and length of any period of involuntary degrowth is highly unpredictable. However, health financing capacity (public or private) likely to be gravely undermined.
Distributional factors	SSE model likely to involve higher income and wealth taxes, luxury taxes; discourage positional consumption; jobs guarantee and/or Universal Basic Income.	Similar to SSE, but less explicitly discussed in degrowth literature beyond calls for Universal Basic Income.	Mass impoverishment likely to coexist with extreme inequality and wealthy elites (even if the latter's wealth is much reduced from today).

(continued)

Table 4.1 Potential Anthropocene-induced economic impacts on health care systems (continued)

Macroeconomic factors	Steady state economy	Voluntary degrowth	Involuntary degrowth
Reduced access to traded goods/services/ labour	Trade volume likely to reduce, mediated via resource controls and import substitution. However, trade would continue to be of substantial importance. Stricter migration controls?	GDP degrowth likely to substantially reduce global trade and migration flows.	Global trade likely to reduce precipitately, and with it access to traded goods. However, distress-driven migration might increase.
Reduced societal/ institutional capacity to support complexity	Limited, deliberate and carefully managed reduction in complexity is conceivable under SSE.	Deliberate and managed reduction of complexity as an aim of policy – but with attendant risks of overshoot and error.	The defining feature of involuntary degrowth – substantial and abrupt reductions in complexity with many negative consequences on most aspects of society and the economy.

and financing of health systems. Some high-level conclusions to be drawn from table 4.1 include the following. Both SSE and VDG models fundamentally entail substantial changes to natural resource extraction, use, and material through-put. This might quite dramatically change relative prices in the economy, with profound impacts for all economic sectors, including health. Whether prices or other rationing mechanisms are used, robust controls on material throughput will necessitate very significant changes in the societal priority afforded to different forms of consumption at the margin, with health care no exception. The relative price of labour (however highly skilled) is likely to change significantly in relation to other non-human inputs, with the potential for more materially resource-intensive "treatments" to become substantially more expensive relative to labour-intensive human "care," even as automation and artificial intelligence continue to impact on demand for labour. Health systems are also likely to feel the impact of significantly deeper controls on pollutants of many forms – most obviously in greenhouse gas emissions, but also as the harmful impacts of environmental releases of pharmaceuticals are increasingly recognized (The Lancet Planetary Health, 2018; UNEP, 2017).

The consequences of the SSE or VDG models for health care financing are clearly significant. What the SSE cannot do – by its nature – is to guarantee the ability to support continued growth in health care expenditure of the type seen in high-income countries since the Second World War. Under SSE, an increasing share of society's resources could continue to be allocated to health care, in theory at least – but this would represent a growing share of a fixed pie, rather than the post-war experience of a growing share of a growing pie. Under VDG, financing capacity for health care is likely to be very significantly challenged. Real GDP degrowth would almost certainly need to involve real reductions in health care spending in high-income countries; the deeper the overall GDP degrowth target, the deeper the concomitant reduction in health care spending. Ecological macroeconomists are beginning to investigate another issue of great significance for health financing policy – namely whether a post-growth SSE or VDG economic model will be inherently stable, or as prone to instability and crisis as the capitalist growth model has been. Using a Minskyan model, Barrett (2018) suggests that growth and no-growth macroeconomic scenarios may display both stable and unstable states, but that zero-growth models appear no more likely to give rise to runaway explosive instability than growth models. Others (e.g. Cahen-Fourot and Lavoie, 2016; Lawn, 2011) have considered whether a stationary or steady state economy can be compatible with capitalism more generally (and money creation via interest-bearing debt specifically), with varying conclusions. Hardt and O'Neill (2017) conclude their survey of ecological macroeconomic models with the suggestion that the question of stability is a critical area for further research.

Table 4.1 also makes clear the fundamental difference between the SSE and VDG scenarios, under which the economy remains under some degree of policy direction and responsiveness, and the Involuntary Degrowth scenario, under which cascading problems pull the economy out of control and into a period of substantial loss of complexity. The likely duration of any such period of IDG is hard to predict, as would be the depth and impact of the attendant reduction in system complexity – but table 4.1 shows many potential points of transmission into the health sector through the economic mechanisms summarized. Just like SSE and VDG, IDG would certainly display absolute and relative scarcity of key resources; under IDG this would be chaotic and essentially unguided by policy. Under IDG, health financing capacity is likely to be severely undermined – both due to macroeconomic constraints, and to degraded institutional capability in both public and private sectors. This loss of institutional capability and complexity would, of course, impact health care systems in many ways beyond financing, ranging from the availability of key technologies through to the ability to continue to train skilled health professionals for the future.

Health Policy Responses to a Steady State or Degrowth Economy

Based on the assessment in table 4.1 and above, it is possible to summarize some critical challenges that any successful health policy would be required to address in an economy transforming towards a steady state or voluntary degrowth model. First, the health care sector would need to minimize its own material throughput and ecological footprint, in response to a macro-policy environment of intense pressure to reduce resource use and emissions and pollution. Second, health systems must reconcile the historical trend towards continuous growth in resources for health care with a potentially zero growth or real degrowth macroeconomic environment. Put crudely, meeting these challenges requires health systems to either greatly increase the efficiency of their resource use (technical efficiency), or to reduce the scale and scope of services produced and provided through active prioritization and resource allocation decisions (allocative efficiency) – or, more likely, to do both simultaneously.

Health Care and Overconsumption

Like all economic activities, it is clear that health care plays its part in driving ecological damage through natural resource use and pollution, and appreciation of this impact is growing. Recent studies point to health care contributing some 4 per cent, 7 per cent and 8–10 per cent of all national greenhouse gas emissions in the UK, Australia and the USA respectively (Malik et al., 2018; Taylor and Mackie, 2017). The imperative need for health care to reduce this emissions footprint has been recognized for some time (Schroeder et al., 2012). Efforts to reduce overall greenhouse emissions and other areas in which health care may contribute to pollution and resource depletion threatening "planetary boundaries" (Steffen, Richardson, et al., 2015) will necessarily involve health systems in making significant changes to reduce consumption of non-renewable resources, even if all the outputs generated by modern health care were viewed unambiguously as beneficial.

However, concern is growing that patients may increasingly be exposed to "too much medicine" (Macdonald and Loder, 2015). Evidence of overdiagnosis (the detection of anomalies that would not have led to clinically significant disease) and overtreatment (treatments providing no clinical benefit and potentially risking harm) has grown rapidly (Carter et al., 2015; Moynihan, Henry, and Moons, 2014; Welch, Schwartz, and Woloshin 2011), as has evidence of overuse (provision of treatments to patients in whom they offer a poor risk to benefit ratio) and "low value care" (Chan et al., 2013; O'Callaghan, Meyer, and Elshaug, 2015). Gabe et al. (2015) and Busfield (2015) describe how "pharmaceuticalisation" increasingly sees drugs employed in ever larger populations of patients, many of whom are increasingly likely not yet to have experienced clinical symptoms. All these phenomena represent both waste (use of resources for little or no benefit) and potential harm (as patients are exposed to the inherent risks of medical treatment).

Meanwhile, quantitative estimates of the scale of waste in health care systems typically yield large numbers. For example, Berwick and Hackbarth (2012) generate a low estimate that 21 per cent of US health care expenditure is wasted in one form or other, with 6–8 per cent of total expenditure representing overtreatment and overuse. Internationally, the OECD (2017) estimates that one-fifth of health care expenditure is wasted, with some 10 per cent of hospital spending reflecting the costs of correcting harms caused to patients by health care. Brownlee et al. (2017) reviewed international evidence on overuse and waste at procedure and intervention level, showing high proportions of common interventions to be inappropriate across many different countries.

Hensher, Tisdell, and Zimitat (2017) have identified that these connected phenomena of overdiagnosis, overtreatment, overuse, and waste in health care are examples of the concepts of both overconsumption and misconsumption developed by Princen (1999), and of Daly's concept of uneconomic growth (Daly, 2006). Princen argues that overconsumption reflects societal consumption choices that, while individually rational, will collectively undermine a species' well-being or survival over time (e.g. via environmental impacts), while misconsumption occurs when individual consumption choices undermine even that individual's well-being (e.g. exposing oneself to harmful treatments with no upside). Growth in non-beneficial health care provides a sectoral example of uneconomic growth, which occurs when continuing increases in production in fact yield net reductions in human well-being through social or environmental harms that outweigh the benefits of that additional production (Daly, 1999, 2006).

Nested within this general problem of overconsumption and misconsumption of health care is the specific phenomenon of antimicrobial resistance (AMR) arising from inappropriate overuse of antibiotics and other antimicrobials. AMR displays features of a negative externality, whereby additional costs (in this case, the loss of efficacy of antimicrobial drugs) fall on actors (society at large) not party to individual treatment transactions (Cecchini and Lee, 2017), and of a common pool resource problem (Ostrom, 2005). AMR is of deep significance not only because it represents highly undesirable current overconsumption, but because of the real risk that a failure to control AMR could undermine decades of progress in reducing mortality from infections, and render many currently routine medical interventions highly risky, costly, or simply impossible (RoAR, 2014; Smith and Coast, 2013). Under resource-constrained future scenarios, and especially under IDG, failure to control AMR risks a profound loss of optionality that future health care systems might never be able to regain.

The preceding discussion suggests that a non-trivial quantum of health care provision in developed countries yields little or no benefit while simultaneously exposing patients to potential harm and generating negative environmental impacts. Any transformative model of health care that seeks to deal with the realities of the Anthropocene era would be well-advised to start with the elimination of unnecessary and low-value care. Doing so yields little or no risk to human health (it may even improve it by reducing iatrogenic harms) while offering substantial opportunities to reduce consumption, material throughput, and environmental harms.

Technical and Allocative Efficiency in a Steady State or Degrowth Health System

Beyond the elimination of unnecessary or harmful overconsumption, any transition away from the traditional economic growth model will require health systems to focus ever more intently on technical, economic, and allocative efficiency. Technical efficiency refers to maximizing outputs for a given set of physical inputs (or minimizing physical inputs for a given output), while economic efficiency refers to maximizing outputs for a given budget (or minimizing costs for a given output); allocative efficiency refers to the achievement of an optimal balance of health care production across society, or producing the best possible mix of services to maximize benefit (Hensher, 2001).

Substantial evidence suggests that a degree of technical inefficiency will obtain at any given time in all health systems (Hensher, 2001). Faced with tougher resource constraints (especially for energy and material throughput), there is no question that post-growth health systems would need to be intently focused on minimizing the resource inputs required to produce desired outputs. As a discipline, health economics has a great deal to offer in this area, albeit with the need to incorporate appropriate measures to reflect "true" or "shadow" prices for key non-renewable or polluting resources. Yet the apparently straightforward need for continuous efficiency improvement carries with it one particular risk – the potential for "rebound" or "Jevons" effects. The Jevons paradox (named after the nineteenth-century English economist William Stanley Jevons, who originated the concept with reference to coal consumption and the efficiency of utilization of coal) proceeds from the observation that improved efficiency in resource use often does not result in a reduction in the use of that resource, but an increase – because improved efficiency has reduced costs, stimulating further production and demand (Alcott, 2005). There appears to be some prima facie evidence that rebound effects are present in health care. Examples include significant decreases in the costs of antidepressant medications being accompanied by large increases in their prescribing (Busfield, 2015), increased demand and utilization following the shifting of services from hospital settings to community-based settings (Hensher, 1997; Sibbald, McDonald, and Roland, 2007), and the post-war historical trend that saw hospital admission rates rise inexorably even as hospital bed numbers shrank continuously in the UK (Hensher and Edwards, 1999). The likelihood and consequences of Jevons effects in health care in a post-growth transition require urgent investigation if they are to be avoided.

Allocative efficiency – attempting to judge the socially optimal mix of interventions to be funded and/or provided – has, through the increasing institutionalization of economic evaluation in many countries, in many ways become the primary business of health economics (e.g. Drummond et al., 2015). There are good reasons to believe that the structural adoption of CEA for Health

Technology Assessment in high-income countries may have inadvertently fallen prey to regulatory capture by industry interests, with the CEA thresholds used for new technologies appearing to be well in excess of those observed in established health care programs (Cairns, 2016; Martin, Rice, and Smith, 2012). In a post-growth world, real scarcity will become the driver of prioritization decisions, not the marketing strategies of pharmaceutical firms. For all its imperfections, CEA has an enormous amount to offer as one important (but not the only) tool in the toolbox for dealing with real scarcity (Mills, 2016). A great deal of experience has been gained in low- and middle-income countries on developing "essential packages of care" using sectoral cost-effectiveness analyses (Jamison, Dean et al., 2006; Jamison, Dean et al., 2018), and a strong supporting data and analytical infrastructure now exists in this space that could easily support different goals for prioritization. A rigorous and critical appraisal of the best of this learning (shorn of the ideological commitments to private financing and provision which have often accompanied these approaches), explicitly translated to degrowth scenarios, would be invaluable. It would also help provide a common frame of reference across nations of differing (current) levels of income and wealth, identifying where growth in health expenditure and provision is needed to deal with the gross underuse and provision that still plagues billions of people (Glasziou et al., 2017), while providing a rather bracing corrective to overuse in the rich world.

One of the ironies of the institutionalization of CEA within Health Technology Assessment programs has been the resulting ascendancy of "market"-based valuation and willingness to pay valuations – which explicitly cast health care as a want (and hence commodifiable), and not as a basic need. Yet the unique problems arising from the commodification of health care and the lack of correspondence between market demand for health care and socially (or even individually) optimal outcomes have been recognized since the very beginnings of health economics (Arrow, 1963; Boulding, 1966). In contrast, much of the work developed for sectoral cost-effectiveness analysis and essential packages can be used directly to support needs-based planning and prioritization, and is ideally suited to the application of more stringent budget constraints under degrowth conditions.

The Health of the Global Poor

Much of the preceding discussion – in common with the broader literature on alternatives to growth – has focused mainly on the health and health care systems of the high-income nations, which have been the greatest beneficiaries of the Great Acceleration. Yet the citizens of these nations make up only a minority of the world population. While it is true that the health and health care enjoyed by many people in upper middle-income countries is moving in a similar direction (and hence these nations should attempt to learn lessons from high income countries, if only to avoid some of their mistakes), health and health care as experienced in the poorest countries is profoundly different. It is therefore necessary to review briefly some aggregate data on global disparities in health status and health expenditure before considering the implications of post-growth macroeconomic models for health in low- and lower-middle income countries.

Figure 4.2 shows the distribution of life expectancy at birth in the years 2000 and 2016, for the 183 countries for which WHO data is available. In 2000, overall global life expectancy stood at 66.5 years. It was highest in Japan, at 81.3 years, and lowest in then conflict-ridden Sierra Leone, at just 39.8 years – indeed, Japanese life expectancy at birth was more than 41 years greater than that in Sierra Leone. Striking gains have been made in the intervening years. Japan still led the world in life expectancy in 2016 at 84.2 years, but the world's lowest life expectancy was now to be found in Lesotho, at 52.9 years. Over that period, life expectancy in Sierra Leone had risen more than 13 years to 53.1. While figure 4.2 shows that life expectancy has continued to rise in the rich world, perhaps more noteworthy is the visible "pivot" upwards of the lowest end of the life expectancy distribution, with the disparity between best and worst performers having reduced by more than ten years. Nonetheless, this leaves a gap of more than thirty years in life expectancy between Japanese and Basotho, with all the differences in life opportunity this implies.

Figure 4.3 displays a similar distribution curve for "health adjusted life expectancy" (HALE) – a measure that adjusts life expectancy at birth with weightings for the period of time lived in poor health (using weightings from the Global Burden of Disease Study). HALE thus provides a more nuanced measure, accounting not only for mortality, but also for non-fatal burden of disease. Health adjusted life expectancy in Japan (then the world leader) was 72.5 years in 2000, and HALE was lowest in Sierra Leone at 35.6 years – the same relative positions as for life expectancy, but with a slightly smaller gap of 36.9 years. By 2016, Singapore had overtaken Japan with the highest HALE of 76.2 years, while the Central African Republic now had the lowest HALE at 44.9 years. Yet, despite the same pivoting upwards of countries with low HALEs, the same thirty-one-year disparity between best and worst performing nations is as apparent for HALE as it is for life expectancy.

In some ways, figure 4.4 (infant mortality rates per 1,000 live births) shows a similar story, especially in the downwards pivot of infant mortality since 2000 in those countries that previously had the highest rates of infant death. Yet this can obscure the reality of the disparity between richest and poorest in this measure. In 2016, a baby born in the Central African Republic was fifty-two times more likely to have died before its first birthday than was a child born in Iceland. Indeed, while the highest *absolute* national IMR fell by over a third

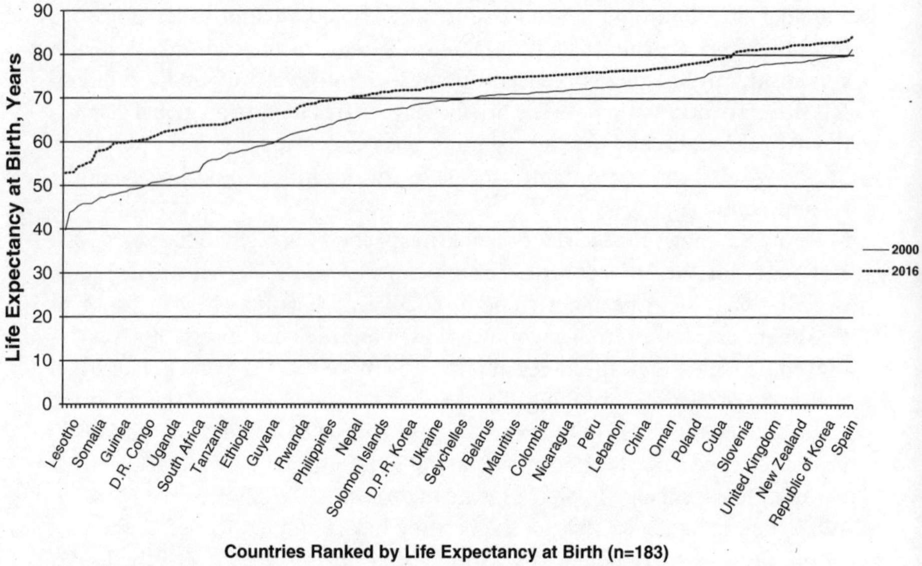

Figure 4.2 Life expectancy distribution by country, 2000 and 2016
(n.b. country names refer to 2016 data).
Source: World Health Organization Global Health Observatory Data Repository, http://apps.who
.int/gho/data/node.main.688?lang=en (accessed 29 September 2018)

between 2000 and 2016, the *disparity* in IMR between highest and lowest countries actually grew, from a multiple of 47 to 52 times.

By contrast, the shape of the distribution of health expenditure per capita shown in figure 4.5 tells an altogether different story. Table 4.2 provides data for the top and bottom five nations, with global mean and median values. Health expenditure per capita (in 2014) shows an extremely skewed distribution, whether measured at current US dollar exchange rates or at Purchasing Power Parities (PPP). Expenditure per capita rises slowly, with half of all nations spending less than $375 per capita (or $668 in PPP terms). Rather strikingly, China sits right next to the median spend on both measures (at $376, immediately next to median nation Dominica's $375 at USD rates, and at $658 next to median nation Grenada's $668 at PPP rates). Fully 136 out of 190 (71 per cent) of nations spent less than the mean global expenditure per capita measured at market exchange rates ($900). But to the right of that mean lies a near exponential increase in spending. The extent of the disparity in health spending per capita is eye-watering. At market exchange rates, top-spending Switzerland spends 562 times more per capita than the bottom-placed Central African Republic. The

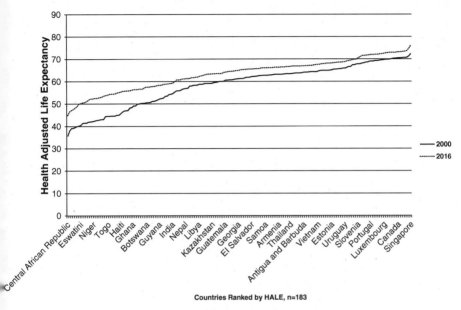

Figure 4.3   Health adjusted life expectancy distribution by country, 2000 and 2016 (n.b. country names refer to 2016 data).
Source: World Health Organization Global Health Observatory Data Repository, http://apps.who.int/gho/data/node.main.HALE?lang=en (accessed 29 September 2018)

use of PPP rates reduces this multiple (now between the US and the CAR) to a factor of a mere 304 times. Clearly, spending per capita cannot tell us everything about the availability of and access to health care resources in different countries; yet these enormous disparities in spending unquestionably represent vast differences in real access to care between the peoples of these nations.

The continued existence of these disparities in health and access to health care between the citizens of rich and poor nations is a challenge that any proposed economic model – including "business as usual" – must be able to address convincingly. The evolution of these disparities unsurprisingly displays some of the same themes that have been remarked upon in recent work on global income and wealth inequalities (e.g. Milanovic, 2016; Ravallion, 2014). The development orthodoxy that has prevailed for many years has posited economic growth as the necessary condition for reducing poverty in lower-income countries, and has more or less explicitly accepted rising inequalities within and between nations as a necessary consequence of rapid economic growth (Ravallion, 2014). Meanwhile, in recent decades, income inequality *between* nations has fallen significantly, with the inequality gap between

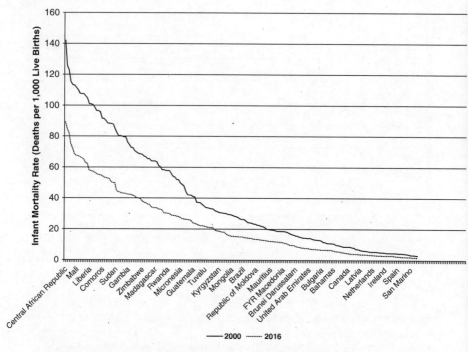

Figure 4.4 Infant mortality rate distribution by country, 2000 and 2016
(n.b. country names refer to 2016 data).
Source: World Health Organization Global Health Observatory Data Repository, http://apps.who
.int/gho/data/node.main.525?lang=en (accessed 29 September 2018)

countries probably reaching its height around 1970 (Milanovic, 2016), even
while inequality *within* nations has increased almost everywhere since that
time. Since then, very significant numbers of people have been lifted out of
extreme poverty with the creation of a new global "middle class." Similarly, in
the health status indicators presented above, there is clear evidence of progress
over time, with progressive reduction in mortality and visible signs of a "level-
ling up" of the middle of the distribution towards the health status of the best-
off countries. Indeed, this hope of a "great convergence" (Jamison, Dean et al.,
2013) has been an explicit aim of global health policy in recent years, especially
in the preparation of the Sustainable Development Goals. Yet the emerging
evidence on global income inequality might give us pause for thought before
we become too excited about a global convergence in health. Much of this "lift
out of poverty" represents a shift of people from the "extreme poverty" category (i.e. living on less than USD$1 or $2 per day) into the "low income" category of $3 or more per day – a change in category that should not be derided,

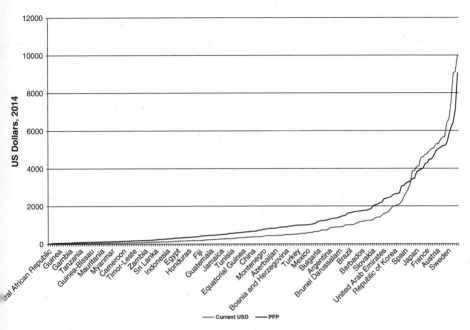

Figure 4.5 Current health expenditure per capita distribution by country, 2014
(n.b. country names refer to current USD data).
Source: World Health Organization Global Health Observatory Data Repository, http://apps.who
.int/gho/data/node.main.GHEDCHFpcUSSHA2011?lang=en (accessed 29 September 2018)

but that is a very different phenomenon from these people becoming "middle class" in any conventional sense of the term (Benatar, 2016). Milanovic (2016) sounds a number of notes of caution which are almost certainly directly transferable to global health inequalities. First, he notes that, while inequality between nations has been falling, the global Gini coefficient (a key measure of inequality) is in fact still higher than the national Gini coefficients of the world's two most unequal societies, South Africa and Colombia. Second – and perhaps most crucially – Milanovic notes that the global income convergence is almost entirely confined to progress made by Asian nations in catching up with the rich world. By contrast, African GDP per capita grew slower between 1970 and 2013 than did GDP in the developed countries, with some countries (e.g. Madagascar, the Democratic Republic of Congo) now actually having a lower real GDP per capita than they did in 1950 (Milanovic, 2016). That many African nations are being left behind in health and health care seems unarguable, given the data on health expenditure in figure 4.5 and table 4.2. Indeed, Benatar (2016) suggests that trying to read these data as providing any strong

Table 4.2 Highest and lowest national health expenditure per capita, 2014

	Current USD exchange rates $		Purchasing power parity $	
Top 5	Switzerland	10,006	United States of America	9,060
	Norway	9,118	Switzerland	7,145
	United States of America	9,060	Luxembourg	6,463
	Luxembourg	7,557	Norway	6,177
	Sweden	6,629	Andorra	5,811
	Global mean	*900*	*Global mean*	*n/a*
	Global median	*375*	*Global median*	*668*
Bottom 5	Ethiopia	23	Guinea	55
	Madagascar	22	Burundi	55
	Burundi	20	South Sudan	53
	Democratic Republic of Congo	19	Democratic Republic of Congo	33
	Central African Republic	18	Central African Republic	30

support for a "grand convergence" in global health outcomes is not only optimistic, but positively evasive.

Moyn (2018) provides an extensive analysis of how the dominant philosophical and policy approaches to problems of inequality, poverty, and meeting the basic needs of the poorest have changed over the last century or more. He describes the ongoing struggle between what he describes as sufficiency and egalitarianism. Approaches built around sufficiency aim to ensure that the poorest have a sufficient level of subsistence to enable them to exist decently, but are unconcerned about relative inequality (as long as the poorest can subsist acceptably, the extreme wealth of the richest is of no moral or policy consequence). Egalitarian approaches, while equally concerned about the lot of the poorest, are also actively concerned with reducing disparities in wealth and income, on the basis that extreme inequalities are viewed as having morally and socially corrosive consequences; extremes of inequality should be reined in by limiting the wealth and power of the richest. Moyn describes how attempts by nations of the Global South to work towards a more explicitly egalitarian "New International Economic order" in the 1970s were overtaken by neoliberalism and replaced by a much more modest focus on meeting "basic needs," which has inadvertently been reinforced by the rise of the international human rights movement. Brown (2015) goes further, in suggesting that the ascendance of what she calls "neoliberal rationality" has gravely undermined the ability of democracies even to conceive of and debate moral alternatives, such as the choice between sufficiency and egalitarianism. In considering how "global health" has been conceptualized under neoliberalism, Benatar (2016) argues that the health of the poorest can only truly be advanced by fundamental changes to the mental models that have guided global economic and health policy for decades:

> The dominant and dominating mind-set of the most privileged people in the world tends to lock us into our particular utopian realms of thinking and action that must surely seem mysterious, untrustworthy and irremediable to those whose lives remain severely restricted by socially constructed causes of poverty and lack of opportunities to flourish. (Benatar, 2016)

Improving the Health of the Poorest in the Anthropocene Era

These would be daunting challenges even without the intrusion of the Anthropocene into the equation. In this case, its most obvious impacts occur via the increasingly well-understood mechanisms by which climate change and the transgression of various other planetary boundaries will have a disproportionately large and adverse effect on the health of the world's poorest (Costello et al., 2009; Watts et al., 2015; Whitmee et al., 2015). Asymmetrically severe health impacts on the poorest will necessarily make the reduction of inequalities harder rather than easier to achieve in purely practical terms. However, the primary focus of the discussion that follows will be to consider whether and how the ecological macroeconomic models described earlier can be used to continue to improve the health of the poor and reduce health inequalities, even in a post-growth world. While these models all to some degree require consumption by the rich to be constrained or reduced (the most fundamental point of departure from the current economic model), this may or may not give rise to any direct redistribution of resources from rich to poor. The tension between sufficiency and egalitarianism may still express itself in a post-growth world order, and any post-growth economic model must meet the needs of the poor, not just the affluent. This brief discussion will attempt to outline some of these issues.

Within most post-growth economic models (e.g. SSE and degrowth), the idea that material consumption may still need to grow in lower-income countries even while consumption is curtailed in the rich world is not especially contentious, and is frequently alluded to. Perhaps the most systematic exposition of this has taken the form of longstanding proposals for "contraction and convergence" (e.g. Stott, 2012), which explicitly posit reductions in carbon emissions by the rich sufficiently large to allow an appropriate degree of increased emissions by the world's poorest. Similarly, Di Giulio and Fuchs (2014) have proposed the idea of "sustainable consumption corridors," under which everyone is guaranteed a minimum "floor" level of consumption to allow them to live a good life, but which also impose consumption "ceilings" (or maxima) to ensure sufficient resources are available to all within an ecologically sustainable envelope.

A great deal of experience has been gained in low- and middle-income countries on developing "essential packages of care" using sectoral cost-effectiveness analyses (Jamison, Dean et al., 2006; Jamison, Dean et al., 2018), and a strong supporting data and analytical infrastructure now exists in this space, which could easily support different goals for prioritization. A rigorous and critical appraisal of the best of this learning (shorn of the ideological commitments to private financing and provision that have often accompanied these approaches), explicitly translated to post-growth scenarios, would be invaluable. It would also help provide a common frame of reference across nations of differing (current) levels of income and wealth, identifying where growth in health expenditure and provision is needed to deal with the gross underuse and provision that still plagues billions of people (Glasziou et al., 2017), while providing a rather bracing corrective to overuse in the rich world. At least in principle, sectoral cost-effectiveness analysis could be modified to develop health sector–specific sustainable consumption corridors that specify both minima and maxima for access to and consumption of health services.

Indeed, recent large-scale modelling exercises emphasize the urgent need for a reinvigorated focus on meeting the basic health needs of the poorest (i.e. in raising the floor of any future sustainable consumption corridor). Stenberg et al. (2017) estimate that, by 2030, an additional USD$371 billion annual health spending will be needed globally to meet the health targets set for Sustainable Development Goal 3 (SDG3, healthy lives and well-being), requiring per capita health spending in the poorest countries of $271 per person (compare this with figure 4.5 and table 4.2 for a crude sense of the change this would entail). Meanwhile, Kruk et al. (2018) estimate that providing universal health coverage to meet the conditions targeted by SDG3 could avert 8.6 million deaths per year in low- and middle-income countries, both by improving access to care and by improving mortality due to poor quality care. These studies, and the many others that have resulted from decades of work on the Global Burden of Disease Project (e.g. WHO, 2019) provide a rigorous infrastructure on which to build the sufficient "floor" for a health-related sustainable consumption corridor. Ironically, much more work is required to develop an equally rigorous framework by which to arrive at a "ceiling" for maximum consumption levels. Work on quantifying the overconsumption of health care has started (Berwick and Hackbarth, 2012; Brownlee et al., 2017; OECD, 2017; Saini et al., 2017), but this work remains tentative and somewhat controversial. Work on defining the sufficient maximum or ceiling for health care consumption in the rich world requires an equivalent investment of resources, talent, and imagination as that devoted to more traditional global health concerns, and it needs to make space for the same techniques of large-scale sectoral cost-effectiveness analysis that are applied without question in lower-income settings.

Even within the frameworks of contraction and convergence or sustainable consumption corridors, some significant questions remain that cannot be solved by technical analysis alone. We might agree on the desirability of a sustainable consumption corridor approach; yet what happens to the resources released by the application of the consumption ceiling in the rich world, and from where do the resources come to meet the consumption floor for the poorest? If we can control or reduce overconsumption of health care in high-income countries, does this release real resources that could be transferred to low-income countries (e.g. health professionals, pharmaceuticals, etc.)? Or does it release funding that could potentially be redistributed through some explicit commitment to a more egalitarian approach to redistributing income and wealth between nations? Under voluntary degrowth in particular, would today's rich nations in fact have any fiscal capacity to transfer resources to the low-income world? Or would ending overconsumption of health care by the rich not transfer any resources per se, but simply open up additional safe space for growth in consumption by the poor? And given the existing problem of persistently low economic growth in the world's poorest nations (especially in Africa), does "space for growth" actually amount to any real improvement, or does it simply offer a hypothetical option that many African nations could not exercise in reality without greatly increased development assistance? Ecological economists and advocates of post-growth economic models must give these questions more attention if they are not also to be found guilty of Benatar's charge of indulging in utopian thinking that fails to meet the needs of the world's poorest (Benatar, 2016).

It is, however, possible to make some more modest suggestions that might help policy formulation even in the absence of resolving these higher-level questions. Despite being recognized for some years as a problem, and with many commitments to action (e.g. Eastwood et al., 2005), the migration of scarce skilled health professionals from the poorest countries remains an issue. While the impacts of climate change may drive further migration, there is a strong argument that post-growth health policies should work harder to stem the ongoing problem of "brain drain." At the same time, access to affordable pharmaceuticals under current intellectual property regimes remains an enormous impediment to global health equity, while attempts to further strengthen monopoly patent protections have continued apace in recent years (Baker, 2016). Indeed, migration, free trade, and intellectual property policy all sit squarely on current fault lines between neoliberalism and the "populist" political wave that has emerged around the world. Intelligent policy for a post-growth era needs to be agile enough to exploit these openings in the pursuit of global justice and sustainability, without debasing its ethical underpinnings.

Finally, study after study has shown that the only effective engine for improving universal health coverage and access to health care in low- and middle-income countries is strengthening government expenditure on health care (Dieleman, et al., 2017; McIntyre, Meheus, and Røttingen, 2017). Even without the need for an overarching global redistributive framework, the jury on health financing for universal coverage is in: only increasing government expenditure can achieve the needed improvements in coverage and access to basic health care for the world's poorest. This will remain true under any post-growth development model, and it is now time to accept that neoliberalism's fixation on marketization and privatization in all sectors has been comprehensively negated by the most recent evidence on health financing. Those planning post-growth alternatives should bear this finding carefully in mind.

Involuntary Degrowth – The Collapse Problem

Failure to act on overshoot and ecological degradation carries the ever-present risk of reaching those system tipping points that might trip society into the trajectory of involuntary degrowth. For rich and poor alike, avoiding the path of involuntary degrowth and collapse is a prerequisite if we are to maintain the capability to promote meaningful human flourishing. Yet the discussion in this chapter also points out that voluntary degrowth – however inadvertently – carries the same risk. It can be quite hard to see how meaningful policy preparations for IDG can really be made in advance. As already noted, two approaches might be relevant. As discussed earlier, the first is to position ourselves to take maximum advantage of the positive opportunities of catagenesis. This avenue is not developed further here. The second approach is to improve resilience, flexibility, and survivability. IDG essentially represents the unplanned and undesired loss of layers of complexity from society and its institutions. IDG would result in significant loss of functionality and capability in modern health care systems; it might take years or decades for these systems to stabilize and rebuild themselves coherently at lower levels of complexity. There is obviously no blueprint that could be offered in response to such a trajectory, and it is exceedingly difficult to apply conventional economic analysis to such a scenario. It is, however, possible to identify a number of areas in which resilience and flexibility could be strengthened today, in order to maximize future options and to minimize losses in a future of involuntary degrowth. Economic analysis tools, such as Real Options Analysis (Buurman and Babovic, 2016), could then potentially be used to assist the incorporation of such actions into policy choices before an irreversible IDG path has taken hold. Three such areas will be identified here: preserving, protecting, and transmitting useful knowledge of appropriate technologies; fostering a professional culture of sufficiency and resilience; and safeguarding critical production technologies.

Great strides have been made in systematizing the capture and dissemination of information on best practice in health care, through such initiatives as the Cochrane Collaboration (Cochrane Library, 2019). Quite reasonably, such efforts almost invariably focus on the current state of knowledge, and on what constitutes the best evidence for action in today's health system. It might be possible to develop more contingent guides, assessing what might represent best feasible management of key conditions given very differing levels of resource availability in future, and to expose health workers to these guides early in their careers – rather like a specialized "where there is no doctor" for health professionals (Werner, 2004). Such guidance would certainly require significant historical input, yet would also need to be maintained and updated in light of changing knowledge both before and, indeed, during IDG. This would require a dedicated, non-market institution, endowed with the resources and the sense of mission to endure under very adverse circumstances.

The professional formation and culture of health workers is essential to how they subsequently work and practice. Contemporary medical and nursing culture has typically equated "best practice" with higher resourcing and more intensive management and intervention, with a tendency to respond to uncertainty by intervening more actively to avoid later regret (Djulbegovic and Paul, 2011). Efforts to build a culture based more on principles of sufficiency ("enough") would not only yield benefits today, but better equip professionals for a future in which resources are scarcer (Hensher, Tisdell, and Zimitat, 2017; Princen, 2003). This could also provide opportunities to expose professionals to the possibility of IDG, and to prepare them both professionally and mentally for a severely resource-constrained future in which they may need to be ready to change their practice substantially.

Currently, most manufacturing of essential drugs, vaccines, medical devices, and consumables is undertaken in the private sector. There are many problems with this arrangement (Goldacre, 2013; Mazzucato, 2013; Rosenthal, 2017), but most relevant here is the ability of manufacturers to exit production of unprofitable products. As a period of involuntary degrowth got started, we might expect great disruption and loss of profitability in all sectors. Private firms will then either fail entirely or be forced to make socially undesirable choices to remain in business, while existing infrastructure, production and distribution models and even skills may become increasingly difficult to sustain as the global consequences of IDG take hold. One possible hedge against this eventuality might be the formation of nonprofit health product manufacturers, owned or controlled as public utilities at national or supra-national levels. The mission of such a health utility would be to develop and improve local, low-cost, and resilient manufacturing processes for key classes of products, especially essential medicines (particularly antibiotics) and vaccines. It might be granted rights under law to obtain, disseminate, and use the intellectual property pertaining to any product that is unavailable (or at risk of unavailability) in the market, or rights to manufacture a product or products from every main category in order to develop broad expertise. As well as being a provider of last resort, this utility would explicitly develop and deploy low-tech and resilient manufacturing technologies, and have legislated rights to take over without compensation the assets (physical and intellectual) and staff of any private provider deemed to be failing. Its mandate would ensure it had little or no interest in traditional new product development, but a keen interest in the development of alternative and appropriate manufacturing and distribution technologies and infrastructure. It would be "hardened" by design to be better able to survive and remain operational in an environment of IDG. Once again, the existence of such a public utility might have significant benefits even in the absence of IDG, with the idea of a pharmaceutical utility being proposed recently in the US (Gaffney, 2018) – however the utility proposed here would not compete with the private sector, but rather stand ready to replace it were IDG to undermine the financial and technical viability of private firms.

Concluding Comments

This chapter has argued that modern health care is an integral component of the Great Acceleration and the growth economy. Health care therefore cannot be insulated from changes to the wider economy – be that the growth of recent decades, some future radical transition to a steady state or voluntary degrowth economy, or a sudden shift to involuntary degrowth. Indeed, health care is now a significant contributor to today's unsustainable economic growth. The chapter has considered the most plausible models from the ecological macroeconomics literature of more fundamental transitions to sustainability, namely the steady state economy and voluntary degrowth, and has outlined what these models might mean for health systems. It has also examined the ever-present risk of involuntary degrowth.

In essence, the promise of limitless abundance that has justified growth economics (despite the conspicuous absence of abundance for much of the world's population) is untenable and illusory. The future is far more likely to be one of scarcity: tightly managed, policy-driven scarcity under SSE or VDG scenarios, or an open-ended, uncontrolled spiral of loss under involuntary degrowth. Scarcity – and the allocation of resources under conditions of scarcity – has always been the central, self-defined mission of economics as a discipline. The close embrace of mainstream economics with the neoliberal ideological project in recent decades has gravely shifted attention away from the central economic problem of justly and efficiently allocating scarce real resources to advance the common good, and instead focused on justifying a particular (and particularly unjust and inefficient) pattern of distribution of wealth and power (Bezemer and Hudson, 2016). Yet economics and economists still have many tools and skills with which to help society navigate the return of scarcity that real sustainability must entail. Many of the tools of health economics can be readily recalibrated to operate effectively and helpfully outside today's narrow neoliberal tramlines, marking a return to its roots in assisting pressing resource allocation decisions, albeit reframed to support future sustainability. Health economists can fruitfully learn a great deal to guide this retooling process from their colleagues in ecological, behavioural, and institutional economics.

This chapter has particularly emphasized a number of areas where health economics might learn from ecological economics – including ecological macroeconomics, overconsumption, and Jevons effects. Two other areas also require attention. While health economics has always made space for questions of equity, the forceful return of inequality to the foreground of economic debate in recent years (Milanovic, 2016; Piketty, 2014) requires urgent attention from health economists, especially when considered through the lenses of sustainability and planetary health. The discussion of global inequalities described above must be matched by a deeper consideration of the importance of health and health care inequalities within societies. A critical insight from behavioural economics is that humans are exquisitely concerned with fairness and comparative position and status. Health economists may therefore need to start investigating the possibility that sustainable health systems may have no place for differential private coverage or access to care – a taboo for many years, and the corollary of the finding that public health expenditure is the engine of achieving better access to care for the poor. Health economics has had much less to say about the place and value of care and caring in health care. It privileges a reductionist view of medical treatments in improving health, and struggles to capture the interpersonal and ethical aspects of caring, compassion and the reduction of suffering (Davis and McMaster, 2015), yet the latter is an area of emerging importance in the degrowth literature (D'Alisa, Deriu, and Demaria, 2015) and will need much better treatment in future economic analyses.

The worldview of health economics and health economists sits uneasily with that of the voluntary degrowth movement. Health economists inhabit a mental world in which institutions and policies are essential to the operation of large and complex systems, while degrowthers emphasize small-scale, local cooperative action, and often have little to say about how their vision might be realized at national or international levels. I would suggest that is not, in fact, a problem. The crucial point of departure on this journey is to recognize that growth (including "green growth") is unlikely to be sustainable, and that a decisive transition to a non-growth path is urgently required – whether that be "agrowth" or "degrowth." Once we have made that step, the widest diversity of voices needs to be heard if we are to stand the best chance of devising a successful pathway for future generations that maximizes their options and does not foreclose their ability to make future choices on how best to protect their health.

REFERENCES

Alcott, B. (2005). Jevons' paradox. *Ecological Economics, 54*(1), 9–21. https://doi.org /10.1016/j.ecolecon.2005.03.020

Alexander, S. (2012). Planned economic contraction: The emerging case for degrowth. *Environmental Politics, 21*(3), 349–68. https://doi.org/10.1080/09644016.2012.671569

Arrow, K. (1963). Uncertainty and the welfare economics of medical care. *American Economic Review, 53*(5) 941–73.

Asara, V., Otero, I., Demaria, F., & Corbera, E. (2015). Socially sustainable degrowth as a social-ecological transformation: Repoliticizing sustainability. *Sustainability Science, 10*(3), 375–84. https://doi.org/10.1007/s11625-015-0321-9

Baker, B. K. (2016) Trans-pacific partnership provisions in intellectual property, transparency, and investment chapters threaten access to medicines in the US and elsewhere. *PLOS Medicine, 13*(3), e1001970. https://doi.org/10.1371/journal .pmed.1001970

Barrett, A. B. (2018). Stability of zero-growth economics analyzed with a Minskyan model. *Ecological Economics, 146*, 228–39. https://doi.org/10.1016/j.ecolecon.2017.10.014

Benatar, S. (2016), Politics, power, poverty and global health: Systems and frames. *International Journal of Health Planning and Management, 5*(10), 599–604. https:// doi.org/10.15171/ijhpm.2016.101

Berwick, D. M., & Hackbarth, A. D. (2012). Eliminating waste in US health care. *JAMA: The Journal of the American Medical Association, 307*(14) 1513–16. https:// doi.org/10.1001/jama.2012.362

Bezemer, D., & Hudson, M. (2016). Finance is not the economy: Reviving the conceptual distinction. *Journal of Economic Issues, 50*(3), 745–68. https://doi.org /10.1080/00213624.2016.1210384

Bithas, K., & Kalimeris, P. (2018). Unmasking decoupling: Redefining the resource intensity of the economy. *Science of the Total Environment, 619–20*, 338–51. https:// doi.org/10.1016/j.scitotenv.2017.11.061

Bonaiuti, M. (2014). *The Great Transition*. Routledge, London: Routledge Studies in Ecological Economics.

Bonaiuti, M. (2018). Are we entering the age of involuntary degrowth? Promethean technologies and declining returns of innovation. *Journal of Cleaner Production, 197*(2), 1800–9. https://doi.org/10.1016/j.jclepro.2017.02.196

Borowy, I., & Aillon, J. L. (2017). Sustainable health and degrowth: Health, health care and society beyond the growth paradigm. *Social Theory and Health, 15*(3) 346–68. https://doi.org/10.1057/s41285-017-0032-7

Boulding, K. E. (1966). The concept of need for health services. *The Millbank Memorial Fund Quarterly, 44*(4), 202–23. https://doi.org/10.2307/3349064

Bowen, A., & Hepburn, C. (2014). Green growth: An assessment. *Oxford Review of Economic Policy, 30*(3), 407–22. https://doi.org/10.1093/oxrep/gru029

Brown, W. (2015). *Undoing the demos: Neoliberalism's stealth revolution.* New York, NY: Zone Books.

Brownlee, S., Chalkidou, K., Doust, J., Elshaug, A. G., Glasziou, P., Heath, I., Nagpal, S., Saini, V., Srivastava, D., Chalmers, K., & Korenstein, D. (2017). Evidence for overuse of medical services around the world. *The Lancet, 390*(10090), 169–77. https://doi.org/10.1016/S0140-6736(16)32585-5

Busfield, J. (2015). Assessing the overuse of medicines. *Social Science and Medicine, 131*, 199–206. https://doi.org/10.1016/j.socscimed.2014.10.061

Buurman, J., & Babovic, V. (2016). Adaptation pathways and real options analysis: An approach to deep uncertainty in climate change adaptation policies. *Policy and Society, 35*(2), 137–50. https://doi.org/10.1016/j.polsoc.2016.05.002

Cahen-Fourot, L., & Lavoie, M. (2016). Ecological monetary economics: A post-Keynesian critique. *Ecological Economics, 126*, 163–8. https://doi.org/10.1016/j.ecolecon.2016.03.007

Cairns, J. (2016). Using cost-effectiveness evidence to inform decisions as to which health services to provide. *Health Systems and Reform, 2*(1), 32–8. https://doi.org/10.1080/23288604.2015.1124172

Capellán-Pérez, I., Mediavilla, M., de Castro, C., Carpintero, Ó., & Miguel, L. J. (2015). More growth? An unfeasible option to overcome critical energy constraints and climate change. *Sustainability Science, 10*(3), 397–411. https://doi.org/10.1007/s11625-015-0299-3

Carter, S. M., Rogers, W., Heath, I., Degeling, C., Doust, J., & Barratt, A. (2015). The challenge of overdiagnosis begins with its definition. *British Medical Journal, 350*, h869. https://doi.org/10.1136/bmj.h869

Cecchini, M., & Lee, S. (2017). Low-value health care with high stakes: Promoting the rational use of antimicrobials. In OECD (Ed.), *Tackling wasteful spending on health* (pp. 115–58). OECD Publishing: Paris. https://doi.org/10.1787/9789264266414-en

Chan, K., Chang, E., Nassery, N., Chang, H.Y., & Segal, J.B. (2013). The state of overuse measurement: A critical review. *Medical Care Research and Review, 70*(5), 473–96. https://doi.org/10.1177/1077558713492202

Cochrane Library. (2019). The Cochrane Library: Trusted evidence, informed decisions, better health. Retrieved from https://www.cochranelibrary.com

Costello, A., Abbas, M., Allen, A., Ball, S., Bell, S., Bellamy, R. et al. (2009). The Lancet Commissions: Managing the health effects of climate change. Lancet and University College London Institute for Global Health Commission. *The Lancet, 373*, 1693–733. https://doi.org/10.1016/S0140-6736(09)60935-1

D'Alisa, G., Deriu, M., & Demaria, F. (2015). Care. In G. D'Alisa, F. Demaria & G. Kallis (Eds), *Degrowth: A vocabulary for a new era.* Abingdon, UK: Routledge.

Daly, H. (1977). *Steady-state economics: The economics of biophysical equilibrium and moral growth*. San Francisco: W. H. Freeman and Co.

Daly, H. (1999). Uneconomic growth: In theory, in fact, in history, and in relation to globalization. In H. Daly (Ed.), *Ecological economics and the ecology of economics: Essays in criticism*, Cheltenham: UK: Edward Elgar.

Daly, H. (2006). Uneconomic growth. In D. A. Clark (Ed.), *The Elgar companion to development studies* (pp. 654–8), Cheltenham: UK: Edward Elgar.

Davis, J. B., & McMaster, R. (2015). Situating care in mainstream health economics: An ethical dilemma? *Journal of Institutional Economics, 11*(4), 749–67. https://doi.org/10.1017/S1744137414000538

Di Giulio, A., & Fuchs, D. (2014). Sustainable consumption corridors: Concept, objections, and responses. *GAIA: Ecological Perspectives for Science & Society, 23*, 184–92. https://doi.org/10.14512/gaia.23.S1.6

Dieleman, J., Campbell, M., Chapin, A., Eldrenkamp, E., Fan, V. Y., Haakenstad, A., Kates, J., Liu, Y. et al. (2017). Evolution and patterns of global health financing 1995–2014: Development assistance for health, and government, prepaid private, and out-of-pocket health spending in 184 countries. *The Lancet, 389*(10083), 1981–2004.

Dieleman, J., Campbell, M., Chapin, A., Eldrenkamp, E., Fan, V. Y., Haakenstad, A., Kates, J., Li, Z. et al. (2017). Future and potential spending on health 2015–40: Development assistance for health, and government, prepaid private, and out-of-pocket health spending in 184 countries. *The Lancet, 389*(10083), 2005–30.

Djulbegovic, B., & Paul, A. (2011). From efficacy to effectiveness in the face of uncertainty: Indication creep and prevention creep. *Journal of the American Medical Association, 305*(19), 2005–6. https://doi.org/10.1001/jama.2011.650

Drummond, M., Schulper, M., Claxton, K., Stoddart, G., & Torrance, G. (2015). *Methods for the economic evaluation of health care programmes* (4th ed.). Oxford, UK: Oxford University Press.

Eastwood, J. B., Conroy, R. E., Naicker, S., West, P. A., Tutt, R. C., & Plange-Rhule, J. (2005). Loss of health professionals from sub-Saharan Africa: The pivotal role of the UK. *The Lancet, 365*(9474), 1893–1900. https://doi.org/10.1016/S0140-6736(05)66623-8

Gabe, J., Williams, S., Martin, P., & Coveney, C. (2015). Pharmaceuticals and society: Power, promises and prospects. *Social Science and Medicine, 131*, 193–8. https://doi.org/10.1016/j.socscimed.2015.02.031

Gaffney, A. (2018). Do we need Pfizer? *Jacobin, 28*, 58–66.

Getzen, T. (2016). Measuring and forecasting global health expenditures. In R.M. Scheffler (Ed.), *World scientific handbook of global health economics and public policy: The economics of health and health systems, 3*, (pp. 177–215). Singapore: World Scientific Publishing. https://doi.org/10.1142/9789813140493_0003

Glasziou, P., Straus, S., Brownlee, S., Trevena, L., Dans, L., Guyatt, G., Elshaug, A. G., Janett, R., & Saini, V. (2017). Evidence for underuse of effective medical services

around the world. *The Lancet, 390*(10090), 169–77. https://doi.org/10.1016
/S0140-6736(16)30946-1

Goldacre, B. (2013). *Bad Pharma: How medicine is broken, and how we can fix it* (2nd ed.). London, UK: Fourth Estate.

Gordon, R. J. (2016). *The rise and fall of American growth: The US standard of living since the Civil War*. Princeton, NJ: Princeton University Press. https://doi .org/10.1515/9781400873302

Hardt, L., & O'Neill, D. W. (2017). Ecological macroeconomic models: Assessing current developments. *Ecological Economics, 134*, 198–211. https://doi.org/10.1016 /j.ecolecon.2016.12.027

Hensher, M. (1997). Improving general practitioner access to physiotherapy: A review of the economic evidence. *Health Services Management Research, 10*(4), 225–30. https://doi.org/10.1177/095148489701000403

Hensher, M. (2001). *Financing health systems through efficiency gains*. Geneva, Switzerland: World Health Organization.

Hensher, M., & Edwards, N. (1999). Hospital provision, activity, and productivity in England since the 1980s. *BMJ: British Medical Journal, 319*(7214), 911–14. https:// doi.org/10.1136/bmj.319.7214.911

Hensher, M., Tisdell, J., & Zimitat, C. (2017). 'Too much medicine': Insights and explanations from economic theory and research. *Social Science & Medicine, 176*, 77–84. https://doi.org/10.1016/j.socscimed.2017.01.020

Homer-Dixon, T. (2006). *The upside of down: Catastrophe, creativity and the renewal of civilization*. Toronto, ON: Vintage Canada.

Jackson, T. (2009). *Prosperity without growth: The transition to a sustainable economy*. London, UK: Routledge,.

Jamison, D., Breman, J. G., Measham, A. R., Alleyne, G., Claeson, M., Evans, D. B., Jha, P., Mills, A., & Musgrove, P. (2006). *Disease control priorities in developing countries* (2nd ed.). New York, NY: Oxford University Press.

Jamison, D., Gelband, H., Horton, S., Jha, P., Laxminarayan, R., Mock, C., & Nugent, R. (2018). *Disease control priorities: Improving health and reducing poverty* (Vol. 9, 3rd ed.). Washington, DC: World Bank.

Jamison, D., Summers, L., Alleyne, G., Arrow, K., Berkley, S., Binagwaho, A. et al. (2013). Global health 2035: A world converging within a generation. *The Lancet, 382*, 1898–955. https://doi.org/10.1016/S0140-6736(13)62105-4

Kallis, G. (2011). In defence of degrowth. *Ecological Economics, 70*(5), 873–80. https:// doi.org/10.1016/j.ecolecon.2010.12.007

Kallis, G., Kerschner, C., & Martinez-Alier, J. (2012). The economics of degrowth. *Ecological Economics, 84*, 172–80. https://doi.org/10.1016/j.ecolecon.2012.08.017

Klein, N. (2014). *This changes everything: Capitalism vs the climate*. New York, NY: Simon & Schuster.

Klitgaard, K. A., & Krall, L. (2012), Ecological economics, degrowth, and institutional change. *Ecological Economics, 84*, 247–53. https://doi.org/10.1016/j.ecolecon.2011.11.008

Kruk, M. E., Gage, A. D., Joseph, N. T., Danaei, G., García-Saisó, S., & Salomon, J. A. (2018). Mortality due to low-quality health systems in the universal health coverage era: A systematic analysis of amenable deaths in 137 countries. *The Lancet, 392*(10160), 2203–12. https://doi.org/10.1016/S0140-6736(18)31668-4

Lawn, P. (2010). Facilitating the transition to a steady-state economy: Some macroeconomic fundamentals. *Ecological Economics, 69*(5), 931–6. https://doi .org/10.1016/j.ecolecon.2009.12.013

Lawn, P. (2011). Is steady-state capitalism viable? A review of the issues and an answer in the affirmative. *Ecological Economics Reviews, 1219*, 1–25, https://doi .org/10.1111/j.1749-6632.2011.05966.x

Macdonald, H., & Loder, E., (2015). Too much medicine: The challenge of finding common ground. *British Medical Journal, 350*, h1163. https://doi.org/10.1136/bmj.h1163

Malik, A., Lenzen, M., McAlister, S., & McGain, F. (2018). The carbon footprint of Australian health care. *The Lancet Planetary Health, 2*(1), e27–e35. https://doi .org/10.1016/S2542-5196(17)30180-8

Malmaeus, J. M., & Alfredsson, E. C. (2017). Potential consequences on the economy of low or no growth – Short and long-term perspectives. *Ecological Economics, 134*, 57–64. https://doi.org/10.1016/j.ecolecon.2016.12.011

Martin, S., Rice, N., & Smith, P. C. (2012). Comparing costs and outcomes across programmes of health care. *Health Economics, 21*(3), 316–37. https://doi .org/10.1002/hec.1716

Mazzucato, M. (2013). *The entrepreneurial state: Debunking public vs private sector myths.* London, UK: Anthem Press,.

McIntyre, D., Meheus, F., & Røttingen, J.-A. (2017). What level of domestic government health expenditure should we aspire to for universal health coverage? *Health Economics, Policy and Law, 12*(2), 125–37. https://doi.org/10.1017 /S1744133116000414

Meadows, D. H., Meadows, D. L., Randers, J., & Behrens, W. W. (1972). *The limits to growth: A report for the Club of Rome's project on the predicament of mankind.* London, UK: Potomac Associates.

Milanovic, B. (2016). *Global inequality: A new approach for the age of globalization.* Cambridge, Mass: The Belknap Press of Harvard University Press.

Mills, A. (2016). The challenges of prioritization. *Health Systems & Reform, 2*(1), 20. https://doi.org/10.1080/23288604.2016.1124173

Moyn, S. (2018). *Not enough: Human rights in an unequal world.* Cambridge, Mass: The Belknap Press of Harvard University Press.

Moynihan, R., Henry, D., & Moons, K. G. M. (2014). Using evidence to combat overdiagnosis and overtreatment: Evaluating treatments, tests, and disease definitions in the time of too much. *PLOS Medicine, 11*(7), e1001655. https://doi.org/10.1371 /journal.pmed.1001655

Newhouse, J. P. (1977). Medical-care expenditure: A cross-national survey. *Journal of Human Resources, 12*(1), 115–25. https://doi.org/10.2307/145602

O'Callaghan, G., Meyer, H., & Elshaug, A. G. (2015). Choosing wisely: The message, messenger and method. *Medical Journal of Australia, 202*(4), 175–8. https://doi .org/10.5694/mja14.00673

O'Neill, D. W., Fanning, A. L., Lamb, W. F., & Steinberger, J. K. (2018). A good life for all within planetary boundaries. *Nature Sustainability, 1*(2), 88–95. https://doi .org/10.1038/s41893-018-0021-4

OECD. (2006). *Projecting OECD health and long-term care expenditures, 477*, OECD Economics Department Working Papers. Paris, France: OECD Publishing.

OECD. (2017). *Tackling wasteful spending on health*. Paris, France: Organisation for Economic Cooperation and Development.

Ostrom, E. (2005). *Unlocking public entrepeneurship and public economies*. Helsinki, Finland: United Nations University – World Institute for Development Economics Research.

Piketty, T. (2014). *Capital in the twenty-first century*. Cambridge, MA: Harvard University Press.

Princen, T. (1999). Consumption and environment: Some conceptual issues. *Ecological Economics, 31*, 347–63. https://doi.org/10.1016/S0921-8009(99)00039-7

Princen, T. (2003). Principles for sustainability: From cooperation and efficiency to sufficiency. *Global Environmental Politics, 3*(1), 33–50. https://doi.org /10.1162/152638003763336374

Ravallion, M. (2014). Income inequality in the developing world. *Science, 344*(6186), 851–5. https://doi.org/10.1126/science.1251875

Raworth, K. (2017). *Doughnut economics: Seven ways to think like a 21st century economist*. London, UK: Random House Business Books.

RoAR. (2014). *Antimicrobial resistance: Tackling a crisis for the health and wealth of nations*. London, UK: Review on Antimicrobial Resistance.

Rosenthal, E. (2017). *An American sickness: How healthcare became big business and how you can take it back*. New York, NY: Penguin Press.

Saini, V., Brownlee, S., Elshaug, A. G., Glasziou, P., & Heath, I. (2017). Addressing overuse and underuse around the world. *The Lancet, 390*(10090), 105–7. https://doi .org/10.1016/S0140-6736(16)32573-9

Schroeder, K., Thompson, T., Frith, K., & Pencheon, D. (2012). *Sustainable healthcare*. London, UK: BMJ Books.

Sibbald, B., McDonald, R., & Roland, M. (2007). Shifting care from hospitals to the community: A review of the evidence on quality and efficiency. *Journal of Health Services Research & Policy, 12*(2), 110–17. https://doi .org/10.1258/135581907780279611

Smith, R. & Coast, J. (2013). The true cost of antimicrobial resistance. *BMJ: British Medical Journal, 346*. https://doi.org/10.1136/bmj.f1493

Steffen, W., Broadgate, W., Deutsch, L., Gaffney, O., & Ludwig, C. (2015). The trajectory of the Anthropocene: The Great Acceleration. *The Anthropocene Review, 2*(1), 81–98. https://doi.org/10.1177/2053019614564785

Steffen, W., Richardson, K., Rockström, J., Cornell, S. E., Fetzer, I., Bennett, E. M. et al. (2015). Planetary boundaries: Guiding human development on a changing planet. *Science, 347*(6223), 736. https://doi.org/10.1126/science.1259855

Stenberg, K., Hanssen, O., Edejer, T. T.-T., Bertram, M., Brindley, C., Meshreky, A. et al. (2017). Financing transformative health systems towards achievement of the health Sustainable Development Goals: A model for projected resource needs in 67 low-income and middle-income countries. *The Lancet Global Health, 5*(9), e875–87. https://doi.org/10.1016/S2214-109X(17)30263-2

Stott, R. (2012). Contraction and convergence: The best possible solution to the twin problems of climate change and inequity. *British Medical Journal, 344*, e1765. https://doi.org/10.1136/bmj.e1765

Streeck, W. (2016). *How will capitalism end? Essays on a failing system.* London, UK: Verso.

Taylor, T., & Mackie, P. (2017). Carbon footprinting in health systems: One small step towards planetary health. *The Lancet Planetary Health, 1*(9), pp. e357–8. https://doi.org/10.1016/S2542-5196(17)30158-4

The Lancet Planetary Heath. (2018). The natural environment and emergence of antibiotic resistance. *The Lancet Planetary Health, 2*(1), e1. https://doi.org/10.1016/S2542-5196(17)30182-1

Tokic, D. (2012). The economic and financial dimensions of degrowth. *Ecological Economics, 84*, 49–56. https://doi.org/10.1016/j.ecolecon.2012.09.011

UN. (2015). *Sustainable Development Goals: 17 goals to transform our world.* Retrieved from http://www.un.org/sustainabledevelopment/sustainable-development-goals/.

UNEP. (2017). *Frontiers 2017 emerging issues of environmental concern.* Nairobi, Kenya: United Nations Environment Program.

van den Bergh, J. C. J. M. (2017). A third option for climate policy within potential limits to growth. *Nature Climate Change, 7*, 107–12. https://doi.org/10.1038/nclimate3113

Ward, J. D., Sutton, P. C., Warner, A. D., Costanza, R., Mohr, S. H., & Simmons, C. T. (2016). Is decoupling GDP growth from environmental impact possible? *PLOS One, 11*(10), 10. https://doi.org/10.1371/journal.pone.0164733

Watts, N., Adger, W. N., Agnolucci, P., Blackstock, J., Byass, P., Cai, W. et al. (2015). Health and climate change: Policy responses to protect public health. *The Lancet, 386*(10006), 1861–914.

Welch, H. G., Schwartz, L. M., & Woloshin, S. (2011). *Over-diagnosed: Making people sick in the pursuit of health.* Boston, MA: Beacon Press.

Werner, D., Thuman, C., & Maxwell, J. (2004). *Where there is no doctor: A village health care handbook* (2nd ed.). London, UK: Macmillan.

Whitmee, S., Haines, A., Beyrer, C., Boltz, F., Capon, A. G., de Souza Dias, B. F. et al. (2015). The Lancet Commissions: Safeguarding human health in the Anthropocene epoch: Report of The Rockefeller Foundation – Lancet Commission

on planetary health. *The Lancet, 386*(10007), 1973–2028. https://doi.org/10.1016/
S0140-6736(15)60901-1

WHO. (2017). *Health expenditure, Total (% of GDP)*.

WHO. (2019). About the Global Burden of Disease (GBD) project. Retrieved from
https://www.who.int/healthinfo/global_burden_disease/about/en/

Zywert, K. & Quilley, S. (2017). Health systems in an era of biophysical limits: The
wicked dilemmas of modernity. *Social Theory and Health, 16*(2), 188–207. https://
doi.org/10.1057/s41285-017-0051-4

5 What about My Pineapples? The Wicked Implications of Nonlinearity, Embedded Systems, and Transformative Social Goals

KAITLIN KISH

In early 2017, I acted as guest editor for a special issue of *Alternatives Journal (A\J)*, a Canadian academic transfer journal for environmental issues. The issue was a follow-up to the Canadian Society for Ecological Economics's 2015 biennial conference in Vancouver, BC. Our main objective was to disseminate the underlying principles and applications of ecological economics to the broader environmental community. During this time, I learned that editors of academic transfer journals have a difficult task; they need to be a certain degree of expert on a different topic for every issue of their journal. The *A\J* editor at the time, Leah Gerber, took this task very seriously. Over the months of development, Gerber and I spent hours talking about degrowth, agrowth, and low-growth economics. We discussed ecological economic philosophy, toolkits, and places where it has been implemented successfully. As our publishing date neared and we were having a final meeting on the structure and organization of the issue, Gerber seemed dissatisfied.

I asked her what she thought was missing. After a moment's pause she turned to me and said: "What about my pineapples?"

The framing of this question has stuck with me ever since. Gerber was tapping into a problem that few environmentalists engage with openly and honestly: what are the trade-offs we'll have to make by living in a more sustainable way? After telling Gerber that her children, or maybe her children's children, are likely to eat pineapple as only a very special treat, if at all, we went on to discuss the wider implications of her question.

It's easy for environmentalists to look at supply chains and see that it might be difficult to have access to pineapples in a sustainable society as we reduce the amount of unnecessary transportation. It is more difficult for environmentalists to see the "supply chain" of abstract concepts that hold a great deal of power and importance in our modern lives such as freedom, individual rights, and relative peace.

This is primarily because, ever since the early 1700s, these concepts have come to define every moment and thought in our modern, Western lives. They have become the ideals that we strive to uphold and maintain. They are the fundamental rights and responsibilities of all citizens. So, it is very difficult to step back and see the evolution of such entrenched and ingrained concepts in our lives, and even more difficult to consider that our well-intentioned sustainability agendas might undermine them.

In this chapter I break this argument down into three pieces. I start by telling the story of how the neoliberal growth agenda has fuelled and empowered our progressive and liberal thoughts. While liberal environmentalists tend to rail against the inequality and biospheric degradation associated with neoliberal economics, it has helped us to obtain unfettered access to pineapples and less innocuous commodities such as child care and health care. Using a complex systems perspective in conjunction with the sociological notion of the base-superstructure heuristic, I then discuss why it is difficult to unwind growth and social progress. Undermining the transportation system that gives us access to pineapples may not lead to any significant discomfort, but undermining the consumer system that funds child care and therefore women's access to the workplace is much more complicated and uncomfortable. This argument was first drawn out by Quilley (2013), who argued that "degrowth is not a liberal agenda" because cultural patterns of thought and institutional structures are not freestanding. I will end with some examples demonstrating the kinds of trade-offs we need to begin to deal with and contemplate.

There are, of course, those with far less privilege who are unable to ask questions about pineapples, transportation systems, child care, and health care. These are questions that befall to those who have benefited the most from progress and contributed the most to associated problems. Canada imports most of their pineapples from Costa Rica, where farming practices are unsustainable, there are regular human and labour abuses, and wages are too low to meet minimum living costs, all to keep costs lower for the top 20 per cent of the population who do not want to pay the real cost of a pineapple (Lawrence, 2010). This is not a problem isolated to pineapples – again and again we see the privileged top 20 per cent of the world use the rest of the world to keep living standards high all while generating the highest ecological footprints.

This chapter represents a challenge to those living in this top 20 per cent. What kinds of discomforts will we need to make our reality to make the world a more sustainable, just, and equitable place?

How Progress Binds Our Thought

Since the Industrial Revolution, growth has dominated world history and human behaviour (Jackson, 2009; Victor, 2008). As the global commitment to growth was solidified, so too were patterns of thought supporting such a system, and institutions to uphold the realization of growth. Growth emerged alongside of, and relied upon, the process of individualization and movement towards individual rights (Beck, 1992; Giddens, 1987). Undercutting complex societal systems (i.e. actions by environmentalists to avoid limits) may undermine the social progress that has come to define a great deal of Western ideals. This history, from the field of sociology, provides a widely accepted framework for understanding the role of social dynamics within discourse and politics.

Karl Polanyi argued that the central dynamic during the early shift into modern society, was the disembedding of economic activities as a distinct domain, separate from cultural ties (1944). As peasants and families moved from farms into cities, livelihoods came to be structured around individual incentives for economic gain, rather than being oriented towards community and kin. In premodern societies the economy was not a separate domain – individual livelihood was motivated by ongoing patterns of social life. Polanyi argued that the disembedding of economic activity "freed" the individual from family and kin obligated relationships. This was a revolution for the rights of the individual. Modernization is characterized by this emergence of new markets:

> Not blood tie, legal compulsion, religious obligation, fealty or magic compel participation in economic life, but specifically economic institutions such as private enterprise and the wage system. (Polanyi, 1971, p. 81)

Separation from land and kin ties allowed for individual mobility, enabling more and more people to become part of the emerging industrial complex. As industrialism and the industrial workforce grew, groups of people began living in conveniently located clusters to access work. This was the early beginning of industrial cities. Cities were filled with "frantic bustle, rife with egoism and alienation from neighbours" (Kumar, 1991, p. 67). Cities created the conditions for multicultural exchanges and tolerance of ideas, faiths, and cultures leading to a growing number of distinct social roles and a shift in the I/We balance, towards the "I" (Elias, 2014).

The combination of migration associated with the enclosure movement and freedom to pursue new activities (such as moving to the city to participate in the industrial revolution) removed any functional attachment to group/kin membership. Peasants were morphed into individualized, free-agent wage labourers who required support and security provided by the state. While individuals had previously been taken care of in times of need by their community and family members, these obligations shifted to the state – starting with labour unions. Individuals needed to create networks to ensure their security, and in doing so shifted the burden towards the state to set up institutions, such as public safety standards and the welfare system. During the industrial revolution we see more intervention of the state on the well-being and livelihood of the individual.

The individual is key. Rights, standards, security, and punishments were no longer family based. The public shaming of one's uncle no longer meant a stain on the family name for decades to come. Such shame was associated only with the individual; the rest of the family could easily distance themselves from that person. This way of thinking started to shape the way that we think about ourselves as members of an equal-access society. This is why, since the Industrial Revolution with exponential growth during the Great Acceleration, there was a rise in indicators of social progress (Pinker, 2012) such as labour laws, animal welfare groups, rights for the disabled, acceptance of alternative lifestyles, and women's emancipation. These indicators of a society firmly committed to acceptance and protection of the individual rose in tandem with consumption patterns, access to telecommunication networks, and environmental degradation. This has become the canon of Western society, and it is tied to the process of disembedding (people needed to move out of families to be considered individuals) and to the generation of the highly complex systems produced by modernization (to take place of the family). Thus, liberal commitments (and ideological attempts to make sense of one's self within the process of modernity – feminism, jihadism, Marxism, environmentalism) are intimately tied to capitalist modernity (Quilley, 2012), and consequently the high energy throughput society associated with industrialism.

The state assisted in setting up systems to ensure that the rights of the individual were upheld, but these systems were not free. Socially progressive systems of welfare and protection require money, infrastructure, and bureaucratic organization – all inputs that in turn require energy and order to create and maintain. These systems are therefore intimately coupled with high energy throughput, as a characteristic of, and supplied by, capital growth. There is a correlation between the hundreds of millions of commodities traded on the internet, the hundreds of thousands of distinct social roles, the mobility of both people and capital, the enormous expansion in regulatory infrastructure of the state, and the social-psychological process of individualization. These systems arose together, intimately entangling social progress with environmental degradation.

Nonlinearity is a key concept in the field of complex systems. Nonlinearity in systems means that we don't always know which way the system will tip – we can nudge a system in a certain direction but the vast complexity within a system as huge as health economics means we have no idea where the system may actually go (Berkes, Boulding, and Folke, 2008). From this standpoint alone, we can assume there will be unintended consequences of change in any system. Beyond that, complex systems studies also tell us that scale and nested complexity is important when considering the reaction of a system. If one subsystem is reliant on another, and that higher-ordered system is disturbed, then the lower-ordered system will also be disturbed. Environmentalists and proponents of a society of simplicity argue for a contraction in the larger system, often not realizing that it is in this larger system that their own arguments and progressive liberal commitments lie.

While the universe has an overall tendency towards unorganized chaos (entropy), pockets of order appear in localized areas. These pockets may have ever-increasing propensities towards organized complexity:

> Certain factors – energy, matter, life, and complexity among them – appear to be self-potentiating: the more of them there is, the more powerful the impetus to the production of yet more. Left to its own devices without let or hindrance, such a tendency is liable to result in exponential growth. (Rescher, 1998, p. 3)

Applying these ideas analogously, it can be said that human culture and current modes of experience (modernity) are one such pocket (Christian, 2011) and that proponents of degrowth need to find a way to internalize constraint in individuals and society to go against this, with two consequences. First, this increasingly ordered complexity requires the constant throughput of energy. For example, industrialization emerges only on the complex and technical repertoire of agrarian civilization, thereby increasing overall complexity. Second, the more complex the pocket becomes, the more energy is required to maintain complexity, making the ordered state fragile and potentially unsustainable. Historically, greater complexity at the level of human culture is, for the most part, achieved at the expense of order elsewhere in the biosphere (Odum, 2007). Complexity in any system always engenders entropic disorder out of that system; complexity and low entropy is achieved by exporting high entropy disorder (Daly, 1990; Georgescu-Roegen, 1975). Daly applies this to the process of production:

> People can measure their throughput, or the rate at which the economy uses them, taking them from low-entropy sources in the ecosystem, transforming them into useful products, and ultimately dumping them back into the environment as high-entropy wastes. (Daly 2005, p. 1)

Degrowth and environmentalism partially hinges on the allocation of low entropy resources between the biosphere and human culture. From a limits perspective, the growth in the scale and complexity of human activities is as astonishing as it is unsustainable. At the dawn of the human Odyssey, the human brain itself was possibly the most complex entity in the universe (Chaisson, 2001). Using a measure of free energy rate density measured in

ERGS per gramme per second, Chaisson contrasts the complexity of a galaxy (0.5), a planet (75), a typical plant (900), an animal body (20,000), a human brain (150,000), and modern society (500,000). He comments that it is "not surprising [sic] a group of brainy organisms working collectively is even more complex than the totality of its individual components" (Chaisson, 2001 p. 139). With language and culture, the network of connected brains engendered a step change in complexity, in turn accelerated by writing and the integration of human societies across the planet.

In an era of limits, this complexification cannot continue indefinitely, and we need to begin picking apart the system that has given us growth; this will mean that we also need to start picking apart and rethinking the system that has given us individual rights and social progress. There are other scholars who begin to touch on this problem. Most recently, Dan O'Neill published a paper that quantified the resource use associated with meeting basic human needs for over 150 countries and compared this to what is globally sustainable (2018). He found that there is currently no country that achieves a good life for its citizens at a level of resource use that could be extended to all people on the planet. Spash (2017) recognizes there is a tension between the idea that individuals have freedom to do whatever they please and the recognition that constraints on that freedom are required to achieve communal goals. Victor et al. recognize that degrowth would mean less investment opportunities, lower government tax revenues, withdrawal of social investment, job loss, and recession, and that this could be solved by investment in the "green economy" (2014). Ecofeminist perspectives recognize that gender relations in a post-growth world are "murky" (Bauhardt, 2014, p. 63) and that the care economy is vital, but the gendered nature of this is not explored in degrowth literatures. Likely, there would be an increase in demand for unpaid work in roles such as education and health care, and consequently a deeper focus on home economics, i.e. cooking and family. The question is – who would this be assigned to? Would it fall to women or would men take on unpaid work traditionally assigned to women? Will the unpaid sector remain undervalued and misunderstood?

Oh, the Thinks You Can't Think!

The first question that comes to mind when the above argument is presented is: why not keep the social progress and throw away the consumer society that makes it so environmentally unsustainable?

Because the two systems evolved together, this is either difficult or impossible. Dr Seuss has misled generations of children with the claim of "oh the thinks you can think if you only try!" Rather, we are are constrained by our cognitive and social reality. Marx expands on this:

> In the social production of their life, men enter into definite relations that are independent of their will, relations of production which correspond to a definite stage of development of their material productive forces.
>
> The sum total of these relations of production constitutes the economic structure of society, the real basis on which rises a legal and political superstructure and to which correspond definite forms of social consciousness. (Marx, 1964)

Our ideas and the way we speak are not random (Marx, 1964). They are intimately connected with one another and with social structures and institutions. How we create things, consume, and relate to one another (the social base) is intimately tied to media, culture, and politics (the superstructure). The base shapes and maintains the superstructure and the superstructure shapes and maintains the base (figure 5.1).

This is a metaphor associated with a brutal form of Marxism but begins to frame the problem of change quite well. While this metaphor suggests a determinism in society, I will frame it for this discussion as the base representing "conditions" or "limits" to the superstructure. Different people have interpreted this metaphor with varying degrees of literalness. Extreme Marxists view the base as a strong and deterministic force of production that "inevitably advance, and that this in turn leads to changes in society" (Harman, 1986, p. 8). In this way, political and ideological struggles are seen as playing little to no role in social change because individuals are products of their circumstance; revolutions, wars, and arguments are already determined. The other side argues that Marx's writing is devoid of fatalistic approaches to history; laying great emphasis on remarks from Engels:

> Political, juridical, philosophical, religious, literary, artistic, etc. development is based on economic development. But these all react on one another and also upon the economic basis. It is not that the economic situation is cause, solely active, while everything else is only passive effect. There is rather interaction on the basis of economic necessity which ultimately always asserts itself. (Engels, in Selsam and Martel, 1963)

Post-1956 new leftists argued that "the terms 'base and superstructure' were simply a metaphor, not to be taken too seriously. The reciprocal influence of the superstructure on the base meant that determination was not to be seen as a strict causal relationship" (Harman, 1986, p. 11). After this, society was seen as having a number of different interacting structures, each developing at their own speed; for example, politics, economics, ideologies, linguistics. All these structures are influenced by the base and influence the base in a reciprocal formation.

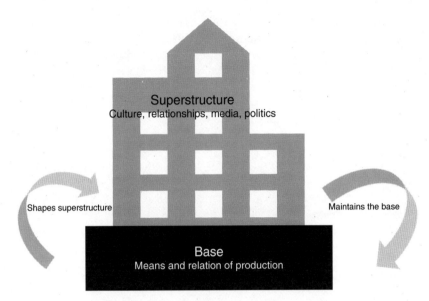

Figure 5.1 The base/superstructure model

For environmentalists, I draw on this less deterministic metaphor of the base/superstructure. Despite the lack of strict determinism, this still means that as we change the material base of society (or shift to a new basin of attraction), our superstructure will also change, likely in unpredictable and non-linear ways. Environmental advocates of simplicity and low/no/degrowth may underestimate the wider implications of their visions for Western liberal society. For example, any large-scale increase in people working in agriculture might engender the kinds of feelings, priorities, and temporal orientations that peasant agriculturalists once had (Quilley, 2013) – that is, a life devoted to work with little consideration or time invested constructing one's identity or contemplating the meaning of one's life.

Progressive forms of social emancipation relating to class, gender, race and ethnicity, disability, and sexuality have been made possible by the base consisting of growth economics and by the expansion of social complexity, which is in turn dependent on harnessing cheap energy. The rights of individuals, characteristic of the enlightenment, mean that someone with a disability has the right to independent living – this requires complex structures of care, emergency communication methods, and complex technological production to provide necessary goods for individuals to be on their own.

All public goods and infrastructure depend upon tax transfers generated, at least partially, by consumption. At the same time, the trajectory of technological innovation that has delivered everything from the internet to antibiotics is also inextricably bound up with expansive consumer capitalism. The patterns of social life, socialization, and identification that reproduce the individuals characteristic of liberal societies – voters, citizens, rights holders, consumers – are themselves engendered by and dependent upon high and expanding flows of energy and materials. Successful environmental activism and/or exogenous shocks sufficient to undermine growth, would reduce the availability of cheap energy (although we would need less energy in general) and potentially force societies to shed layers of complexity (Kish and Quilley, 2017; Quilley, 2013; Zywert and Quilley, 2017). This would be devastating for taken for granted and cherished forms of social emancipation.

Anyone who takes limits to growth seriously and as such supports an agenda of low/no/degrowth seeks to alter the base while enjoying a great deal of the progressive superstructure. But the base and superstructure may coexist in a mutually defining feedback cycle.

The Complexity of Simplicity

Environmental advocates of simplicity or a low-growth system underestimate the wider implications for societies if their visions are realized. Progressive forms of social emancipation relating to gender, multiculturalism, disabilities, and sexuality are made possible, and upheld, by growth economics and the harnessing of cheap energy. Successful environmental activism and/or exogenous shocks that undermine growth reduce the availability of cheap energy and force societies to shed layers of complexity.

In this section I very briefly explore a few implications for Westerners of the above reasoning, particularly for women's emancipation. This discussion is not to say that women's emancipation and sustainability are necessarily mutually exclusive – rather, it is a challenge for simplicity advocates to think more broadly about the implications of their work and arguments on important areas of society. These are privileged challenges that we need to become critical of to decide what we really need and what we're willing to trade or make different.

In table 5.1 I have laid out modern social norms alongside the modern requirements that uphold them; any simplicity activism that undermines the modern requirements is threatening the norm. For a more detailed discussion of these relationships, see the paper "Wicked Dilemmas of Scale and Complexity in the Politics of Degrowth," in which Quilley and I (2017) discuss these modern progressive norms that would potentially be undermined by low growth economics. Related and interesting discussions with far greater detail come most notably from Norbert Elias (2000) in *The Civilizing Process*, Steven Pinker (2012; 2018) in *The Better Angels of Our Nature* and his newest book *Enlightenment Now*, and Jeremy Rifkin (2009) in *The Empathic Civilization*.

Table 5.1 Cherished modern norms and the social processes that uphold them

Norm	Definition	Developmental requirement	Modern requirement
Internal peace and security	State's monopoly of violence; a general assumption of safety and state control of violence.	Effective nation-state (Elias, 2014); Imagined community (Anderson, 1991)	Police institutions; state funding; tax systems
Capital growth	Large trading partners and the right to accumulate wealth.	Individualization (Beck and Beck-Gernsheim, 2002) Citizenship (membership based/ exclusive) and/in tension with human rights	Capitalism; high energy throughput; extended empathy
Social progress and rights	Increasing respect for marginalized groups.		Gender emancipation; state child support; tax systems; birth control; secularization
Cosmopolitanism	Everyone is a member of a shared community with shared morality. Rise in literacy, mobility, and mass media.	Literacy, mobility, mass media (Giddens, 1990; Gellner, 1983) Effective states/ markets	Cities; disembedding; individualization; educational institutions; bureaucracy
Science and rationality	Intensifying application of rationality, knowledge, and technological development.	Detribalization (Gellner, 1983) Integrated system of nation-states (Giddens, 1990)	Rationalization; secularization; educational institutions; bureaucracy; time/space abstraction; disembedding

Innovation, Health Care, and Women

Consumerism has become part and parcel of the very fabric of life in developed countries. Areas of life that are integral to livelihood that were once free of the marketplace, such as religion and family, now compete with consumerism. What we consume defines who we are as individuals, helping us to curate an identity that may once have been fully informed by our place in our community. As free-floating individuals, we are no longer prescribed an identity and so we spend a great deal of our lives struggling with what it means to be one's self. Corporations have seized this opportunity and capitalized on the deep insecurities of the modern individual, promising with each swipe of the credit card that they'll feel better about themselves. Consumerism has become the primary way in which people develop self-esteem and curate their world views (Arndt et al., 2004; Solomon, Greenberg, and Pyszczynski, 2004).

Consumer capitalism has proven itself very resilient, altered by corporations and advertising companies as times change. Companies are constantly required to focus on innovation to remain relevant and provide new products for consumers. One could see this as an honest pursuit of a better product for consumers or from a slightly more cynical perception that it is simply to make more money – an argument that is especially convincing when we look at new generations of iPhones and consider the extent to which the product was actually improved. Either way, innovation has become so important that it is touted by the world's top universities as their primary objective, and corporations will hire heads of innovation to ensure they're at the cutting edge. Innovation drives capitalism and capitalism supports innovation (Hans-Ruediger, 2014).

Problematically for environmentalists, the trajectory of technological innovation that has delivered useless iterations of the iPhone has also helped to produce antibiotics, state-of-the-art MRI machines, perfected the tools necessary for successful organ transplants, and much more. Innovation labs for health sciences are immensely energy intensive and expensive, making them inextricably bound up with expansive consumer capitalism (Zywert and Quilley, 2017). It is unlikely that we can separate consumer innovation from necessary and life-saving or emancipatory innovation. Therefore, it stands to reason that a more localized economy may see the loss of sophisticated (read: "high energy") medications and health services such as birth control, which has given women enormous freedom over their bodies and lives. An IUD requires the creation of plastic and mining of copper, and pills require exact measurements of hormones in a laboratory – all of which require a lot of energy.

One could easily argue that there are very simple ways to have a reduced form of birth control, i.e. cycle tracking. Leaving aside the fact that this is just one example of many that will not have such a straightforward low-energy alternative, this energy footprint is not just embodied in the particular artefact or processes of development. The energy footprint of birth control is also distributed across the entire network of socioeconomic systems that are necessary platforms for their production – for example, these forms of birth control are highly associated with women's liberation and entry into the workforce (Heer and Grossbard-Shechtman, 1981; Goldin and Katz, 2002). They are, in other words, associated with what Odum refers to as high transformity values (Odum, 2007): "the systems of nature and society are interconnected in webs of energy flow" (M. T. Brown and Ulgiati, 2004, p. 92). The transformity is the amount of one kind of energy that is required to make another kind of energy within that web.

This isn't the only way that women's rights could potentially be threatened by simplicity advocates. In Canada, provinces provide varying levels of child care subsidies or monthly child benefits. Most of the budget for this comes from tax revenues provided by citizens and consumers. If we limit the amount of consumption and scale back the economy, we can expect to see a reduction in tax revenues; even if we increase tax rates or innovate how taxes work, we will still almost certainly see less available income from social service spending. In this case, the government may no longer be able to provide subsidies for child care and/or child rearing. Child care has given women a great deal of freedom for returning to work and pursuing their careers. If, in a low-growth society, the government can no longer provide these subsidies, there would be fewer families with both parents working, or an urgent call for the re-emergence of "the village" in parenting. Since parents are·often tied to the house, this role is typically associated with a reduction in freedom and the inability to pursue one's individual need to self-explore, or as a less empowered option than joining the workforce. Simplicity advocates need to a) attempt to reframe this discourse, arguing instead that staying at home is a radical act as one removes themselves from the constraints of capitalism and work, and b) talk more openly about the relationship between a return to domestic work and environmental sustainability.

Conclusion

There are, of course, many creative and innovative ways to solve the problems I briefly engage with above. Women could end up better off in a low-growth scenario – we don't know how this will shake out. Perhaps women will run governance structures or perhaps feminism will expand to include different forms of womanhood as empowering. However, only by facing these difficult questions head-on and recognizing that there will be trade-offs will we finally be able to talk about what a sustainable future really looks like. The actual consequences of a low growth economy are undeterminable, but examples like those above raise an interesting question: what is the smallest possible ecological footprint we can have that will support a minimum acceptable level of liberal and technological social progress?

This is a difficult question to answer, and we are unlikely to know before change is imperative. While these are real challenges, and low growth economics might be associated with the loss of some liberal institutions and technologies, there are possibly ways to prioritize. First, the loss of certain kinds of liberal freedoms could have both positive and negative consequences. For example, losing the right to unfettered mobility may limit an individual's freedom, but may also increase a person's sense of place, which develops ecological identity and extended empathy for a specific region. Ecological economics and degrowth are often associated with outcomes that make it difficult to know how these problems with change will manifest, such as decreases in issues of mental health (stress and anxiety), "the village" re-emerging in parenting, work taking a back seat to family, and overpasses turned into gardens as we limit car use.

By facing this difficult question, and exploring what we really value about life, we can begin to consider what kinds of trade-offs we might face in exchange for living in a more sustainable future.

REFERENCES

Anderson, B. (1991). *Imagined communities: Reflections on the origin and spread of nationalism*. New York, NY: Verso.

Arndt, J., Solomon, S., Kasser, T., & Sheldon, K. M. (2004). The urge to splurge: A terror management account of materialism and consumer behavior. *Journal of Consumer Psychology, 14*(3), 198–212. https://doi.org/10.1207/s15327663jcp1403_2

Bauhardt, C. (2014). Solutions to the crisis? The green deal, degrowth, and the solidarity economy: Alternatives to the capitalist growth economy from an ecofeminist economics perspective. *Ecological Economics, 102*, 60–8. https://doi.org/10.1016/j.ecolecon.2014.03.015

Beck, U. (1992). *Risk society: Towards a new modernity*. Thousand Oak, CA: SAGE.

Beck, U., & Beck-Gernsheim, E. (2002). *Individualization: Institutionalized individualism and its social and political consequences* (1st ed.). London; Thousand Oaks, CA: SAGE Publications Ltd.

Berkes, F., Colding, J., & Folke, C., Eds (2008). *Navigating social-ecological systems: Building resilience for complexity and change* (1st ed.). Cambridge, UK: Cambridge University Press.

Brown, M. T., & Ulgiati, S. (2004). Energy quality, emergy, and transformity: H.T. Odum's contributions to quantifying and understanding systems. *Ecological Modelling, through the MACROSCOPE: The Legacy of H.T. Odum, 178*(1), 201–13. https://doi.org/10.1016/j.ecolmodel.2004.03.002

Chaisson, E. (2001). *Cosmic evolution: The rise of complexity in nature*. Cambridge, MA: Harvard University Press.

Christian, D. (2011). *Maps of time: An introduction to big history*. Berkeley, CA: University of California Press.

Daly, H. E. (1990). Toward some operational principles of sustainable development. *Ecological Economics 2*(1), 1–6. https://doi.org/10.1016/0921-8009(90)90010-R

Daly, H. E. (2005). Economics in a full world. *Scientific American, 293*, 100–7. https://doi.org/10.1038/scientificamerican0905-100

Elias, N. (2000). *The civilizing process: Sociogenetic and psychogenetic investigations* (2nd ed.). Oxford; Malden, Mass: Wiley-Blackwell.

Elias, N. (2014). *The collected works of Norbert Elias*. (Revised ed.). Dublin, Ireland: University College Dublin Press.

Gellner, E. (1983). *Nations and nationalism*. Ithaca, NY: Cornell University Press.

Georgescu-Roegen, N. (1975). Energy and economic myths. *Southern Economic Journal, 41*(3), 347. https://doi.org/10.2307/1056148

Giddens, A. (1987). *Social theory and modern sociology*. Stanford, CA: Stanford University Press.

Giddens, A. (1990). *The consequences of modernity*. Stanford, CA: Stanford University Press.

Goldin, C., & Katz, L. F., (2002). The power of the pill: Oral contraceptives and women's career and marriage decisions. *Journal of Political Economy 110*(4), 730–70. https://doi.org/10.1086/340778

Hans-Ruediger, K. (2014). Handbook of research on consumerism in business and marketing: Concepts and practices. *IGI Global*. https://doi .org/10.4018/978-1-4666-5880-6

Harman, C. (1986). Base and superstructure. *International Socialism, 2*(32): 3–44.

Heer, D. M., & Grossbard-Shechtman, A. (1981). The impact of the female marriage squeeze and the contraceptive revolution on sex roles and the Women's Liberation movement in the United States, 1960 to 1975. *Journal of Marriage and Family, 43*(1): 49–65. https://doi.org/10.2307/351416

Jackson, T. (2009). *Prosperity without growth: Economics for a finite planet.* London; New York: Earthscan.

Kish, K., & Quilley, S. (2017). Wicked dilemmas of scale and complexity in the politics of degrowth. *Ecological Economics, 44.* https://doi.org/10.1016/j.ecolecon.2017.08.008

Kumar, K. (1991). *Prophecy and progress: Sociology of industrial and post-industrial society.* Harmondsworth: Penguin Books Ltd.

Lawrence, F. (2010). Costa Rica needs a new way of farming. *The Guardian.* Retrieved from https://www.theguardian.com/global-development/poverty-matters/2010 /oct/07/costa-rica-agriculture-development-pineapples

Marx, K. (1844). *The economic and philosophic manuscripts of 1844 and The Communist Manifesto* (1st ed.). Amherst, NY: Prometheus Books.

Marx, K. (1964). *Karl Marx: Early writings.* New York, NY: McGraw-Hill.

O'Neill, D. W. (2017). The proximity of nations to a socially sustainable steady-state economy. *Journal of Cleaner Production, 108*(A), 1213–31. https://doi.org/10.1016 /j.jclepro.2015.07.116

Odum, H. T. (2007). *Environment, power, and society for the twenty-first century: The hierarchy of energy.* New York, NY: Columbia University Press.

Pinker, S. (2012). *The better angels of our nature: Why violence has declined.* (MP3 Una ed.). Brilliance Audio on MP3-CD.

Pinker, S. (2018). *Enlightenment now: The case for reason, science, humanism, and progress.* New York, NY: Viking.

Polanyi, K. (1944). *The Great Transformation: The political and economic origins of our time.* Garden City, NY: Beacon Press.

Polanyi, K. (1971). *Primitive, archaic, and modern economies: Essays of Karl Polanyi.* Garden City, NY: Beacon Press.

Quilley, S. (2012). System innovation and a new 'Great Transformation': Re-embedding economic life in the context of 'de-growth.' *Journal of Social Entrepreneurship, 3*(2), 206–29. https://doi.org/10.1080/19420676.2012.725823

Quilley, S. 2013. De-growth is not a liberal agenda: Relocalisation and the limits to low energy cosmopolitanism. *Environmental Values, 22*(2), 261–85. https://doi.org /10.3197/096327113X13581561725310

Rescher, N. (1998). *Complexity: A philosophical overview*. Piscataway, NJ: Transaction Publishers.

Rifkin, J. (2009). *The empathic civilization: The race to global consciousness in a world in crisis.* (1st ed.). New York, NY: Tarcher.

Selsam, H., & Martel, H. (1963). *Reader in Marxist philosophy*. New York, NY: International Publishers Co.

Solomon, S., Greenberg, J. L., & Pyszczynski, T. A. (2004). Lethal consumption: Death-denying materialism. In T. Kasser and A. D. Kanner (Eds), *Psychology and consumer culture: The struggle for a good life in a materialistic world*, (pp. 127–46). Washington, DC: American Psychological Association. https://doi.org/10.1037/10658-008

Spash, C. L. (2017). The need for and meaning of social ecological economics. SRE-Disc sre-disc-2017_02, Institute for Multilevel Governance and Development, Department of Socioeconomics, Vienna University of Economics and Business.

Victor, P. A. (2008). *Managing without growth: Slower by design, not disaster*. Cheltenham, UK; Northampton, MA: Edward Elgar.

Victor, P., Jackson, T., Drake, B., Kratena, K., & Sommer, M. (2014). Foundations for an ecological macroeconomics: Literature review and model development. WWWforEurope Working Paper, no. 65. Retrieved from http://hdl.handle.net/10419/125724.

Zywert, K., & Quilley, S. (2017). Health systems in an era of biophysical limits: The wicked dilemmas of modernity. *Social Theory & Health*, *16*(2), 188–207. https://doi.org/10.1057/s41285-017-0051-4

6 Imagining Health Systems 150 Years from Now: Best and Worst-Case Scenarios for the Future of Human Health

KATHARINE ZYWERT

We must place the future, like the unborn child in the womb of a woman, within a community of men, women, and children, among us, already here, already to be nourished and succored and protected, already in need of things for which, if they are not prepared before it is born, it will be too late.

—Margaret Mead, 1970

To grasp this metamorphosis of the world it is necessary to explore new beginnings, to focus on what is emerging from the old and seek to grasp future structures and norms in the turmoil of the present.

—Ulrich Beck, 2016

Contemplating the Future in the Contingency of the Anthropocene

When I ask researchers, practitioners, and social innovation participants about the future of health systems, it is usually in a tentative way. I am serious about the question, and of all the questions I ask, this is the one I am most curious about. I also realize, though, that the way I have chosen to frame the question strikes some as absurd. I have asked people to consider the future of health systems *150 years* from now. This places us around the year 2170, nearly 70 years after the turn of the next century, the benchmark year 2100 that is often referenced by researchers when they present scenarios for the future. For this reason, it might have been simpler to ask people what health systems might be like in the year 2100, and yet I wanted to push the boundaries of imagination even further, into territory that is usually beyond its reach. In the year 2170, any children or grandchildren that I have will be gone. My great-grandchildren, assuming they were born in the first place, will be in their eighties or nineties if they are long-lived, or will already have passed. For those of us born into modern, globalized, technologically rich cultures who lived through the rise of digital technology or who never knew a world without it, it is easy to think that life in 2170 will be nearly unrecognizable. Most of us share the assumption that each new generation will lead lives that are fundamentally different than their parents. After all, this has been the case for at least 150 years already. We forget that for thousands of years in most parts of the world, generational continuity was the rule, mobility and change the exception.

In 1970, Margaret Mead published a small book, *Culture and Commitment*, based on a series of lectures she delivered at the American Museum of Natural History in the spring of 1969. The book's subtitle, "A study of the generation gap," speaks to a pressing question of the 1960s and 70s: how to cope with the growing divide between a generation that came of age through two world wars, and a rising youth subculture that didn't trust anyone over thirty. Yet the core of *Culture and Commitment* is a theory of cultural change that aims to account for transitions in the social relationships between elders, adults, and children from premodern cultures through the industrial revolution into a globally connected present. Mead proposes that cultures can be categorized as one of three types. Post-figurative cultures are place-based premodern societies in which knowledge and tradition are passed from elders to their children in unbroken continuity. In post-figurative cultures, authority comes from the past, reinforced by the presence and engagement of three or more generations in daily life. Post-figurative cultures are largely ascriptive: "The answers to the questions: *Who am I? What is the nature of my life as a member of my culture ...* are experienced as predetermined" (Mead, 1970, p. 6). Change occurs slowly in post-figurative cultures, and for the most part, a child's future can be reasonably expected to resemble the lives of their parents, grandparents, and more distant elders who lived in the same place and encountered the same lakes or mountains or herds of animals.

In cofigurative cultures, the hold of the past is weakened. Behaviour patterns are no longer defined by one's elders, but by one's peers. While elders still influence cultural norms, it becomes accepted that the lives of successive generations will differ significantly from those that have come before. The cofigurative mode arises when post-figurative cultures are disrupted by colonization, forced migration, disasters that wipe out or otherwise divide elders from adults, or the introduction of new technologies that are adopted by the young but not by the old. Cofiguration became the dominant cultural mode as societies gained access to more resources and civilizations developed the means to subjugate other cultures on a large scale, and later as individuals became more mobile geographically and economically. In cofigurative cultures, elders are unable to provide relevant models for life, and younger generations must develop these for themselves by adapting to the circumstances of the moment.

In an era of global connectivity, Mead proposes that a third cultural type has emerged, the prefigurative culture oriented towards the future, in which children must also teach adults how to get by in a changing world. In prefigurative cultures, the presumption of ongoing technological, economic, and social change leaves adults feeling as though they can provide only limited guidance to their children, who will need to be directly engaged in the development of workable ways of living for unsettled times. In this context, Mead writes: "We must create new models for adults who can teach their children not what to learn, but how to learn and not what they should be committed to, but the value of commitment" (1970, p. 92).

Although anthropologists have for the most part moved away from efforts to categorize human cultural development, Mead's continuum of post-figurative to cofigurative to prefigurative cultures has renewed relevance when we consider social-ecological change from the perspective of deep time. The Anthropocene brings with it new ecological dynamics that are already beginning to shape human society. Climate change, loss of biodiversity, population growth, and the threat of nuclear catastrophe, among other global-scale threats, alter the possibilities for human survival (Beck, 2016; Lovelock, 2014; Greer, 2009). This leads Ulrich Beck to propose that our current conceptualizations of social change are inadequate explanatory frameworks for the kind of change we are currently living through (2016). Today, change is not a process of transformation or evolution, but one of "metamorphosis" in which "what was unthinkable yesterday is real and possible today" (Beck, 2016, p. xii). Metamorphosis is unprecedented, nonlinear, and rife with unintended consequences, both negative and positive. It is a kind of change that "explodes the anthropological constants of our previous existence" (Beck, 2016, p. xi). Although there are no apparent connections between Mead's *Culture and Commitment* and Beck's *The Metamorphosis of the World*, they share a similar vision of the future as one that must be navigated by adopting a future-oriented worldview that remains open and adaptive, drawing connections between emerging possibilities in the present to walk into uncertain terrain.

It remains rare, however, for people in most walks of life in the modern world to think about deep time, either past or future. As Mead describes, geographic and cultural ruptures between the generations mean that many of us don't know the first names of our great-grandparents, let alone the details of their daily lives. When it comes to thinking about the future, those who do engage in structured planning often do so in the context of strategic planning or policy development. In most organizations, future-oriented planning is limited to time frames shorter than a decade. While the rare business or department may have ten-year strategic plans, the majority of planning cycles consider the next two to five years. Most of us who think about the *deep* future, that span of time that begins after everyone we know has passed on, are generally engaged in creative pursuits of one kind or another, from science-fiction writing to speculative art, theoretical physics, and other pockets of academia in the social sciences, ecology, and humanities. In a rhetorical sense, the Anthropocene opens up space to think about the future. Beck describes climate change as "a strong source of future-oriented meanings, in everyday life and for legitimation of political action (reforms or even revolutions)" (2016, p. 46). For human health, this potential is materializing in growing mainstream attention to the effects of climate change on health (Watts et al., 2018), the implications of the Anthropocene epoch for long-term patterns of health and well-being on a global scale (Whitmee et al., 2015), and ecological determinants of health (CPHA, 2015). Health is also a prominent concern in the Sustainable Development Goals (United Nations, 2015) and is mentioned in the Paris Agreement (UNFCCC, 2015).

However, the climate crisis; the mainstream denial of ecological limits to economic growth, energy use, and material consumption; and the sheer scale of the environmental destruction wrought in the past century (Meadows, Randers, and Meadows, 2004; Rockström et al., 2009; Jackson, 2009; D'Alisa, Demaria, and Kallis, 2014) are testaments to ongoing shortsightedness. I hesitate to say *human* shortsightedness because of the great disparity that exists between those most responsible for global social-ecological challenges and those most likely to experience their effects (Steffen et al., 2015). Since the industrial revolution, affluent countries have taken more than their share of the rewards of growing environmental exploitation, further entrenching the vulnerabilities of low-income areas to ecological catastrophes caused by global biophysical changes (e.g. the effects of climate change) and local overshoot (see Butler, this volume). On a global level, "we have been mortgaging the health of future generations to realize economic and development gains in the present" (Whitmee et al., 2015, p. 1973). Where social-ecological health is concerned, mainstream society has not effectively harnessed its capacity to think and act with the future in mind. There are some ways in which our society is oriented towards the future, for instance, in our anticipation that technological developments will solve environmental problems (see Dryzek, 2013). However, this kind of future orientation represents more of a blind faith in human ingenuity than a genuine attempt to "grasp future structures and norms in the turmoil of the present" (Beck, 2016, p. 3). Societal confidence in the power of new technologies is also a far cry from a meaningful effort to "place the future, like the unborn child in the womb of a woman, within a community of men, women, and children, among us, already here" (Mead, 1970, p. 97).

With the goal of bringing the future of human health into clearer focus within existing communities of researchers, practitioners, and social innovators, I decided to ask my research participants what they think health systems might look like in 150 years. In doing so, I seek to contribute to a growing dialogue about the effects of long-term social-ecological change on human health (e.g. McMichael, 2017; Whitmee et al., 2015; CPHA, 2015) and begin to draw the outlines of potential alternative futures.

Health System Futures

Between July 2017 and December 2017, I conducted semi-structured interviews with researchers, health practitioners, and social innovation participants whose work has implications for health systems in the Anthropocene. Each interview explored characteristics of the participant's research or practice, asked about emerging social-ecological challenges to health and health systems, and considered potential solutions according to the participant's area of expertise. This article focuses on responses to the following question concerning the long-term future of health systems, presenting findings from a sample of fourteen interviews:

> I'm going to ask you now to imagine that we are 150 years in the future. What kind of health system do you think will exist then? Try to answer by sharing both a worst-case scenario that represents your greatest fears and a best-case scenario that represents your greatest hopes for health systems.

Participants included academic researchers in the fields of planetary health, public health, horticultural therapy, degrowth, and anthropology. Health practitioners and participants in social innovations were also interviewed, including a medical doctor, psychologist, alternative health practitioner, and one ecovillage resident (see table 6.1 for a breakdown of participants' backgrounds, expertise, and gender). Potential participants were invited to take part in a research interview based on a wide-ranging literature review summarizing challenges to and promising approaches for health in the Anthropocene (see Zywert, 2017 for a variation of this review). Interviews ranged from forty minutes to two hours in duration and were audio-recorded and transcribed. Responses to the question presented above were then coded thematically using Quirkos to identify common threads in participants' visions of the future of health systems (see tables 6.2 and 6.3).

The participants interviewed in this study presented diverse perspectives on potential alternate futures for health systems 150 years from now. Within the broad categories of "worst-case scenario" and "best-case scenario," however, a number of themes could be discerned (see table 6.2 for complete list of themes and their incidence).

Within this list, it was also possible to identify cross-cutting themes discussed in both best- and worst-case health system futures (table 6.3). The next section explores these cross-cutting themes and their significance in greater detail, illustrating each with direct quotations.

Table 6.1 Summary of interviewees

Professional background		Discipline/area of practice		Gender	
				Female	Male
Academic researcher	10 (71%)	Planetary health	2 (14%)	4 (29%)	6 (43%)
		Public health	4 (29%)		
		Horticultural therapies	2 (14%)		
		Degrowth	1 (7%)		
		Anthropology	1 (7%)		
Health practitioner	3 (21%)	Medical doctor	1 (7%)	1 (7%)	2 (14%)
		Psychologist	1 (7%)		
		Alternative health practitioner	1 (7%)		
Social innovation participant	1 (7%)	Ecovillage resident	1 (7%)	1 (7%)	0
Total	**14**			**6 (43%)**	**8 (57%)**

Table 6.2 Themes identified in best-case and worst-case health system futures

Worst-case scenario		Best-case scenario	
Theme	# of participants	Theme	# of participants
Civilizational collapses of varying severity impact the structure and accessibility of health systems (e.g. through lost knowledge, dramatic losses of population, fragmentation of civilization, a return to violence and warlordism)	6	Health systems incorporate greater understanding of the importance of social connection and connection with nature to human health and well-being	6
Existing inequalities become exacerbated; health systems offer high-quality services to the rich and privileged, while socioeconomically disadvantaged populations are excluded	6	Public and preventative health are emphasized and become the organizing framework for health systems	6
Energy and resource shortages limit the capacity of health systems	5	Health systems adapt with reasonable success to partial collapses of human civilization	5
Climate change exerts a stronger negative influence on human health and health systems	5	Technology is used in more limited, strategic ways	5

(continued)

Table 6.2 Themes identified in best-case and worst-case health system futures (continued)

Worst-case scenario		Best-case scenario	
Theme	# of participants	Theme	# of participants
Disconnection (e.g. from nature, the social world, our own humanness, and the complex systems on which well-being depends)	4	Existing health system inequalities are overcome, and health systems are universally accessible regardless of socioeconomic status	4
Genetic engineering and high-technology approaches to health create negative outcomes	3	Technological advances improve health outcomes	3
Long-term human survival is threatened	3		

Table 6.3 Cross-cutting themes in health system futures

Adaptation of health systems to deep or shallow civilizational collapses

Equity in health systems

Connection to nature and social networks are central to human well-being

Implications of technology for human health outcomes

A return to past modes of health system organization

Adaptation of Health Systems to Deep or Shallow Civilizational Collapses

Discussions of civilizational collapses of varying severity presented in both worst-case (6) and best-case (5) scenarios. In the worst-case scenarios, three participants suggested that long-term human survival hangs in the balance. The majority of participants, however, did not suggest that collapse would be total or that it would represent the annihilation of humanity, but rather that social-ecological challenges would result in partial, local, and/or slow reductions in the levels of complexity that could be maintained in human societies as a whole and health systems in particular.

> We will have to have a very heavily public health-oriented system. There will be some pockets of acute care. Perhaps there will be a local doctor that can provide fundamental basic medical care, there may be the odd center that is a bit more advanced. I doubt that there would be many centers at the level of say a modern general hospital, but there would be some. Maybe I'm a bit more pessimistic than I should be there, but I don't think particularly. —Don Spady, adjunct professor, School of Public Health, University of Alberta

Reductions of human population through famine, resource-based geopolitical conflict, epidemics, declining living conditions, and interpersonal violence was a common element of collapse scenarios.

> Well, die-backs are die-backs. [The hope is] that it's not too severe. Well, it will be severe, but that in certain places in the world, populations will survive, and, this is the big hope, will be able to incorporate into the culture a true understanding of our place in the biosphere.... That the actual understanding of limits to growth will be incorporated into the species and that our propensity for solidarity will come out, because my greatest fear would be that you descend into warlordism. —Dan Bednarz, assistant professor at Bristol Community College and founder of the blog *Health after Oil*

These discussions portray a future in which suffering is not avoided, but eventually overcome as human societies learn to live sustainably within ecological constraints. The quotations above and below propose that our capacity to retain and incorporate the knowledge we have accumulated about human impacts on earth systems will be crucial in this effort.

> My worst fear is that the combination of energy decline and dangerous climate change, which I think are already overlapping, are going to create a lot of difficult and unprecedented challenges over the next 50 years, and likely far beyond. If we fail to reduce GHG emissions, climate change alone is liable to make uninhabitable many of the places where people now are thriving and wreak economic harm in many others, while overshoot proceeds in other environmental areas, challenging our expectations of civilizational progress. I think there will be some very difficult times getting through the coming bottleneck. I think parts of humanity will survive it, but there will be a much smaller population after all is said and done. Hopefully they will have learned some of the lessons and will be living much more sustainable lifestyles in a world that's going to remain climatologically and biologically damaged for a long long time. —Hank Weiss, epidemiologist and former founder and coordinator of the injury prevention program at the Wisconsin Department of Health Services

Equity in Health Systems

Rising inequality was discussed by six participants as a worst-case scenario for health systems in the future, while overcoming inequality was a central component of four best-case scenarios. Most participants who discussed equity were primarily concerned about economic disparities. However, racial and social equity were also seen to be significant.

> In the best-case scenario you would see health care facilities that are more focused on health: there is more salutogenic design, there's a much greater focus on

wellness, there's a much greater focus on inequality, or trying to get equality ... it doesn't matter how much you make or what colour your skin is or who you love, it's just health and health care is a right, not a privilege. —Naomi Sachs, post-doctoral associate, Cornell University, and founding director of the Therapeutic Landscapes Network

The extent to which equity will exist in the health systems of the future was seen to be dependent on broader dynamics of social and environmental equity on a global scale, including our capacity to adopt policies that emphasize intergenerational equity.

The worst-case scenario is a system with increased inequities where the poor and vulnerable are bearing the brunt of the impacts of the high consumers in the population.... The inequalities are increased, and you have essentially a fragmented and divergent society ... rather than seeing a kind of collaborative and supportive approach in which health is a shared aspiration for everyone. [In a best-case scenario] the emphasis is on the prevention of ill health in the context of environmental sustainability, with a strong ethical commitment to considering the impact of today's activities on future generations. And strong policies for equity, not just within the current population, but also thinking about intergenerational equity as well. —Sir Andy Haines, professor, London School of Hygiene and Tropical Medicine and Chair of the Rockefeller Foundation/Lancet Commission on Planetary Health

Connection to Nature and Social Networks as a Central Component of Human Well-Being

Incorporating greater recognition of the importance of social connection and connection to nature was discussed in six best-case scenarios, while four people warned of the dangers of ignoring these aspects of well-being. In the best-case scenarios, participants emphasized that we have accumulated significant knowledge about the beneficial effects of connection, and that these avenues represent low-cost, high-impact approaches in a context of growing ecological constraints:

I think we actually know a great deal about how to get really good health for a large number of people with really good diet, exercise, social connections, contact with nature. There's a whole lot of things and they don't actually require a lot of money. —Colin Butler, principal research fellow, College of Arts, Humanities and Social Sciences, Flinders University, Australia, and adjunct professor, Health Research Institute, University of Canberra, Australia

Placing connection at the centre of health systems would require new ways of thinking about health.

> I would say that my idea of an ideal health system would be something where there is a more holistic view of health taken, and the natural environment is integrated more into the thinking about how people can live healthier lives, and people could be prescribed more access to green spaces. —Sarah Whitmee, postdoctoral researcher, University College London and lead author on the Lancet Commission on Planetary Health report, "Safeguarding human health in the Anthropocene epoch"

One participant raised concerns that with the rise of digital technology, disconnection from one another is increasing. She proposed that this could have long-term implications for cognitive development and the capacity to work together in a world beset by social-ecological instabilities that will require enhanced cooperation to address.

> I think the other piece of my worst-case scenario is that social and environmental conditions impact our mental functioning in various ways that put us in a space where we can't think our way out of the troubles that we're in.... For the past couple years I've been working in schools and teachers are in a state of shock as to what's going on, that this new generation of kids is relatively non-functional in group activities in a way that they've never seen before. There are a few possible reasons that are kicking around. One is that with the advent of handheld phones mothers stopped looking at their children while they're breastfeeding. That basic mammalian connection response – which is a chemical response – is missing. Which is kind of horrifying. Another factor that could limit our ability to think is the impact of glyphosate and other antibiotics on our gut microbiome, which turns on our brain development and produces neurotransmitters. Also, society doesn't provide information, framing, or access to the tools and strategies necessary for people to create the relational support systems they need to process the challenging circumstances we face as capitalism collapses and the environmental conditions shift. Without those simple tools and strategies, our instinctual fear-based reactions of freeze, appease, fight, flight, and play dead take over, we turn to addictions and patterned reactive behaviors, and we don't have access to our full intelligence, resilience, and responsiveness. —Didi Pershouse, founder of the Center for Sustainable Medicine and author of *The Ecology of Care: Medicine, Agriculture, and the Quiet Power of Microbial Communities*

Implications of Technology for Human Health Outcomes

Technology was a common theme across worst- and best-case scenarios for health. Participants were hopeful that technological advances such as personalized medicine and genetic engineering could improve population-level health outcomes. However, they were wary of health systems becoming overly reliant on new technologies that were more about making a profit than delivering real benefits for health.

At the same time we would have improvements in technology, but with technologies that serve to better our life condition rather than serving only the imperative to buy more. —Eduardo Missoni, medical doctor and professor, Department of Sociology and Social Research, Bocconi University

Participants shared the sense that although technology is useful in many circumstances, a healthier future may be one in which technological interventions are limited to cases where they are deemed to be essential.

We start trusting natural processes more than we trust technology, and technology is really limited. If somebody gets in a horrible car accident and they need an artificial limb, fine, that's a great use of technology. Use of high-end technology is limited primarily to those cases where we can maybe save a life or make someone's life far better through the use of technology, but it's not used for routine health care at all. Instead we use preventative health care based on whole systems thinking, individual and family support systems for people to make the behavioral changes they need to live healthier lives, and a shift in our food production systems to ones in which all food that is grown is nutrient dense and free of toxic biocides, among other strategies. —Didi Pershouse, founder of the Center for Sustainable Medicine and author of *The Ecology of Care: Medicine, Agriculture, and the Quiet Power of Microbial Communities*

In this context, public health measures and behavioural interventions would take the place of high-technology treatments.

We'd cut out unnecessary tests, have people more focused on making healthy lifestyle choices than just treating everything with a medication. —Ecovillage resident

A Return to Past Modes of Health System Organization

When many participants imagined the future of health systems, they made comparisons to modes of organization that existed in the past. These were not necessarily perceived to be regressive, nor to signify a return to a golden age of medicine. Rather, they represent potential adaptations to limited resources and losses of social complexity that make use of an existing repertoire of structural knowledge that resides within communities.

Well, 150 years ahead, I think best-case scenario is that you have an organized community. Let's say a large village, a small town of a few thousand people. The doctor would be one of a number of specialists in the town, and specialist trades-people are included in that. I'm thinking that the town would have a doctor, a blacksmith, a carpenter, a tailor, a shoemaker, and they would be surrounded by an agricultural area. I guess I'm pretty much thinking about the model of a typical medieval English town. I think payment for the doctor's services would be on a fee-for-service basis, but with the doctor charging reasonable fees. The doctor's hourly rate is going to have to be something similar to the blacksmith's, carpenter's and tailor's really, because that's what people can afford. You might also have a bit of locally based insurance where the doctor collects a weekly or a monthly sub-scription and then treats free at the point of service. —Family physician Peter Gray

It was also suggested that various models from the past might exist simultane-ously depending on local ecological conditions and the scale and speed at which reductions in social complexity occur. In this future, some health systems may resemble those of the present day (though with less access to resources), while other areas could be more like the Dark Ages or the days of hunters and gatherers.

I think humans will survive and I think there will be pockets of advanced civiliza-tion. Even in a worst case. Not an extremely worst case, but if we're talking about a distribution and 95–100 is a worst case and 99 is global nuclear winter and the end of civilization as we know it. A 95–9[8] gloomy scenario is of a sort of fragmented world with civilization just hanging on in a few ordered areas, a bit like the Dark Ages were, with people living in monasteries. I think that's a plausible future, in which case many people in the world would have very little. They'd go back to their traditional witch doctors and getting herbs or elephant horns or something.... In that world in some parts of the world there could be a reasonable health system, but maybe not as good as we've got now, because it depends on this whole, all these global inputs. —Colin Butler, principal research fellow, College of Arts, Hu-manities and Social Sciences, Flinders University, Australia, and adjunct professor, Health Research Institute, University of Canberra, Australia

There was a great deal of ambivalence about these potential futures, and at times participants found it difficult to discern whether they represented worst- or best-case scenarios.

I imagine the trajectory is that health care just becomes so much more inacces-sible that basically people just start practicing renegade healing. People develop skills outside of the mainstream and even in a way outside of the alternative. You know, people learn how to do their own stitches, or they learn how to do menstrual extraction. Then basically we return to what I imagine was true however many hundreds of years ago, where there was one person or a few people in an area, and everybody knew that's who you go to when you have a health issue and that person would just do that thing for you or you'd barter. And partly I want that. I want humans to empower themselves to have those skills and to share them with each other. —Ecovillage resident

It was generally acknowledged that a future that shares characteristics with the distant human past would be more difficult in many ways. However, there was also the sense that these potential futures could provide people with greater community connectedness, meaning, and purpose.

> I would like to think that, because we won't have the ability to have as much con-sumption as we do today, that we will develop much better community resources and community entertainment and community cultures that will give people motivation and hope, and a structure to their lives. You've got to remember that if you look at the Greek philosophers, or even people living in the early Renaissance, they didn't have much energy, and yet look at the incredible things they built and ideas they generated and philosophies they created and art they made, and music. So it's a different kind of life, but it's not necessarily a bleak life at all. It would be harder, for sure. But I don't think it has to be a terrible life. But we have to accept that our lives are going to change. And that's what we have to do. I mean, you're talking about 150 years in the future when all of us are dead. So our actions may predicate what those people's lives are like. Our actions predicate the deep black-ness or perhaps the grey dawn. —Don Spady, adjunct professor, School of Public Health, University of Alberta

To Contingency and Back Again

The health system futures articulated by researchers and practitioners in this study express the profound contingency of human health in the present moment. If any sense of certainty arose in our discussions of the unknown future, it was that the next century and a half is likely to be a period of adaptation, of collapse and creative destruction, of nonlinear changes that drastically reorient the tra-jectory of human societies. Modernity ingrains the ideal of relentless progress in the individuals who inhabit its fragile complexity (Giddens, 1990; Bauman, 2012) while the Anthropocene makes capitalist modernity's particular brand of progress untenable. The geological epoch of human impact attributes new and potentially devastating meanings to material consumption, to the expan-sion of technology, and even to the pursuit of health through modern medi-cine, which has been demonstrated to displace risks onto future generations (Whitmee at al., 2015; Butler, 2016). Participants in this study presented poten-tial alternative futures for health systems that spoke not only to humanity's capacity for innovation, but to our ability to repurpose the social arrangements of the past. These modes of organization, though partially forgotten, remain available to the human imagination, especially in moments of contingency (Quilley, 2012). The health system futures presented in this article therefore create space for us to consider the kind of culture that might exist if human societies successfully navigate the precarity of the Anthropocene. Mead suggests that even post-figurative cultures have been "reestablished after periods of self-conscious turmoil" (1970, p. 28). While we currently exist in a time when cultivating the future-orientation of human society is necessary if we are to cope with the changes accelerated and intensified by social-ecological systems transformations unfolding in the Anthropocene, it is possible to contemplate the emergence of a different kind of society beyond the contingencies of the present. Perhaps there is a circularity to Mead's typology. Perhaps it will be possible to "place the future ... within a community of men, women, and children" at the same time as we reestablish elements of place-based, ecologically constrained cultures in which grandparents, holding their grandchildren in their arms, see their own past reflected in the future (Mead, 1970, p. 97). Perhaps, if we hope to secure human health 150 years or more into the future, it will need to be possible.

REFERENCES

Bauman, Z. (2012). *Liquid modernity*. Cambridge: Polity Press.

Beck, U. (2016). *The metamorphosis of the world*. Cambridge: Polity Press.

Butler, C. (2016). Sounding the alarm: Health in the Anthropocene. *International Journal of Environmental Research and Public Health, 13*, 1–15.

Canadian Public Health Association. (2015). *Global change and public health: Addressing the ecological determinants of health*. Ottawa: Canadian Public Health Association.

D'Alisa, G., Demaria, F., & Kallis, G. (2014). *Degrowth: A vocabulary for a new era*. New York, NY: Routledge.

Dryzek, J. (2013). *The politics of the earth: Environmental discourses*. Oxford, UK: Oxford University Press.

Giddens, A. (1990). *The consequences of modernity*. Stanford, CT: Stanford University Press.

Greer, J. M. (2009). *The ecotechnic future: Envisioning a post-peak world*. Gabriola Island: New Society Publishers.

Jackson, T. (2009). *Prosperity without growth: Economics for a finite planet*. London: Earthscan.

Lovelock, J. (2014). *A rough ride to the future*. New York: The Overlook Press.

McMichael, A. (2017). *Climate change and the health of nations: Famines, fevers, and the fate of populations*. Oxford: Oxford University Press.

Mead, M. (1970). *Culture and commitment: A study of the generation gap*. New York: Natural History Press/Doubleday & Company, Inc.

Meadows, D., Randers, J., & Meadows, D. (2004). *Limits to growth: The 30-year update.* White River Junction, VT: Chelsea Green Publishing Company.

Quilley, S. (2012). System innovation and a new 'Great Transformation': Re-embedding economic life in the context of 'de-growth.' *Journal of Social Entrepreneurship, 3*(2), 206–29.

Rockström, J. et al. (2009). A safe operating space for humanity. *Nature 461,* 472–5.

Steffen, W. et al. (2015). The trajectory of the Anthropocene: The Great Acceleration. *The Anthropocene Review, 2*(1), 81–98.

United Nations (2015). *Transforming our world: The 2030 agenda for sustainable development.* Retrieved from https://sustainabledevelopment.un.org/post2015/transformingourworld/publication

United Nations Framework Convention on Climate Change. (2015). *Paris agreement.* Retrieved from http://unfccc.int/paris_agreement/items/9485.php

Watts, N. et al. (2018). The Lancet Countdown on health and climate change: From 25 years of inaction to a global transformation for public health. *The Lancet, 391*(10120), 581–630.

Whitmee, S. et al. (2015). Safeguarding human health in the Anthropocene epoch: Report of The Rockefeller Foundation – Lancet Commission on planetary health. *The Lancet, 386,* 1973–2028.

Zywert, K. (2017). Human health and social-ecological systems change: Rethinking health in the Anthropocene. *The Anthropocene Review, 4*(3), 216–38.

7 A Changing Role for Public Health in the Anthropocene: The Contribution of Scenario Thinking for Reimagining the Future

BLAKE POLAND, MARGOT W. PARKES, TREVOR
HANCOCK, GEORGE McKIBBON, AND ANDREA CHIRCOP

We cannot solve the world's problems with the same level of thinking that created them in the first place.

—Albert Einstein (1879–1955)

A map of the world that does not include Utopia is not worth even glancing at.

—Oscar Wilde (1854–1900)

Introduction

Our current reality reflects a new phase of struggle and transformation. Korten (2005) frames this as a "Great Turning:" a shift from a paradigm of domination towards a life-centred or "ecozoic" reality. The implications for professional practice are immense, as are the potential repercussions for society and existing institutions. In this chapter, we focus on public health as a particular area of practice that will be among the "first responders" in an unpredictable future driven by challenges like climate change (Frumkin et al., 2007, 2008) and other implications of living in the Anthropocene (Whitmee et al., 2015). We recommend a fulsome response to these challenges (Hancock et al., 2015) and the associated educational reform and training needs (Parkes et al., 2018; Yassi & Hancock, 2017), by considering implications for professional practices.

Risk management is well entrenched within the field of public health, characterized by a modus operandi of "predict and control." While successful in managing many risks (infectious outbreaks, foodborne illness, sanitation, smoking), its orientation is to incremental improvements in public health and the safe return to "normal." However, "normal" is ecologically and socially unsustainable. Rather than "bouncing back" from adversity, we need to consider how we can embrace change and "bounce forward" into new ways of thinking, doing, and being (Poland et al., 2011; URP, 2015). This requires openness to new ways of thinking and working.

It also requires a (re)imagining and (re)storying of the future, to widen the scope of possibilities for co-creating something different. This chapter explores different futures scenarios to stimulate critical reflection, imagination, and creativity about the role of public health. Three alternatives are presented, followed by a hybrid case example of how the future might play out as a bricolage or mosaic.

Stories, Scenarios, and the Future of Public Health

Experience is a mixture of intention and perception. The stories we tell ourselves – and each other – about who we are, where we are, and where we're headed steer what we do, how we feel, and whether (and how) we are empowered (or not) to participate in co-creating a more desirable future (Baldwin, 2005; Huston, 2007; Leonard, 2010; Polk, 2015; de Leeuw et al., 2017). The "co-creation" part is key, insofar as it's clear that public health cannot go it alone, but rather is one party in intersecting fields of practice, discourse, deliberation, and constituencies: government, private sector, not-for-profits, community interests, and public activists.

As Kickbusch and Gleicher aptly put it: "co-production of health implies co-production of knowledge" (2012, p. 14). It is necessary to include as many viewpoints as possible to avoid framing biases, and also to be open to the disruption and disturbance that may result from engaging with viewpoints, perspectives, and narratives. Public health's role will shift as it grapples with "participatory governance" (Otsuki, 2015), and engages with "unusual allies" associated with social determinants of health, as well as those associated with ecological and biophysical dynamics of built environments, agriculture and food security, natural resource extraction, forestry, and related issues (Northern Health, 2012; Parkes, 2016). Public health is challenged to reconsider what actors, which knowledge and evidence are needed, and how understanding and governing the public's health and addressing the social and ecological factors that influence this will change (see Parkes et al., 2010).

Appeals for inclusion or technical solutions (e.g. governance mechanisms and structures) won't be sufficient, as long as inequitable power relations, wealth accumulation, and exploitation remain unaddressed (Baum & Fisher, 2010; Baum & Sanders, 2011; Birn, Pinay & Holtz, 2017; Blas et al., 2008; Coburn, 2000, 2004; Navarro, 2007). We need spaces for meaningful dialogue where we can address who benefits from systems, laws, policies, and practices that have been tailored over time to benefit some more than others, and to recognize that powerful vested interests frequently are mobilized to block changes designed to bring about greater social equity and ecological sustainability.

That said, we acknowledge that allies can be found in every sector of society, and the enjoinder to find and work with "unusual allies" potentially includes them all.

Working with narratives of alternative futures enables people to explore and understand the forces that shape us, express their values in a vision, and then work to create that future. Futures thinking and approaches (Hancock, 1985; Bezold and Hancock, 1994) have been applied, including by WHO (Bezold and Hancock, 1993), in health promotion (Bezold and Hancock, 1997), in public health (Institute for Alternative Futures, 2014), and in healthy communities work (Bezold and Hancock, 2014). Futures thinking is also used in sustainable development planning (Cook, 2004; James and Lahti, 2004; Lyons et al., 2013; Robinson et al., 2011; Sheppard et al., 2011; Swart, Raskin, and Robinson, 2004).

The Canadian futurist Norman Henchey (1978) identified four alternative futures:

- The "probable future," what most people and organizations think will likely happen, often described as "business as usual," in which life continues much as it is, but more so (although in some cases the probable future is seen as more of a "gloom and doom" or even doomsday scenario).
- The "possible future," all the things we can dream of, our flights of fancy, often straining the limits of imagination, even defying the known or accepted laws of physics; think of science fiction.
- The "plausible future," a narrower zone within the realm of possible futures, more constrained by what we think is reasonable, but well beyond what we think is probable. Often a set of scenarios are developed that lay out a range of plausible scenarios that usually includes a "business as usual" future, a more high-tech optimistic future, a decline or collapse scenario and a transformative/alternative vision (usually 'green' and with high levels of human development).
- The "preferable future," the way we would like the future to be for ourselves and our descendants.

Plausible and preferable future scenarios can be empowering and have the potential to disrupt established unquestioned patterns of power and established senses of likely trajectories of change (or inaction). The stories we tell and encounter in the media and politics are also powerful determinants of action or inaction, often reflecting well-established patterns of governance, development, and power that underpin the dynamics of social and ecological change but also the implications for health and well-being (Parkes et al., 2003).

Scenario reflections have the potential to uncover powerful cognitive dissonance between the future that people think is probable and the future they find preferable. In a futures project on public health in the United States (Institute for Alternative Futures, 2014), leaders and experts participating in a national workshop:

- rated the probable future (titled "One Step Forward, Half a Step Back") as the most likely to occur (62 per cent) but not very desirable (only 29 per cent);
- gave a high probability (50 per cent) to a "bad news" scenario ("Overwhelmed, Under-Resourced") but not surprisingly found it to be very undesirable;
- found the two versions of an aspirational future ("Sea Change for Health Equity" and "Community-Driven Health and Equity") to be quite unlikely (only 43 per cent and 35 per cent, respectively) but highly desirable (82 per cent and 84 per cent).

These scenarios revealed dissonance between the futures people thought would happen and the preferable futures. These differences can spur action.

The use of scenarios to inform public health practice is consistent with a range of literature across the health, environment, and community spectrum (Shaw et al., 2009, Varum and Melo, 2010; Sheppard et al., 2011). Though several conceptions exist, scenario development in the context of public health has been described as an approach to developing and sharing collections of relevant and plausible narratives in order to explore and compare different possible futures (Public Health Agency of Canada, 2011).

The use of scenarios and narratives is consistent with the role of collective "imagination" and learning, an integral feature of Brown's "d4-p4" collective learning cycle (develop/principles; describe/parameters, design/potential and do/practice/develop, describe, design) and a response to the "wicked problems" of our times (Brown, 2007; Brown, Harris, and Russell, 2010). Scenarios and narratives are well-suited to moving beyond the constraints of "what is," helping to inform and frame "what should be," and then moving towards designing and engaging "what could be" as a precursor to "what can be" (Brown et al., 2010).

We now explore the idea of "next generation" public health through three possible futures. Each narrative unfolds in different directions; each offer different guides. None hold all the answers: they create a space for thinking.

Three Narratives: Making Sense of What Is Happening and What Is Possible

The three narratives presented here are not so much predictions of possible futures as they are stories that help us make sense of what is happening and where we could be headed. We acknowledge that each story embodies different aspirations and different contested assumptions about what these challenges mean, how they develop, and what needs to be done.

The three narratives are "Doing the same things" (business as usual), "doing the same things better" (risk management) and "doing better things" (transition).[1] The scenarios reflect the idea that "every system is designed to achieve the results it gets."[2] The design of our present system is the result of centuries of domination and exploitation by privileged players who stand to benefit the most from this system. The result is rising social inequity, depleted natural capital, and declining ecosystem functioning. The narratives help us reconstruct what is required to create a different system, one that generates socially just and ecologically sustainable human development.

The narratives are written from the perspective of someone in Canada looking back from a dozen years in the future (~2030), informed by population health trajectories and transition points discussed by Hancock et al. (2015). They are also informed by our understanding of existing planning cycles required to ensure mitigation and adaptation. These narratives are offered with the understanding that others might have framed them differently. Narrative 1 (business as usual) is perhaps the least controversial, as the contours of the dominant paradigm are evident to all who care to look. Narrative 2 (risk management) represents a predictable intensification of currently mainstream approaches to dealing with crisis and adversity. Risk management is a particularly well-entrenched way of thinking and responding in the public health field, and it goes largely unquestioned as an approach to address public health challenges. Narrative 3 (transition) represents the most radical departure, or paradigm shift, from the previous two. It is informed by sustained engagement with social movements and literatures, from Transition Towns (Hopkins, 2008) to relocalization (deYoung and Prinzen, 2012; Hines, 2000; North and Featherstone, 2017) and degrowth (Bednarz and Beavis, 2012; Demaria et al., 2013; Victor, 2012), that charts a very different course for society that presupposes a capacity to embrace other ways of seeing and doing. The reader is reminded that the scenario presented in Narrative 3 requires threading a fine balance between believability and "thinking outside the box," informed by social movements and authors who've devoted considerable time and energy to articulating what needs to change and to come for us to embrace deep sustainability and transformative resilience. The three narratives presented here are intended to provoke our imagination (Brown et al., 2010) – encouraging us not only to consider a range of possible future trajectories and, potentially, to envision others beyond what are presented here, but also to consider the different pathways and actions that may be required to re-imagine, drive, and manifest these different future scenarios.

Narrative 1. Business as Usual: "Doing the Same Things"

In the early 2020s, governments struggled to maintain public confidence and economic growth in the midst of spreading economic malaise and growing public and private debt. Attempts to balance fiscal austerity with the cost of significant investments in "security" infrastructure resulted in alarming increases in social inequality, and with it growing social unrest that was seen to justify further "security" measures. Economic woes were compounded by rising energy costs, aging infrastructure, and delayed investments in infrastructure renewal, compounded by the emergence of more severe destructive extreme weather events unleashed on an aging and outdated infrastructure. During the 2020s governments in the Global North redoubled their efforts to restart economic growth, reassuring populations that technological innovation would offer breakthroughs that would enable populations to continue their current ways of life, albeit with some "belt-tightening."

Think tanks proliferated and studies were commissioned, but the solutions offered proved difficult to implement in the context of increasingly acrimonious debate, finger-pointing, partisan politics, short-term political focus, and constrained finances. Despite the promise of international agreements, negotiations on climate change at the national level only made incremental gains that were increasingly out of step with the growing urgency felt by scientists and many social groups. Lack of trust, growing anxiety, and a scarcity mentality translated into a lack of political will at every level. Growth faltered, public confidence was shaken, and we discovered that we had lost much of our earlier capacity for meaningful public dialogue. Canada fared better than many countries, but was not immune from the worsening global economy, increasingly chaotic climate, and growing social polarization. Public health struggled valiantly to address worsening social determinants of health, drawing attention to the links between social exclusion and health, and redoubling their efforts especially in proliferating "priority neighbourhoods" and areas hard-hit by economic and ecological change. This proved challenging, meeting growing needs while dealing with successive budget cuts and rising costs, and staff burnout became a pressing problem with significant numbers on mental health leave. Even public health "successes" proved problematic. For example, as is the case with many health interventions, attempts to promote health and to build links between social and environmental determinants of health were taken up unevenly and in ways that exacerbated inequalities. This was seen not only in traditional public health areas like tobacco control and nutrition, but also with newer innovations such as the promotion of walkable neighbourhoods and active transportation. Despite their good intentions, such initiatives contributed to gentrification and the suburbanization of poverty, which left excluded groups with diminished access to public transit and other urban amenities as they were displaced by more affluent groups drawn to move back into the city as downtown neighbourhoods became more "attractive," well-resourced, and valued for the proximity of amenities, "community spirit," and socially/physically active lifestyles. Rural and remote communities were even harder hit, as they dealt with growing environmental, social, and economic crises with ever-diminishing resources. Often this felt like "one step forward, two steps back."

Thus, sadly, business as usual represented a failure to meet emerging challenges with sufficient collaboration, innovation, foresight, political will, and integrated consideration of social and ecological determinants. The general mood among the public and many health and social service workers was that the future looked increasingly gloomy and neither governments nor the private sector were able to meet emerging challenges with anything close to the scale, speed, and audacity required.

Narrative 2. Risk Management: "Doing the Same Things Better"

Worsening economic, social, and ecological conditions in the 2010s and early 2020s, coupled with public impatience with government inaction and finger-pointing eventually led to significant political change and an emerging social consensus on the need for concerted action to address emerging challenges. A new era of collaboration enabled long-overdue investments in public infrastructure (water/sanitation/public transit), urban renewal, and climate change adaptation measures based on the best available evidence and a renewed commitment to public participation and intersectoral collaboration. Whole-of-government approaches enabled hitherto elusive synchronicities in what different departments were doing, sparking renewed public faith in the capacities of government to respond meaningfully to emerging challenges. Policies and programs were developed for key settings (schools, workplaces, hospitals, communities) addressing sustainability and health.

Special attention was paid to the social distribution of costs and benefits, recognizing that the old neoliberal adage that "a rising tide lifts all boats" was more fiction than fact, and that progress on ecological issues would be blocked without corresponding attentiveness to social inclusion and social justice. New monitoring, regulatory, and evaluation mechanisms reflected the best of what contemporary risk management approaches had to offer. Increasingly, experience moving from policy-making to implementation enabled the wider adoption of more consultative and participatory approaches that could proactively identify and address potential sources of resistance while building genuine consensus, shared vision, teamwork, and community. Ideas of systems resilience also took hold, operationalized primarily in terms of shoring up the capacity to "bounce back" from adversity. Public health played an active role, since it was well positioned to make the links between social and ecological determinants of health and issues of social exclusion and health equity. Public health professionals, energized by a broadened social mandate and social legitimacy, seized opportunities to work with professionals in other sectors as well as many actors in civil society. New alignments with emerging vibrant social movements enabled progress on multiple fronts related to cultural, political, social, and policy change at the local, regional, and national level.

Initially these produced favourable results, which fuelled additional investments in public health and social determinants of health, legislation to address social disparities, and the reformulation of environmental policies with fuller attention to the precautionary principle and environmental justice. Social justice and environmental groups discovered common ground and worked together with a shared vision for social equity and sustainability. Despite rising energy costs, a worsening global economy, accelerated ecological decline, and worrying signs we had passed crucial climatic tipping points, many people remained hopeful, buoyed by a renewed faith in public dialogue, collaboration, and shared fate. Still, progress was slower than many people wanted, in part because the evidence base was lacking in several key areas and took time to accumulate; realignments around new values of sustainability took time to work their way through the political process into policy and practice, creating new winners and losers who mobilized to protect their interests; and phase-in periods meant that the actual implementation of change was incremental. In short, the sense of movement and collaboration was also coupled with growing frustration about the mismatch between a growing sense of urgency and the time required to phase in new regulations to appease affected parties (e.g. real and immediate reductions in carbon emissions, vehicle fuel economy requirements, and the control and/or banning of key pollutants).

Narrative 3. Transition: "Doing Better Things"

As emerging threats (climate change, peak oil/energy insecurity, declining ecosystem functioning, rising inequalities, economic instability and their ripple effects – social unrest, energy and food shortages, etc.) became harder to ignore in the early 2020s, governments were forced to abandon commitments to "restarting economic growth at all costs." It was becoming obvious that sustained economic growth was a thing of the past, and no longer a viable option around which to build either domestic or foreign economic, social, and environmental policy. The age of limits was biting hard. Core cultural narratives of "progress" and "growth" were increasingly questioned, along with notions of "making it," and "getting ahead."

A more aggressive approach to risk management that had seemed so promising in the early 2010s, whose early achievements justified the huge incremental costs of setting up elaborate regulatory and enforcement mechanisms for "driving change" through multiple systems and settings (and monitoring/evaluating impacts), proved increasingly ineffective at managing change in an increasingly unpredictable world. Further, it was becoming evident that the main function of risk management had been to "manage" the problems arising from industrial growth society in a way that would allow it to continue, the problem being that even with significantly reduced economic growth, the more dysfunctional elements of globalized capitalism continued to wreak havoc and misery for many, especially the world's poorest, accompanied by tendencies towards the concentration of wealth and power that progressive tax reform only partially addressed. Furthermore, in a diversity of fields from agriculture to energy production to watershed and ecosystem management, risk management was increasingly recognized to have concerned itself with maximum sustainable yield, efficiency, stability/equilibrium, and adversity to risk rather than proactive adaptation to change.

Since the 1990s those dedicated to understanding the behaviour of complex adaptive systems had been warning that traditional risk management approaches tended to lock systems into development paths that eroded resilience over time and predisposed systems to collapse. The collapse of the east coast cod fishery was an early example of the failure of well-developed permitting, quota, and monitoring systems to forestall ecosystem collapse, but the collapse of the west coast salmon fishery, followed by many of the world's marine fisheries despite increasingly rigorous attempts at monitoring, management, and enforcement, forced a re-evaluation of the assumptions and limitations of risk management. Risk management, it turns out, had largely concerned itself with mitigating the worst effects of the dominant social-economic system, without fundamentally calling this system into question. By the late 2010s it was becoming evident that deeper change was required. Many who had previously believed there was no viable alternative to late-capitalist economic globalization were forced to reconsider their stance. The significant costs incurred in creating a sophisticated risk management apparatus made this an especially difficult and bitter pill to swallow.

Increasingly resilience was redefined not as the capacity to "bounce back" from adversity to some imagined (but increasingly dysfunctional) "normal," but rather as the capacity to embrace (rather than resist) change and to "bounce forward" into new ways of thinking and doing. Innovative new ways were explored for understanding the "animate earth," sensing the changes wanting and needing to come, harnessing collective wisdom and diversity, and "engaging emergence." Emerging from movements and groups working on progressive alternatives to the status quo (such as ecovillages, Transition Towns, community watershed councils, bioregionalism, permaculture, degrowth, and Slow Food/Money), those with the capacity to identify synergies between community development, social justice, and ecological harmony/renewal found themselves catapulted into the forefront of public attention, and were nearly overwhelmed by the outpouring of interest and engagement that followed, as people eagerly explored alternatives that resonated with deeper longings for connection and harmony. Interest in Indigenous and Global South ways of thinking and doing grew significantly. Much was learned, although attempts at paradigm "integration" proved challenging. Progress in addressing the results of colonization was evident in a closing of health disparities between Indigenous and non-Indigenous peoples after decades of deterioration.

In short, by the mid 2020s, what had been seen as a marginalized world view a decade or two earlier was widely accepted: like it or not, we were already in the midst of a massive societal transition from an industrial growth paradigm (a way of relating to the world based on economic growth, competition, exploitation, fear, acquisitiveness, and the impulse to control, "manage," and impose order – enabled by 100 years of cheap fossil fuels) to a life-centred paradigm where human flourishing is based on interdependence, deep respect and reverence for all life, and the capacity to listen to and work with nature and with each other.

Ultimately, and perhaps most ironically, the transition was propelled not by growing fear but by the compelling nature of the new cultural narratives and practices that enabled people to proactively and collectively build better futures together.

In this context, public health work flourished in many forms. Many aspects of traditional public health work continued (school nurses, public health inspections, well-baby clinics), though the work itself shifted as the new paradigm took root. Those within public health who had been leaders in interdisciplinary, bridge-building, intersectoral collaboration, and participatory governance found many new opportunities for leadership and co-creation.

Moving from Theory to Practice: Challenges and Potential

Viewing all three narratives together prompts reflection that, to a certain extent, all three are already in play, and public health is already engaging implicitly or explicitly with these different potential trajectories, and that there are insights to be gained by distinguishing and comparing patterns of characteristics among the different narratives (table 7.1). The three sets of characteristics in table 7.1 raise questions about progress, power, and sequencing. "Re-imagining the future" does not necessarily involve or flow from left to right in this table. Even so, the characteristics presented in table 7.1 help us to recognize patterns, path-dependencies and obstacles to doing better things. Aspects of this parallel what Chelleri et al. (2015) describe as overlapping stages of resilience: recovery, adaptation, and transformation. Whether an incremental approach ends up resulting in "too little too late" remains to be seen. In considering these different

Table 7.1 Characteristics of the three alternative narratives[a]

Narrative 1: Business as usual	Narrative 2: Risk management	Narrative 3: Transition
You know what you know	There are things you know you don't know	There are things you don't know you don't know
You are working in your policy/legislative mandate	You are working with other departments/professions on shared policy/legislative mandates/programs	You are working with a host of other departments/professions/stakeholders on shared concerns where policy/legislative mandates may not exist
You are delivering a program	You are working with risk-based/actuarial concerns	You are working on matters beyond the "tipping point"
Established power dynamics and systems of exploitation are an unquestioned part of business as usual	The risk associated with inequities of established power dynamics and exploitative institutional practices are "managed"	Disruption of established power dynamics and alternatives to exploitative practices are essential features of co-creating a positive future with our planetary home
Program delivery by linear measurement and a defined narrative	Program delivery involves increasing inability to predict rare events and broken narratives exist where rare events are concerned	You are working with asymmetries, sensing into and aligning with the emerging future
Fragile[b]	Robust	Gains from disorder
Vulnerable (lack of resilience)	Resilience as capacity to "bounce back"	Resilience as capacity to "bounce forward" into new ways of thinking and doing
Forecasting as projection of current stability	Increasing uncertainty involved with forecasting	Engaging emergence[c]
Working with theory of general application	Working with theory and place	Working with place and developing theory and new relationships
Doing the same things	Doing the same things better	Doing better things

Notes: [a] The table draws on our discussions while drafting chapter 6 in Hancock et al. (2015), as well as reflections on the writing of Stewart Brand, Nassim Nicholas Taleb, William R. Catton Jr, Clive Hamilton, David Tacey, James Lovelock, Al Gore, Brian Walker, and David Salt as well as our public health and environmental planning practices.
[b] The terms in this row (Fragile, Robust, and Gains from Disorder) are explained in more detail in Taleb (2012).
[c] Holman (2010).

narratives it is important to recognize the power dynamics and practices that are at play and may actively block proactive attempts to move towards what Korten (2005) and others refer to as the "Great Turning." The ideas presented in table 7.1 fuel recognition of the ways in which our patterns of thought influence our options for change (Senge et al., 2004). Doing the same things is leaving us ill-equipped (cognitively and culturally) to assess the real dangers and implications of climate change and the Anthropocene (Kahneman, 2011, Stocknes, 2015; Taleb, 2012). While we may safely project the occurrence of extreme events, many of the standards by which we design our social, cultural, and physical infrastructures are based upon our collective memory of rare events that have occurred in the past and the risks associated with these occurrences – the concept of the "hundred-year flood" reflects this way of thinking. Further, Mullainathan and Shafir (2013) observe that infrastructure managers, overworked and overstrained with the challenges of maintaining, operating, and replacing spent facilities with limited resources, often "tunnel" into their tasks, ignoring important information that would point to the need for more fundamental systems change.

With the occurrence of each challenging event, the opportunity exists to make that event a learning moment from which we can transition into doing better things. We argue that the creativity with which public health and allied professions need to approach this challenge will be both rewarding and perhaps surprising! Indeed, fostering our imagination is critical to living in an alternative future that addresses complex "wicked" challenges at the interface of health, ecosystems, and society (Brown et al., 2010). Narrative 4 below presents an example of how the range of considerations, opportunities, and tensions evident in the three narratives and preceding discussion could manifest in the daily practice of a public health nurse.

Narrative 4. Imagining the Future: Everyday Practice for a Public Health Nurse in 2030

A public health nurse (PHN) works as part of an interdisciplinary team (community residents, NGOs, First Nations, political scientist, public relations officer, medical officer of health, environmental health inspector, engineers, research coordinator, nutritionist, dental hygienist, social worker, legal aid, economist, industrial liaison, data management officer, community development worker, artists, etc.) based in a multipurpose community health centre in a rural, suburban or urban neighbourhood set up in a storefront fashion and/or as a mobile unit to maximize visibility and accessibility for the community.

A typical day starts with a team conference to determine collaborative approaches to health issues identified by the community through Scenario Thinking. Next, the public health nurse's day may head into the community for a "home environmental assessment" as a routine part of a newborn family visit. One of the goals of the visit is to facilitate social and ecological wellness in participation with the family. En route to the family's home the PHN continues an ongoing practice of collecting relevant data about the physical neighbour-hood environment through an air monitor attached to her renewable energy powered scooter. Neighbourhoods along the coast had to be relocated and re-designed due to sea-level rise and coastal erosion. As part of the home and family assessment, the PHN offers information about green spaces in the new Transition Town neighbourhood, community gardens, farming co-operatives and publicly funded alternative transportation. The PHN also uses an exercise based on the "ecological footprint" concept to provide information about en-vironmental effects of consumer products and daily practices and to encour-age ecosystem friendly practices of reusing, recycling, and reducing. Noting the newborn's grandparents living in the home, the PHN discusses options for community day care for children as well as for the elderly, and other services provided by public and private organizations that support the care work of fam-ilies. Public health standards of practice include a health equity lens and the integration of co-health benefits in all levels of prevention.

Next, the PHN visits one of the district high schools to meet with the nurse practitioner of the teen health centre together with the school's principal, guid-ance counsellor and student representatives. In addition to discussing the im-munization schedule for the coming school year, the group continues to discuss a future school event about climate change and mental health effects for young adults, and student demands for a greater ethnocultural diversity of crops in the school food garden.

Upon returning to the community health centre the PHN briefs the data management officer, who enters the quantitative and qualitative data collected through home visits and neighbourhood surveillance in a comprehensive data-base, including the Genuine Progress Index and Canadian Index of Wellbeing to inform policy. In the afternoon, the PHN participates on a municipal Health Equity Impact Assessment committee to discuss a draft policy for a pro-posed residential and commercial development adjacent to her/his district/ neighbourhood.

Before the end of the day the PHN participates in design and planning work to renovate an old public housing complex built in the 1970s into a state-of-the-art, fully accessible home for single parents, with integrated em-ployment, social, and childcare services, community garden and kitchen, in-tegrated renewable energy source and wastewater system, and local non-toxic building materials. The group is finalizing a funding proposal and draft policy brief to be submitted to the governance board, including intergovernmental ministers, diverse community representatives, and NGO coalitions.

The work of a PHN is integrated across sectors, scales, and policy-making levels and informed by a practice rooted in communities. It is not about judging an individual's decision-making as good or bad; rather it is concerned with engaging local knowledge to inform advocacy work towards healthy public policy and health equity for future populations.

We note that the imagined future in Narrative 4 contains some elements of each of the three narratives presented earlier, and that a realistic depiction of the future may well be best imagined as a "mosaic" of plausible alternative futures. Irrespective of the specific trajectory, it is clear that reimagining our future will require new ways of thinking, acting, and relating – and this is a challenge that will require public health to work with others, and in ways that go beyond the limits of our current conceptions. We submit that the creative use of future scenarios can be used by and with public health practitioners and others to (a) imagine the potential of a variety of possible futures, (b) highlight the difference between "plausible" and "preferred" futures, as a spur to action, (c) underscore the challenges and limitations of conventional thinking and of "redoubling our efforts" in risk management as a default response to emerging and intensifying threats, (d) uncover latent beliefs and assumptions about what is happening and what is possible for healthy discussion and reflection including within public health practices, and (e) aid in the identification of key choice points and potential levers of change for the co-creation of a more desirable future.

We recognize, in closing, that this work has enormous implications for the education and training of public health professionals, most of whom are not exposed to these issues as a regular feature of current master's of public health (MPH) programs in Canada. Addressing these lacunae has become the core mandate of the Ecological Determinants Group on Education (EDGE), an outgrowth of the previously cited 2015 CPHA Discussion paper (Hancock et al, 2015), working in tandem with key partners across the country (the Canadian Public Health Association, the Network of Schools of Population and Public Health, the Canadian Association of Physicians for the Environment, the National Collaborating Centre on Aboriginal Health, and the National Collaborating Centre on Environment and Health).[3]

NOTES

1 For comparison, readers might like to look at the four scenarios used in the Institute for Alternative Future's (2014) report on alternative futures for public health in the USA in 2030. Of note is the relative absence of the ecological determinants (of health and well-being) in those scenarios.

2   Generally attributed to Dr Don Berwick, past president and CEO of the Institute for
    Healthcare Improvement in the USA, but also to W. Edward Demings, a founder
    and leader in quality improvement approaches.
3   For more information on the work of EDGE, go to https://www.cpha.ca/EDGE.

REFERENCES

Baldwin, C. (2005). *Storycatcher: Making sense of our lives through the power and
    practice of story.* Novato, CA: New World Library.
Baum, F., & Fisher, M. (2010). Health equity and sustainability: Extending the work of
    the Commission on the Social Determinants of Health. *Critical Public Health, 20*(3),
    311–22. https://doi.org/10.1080/09581596.2010.503266
Baum, F., & Sanders, D. (2011). Ottawa 25 years on: A more radical agenda for health
    equity is still required. *Health Promotion International, 26*(S2), ii253–7. https://doi
    .org/10.1093/heapro/dar078
Bednarz, D., & Beavis, A. (2012). Neoliberalism, degrowth and the fate of health
    systems. Retrieved from: http://www.energybulletin.net/stories/2012-09-14
    /neoliberalism-degrowth-and-fate-health-systems
Bezold, C., & Hancock, T. (1993). *An overview of the health futures field (background
    paper for the WHO Health Futures Consultation) Appendix 5 in health futures in
    support of health for all.* Geneva: World Health Organization.
Bezold, C., & Hancock, T. (1994). Possible futures, preferable futures. *Healthcare
    Forum Journal, 37*(2), 23–9.
Bezold, C., & Hancock, T. (1997). *Health promotion futures, World Health 2020:
    Global scenarios for health promotion (conference working paper, 4th International
    Conference on Health Promotion, Jakarta, Indonesia, July 1997).* Geneva: World
    Health Organization.
Bezold, C., & Hancock, T. (2014). The futures of the healthy cities and communities.
    Movement National Civic Review, 103(1), 66–70. https://doi.org/10.1002/ncr.21182
Birn, A., Pillay, Y., & Holtz, T. H. (2017). Health and the environment. In *Textbook of
    global health* (pp. 425–76). Oxford UK: Oxford University Press.
Blas, E., Gilson, L., Kelly, M., Labonte, R., Lapitan, J., Muntaner, C., Ostlin, P., Popay,
    J., Sandana, R., Sen, G., Schrecker, T., & Vaghri, Z. (2008). Addressing social
    determinants of health inequities: What can the state and civil society do? *The
    Lancet, 372*(9650), 1684–9. https://doi.org/10.1016/S0140-6736(08)61693-1
Brown, V. (2007). Collective decision-making bridging public health, sustainability
    governance and environmental management. In C. Soskolne, L. Setra, L. Kotzé, B.
    Mackey, W. Rees, & R. Westra, *Sustaining life on earth: Environmental and human
    health through global governance.* Lanham, MD: Lexington Books.
Brown, V., Harris, J., & Russel, J. (2010). *Tackling wicked problems: Through the
    transdisciplinary imagination.* Oxford: Earthscan.

Chelleri, L., Waters, J. J., Olazabal, M., & Minucci, G. (2015). Resilience trade-offs: Addressing multiple scales and temporal aspects of urban resilience. *Environment & Urbanization, 27*(1), 181–98. https://doi.org/10.1177/0956247814550780

Coburn, D. (2000). Income inequality, social cohesion and the health status of populations: The role of neo-liberalism. *Social Science and Medicine, 51*(1), 135–46. https://doi.org/10.1016/S0277-9536(99)00445-1

Coburn, D. (2004). Beyond the income inequality hypothesis: Class, neo-liberalism and health inequalities. *Social Science and Medicine, 58*(1), 41–56. https://doi.org/10.1016/S0277-9536(03)00159-X

Cook, D. (2004). *The natural step: Towards a sustainable society.* Totnes, UK: Green Books.

de Leeuw, S., Parkes, M. W., Sloan Morgan, V., Christensen, J., Nicole, L., Mitchell Foster, K., & Russell Jozkow, J. (2017). Going unscripted: A call to critically engage storytelling methods and methodologies in geography and the medical-health sciences. *The Canadian Geographer / Le Géographe Canadien, 61*(2), 152–64. https://doi.org/https://doi.org/10.1111/cag.12337

Demaria, F., Schneider, F., Sekulova, F., & Martinez-Alier, J. (2013). What is degrowth? From an activist slogan to a social movement. *Environmental Values, 22*(2), 191–215. https://doi.org/10.3197/096327113X13581561725194

De Young, R., & Princen, T. (Eds) (2012). *The localization reader: Adapting to the coming downshift.* Cumberland, RI: MIT Press.

Frumkin, H., Hess, J. J., & Vindigni, S. (2007). Peak petroleum and public health. *JAMA, 298*(14), 1688–90. https://doi.org/10.1001/jama.298.14.1688

Frumkin, H., McMichael, A., & Hess, J. J. (2008). Climate change and the health of the public. *American Journal of Preventive Medicine, 35*(5), 401–2. https://doi.org/10.1016/j.amepre.2008.08.031

Hancock, T., Spady, D. W., & Soskolne, C. L. (Eds) (2015). *Global change and public health: Addressing the ecological determinants of health – The report in brief.* Ottawa, ON: Canadian Public Health Association. Retrieved from https://www.cpha.ca/sites/default/files/assets/policy/edh-discussion_e.pdf

Hancock, T. (1985). An introduction to health futurism. *Health Care Management Forum, 6*(1), 18–25

Henchey, N. (1978). Making sense of future studies. *Alternatives, 7,* 24–9.

Hines, C. (2000). *Localisation: A global manifesto.* London: Routledge.

Holman, P. (2010). *Engaging emergence: Turning upheaval into opportunity.* San Francisco, CA: Berret-Koehler.

Hopkins, R. (2008). *The transition handbook: From oil dependency to local resilience.* Devon, UK: Green Books.

Huston, T. (2007). Inside/out: Stories and methods for generating collective will to create the future we want. SoL (Society for Organizational Learning).

Institute for Alternative Futures. (2014). Public health 2030: A scenario exploration. Alexandria, VA: The Institute. Retrieved from www.altfutures.org/pubs/PH2030/IAF-PublicHealth2030Scenarios.pdf

James, S., & Lahti, T. (2004). *The natural step for communities: How cities and towns can change to sustainable practices.* Gabriola Island, BC: New Society Publishers.

Kahneman, D. (2011). *Thinking fast and slow.* New York, NY: Farrar Straus and Giroux.

Kickbusch I., & Gleicher D. (2012). Governance for health in the 21st century: A study conducted for the WHO Regional Office for Europe. Copenhagen, WHO Regional Office for Europe. Retrieved from http://www.euro.who.int/__data/assets /pdf_file/0010/148951/RC61_InfDoc6.pdf

Korten, D. C. (2006). *The great turning: From empire to earth community.* Bloomfield, CT: Kumarian Press.

Leonard, A. (2010). *The story of stuff: How our obsession with stuff is trashing the planet, our communities, and our health – and a vision for change.* Toronto, ON: Free Press.

Lyons, S. H., Walsh, M., Aleman, E., & Robinson, J. (2013). Exploring regional futures: Lessons from metropolitan Chicago's online Metroquest. *Technological Forecasting and Social Change, 82,* 22–33. https://doi.org/10.1016/j.techfore.2013.05.009

Mullainathan, S., & Shafir, E. (2013). *Scarcity: Why having too little means so much.* New York, NY: Times Books.

Navarro, V. (2007). *Neoliberalism, globalization and inequalities: Consequences for health and quality of life.* Amityville, NY: Baywood.

North, P., & Featherstone, D. (2017). Localisation as radical praxis and the new politics of climate change. In J. Sen (Ed.), *The movements of movements. Part I: What makes us move?* (pp. 535–56). Oakland, CA: PM Press.

Northern Health. (2012). *Position on the environment as a context for health: An integrated settings approach – Version 2.0).* Prince George, BC: Northern Health

Otsuki, K. (2015). *Transformative sustainable development: Participation, reflection and change.* Abingdon, UK: Routledge.

Parkes, M., Panelli, R., & Weinstein, P. (2003). Converging paradigms for environmental health theory and practice. *Environmental Health Perspectives, 111*(5), 669–75.

Parkes, M., Bienen, L., Breilh, J., Hsu, L., McDonald, M., Patz, J. et al. (2005). All hands on deck: Transdisciplinary approaches to emerging infectious disease. *EcoHealth, 2*(4), 258–72. https://doi.org/10.1007/s10393-005-8387-y

Parkes, M. W., Morrison, K. E., Bunch, M. J., Hallström, L. K., Neudoerffer, R. C., Venema, H. D., & Waltner-Toews, D. (2010). Towards integrated governance for water, health and social-ecological systems: The watershed governance prism. *Global Environmental Change, 20*(4), 693–704. https://doi.org/10.1016 /j.gloenvcha.2010.06.001

Parkes, M. W. (2016). Cumulative determinants of health impacts in rural, remote, and resource-dependent communities. In M. P. Gillingham, G. R. Halseth, C. J. Johnson, M.W. Parkes (Eds), *The integration imperative: Cumulative environmental, community and health effects of multiple natural resource developments* (pp. 117–52). New York, NY: Springer International Publishing AG.

Parkes, M. M. W., Poland, B. D., Allison, S., Cole, D., Culbert, I., de Leeuw, S. et al. (2018). Ecological determinants of health in public health education in Canada: A scan of needs, challenges and assets. Retrieved from https://www.cpha.ca/sites /default/files/uploads/about/cmte/EDGE-scan-needs-challenges-assets-2018-final .pdf

Poland, B., Dooris, M., & Haluza-DeLay, R. (2011). Securing 'supportive environments' for health in the face of ecosystem collapse: Meeting the triple threat with a sociology of creative transformation. *Health Promotion International, 26*(S2), ii202–15. https://doi.org/10.1093/heapro/dar073

Polk, E. (2015). *Communicating global to local resiliency: A case study of the transition movement.* Lanham, MD: Lexington Books.

Public Health Agency of Canada. (2011). *Children and physical activity scenarios project: Evidence-based visions of the future, executive summary.* Ottawa: Health Canada.

Robinson, J., Burch, S., Talwar, S., O'Shea, M., & Walsh, M. (2011). Envisioning sustainability: Recent progress in the use of participatory backcasting approaches for sustainability research. *Technological forecasting and social change, 78*(5), 756–68. https://doi.org/10.1016/j.techfore.2010.12.006

Senge, P., Otto Scharmer, C., Jaworski, J. & Flowers, B. S. (2004). *Presence: An exploration of profound change in people, organizations, and society.* New York, NY: Currency/Doubleday/Random House.

Shaw, A., Sheppard, S., Burch, S., Flanders, D., Wiek, A., Carmichael, J., ... Cohen, S. (2009). Making local futures tangible: Synthesizing, downscaling, and visualizing climate change scenarios for participatory capacity building. *Global Environmental Change, 19*(4), 447–63. https://doi.org/10.1016/j.gloenvcha.2009.04.002

Sheppard, S. R. J., Shaw, A., Flanders, D., Burch, S., Wiek, A., Carmichael, J., Robinson, J, & Cohen, S. (2011). Future visioning of local climate change: A framework for community engagement and planning with scenarios and visualisation. *Futures, 43*(4), 400–12. https://doi.org/10.1016/j.futures.2011.01.009

Stoknes, P. E. (2015). *What we think about when we try not to think about global warming: Toward a new psychology of climate action.* White River Junction, Vermont: Chelsea Green.

Swart, R. J., Raskin P., & Robinson, J. L. (2004). The problem of the future: Sustainability science and scenario analysis. *Global Environmental Change, 14*(2), 137–46. https://doi.org/10.1016/j.gloenvcha.2003.10.002

Taleb, N. N. (2012). *Antifragile: Things that gain from disorder.* New York, NY: Random House.

Urban Resilience Project. (2015). *Bounce forward: Urban resilience in the era of climate change.* Washington, DC: Island Press & The Kresge Foundation.

Varum, C. A., & Melo, C. (2010). Directions in scenario planning literature: A review of the past decades. *Futures, 42*(4), 355–69. https://doi.org/10.1016 /j.futures.2009.11.021

Victor, P.A. (2012). Growth, degrowth and climate change: A scenario analysis. *Ecological Economics*, *84*, 206–12. https://doi.org/10.1016/j.ecolecon.2011.04.013

Whitmee, S., Haines, A., Beyrer, C., Boltz, F., Capon, A. G., de Sousa Dias, B. F., Ezeh, A., Frumkin, H., Gong, P., Head, P., Horton, R., Mace, G. M., Marten, R., Myers, S. S., Nishtar, S., Osofsky, S. A., Pattanayak, S. K., Ponsiri, M. J., Romanelli, C., Soucat, A., Vega, J., & Yach, D. (2015). Safeguarding human health in the Anthropocene epoch: Report of the Rockefeller Foundation – Lancet Commission on Planetary Health. *The Lancet*, *386*(10007), 1973–2028. https://doi.org/10.1016/S0140-6736(15)60901-1

Yassi, A., Lockhart, K., Gray, P., & Hancock, T. (2019). Is public health training in Canada meeting current needs? Defrosting the paradigm freeze to respond to the post-truth era. *Critical Public Health*, *29*(1), 40–7.

PART II

Emerging Social Innovations for Health and Well-Being: Prefiguring Viable Health Systems for the Anthropocene

The papers in this collection step outside conventional theories of change that place their trust in technological innovation, education and knowledge sharing, multilateral agreements, and other forms of global governance as primary avenues for sustainable behaviour change. We begin, rather, from the premise that these mainstream mechanisms are not designed to negotiate the wicked tensions between human health and economic growth in the Anthropocene. As such, they are unlikely to lead to change at the scale required to reconcile human health and ecological integrity, nor address adequately the contingencies of the current social-ecological transition (Zywert and Quilley, 2017; Zywert, 2017). This assumption is borne out by the evidence. Since the 1970s, scientific knowledge about environmental issues has diffused into the general population, universities and governments have invested billions in environmental research and action plans, and "sustainable development" has become common parlance (Quilley, 2017). In the past two decades, a rising number of corporations have also embraced sustainability, generating "green" product lines with the intention to meet the demands of an increasingly environmentally aware consumer (Ottman, 2011). In spite of this, at a global scale, we have gained almost no traction on humanity's growing environmental impact. At the end of the second decade of the twenty-first century, the Great Acceleration continues, pushing us across planetary boundaries and beyond the ecological thresholds that have supported human flourishing throughout the Holocene (McNeill and Engelke, 2016; Steffen et al, 2015). Part of the problem with conventional theories of change is that their managerial approach is ill-suited to addressing the complexity of current challenges. They attempt to "solve" wicked problems either by denying their "wickedness" (downplaying or underestimating the significance of the paradoxes they invoke) or by simplifying complex interactions to make the problem more amenable to intervention. The most successful inroads into wicked problems, in contrast, are made when paradoxes are engaged head-on and meaningfully negotiated to create space for unprecedented innovations (Homer-Dixon, 2006; Meadows, 2008; Zywert and Quilley, 2017). Solutions that acknowledge paradoxes more directly often contain uncomfortable elements. They may not fit squarely within the frame of mainstream discourses and value systems, or appeal at first glance to society at large (Kish and Quilley, 2017). However, by addressing foundational tensions and blending unconventional elements, we argue that these niche innovations are more likely to generate mutual benefits for human health and the planetary biophysical systems upon which health depends.

Many of the most promising innovations can be classified as "prefigurative" in their approach and impact. Prefigurative practices are experimental and function to seed the cultural and political landscape with a broader range of conceivable (but hitherto unarticulated) approaches or solutions; alternatives that can then be ready and waiting for a future when the social-ecological system begins to shift (Westley et al., 2011). They are enacted by social movements seeking to embody new ways of living and seeing the world in order to lay the foundation for more widespread social transformations (Leach, 2013). Often, prefigurative alternatives are radical, diverging so starkly from the conditions of the existing system that they are unlikely to gain much traction within the dominant regime (Cornish et al., 2016). They are, however, well-placed to demonstrate the successes of alternative ways of being and thinking as the dominant system loses its resilience and people begin searching for ways to cope with profound change.

Heuristics from complexity science are useful for illustrating the significance of the kinds of prefigurative practices discussed in the following chapters. Complexity science perceives social-ecological systems to exist in one or more steady states that can be conceptualized using a state-space metaphor in which each attractor, or steady state, represents a deep valley on a three-dimensional plane. These valleys are known as "basins of attraction" (see figure P2.1). In the Navigators of the Anthropocene research group led by Stephen Quilley at the University of Waterloo, we have identified three primary potential basins of attraction for the existing global social-ecological system. The first is the basin in which we currently find ourselves: the basin of consumer capitalism. Since the industrial revolution, this basin has deepened and has come to dominate the global political economy, mainstream culture, and the interactions of most modern people with the natural world. The basin of consumer capitalism has proved incredibly resilient and resistant to change. It has been responsible for many significant improvements to quality of life around the world (e.g. expanding access to education, energy, health care, gender equity) (Quilley, this volume; Kish, this volume). It has also been responsible for what critics of modernity have described as widespread disenchantment and individualization

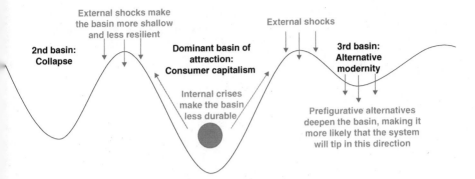

Figure P2.1 The three basins of attraction of the global social-ecological system

(Weber, 1968), alienation (Marx, 1992), anomie (Durkheim, 1897), community disintegration (Tönnies, 1887), the expansion of the economic sphere at the cost of more meaningful social ties (Polanyi, 1944), narcissism and mental instability (Lasch, 1979; Laing, 1969), and more recently the erosion of social capital (Putnam, 2000). The dominant basin is now increasingly running up against the ecological limits to economic growth (Meadows et al, 2004). The quality of life gains that have been won by consumer capitalism have come at the cost of ecological devastation, biodiversity loss, and worsening climate instabilities that may increasingly compromise the well-being of future generations (Whitmee et al., 2015; Zywert and Quilley, 2017; Quilley, this volume). Although remarkably durable, ecological crises will eventually lower the threshold between this dominant basin of attraction and other adjacent basins until the system tips into a new equilibrium.

As consumer capitalism fails, we propose that the social-ecological regime will be drawn towards one out of two potential alternative basins or attractors. The most undesirable scenario is what we call the "second basin," representing a deep collapse of the dominant regime (e.g. Tainter, 1988). The second basin of attraction would present as a wholesale breakdown of the global economy, in other words a contraction in trade and economic activity much more catastrophic and sustained than the Great Depression. Such a collapse would be likely to be accompanied by a significant loss of ecosystem functions (for instance, much of the African continent becoming uninhabitable), widespread socio-political chaos (deepening immigration crises, loss of faith in democratic institutions, rising inter-group violence), and geopolitical conflict including regional wars. Although the second basin of attraction may appear to be the stuff of dystopian science fiction, we are already on the on ramp towards this future, with many of these realities seeming not far off at all (Tainter, 2014; Kaplan, 2012; Dyer, 2009; Braucha and Scheffran, 2012).

Instead of tipping into the collapse scenario of the second basin, we argue that our goal should be to transition towards a third basin of attraction, an "alternative modernity" that preserves some of the benefits of modern societies while operating within ecological constraints. The transition towards this alternative modernity will not proceed without some losses of cherished aspects of the current regime (Kish and Quilley, 2017; Quilley, 2013; Quilley, this volume; Kish, this volume). It will likely involve some localized collapses that would enable what Homer-Dixon (2006) refers to as "catagenesis," the positive transformations that become possible when resources previously sequestered by the dominant regime are freed up to be put to new uses. In such a third basin of attraction, we would undoubtedly still see our societies shed layers of social complexity, with significant implications for health care and social welfare systems. Such a trajectory might at the same time allow for more creative responses to some of the more problematic concomitants of modernity, such as disconnection from nature and the breakdown of community life – processes that may well move into reverse gear as a matter of necessity (Kish, this volume; Aillon, this volume; Hopkins, 2009; Ophuls, 2011; Böhm et al., 2015).

The papers in this section present a range of promising social innovations for health in the Anthropocene. Blake Poland and colleagues begin with a chapter that explores the Transition movement as a site of adaptation to a post-carbon future. The Transition movement aims to build more resilient communities by meeting our needs for food, energy, health, and well-being through alternative, relocalized systems. Positioning the movement as a "trojan horse" for societal transformation, the chapter presents an in-depth study of the movement within Canada and shares lessons learned. Building on the potential of grassroots social movements to improve health through local action, Lisa Mychajluk considers how ecovillages can cultivate human and planetary health by developing regenerative food systems. Food is a central concern for ecovillages, which seek to establish sustainable communities within the constraints of a single planet. By exploring how ecovillages approach cycles of growing, acquiring, eating, and recycling their food, Mychajluk presents ecovillage food systems as a model for a healthier approach. Next, Marjolein Elings examines the history of the care farming movement in the Netherlands. Care farms combine agricultural activities and care for people with diverse needs, including elderly people with dementia, youth with behavioural problems, and adults experiencing mental health and addiction issues. The growth of the movement can be attributed to broader shifts in health systems such as retrenchment of government funding and rapid urbanization. In generating mutual benefits for people and the land, care farms offer new pathways for addressing serious health concerns, creating meaningful work in rural areas, and regenerating ecosystems.

Two chapters then consider how people can work more closely with nature to improve health and environmental resilience. Sonya Jakubec and colleagues discuss the role that parks and nature play in end of life care and death.

Drawing on results from a 2015 study, Jakubec proposes that death brings people to nature, that nature can help teach people to grieve in healthy ways, and that parks and nature are perceived as sites of life and death, revealing wisdom about the life course. In "Nature as Partner," Mary Jane Yates then explores how nature has (and has not) been included in mainstream models of human health and health promotion. She discusses the positive health outcomes associated with greater connection to nature and considers how public health can effectively engage nature in health promotion, applying theories of partnership and intersectoral collaboration to the natural world.

The last two chapters in the section bring further attention to the embeddedness of health within broader social-ecological systems. Shifting from working with individuals as a holistic health practitioner to educating farmers about how to cultivate a living soil sponge matrix that is resilient to drought and flooding, Didi Pershouse proposes that collaborating with other species is central to optimizing public and environmental health. She suggests that while the work done by the microbiomes in the soil and in our guts is often neglected, attending to these intelligent community networks is an important leverage point for both improving human well-being and mitigating the negative effects of climate change. To conclude, Katharine Zywert and William Sutherland apply insights from the study of complex adaptive systems to the practice of medicine. They propose that no single approach to medicine can effectively respond to ill health in our bodies, environments, and cultures, especially as we enter increasingly precarious times. Instead, it will be necessary to develop meta-medicines that can work across scales to promote health not only within individuals, but within broader complex adaptive systems. Taken as a whole, the chapters in part 2 present a diverse range of prefigurative social innovations that together demarcate an alternate route towards a future social-ecological regime that will allow us to live well within the ecological constraints of a finite planet.

REFERENCES

Böhm, S., Pervez Bharucha, Z., & Pretty, J. (2015). *Ecocultures: Blueprints for sustainable communities.* Abingdon, Oxon; New York, NY: Routledge.
Brauch H. G., & Scheffran J. (2012). Introduction: Climate change, human security, and violent conflict in the Anthropocene. In J. Scheffran, M. Brzoska, H. Brauch, P. Link, J. Schilling (Eds), *Climate change, human security and violent conflict.* Hexagon series on human and environmental security and peace, vol. 8. Berlin, Heidelberg: Springer.
Cornish, F. et al. (2016). Rethinking prefigurative politics: Introduction to the special thematic section. *Journal of Social and Political Psychology, 4*(1), 114–27. https://doi.org/10.5964/jspp.v4i1.640
Durkheim, E. (1897). *Suicide: A study in sociology.* Glencoe, Ill.: The Free Press.

Dyer, G. (2008). *Climate wars*. Toronto: Random House Canada.

Homer-Dixon, T. (2007). *The upside of down: Catastrophe, creativity and the renewal of civilization*. Toronto: Vintage Canada.

Hopkins, R. (2009). *The transition handbook: From oil dependency to local resilience*. White River Junction, VT: Chelsea Green Pub.

Kaplan, R. (2012). *The revenge of geography: What the map tells us about coming conflicts and the battle against fate*. New York: Random House.

Kish, K. and Quilley, S. (2017). Wicked dilemmas of scale and complexity in the politics of degrowth. *Ecological Economics, 142*, 306–17. https://doi.org/10.1016/j .ecolecon.2017.08.008

Laing, R. (1969). *The divided self*. New York: Pantheon Books.

Lasch, C. (1979). *The culture of narcissism: American life in an age of diminishing expectations*. New York: Norton.

Leach, D. K. (2013). Prefigurative politics. In D. A. Snow, D. della Porta, B. Klandermans, & D. McAdam (Eds), *The Wiley-Blackwell encyclopedia of social and political movements*. Malden, MA: Wiley.

Marx, K. (1992). Economic and philosophical manuscripts. In *Early writings* (Penguin classics). Harmondsworth, England: Penguin Books.

McNeill, J. R., & Engelke, P. (2016). *The Great Acceleration*. Cambridge, MA: Harvard University Press.

Meadows, D. (2008). *Thinking in systems: A primer*. White River Junction, VT: Chelsea Green Publishing Company.

Meadows, D. H., Randers, J., & Meadows, D. L. (2004). *Limits to growth: The 30-year update*. White River Junction, VT: Chelsea Green Publishing Company.

Ophuls, W., & Ebrary, Inc. (2011). *Plato's revenge: Politics in the age of ecology*. Cambridge, Massachusetts: MIT Press.

Ottman, J. A. (2011). *The new rules of green marketing*. Berrett-Koehler Publishers, Inc.: San Francisco, CA.

Polanyi, K. (2001). *The Great Transformation: The political and economic origins of our time*. Beacon Press: Boston.

Putnam, R. (2000). *Bowling alone: The collapse and revival of American community*. New York: Simon & Schuster.

Quilley, S. (2013). De-growth is not a liberal agenda: Relocalisation and the limits to low energy cosmopolitanism. *Environmental Values, 22*(2), 261–85. https://doi.org /10.3197/096327113X13581561725310

Quilley, S. (2017). Navigating the Anthropocene: Environmental politics and complexity in an era of limits. In P. A. Victor, B. Dolter (Eds), *Handbook on growth and sustainability* (pp. 439–70). Cheltenham, UK: Edward Elgar.

Steffen, W. et al. (2015). The trajectory of the Anthropocene: The Great Acceleration. *The Anthropocene Review, 2*(1), 81–98. https://doi.org/10.1177/2053019614564785

Tainter. J. A. (1988). *The collapse of complex societies*. Cambridge: Cambridge University Press.

Tainter. J. A. (2014). Collapse and sustainability: Rome, the Maya, and the modern world. *Archeological Papers of the American Anthropological Association, 24*(1), 201–14. https://doi.org/10.1111/apaa.12038

Tönnies, F., & Loomis, C. P. (1887). *Community and society = Gemeinschaft und gesellschaft.* Mineola, NY: Dover Publications.

Weber, M. (1968). *Economy and society; An outline of interpretive sociology.* G. Roth & C. Wittich (Eds). (E. Fischoff and others, Trans.). New York: Bedminster Press.

Westley, F., Olsson, P., Folke, C., Homer-Dixon, T., Vredenburg, H., Loorbach, D., Thompson, J., Nilsson, M., Lambin, E., Sendzimir, J., Banerjee, B., Galaz, V., van der Leeuw, S. (2011). Tipping toward sustainability: Emerging pathways of transformation. *Ambio, 40,* 762–80. https://doi.org/ 10.1007/s13280-011-0186-9

Whitmee, S. et al. (2015). Safeguarding human health in the Anthropocene epoch: Report of The Rockefeller Foundation – Lancet Commission on planetary health. *The Lancet, 386,* 1973–2028. https://doi.org/10.1016/S0140-6736(15)60901-1

Zywert, K. (2017). Human health and social-ecological systems change: Rethinking health in the Anthropocene. *The Anthropocene Review, 4*(3), 216–38. https://doi.org/10.1177/2053019617739640

Zywert, K. & Quilley, S. (2017). Health systems in an era of biophysical limits: The wicked dilemmas of modernity. *Social Theory & Health, 16*(2), 188–207. https://doi.org/10.1057/s41285-017-0051-4

8 The Role of Grassroots Social Movements as Agents of Change for Societal Transformation: The Example of the Transition Movement

BLAKE POLAND AND THE TRANSITION EMERGING STUDY
RESEARCH TEAM (CHRIS BUSE, RANDY HALUZA-DELAY,
CHRIS LING, LENORE NEWMAN, ANDRÉ-ANNE PARENT,
CHERYL TEELUCKSINGH, REBECCA HASDELL, AND
KATIE HAYES)

Whereas much discussion of energy transition in the popular press and in academic research assumes a largely technical and economic stance, imagining that transition is contingent on finding the "right" combination of technological innovation and economic incentive structures, following Grandin et al. (2018) and others, we take a different approach, emphasizing that social and political dynamics are determinative of the progress towards deep sustainability transition (or lack thereof). Put differently, the "perfect storm" of emerging challenges to health equity (climate change, resource depletion, ecological degradation, rising socioeconomic inequality), and our myriad responses to it (sometimes effective, often not), are not primarily a "technical" problem, but a social and political one (Poland et al., 2011).

Transformative social change, we argue, is thus primarily the domain of everyday practice, power politics, structured inequality, social movement organizing, and governance. While the latter has received considerable attention in the literature(s) on the governance of social-ecological systems (Berkes et al., 2003; Patterson et al., 2016) and what governments and the private sector do to block or support transition matters enormously, it is the role of civil society in its various forms that primarily interests us here.

Our emphasis on civil society and social movements stems from several observations. First, social movements have been significant agents of change in the last one hundred years, in the health field (Brown and Zavestoski, 2004) and more broadly (Smith et al., 2017). Whether it's #MeToo, Black Lives Matter, Idle No More, "Occupy," ACORN, the women's movement, 350.org, consumer survivor, gay rights, cycling advocacy, or, reaching back a bit further in time, the suffragettes, these movements have helped shape discourse and practice in contemporary social policy. So too, of course, have movements like the Ku Klux Klan, the alt-Right, neo-Nazism, white supremacy and others decidedly outside the progressive left, also shaped the political and social landscape. Our point is simply that social movements are powerful agents of change. Whatever might and has been said about their tactics and impact, the Occupy movement, for example, singlehandedly catapulted issues of social inequality onto the lips of most politicians and journalists in ways that twenty-five-plus years of research had not, and the popularized notion of the 1 per cent lives on well after the movement has waned. Second, while the role of academics could be debated at length in these movements (and there is a longstanding tradition of "socially engaged scholarship" – see Beaulieu et al., 2018), these are primarily led by civil society actors, and despite claims to the contrary, "data" and "evidence" by themselves are rarely decisive. Movements may build on and make use of research, but research remains secondary to activist organizing, and as we've shown elsewhere, allies within public health and other systems ("on the inside") rely on the activism of social movements to push the political agenda further than they could themselves (Poland et al., 2000).

Thus, having argued for a focus on social movements, in this chapter we narrow the scope further by zeroing in on the role of community organizations at the local level, recognizing that humanity is increasingly an urban species (WHO, 2016), and that in many jurisdictions it is cities that have led the way in climate adaptation and mitigation, where national governments and binding international negotiations have lagged (Gardner and Noble, 2008; Lo, 2014; Kousky and Schneider, 2003; Shi et al., 2015). Indeed, there has been a veritable explosion of interest in "community resilience" (Berkes and Ross, 2013; Lerch, 2017; Henfrey et al., 2017; Wilson, 2012b), both as the capacity to "bounce back" from adversities such as extreme weather events (Lalone, 2012; Morello-Frosch et al., 2011; Norris et al., 2008) or economic downturn (Colussi and Rowcliffe, 2000), but also in terms of the capacity to "bounce forward" into new ways of thinking and doing (Fazey et al., 2018; Manyena et al., 2011; URP, 2015). This latter aspect is our primary focus here, examining how movements take hold in civil society in urban contexts. We observe that movements such as maker culture, the sharing economy (before its recent corporate colonization), voluntary simplicity, permaculture, clothing swaps, community gardens, Freecycle, cycling advocacy groups, repair cafés, tiny houses, car sharing, bike share, guerrilla gardening, and other initiatives, while trans-local in scope, function to instantiate sustainability as social innovations in everyday practice in particular urban and suburban neighbourhoods, and rural settlements. They function as "communities of practice" (Bradbury & Middlemiss, 2015; Ingram et al., 2014) that promote, socialize, and normalize ways of living that are decidedly alternative to the mainstream culture's emphasis on consumerism (Carlsson, 2008; Poland et al., 2011; Schor and Thompson, 2014). Indeed, our case example, the Transition movement, illustrates this point.

Originating in the UK in 2006, the Transition movement is oriented to local grassroots citizen-led efforts that prepare for and support a societal energy transition to a low- or post-carbon future in response to climate change, peak oil, ecological degradation, and economic instability (www.transitionnetwork.org). Overlapping significantly with larger relocalization, degrowth/slow growth, local food, and related movements, and based on permaculture principles and a distributed network model, it embraces the opportunity to turn crisis into an opportunity to build more resilient, convivial, and vibrant local communities, declaring that "if it's not fun, it's not sustainable" (Hopkins, 2008). The movement recognizes that many of the systems we rely on for global food production, energy distribution, and advanced health care can no longer be counted on to deliver in the future, and the challenge is to creatively explore what it is possible to produce locally and do differently in an energy-constrained future, and to build community, health and well-being in the process. The Transition approach has spread rapidly, with initiatives in over 1,200 cities around the world and 100 communities and cities in Canada (www.transitionnetwork.org; Poland et al., 2018).

Utilizing a practice theory lens and drawing on an extensive web-scan of the movement's online presence, a survey and interviews with initiative (co) founders, an e-survey of Transition members/participants, regional "structured story dialogue" workshops, and key informant interviews, and informed by input from a Movement Advisory Group, from 2012 to 2017 we undertook a Canadian community-engaged research study aimed at understanding how and where the movement has taken root across the country, what Transition practice looks like, challenges and opportunities encountered, and lessons learned that could be applied within the movement and by others interested in the role of citizen-led initiatives for sustainability transition (Poland et al., 2017). We briefly summarize a few of the key findings before addressing the "burning question" of impact. We pay particular attention to the ways in which the Transition movement acts as a "niche" of social innovation and a "Trojan horse" for an "alternate route" to societal transformation that emphasizes community-level change, and the building of community resilience that is framed less in the conventional sense of the ability to "bounce back" from adversity and more in terms of the capacity to embrace change and "bounce forward" into new ways of seeing, doing, and being.

In Canada, the Transition movement first took hold in Ontario in 2008, spreading rapidly across the country before tapering off in growth in 2011. Our research shows that 101 communities self-declared as Transition Towns from 2008–15; 29 of these were recognized by the UK office to have met their criteria for "official" status, the rest being at earlier stages of development or choosing not to register or apply for official status. Half of all Transition initiatives are found in Ontario, with the remainder split between BC and the rest of the country. Using Statistics Canada criteria, slightly more than half of these can be considered suburban. In Canada, as elsewhere, the movement has grown beyond its initial emphasis on small(ish) towns to include large metropolitan areas like Vancouver and Toronto, and has thus dropped the "Transition Town" moniker. Movement practice, while taking inspiration from *The Transition Handbook* (Hopkins, 2008), varies from place to place, with food as a key area of focus that includes community gardens, permaculture workshops, edible seedling giveaways, 100-mile potlucks, harvest suppers, local food festivals, locavore breakfasts, canning and food preserving workshops, community-supported agriculture (CSA) initiatives, beekeeping, backyard chickens, and more. One of the hallmarks of the Transition movement is a focus on co-creating a vibrant local economy. This takes several forms, including the creation of local farm maps, buy-local guides, the formation of co-operatives, and the development of local currencies. Several communities also organize annual "resilience festivals," work bees, and community energy projects (e.g. http://guelphresiliencefestival.ca). Other hallmarks of the Transition movement include an emphasis on community-building, awareness-raising (often through film screenings followed by discussion), and "re-skilling" workshops. Initiatives are typically led by a small self-appointed steering committee and a series of work groups on different topic areas (food, energy, local economy, awareness-raising, heart and soul of transition, etc.) that act as sub-committees for event planning and project management.

Our research indicates that movement leaders tend to be older, well-educated, and white. Indeed, while diversity and social inclusion are oft-repeated priorities in movement literature (Alloun and Alexander, 2014; Nicolosi and Feola, 2016; Pickering, 2011) and among many local initiative founders, what little specific guidance there is for those without the requisite background, skills, and experience (e.g. Pickering, 2011) is not well publicized, and diversity is often redefined by local leaders to mean diversity of ideas, perspectives, age groups, and the like, rather than addressing potential barriers to the inclusion of racialized, marginalized, low-income, and Indigenous peoples; although, to be fair, there are also several promising discussions and initiatives that are starting to tackle these issues.

While much more could be said about the Transition movement experience in Canada (see Poland et al., 2017 & 2018), we highlight here several observations and "lessons learned" that are particularly germane for those interested in the role of citizen-led initiatives for sustainability transition. First, we were intrigued to see that the movement took hold not only in "progressive" communities (as one might have expected) but also in ones rated as more politically and socially "conservative" by those in the movement. In the latter case, they become a welcome gathering point for those disenfranchised by the local status quo, enabling a sense of belonging that may have been previously missing. Regardless of the progressiveness of the local culture, breaking out of an all-too-familiar dynamic of "preaching to the choir" is quite a challenge for most initiatives. Thus, our second observation is that although the Transition movement enjoys the advantage of not emphasizing ideological alignment as a prerequisite for participation, and instead bringing a positive message of working together to build community resilience (recall the slogan "if it's not fun, it's not sustainable"), most initiatives quickly "tap out the market" of those already predisposed to the Transition message, and have difficulty breaking into other social circles. In practice, this means that although the appearance of a new initiative often generates a groundswell of initial interest, sustaining that growth over time is a challenge for most initiatives. And third, the "part-time" nature of the movement (which enables people to engage selectively alongside full-time employment and other family and community commitments) (Bailey et al., 2010) means that many people may be peripherally involved, but few will be clearly changed, and few will become active volunteers and co-creators of change. This means the bulk of the actual work falls to a handful of the most committed steering committee members who put in significant amounts of time and energy into sustaining and growing the initiative. While this can be meaningful and even life-changing work, it can (and often is) also demoralizing for movement leaders who frequently bemoan the lack of active volunteers willing to take on portions of the work. Another challenge is that when the most promising projects go well and scale up to be significant in their own right, they often spin off into their own thing and lose observable connection to the initial Transition initiative from which they were spawned. Rob Hopkins, founder of the movement, refers to this as the "donut effect," where projects end up consuming all the attention, focus, resources, and person hours, and "no-one is left holding the centre" (Hopkins, personal communication, 2014).

We observed a certain "life cycle" of a Transition initiative that goes something like this: someone (who is often already active on climate change, peak oil, or related issues) learns about the Transition movement and tells a few friends; together they decide to see if there's interest in starting a local initiative; they host a screening of a movie (*End of Suburbia* and *In Transition* are popular choices), followed by discussion and invited expressions of interest in starting a local initiative; they get something under way, get themselves listed on the Transition Network (www.transitionnetwork.org), form working groups on particular topics (e.g. food, local economy, etc.); host monthly meetings and a number of events each year, often in collaboration with other like-minded groups; email lists of participants grows over time, as does the initiative's online profile; personality clashes or differences of opinion surface over strategy and emphasis, which are experienced by some as draining, unproductive, or overwhelming, leading to their withdrawal from the initiative, and that are eventually resolved, despite considerable angst, in ways that draw the remaining initiative leaders together; attendance and email list growth plateaus, and despite some inroads in visibility of the movement, the dominant growth paradigm continues to prevail, leading some movement leaders and co-founders to become discouraged; after four to five years of sustained effort, some leaders burn out or experience life changes that cause them to pull back. Having not been very successful at cultivating new leadership for succession, many initiatives falter at this point. Indeed, although it is difficult to surmise exactly, our impression is that nearly half of all initiatives that ever gain some traction continue to sustain after the five-year mark. That movement co-founders come into leadership out of passion for change and often do not have the requisite skills and experience in community development, conflict resolution, or inclusive governance practice means that initiatives are prone to specific kinds of "failure" that have to do with predictable challenges of the sort mentioned above (personality conflicts, group process issues, discouragement over perceived failure to decisively shift local sustainability culture, difficulties with leadership succession, etc.). The larger Transition movement, with its international office in the UK (Totnes), has worked hard to identify these issues and support movement leaders as they mature beyond initial startup, but their success at supporting initiatives in Canada is tempered by the fact that this is not a "franchise" model, and local initiative leaders remain variably (dis)connected from the central office, preoccupied with local issues rather than staying on top of online discussion forums and the availability of central resources (in terms of ideas, documents, and stories).

One interesting issue that surfaced repeatedly in the narratives of local Transition movement leaders was an apparent tension between members oriented more to "process" and those oriented more to "outcome." Like some of the other dynamics discussed above, this will be familiar to anyone who has engaged in community development work. It refers to the fact that some members are keen to discuss what's wrong with the world and what needs to change at length, and are often also keen to put considerable emphasis on group process. Others, in contrast, find such preoccupations tiresome, and are anxious to move into "action" and doing. Structuring meetings and opportunities that appeal to both types, rather than simply reflecting the predilections of movement leaders, can often be a challenge, and failure to do so can result in the loss of one or another of these groups over time, to the detriment of the initiative overall. To some extent, a similar tension prevailed between those predisposed to "activism" on key issues of concern, and those motivated to "get on with" positive actions they felt would make a more practical contribution to the community. Occasionally, local movement leaders or participants perceived to be using Transition to push their own agenda to the detriment of other ideas or a process of co-creation generated tensions that were at times quite painful and led to loss of members, leaders, and momentum, or even the collapse of the initiative.

The preceding discussion inevitably raises questions about the impacts of the Transition movement over time, especially where efforts are not sustained, but even when and where they are. Indeed the impact of the Transition movement, and grassroots citizen initiatives, has been widely discussed (Feola and Nunes, 2014; Forrest and Wiek, 2014; Middlemiss, 2011; Nicolosi and Feola, 2016; North, 2013; Richardson et al., 2012; Wilson, 2012a). Even the leaders of local initiatives widely judged to have been "successful" and more active than the movement norm were not exempt from periods of soul-searching doubt about the ultimate impact of their considerable efforts. Our discussions with movement leaders enabled us to better understand how they came to reframe success and impact over time. Initially motivated to make substantial change in local sustainability culture and community resilience, most movement leaders were forced over time to conclude that effecting change in everything from routine residential development decisions to consumer culture and community-wide food sovereignty remains something akin to "redirecting the Queen Mary": the effect of considerable effort can be remarkably difficult to detect. Those who "stuck it out" found themselves redefining success in a variety of ways. For some, the impact the initiative had on their own lives and those of the most active steering committee members became a source of ongoing inspiration. These are where social links were the strongest and where people were the most invested, and they typically took inspiration from each other's efforts, egging each other on, as it were, to adopt practices (solar energy, homesteading, water conservation, permaculture, urban agriculture) that were not "mainstream" in the wider social context. This aligns with a "practice theory" lens (Shove et al., 2012), which we employed in the Transition Emerging Study to recast localized social movements as "communities of practice" for normalizing new ways of thinking and doing, and the co-construction of an "ecological habitus" (Haluza-Delay, 2008; Haluza-Delay and Berezan, 2013; Kasper, 2009; Kirby, 2017; Poland et al., 2011). From this perspective, Transition initiatives are less straightforwardly "drivers" of change, but rather, in the context of complex adaptive systems, containers that support co-founders in staying connected to like-minded others and hopeful about the future, as an outlet and social space in which to pour action-oriented energy as a tangible alternative to fear and anxiety about the future, and as social spaces for trying on new things and co-mentorship in "living well" in alignment with the earth (in much the same way as, for example, wine-tasting clubs function as spaces for learning about the fine art of wine appreciation).

Our in-depth interviews with local Transition co-founders, as well as sustained discussion of these issues in our regional "dialogical workshops" with movement leaders (Poland and Cohen, 2017) revealed shifting logics over time, such that conventional ways of framing impact (numbers reached and "converted," changes in local practices such as suburban growth and purchasing/consumption) were increasingly replaced with narratives that emphasized the importance of "planting seeds" that may only "bear fruit" in the longer term, and that framed social change work as long-term and non-linear. The Transition movement became as much about holding a vision and compelling narrative as it was about building community connections, as well as practical examples of what is possible. Indicators of success included when the work "gets easier," such as:

> Getting yeses when we put out asks; when we hear others talking about our work, or using the discourse we promote; when municipalities and other groups and people come to us for ideas and advice; and, when others are doing the work we set out to do, whether they call it 'Transition' or not. (Guelph TES Regional Forum, October 2016)

Impact thus came to be redefined by many within the movement as a process rather than an outcome: a becoming. The importance of holding a space for alternative visions of the future, and a space to experiment with new ways of thinking and doing, was emphasized.

A third perspective on the impact of the Transition movement, anchored in the study of socio-technical systems change, is that of sustainability transitions theory, and specifically the "multi-level perspective" (MLP) (Geels, 2010; Hargreaves et al., 2013; Markard et al., 2012). Different in perspective and content than either conventional evaluation paradigms or social practice perspectives (though there are overlaps; see table 8.1), the multi-level perspective examines the dynamic interplay between relatively protected "niches" of innovation (business incubators, think tanks, pilot projects, ecovillages and other social innovation spaces), dominant "regimes," and wider landscape pressures (e.g. climate change, economic trends, etc.), with specific emphasis on the conditions under which "niche" innovations can scale up and out and ultimately effect regime change through a combination of naturally occurring conditions and more intentional "strategic niche management" via learning, network development, incentive structures, and other practices and policy levers (Markard et al., 2012; Seyfang and Haxeltine, 2012). Sustainability transitions theory and MLP have emerged as relatively new lenses for understanding the role of civil society as grassroots niches of innovation, as opposed to market-based technological innovation (Seyfang and Haxeltine, 2012; Seyfang and Longhurst, 2013). The argument is that Transition movements, and other related movements (maker culture, relocalization, urban agriculture, etc.) have a potentially important role to play in sustainability/energy transition.

Table 8.1 Alternative framings of "success" and "impact"

	What the Transition movement is seen to be doing	What the impact of the Transition movement is anticipated to be
Conventional dominant paradigm	Raising awareness, convincing people of the need for change, rallying support for proposed "solutions" and projects in the form of endorsements from community leaders, funding, media coverage, public support, and community engagement.	Sustained growth in number of people engaged, new projects, media coverage, endorsements. Changing environmentally oriented behaviours (recycling, consumerism, voting, flying, etc.). Success in obtaining external funding.
Social practice theory perspective	Influencing constellations of social practices at the intersection of materials, meanings, and skills/performative accomplishments. Creating "communities of practice" for normalizing sustainable living in an unsustainable society.	Extent to which movements provide members with the requisite skills, meanings and materials to nurture the development of an "ecological habitus." Shifts in the everyday social practices of groups.
Sustainability transition theory "multi-level perspective"	Creating niches for social innovation and local "experiments" relatively unconstrained by the dominant "landscape" or "regime."	Vibrancy of local niches of innovation. Capacity to diffuse innovative practices through replication, scaling up, and translation.

Our observations mirror those of others insofar as the evidence of impact remains equivocal and highly dependent on one's frame of reference and understanding of how impact is to be conceptualized and measured in the context of complex adaptive systems, non-linear change, and multiplicity of allied and competing forces. Some, echoing a broader call for sustainability transitions theory to pay attention to power relations (Ahlborg, 2017; Avelino et al., 2016; Geels, 2014; Lawhon and Murphy, 2012), critique the movement for eschewing activism and the politics of change and the analysis of root causes (Chatterton and Cutler, 2008), as well as the potential for communities to be co-opted into the downloading of government responsibility for environmental governance to the local level (Aiken, 2015). While not discounting the very real dangers pointed to by these critics, we argue that Transition Towns could also be seen as a kind of "Trojan horse," whereby the middle classes of the Global North are shaken of their confidence in the status quo (including mainstream appeals to ecological modernization) and instead enlisted in radical acts of reinventing a very different future without the usual appeals to ideologies of outrage and political protest.

Ultimately, history will be the judge of the relative success of the Transition movement, whether success is framed in terms of energy transition, community resilience, re-skilling, or re-localization. It seems unfair to burden the move-ment with unrealistic expectations. But taken alongside the confluence of like-minded movements or social and environmental justice (which Paul Hawken estimates to be in the hundreds of thousands; Hawken, 2007), we can be confident that social movements have an important role to play in the tran-sition from Anthropocene or Capitalocene (Moore, 2017) to the Symbiocene (Albrecht, 2016), and that the Transition movement will have played a part.

REFERENCES

Ahlborg, H. (2017). Towards a conceptualization of power in energy transitions. *Environmental Innovation and Societal Transitions, 25,* 122–41. https://doi.org /10.1016/j.eist.2017.01.004

Aiken, G. T. (2015). (Local-) community for global challenges: Carbon conversations, transition towns and government elisions. *Local Environment, 20*(7), 764–81. https:// doi.org/10.1080/13549839.2013.870142

Albrecht, G. A. (2016). Exiting the Anthropocene and entering the Symbiocene. *Minding Nature, 9*(2), 12–16.

Alloun, E., & Alexander, S. (2014). The Transition Movement: Questions of diversity, power and affluence. Simplicity Institute Report 14G. The Simplicity Institute.

Avelino, F., Grin, J., Pel, B., & Jhagroe, S. (2016). The politics of sustainability transitions. *Journal of Environmental Policy & Planning, 18*(5), 557–67. https://doi .org/10.1080/1523908X.2016.1216782

Bailey, I., Hopkins, R., & Wilson, G. (2010). Some things old, some things new: The spatial representations and politics of change of the peak oil relocalisation movement. *Geoforum, 41*(4), 595–605. https://doi.org/10.1016/j.geoforum.2009.08.007

Beaulieu, M., Breton, M., & Brousselle, A. (2018). Conceptualizing 20 years of engaged scholarship: A scoping review. *PLOS One, 13*(2), e0193201. https://doi.org/10.1371 /journal.pone.0193201

Berkes, F., Colding, J., & Folke, C. (Eds) (2003). *Navigating social-ecological systems: Building resilience for complexity and change.* Cambridge, UK: Cambridge University Press.

Berkes, F., & Ross, H. (2013). Community resilience: Toward an integrated approach. *Society & Natural Resources, 26*(1), 5–20. https://doi.org/10.1080/08941920.2012.736605

Bradbury, S., & Middlemiss, L. (2015). The role of learning in sustainable communities of practice. *Local Environment, 20*(7), 796–810. https://doi.org/10.1080/13549839 .2013.872091

Brown, P., & Zavestoski, S. (2004). Social movements in health: An introduction. *Sociology of Health & Illness, 26*(6), 679–94. https://doi.org/10.1111/j.0141-9889 .2004.00413.x

Carlsson, C. (2008). *Nowtopia: How pirate programmers, outlaw bicyclists, and vacant-lot gardeners are inventing the future today!* Oakland, CA: AK Press.

206 Emerging Social Innovations for Health and Well-Being

Chatterton, P., & Cutler, A. (2008). *The rocky road to a real transition: The Transition Towns movement and what it means for social change.* Trapese Popular Education Collective. Retrieved from http://trapese.clearerchannel.org/resources/rocky-road-a5-web.pdf

Colussi, M., & Rowcliffe, P. (2000). *The community resilience manual: A resource for rural recovery & renewal.* Port Alberni, BC: Canadian Centre for Community Renewal.

Fazey, I., Schapke, N., Caniglia, G., Patterson, J., Hultman, J., van Mierlo, B. et al. (2018). Ten essentials for action-oriented and second order energy transitions, transformations and climate change research. *Energy Research & Social Science, 40,* 54–70.

Feola, G., & Nunes, R. (2014). Success and failure of grassroots innovations for addressing climate change: The Transition Movement. *Global Environmental Change, 24,* 232–50. https://doi.org/10.1016/j.gloenvcha.2013.11.011

Forrest, N., & Wiek, A. (2014). Learning from success: Toward evidence-informed sustainability transitions in communities. *Environmental Innovation and Societal Transitions, 12,* 66–88. https://doi.org/10.1016/j.eist.2014.01.003

Gardner, S. M., & Noble, D. (2008). *Stepping up to the climate change challenge: Perspectives on local government leadership, policy and practice in Canada.* St Thomas, ON: Municipal World.

Geels, F. W. (2010). Ontologies, socio-technical transitions (to sustainability), and the multi-level perspective. *Research Policy, 39*(4), 495–510. https://doi.org/10.1016/j.respol.2010.01.022

Geels, F. W. (2014). Regime resistance against low-carbon transitions: Introducing politics and power into the multi-level perspective. *Theory, Culture & Society, 31*(5), 21–40. https://doi.org/10.1177/0263276414531627

Grandin, J., Haarstad, H., Kjaeras, K., & Bouzarovski, S. (2018). The politics of rapid urban transformation. *Current Opinion in Environmental Sustainability, 31,* 16–22. https://doi.org/10.1016/j.cosust.2017.12.002

Haluza-DeLay, R. (2008). A theory of practice for social movements: Environmentalism and ecological habitus. *Mobilization: The International Quarterly, 13*(2), 205–18.

Haluza-DeLay, R., & Berezan, R. (2013). Permaculture in the city: Ecological habitus and the distributed eco-village. In J. Lockyear & J. Veteto (Eds), *Localizing environmental anthropology: Bioregionalism, permaculture, and ecovillage design for a sustainable future* (pp. 130–45). New York, NY: Berghahn Books.

Hargreaves, T., Longhurst, N., & Seyfang, G. (2013). Up, down, round and round: Connecting regimes and practices in innovation for sustainability. *Environment and Planning A, 45*(2), 402–20. https://doi.org/10.1068/a45124

Hawken, P. (2007). *Blessed unrest: How the largest movement in the world came into being, and why no one saw it coming.* New York, NY: Viking Books.

Henfrey, T., Maschkowski, G., & Penha-Lopes, G. (Eds) (2017*). Resilience, community action & societal transformation: People, place, practice, power, politics & possibility in transition.* Devon, UK: Chelsea Green.

Hopkins, R. (2008). *The Transition handbook: From oil dependency to local resilience.* Devon, UK: Chelsea Green.

Ingram, J., Maye, D., Kirwan, J., Curry, N., & Kubinakova, K. (2014). Learning in the permaculture community of practice in England: An analysis of the relationship between core practices and boundary processes. *Journal of Agricultural Education and Extension, 20*(3), 275–90. https://doi.org/10.1080/1389224X.2014.887756

Kasper, D. V. S. (2009). Ecological habitus: Toward a better understanding of socioecological relations. *Organization & Environment, 22*(3), 311–26. https://doi.org/10.1177/1086026609343098

Kirby, J. (2017). Fleshing out an ecological habitus: Field and capitals of radical environmental movements. *Nature + Culture, 12*(2), 89–114. https://doi.org/10.3167/nc.2017.120201

Kousky, C., & Schneider, S. H. (2003). Global climate policy: Will cities lead the way? *Climate Policy, 3*(4), 359–72. https://doi.org/10.1016/j.clipol.2003.08.002

LaLone, M. B. (2012). Neighbors helping neighbors: An examination of the social capital mobilization process for community resilience to environmental disasters. *Journal of Applied Social Science, 6*(2), 209–37. https://doi.org/10.1177/1936724412458483

Lawhon, M., & Murphy, J. T. (2012). Socio-technical regimes and sustainability transitions: Insights from political ecology. *Progress in Human Geography, 36*(3), 354–78. https://doi.org/10.1177/0309132511427960

Lerch, D. (ed.). (2017). *The community resilience reader: Essential resources for an era of upheaval.* Washington, DC: Island Press.

Lo, K. (2014). Urban carbon governance and the transition toward low-carbon urbanism: Review of a global phenomenon. *Carbon Management, 5*(3), 269–83. https://doi.org/10.1080/17583004.2014.981384

Manyena, S. B., O'Brian, G., O'Keefe, P., & Rose, J. (2011). Disaster resilience: A bounce back or bounce forward ability? *Local Environment, 16*(5), 417–24. https://doi.org/10.1080/13549839.2011.583049

Markard, J., Raven, R., & Truffer, B. (2012). Sustainability transitions: An emerging field of research and its prospects. *Research Policy, 41*(6), 955–67. https://doi.org/10.1016/j.respol.2012.02.013

Middlemiss, L. (2011). The effects of community-based action for sustainability on participants' lifestyles. *Local Environment, 16*(3), 265–80. https://doi.org/10.1080/13549839.2011.566850

Moore, J. W. (2017). The Capitalocene, part 1: On the nature and origins of our ecological crisis. *Journal of Peasant Studies, 44*(3), 594–630. https://doi.org/10.1080/03066150.2016.1235036

Morello-Frosch, R., Brown, P., Lyson, M., Cohen, A., & Krupa, K. (2011). Community voice, vision, and resilience in post-Katrina recovery. *Environmental Justice, 4*(1), 71–80. https://doi.org/10.1089/env.2010.0029

Nicolosi, E., & Feola, G. (2016). Transition in place: Dynamics, possibilities, and constraints. *Geoforum, 76*, 153–63. https://doi.org/10.1016/j.geoforum.2016.09.017

Norris, F. H., Stevens, S. P., Pfefferbaum, B., Wyche, K. F., & Pfefferbaum, R. L. (2008). Community resilience as a metaphor, theory, set of capacities, and strategy for disaster readiness. *American Journal of Community Psychology, 41*(1–2), 127–50. https://doi.org/10.1007/s10464-007-9156-6

North, P. (2013). Knowledge exchange, 'impact' and engagement: Exploring low carbon urban transitions. *The Geographical Journal, 179*(3), 211–20. https://doi.org /10.1111/j.1475-4959.2012.004 88.x.

Patterson, J., Schulz, K., Vervoort, J., van der Hel, S., Widerberg, O., Adler, C. et al. (2016). Exploring the governance and politics of transformations towards sustainability. *Environmental Innovation and Societal Transitions, 24*, 1–16. http:// doi.org/10.1016/j.eist.2016.09.001

Pickering, C. (2011). *7 ingredients for a just, fair and inclusive transition: A transition network guide.* Totnes, UK: Transition Network. Retrieved from https:// transitionnetwork.org/wp-content/uploads/2016/09/Diversity-and-Social-Justice -Resource-Final.pdf

Poland, B., Boutilier, M., Tobin, S., & Badgley, R. (2000). The policy context for community development practice in public health: A Canadian case study. *Journal of Public Health Policy, 21*(1), 5–19. https://doi.org/10.2307/3343471

Poland, B. D., & Cohen, R. (2017). Adaptation of a structured story-dialogue method for action research with social movement activists. *Action Research, 15*(4), 1476750317745955. https://doi.org/10.1177/1476750317745955

Poland, B., Buse, C., Antze, P., Haluza-Delay, R., Ling, C., Newman, L., Teelucksingh, C., Cohen, R., Elton, S., Hasdell, R., Hayes, K., Massot, S., Zook, M. (2017). *The transition emerging study: Final report.* University of Toronto: Dalla Lana School of Public Health.

Poland, B., Buse, C., Antze, P., Haluza- DeLay, R., Ling, C., Newman, L. et al. (2018). The emergence of the Transition movement in Canada: Success and impact through the eyes of initiative leaders. *Local Environment, 24*(3), 180–200.

Poland, B., Dooris, M., & Haluza-DeLay, R. (2011). Securing 'supportive environments' for health in the face of ecosystem collapse: Meeting the triple threat with a sociology of creative transformation. *Health Promotion International, 26*(S2), ii202–15. https://doi.org/10.1093/heapro/dar073

Richardson, J., Nichols, A., & Henry, T. (2012). Do transition towns have the potential to promote health and well-being? A health impact assessment of a transition town initiative. *Public Health, 126*(11), 982–9. https://doi.org/10.1016/j.puhe.2012.07.009

Seyfang, G., & Haxeltine, A. (2012). Growing grassroots innovations: Exploring the role of community-based initiatives in governing sustainable energy transitions. *Environment & Planning C, 30*, 381–400. https://doi.org/10.1068/c10222

Seyfang, G., & Longhurst, N. (2013). Desperately seeking niches: Grassroots innovations and niche development in the community currency field. *Global Environmental Change, 23*(5), 881–91. https://doi.org/10.1016/j .gloenvcha.2013.02.007

Shi, L., Chu, E., & Debats, J. (2015). Explaining progress in climate adaptation planning across 156 U.S. municipalities. *Journal of the American Planning Association, 81*(3), 191–202. https://doi.org/10.1080/01944363.2015.1074526

Schor, J. B., & Thompson, C. J. (Eds) (2014). *Sustainable lifestyles and the quest for plenitude: Case studies of the new economy*. New Haven, CT: Yale University Press.

Shove, E., Pantzar, M., & Watson, M. (2012). *The dynamics of social practice: Everyday life and how it changes*. Thousand Oaks, CA: Sage.

Smith, J., Goodhart, M., Manning, P., & Markoff, J. (Eds) (2017). *Social movements and world-system transformation*. Abingdon, UK: Routledge.

URP. (2015). *Bounce forward: Urban resilience in the era of climate change*. Island Press & The Kresge Foundation: Urban Resilience Project

WHO. (2016). Global report on urban health: Equitable, healthier cities for sustainable development. Kobe, Japan: World Health Organization Centre for Health Development (WHO Kobe Centre).

Wilson, G. (2012a). Community resilience, globalization, and transitional pathways of decision-making. *Geoforum, 43*(6), 1218–31. https://doi.org/10.1016/j.geoforum.2012.03.008

Wilson, G. (2012b). *Community resilience and environmental transitions*. Abingdon, UK: Routledge.

9 "Food as Thy Medicine": How Ecovillages Foster Population and Planetary Health through Regenerative Food Systems

LISA MYCHAJLUK

Introduction

Could there be a more intimate act than eating? When we eat, the food that we put into our bodies is ingested and incorporated – it becomes a part of us. In popular parlance, "you are what you eat." However, the food that we eat is becoming increasingly unhealthy – for our bodies, due to poor dietary choices (e.g. highly processed "fast" foods with low nutrition density); for the health of food workers; for the environment (and subsequently human health); and for the food insecure, as a result of how food is produced and distributed (or not) in the global food system (IPES-Food, 2017). Eating is something that most of us do several times a day, which is part of the reason the health impacts are so profound. However, the regularity of food consumption is also an opportunity for every eater to contribute to food system transformation, because eating is both an agricultural act (Berry, 1990) and a political act (Pollan, 2006). This chapter considers how ecovillages – grassroots, sustainable community initiatives (Dawson, 2006; Litfin, 2014) – act to improve population and planetary health through their choices around eating. Furthermore, this chapter utilizes a systems approach to recognize that eating involves connected activity – to food production, acquisition, and recycling. Through this systematic approach, a broad array of ecovillage strategies and practices are identified. In addition, I suggest that ecovillages are themselves modelling (and experimenting with the design and implementation of) "regenerative" food systems (DeLind, 2011). Taken collectively, the ecovillage examples in this chapter (and the many more that exist that are not documented here) could perhaps be considered a remedy for the maladies of the industrialized and globalized food system.

What Is Wrong with Our Food System? The Food-Health Nexus

Food is a basic human need, but modern processes of food production and practices of consumption can be destructive to our health – physically and spiritually, environmentally, socially, and economically. The opening statement of the report by the International Panel of Experts on Sustainable Food Systems (IPES-Food) and the Global Alliance for the Future of Food, "Unravelling the Food-Health Nexus: Addressing Practices, Political Economy, and Power Relations to Build Healthier Food Systems," illustrates the breadth of the issue:

> Good food is a cornerstone of good health, and this fundamental relationship is widely understood. Yet profound changes in global food systems over the last decades have resulted in significant negative impacts on health and well-being that range from food insecurity to chronic disease, and from environmental degradation to diminished economic opportunity and the erosion of culture. (IPES-Food, 2017, p. 1)

Applying a political economy lens is one way to understand the population and planetary health implications of the global food system. The global food system is destructive for two primary reasons: 1) it relies on significant inputs of fossil fuels (McKibben, 2007) (the environmental, social, and political consequences of their extraction, sale, and use being, of course, well-documented) and 2) food is produced foremost as a tradable commodity, not to feed people (Sumner and Mair, 2008).

Taking into consideration all aspects of the food chain – farm production, food processing, packaging, transportation, retail, food service, and household consumption – the North American food system is a significant and intensive user of fossil fuels (c.f. Canning et al., 2017; Pimentel et al., 2008). Furthermore, an oft-repeated factoid in sustainable food activism circles, that "it takes ten calories of fossil fuel to produce a single calorie of modern supermarket food" (Walker, 2010, p. 29), points to a common perception of the fundamental unsustainability of the industrialized food system. While the energy intensity of the food system poses a major concern with respect to greenhouse gas emissions – and climate change – this dependence on fossil fuels is also of economic concern, due to the volatility in fuel prices and concerns about supply. Furthermore, as the climate changes, the resilience of global food systems is called into question, and the implications may be far-reaching. Consider, for example, the suggestion that the civil war in Syria was fuelled, in part, by climate-induced drought and food shortage, combined with neoliberal agricultural policies (Friedman, 2013). In addition, a fossil fuel-intensive agricultural system, based on trade, has other significant environmental impacts, such as soil degradation and loss of biodiversity, largely perpetuated by the monocropping system, which is used to maximize the profitability of tradable commodities. Rees calls this system a "self-consuming quasi-parasitic system that sheds biodiversity, dissipate[s] energy and nutrients and convert[s] natural cycles into terminal throughput" (quoted in Sumner and Mair, 2008, p. 62).

This loss of soil health and biodiversity is a significant threat to sustained human life on earth (Ohlson, 2014; Shiva, 2015; Steffen et al., 2015).

Bang neatly sums up the economic and social health implications of "food as tradable commodity" in a globalized food system:

> Agriculture today is about power, not feeding people. It is an industry that takes responsibility from people and makes them dependent and powerless, turning power into profits for the few, essentially multinational corporations.... In the US today only 10 cents of each dollar of disposable income is spent on food. Of that 10 cents, only 1 cent actually reaches the farmer, the producer. The other 9 are lost on food processing and food kilometers (transport) ... Even though we grow enough food to feed everyone in the world, there are 800 million people starving. Farming itself is producing enough; it is the economics surrounding farming that is incapable of getting the products to the right people in the right quantities. (2005, p. 136)

Bang touches on quite a few maladies of the global food system: that multinational corporations, rather than farmers, profit through this system; that most people are dependent on this system, and are not able to provide food for themselves; that the food is cheap for those who can get it (though he makes no mention of all the externalized costs, such as pollution, dangerous working conditions, poor treatment of animals, and increased food safety concerns – c.f. McKibben, 2007; Roberts, 2008); and that food insecurity is largely the result of financial insecurity and food distribution, and not a production issue.

Healthy communities are also victims of the modern food system. Rural communities, for instance, have declined as the economics of the globalized food system has caused farm consolidation across much of the industrialized world, almost eliminating the "family farm" and drastically changing the face of the rural landscape (McKibben, 2007). With corporate innovation focused on convenience and product diversity, this food system also supports modern, hyper-individualized lifestyles – characterized by disconnection from others (i.e. social isolation) and nature (Louv, 2011) – which is increasingly being blamed for many of our societal ills, such as overconsumption and depression resulting from social isolation (McKibben, 2007).

Sumner and Mair (2008) argue that the process of commodification blinds us from seeing the environmental, social, and economic maladies wrought by the global food system. However, if we "lift the veil of ignorance surrounding the food we eat" (Sumner and Mair, 2008, p. 67), they say we will see not a life-supporting system, but one that destroys the very elements on which life depends: a healthy environment, access to one of life's most basic needs, and supportive human relationships.

While the links between food and health are clearly vast and complex (as are the challenges in being able to address these issues), the message, in short, is that "food systems are making us sick" (IPES-Food, 2017). Ultimately, the IPES-Food report calls for transformative food system change in order to "strengthen the fundamental role that food systems play in creating and sustaining health and well-being in all communities and populations" (2017, p. 1). Sumner and Mair suggest that "lifting the veil" to reveal how food systems are currently operating may help us to better comprehend how the food system *could* operate, and open a window for the "politics of the possible" to thrive (2008, p. 67). However, when dealing with complex system transformation, perhaps what is also necessary is for the possibilities to be brought to light (IPES-Food, 2017), tested, and tried.

Unveiling the Possibility of an Alternative, "Regenerative" Food System

According to McMichael, "there is a counter-movement towards community agriculture and fresh organic food that corresponds to the excesses of industrialization" (2000, pp. 21–2). Likewise, there is a growing "local food" movement, which DeLind calls, "at once a social movement, a diet, and an economic strategy – a popular solution – to a global food system in great distress" (2011, p. 273). Largely emerging from the grassroots community level, in both rural and urban areas, the "relocalization" of the food system manifests in a variety of forms, including farmers' markets, community-supported agriculture, urban agriculture, and food cooperatives (production and retail) (Lyson, 2012). According to proponents, the benefits of relocalization of food systems include being less ecologically disruptive, being better able to weather shocks (environmental and economic), and greater life satisfaction through a rebuilding of community and overall improved socioeconomic well-being (c. f. McKibben, 2007; Lyson, 2012).

Despite these benefits, in reflecting on the state of the local food movement today, DeLind posits that relocalization of food production is not sufficient to achieve a truly sustainable food system. Rather, she envisions a sustainable food system to resemble Dahlberg's earlier notions of a "regenerative food system" based on understanding of place; the use and restoration of the natural resource base; the recognition of our kinship to all other life forms; and the fair distribution of resources, voice, and power (as described in DeLind, 2011). DeLind (2011) reasons that much of the original ideology of the local food movement has been lost in practice, as local food pursuits have focused narrowly on economic potential and failed to promote the broader regenerative values that Dahlberg advocated, related to ecology, cultural and biological diversity, power, justice, and spirituality. This reductionist approach, critiques DeLind (2011), more keenly serves the status quo – the individual, the industrial, the generic – and loses much of its potential for systemic resiliency, without which a truly sustainable system cannot be realized. What is needed, argues DeLind (2011), is a food system approach with a much broader focus – one that is particular, democratic and collaborative, and that is based on the community building relationships and processes that hold people to place and to shared responsibility. Such a "sustainable" food system is described by Feenstra to be "a collaborative effort to build more locally-based, self-reliant food economies – one in which sustainable food production, processing, distribution, and consumption [are] integrated to enhance the economic, environmental, and local health of a particular place" (quoted in DeLind, 2011, p. 274).

In this chapter, I posit that ecovillage food systems are responding to the maladies of the global food system by modelling regenerative and sustainable food systems (DeLind, 2011) and food practices. Ecovillage food systems are place-based and just, and serve the life needs of particular places (its people and its ecology), including by building community (DeLind, 2011). Furthermore, such food systems achieve what the IPES-Food report calls for by recognizing the fundamental role that food plays in the health and well-being of the community in all its forms.

Modelling the Alternative: The Ecovillage Food System

Ecovillages are a form of intentional community – a group of people who choose to live and work together towards a common aim, which for ecovillages entails realizing a "sustainable or environmentally virtuous way of life" (Sargisson, 2012, p. 130). Ecovillages exist around the globe (Litfin, 2014), and are largely grassroots initiatives that receive little to no government support (Dawson, 2006), despite being recognized by the United Nations as a promising form of alternative human settlement to address the most pressing social, economic, and ecological crises of our times (Litfin, 2014). Ecovillages have often been described as experiments and models for alternative systems (Dawson, 2006). Furthermore, while each ecovillage is arguably is own "socionature" (Lockyer and Veteto, 2013) (suggesting no single one can, or should, be replicated exactly), food is a central feature and concern for all ecovillages (Liftin, 2014), and a fundamental way that ecovillagers translate their values into practices (Sanford, 2014). As such, understanding the strategies and practices of ecovillages in enacting alternative food systems, including the challenges that they face when doing so, can illuminate possibilities for broader societal and system change.

The remainder of this chapter journeys through the ecovillage food system in order to "bring the alternatives to light" (IPES-Food, 2017, p. 82). A range of academic, grey, and popular literature sources were reviewed in order to identify exemplars of ecovillage food system practices related to food growing, acquiring, eating, and recycling.[1] Taking a systems approach poses a challenge for deciding how to begin. However, given the focus of this chapter, perhaps it is logical to start with "growing" – which begins with the seed.

Growing

Applying a "permaculture" approach to food production appears to be a fairly ubiquitous ecovillage strategy (Litfin, 2014). The concept of permaculture was originally introduced by Mollison and Holmgren (1978) as a set of design principles intended to create agricultural systems that mimic and integrate with ecological systems. Furthermore, grounded in the ethics of "earth care," "people care," and "fair share," permaculture results in a holistic approach that recognizes the fundamental interdependence of economic viability, social justice, and a functioning ecology (Lockyer and Veteto, 2013). In practical terms, J.M. Bang posits that permaculture necessitates thinking "carefully about our environment, our use of resources and how we supply our needs ... [and] to be resourceful and self-reliant and to become a conscious part of the solution to the many problems which face us both locally and globally" (2005, p. 49). The following examples illustrate permaculture in practice in the growing of food within ecovillages. However, as will become evident in subsequent subsections, permaculture, as a systemic concept, permeates through the examples provided to illustrate other aspects of the ecovillage food system. In fact, the first example provided here shows how permaculture is not only an important concept for the ecovillage food system, but also an integral part of the design of the ecovillage landscape:

> Permaculture infuses the landscape at LA Ecovillage [California, USA]: the common green space behind their buildings is a jungle of fruit trees, plants, vegetables and flowers all planted in circular patterns. Here biodiversity gives rise to natural insecticides and fertilizers. And woven into all of this ecological abundance are elements of the human world. (Fosket and Malmo, 2009, p. 72)

The next two examples come from La'akea Ecovillage on the Big Island of Hawaii (USA). These examples illustrate how permaculture is used to design food production systems in an ecologically integrated manner that is mindful of local biodiversity and landscapes, and that considers its impact on interrelated systems, such as energy. La'akea Ecovillage also shares what appears to be a common ecovillage objective – striving for self-sufficiency in food production and achieving a more sustainable way of life through food practices (Sanford, 2014).

> Food, a primary focus of our sustainability efforts, averages about 70 per cent from our land. The leafy greens and the annual vegetables come from an organic garden with raised beds. The remainder comes from food forests which mimic natural ecosystems. Tall palm trees coexist with shorter fruit and nut trees and bananas, interplanted with spindly cassava plants, berry bushes, kava, coffee, and cacao.

Vanilla orchids and air potatoes climb up the trees. Squash grows around the edge of the food forest.

When we arrived at Laʻakea the jungle was higher than the fruit trees in our orchards. Foliage in a rain forest grows very fast. Saws and weed whackers were wasteful and intensive not only of fossil fuel, but of human energy. So we partnered with sheep to keep the orchards mowed and fertilized, and the nitrogen-fixing trees under control (maintaining just the right number of sheep so pastures are not overgrazed). (Matfin, 2011, pp. 46–7)

The final example in this section, from Earthaven ecovillage (North Carolina, USA), outlines a vision for food growing that appears to embody the notions of both permaculture and regeneration:

We intend to use agriculture to provide sustenance and livelihood for ourselves, through a regenerative relationship with Earth, peaceful trade with our neighbors, and demonstration of our values. Our agriculture will enhance, rather than diminish the fertility of the soil and the biodiversity of our ecosystem. (Earthaven Ecovillage, 2018)

There are a variety of food production enterprises at Earthaven that exemplify this vision, including:

- Gateway Farm: a five-acre growing demonstration of integrated agriculture, incorporating pasture-raised sheep and poultry, annual and perennial plants, forestry, and biofuel production.
- Useful Plants Nursery: a small, permaculture-based nursery selling to a retail market, specializing in useful, phytonutritional food and medicine plants well-adapted to surrounding bioregions.
- Yellowroot Farm: part of a collective of local farmers called Foothills Family Farms, where they market some of their pork and vegetables.
- The forest garden: an example of a style of gardening that mimics nature while emphasizing production of food, fibre, fuel, and other useful products (Earthaven Ecovillage, 2018).

Through application of a permaculture approach that works with nature rather than against it, these ecovillages are striving for a regenerative, holistic food production system that is dynamic and diverse. Furthermore, the food-growing practices at the ecovillages presented in this section offer a stark alternative to industrialized, chemical farming, with its focus on productivity through the intensive application of fossil fuel inputs and tendency to threaten the health of natural systems.

Acquisition

The next section considers how ecovillagers "get" or "acquire" food, apart from producing it themselves. Ira, a resident at Acorn community (Virginia, USA), describes their approach to food acquisition as such: "We grow some of our own things, but we also want to buy food from organic and sustainable sources" (quoted in Healy, 2011, p. 22). Furthermore, Levkoe (2006) provides the umbrella concept of "community food security" (CFS), which may usefully be applied to understand, in part, the spirit of food acquisition practices at ecovillages. Levkoe describes CFS as aiming to be "supportive of the needs of the whole community and to assure equitable food access created through democratic decision-making" (2006, p. 91). There are a variety of activities at ecovillages that appear to build CFS, including: community gardens, community-supported agriculture (CSA), co-ops, barter and community currency systems, and donations (Litfin, 2014). Furthermore, as is demonstrated in this section, for ecovillagers, building community food security is an activity that extends beyond the geographic borders of the ecovillage. The examples provided here illustrate deliberate attempts to build regenerative and sustainable local food systems.

Ecovillage at Ithaca (EVI) (New York, USA) exemplifies the varied food acquisition activities at ecovillages that, collectively, support community food security and regenerative food systems. Food at EVI comes from community gardens, as well as a privately run ten-acre organic farm that operates a CSA program open to both ecovillagers and the broader community. Food grown at EVI is also made available to the surrounding community through the Ithaca farmers market and a local food cooperative. Surplus food is donated to a local food rescue group, the Friendship Donations Network (FDN), a volunteer-run operation that feeds 2,000 people a week by re-distributing donations to a soup kitchen, food pantries, and work sites employing low-income workers (Walker, 2005).

Another exemplar of regenerative food acquisition practices is Tamera, a peace-based community in Southern Portugal. Tamera aims to ensure that all of its members have their basic food needs met, as the community believes that once members are relieved of the need to focus on "survival" practices, they are then freed to (and become open to) contributing to the community's gift economy, and to serve the community as a whole (Tamera, 2018a). In addition, Tamera decided that it would stop buying supermarket food by the end of 2010, because "industrial production of food is a sort of war ... Behind nearly every product you will find suffering, ignorance, and violence" (Dregger, 2010, p. 27). To this end, the community developed a strategy for a regenerative, regional food autonomy network, which included gradually increasing their own food production efforts and partnering with local farmers (Esteves, 2017; Tamera, 2018b). Tamera's efforts to partner with farmers in the region has created a win-win-win situation, with Tamera getting organic food at a reasonable cost and local farmers producing independent of the global market (which has not served the region well, economically), while supporting regional environmental health. For example, Tamera buys organic honey from a local farmer at a much cheaper price than the supermarket, yet the farmer earns nearly double what s/he would if producing for industry. In addition, the presence of bees in the area adds to the permaculture landscape – pollinating the community's fruit trees. These partnerships have helped area farmers move away from unsustainable farming practices, such as large-scale livestock production (Dregger, 2010). Also, Tamera has been credited with bringing economic viability to area farmers, and at the same time, playing a part – through their food acquisition practices – in transforming not only agricultural practices, but also bringing alternative food production (e.g. organic bread) and eating practices (e.g. vegetarianism) to the local region (Kunze and Avelino, 2015). This example of "getting" food by Tamera demonstrates how through ethically informed buying decisions, an ecovillage can support its bioregion neighbours and the local environment while diminishing their collective reliance on the global food system.

The final example in this section highlights one of many community food security activities of Los Angeles Ecovillage (LAEV), a community in a low-income, racially and ethnically diverse neighbourhood in Central Los Angeles. This example demonstrates how ecovillages might consider the food acquisition needs of the surrounding community. To illustrate: LAEV's founders faced the challenge of how to develop trust among neighbours who were steadfastly fearful of one another. They started by organizing a community brunch. At the brunch they invited all of the neighbourhood children to taste different kinds of fruit, and then they asked them which were their favourites. Trees were planted based on the children's choices. Once planted, community members were invited to hold hands, encircling the new additions to the neighbourhood, and talk about the future they symbolized. Furthermore, to the kids living in this neighbourhood, the availability of free fruit hanging from trees holds more than symbolic value. Today, LAEV estimates that they have planted over 100 fruit-producing trees in the two-block radius they call home (Fosket and Malmo, 2009). In bringing people together, transforming the concrete neighbourhood into something greener, and choosing edible trees, the founders of LAEV and others who joined were enacting what has come to be an important part of LAEV: making connections among ecological, social, and economic systems.

Few ecovillages are 100 per cent food self-sufficient, which requires making decisions about how to acquire the food that they don't grow. While no two ecovillages are exactly alike, the above examples show how they may be actively engaged in building community food security within the ecovillage itself and in local communities and regional areas. Through a variety of food acquisition activities, ecovillages demonstrate value-laden decision-making, influenced by a commitment to place and shared responsibility, which enables "stepping out" of the global food economy, and in doing so, supporting the development of a healthier, regional alternative. Furthermore, in illustrating how dietary choices are integral to the shape and functioning of the food system, and also how food-related decisions can influence community-building more broadly, the examples in this section provide a link to the next stage of the ecovillage food system cycle – "eating."

Eating

The examples provided in this section further demonstrate how ecovillage food choices, and also the collective manner in which ecovillagers often choose to consume food (i.e. communal meals), are driven by a variety of environmental, personal, social, and economic health concerns.

O.U.R. Ecovillage (British Columbia, Canada) provides an excellent example of mindful dietary choices, as evidenced by some of the provisions in their *Food Manifesto*[2]:

- We try to keep O.U.R. food affordable, accessible and healthy. O.U.R. ideal is to eat organic and GMO-free.
- We strive towards eating a nourishing diet of natural, whole foods, prepared for maximal enjoyment and appropriate nutrition, inspired by traditional cooking wisdom.
- We work to grow O.U.R. own organic foods in line with traditional and contemporary wisdom, towards regeneration of the land and wholesome nourishment of O.U.R.selves as Eaters.
- We do O.U.R. best to support small-scale, local and organic food systems when we are unable to provide for O.U.R. needs on this land.
- We honour the role that plant-based eating plays within the multi-faceted spectrum of personal and planetary healing.
- We value collective eating as a community building practice, an antidote to many of O.U.R. world's ills (O.U.R. Ecovillage, 2018).

The perceived connection between food and health/healing is also made clear in O.U.R. Ecovillage's Food Manifesto. Furthermore, the example of La'akea Ecovillage (Hawaii, USA), below, demonstrates that to align dietary choices with a healthy, local food system means reconnecting with what can be grown in the bioregion and adjusting consumption accordingly – which, arguably, is a radical notion for the modern eater.

Three years ago, several members dedicated a month to eating 100 per cent locally from the big island. While they were successful, one challenge was getting enough starch. What to eat if not rice, wheat or other grains? Grains do not grow well in the tropics. So the fourth year we opened our eyes to alternative starches. We already had taro, and to this we added cassava, peach palm fruit, air potatoes, squash, and beyjool seeds. Year 5, two of us went 100 per cent local again. The diet nurtured us psychically and physically, producing very little non-compostable waste. After six years, we have enough food to survive. The land is not lacking. It is our taste buds and preferences for what is familiar that need to change. (Matfin, 2011, p. 46)

As La'akea demonstrates, eating mindfully may require a re/learning of local food knowledge, and it may also involve learning new skills, such as how to cook unfamiliar foods, and how to preserve foods for the less abundant seasons (Sanford, 2014).

The literature on ecovillages is also ripe with examples of how eating choices – in particular, the practice of eating together at communal meals – are important contributors to the making of the "community glue" that supports members in living and working together (Jongkind, 2015; Litfin, 2014; Metcalf, 1995). The following examples are illustrative of what is involved in eating together:

At Twin Oaks in Virginia, USA, a food team is in place each week to coordinate meal preparation and make decisions about purchases to supplement what is produced by the community. Lunch and dinner are served daily, and brunch is served on the weekends. (Fosket and Malmo, 2009, p. 24)

At EcoVillage at Ithaca community dinners are held four times a week throughout the year. Typically, there are between 40–80 people gathering for a meal cooked by a volunteer team. Cooks plan their meals around what is seasonably available from the EcoVillage farms and other local farms. (Walker, 2010, p. 41)

As is clear, these communal meals are, in part, a natural extension of communal food growing and acquisition, but they also serve other important functions for individuals living in community, and for the community as a whole. For instance, communal meals provide residents an opportunity to work together – saving time and energy (Ludwig, 2017), and thereby facilitating more regular consumption of fresh, healthy meals rather than packaged or fast food. This is an important social support, as "simple" eating can often prove to be anything but simple – taking much time and effort for the individual to do on their own (Sanford, 2014). In this manner, the act of collective eating supports ecovillagers in living out values of place-based eating and sustainable food.

Furthermore, eating together provides opportunities to socialize and connect, which contrasts sharply with the modern eating experience that has become isolated for many.[3] The literature on ecovillages is abundant with examples of how eating together contributes to a multiplicity of interconnected health benefits, including physical, mental, social, and spiritual well-being. For instance, members of Songaia, a community in Bothell, Washington, experience daily dinners as an opportunity for families to come together, for coworkers in the organic garden to chat about the day's work, and a chance to celebrate (Lanphear, 2014). Similarly, members of Maitreya Mountain Village in Northern California see their communal eating space as vital to community-building, including contributing to a sense of comradeship, conviviality, and contentment (Moran, 2015). And, as Devon Bonady (2015), a resident of a rural intentional community in the Pacific Northwest, points out, eating together is a way to connect people in the community to each other, and to physically nourishing food, while also connecting to the Earth community from which the food is derived – a reconnection that can be spiritually fulfilling. These types of reconnections – to people and to nature – are being recognized for their potential physical and mental health benefits. Consider, for instance, the results of a four-year study of Ontario high school students by Khoury et al. (2015), which suggest that eating with family may be positively associated with cardiometabolic health. Or the myriad of restorative psychological health benefits evidenced as a result of spending time in natural environments (Louv, 2011). Thus, communal eating can be seen as an important contributor to overall health and well-being in ecovillages.

As is evidenced by these examples, ecovillages are motivated to eat locally and organically, but unlike individuals with similar motivations, the communal approach to eating within ecovillages can overcome the constraints of available time and resources to actualize these values on a daily basis. Consequently, ecovillages may be better positioned to achieve a multiplicity of aims of the mindful diet, including: supporting a local, organic food economy; eating healthy meals in a socially fulfilling environment, which can nourish body and spirit; and reducing the environmental impact of the food eaten, for instance, by reducing its carbon intensity (organic; grown close to home), and by consuming food that is seasonal and regionally appropriate. In these ways, the act of eating in ecovillages becomes an "antidote to many of [the] world's ills" (O.U.R. Ecovillage, 2018).

Recycling

In this final stage of the journey through the ecovillage food system – the by-products of the other stages – growing, getting, and eating – are dealt with. However, calling it "final" is somewhat of a misnomer, as there is no end to a regenerative system. Accordingly, I have called this section "recycling," in the spirit of permaculture principle number six, "Produce no waste" (Roth, 2011, p. 10). In many of the previous stages of the system, this principle is embedded – reducing the creation of "waste" in the first place; for example, by eliminating packaging through the self-provision of food, and buying collectively in bulk. However, inevitably, there will be by-products of production and consumption;

the following examples provide a glimpse at how these by-products are used as nourishment, to replenish soils, and create a healthy foundation for a regenerative food system.

This example from Ecovillage at Ithaca (New York, USA) illustrates how food waste may be handled:

> I dumped my contribution of kitchen scraps into the wire mesh enclosed bin and placed brown leaves on top, to help make the compost cook at a high temperature. We have an agreement with the Town of Ithaca to dump leaves here in the fall. It keeps the leaves out of the landfill and offers us a much-needed brown material to mix with kitchen scraps. As a community we are able to compost all of our kitchen waste (except for meat scraps), and I feel good that it goes right back to our gardens to start the cycle of growing food once again. (Walker, 2010, p. 184)

And of course, there are other ways that food becomes "waste," but still may be used for beneficial purpose:

> Ecovillages also recycle greywater (e.g. from kitchen sinks and showers) and blackwater (human wastes from toilets) through a variety of constructed systems such as composting toilets and wetland wastewater treatment. By reclaiming and recycling these "wastes" ecovillage systems can recover for agricultural purposes up to 90% of the nutrients in domestic wastewater. (Bang, 2005, p. 164)

And so, the "end" of the food system becomes the beginning.

Conclusion

The IPES-Food report posited that "good food" is the cornerstone to "good health", but the global food system appears to be failing both of these objectives. The maladies of the global food system are vast: quasi-parasitic from an ecological perspective (Sumner and Mair, 2008); economically unhealthy for farmers; and socially destructive for communities. From permaculture to co-ops, community meals to composting toilets, the ecovillage food system differs significantly from the modern, industrialized, and globalized food system. It is a dynamic system designed to harmonize with the place where the ecovillage is located; to work with and respect nature; and to provide community food security (Levkoe, 2006), both for ecovillagers and their neighbours. At the same time, ecovillage food strategies and practices demonstrate an awareness of the exploitive and destructive nature of the global food system, and reveal a desire to counteract that system with a commitment to place and shared responsibility (DeLind, 2011). Through conscious decisions about food production and consumption, ecovillages aim to remedy the maladies (Dawson, 2006) of the global food system – an intention that is embodied in the opening line of O.U.R. Ecovillage's *Food Manifesto* (2018): "O.U.R. Vision is to joyfully share food as medicine for O.U.R.selves, O.U.R. land and for O.U.R. broader world's socioeconomic, ecological and political systems." Such a vision is not achieved without challenges: there are trade-offs (growing food for sustenance or livelihood?); the need to rethink abundance and tastes; re/learning food skills; finding the time to eat mindfully. However, it is "in community" – built on shared food values – that ecovillagers find the support necessary to face these challenges. If "you are what you eat," then ecovillagers are mindful community members and global citizens, enacting the practices of a regenerative food system and nourishing population and planetary health with every morsel that passes their lips.

NOTES

1 The ecovillage practices in this chapter are drawn from examples of ecovillages in Western countries, e.g. Canada, the United States, and European countries. As such, these practices may or may not be applicable/relevant to non-Western countries.
2 This is not the complete manifesto. It can be read in its entirety here: https://ourecovillage.org/our-policies/#food
3 A recent American study reported 46 per cent of adult eating occasions, including 25 per cent of dinners, are done alone (Ludwig, 2017).

REFERENCES

Bang, J. M. (2005). *Ecovillages: A practical guide to sustainable communities.* Gabriola Island, BC: New Society Publishers.

Berry, W. (1990). *What are people for? Essays.* San Francisco: North Point Press.

Bonady, D. (2015). How the kitchen is the heart of a community. *Communities,* Summer 2015: 10–11.

Canning, P., Rehkamp, S., Waters, A., & Etemadnia, H. (2017, January). The role of fossil fuels in the US food system and the American diet, ERR-224, US Department of Agriculture, Economic Research Service.

Dawson, J. (2006). *Ecovillages: New frontiers for sustainability.* White River Junction, VT: Chelsea Green Pub. Co.

DeLind, L. B. (2011). Are local food and the local food movement taking us where we want to go? Or are we hitching our wagons to the wrong stars? *Agriculture and Human Values, 28,* 273–83. https://doi.org/10.1007/s10460-010-9263-0

Dregger, L. (2010). To learn sustainability is to learn community – An example from South Portugal. *Communities,* Summer 2010, 26–9.

Earthaven Ecovillage. (2018). Farms and gardens at Earthaven. Retrieved from http://www.earthaven.org/farms-and-gardens/

Esteves, A. M. (2017). Radical environmentalism and 'commoning': Synergies between ecosystem regeneration and social governance at Tamera Ecovillage, Portugal. *Antipode, 49*(2), 357–76. https://doi.org/10.1111/anti.12278

Fosket, J., & Malmo, L. (2009). *Living green – Communities that sustain.* Gabriola Island, BC: New Society Publishers.

Friedman, T. L. (2013, May 18). Without water, revolution. *The New York Times.*

Healy, J. (2011). Balancing act: How much are you willing to share. *Communities, 152,* 20–3.

IPES-Food. (2017). Thematic Report 2 (October 2017): Unravelling the food-health nexus: Addressing practices, political economy, and power relations to build healthier food systems. Retrieved from http://www.ipes-food.org/publications.

Jongkind, J. (2015). Celebrating the local, shared bounty at Groundswell Cohousing. *Communities, 167,* 63.

Khoury, M. et al. (2015). Evaluating the associations between buying lunch at school, eating at restaurants, and eating together as a family and cardiometabolic risk in adolescents. *Canadian Journal of Cardiology, 31*(10), S266–7. https://doi.org/10.1016/j.cjca.2015.07.714

Kunze, I., & Avelino, F. (2015). Social innovation and the global ecovillage network. Research report, TRANSIT: EU SSH.2013.3.2-1 Grant agreement no: 613169.

Lanphear, F. (2014). *Songaia: An unfolding dream, the story of a community's journey into being.* Bothell, WA: Songaia Press.

Levkoe, C. Z. (2006). Learning democracy through food justice movements. *Agriculture and Human Values, 23,* 89–98. https://doi.org/10.1007/s10460-005-5871-5

Lockyer, J., & Veteto, J. R. (2013). *Environmental anthropology engaging ecotopia: Bioregionalism, permaculture, and ecovillages.* New York, NY: Berghahn Books.

Louv, R. (2011). *The nature principle: Human restoration and the end of nature-deficit disorder.* Chapel Hill, NC: Algonquin Books of Chapel Hill.

Litfin, K. (2014). *Ecovillages: Lessons for sustainable community.* Cambridge: Polity Press.

Ludwig, M. (2017). *Together resilient: Building community in the age of climate disruption.* Rutledge, MO: Fellowship for Intentional Community.

Lyson, T. A. (2012). Civic agriculture. In R. De Young, & T. Princen (Eds), *The localization reader: Adapting to the coming downshift* (pp. 117–27). Cambridge, MA: MIT Press.

Matfin, T. (2011). Doing it, or are we? *Communities,* Winter 2011, 46–7.

McKibben, B. (2007). *Deep economy: The wealth of communities and the durable future.* New York, NY: Times Books.

McMichael, P. (2000). The power of food. *Agriculture and Human Values, 17,* 21–33. https://doi.org/10.1023/A:1007684827140

Metcalf, B. (1995). *From utopian dreaming to communal reality – Co-operative lifestyles in Australia*. Randwick: University of New South Wales Press.

Mollison, B., & Holmgren, D. (1978). *Permaculture 1: A perennial agricultural system for human settlements*. Melbourne: Transworld Publishers.

Moran, J. (2015). Make food, make *hygge*, make happy. *Communities*, Summer 2015, 26–7.

Ohlson, K. (2014). *The soil will save us! How scientists, farmers, and foodies are healing the soil to save the planet*. New York, NY: Rodale.

O.U.R. Ecovillage. (2018). Food manifesto. Retrieved from https://ourecovillage.org/our-policies/#food

Pimentel, D., Williamson, S., Alexander, C. E., Gonzalez-Pagan, O., Kontak, C., & Mulkey, S. E. (2008). Reducing energy inputs in the US food system. *Human Ecology, 36*(4), 459–71. https://doi.org/10.1007/s10745-008-9184-3

Pollan, M. (2006). *The omnivore's dilemma: A natural history of four meals*. New York, NY: Penguin Press.

Roberts, W. (2008). *The no-nonsense guide to world food.* Toronto: New Internationalist/Between the Lines.

Roth, C. (2011). Permaculture 101, *Communities, 153*, 10–13.

Sanford, A. W. (2014). Being the change: Food, nonviolence, and self-sufficiency in contemporary intentional communities. *Communal Societies Journal, 34*(1), 28–52.

Sargisson, L. (2012). *Fool's gold? Utopianism in the twenty-first century*. New York, NY: Palgrave Macmillan.

Shiva, V. (2015). Vandana shiva: 'All life depends on soil'. *EcoWatch*. Retrieved from https://www.ecowatch.com/vandana-shiva-all-life-depends-on-soil-1882012429.html

Steffen, W. et al. (2015). Planetary boundaries: Guiding human development on a changing planet. *Science, 347*(6223), 1259855. https://doi.org/10.1126/science.1259855

Sumner, J., & Mair, H. (2008). Setting the table: The political economy of food. In M. Koc, R. MacRae, & K. Bronson (Eds), *Interdisciplinary perspectives in food studies*. Toronto: McGraw-Hill Ryerson Limited.

Tamera. (2018a). Communitarian economy. Retrieved from https://www.tamera.org/communitarian-economy/

Tamera. (2018b). Food sovereignty. Retrieved from https://www.tamera.org/food-sovereignty/

Walker, L. (2005). *EcoVillage at Ithaca – Pioneering a sustainable culture*. Gabriola Island, BC: New Society Publishers.

Walker, L. (2010). *Choosing a sustainable future: Ideas and inspiration from Ithaca, NY*. Gabriola Island, BC: New Society Publishers.

10 Care Farming: Making a Meaningful Connection between Agriculture, Health Care, and Society

MARJOLEIN ELINGS

Care farming or social farming is an established sector in the Netherlands and a fast-growing sector across Europe. It is an innovative practice in health care in which agricultural production is combined with health and social services (Hassink, 2017). Care farms incorporate aspects of both agriculture and health care, using agricultural production to provide care to different client groups (Hassink, 2017; Elings, 2011). Client groups vary from people with learning disabilities to elderly people with dementia or youth with behavioural problems. This chapter will mainly focus on the Dutch social farming sector and its role in the Dutch health care system.

If we look at the social farming sector in the Netherlands, we see that the number of care farms increased from 75 in 1998 to more than 1,100 in 2014 (Elings, 2011; Hassink, 2017). Many of these care farms were initiated by farmers and their partners. Others were started by former health care workers who were interested in starting their own care farm, independent of the care institutions they worked for (Hassink, 2017).

In their paper "Changing Role of Agriculture in Dutch Society," the authors outline how Dutch agriculture in the past century, like in the rest of Europe, has undergone significant changes: "Due to economics of scale and in order to remain economically profitable, it became necessary for farmers to increase farm size, efficiency and external inputs, while minimizing labour use per hectare" (Meerburg et al., 2009, p. 511). In Dutch agriculture, some of the farmers disagreed with the idea of intensification and growth. Further, urbanization of the landscape increased competition for available space and had a negative effect on the ability of farmers to continue farming (Opdam et al., 2001). From the mid-1970s onwards, farm incomes did not keep pace with those in other sectors (Meerburg et al., 2009). Small-scale farmers especially were looking for ways to increase their farm income. As an alternative, farmers could combine farming with other rural activities, becoming multifunctional (Vereijken, 2003). Social farming or care farming was one of the options.

From a historical point of view, care farms have existed for decades. One of the oldest examples of a care farming program was founded around 1350 in Gheel, Flanders (Roosen, 2007; Elings, 2011). In rural areas it was quite common for vulnerable people to work along with families from the village as part of a daily routine and structure. The program in Gheel is one of the first examples of what is called a therapeutic living and working community. During the 1940s more therapeutic living and working communities were founded, where nature was considered an important element in therapy. Examples can also be found in the Camphill movement, particularly in Ireland and the UK (Elings, 2011). In the 1950s and 1960s in the Netherlands there was also an increase in therapeutic communities where people with a disability received shelter and support. Most often these communities started as small-scale projects that featured agriculture as a central part of daily activities. Those communities were usually founded as protest against large care institutions (Ketelaars, 2001). In the Netherlands, many farmers welcomed vulnerable people onto their farms for idealistic reasons, before care farms even became a concept.

The Swift Development of the Care Farming Sector in the Netherlands

In his PhD thesis "Understanding Care Farming as a Swiftly Developing Sector in the Netherlands," Hassink (2017) noticed that it is quite a challenge for farmers to take a different direction than the majority of farmers who choose intensification and enlargement of agricultural production. This difficulty was amplified because care farmers collaborate with other sectors and were newcomers to the health care field: "They were pioneers who faced challenges like a lack of cognitive and socio-political legitimacy and a mismatch with financing structures in the health care sector" (Hassink, 2017, p. 275–6). Like any other newcomers, care farmers needed to narrow the gap between the two sectors, building legitimacy and setting up a professional organization with a sustainable financing structure for care farm services (Hassink, 2017).

Looking at the development of the care farming sector in the Netherlands there are some key milestones. First in 1999 there was the start of the National Support Centre. This centre was funded by both the Ministry of Agriculture and the Ministry of Health Care and Wellbeing. The centre had the task of supporting new and existing care farmers, and initiated a website, a database, and a quality system. These activities increased familiarity with care farms as well as acceptance of the concept in the health care sector (Hassink, 2017). The number of clients on care farms increased around 2003 when the introduction of personal budgets gave clients the possibility to choose their own care and day activities. These personal health care budgets are provided by the Dutch government for people who receive continuing care in order to give clients more control over the care they receive. Additionally, the liberalization of long-term health care in 2005 meant that care farmers or regional organizations of care farmers could receive an AWBZ (General Law on Special Health Care Costs) accreditation and enter into a direct agreement with the government to provide care (Hassink, 2017; Elings, 2011). This made it easier for care farmers to work independently from other care organizations. From then on, there has also been increased engagement of more varied client groups that visit care farms and a rise in the number of care farms around cities. Hassink (2017) mentions that at first care farmers presented themselves as a counter-movement. Their legitimacy in the health care sector increased by a specially developed quality system for care farms and cooperation with regular care organizations (Hassink, 2017).

The Broader European Perspective

Not only in the Netherlands, but also in other European countries like Norway, Belgium, Italy, and the UK, there has been an increase in the number of care farms or social farms. Care farming can be seen as part of the green care movement. Green care is the umbrella term for all care or health promotion activities conducted with or in nature. Haubenhofer et al. (2010) developed an overview of diverse green care activities (figure 10.1).

The overview shows that care farms can offer health promotion, therapy, and labour reintegration. Over the last few years vocational training and education has become a common feature on care farms as well. In this way, care farms can offer a variety of activities depending on the target group. For instance, vulnerable people who have experienced exclusion from the labour market can be part of a labour reintegration program in which they learn new skills and obtain work experiences. Likewise, on a care farm serving elderly people with dementia, the focus is on accommodating social farm activities.

While the Netherlands has the National Support Centre and Federation of Care Farmers, Norway, Belgium, and the UK also have national care farm initiatives that oversee the general interests of care farmers. However, the financial support available to care farmers varies significantly between EU countries. For example, in Italy vulnerable people are paid for working on so-called "social cooperative farms," while on care farms in Flanders (Belgium), farmers are paid by the Ministry of Agriculture to welcome people with a disability onto their farm (Di Iacovo and O'Connor, 2009).

The Dutch Care Farm Does Not Exist

During focus group meetings with care farmers, they emphasized that *the* care farm does not exist. There are big differences between care farms: in size (the number of clients), client group, type of agricultural production, and type of

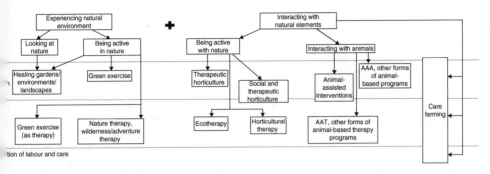

Figure 10.1 Overview of green care activities (Haubenhofer, Elings, and Hine, 2010)

care offered (day activity, 24/7 care, educational programs) (ZONMW, 2018). The main client groups are youth, people with learning difficulties, people with mental health issues (including people with an addiction and burnout), and people with dementia. Within those client groups, there are great differences in the severity of the disabilities. Also, many care farmers welcome a variety of client groups onto their farm. Often this is a specific choice; the idea is that having a variety of client groups on a care farm reflects society best (ZONMW, 2018). The Federation of Care Farmers in the Netherlands does not have a clear overview of which client groups visit which care farms. Thorough data such as the exact number of care farms in the Netherlands is also unavailable, though the Federation estimates that there are between 1,100–1,200 care farms in total. Around 820 care farms are members of the Federation. The average number of clients visiting a care farm is estimated to be between 15–20 each week. However, not all clients come on a daily basis (ZONMW, 2018). The nature and setup of care farms also differ greatly. There are care farms where agricultural production plays an important role and clients and the farmer work together to achieve that production. On the other end of the spectrum, there are care farms that are small care organizations or part of a larger care organization. Agriculture on these care farms is usually there solely for the benefit of care and experience for the clients (ZONMW, 2018). Officially there are no requirements for the education or training of care farmers and their co-workers. The Federation of Care Farmers instead developed a quality system that checks and presents the quality mark to care farmers. In the Netherlands, around 700 care farms have this quality mark (ZONMW, 2018).

Effects and Qualities of Care Farms for Different Client Groups

Research has been done to explore the effects of care farms on specific client groups. Some of these reviews had a quasi-experimental study design in which they compared care on farms with care in regular day care facilities. For the main four client groups (youth, people with mental health issues, people with learning disabilities, and dementia patients), studies show a range of positive effects (Hassink et al., 2017; Elings, 2011).

Children and Youth

Youth care farms offer weekend and after-school care mostly for children between five and sixteen years old. In particular, children with autism experience positive effects from working with animals (Ferwerda et al., 2012). Parents have observed that the farm is a place where their child can be him or herself, can play with other children, and participate in appealing activities (Veerman et al., 2016). Parents also feel that they and their family are able to find moments of relief when their children visit the farms. Further, youth care practitioners think that offering care on the farm causes a decline in the need to place youth in institutional care facilities (Veerman et al., 2016).

There are also special individual live and work programs for youth with severe behavioural problems. In these programs, adolescents live in a residential unit on the farm, which they are expected to maintain. They help the farmer with farm work and eat together with the farmer's family. The program takes one year, half of which is spent on the farm and the other half at home with a post-support program (Hassink et al., 2011). Both the adolescents and the parents receive remote support. More than 100 adolescents signed up for the program and 69 per cent completed it as planned on different care farms. Research results from Hassink and colleagues (2011) show that the farm program had a positive effect on the behavioural issues and youth's self-respect. These positive effects remained a year after finishing the farm program. The program also led to improved relationships between the adolescent and their family and improved their self-esteem and well-being (Hassink et al., 2011). In many situations, school performance improved or the young person became re-engaged in school or work. For the older participants, the researchers found a strong decrease in use of drugs (Hassink et al., 2011). Young people reported less aggression and disruptive stimuli at the farm compared to regular care facilities or school. Overall, there were also fewer interpersonal conflicts, a finding that social workers attribute to the higher concentration of youth with behavioural issues in regular facilities, which creates more opportunities for conflict (Hassink et al., 2011).

People with Mental Health Issues

Care farms offer people with mental health issues a safe workplace. Research results show that people experience the farm as an informal non-care context between illness, the labour market, and society (Elings et al., 2005). The farm is a place where they learn to socialize and can practice their skills. Although the farm activities are the main objective on the care farm, the farmer and co-workers do recognize the problems of the participants, and farm work can be used to cope with their specific feelings and issues (Elings et al., 2011; Iancu et al., 2014). Working on the farm increased self-esteem, self-respect, perseverance, responsibility, and improved health (Elings and Hassink, 2008). For people with a history of alcohol and drug addiction, social workers additionally observed that clients become more social and show more solidarity and empathy compared to their behaviour in regular facilities. For instance, participants encourage each other in the mornings to come to the farm and have different conversations. Also, the physical condition of people with alcohol or drug addiction issues improves: they feel fitter, eat better, and their body gets time to recover. International research similarly shows a positive effect of being in a green environment on people with mental health issues (Dalskau et al., 2016; Kogstad et al., 2014; Hassink et al., 2017).

People with Learning Disabilities

Although one of the largest groups of clients coming to care farms are people with learning difficulties, not much research has been done on the impact of working on the farm for this target group (Elings, 2004). This probably has to do with difficulties in doing research; for example, a lack of appropriate surveys that can be filled out by this client group (Elings, 2004). From a qualitative study, it became clear that the farmer is of great importance to people with learning difficulties. He is a role model and has the skills and knowledge related to farm activities. Next to that, he is an entrepreneur and has the creative skills to improvise if necessary. For instance, a care farmer developed a system that enables the participants to feed the pigs independently (Elings, 2004). Knowledge of agriculture gives farmers and care workers the ability to fit the activities to the capacity of clients. It helps them to be flexible if unexpected circumstances appear (Elings, 2004). This is especially important for this client group that often lives and works on the same institution ground, as the care farm can offer a different setting during working hours, where they meet other people like the farmer's family, other colleagues, volunteers, and visitors on the farm. This also expands their social network (Elings, 2008; Van Oorsouw et al., 2015).

People with Dementia

People with dementia can attend day programs on care farms. Some of the care farms also offer residential facilities where elderly people can live full-time. These residential care farms are an example of innovative small-scaled housing that are an alternative to being admitted into a nursing home (De Boer et al., 2015; Hassink et al., 2017). Care farms can offer people with dementia a structured day in an informal family setting in which they have the chance to participate in outdoor activities like gardening, nursing the pets, and walking, as well as household activities like cooking together (De Bruin, 2010). An effect study by De Bruin (2009) showed that people with dementia that had day care on a farm took part in more activities, were more physically active, and spent more time outside than people with dementia in regular day care facilities (De Bruin et al., 2009). The elderly on care farms also have more social interactions (De Boer et al., 2017). Further, people with dementia on care farms have a higher intake of energy, carbohydrates, and fluid than their peers in regular day care facilities (De Bruin, 2010). Care farms can contribute to the socialization of people with dementia because they stimulate social interactions and give people with dementia the feeling of making a useful contribution to society (De Bruin et al., 2015). Research from De Boer (2017) shows similar effects for elderly people with dementia in residential care farms. In comparison with regular nursing homes, they are more involved in household tasks, activities outside, and other activities related to nature. This is significant because people with dementia have been shown to experience greater well-being when they are outside or when they are engaged in activities (Beerens et al., 2016; Hassink, et al., 2017).

Qualities of Care Farms

Numerous studies show that care farms can make a positive contribution to the lives of participants that work or live on the farm. From these studies it becomes clear that care farms can greatly increase the options of day care facilities clients can choose from. Care farms differ from regular facilities because care or education are not the main objectives; instead, the focus is on living and working together with the common goal of agricultural production. On a care farm the farmer does not speak about clients but about participants or co-workers; the farmer, his family and the participants work together. The farmer talks to participants about his or her opportunities and responsibilities. In this way, care farms possess many qualities that make them a unique informal non-care context (Elings, 2011; Hassink, et al., 2007). These qualities can be classified into five main groups:

- *Personal engagement of the farmer*: On care farms there is personal attention paid to the interests and wishes of the individual. The farmer tries to tailor the work and activities to the abilities of the participant (Hassink et al., 2017). Research demonstrates that participants value the involvement of the farmer and the relationships they develop with him and his family (Elings, 2004; Hassink et al., 2017).
- *Social contact and support*: Care farm participants are part of a social community consisting of the farmers, the farmer's family, volunteers, and

other colleagues (Elings, 2011). Participants can build up their social network and get support and recognition for the work they do.

- *Useful and diverse activities*: Participants can take part in a variety of agricultural activities such as taking care of the animals, gardening, and working on the land, all of which are useful (Elings et al., 2011; Hassink et al., 2007; Elings, 2004). Taking care of the animals can lead to an emotional bond and can give the participant a feeling of support. People can also contribute to the household through activities like cooking or cleaning (Hassink et al., 2017).
- *Green environment*: On care farms people come into contact with nature. The Health Council of the Netherlands concluded in a study that people's contact with nature is decreasing. Around the same time, an increasing number of studies showed that contact with nature can lead to improved health and well-being (Health Council of the Netherlands, 2004; Elings, 2011). The physical green space on a care farm can give participants the experience of peace and offer opportunities for (existential) reflection (Hassink et al., 2017).
- *Informal family context*: Most often care farms have an informal family setup that can help participants to quickly feel at ease. Participating in household duties also helps participants to feel comfortable on the farm (Hassink et al., 2017).

Figure 10.2 provides an overview of the main qualities that make care farms attractive day care settings for a variety of client groups.

Future Developments

The number of new care farms starting up has dwindled, as the market is now saturated. The care farming sector started as a counter movement (Hassink, 2017) but increased its legitimacy; at the moment care farms are part of the health care landscape in the Netherlands. The question is: How can they remain relevant and align with future developments in health care and society?

Improve Quality of Care Farms

In 2017 the Dutch Organisation for Health Research and Development finished a research program about care farming. Part of the goal of this program was to implement the research results in practice, for instance, by giving workshops to care farmers and discussing together how the results could be used to provide better care to their clients (ZonMw, 2018). The workshops made it clear that care farms are working with clients who have increasingly complicated problems. For example, participants with dementia have been demonstrated to present with more complex problems today than they did several years ago

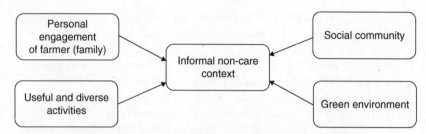

Figure 10.2 Qualities of care farms in the Netherlands (adapted from Hassink, 2010)

(ZonMw, 2017). Facing these rising demands for care, some care farms struggle to determine the right inclusion criteria, size, and scope for their programs. Farmers are also worried that the unique character of care farms may be at risk due to the need to adhere to general health care rules and systems. If they follow all the rules and bureaucratic requirements of the formal health care system, will it still be possible to maintain the individual character that typifies care farms?

Inclusion and participation in society are important for vulnerable people and are also the main goals of the Dutch government's health care policy. In what ways do care farms contribute to these goals? Do they provide a better environment for inclusion than regular care facilities? And which innovative services from the care farming sector can be adopted by regular care organizations? For example, can elderly people with dementia in cities experience being in nature in similar ways to their peers on care farms? (ZonMw, 2017).

For the development of the care farming sector, research on cost effectiveness could give care farmers more insights into the costs and assets of care farms compared to other care facilities. Researchers think that care farms can be successful in preventing heavy care in the future, for instance by relieving informal caretakers (ZonMw, 2017).

Contribution of Care Farms to Developments in Dutch Society

If we look at the development of Dutch society, it is clear that people are looking for connection. There is an increase in the number of citizens' initiatives. Citizens like to contribute to their neighbourhood, city, or region. However, the growth in citizens' initiatives is also due to the stepping back of the Dutch government in the public domain, urging citizens to pick up activities in their local communities. This "participation society" has become particularly prevalent in health care, for example, when children give informal care to their parents so they can prolong their time at home rather than moving into a nursing home. Care farms can contribute to this participation society by relieving informal caregivers and giving elderly people or children day activities to attend. In the

1990s, before the rise of the participation society, the concept of community care, or care in and by society, began to be integrated into the Dutch health care sector. However, it was not an overall success (Elings and Goede, 2012). The idea of vulnerable people living in society instead of in care institutions is not always feasible in practice. Research demonstrates that care farms can offer a place for vulnerable people to live or work in society (Elings and Hassink, 2008). Additionally, quite a lot of volunteers work on care farms, and without this opportunity, those volunteers may remain at home. The work on the farm also gives this group of people an activating and meaningful day activity.

In the Netherlands we see a growing number of social entrepreneurs and social enterprises. Social enterprises are independent companies that provide a product or service and thereby primarily or explicitly pursue a social objective (SER, 2015). Often these companies employ vulnerable people, such as those who struggle to compete in the labour market (Elings et al., 2017). Social enterprises in (urban) agriculture and on care farms are a good example of the rising prevalence of this new socially oriented business model (Elings et al., 2017). In the Dutch labour sector, on one hand semi- and unskilled jobs are disappearing. On the other hand, the new Participation Law, enacted in 2016, obliges employers to create jobs for people lacking sufficient qualifications for the job market (Smit et al., 2016).

In the Dutch agricultural sector, farmers are forced to leave their farms every day. When they do so, it is not only the agricultural production that is lost; they also stop maintaining their land. Municipalities add to this problem by not considering the maintenance of green space as their task anymore, leading to the neglect of public gardens and green spaces (Elings et al., 2017). In the near future, this challenge could be taken on by green social enterprises like care farmers. Care farmers can employ low-skilled people and offer them a useful job, providing meaningful employment while also adding to the quality of life of the local community (Elings et al., 2017).

The Changing Role of Agriculture in Dutch Society

As the number of farmers in the Netherlands decline, there are fewer people who have a farming background or roots in rural areas. This has led to weaker links between agriculture and society (Meerburg et al., 2009). The societal knowledge about (modern) agriculture and how food is produced has also weakened. However, the acceptance of society for large-scale production has also slowly decreased. Because of outbreaks of contagious animal diseases and food safety scandals in the 1990s, the societal acceptance reduced even further (Meerburg et al., 2009). The resistance against overproduction, promotion of animal welfare, and acknowledgment of environmental pollution added to negative attitudes towards modern agriculture. In interviews with care farmers, they talked about a change of image within the neighbourhood regarding their farming practice. Also, the increasing profile of urban agriculture and care farms around urbanized areas is encouraging citizens to reassess their image of farmers and of agriculture more broadly. Because of the lack of green spaces in cities, city dwellers are looking outside the city for recreation. Multifunctional agriculture and specific care farms can add to these kinds of green and rural recreational activities.

We see also that more attention is being paid to locally produced food, especially in urban areas. This renewed acquaintance with how food is produced fits in with the activities of care farms including offering food workshops, having a farm shop or picking fresh vegetables from the gardens. In this way care farms can contribute to a healthy lifestyle for diverse groups of citizens (Elings et al., 2017). On top of this, care farms can also add to the quality of life of the rural population. In some rural parts of the Netherlands there is a declining population; young people are leaving to find better employment opportunities in more economically favourable regions like the highly urbanized Western part of the Netherlands (Breman and Vogelzang, 2012). In these "shrinkage regions," care farms can also serve a function by offering the rural population a vibrant place to meet. For instance, the opening of a farm shop can provide activities for volunteers but can also offer employment for the local population.

Positive Health

The way of viewing patients or clients has changed over the last decades. Nowadays social workers are trying to empower clients and think in terms of their possibilities instead of their disabilities or illness (Hassink et al., 2007). Especially for people with chronic illness, the medical model of pathogenesis has not proven to be an effective solution (Hassink et al., 2007). Hubert and colleagues write in their paper "How should we define health?" that the current WHO definition of health describes it as "a state of complete physical, mental and social well-being" (Hubert et al., 2011, p. 1). In their paper they suggest that the current definition of health should be replaced by a new conceptual framework of health (Hubert et al., 2011). From research with chronically ill patients, Hubert emphasizes the importance of seeing health as a broader concept than psychical health. Her model of positive health describes six pillars of health: body, mental status, sense of purpose, quality of life, daily life functioning, and social participation (Hubert, 2014). The research demonstrates that care farms give a variety of people a place to work within agriculture and nature. Care farms can offer people useful and diverse activities through which they can learn new skills and have positive experiences. Participants often experience the care farm as a safe community where they can work on their personal development.

It is an environment where the farmers and other workers understand their clients' backgrounds, enabling them to just be themselves while working. Above all, clients are appreciated (Elings and Hassink, 2008; Elings, 2011). Care farms are an example of an innovation that brings different sectors and people together, making a meaningful and sustainable connection within society.

REFERENCES

Beerens, H. C., de Boer, B., Zwakhalen, S. M., Tan, F. E., Ruwaard, D., Hamers, J. P. H., & Verbeek, H. (2016). The association between aspects of daily life and quality of life of people with dementia living in long-term care facilities: A momentary assessment study. *International Psychogeriatrics, 28*(8), 1323–31. https://doi.org/10.1017/S1041610216000466

Breman, B., & Vogelzang, T.. 2012. Krimp! Synthese van beleidsondersteunend onderzoek voor het Ministerie van EL&I 2010–2012 (Shrinkage regions: Synthesis of policy in the period of 2010–2012). Wageningen: Wageningen University & Research. Retrieved from https://edepot.wur.nl/214584

De Boer, B., Hamers, J. P. H., Beerens, H. C., Zwakhalen, S. M. G., & Verbeek, H. (2015). Living at the farm, innovative nursing home care for people with dementia – Study protocol of an observational longitudinal study. *BMC Geriatrics, 15*, 144. https://doi.org/10.1186/s12877-015-0141-x

De Boer, B., Hamers, J. P. H., Beerens, H. C., Zwakhalen S. M. G., & Verbeek, H. (2017). Green care farms as innovative nursing homes, promoting activities and social interaction for people with dementia. *Journal of the American Medical Directors Association, 18*(1), 40–6. https://doi.org/10.1016/j.jamda.2016.10.013

De Bruin, S., Oosting, S., Tobi, H., Schols, J., & de Groot, L. (2010). Day care at green care farms: A novel way to stimulate dietary intake of community-dwelling older people with dementia? *The Journal of Nutrition, Health and Aging, 14*(5), 352–7. https://doi.org/10.1007/s12603-009-0223-6

De Bruin, S. R. (2009). Sowing in the autumn season. Exploring benefits of green care farms for dementia patients. (Doctoral dissertation). Wageningen University & Research, Wageningen, Netherlands.

De Bruin, S., Oosting, S. J., Kuin, Y., Hoefnagels, E. C. M., Blauw, Y. H., De Groot, L. C. P. G. M., & Schols, J. M. G. A. (2009). Green care farms promote activity among elderly people with dementia. *Journal of Housing for the Elderly, 23*(4), 368–89. https://doi.org/10.1080/02763890903327275

De Bruin, S. R., Stoop, A., Molema, C. C. M., Vaandrager, L., Hop, P. J. W. M., & Baan, C. A. (2015). Green care farms: An innovative type of adult day service to stimulate social participation of people with dementia. *Gerontology and Geriatric Medicine, 1*, 233372141560783. https://doi.org/10.1177/2333721415607833

Di Iavoco, F., & O'Connor, D. (Eds) (2009). *Supporting policies for social farming in Europe. Progressing multifunctionality in responsive rural areas.* Firenze: Arsia (EU project 022682 So Far: Social Services in Multifunctional Farms).

Elings, M. (2004). *Boer zorg dat je boer blijft (Importance of staying a real farmer for people with learning disabilities working on care farms).* Wageningen: Wageningen University & Research. Retrieved from http://library.wur.nl/WebQuery/wurpubs /337490

Elings, M. (2011). Effects of care farms: Scientific research on the benefits of care farms for clients. Wageningen: Taskforce Multifunctional Agriculture, Wageningen University & Research and Trimbos-institute (Netherlands Institute of Mental Health and Addiction). Retrieved from http://library.wur.nl/WebQuery/wurpubs/450976

Elings, M., & Hassink, J. (2008). Green care farms, a safe community between illness or addiction and the wider society. *Therapeutic communities, 29*(3), 310–23.

Elings, M., van Erp, N., & van Hoof, F. (2005). *De waarde van zorgboerderijen voor mensen met een psychiatrische of verslavingsachtergrond (The added value of care farms for people with mental health issues and addiction history).* Wageningen: Wageningen University & Research and Trimbos-institute. Retrieved from http://edepot.wur.nl/39437

Elings, M., Vijn, M., & Kruit, J. (2017). Sociaal ondernemerschap in de zorglandbouw. Voorwaarden voor een kansrijke start (Social entrepreneurship in the social farming sector. Conditions for starting up a social enterprise.) Wageningen: Wageningen University & Research. Retrieved from http://edepot.wur.nl/410110.

Ellingsen-Dalskau, L. H., Morken Kolsø, M. Berget, B., & Pedersen, I. (2016). Autonomy support and need satisfaction in prevocational programs on care farms: The self-determination theory perspective. *Work: A Journal of Prevention, Assessment and Rehabilitation, 53*(1), 73–85. https://doi.org/10.3233/WOR-152217

Ferwerda-Van, Z., Reina, T., Oosting, S. J. & Kijlstra, A. (2012). Care farms as a short-break service for children with Autism Spectrum Disorders. *NJAS-Wageningen Journal of Life Sciences, 59*(1–2), 35–40. https:doi.org/10.1016/j.njas.2012.01.001

Goede, M., & Elings, M. (2012). *Ontmoeting tussen Boer & Zorg (Encounter of farmer & care).* Amsterdam: Applied University of Amsterdam, department of Community Care and Wageningen University & Research.

Hassink, J. (2017). Understanding care farming as a swiftly developing sector in the Netherlands. (Doctoral dissertation). University of Amsterdam, Amsterdam

Hassink, J., Elings, M., Ferwerda, R., & Rommers, J. (2007). *Meerwaarde Landbouw en Zorg (The added value of care farms).* Wageningen: Wageningen University & Research.

Hassink, J., de Bruin, S., Verbeek, H., & Buist, Y. (2017). *Factsheet Betekenis van zorgboerderijen voor verschillende doelgroepen (Factsheet: The meaning of care farms for different client groups).* Wageningen: Wageningen University & Research, National Institute for Public Health and the Environment, Ministry of Health, Welfare and Sport, Maastricht University.

Hassink, J., de Meyer, R., van de Sman, P., & Willem Veerman, J. (2011). Effectiviteit van ervarend leren op de boerderij. *Orthopedagogiek: Onderzoek en Praktijk, 50*(2), 51–63.

Hassink, J., Elings, M., Zweekhorst, M., van den Nieuwenhuizen, N., & Smit, A. (2010). Care farms in the Netherlands: Attractive empowerment-oriented and strengths-based practices in the community. *Health & Place, 16*(3), 423–30. https://doi.org/10.1016/j.healthplace.2009.10.016

Haubenhofer, D. K., Elings, M., Hassink, J., & Bragg, R. E. (2010). The development of green care in western European countries. *Explore the Journal of Science and Healing, 6*(2), 106–11. https://doi.org/10.1016/j.explore.2009.12.002

Health Council of the Netherlands. (2004). Natuur en gezondheid. Invloed van natuur op sociaal, psychisch en lichamelijk welbevinden. The Hague: Health Council of the Netherlands.

Huber, M., Knottnerus, J. A., Green, L., van der Horst, H., Jadad, A. R., Kromhout, D., Leonard, B., Lorig, K., Loureiro, M. I., van der Meer, J. W .M. Schnabel, P., Smith, R., van Weel, C., Smid, H. (2011). How should we define health? *BMJ 2011, 343*, d4163. https://doi.org/10.1136/bmj.d4163

Huber, M. (2014). Towards a new, dynamic concept of health. Its operationalisation and use in public health and healthcare, and in evaluating health effects of food. (Doctoral dissertation). Maastricht University, Maastricht

Iancu, S. C., Zweekhorst, M. B. M., Veltman, D. J., van Balkom, A. J. L. M., & Bunders-Aelen, J. G. F. (2014). Mental health recovery on care farms and day centres: A qualitative comparative study of users' perspectives. *Disability and Rehabilitation, 36*(7), 573–83. https://doi.org/10.3109/09638288.2013.804595

Ketelaars, D., Baars, E., & Kroon, H. (2001). *Healing through working: A study of therapeutic communities for persons with psychiatric problems.* Dronten: Foundation Omslag and Trimbos-institute (Netherlands Institute of Mental Health and Addiction).

Kogstad, R. E., Agdal, R., & Hopfenbeck, M. S. (2014). Narratives of natural recovery: Youth experience of social inclusion through green care. *International Journal of Environmental Research and Public Health, 11*(6), 6052–68. https://doi.org/10.3390/ijerph110606052

Meerburg, B. G., Korevaar, H., Haubenhofer, D. K., Blom-Zandstra, G., & van Keulen, H. 2009. The changing role of agriculture in Dutch society. *Journal of Agricultural Science, 147*, 511–21. https://doi.org/10.1017/S0021859609990049

Oorsouw, W. M. W. J., Hassink, J., Elings, M., & Embregts, P. J. C. M. (2015). (Kosten) effectiviteit van zorglandbouw bij mensen met een verstandelijke beperking (Cost effectiveness of care farms for people with learning difficulties). Tilburg: Tilburg University and Wageningen University & Research. Retrieved from http://library.wur.nl/WebQuery/wurpubs/490491

Opdam, P., Ruud, F., & Vos, C. (2001). Bridging the gap between ecology and spatial planning in landscape ecology. *Landscape Ecology, 16*, 767–79. https://doi.org/10.1023/A:1014475908949

Roosens, E., & van de Walle, L. (2007). *Geel revisted. After centuries of mental rehabilitation.* Antwerpen-Apeldoorn: Garant Publishers.

Smit, A., Hassink, J., Dijkshoorn-Dekker, M., Michels, R., de Vries, S., & Jeroen, K. (2016). *Groen als banenmotor? Verkennend onderzoek in opdracht van het Ministerie van Economische Zaken (Green environment generating new job opportunities? An explorative study for the Ministry of Economic Affairs).* Wageningen: Wageningen University & Research.

Social and Economic Council of the Netherlands (SER). (2015). *Sociale ondernemingen: een verkennend advies (Social enterprises: A feasibility study).* The Hague: SER.

Veerman, J. W., De Meyer, R., Hassink, J., Berghuis, E., & Kienhuis, J. (2016). *Onderzoek naar de effectiviteit van jeugdzorgboerderijen in Overijssel en Gelderland (Research on the effects of youth care farms in the provinces of Overijssel and Gelderland).* Nijmegen/ Wageningen: Praktikon and Wageningen University & Research

Verreijken, P. H. (2003). Transition to multifunctional land use and agriculture. *NJAS-Wageningen Journal of Life Sciences, 50,* 171–9. https://doi.org/10.1016/S1573 -5214(03)80005-2

ZonMw, The Netherlands Organisation for Health Research and Development. (2018). *Programma Landbouw en Zorg 2011–2017 (Research program: Agriculture and care).* The Hague: ZonMw.

11 Grieving Nature – Grieving in Nature: The Place of Parks and Natural Places in Palliative and Grief Care

SONYA L. JAKUBEC, DON CARRUTHERS DEN HOED,
HEATHER RAY, AND ASHOK KRISHNAMURTHY

There are thousands of ways to talk about the tragedies of the Anthropocene – and about human death and loss. There are ways that lay blame, provide analysis, pursue solutions, and some that seek recognition of loss with a willingness to look deeply at the pain. This chapter undertakes this deliberate journey along the bumpy road of pain of loss. Through the journey we establish a profound recognition of the ways that mourning publicly, in natural places, serves to support the integration of personal and ecological grief.

For many without this connection, there is little opportunity to make linkages back to coherence and meaning in context and place; instead, there may be denial and a sense of being stuck or unable to navigate the imbalance of the new ground on which one walks in loss and grief (Wolfelt, 2007). Modern death practices have influenced grief by removing all cues of death – bodies, public grieving, even funerals are stripped of honest recognition of the realities of loss (for instance, we now refer to "celebrations of life") (Warraich, 2017). Even the basic hospitality and compassion of recognizing another's true pain of grief through public mourning are carefully removed in our contemporary suppression and repression of grief (Burton-Christie, 2011).

In this chapter, we delve into the landscape and pain of mourning human loss and experiencing grief *in* parks and nature. Research with Alberta Parks and an interdisciplinary/intersectoral team has recently examined the place of parks and nature at end of life through survey and narrative research, and with palliative care and grief/loss support program implementation. Lessons learned from these groundbreaking programs shine a light on the value of public spaces, public health, and public mourning, and are explored here with a connection to grieving in nature and grieving ecological loss.

"The Wilderness of Grief": Background and Conceptual/Contextual Framing of a Collaborative Research Project

The metaphor of entering the "wilderness of grief" is an approach to grief and mourning established by Wolfelt (2007) that suggests a path through grief can be likened to travelling in uncharted territory. The sustained emotion experienced in ecological loss described by Cunsolo (2018) and Cunsolo and Neville (2018) also resonates with Wolfelt's view of the uncharted wilderness of grief. Cunsolo and Landman's (2017) edited book provides additional framing of a broader exploration of the place of parks and natural places in grief and loss. Other theorists and practitioners of ecotherapy (Fisher, 2013), as well as spiritual and contemplative ecology (Ellison and Weingast, 2016; Macy and Brown, 1998) extend perspectives beyond a material analysis. Grieving publicly and mourning in and for natural places in the broader view of these theorists and practitioners establishes both a philosophy and practice of making meaning, and entering the wilderness of grief. Indeed, more evidence is becoming known about how natural environments impact both our physical and spiritual well-being (Williams et al., 2017). Yet little is known specifically about the place of parks and natural places at end of life, or the impact of parks and nature on quality of life during palliative care or bereavement experiences (Kearney, 2009).

Existing evidence shows that multiple agencies and disciplines are beginning to understand that health, quality of life, and nature are interrelated (Maller et al., 2008). Alberta Parks, for example, is interested in understanding how to better provide access for all those wishing to experience nature – for all people and at all life stages, from the beginning to the end of life. This interest is articulated in the Alberta government's current research and program priorities (Alberta Parks, 2014; Hallstrom et al., 2019).

While there exists a large volume of literature in the multiple related topics of quality of life and nature/parks inclusion, we found no literature that specifically explored the concept of end-of-life experience and parks. The topic is of particular practical interest to Alberta Parks with their anecdotal accounts of traumatic deaths and deaths by suicide in parks, as well as people choosing end-of-life activities (such as final end-of-life wishes at lodges or campsites, and memorialization activities such as scattering of ashes, or park bench or tree memorials). With limited data or understanding about experiences and perceptions of connecting with parks and nature at the end of life, a broad exploration of the topic is required.

The purpose of this study was to develop initial foundations for planning and programming within parks that support the access to and enjoyment of parks for people during end-of-life experiences. Thus an emergent, explorative, qualitative study conducted using a narrative approach (Frank, 2006) as its primary methodology was well aligned with the purpose and goals at this stage of knowledge development. This study aimed to develop a better understanding of what adults who identified as palliative (and their caregivers or significant others) experienced and believed about connecting parks and natural places at the end of life.

The Palliative-Grief Parks Project

This study incorporated a mixed method approach, with an initial survey of demographics, perceptions and comments about connecting parks and end of life. The qualitative aspect of the study is intended to be a narrative exploration of the experiences, stories, and values perceived by a small sample of volunteers drawn from the initial survey participants. The qualitative enquiry exploring personal experiences and the meaning of nature in park settings at the end of life used a narrative approach. Narrative research approaches have particular merit in exploratory studies where little is currently known about a topic or problem (Frank, 1993, 2006, 2014). Taking a narrative approach, the accounts of participants function as a sense-making exercise for those participating and provide a broader contextual understanding. Storytelling interview opportunities can sometimes help participants to share emotionally, and offer an avenue for structuring their perceptions and life experiences (Bingley et al., 2008). In this study participants were invited to tell their stories in one-to-one in-depth interviews about experiences in parks and with nature during the last phases of life. Narrative analysis of these stories was the primary analytic approach. Narrative analysis has been found to be useful in this exploratory stage of understanding of illness (Frank, 2006, 2014) as well as in palliative and end-of-life experiences (Southall, 2011).

Methods

Data gathering for this study occurred in two phases, using both a quantitative survey method and qualitative storytelling interviews. Data was firstly gathered in demographic and survey format to pursue information about perceptions and beliefs related to parks and end-of-life experiences. Participation in the online survey was anonymous, though participants were asked to enter the first three numbers of their postal code to assist in some analysis of neighbourhood trends. The survey invitation was available through electronic newsletters with Alberta Parks's community partners and social media. At the end of the survey, participants were asked to indicate if they would be willing/interested in participating further in an in-depth interview. Those who indicated they were willing to participate and able to consent were invited to an interview. Interviews were held in person or by phone and were held at hospices, home settings, or parks/recreation centres according to individual preferences. Ethical approval for this study was granted from a university research ethics board and participants consented to the dissemination of their stories collected in audio and video and transcribed.

During the exploratory in-depth interviews, we enquired about the value of nature and parks to their quality of life as they journey towards the end of life. Interviews were intended to be personally directed and open-ended with minimal probing structure from interviewers to focus on the participant's own story, experiences, perceptions, and beliefs about nature and parks and the end-of-life experience. A free and collaborative negotiation and journey through a storytelling exchange occurred (Bingley et al., 2008). Participants were asked about the beginning (how they arrived at choosing to participate in the study), middle (the key experiences and chapters or turning points that they wanted to reflect on), and finally the end (recommendations and a final title they might want to assign to their story of connecting parks and end of life). Field notes by the primary investigators were composed during the study, and were included as a reflexive process, building insights into the narrative analysis.

Analysis

Methods for analysis of the survey data included basic descriptive statistics with an interest in observing trends and identifying potential informants for the storytelling/interview portion of the study. Our data analysis of the storytelling interview audio/video transcripts and interviewer field notes employed nonlinear, iterative, and ongoing narrative analysis. Transcribed, the data was reviewed by the principle investigators individually to establish the narrative and the broader story to be told – a composition that was also shared back, confirmed, and verified for intended meaning by those interviewed for the study. Field notes by the principle investigators were composed during the study and these notes were included as data, employing a reflexive process, building insights into the narrative analysis.

Discoveries and Developments

Only about 3 per cent of the respondents were palliative patients; the remainder were caregivers (described as family or friend or professional). About 91 per cent of the respondents agreed or strongly agreed that parks can provide physical comfort (e.g. pain relief, activity, physical relaxation) at the end of life. About 93 per cent of the respondents agreed or strongly agreed that parks can provide emotional comfort (e.g. solitary calm or social or family reunion) at the end of life. About 92 per cent of the respondents agreed or strongly agreed that parks can provide spiritual comfort (e.g. feeling of spiritual connection and peace) at the end of life (Jakubec et al., 2016a).

Animal companions (e.g. "we snuck a baby goat into my grandmother's hospice room"), observing the cycles of natural decay and renewal, and observations of nature as something bigger than death (e.g. "if the park could survive the flood, I know we too will endure our loss") were all emphasized in the rich and lengthy comments reported in open-ended survey questions and comments. These comments concentrated on the perspectives of respondents about the above dimensions of comfort provided at end of life in parks and nature, views and desires about memorialization in parks, as well as other demographic factors such as religion and culture (which did not have any significant correlation with responses). In total, views on memorialization were largely positive and desirable with comments such as "I like to take time to look at memorial benches. I think about the lives of those who may have sat in this same place." A few complained about our human interest and need to "put our names all over everything – to take over – even out in nature."

Extending into the narrative components of the study, there are stories of intense suffering, renewal, and activism from informants: fifteen people, men and women from various walks of life and all ages from young adult to older adult. These people generously shared their stories of terminal illness, palliative and hospice care, family caregiving, spiritual and ceremonial practices, natural burial, memorial experiences in parks as well as connections with parks and natural places for all manner of losses (including job loss and relationship demise). One informant's story richly illustrates the themes uncovered in our study: 1) parks and natural places connect people to grief and loss, 2) grief and loss connect people to parks and natural places, and 3) nature teaches people to grieve. We excerpt from her story to illustrate our findings and to extend our discussion of ecological grief and mourning.

"My pet shark": Natural Places Connect Us to Loss and Grief

When something you love contributes to the death of someone or something else you love (thinking here of the traumatic deaths in mountain parks or waters, or the tragedy of loss through climate change), there is a further complexity and often conflict that can add additional bumps in the journey of grief and mourning. Anita (pseudonym) explained her struggles to reconcile the traumatic deaths of friends in the mountain parks she loved. Asked to give her story a title, Anita called it "My pet shark," capturing the complexity of life and death that, for her, coexisted in the mountain parks.

> My story of this life and death has always been really close. I got involved in rock climbing at the gym and I went outside and the mountains got bigger and I got into mountaineering. This landscape is very much a part of my family, it's like a loved one. I just have so much passion for the area, for the landscape. Through that lifestyle I lost some friends, so death has been close in this journey through the mountains. There have been some accidents that have happened right from the beginning. The fellow who taught us died a year or two after we got into it.

A young beautiful man. Right at the beginning of the story. That doesn't happen to everybody who gets involved in the mountains. It's a risky sport but it doesn't happen to everyone. The context of having such a vibrant life here and then having death side by side, it enriches it. That's what brings the richness into paradox. All of a sudden I go to the mountains and death isn't just something that happens to old people, it happens to everybody.

I felt it's like you have this pet shark you really love and it eats your buddy. How do you come to terms with that? I don't know if I can articulate it. It's the paradox of what you risk, and I'm not into adventure sports and certainly don't want to die. As I get older I don't have to ice climb anymore to be happy. There was a time when I did. I needed the drugs you get in your body or the amazing relationships you get when you do these things with them. I'm not sure what being out in nature has to do with it. I don't know how to answer that. I can have that happen when people don't die outside, right? You can still get that shark bite from anything and that presence of just being with people at the end of their lives.

"It's like a bridge to there [the sacred]": Loss and Grief Connects People to Natural Places

Anita went on to articulate the connection or bridge that loss and grief provided to the mountain parks and to a sense of the sacred in natural places. Her story, told in retrospect, is one of learning and understanding personal loss in the context of the traumatic losses occurring in the Anthropocene. The bridge between loss and natural places enabled Anita to regain her footing on the bumpy road of grief. This more solid footing has given her perspective in understanding ecological loss as well as her own losses.

One of the first accidents I was directly involved with was Cascade Icefall. I drive past that every day on the way to work. I've noticed over 15 years how my emotions have changed. It's been so long. It's just life. I'm a different person now, I'm older. Back then I was so angry, I was really angry at the mountains. I just loved the mountains, but they killed my friends and I was angry at them – and at myself. Then you move on through the phases. Those spots are a reminder of how fragile life is. You can get complacent about life and get bored. I hate that place. Then the negativity and questions: how good am I? What am I doing here? To get to those places, it took me ten years of therapy to figure things out.

Therapy did reconcile the nature and deep love and trauma and sacred place – some of it. But you do get to a place with your faith and spirituality – it's like a bridge to there. For me it was. It's not easy by any means. The interesting thing now is, where are we with parks in the bigger picture? We've swung right from parks need to be wild and untouched by humans, back to we need to have humans be part of nature, and back to what is the bottom line? I'm sure these are all issues you can relate to. As we bring death more into life, and enrich and mature our societies because we're starting to look at it. The planet is dying too so that's a whole other issue. There are more reasons than just the ones we've talked about. Humanity, we have to look at the destruction of our planet. Looking to reconnect people to nature is going to do more for the environment than anything. I think there are places in the world we could keep wild, I don't know if we can do that because there's so many of us. At this stage of my life, I used to think parks should be wild because humans just destroy them. I used to think that way. Now it's about education and connecting through the landscapes – right through to the end.

"Nature is like watching a film on how we deal with death": Parks and Natural Places Teach People to Grieve

Of the final theme uncovered in our broader narrative analysis of all study informants, an overarching story that nature teaches people to grieve stood out strongly. Whether through companion animals, witnessing the seasonality of decay and renewal, or changes in the environment, grief and loss were ever-present teachers and the classrooms were constantly changing. Anita said it in this way:

Nature is like watching a film on how we deal with death. You think of the salmon in the fall. They're chasing their deaths basically. What becomes of that? They give life, they lay their eggs and they feed all of the wildlife. Their bones decompose and give us all that rich mineral soil. And just to witness that, without bringing your ego into it, you're just this human and you're part of it. By being part of it, you're important and to witness that, it's all right there. It's like watching a film that's educating you. I haven't personally been taking people out to nature. But I've heard people craving that, just being out there – instead of the antiseptic hospital.

Discussion and Conclusions: A Natural Connection of Nature and Grief

The significant work that has been done around how to manage grief in the arena of death and dying has something to offer to those experiencing grief in response to ecological crises. (Eaton, 2012, p. 1)

The study reported in this chapter sought to understand individual perspectives and values of the place of parks and nature at end of life. A narrative process and the stories of people like Anita and others uncovered three dominant themes: 1) death brings people to parks and nature, 2) parks and nature reveal death and life, and finally 3) nature teaches people to grieve. These discoveries have provided the foundation for policy and practice across parks and ·

health sectors that promote access to and enjoyment of parks and nature for people during end-of-life experiences. Specifically, novel grief and loss walking programs, parks access audits, and the 2017 expansion of volunteer and staff curriculum and support have been developed for Alberta Parks as informed by the study. "Place-based interventions" such as these, as well as adventure therapy (Brewer and Sparkes, 2011), animal assisted therapies (Hartwig and Smelser, 2018), and gardening or care farming (Gorman and Cacciatore, 2017) are gaining popularity for their social and non-medicalized approach to mourning and grief.

Experiences in parks and natural settings have previously been found to offer support, enhance mood, and contribute to sensory and social benefits for adults with disabilities and their caregivers (Jakubec et al., 2014; Jakubec et al., 2016b). These are experiences that shift focus from the medical sector and relocate people and their circumstances into the public, into a social domain. They also welcome the universal, existential, and sacred into the ecological sphere of being human in a world of suffering (Weller, 2015). Shaw and Bonnett (2016) reflect on this work of grief, and what Wolfelt (2003, 2007) and others articulate as public mourning as an antidote to the distress of the Anthropocene. They propose processes of "rewilding," and entering into the messy practice of "bewilderment, denial and also creative re-imaginings" provoked by the experience of grief for human and non-human loss (p. 565).

We discovered that mourning and facing the pain of human loss with others in public spaces enables both people at end of life and their caregivers to integrate and respond to the conflict – rather than prolonging it, holding on to the distress, and, perhaps, the overwhelming feelings that halt engagement and movement. Through our narrative analysis, we found that mourning publicly in and with parks and natural places enables the integration of a forever changed landscape of personal and, we believe, ecological loss. We found that nature teaches people to grieve. Just as public mourning and connection with parks and nature can productively allow grief to be integrated into the fabric of our lives, the same practices can become part of the integration of ecological loss into our lives – to recognize and respond. Grief changes what we love, and enables us to be changed – and it must.

ACKNOWLEDGMENTS

The authors would like to recognize Alberta Environment and Parks, who generously funded the study reported on in this chapter, as well as Dr Mike Quinn at Mount Royal University, who was part of the original research team. Most importantly, we acknowledge the fifteen people who shared their stories of grief, loss, and natural places with us.

REFERENCES

Alberta Parks. (2014). *Everyone belongs outside: Alberta's plan for parks: Inclusion plan.* Edmonton, AB: Government of Alberta.

Bingley, A. F., Claudewell, T., Heller Brown, J., Reeve, J., & Payne, S. (2008). Developing narrative research in supportive and palliative care: The focus on illness narratives. *Palliative Medicine, 22*(5), 653–8. https://doi.org/10.1177/0269216308089842

Brewer, J., & Sparkes, A. C. (2011). The meanings of outdoor physical activity for parentally bereaved young people in the United Kingdom: Insights from an ethnographic study. *Journal of Adventure Education & Outdoor Learning, 11*(2), 127–43. https://doi.org/10.1080/14729679.2011.633382

Burton-Christie, D. (2011). The gift of tears: Loss, mourning and the work of ecological restoration. *Worldviews: Global Religions, Culture, and Ecology, 15*(1), 29–46. https://doi.org/10.1163/156853511X553787

Cunsolo, A. (2018). To grieve or not to grieve. Retrieved from http://niche-canada .org/2018/01/19/to-grieve-or-not-to-grieve

Cunsolo, A., & Ellis, N. (2018). Ecological grief as a mental health response to climate change-related loss. *Nature – Climate Change, 8*, 275–81 https://doi.org/10.1038 /s41558-018-0092-2

Cunsolo, A., & Landman, K. (2017). *Mourning nature: Hope at the heart of ecological loss and grief.* Montreal: McGill-Queen's University Press.

Eaton, M. (2012). Environmental trauma and grief. Retrieved from https://serc .carleton.edu/bioregion/sustain_contemp_lc/essays/67207.html

Ellison, K. P., & Weingast, M. (2016). *Awake at the bedside: Contemplative teachings on palliative and end-of-life care.* Somerville: Wisdom Publication.

Fisher, A. (2013). *Radical ecopsychology: Psychology in the service of life.* 2nd ed. Albany: State University of New York Press.

Frank, A. (1993). The rhetoric of self-change: Illness experience as narrative. *The Sociological Quarterly, 34*(1), 39–52. https://doi.org/10.1111/j.1533-8525.1993 .tb00129.x

Frank, A. (2006). Health stories as connectors and subjectifiers. *Health, 10*(4), 421–40. https://doi.org/10.1177/1363459306067312

Frank, A. (2014). Narrative ethics as dialogical story-telling. *The Hastings Center Report, 44*(s1), S16–20. https://doi.org/10.1002/hast.263

Gorman, R., & Cacciatore, J. (2017). Cultivating our humanity: A systematic review of care farming & traumatic grief. *Health and Place, 47*, 12–21. https://doi .org/10.1016/j.healthplace.2017.06.006

Hallstrom, L. K., Hvenegaard, G., Gould, J., & Joubert, B. (2019). Prioritizing research questions for protected area agencies: A case study of provincial parks in Alberta, Canada. *The Journal of Park and Recreation Administration, 37*(3). https://doi .org/10.18666/JPRA-2019-9434

Hartwig, E. K., & Quinn, K. S. (2018). Practitioner perspectives on animal-assisted counseling. *Journal of Mental Health Counseling, 40*(1), 43–57. https://doi.org /10.17744/mehc.40.1.04

Jakubec, S. L., Carruthers Den Hoed, D., Krishnamurthy, A., Ray, H., & Quinn, M. (2016a). Research snapshot – Nature teaches us to grieve: The place of parks and nature at end of life. Retrieved from https://mruir.mtroyal.ca/xmlui/handle/11205/273.

Jakubec, S. L., Carruthers Den Hoed, D., Krishnamurthy, A., Ray, H., & Quinn, M. (2016b). Mental well-being and quality of life benefits of inclusion in nature for adults with disabilities and their caregivers. *Landscape Research, 41*(6), 616–27. https://doi.org/ 10.1080/01426397.2016.1197190

Jakubec, S. L., Carruthers Den Hoed, D., & Ray, H. (2014). 'I can reinvent myself out here': Experiences of nature inclusion and mental well-being. In B. M. Altman, S. N. Barnartt (Eds), *Research in social science and disability (Environmental contexts and disability, volume 8)* (pp. 213–29). Bingley, UK: Emerald Group Publishing Limited.

Kearney, M. (2009). *A place of healing: Working with nature & soul at the end of life.* New York, NY: Spring Journal Publishers.

Macy, J., & Young Brown, M. (1998). *Coming back to life: Practices to reconnect our lives, our world.* Gabriola Island: New Society Publishers.

Maller, C., Townsend, M., St Leger, L., Henderson-Wilson, C., Pryor, A., Prosser, L., & Moore, M. (2008). *Healthy parks healthy people: The health benefits of contact with nature in a park setting.* Victoria, Australia: Deakin University and Parks Victoria.

Shaw, W. S., & Bonnett, A. (2016). Environmental crisis, narcissism and the work of grief. *Cultural Geographies, 23*(4), 565–79. https://doi.org/10.1177 /1474474016638042

Southall, D. J. (2011). Creating new worlds: The importance of narrative in palliative care. *Journal of Palliative Care, 27*(4), 310. https://doi.org/10.1177 /082585971102700408

Warraich, H. (2017). *Modern death: How medicine changed the end of life.* Berkeley: North Atlantic Books.

Weller, F. (2015). *The wild edge of sorrow: Rituals of renewal and the sacred work of grief.* New York: St Martin's Press.

Williams, F. (2017). *The nature fix: Why nature makes us happier, healthier and more creative.* New York: W.W. Norton & Company.

Wolfelt, A. (2003). *Understanding your grief: Ten essential touchstones for finding hope and healing your heart.* Fort Collins: Companion Press.

Wolfelt, A. (2007). *Living in the shadow of the ghosts of grief: Step into the light.* Fort Collins: Companion Press.

Wolfelt, A. (2014). *The wilderness of suicide grief: Finding your way.* Fort Collins: Companion.

12 Nature as Partner: Rethinking Intersectoral Action for Health in the Anthropocene Era

MARY JANE YATES

Introduction: A Scenario

Imagine you are director of a large public health organization that has just convened a meeting to develop a response to the rising rates of opioid overdose and mental illness in your nation's youth. You have gathered experts from across the country to share their views on what can be done, including several elders from First Nations communities and even a few youth who have themselves suffered from mental health and addictions issues. The first day of your meeting ends with many shaking their heads in frustration at the differing opinions and obvious roadblocks there may be to developing tangible solutions to the problem. Recognizing this frustration, you invite one of the elders in attendance to help you plan an opening activity for day two of your gathering. The elder agrees on only one condition: that the session take place outside in a nearby park, where everyone would be instructed to sit for at least ten minutes in complete silence before any further conversation can take place.

Sound familiar? And if so, what was your response? Did you go along with the elder's suggestion, recognizing the wisdom of it? Or did you immediately think of the logistical problems there would be with facilitating this activity and decide to stick with your original agenda instead?

For those of us who have been trained and now work in public health settings in Canada and elsewhere, the first part of this scenario may be all too familiar. But the elder's presence at the meeting may not be all that familiar, nor would his unusual request. As a result, we may have no idea how to respond. It is this "not knowing" that I hope to address in this chapter. For while many of us know intuitively that such a request might make sense, we have not yet explored to any depth how such an activity might serve to strengthen our capacity to work with others, and how time spent in nature might be essential for both understanding and acting on the complex issues of our time.

Why Partner with Nature?

To answer the question of why partner with nature in taking action on public health issues, I will first briefly review the history and theory behind public health and health promotion and how their ontological underpinnings might inform a more proactive approach to working *with* nature rather than *for* or *on* her. This will be followed by a brief summary of the growing body of evidence there is to demonstrate the positive effects of a connection with nature on both individual and community health.

Public health as a profession has its origins in understanding and acting on the relationships between human beings and their environment. As the classic example, most contemporary practitioners identify the work of English physician John Snow as pivotal in shaping the profession, with his discovery of the link between a cholera epidemic and the water coming from the Broad Street pump in the Soho district of London in 1854 (Smith, 2002). Since that time, the study of "environmental health" has largely focussed on the *adverse* effects of human relationships with the environment, with the purpose of "preventing adverse health conditions by limiting exposure to biological, chemical, or physical hazards in specific settings such as the workplace, home or community" (Buse et al., 2017, p. 2). And while millions of lives have been saved and diseases even eradicated because of this work, an unfortunate side effect has perhaps been the increasing dissociation and "mistrust" between human beings and their natural environments. A classic example of this in contemporary Canadian cities is how a concern for injury prevention and "safe" environments has resulted in the proliferation of asphalt surfaces and synthetic equipment in children's playgrounds – thereby replacing the more natural elements of sand, wood, and water that we now know may have a much more beneficial effect on children's stress levels and cognitive development (Strife and Downey, 2009).

While the health promotion movement beginning in the 1980s in Canada served to shift the focus in public health to more positive views of health and the environment, much work has yet to be done. Take for example the original definition of health promotion from the Ottawa Charter:

> Health promotion is the process of enabling people to increase control over, and to improve, their health. To reach a state of complete physical, mental and social well-being, an individual or group must be able to identify and to realize aspirations, to satisfy needs, and **to change or cope with the environment**. (World Health Organization, 1986)

Despite the broader concept of health embedded in this definition (i.e. "a state of complete physical, mental and social well-being"), the definition overall is still clearly embedded in an anthropocentric worldview, with the assumption being that humans have (or should have) *control over* their health, which in part means to *be able to change or cope with their environment.* Hardly a place to start in terms of respecting and valuing the *positive* attributes of nature as partner.

Underlying a health promotion framework, however, is also the theory of salutogenesis and its related emphasis on *assets* or strengths-based approaches to understanding health and its origins (McKnight and Kretzmann, 2012; Morgan and Ziglio, 2007). Added to this is the strong emphasis health promotion has contributed to understanding the importance of *intersectoral action* and partnering with others *outside the health sector* for effective public health action (Prevention Institute, 2003; Public Health Agency of Canada, 2007). Again, these practice elements are clearly rooted in the original Ottawa Charter, which further explains:

> Health is a positive concept emphasizing social and personal resources, as well as physical capacities. Therefore, health promotion is not just the responsibility of the health sector but goes beyond healthy life-styles to well-being. (WHO, 1986)

These two principles combined (salutogenic and intersectoral approaches) clearly support a further shift in public health practice to a more holistic consideration of the *reciprocal* relationships between people, animals, and ecosystems. And the proliferation of frameworks and papers on this topic in recent decades certainly illustrates that the broader public health community is now taking these relationships more seriously. As an example, the discussion paper released by the Canadian Public Health Association (CPHA, 2015) clearly places the environment and environmental determinants of health at the forefront of the public health agenda. Interestingly, however, this document focuses largely on the detrimental effects of climate change on human health rather than the *positive* contributions of nature to human well-being. Nonetheless, the work of these authors and numerous others highlight "the need to question the role of dominant anthropocentric narratives" and commit to an "epistemological diversity" that will support "true engagement with ecological systems as living entities" (Buse et al., 2017 p. 3–4). The question then presents itself *how* to achieve this engagement, which I think in part needs to begin with a solid understanding of the positive contributions of nature to well-being in order to avoid the typically "pathogenic" views taken by practitioners in the past. To solidify this understanding then, a brief review of the positive effects of nature on human health is provided below, including its salutogenic effect on the physical, psychological, social, and spiritual dimensions of human well-being.

Nature's Role in Promoting Health

As Indigenous cultures tell us, the connection between Earth and the well-being of humans has been known intuitively since time immemorial. In recent decades there has been increasing attention to this connection and an effort to explore and quantify this relationship (Booth, 2016; Rudnev, 2015; Kimmerer, 2013). A few of these research findings are highlighted below as a way of illustrating how nature is indeed an essential partner in both preventing and alleviating some of the world's most challenging public health problems.

First, numerous studies have demonstrated that proximity to natural environments is a key predictor of people's physical activity, "more so than proximity to community centres or indoor gyms" (Parks Canada, 2014, p. 12). Childhood play in natural environments has also been shown to be essential to the development of core cognitive skills such as observation, problem-solving, and creativity (Parks Canada, 2014, p. 17). Wells and Lekies explain in their 2006 article "Nature and the life course: pathways from childhood nature experiences to adult environmentalism" (cited by Parks Canada, 2014):

> Nature is hands on – playing in dirt, navigating rough terrain, examining insects and climbing trees. Natural spaces are dynamic, changing, complex, places to explore, disorderly, free-range, untidy. There is nothing in the built environment that mimics it.

Importantly, playing in nature has also been shown to nurture the development of empathy and self-awareness in both children and adults. In their 2003 study, Malone and Tranter found that playing in nature helped to remove the social hierarchy among children and reduce instances of bullying (Malone and Tranter, 2003). In natural play areas, researchers have noted a diversity of play activities – including fantasy and creative play – that contribute to rotating leadership positions and better collaboration among children (Parks Canada, 2014, p. 20).

And finally, the literature acknowledges the essential connection between the *spiritual* dimension of human health and a connection with nature:

> Modern studies in a range of disciplines have all come to the same conclusion: nature offers something spiritual that is good for the soul. In nature, we can experience wonder, joy, thrill, and satisfaction all in a single hike in the woods. Aesthetics of the natural world, particularly those provided by mountains, deserts, waterfalls, forests and oceans have been shown to inspire episodes of ultimate happiness and spiritual fulfillment. The more natural the environment the more restorative power it has. The heightened sensory awareness acquired through contact with nature, especially wilderness, is associated with "peak experiences" – where people

lose themselves in the wonder and awe of the moment. These experiences are akin to the vision quests in ancient cultures. (Parks Canada, 2014, p. 15)

Given the range of benefits provided to us by nature and the imperative to part-ner with sectors well beyond the health sector, can there be any doubt that nature may provide just the incentive we need to do so?

How to Partner with Nature?

Theory/Models of Partnership, Intersectoral Collaboration

In order to explore the question of how to partner with nature, I will first pro-vide a brief review of the literature on what constitutes "successful" partner-ship development and intersectoral collaboration. Not surprisingly, some of the leading research in this area comes from the business world, an example of which is the "phases of partnership" model outlined by Kanter (1994) from her extensive study of partnerships through the Harvard School of Business. It is also perhaps not surprising to recognize that the stages of partnership outlined by Kanter closely parallel those experienced by partners in any type of human relationship: courtship, engagement, housekeeping, learning to collaborate, and change within. These will each be described in brief as a means of framing the recommendations I make in the remainder of the chapter.

First, according to Kanter, the "courtship" stage of partnering involves the experience of some initial excitement or "spark" when partners first meet, an experience that I think many of us can say has certainly been part of the human side of our encounters with aspects of the natural world. The challenge then, is in thinking about how and when humans, and specifically public health prac-titioners, and the natural world have an opportunity to meet, and whether this "initial spark" is experienced on both sides.

Second, once the courtship phase has occurred, Kanter describes a stage of partnership in which partners perform some sort of "ceremony" or official act in which the partners declare their intentions to work with each other in a more intimate fashion. Kanter compares this "engagement" stage of partnership to "meeting the family" in a human romantic relationship. Using this analogy to examine the relationship of the public health sector with the natural world, we can clearly see that many in our public health community have publicly declared their intentions to partner more intentionally in both understanding and solving some of today's most complex public health issues. The CPHA po-sition paper (2015) is one example of this type of declaration, as is the prolifer-ation of networks and training events related to "ecohealth," "one health," and "planetary health" that have emerged in Canada and around the world in recent decades. Surely these developments represent a type of open declaration on the part of public health practitioners that could be compared to the "wedding vow" stage of partnership as described by Kanters.

So the "spark" and the "commitment" may have been achieved, but now what? The next two phases of Kanter's typology describe some of the hard work and not so glamourous aspects of partnership building that need to occur. In the "housekeeping" phase, partners begin to realize the realities of working together and some of the profound differences that exist in the way each views their role and how they plan to contribute to the "marriage." In the "learning to collaborate" phase, partners find creative ways of working with these differences and actually shift some of their structures and processes to enable more effective action. This type of integration can be a slow and painful process and, interestingly, both Kanter and others talk about the shift in values or "change within" that needs to take place in order for partnerships to reach what is considered true collaboration.

Understanding then, that effective partnerships are really about relationship development and "change within," the next section describes some practical steps for how public health professionals might begin to operationalize the "engagement" we have declared should be so important to our work.

Get Outside!

At the risk of sounding obvious, one recommendation for engaging more intentionally with nature is for public health practitioners to spend more time outdoors, both in their personal and professional lives. This suggestion is especially relevant to the "courtship" stage of partnering, though it is integral as well to all other stages as it is the most direct method for communicating with and listening to this partner, whose language and ways of being can be so immensely different from ours. While the suggestion to get outside may sound easy, evidence on the amount of time people in North America spend outdoors seems to tell us otherwise. As far back as 1989, the United States Environmental Protection Agency (EPA) was reporting that its citizens were spending up to 90 per cent of their time indoors. (EPA, 1989). A more recent study conducted by Angus Reid for the Coleman Canada Outdoor report found that 29 per cent of Canadians, almost three in ten, say they spend less than a half hour per week outside, while 64 per cent enjoy the open air for less than two hours a week (BusinessWire, 2017). And while these statistics do not describe how much time people spend outdoors in a work setting, I think it is safe to assume that the majority of public health professionals in North America today spend little to no time outdoors in the course of their everyday employment. The exception to this may be those employed in the area of environmental health, but even then, the purpose of these outdoor excursions is likely not so much to "court" nature but to examine, prod, and diagnose any number of symptoms that are currently ailing her. Not exactly activities designed to "ignite the spark" and nurture a love for nature and the outdoors!

This suggestion to get outside means that collectively we as a profession start to ask ourselves, "What is the relationship we want with the earth?" As Margaret Wheatley suggests, this question is a key one for creating hope for our world:

> I believe the easiest way to become partners with life is to get outside, to be in nature and let her teach us. About half of us no longer have this option. Half of the world's population lives in large cities, breathing polluted air, unable to see the stars, never knowing peace or quiet. I grieve for those of us who cannot know the feel of wild places, the sound of a small stream, the shade of a grove of trees. But for those of us who still have nature available to us, it is even more important that we get outside. We need to experience the power and beauty of life on behalf of all humans who no longer can do this themselves. (Wheatley, 2009, p. 112)

One extremely promising model for achieving more time outdoors in training public health practitioners has been developed by the Canadian Community of Practice for Ecohealth (CoPEH Canada) in the short courses and summer "field schools" they have been offering since 2008. Designed collaboratively by scholars and practitioners from a wide array of perspectives, these courses have convened a diverse group of graduate students and practitioners for an intensive learning opportunity including case studies, fieldwork, and interdisciplinary group work. An example of topics covered in the course include "land-based learning as a response to environmental and health equity challenges" and "universities in their watersheds" (CoPEH Canada, n.d.) A key focus for these field schools is to have participants spend extended periods of time outside; even when activities occur indoors a very "real-life" engagement with the non-human world is encouraged. For example, in an activity that was part of the 2013 field school, one participant played the role of a pregnant moose in helping the rest of the (human) group to define the term "health." And in another, participants were assigned the task of sitting silently for a while to "hear, smell, taste, and visualize" the life of the water pushing past in the Nechako River nearby. These kinds of experiences leave a lasting impression on practitioners and can easily be implemented in other settings – for example, in the curriculum of more standard academic programs or a variety of public health workplaces, wherever there is even a small area of green space nearby such as a rooftop garden, park bench, or view from a riverbank.

Learn from Indigenous Teachers

Given how clearly Indigenous cultures value the natural world, I suggest a second way to engage with nature is to partner more intentionally with Indigenous colleagues and learn from them both the practices and "ways of knowing" that can connect us more closely with the natural world. This step is essential especially for those who have been educated and acculturated primarily in Western, colonial settings – which again will likely describe many of those currently working in public health settings in North America. While partnering with Indigenous colleagues may seem one step away from engaging directly with nature, I would say it parallels the act of engaging a translator when the language being spoken by your beloved is not one that you know. This approach is in fact one that has been adopted by the legal community in several landmark cases where the "rights" of nature are now being recognized. In the case of the Whanganui River in New Zealand, for example, the "rights of personhood" that were granted in March 2017 are now represented in part by a committee composed of representatives of the Indigenous community that fought for these rights (Tanasescu, 2017). Examples like this tell us that a connection with Indigenous communities may indeed be an essential one in understanding the interests and views of nature as person.

To connect more intentionally with Indigenous colleagues, learning even a few words of a native language might be a place to start, as even a rudimentary understanding of Indigenous languages can tell us much about a connection with nature. This is because native languages in themselves often mimic the sounds of the landscapes where they originate. As described by Abrams (1996):

> If we listen, first to the sounds of an oral language – to the rhythms, tones, and inflections that play through the speech of an oral culture – we will likely find that these elements are attuned, in multiple and subtle ways, to the contour and scale of the local landscape, to the depth of its valleys or the open stretch of its distances, to the visual rhythms of the local topography.... Such attunement is simply imperative for any culture still dependent upon foraging for its subsistence. (Abrams, 1996, p. 140)

And beyond the sounds of a native language, its grammar teaches us about alternative, non-anthropocentric ways of relating with nature. In a vibrant description of efforts to learn her native Potawatomi, botanist Robin Kimmerer says the following:

> This is the grammar of animacy. Imagine seeing your grandmother standing at the stove in her apron and then saying of her, "Look, it is making soup. It has gray hair." We might snicker at such a mistake, but we also recoil from it. In English, we never refer to a member of our family, or indeed to any person, as "it." That would be a profound act of disrespect. "It" robs a person of selfhood and kinship, reducing a person to a mere thing. So it is that in Potowatomi and most other indigenous

languages, we use the same words to address the living world as we use for our family. Because they are our family. (Kimmerer, 2013, 55)

In addition to reading Indigenous authors and perhaps learning a few phrases of Cree or Potawatomi, public health practitioners can look for some of the many opportunities there are to link with Indigenous colleagues through their research and practice settings. Thanks to the work of the Truth and Reconciliation Commission (TRC) of Canada, these connections are easier to make today than they were a decade ago. For example, in response to the TRC Call to "provide the necessary funding to post-secondary institutions to educate teachers on how to integrate Indigenous knowledge and teaching methods into classrooms" (TRC, 2015, p. 7), the University of Alberta has now hired a "culture educational developer" whose job it is to promote the use of Indigenous epistemologies and pedagogies in U of A courses and curricula (University of Alberta Centre for Teaching and Learning, n.d.). As a result, faculty and staff have regular opportunities to engage with Indigenous educators in an ongoing dialogue about Indigenous ways of knowing and how they might contribute to more effective teaching and learning experiences. This initiative is just one of many that are developing across Canada in response to the TRC's call to action. A simple step for practitioners and researchers is to connect with similar events within their geographic area and use them as a platform to continue to foster these connections.

Practice Silence

The day will come when man will have to fight noise as inexorably as cholera and the plague. (Koch, 1905, cited in Hempton and Grossman, 2009)

Related to the steps of both "getting outside" and "connecting with Indigenous teaching," the practice of silence is an essential one for furthering our relationship with nature. Anyone who has spent even a small amount of time in a wilderness setting quickly realizes the importance of sitting still and shutting up in order to truly hear the "presence" of the plants, water, and rocks that surround them. And Indigenous ways of communicating also model silence for us; for example, in the pause to offer prayers or burn sweetgrass before gatherings and the silences that are then welcomed as part of talking circle practice (Lane, 1992; Regnier, 1994).

While silence may be something that humans know intuitively is a part of our connection with nature, few of us in this Anthropocene age may have had the opportunity to actually experience it. As audio ecologist Gordon Hempton (Hempton and Grossman, 2009) puts it, silence is defined "not merely as the absence of noise, but the complete absence of *all audible mechanical vibrations,* leaving only the sounds of nature at her most natural. Silence is the presence of everything, undisturbed" (Hempton and Grossman, 2009, p. 2). The "practice of silence" then, means creating places for ourselves and others where audible *human-made* vibrations are absent, or at least minimized to the fullest extent possible.

So how might we do this, you ask – especially in an age when technological innovations and their associated vibrations are present in almost every square inch of our world (Hempton and Grossman, 2009)? Is there really a way to practice the kind of silence that will allow us to experience the "presence of everything" as Hempton and Grossman describe it? I would suggest that this type of silence can be cultivated not only through minimizing the *external* sound that is so ubiquitous to daily life, but also the *internal* noise that accompanies us in the form of incessant thinking and reflection. Minimizing this type of noise through some type of meditation practice can connect us with the non-human world in a way that even a trip to the wilderness might not do if our mind is constantly distracted by thoughts and interior noise. How meditation and interior silence connect us with nature has been described by great teachers and mystics of all religions. Take for example these words of Thomas Merton, a Trappist monk from Kentucky:

> When your tongue is silent, you can rest in the silence of the forest. When your imagination is silent, the forest speaks to you.... But when your mind is silent, then the forest suddenly becomes magnificently real and blazes transparently with the Reality of God. (Merton, 1997)

Surely these words reflect the "courtship" element of partnership building referred to by Kanters as the initial excitement or "spark" when partners first meet!

The practice of silence however, does much more to enhance our ability to partner with nature than to "ignite the first spark." Probably to a much greater extent than getting outside or learning from Indigenous teachers, this practice plays a critical role in negotiating the deeper challenges of learning to collaborate referred to by Kanters and others; in other words, the "shift in structures and processes" and "change within" that is needed for effective action. This belief seems to be shared by several leading leadership theorists of our time. After extensive experience in both attempting to lead and teach others the skills needed for effective public health leadership, I have compiled an impressive list of authors who speak of the importance of regular practice of silence and interior listening. These include: Senge (1990); Wheatley (2002); Kouzes and Posner (2012); Senge, Scharmer, Jaworski, and Flowers (2004). Using Senge's definition, this practice consists of "some form of meditation, such as contemplative prayer or a method to quiet the conscious mind" (Senge, 1990, p. 153).

These authors further hypothesize that this type of silence and listening is also needed on a collective basis as part of the "letting go and letting come" process that needs to occur in order for true transformation to take place. Describing the concept of "presencing" and the movements of "Theory U," Scharmer explains:

> The first movement he called "observe, observe, observe." It means to stop down-loading and start listening. It means to stop our habitual ways of operating and immerse ourselves in the places of most potential, the places that matter most to the situation we are dealing with. (Scharmer, 2007, p. 5)

As Scharmer and others point out, this kind of silence or contemplative practice can be especially helpful in working with partners whose mindsets and viewpoints are extremely different from our own. This is because the meditation practice itself consists of a "letting come and letting go" in relation to any thoughts, feelings, sensations, or experiences that occur during our sitting period. And over time, the effects of this kind of meditation, if practiced on a regular basis, can be seen during our daily lives and interactions with others. A recent systematic review and meta-analysis of the effects of meditation revealed "a moderate increase in prosociality following meditation" – albeit an effect that was observed only in the domains of compassion and empathy, but not on aggression, connectedness, or prejudice (Kreplin, Farias, and Brazil 2017, p. 1). Interestingly, however, a longitudinal study conducted by Hölzel et al., (2011) demonstrated actual "changes in gray matter concentration in brain regions involved in learning and memory processes, emotion regulation, self-referential processing, and perspective taking" (p. 1). The practice of silence in this context consisted of participants engaging in an eight-week mindfulness-based stress-reduction course which included daily practice of a body scan, mindful yoga, and sitting meditation (Holzel et al., 2011).

Given that there is some evidence to demonstrate the importance of "practicing silence" in supporting our efforts to partner with both nature and others, how might we begin to experience this in both our work and personal lives? Again, recent initiatives and broader societal movements in the Western world make it easier to begin and maintain a practice of silence than would have been the case even a few decades ago. In most urban centres across Canada and the US there has been a proliferation of local meditation and mindfulness groups emerging in the last several years. As an example, on the University of Alberta campus alone, there are four different silent prayer or meditation groups who meet on campus each week, along with several undergraduate psychology courses where mindfulness meditation is taught as part of the curricula. And on a broader level, there now exist organizations such as the Center for Contemplative Mind in Society (http://www.contemplativemind.org),

Contemplative Outreach Ltd (http://www.contemplativeoutreach.org), and others that provide a host of resources and the opportunity to connect with both online and "real-time" communities of practice. Other supports to practice "collective listening" include authors such as Christina Baldwin and Ann Linnea and their work to introduce circle practice to groups and organizations worldwide (see https://peerspirit.com/the-circle-way) as well as Margaret Wheatley and Toke Moeller's work to establish the Art of Hosting community of practice (see http://www.artofhosting.org).

Conclusion

Now that we have considered both the "why" and "how" of partnering with nature, I invite you to return to the scenario with which this chapter began. Imagine you are now ready to work with your Indigenous colleague to open your gathering with a period of silence in the park nearby. As participants settle into their places, your elder friend begins with this invitation:

> I have noticed in my life that all of us have a liking for some special animal, tree, plant, or spot of earth. I am asking you now to close your eyes and bring to mind a favourite plant, tree, or animal that you can hear nearby in the landscape around you. Make a study of it, learning its innocent ways.
>
> Once you have this being fully in your mind, let her tell you what she thinks about what is going on with the youth in our country. See if you can hear what she thinks can be done about it. And finally, seek what is best to do in order to make yourself worthy of that to which you find yourself so attracted. (adapted from a saying by Brave Buffalo, Teton Sioux, late nineteenth century, cited in Jean, 2003, 15 March reading)

At the end of the silent period, participants begin to talk in new ways about the opioid crisis and how it might be linked to the generations of loss and disconnection from the land experienced by both settler and First Nations communities. They also begin to envision new ways of restoring this connection, especially for those who are most vulnerable in both the human and natural domain. They begin to realize that both these realms must be considered together; that healing for one cannot happen without healing the other.

REFERENCES

Abram, D. (1996). *The spell of the sensuous: Perception and language in a more-than-human world.* New York, NY: Vintage Books.

Booth, A. L. (2016). Environment and nature: The natural environment in Native American thought. In H. Selin (Ed.). *Encyclopaedia of the history of science, technology, and medicine in non-Western cultures.* Springer: Dordrecht.

BusinessWire. (2017). Canadian adults and kids spending less time in nature, poll finds. Retrieved from https://www.businesswire.com/news/home/20170614005351/en/Canadian-Adults-Kids-Spending-Time-Nature-Poll

Buse, C. G., Oestreicher, J. S., Ellis, N. R. et al. (2017). Public health guide to field developments linking ecosystems, environments and health in the Anthropocene. *Journal of Epidemiology and Community Health, 72*(5), 420–5. https://dx.doi.org/10.1136/jech2017-210082

CPHA. (2015). Global change and public health: Addressing the ecological determinants of health. Retrieved from https://www.cpha.ca/sites/default/files/assets/policy/edh-discussion_e.pdf

Community of Practice in Ecosystem Approaches to Health (CoPEH) – Canada (n.d.): Retrieved from http://www.copeh-canada.org/en/key-areas/training-and-capacity-building.html

Hempton, G., & Grossman, J. (2009). *One square inch of silence: One man's search for natural silence in a noisy world.* New York, NY: Free Press.

Hölzel, B. K., Carmodyc, J., Vangela, M., Congletona, C., Yerramsettia, S. M., Garda, T., & Lazara, S. W. (2011). Mindfulness practice leads to increases in regional brain gray matter density. *Psychiatry Research, 191*(1), 36–43. https://doi.org/10.1016/j.pscychresns.2010.08.006

Jean, T. (2003). *365 days of walking the red road: The Native American path to leading a spiritual life every day.* Avon, Minnesota: Adams Media.

Kanter, R. M. (1994). Collaborative advantage: The art of alliances. *Harvard Business Review on Strategic Alliances.* Harvard Business School Press. Retrieved from https://hbr.org/1994/07/collaborative-advantage-the-art-of-alliances

Kimmerer, R. (2013). *Braiding sweetgrass: Indigenous wisdom, scientific knowledge, and the teachings of plants.* Minneapolis, Minnesota: Milkweed Editions.

Kouzes, J., & Posner, B. Z. (2012). *The leadership challenge.* (5th ed.) San Francisco, CA: Jossey-Bass.

Kreplin, U., Farias, M., & Brazil, I. A. (2017). The limited prosocial effects of meditation: A systematic review and meta-analysis. *Scientific Reports, 8*(2403). https://doi.org/10.1038/s41598-018-20299-z

Lane, P. (1992). Guiding principles for healing circles and principles of consultation. Four Worlds International Institute. Retrieved from http://www.fwii.net/profiles/blogs/guidelines-for-talking-healing-and-sharing-circles-and-principles

Malone, K., & Tranter, P. (2003). Children's environmental learning and the use, design and management of school grounds. *Children, Youth and Environments, 13*(2), 87–137.

McKnight, J., & Kretzmann, J. (2012). Mapping community capacity. In M. Minkler (Ed.). *Community organizing and community building for health and welfare* (3rd ed.) (pp. 171–86). New Brunswick, NJ: Rutgers University Press.

Merton, T. (1997). *Entering the silence: Becoming a monk and a writer. Thomas Merton journals, volume 2.* J. Montaldo (Ed.). San Francisco, CA: HarperCollins.

Morgan, A., & Ziglio, E. (2007). Revitalizing the evidence base for public health: An assets model. *Promotion & Education*, Supplement 2, 17–22. https://doi.org/10.1177/10253823070140020701x

Parks Canada Agency. (2014). *Connecting Canadians with nature – An investment in the well-being of our citizens.* Ottawa, ON: Parks Canada. Retrieved from http://www.parks-parcs.ca/english/ConnectingCanadians-English_web.pdf

Prevention Institute. (2003). *The tension of turf: Making it work for the coalition.* Retrieved from http://www.preventioninstitute.org/pdf/TURF_1S.pdf

Public Health Agency of Canada. (2007). *Crossing sectors – Experiences in intersectoral action, public policy and health.* Retrieved from http://www.phac-aspc.gc.ca/publicat/2007/cro-sec/pdf/cro-sec_e.pdf

Regnier, R. (1994). The sacred circle: A process pedagogy of healing. *Interchange*, 25(2), 129–44. https://doi.org/10.1007/BF01534540

Rudnev. V. (2015). Indigenous knowledge: Searching for a model of sustainable development for humankind. *Global Bioethics*, 26(2), 46–51. https://doi.org/10.1080/11287462.2015.1038099

Scharmer, C. O. (2007). *Addressing the blind spot of our time: An executive summary of the book Theory u: Leading from the future as it emerges.* Cambridge, MA: Society for Organizational Learning. Retrieved from https://www.presencing.com/sites/default/files/page-files/Theory_U_Exec_Summary.pdfs

Senge, P. (1990). *The fifth discipline: The art and practice of the learning organization.* New York, NY: Currency.

Senge, P, Scharmer, C. O., Jaworski, J., & Flowers, B. S. (2004). *Presence: Human purpose and the field of the future.* New York: Random House.

Smith, G. D. (2002). Commentary: Behind the Broad Street pump: Aetiology, epidemiology and prevention of cholera in mid-19th century Britain. *International Journal of Epidemiology*, 31(5), 920–32. https://doi.org/10.1093/ije/31.5.920

Strife, S., & Downey, L. (2009). Childhood development and access to nature: A new direction for environmental inequality research. *Organization & Environment*, 22(1), 99–122. http://doi.org/10.1177/1086026609333340

Tanasescu, M. (2017, June 19). Rivers get human rights: They can sue to protect themselves. *Scientific American*. Retrieved from https://www.scientificamerican.com/article/rivers-get-human-rights-they-can-sue-to-protect-themselves/

Truth and Reconciliation Commission of Canada. (2015). *Calls to action.* Retrieved from http://www.trc.ca/websites/trcinstitution/File/2015/Findings/Calls_to_Action_English2.pdf

University of Alberta Centre for Teaching and Learning (n.d.) *About us.* Retrieved from https://www.ualberta.ca/centre-for-teaching-and-learning/about/people

US Environmental Protection Agency. (1989). *Report to Congress on indoor air quality* — *Vol. II: Assessment and control of indoor air pollution. EPA/400/1-89/001C.* Washington, DC: US EPA. Retrieved from tinyurl.com/CCN-2013-R017E.

Wheatley, M. J. (2002). Leadership in turbulent times is spiritual. Retrieved from http://www.margaretwheatley.com/articles/turbulenttimes.html

Wheatley, M. J. (2009). *Turning to one another: Simple conversations to restore hope to the future.* San Francisco: Berrett-Koehler Publishers.

World Health Organization. (1986). Ottawa charter for health promotion. Retrieved from http://www.phac-aspc.gc.ca/ph-sp/phdd/pdf/charter.pdf

13 The Soil Sponge: Collaborating with the Work of Other Species to Improve Public Health, Climate Change, and Resilience

DIDI PERSHOUSE

Introduction

In small creative pockets around the world, farmers and ranchers are working to address major public health and environmental challenges based on a new understanding of biological work.

Like the working class, the work of microbes is particularly quiet and hidden from view. Yet these workers, and their plant and animal symbionts, provide essential goods and services we rely on for daily life. Their ability to do this work, or not, determines nearly everything we depend on to thrive and survive: from our metabolic and brain function, to water quality, to disaster preparedness, to the nutrient density of crops.

Many people are now familiar with the concept of the microbiome – communities of beneficial organisms that live in, on, and around our bodies. Though the health care system has been slow to adapt, most health care workers and many patients now understand that our health is far more dependent on the work of our microbial companions than we ever thought possible. For those who are paying attention, our understanding of the work of microbes in our inner landscapes has turned the germ theory of disease inside out, flipped our anthropocentric view on its head, and continues to bring up a nearly endless string of questions about the future of medicine (Nicholson et al., 2005; Pershouse, 2016).

Fewer people, however, are aware of the importance of the biological work that happens in soils, and how large of an impact "soil health" has on public health – in ways we can hardly imagine. Plants, soil microbes, and all other species do work to build the soil sponge matrix that makes life on land possible, by influencing flows of water, carbon, and nutrients; creating and defining the structure and function of every landscape; and regulating the temperatures and weather patterns on Earth.

Between 2006 and 2014, I began to see that the soil microbiome and the gut microbiome both work as intelligent community networks that provide the structural and functional basis for health, intelligence, and resilience in the organisms they are connected to – and that only by paying attention to these realms could we have any hope of creating healthy communities in the long term. I shifted my career in health care away from treating individuals and towards writing and teaching about opportunities to collaborate with other species to improve public and environmental health on personal, local, regional, and global scales (Pershouse, 2016, 2017).

Modern humans have rarely acknowledged even the slightest dependence on the work of other species (with occasional exceptions, like pollinators, who are treated as unpaid migrant workers in the nut and fruit industries).[1] Our blindness to biological work has impacted our inner and outer landscapes. Nearly every major crisis we are facing today, from the explosion of chronic diseases to desertification, can be traced back to a lack of respect for biological work.

Those who don't recognize the role of other species as essential workers end up creating conditions in which those organisms cannot do their work or even survive – exposing them to unnecessary "occupational hazards." We kill the workers in our interior and exterior landscapes when we give antibiotics to animals (including ourselves) whose health depends on a healthy gut microbiome; cut and burn grasslands and forests that all land dwellers need for cooling and rainfall; spray lethal chemicals targeting fungi, insects, and plants across farms, parks, and soccer fields; expose soil microorganisms to life-threatening temperatures through tillage and bare soil; patent new organisms that *can* tolerate our mistreatment, then terminate "weeds" that attempt to help provide shade, cover, and food for the failing system.[2]

Our capacity to survive and thrive during and beyond the Anthropocene will require us to learn to collaborate with non-human communities – not to dominate, organize, and patent them – but to work with them *on their own terms*.

To do this, we need to shift from the usual hierarchical, anthropocentric, single-species-at-a-time-focused ("humans can save the spotted owl") environmental perspective to something much more complex and community based. We need to learn what work other species do, what conditions they need in their own communities in order to work together, and then we need find our place within their communities so we aren't getting in their way. *Yet we need to make this shift while most of us are still living and working within a top-down, highly compartmentalized social system that promises to reward us for exactly the opposite behaviours, and which is currently undergoing collapse.*

Biological Work in the Microbiome

Our dependence on other species starts before we even enter the world: with beneficial microorganisms arriving in utero (Kai-Larsen et al., 2014). We receive another major inoculation of microbes in the birth canal and continue our symbiotic initiation with a huge rush of hundreds of species of allies streaming into our bodies with every sip of breast milk (Quinn, 2014).

The microorganisms that we inherit from our mothers, and later ingest in our food and collect from our surroundings, do much of the work that we take credit for ourselves. They carry out and direct many of the essential processes that enable us to think, play, reproduce, digest, grow, survive, and work in daily life (Kinross et al., 2011b).

We've learned (just in the past few decades) that the microbial workers in and on our bodies:

- Teach our immune systems how to behave and regulate immunity (Lozupone, 2018)
- Digest our food, creating and offering us nutrients we can't make ourselves
- Influence neuroendocrine and circulatory functions (Dethlefsen, Mcfall-Ngai, and Relman, 2007)
- Form barricades against disease-causing bacteria
- Determine how we metabolize drugs and other toxins and whether or not we have side effects[3] (Clayton et al., 2006)
- Influence dietary calorific bioavailability (i.e. how quickly we gain weight) (Hooper, 2001)
- Influence post-surgical recovery times (Kinross et al., 2011a)
- Make most of our neurotransmitters
- Turn on brain development (Heijtz et al., 2011)

During extreme disease states, and after death, other microbes take charge of making sure our bodies shut down their functioning, decompose properly, and are recycled – so that the carbon, water, calcium, and other elements we are made of can be reused to create more life.

Biological Work in the Land, Sea, and Sky

Like the microbes that work within us, all species participate as workers within a larger body: the body of the Earth.

For example, plants create the oxygen necessary for most of life, transpire water that cools the local climate, and feed everyone, above and below ground, directly or indirectly. (None of us would exist without photosynthesis.) Herds of grazing animals, insects, and flocks of birds move microorganisms, seeds, and nutrients up and over mountains and across continents as they eat, move, and excrete. (Without them, all mountains would be bare, and grasslands would turn to deserts.)

Beavers create dams to slow and filter the flow of water through the landscape, and the diggers – prairie dogs, wolves, snakes, worms, turtles, and beetles, just to name a few – create tunnels that help capture and hold water to kick-start the water cycle after a drought. Saprophytic organisms – like certain fungi, yeasts, bacteria, and moulds – do the work of breaking down dead organic matter. Without them, we would be surrounded by huge (miles high) piles of fallen trees, leaves, and dead animals waiting for slow oxidation by sunlight.

Biological Work in the Atmosphere

Biological work is also largely responsible for rain and snowfall. Algae living in the ocean emit volatile compounds (including dimethyl sulfide) that allow evaporated water vapour to form hazes in the air above oceans, which airborne ocean salts can then coalesce into clouds and rain (Jehne, 2016). Forests and grasslands create cool, moist low-pressure zones through transpiration that pull those atmospheric rivers of water vapour onto and across continents (Jehne, 2016; Kravčík et al., 2007). Trees and other plants emit their own volatile compounds like pinenes and terpenes that allow transpired water vapour to form hazes above land.

Many trees form symbiotic relationships with tiny microorganisms that grow inside the stomata of leaves, and are light enough to float off into the air with the transpiration stream to form microbiomes in the air above forests. The airborne microorganisms act as precipitation nuclei coalescing enough water around themselves to turn haze droplets into raindrops heavy enough to fall out of the sky (Jehne, 2016).

The Soil Sponge

One of the primary jobs of plants, soil microbes, grazing animals, predators, insects, worms, and other above- and below-ground workers is to create the living matrix of the soil carbon sponge: the kind of healthy, intact topsoil that grows in a natural grassland or forest, and can be regrown with appropriate farming techniques. This sponge is the basic infrastructure that makes life on land possible. We cannot survive without it.

Soil without biological work is just powdery broken-down rocks, which, when in contact with wind or water act like flour: blowing away, eroding, and resisting any attempts of the water to soak in. Rainwater will run sideways across a sloping surface, creating flooding, followed by drought, and evaporate quickly on flat degraded landscapes (Pershouse, 2017).

When plants grow in undisturbed landscapes, they feed underground life that changes the structure and function of those mineral particles into a sponge that soaks up rain and filters water. The underground life (like all of us) exudes slimes and glues that stick together sand, silt, and clay particles to create soil aggregates (tiny clumps) with spaces in between (Ingham, 2014). Thread-like roots and fungal hyphae weave these clumps together and then shrivel up, leaving open channels. Organisms of all sizes move, burrow, and dig, creating additional pore spaces and channels. This combination of activities together form a porous, flexible, strong, highly absorbent yet also water resistant structure (similar to a kitchen sponge).

If we look at the earth as a single body, the soil sponge functions as the primary mucosal membrane of the earth: providing a microbially rich, safe space for nutrient sorting and absorption, fluid regulation, respiration, immune function, and reproduction (Pershouse, 2016). A membrane is the most essential and most basic form of intelligence, and is necessary for life. Even the most basic membrane of a single cellular organism decides which elements to let in, and which to keep out.

The porous structure of a healthy soil sponge is a foundation for three primary cycles of life: the water, carbon, and nutrient cycles. The soil sponge:

- Absorbs vast amounts of water when it rains, preventing flooding and drought. (Imagine pouring water onto bread slices, rather than flour.) (Pershouse, 2017)
- Provides a stable yet porous structure within which roots can grow down to reach water at varying depths, and from which plants can grow upward to transpire water vapour back into the atmosphere (Jehne, 2018b).
- Provides clean water for humans and other living things by physically filtering out particulates, biologically decomposing poisons and pollutants, (Haggblom, 1992), and binding heavy metals to make them less water soluble.
- Holds water in place, protected from evaporation, freely available to all, when and where plants and other living things need it throughout continents (Jehne, 2018a). (Rather than guarded – often by vested interests – in dams or pipes, or flowing entirely into oceans.[4])
- Provides the foundation for the numerous hydrological cycles that largely determine the heating and cooling dynamics of our planet, influencing local, regional, and global temperatures, precipitation, methane removal from atmosphere, and weather patterns (Jehne, 2015, 2018a).
- Accumulates and stores carbon, in living, dead, and very dead forms. These labile, stable, and semi-stable pools of carbon provide conditions that allow the remaining carbon to cycle in relatively organized and predictable ways – photosynthesized into, and respired out of, the bodies of living things, and (along with hydrological cycles) creating an atmosphere that is neither too cold nor too warm for our current community of living things (Pershouse, 2016).
- Prevents our farms, forests, and prairies from blowing away, or washing into rivers and oceans, leaving nothing but grand canyons and bare rocks (Pershouse, 2017).

- Provides space for oxygen to reach underground aerobic organisms (Ingham, 2014).
- Increases the available surface area of soil particles, making it easier for plants and their microbial symbionts to access, solubilize, and transport nutrients (Jehne, 2018b).
- Provides an intelligent mycorrhizal interface that finds and sorts those nutrients into appropriate ratios and quantities providing optimum health *for the entire food chain that grows from it* (Jehne, 2018a; Finlay, 2008).

One third of the globe's productive land – the soil sponge – is now severely degraded, and fertile soil is being lost at the rate of 24 billion tonnes a year, according to a 2017 study backed by the United Nations (Watts, 2017).

Dangers of Interfering with Biological Work

When biological work is not allowed to function in a landscape (fields are left bare or paved over; forests are cut; the sponge is broken up and compacted with tillage; pesticides and other chemicals kill off soil biology, insects, etc.), the soil sponge deteriorates and public health is impacted (Pershouse, 2016).

Fewer nutrients are available to plants without microbial workers to break them down and transport them to their roots. Without microbial work, whatever *is* available in the root zone is soaked up by plant roots through simple physics like a straw – with no intelligence, no sorting out of what is toxic or not, no way to know proper amounts, timing, or ratios (Jehne, 2018a). The entire food chain that grows from a degraded soil system becomes a random mishmash of human-added or naturally occurring chemicals sucked up into plants, with no relationship to what those who eat from that food chain (whether insects, cows, or humans) need to thrive or survive. The nutrient density of common foods has decreased dramatically over the past fifty years (Davis, 2009), and toxins in the food chain have accumulated (Indyk and Woollard, 2011): this is a failure of our ability to maintain conditions for a healthy and intelligent soil sponge.

Without a sponge, water evaporates from the hot desertified surface of the soil or pavement throughout the daytime hours and collects around dust, soot, exhaust, and other haze particles. Lacking precipitation nuclei to aggregate the hazes and clouds into actual raindrops, afternoon showers never happen. Instead, the water remains in the air as smog and humid hazes. Humid haze above the land makes it difficult for heat to escape from the land at night, driving temperatures upward, drying out the land even further (Jehne, 2016).

In the Middle East and Asia exceedingly high temperatures with 90 per cent humidity are becoming more common, and are projected to reach conditions in which sweat will no longer evaporate and humans cannot survive without air conditioning (Carrington, 2017). With humid hazes, although there is plenty of water in the air above, the landscape below dries out, creating more dust, which creates even more haze. Air quality deteriorates, increasing respiratory diseases. These diseases include common concerns like asthma, dust pneumonia, and COPD, which is on the rise in countries like China, as well as newly discovered concerns such as the spread of airborne antibiotic resistant bacteria from feedlots in the United States (McEachran et al., 2015).

Without the work of forests and grasslands in the centre of continents like the United States, atmospheric rivers cannot move around high-pressure heat domes, and the "biotic pump" changes its patterns. Megastorms develop in coastal areas, knocking out power and water, while inland areas wait for rain, and crops fail (Makarieva and Gorshkov, 2010).

Without a natural filtration system throughout the land, and with increased use of agricultural inputs to make up for loss of function, water quality deteriorates rapidly as well. For example, the High Plains aquifer (which provides water for eight US states) contains nitrate concentrations up to 189 times greater than the EPA standard, and uranium concentrations up to 89 times greater, because nitrate in water, from agricultural practices, solubilizes uranium and increases its concentration in water supplies as well. The uranium and nitrate levels of the California-based Central Valley aquifer measured up to 180 and 34 times their respective EPA thresholds (Nolan and Weber, 2015).

Land that is under stress from flooding, erosion, mudslides, algal blooms, heat waves, unavailability of safe water supplies, and wildfires causes acute and chronic stress and illness for those who live in the region. It shifts spending away from preventative and routine health care towards externality costs of emergency care in natural disasters, environmental illness, and stress-based illness, and away from growing solid local economies and towards billions of dollars worth of assistance, bailouts, insurance payments, and federal, state, local, and personal funds paying the ongoing costs of infrastructure damages and crop failures (Pershouse, 2016; Dorner, Porter, and Metzka 2008; Kwaad, 2018).

Professor Richard Cruse of Iowa State University's Iowa Water Center estimates that for each pound of corn harvested in Iowa, the farm loses over a pound of topsoil, and for each pound of soybeans, the farm loses more than two pounds of topsoil (Cruse, 2018). At a speech in Rome in 2014, the deputy director of the United Nations FAO estimated that at current soil loss rates, we have fewer than sixty harvests left (Arsenault, n.d.).

Society destabilizes quickly when land and water systems fail (Montgomery, 2012). Syria is a case in point. For thousands of years, it was the fertile crescent, the cradle of Western agriculture, with continuous production. For the last forty years, under the Green Revolution, industrial agricultural practices destroyed the soil sponge, which contributed to conflict and destabilization as farmers walked off previously fertile land in search of food and water (Jehne, 2018a).

For all of the above reasons, our future health, social stability, economies, and survival are utterly dependent on each region's capacity to manage land in ways that regenerate the soil sponge and the biological drivers of weather and climate.

Sterile vs Fertile Paradigms of Care

The industrial farming model – in which we put an animal in a box, away from its natural environment, give it antibiotics and hormones, and then try to determine what nutrients it needs to be maximally productive, or we put a seed into "sterilized" dirt, kill off all the weeds and bugs with chemicals, and try to figure out what artificial fertilizer the seed needs to be maximally productive— is strangely similar to the industrial medical model.

In *The Ecology of Care*, I described both of these models as "sterile" paradigms of care in which the object is to kill off what we don't want and maximize profits. As we have changed our outer landscape with industrial agriculture and changed our inner landscape with industrial medicine, we have created problems that never existed before – many of them intertwined in the ongoing relationships between food and health, and health care and the environment.

Glyphosate (a chemical used as an herbicide on many farms and lawns) is perhaps the darkest point at the centre of these two intersecting circles. Initially patented as an industrial descalant because it binds to minerals, it was then patented as an herbicide. Because of its capacity to bind minerals, if you spray it on a plant, it will shut down the plant's capacity to perform basic life functions that require those minerals by interfering with the shikimate pathway, a physiologic pathway that exists only in plants, bacteria, fungi, and algae. Glyphosate was then patented as a broad-spectrum antibacterial and then as a general biocide due to its capacity to inhibit an organism's ability to biosynthesize vitamins, hormones, and amino acids, but it never went to market under those labels (Abraham, 2010).

Because the shikimate pathway doesn't exist in humans, one might believe that glyphosate couldn't possibly affect human health. Genetically modified crops were developed that could withstand glyphosate so that a farmer could spray it not just on the weeds but all over the crop itself to kill weeds around it. Finally it was approved for use as a dessicant, to dry crops like barley and hops right before harvest (Pershouse, 2016).

The use of glyphosate has skyrocketed since 1996, increasing fifteen-fold worldwide by 2016, making it the most used (human made) agricultural chemical in the history of the world (Main, 2016). During that same period, more or less, scientists began to understand the work of the microbiome: that microbes turn on our brain development, make our brain chemicals, and direct most of the essential physical processes in our bodies, and in the bodies of birds, bees, sheep, wolves, and to a large extent, the land itself ...

What happens when an entire wild and domesticated food chain ingests a broad spectrum antimicrobial that binds essential minerals and prevents the capacity of microbiomes to synthesize vitamins, hormones, and amino acids? We are just starting to find out. Don Huber and Thierry Vrain point out R-values of .96 to .99 when looking at correlations between increases in glyphosate use and increases in autism, obesity, dementia, liver cancers, and many other diseases that are on the rise (Vrain, 2014).

When we change the biology, chemistry, genetics, and even the physics around us, we change the systems that we rely on for health and survival. As we begin to fathom the interconnectedness of life, it makes sense to shift to a "fertile" model of care, in which we re-learn how to participate and collaborate with other species to create inner and outer landscapes that help inhabitants to survive and thrive.

Opportunities to Step Out of the Current Climate Narrative and into One That Will Actually Work

Working with other species to restore the soil sponge also offers us an entirely new framework for addressing climate resilience (adapting our behaviours, social systems and infrastructure so that they can withstand extreme weather and other climate-related events) and climate mitigation (participating in the actual restoration of the climate that our bodies and biosystems are already adapted to).

We can allow conditions that maximize the capture of solar energy and atmospheric CO_2 via photosynthesis and then step back and allow plant/microbial communities to put that beautiful combination of sunlight and carbon to work creating healthy living systems that naturally correct climate extremes. These natural systems have successfully operated for all of human existence until the Anthropocene. Because of the complexity of the ongoing relationships we do have, and will need to have with other species, this approach to climate mitigation and resilience is by nature a creative endeavour that involves collaborating with all of life.

This is a very different story than the frequent climate narrative that leaves people imagining that carbon is a problem, and solar energy is a solution – as if the two parents of life on earth had never spoken, never met, and never danced, had never given birth to us and all other life.

That same climate narrative often tells us that our best ways of escaping crisis are to:

1. **Stop doing things:** drive less, turn off lights, consume less meat.
2. **Buy things (especially technology):** electric cars, new light bulbs, solar panels for our houses.

3. **Fight:** barricade pipelines, hold protests, demand policy changes, argue with climate deniers and meat eaters, etc.
4. **Escape:** find alternate planets or high-tech solutions to bury carbon in the ground.

Many of these approaches may fail because they are fuelling the same passive, addictive, escapist, and competitive behaviours (fight, flight, freeze, appease, and play dead) that have brought us to the brink of collapse. Many climate groups now realize that any widespread shift in our environment will have to have a profound respect for relationships and the complexity of natural systems at their foundation in order to succeed. However, the media coverage, corporate greenwashing, and political narrative have tended to corroborate the above-mentioned reactive stress-based (and stress-inducing) strategies.

These strategies also don't suit our true natures as creative mammals who love to think and do, and who love plants and animals and other people. Living things and relationships are endlessly interesting to humans – even dull eyes fixated on a computer screen will naturally gravitate towards the animal, the tree, or the person in a picture: this is biophilia (Kellert and Wilson, 1993). We yearn to understand, live, and work intimately and collaboratively with other living beings: look how much attention we give to our dogs, our house plants, lawns, and gardens, and our intimate relationships.

One could make a similar comparison with the current health narrative (buy drugs and water purifiers, stop eating fat, etc.) versus the potential of working with other species to create a landscape that naturally provides physical and emotional health and safety to its inhabitants (Pershouse, 2016).

Innovation and Oppression in the Farming Community

Farmers, ranchers, and agronomists around the world are experimenting with managing land in ways that mimic nature to prevent flooding and drought, reduce erosion, improve the health of their animals, crops, and families, improve nutrient density of food, reduce dependence on corporations and their products, clean up rivers, and restore the biodiversity of birds, insects, and other wildlife. In much of the corn, soy, wheat, and beef growing areas of the United States, this movement is called the soil health movement and the regenerative agriculture movement.[5]

The observations in this section are drawn from conversations I have had with individual farmers, ranchers, and agronomists while monitoring land and watershed function on farms and ranches with the Soil Carbon Coalition, and while attending and/or speaking at dozens of agricultural and ranching conferences across North America from 2014 to 2018.

The core principles of soil health (based on observations of natural systems) emerged out of relationships and loosely organized collaborative learning groups going back to 1990 in Burleigh County, North Dakota, that included USDA-Natural Resources Conservation Service agronomist Jay Fuhrer, farmer/rancher Gabe Brown, and others. In an interview with me, Jay Fuhrer described his shift from teaching soil conservation towards teaching soil health as "I got tired of trying to teach people how to conserve a degraded resource."

The NRCS now has a small national Soil Health Team, which publishes a version of the Soil Health Principles to help guide the innovation of these farmers. The principles themselves are often reworded, expanded on, or added to by various speakers, farmers, and writers in the soil health movement,[6] but the official NRCS version of these principles are:

• Minimize disturbance
• Maximize soil cover
• Maximize biodiversity
• Maximize presence of continuous living roots

An often-added principle is:

• Integrate animals in crop production

These principles help guide farmers as they experiment with new practices that promote the regeneration of healthy soil microbial communities to regrow the soil sponge. This principles-based teaching approach is also a radical departure from the Best Management Practices approach that has been used in standard agricultural extension programs.

What drives the initial shift towards regenerative farming for many individual farmers is the collapse of the conventional commodity market. Rising costs of industrial inputs (fertilizer, pesticides, genetically modified seeds, etc.) and equipment make it impossible to make a profit within an increasingly corporate and global commodity market. According to USDA-ERS farm household income data, more than half of all the farms in the United States are losing money.

Farmers (in general) are more likely to commit suicide than any other group, and the stresses of modern farming are extremely high.[7] Environmental laws and policies are often at odds with how farmers are taught to farm, and with what chemical companies tell them will work best. Farmers get caught in the middle. People who work on industrial farms are exposed to many chemicals in their work – sometimes creating severe health issues for them and their families. Many farmers know what they want to be doing to help improve their own health and the health of the land, but they have a hard time finding a way out of the debt, the cultural expectations, what they call the "addiction to chemical farming," the dependence on crop insurance subsidies, and the social pressures from family friends and neighbours to do things the way they have "always been done" (Davis, 2011; Davis and Winslett, 2014[8]).

Being on the verge of bankruptcy leads many to give up farming altogether, and others to take their lives, but some brave souls decide to try something new that they have been reading about in their farm journals. They experiment with using the soil health principles. They stop tilling their land to preserve the structure and function of the soil, and plant mixed-species cover crops to break up compaction, feed underground life, attract beneficial insects, and provide natural nitrogen fixation. They reduce or eliminate their use of biocides, fertilizers, and GM seeds. Some of them use cows or sheep to graze the corn stubble or other plant residue rather than tilling or "burning it down" with glyphosate, atrazine, or other toxic chemicals. Often the land needs a couple of years to adapt to the new management before it starts "humming" with new life, and many farmers lose their nerve and turn back during this period. Those who do stick with it, however, are rewarded in many ways: with increased net profits, reduced pests, and freedom from the "addictions" to chemical inputs and crop insurance subsidies (LaCanne and Lundgren, 2018; Ohlsen, 2016).

Innovative farmers who switch to regenerative practices are frequently targeted within their own communities for being different (some of them call themselves "herd quitters"). In the very small, often failing, rural towns where they live, social norms are seen as crucial to maintaining what is left of the community.

It is worth noting (for those readers who imagine these "herd quitting" innovators as being liberal hippie types) that many or most of the leading innovators in the soil health movement are conservative Christians. (Some are Amish or Mennonite – but more often they are Evangelical.) Not all are Republicans, but many are. Joel Salatin's book *The Marvellous Pigness of Pigs*, and Keith Berns' YouTube talk "Rebuilding Our Soils" from the Southern Soil Health Conference will give the liberal reader an idea of how the conservative Christian voice can speak powerfully for regenerative farming. But the fact that they attend the same churches as their neighbours doesn't necessarily help bridge the gap.

Neighbouring farmers view the new fields bursting with blooms of mixed species cover crops (and buzzing with beneficial insects) as being "messy" and fear that the seeds and insects will come onto their land and invade their monocrop of corn, soy, or wheat. Local crop advisors who often represent chemical companies fear the movement away from chemical inputs will spread, losing them business. And many people think it is just plain weird to let cows into a cornfield.

Even those farmers and ranchers who are paid highly as speakers at soil health conferences and are extremely successful at crop production are often shunned by their closest neighbours (which is ironic, because farmers from *other* regions will drive hundreds of miles to visit these regenerative farms and ranches for field days and workshops). Many people who made the switch to regenerative agriculture have told me that the only days of the year that they feel "normal" is when they attend conferences for regenerative agriculture.

The oppression plays out in various ways:

1. The farmer or rancher walks into the (only) coffee shop and someone says something harsh to them, or everyone literally turns their backs and refuses to speak to them.
2. They are often caught in difficult situations when their parents or siblings or spouses who share the farm don't agree with their choices. There is a lot of pressure to keep doing things the way they have "always been done."
3. Their close friendships become strained. One farmer told me that his best friend was the fertilizer salesperson for the town. When the farmer stopped using fertilizer, his friend was worried that his farm would fail and kept pressuring him to use it. When his farm didn't fail, and the farmer talked to other farmers about his choice to use natural processes rather than chemical fertilizer, his friend the fertilizer salesman was upset, because he felt that the farmer was convincing people to stop using fertilizer and that he would lose his business.
4. When environmental groups write articles about the innovative farmers or give them awards, intending to do something good for the farmer and the environment, it often backfires. The neighbouring conventional farmers feel as if they are being indirectly criticized for doing things the more conventional way, and they respond by saying that the innovative farmer thinks they are "better than everyone else."
5. Professional agronomists and scientists who advise farmers through university extension programs (or teach and develop curriculum for 4H and FFA programs to younger generations) and the USDA-NRCS have had many years of training in conventional farming practices, and will often serve the role of "experts" who unintentionally fuel conflict by corroborating the neighbours' negative views.
6. Crop insurance won't cover farmers who do things in ways that are considered non-standard because it is considered "risky."
7. Without crop insurance, banks often won't give those farmers loans.

For all these reasons and more, regenerative farmers often don't toot their own horns, but simply work hard at trying new things until they quietly figure them out.

Farmers aren't the only ones who get pressured to stick with the doomed-to-fail industrial norm. The big agriculture corporations finance much of the university-based research in agriculture, and help create STEM and agricultural education curricula for all ages (McColl, 2017; Monsanto, 2018).[9] Scientists and agronomists who push back against these corporate influences, or who do research that shows that agricultural chemicals are harmful, can be harassed at work, lose their jobs, and lose access to publishing in peer-reviewed journals, as happened to award-winning USDA scientist Jonathan Lundgren when he refused to be silenced about the effects of pesticides on pollinators. Some of them are having their lives threatened.

The people who are successfully collaborating with other species to regenerate land function are often farmers and ranchers who work quietly under the radar as they do groundbreaking work. The more liberal environmental movement is often unaware of them because they don't fit the profile. Many of them are quite conservative, or quiet, private humble folks just trying to do what they view as restoring God's creation, and they feel at odds with the typical "liberal agenda."

Yet just because their work (like that of microbes) is hidden from the public view, unseen, and unappreciated, doesn't mean it isn't significant, and doesn't mean that they are working alone. A key element in the success of regenerative farmers and ranchers, and the scientists who support their work, appears to be the support groups, gatherings, online discussion groups, and mentorship networks they are forming with each other, sometimes across many miles.[10]

Case in point, a group of about seven farming families practicing Holistic Decision Making in the prairies of Saskatchewan, and all of whose farms are gaining carbon (restoring their soil carbon sponge) at a rate far faster than other farms who were remonitored during the Soil Carbon Coalition's challenge. These families have been meeting together in a monthly support group for over fifteen years to study together, experiment, support each other during marital stresses and other crises, and learn from each other's successes and failures. In the process they have learned to manage land holistically in a way that supports soil and watershed health, microbial work, photosynthesis, public health and biological diversity while also reaching their personal and economic goals.

Ralph and Lynda Corcoran are managing one of those farms in such a way that it is gaining over thirteen tons of soil carbon (via photosynthesis and microbial work) per hectare each year. Over a square mile, that would translate to their land taking in the equivalent of the annual CO_2 emissions of 800 Canadian citizens every year, and turning it into a soil sponge that supports a biologically diverse landscape of plants and animals, soaks in the rain, and filters water, while providing high-quality, nutrient-dense food for their community.

In 2014 there were huge problems with flooding in Saskatchewan – farmers lost their crops as seeds rotted in the muddy ground, and lost a lot of soil downriver too – but the Corcorans and the other farmers in their support group had no trouble with flooding, erosion, or runoff of agricultural chemicals into the rivers. The healthy carbon-rich soil sponge on their farms soaked up the water and filtered it cleanly and safely down into the in-soil reservoir, saving it for later use.

This is one of many examples I have witnessed of the power of collaborative work between people and other species, in the context of mutual support within a community of practice.

Where Do Humans Fit into the Whole?

Unlike other biological work, most human work for the past few hundred years is strangely hard to categorize when we look at the natural functioning of the whole. Not only are we not helping much, but our failure to recognize the importance of the work of other species in our bodies and landscapes may well be behind nearly all of the symptoms our world is currently facing. This is not unlike the situation of the factory owner who prides himself on his production, until the workers go on strike and he realizes he doesn't actually make anything at all.

Our relationship to and purpose within the whole is no longer clear to us (or, as a friend put it: "We are no longer lion food, so what are we?") One can make a case that we have been acting as oppressors and that we need to shift our roles to something more collaborative if we want the biosphere, and our own bodies, to survive.

The concept that we rely almost entirely on the quiet work of other species for the health, productivity, and functionality of our inner and outer landscapes presents us with some fascinating challenges. Who, if anyone, is in charge? Can we trust in the wisdom of other species to do the right thing? Should we try to manage these workers? How do we (or they) create working conditions in which they can do their jobs? And how do we teach, learn, and make decisions as humans within the complexity of local contexts and community dynamics?

These questions are similar to the questions facing other groups who are trying to shift from acting as oppressors to acting as allies. What is appropriate aid? What are appropriate reparations? Can a community that has been partially destroyed recreate itself without outside help? Can you be an ally without creating dependencies? What are the conditions that allow systems to be self-organizing?

Human lives are deeply interwoven with the lives and work of other species. Anthropocentrism has damaged other species, but it is time to admit that it has also damaged humans: because it has hurt our relationships with, and separated us from all of our symbionts – including, it turns out, each other. It is very possible that by stepping out of the anthropocentric paradigm and into collaborative work with other species, our relationships and lives will not only be healthier, but also fuller and more interesting.

NOTES

1 The increasing use of the term "ecosystem services" is a step in the right direction, but it's often still framed as a somewhat vaguely defined system that can be tapped, tracked, or valued for the benefit of carbon markets and other human economies. Therefore I prefer the term "biological work."

2 Weeds are sometimes called "first responders" in the regenerative paradigm for their capacity to photosynthesize in terrible conditions, and begin restoring the

function of a highly degraded landscape, breaking up compaction, protecting bare soils from further drying out, and pumping sugars down to feed and revive the remnant microbial communities.

3   This offers a tantalizing new branch of medicine just waiting to emerge...which the Chinese have been onto for years, with their practice of using tongue diagnosis, a snapshot of a microbial landscape, to determine dosages of ingredients in herbal formulas.

4   Hydrologist Michal Kravčík and colleagues estimate that most of current ocean rise is due to water running off of impermeable surfaces – including compacted soils (Kravčík et al., 2007).

5   Holistic decision-making, agroecology, carbon farming, and permaculture are some of the other terms that are used to describe variations on this, though the latter two terms in particular are generally used by a more liberal coastal crowd in the United States.

6   See expansions on these principles at https://www.didipershouse.com/ soil-health-principles.html and http://soilcarboncoalition.org/learn.

7   When national milk prices dropped to $16 per gallon, less than the cost of producing milk in Vermont, the Agri-mark milk co-op set up a suicide hotline for farmers (Wolfe, 2018).

8   I highly recommend the brilliant (and spartanly edited – in a way that will challenge the classism of many academics) writing of rancher and regenerative farming guru Walt Davis. He gives a clear view of the true challenges of farming and ranching and how complex natural systems are destroyed by industrial ones.

9   For example, Next Generation Science Standards in the United States now include lessons in genetic engineering for all high school students, and Monsanto STEM Engagement Leaders provide workshops for agricultural educators looking at the "benefits and challenges" of GMOs at the National Ag in the Classroom Conference.

10 See, for example, the North Dakota Grazinglands Coalition free mentorship network (https://www.ndglc.com/mentor-network.html), the numerous Facebook discussion groups that have formed around Soil Health and Regenerative Agriculture, as well as YouTube videos, conferences, and other gatherings.

REFERENCES

Abraham, W. (2010, August 10). Glyphosate formulations and their use for the inhibition of 5-enolpyruvylshikimate-3-phosphate synthase. United States patent no. US7771736B2. Retrieved from: https://patents.google.com/patent/US7771736B2/en

Arsenault, C. (n.d). Only 60 years of farming left if soil degradation continues. *Scientific American*. Retrieved from https://www.scientificamerican.com/article /only-60-years-of-farming-left-if-soil-degradation-continues

Carrington, D. (2017, August 2). Climate change to cause humid heatwaves that will kill even healthy people. *The Guardian*. Retrieved from https://www.theguardian .com/environment/2017/aug/02/climate-change-to-cause-humid-heatwaves-that -will-kill-even-healthy-people.

Clayton, T. A., Lindon, J. C., Cloarec, O., Antti, H., Charuel, C., Hanton, G., Provost, J.-P. et al. (2006). Pharmaco-metabonomic phenotyping and personalized drug treatment. *Nature, 440*(7087) 1073–7. https://doi.org/10.1038 /nature04648

Cruse, R. Soil Loss. Email, May 19, 2018.

Davis, D. R. (2009). Declining fruit and vegetable nutrient composition: What is the evidence? *Horticultural Science, 44*(1), 15–19. https://doi.org/10.21273 /HORTSCI.44.1.15

Davis, W. (2011). *How to not go broke ranching*. Scotts Valley, CA: CreateSpace.

Davis, W., & Winslett, T. (2014). *The green revolution delusion: The false promise of industrial agriculture*. Scotts Valley, CA: CreateSpace.

Dethlefsen, L., Mcfall-Ngai, M., & Relman, D. A. (2007). An ecological and evolutionary perspective on human-microbe mutualism and disease. *Nature, 449*(7164), 811–18. https://doi.org/10.1038/nature06245.

Dorner, W., Porter, M., & Metzka, R. (2008). Proceedings from Interpraevent 2008: Economic assessment of natural flood detention measures – Scientific approaches to identify flood related land use externalities. Dornbirn, Vorarlberg, Austria: International Research Society INTERPRAEVENT.

Finlay, R. D. (2008). Ecological aspects of mycorrhizal symbiosis: With special emphasis on the functional diversity of interactions involving the extraradical mycelium. *Journal of Experimental Botany, 59*(5), 1115–26. https://doi.org/10.1093/jxb/ern059

Haggblom, M. M. (1992). Microbial breakdown of halogenated aromatic pesticides and related compounds. *FEMS Microbiology Letters, 103*(1) 29–72. https://doi .org/10.1111/j.1574-6968.1992.tb05823.x

Heijtz, R. D., Wang, S., Anuar, F., Qian, Y., Bjorkholm, B., Samuelsson, A., Hibberd, M. L., Forssberg, H., & Pettersson, S. (2011). Normal gut microbiota modulates brain development and behavior. *Proceedings of the National Academy of Sciences, 108*(7), 3047–52. https://doi.org/10.1073/pnas.1010529108

Hooper, L. V. (2001). Commensal host-bacterial relationships in the gut. *Science, 292*(5519), 1115–18. https://doi.org/10.1126/science.1058709

Indyk, H. E., & Woollard, D. C. (2011). Contaminants of milk and dairy products | Nitrates and nitrites as contaminants. *Encyclopedia of Dairy Sciences, 1*(2), 906–11. https://doi.org/10.1016/b978-0-12-374407-4.00106-0

Ingham, E. (2014). Proceedings from Northeast Organic Farming Association Summer Conference: Soil carbon workshops and keynote lecture. Amherst, MA: NOFA.

Jehne, W. (2015). Restoring water cycles to naturally cool climates and reverse global warming. Global Cooling Earth. Retrieved from http://www.globalcoolingearth.org /cooling/.

Jehne, W. (2016). Restoring water cycles to naturally cool climates and reverse global warming [video file]. Retrieved from https://www.youtube.com /watch?v=K4ygsdHJjdI

Jehne, W. (2018a). Proceedings from the 2018 Soil Sponge Seminar. Fairlee, Vermont.

Jehne, W. (2018b). The soil carbon sponge, climate solutions and healthy water cycles [video file]. Retrieved from https://www.youtube.com/watch?v=123y7jDdbfY

Kai-Larsen, Y., Gudmundsson, G. H., & Agerberth, B. (2014). A review of the innate immune defence of the human foetus and newborn, with the emphasis on antimicrobial peptides. *Acta Paediatrica, 103*(10), 1000–8. https://doi.org/10.1111/apa.12700.

Kellert, S. R., & Wilson, E. O. (1993). *The biophilia hypothesis.* Washington, DC: Island Press.

Kinross, J. M., Alkhamesi, N., Barton, R. H., Silk, D. B., Yap, I. K. S., Darzi, A. W., Holmes, E., & Nicholson, J. K. (2011a). Global metabolic phenotyping in an experimental laparotomy model of surgical trauma. *Journal of Proteome Research, 10*(1), 277–87. https://doi.org/10.1021/pr1003278.s

Kinross, J. M., Darzi, A. W., & Nicholson, J. K. (2011b). Gut microbiome-host interactions in health and disease. *Genome Medicine, 3*(3). https://doi.org/10.1186/gm228

Kravčík M., Pokorný, J., Kohutiar, J., Kováč, M., Tóth, E. (2007). *Water for the recovery of the climate: A new water paradigm.* Žilina, Slovakia: Krupa Print.

Kwaad, F. J. P. M. (2018). Economic costs of soil erosion. Retrieved from http://www .kwaad.net/EconomicCostsOfSoilErosion.html

LaCanne, C. E., & Lundgren, J. G. (2018). Regenerative agriculture: Merging farming and natural resource conservation profitably. *PeerJ.* https://doi.org/10.7717/peerj.4428

Lozupone, C. A. (2018). Unraveling interactions between the microbiome and the host immune system to decipher mechanisms of disease. *MSystems, 3*(2). https://doi .org/10.1128/msystems.00183-17.

Main, D. (2016, May 19). Glyphosate now the most-used agricultural chemical ever. *Newsweek.* Retrieved from http://www.newsweek.com/glyphosate-now-most -used-agricultural-chemical-ever-422419

Makarieva, A. M., & Gorshkov, V. G. (2010). The biotic pump: Condensation, atmospheric dynamics and climate. *International Journal of Water, 5*(4), 365–85. https://doi.org/10.1504/ijw.2010.038729

McColl, S. (2017, July 25). 4-H: Indoctrination nation. *Modern Farmer.* Retrieved from https://modernfarmer.com/2017/07/4-h-indoctrination-nation/

Mceachran, A. D., Blackwell, B. R., Hanson, J. D., Wooten, K. J., Mayer, G. D., Cox, S. B., & Smith, P. N. (2015). Antibiotics, bacteria, and antibiotic resistance genes: Aerial transport from cattle feed yards via particulate matter. *Environmental Health Perspectives, 123*(4). https://doi.org/10.1289/ehp.1408555.

Monsanto. (2018). Connecting curious minds to modern agriculture. Retrieved from https://monsanto.com/app/uploads/2018/02/NSTA_Backpack-Update_FINAL.pdf

Montgomery, D. R. (2012). *Dirt: The erosion of civilizations.* Berkeley, CA: University of California Press.

Nicholson, J. K., Holmes, E., & Wilson, I. D. (2005). Gut microorganisms, mammalian metabolism and personalized health care. *Nature Reviews Microbiology, 3*(5), 431–8. https://doi.org/10.1038/nrmicro1152

Nolan, J., & Weber, K. A. (2015). Natural uranium contamination in major U.S. aquifers linked to nitrate. *Environmental Science & Technology Letters, 2*(8), 215–20. https://doi.org/10.1021/acs.estlett.5b00174

Ohlson, K. (2016, December 5). This Kansas farmer fought a government program to keep his farm sustainable. *Ensia.* Retrieved from https://ensia.com/features /sustainable-farm-crop-insurance/

Pershouse, D. (2016). *The ecology of care: Medicine, agriculture, money, and the quiet power of human and microbial communities.* Thetford Center, VT: Mycelium Books.

Pershouse, D. (2017). Understanding soil health and watershed function: A teacher's manual. Retrieved from http://soilcarboncoalition.org/learn

Quinn, E. A. (2014, December 14). Biomarkers & milk. Retrieved from http:// biomarkersandmilk.blogspot.com/2014/12/human-milk-has-microbiome-and -bacteria.html.

Vrain, T. (2014, March 8). Engineered foods and your health: The nutritional status of GMOs [video file]. Retrieved from https://www.youtube.com/watch?v=yiU3Ndi6itk

Watts, J. (2017, September 12). Third of Earth's soil is acutely degraded due to agriculture. *The Guardian.* Retrieved from https://www.theguardian.com /environment/2017/sep/12/third-of-earths-soil-acutely-degraded-due-to-agriculture -study#img-1

Wolfe, R. (2018, February 7). Dairy co-op sends farmers suicide hotline numbers after milk prices plummet. *Valley News.* Retrieved from http://www.vnews.com/Dairy -co-op-Agri-Mark-sends-farmers-suicide-prevention-hotline-numbers-as-milk -prices-drop-15398364

14 Making Medicine Work in the Anthropocene: Tenets of a Meta-medicine for Complex Adaptive Systems in Precarious Times

KATHARINE ZYWERT AND WILLIAM SUTHERLAND

Introduction

Ill health is a pressing truth of our times. Around the world people from all walks of life experience illness as a result of behavioural choices, genetic predispositions, social vulnerabilities, environmental exposure and degradation, or the synergistic interactions between these etiological pathways. In modern societies, gains in health and well-being are fundamentally paradoxical. Lack of access to medical care is a central cause of morbidity and mortality, particularly in low- and middle-income countries (WHO, 2015), while iatrogenic illnesses (the adverse health effects of medical treatments) are also on the rise, causing close to 142,000 deaths worldwide in 2013 (GBD, 2013). On the whole we are living longer but not necessarily better, with our aging populations increasingly afflicted by dementia and other noncommunicable diseases (NCDs) (WHO, 2015). Increasingly it appears that in low-income areas people are ill because of what they lack, while in high-income areas, they are ill from overabundance (Aillon, this volume).

At a global scale, the gains in life expectancy and health outcomes we have experienced since the industrial revolution have been won at the expense of the planet's biophysical systems, which have been altered, depleted, and polluted by the sheer scale of human economic activity (McMichael, 2014; Whitmee et al., 2015). Climate change is now one of the most significant long-term threats to human health (McMichael, 2014). Rising temperatures speed up the life cycles of mosquitoes and zoonotic carriers of disease, enable the rapid growth of allergenic plants, and suppress the human immune system (Singer, 2009). Climate change is associated with widespread mental health issues including psychological trauma due to environmental disasters, high levels of anxiety and fear at the prospect of impending ecological catastrophe, and solastalgia, mental distress caused by the loss of natural landscapes (Doherty and Clayton, 2011). Perhaps most troubling, climate change poses substantial risks to global food security, with environmental changes threatening not only the quantity of food produced and its accessibility within food systems, but also the nutritional content of the food itself (Whitmee et al., 2015).

In places experiencing war and social unrest, we can observe the fragility of our health systems and the extent to which our control over disease is contingent on socioeconomic stability. In conflict zones like Syria, hospitals and health workers have become targets for destruction. Doctors work in blown-out buildings without electricity, holding up their cell phones to light emergency surgeries (Fouad et al., 2017). An outbreak of cholera in Yemen has seen close to 74,000 reported cases since April 2017, an unmanageable crisis in a country where more than half of its hospitals are non-operational or functioning with severely limited supplies (Zwizwai, 2017). In 2017, it was estimate that estimated that 30,000 health workers in Yemen had been serving their communities without receiving pay for eight months, selling any remaining personal valuables to feed themselves and their families (Shankar Balakrishnan, 2017).

On a global scale, our defences against disease are weak and are becoming more precarious. The trajectory of the AIDS epidemic since the 1980s or the more recent spread of the Ebola virus across international borders (see Honigsbaum, 2017) demonstrate that geopolitical boundaries cannot save us from the spread of infectious disease. On the contrary, our tightly interconnected globalized society creates conditions that favour the movement of pathogens through increasingly concentrated urban populations (Homer-Dixon, 2006). Moreover, environmental toxins, which disproportionately affect vulnerable populations, including people living in poverty, the undernourished, the elderly, and unborn children, know no borders, drifting in the air and through our water systems, concentrated in our food chains and appearing in our breast milk (Whitmee et al., 2015).

Modern medicine is ill-equipped to respond to these myriad challenges, many of which represent the health effects of our transition into the Anthropocene (McMichael, 2014; Whitmee et al., 2015; Butler, 2016). It remains to be seen whether humanity as a species can adapt to existence in the Anthropocene world we have created (Lovelock, 2014). The health effects of social-ecological precariousness are both profound and wide-ranging, spanning the globe while at the same time reaching in to affect our bodies, our genes, and our minds. In the Anthropocene, the causes of ill health and the challenges that face health systems around the world are not confined to any one scale (McMichael, 2014). "Health" cannot be achieved only by ensuring that interventions for individual patients are adequate and appropriate, by redressing structural problems related to access and affordability of care, or by improving environmental integrity alone. Health is determined at the intersection of personal circumstances, sociocultural forces, and environmental conditions. Perceiving any one of these scales to be independent or insignificant is not only unhelpful, it has become increasingly dangerous to us all as inhabitants of a planet in crisis.

This paper applies insights from the study of complex adaptive systems to develop tenets of a meta-medicine that operates across scales to respond to ill health in our bodies, our cultures, and our environments. We say "meta-medicine" to explicitly recognize that although medical science is often best suited to curing or treating the diseases that afflict individual human bodies, other domains of action ranging from public health measures to city planning, economic policy, agriculture, housing, and education also determine population-level health outcomes. Culture, with its assemblages of belief systems, embodiments, and ways of creating collective meaning, also defines human-environment interactions, patterns of social relations, and behaviours that either promote or contravene health. These domains outside of formal medical systems have wide-ranging implications for the health of complex adaptive systems including individual human beings, societies, and ecosystems. As a result, these approaches must be encompassed within the medicines we use in precarious times.

Understanding Health within Complex Adaptive Systems

Across cultures and historical periods, people define health in ways that reflect their contextual understandings of well-being and the nature of prevalent risks to wellness (Baer, Singer, and Susser, 2013). When we speak about health from the perspective of complex adaptive systems, we are not simply referring to the absence of disease within an individual organism. Rather, we propose that a robust conceptualization of health in the Anthropocene should aim to be inclusive of the various conditions that promote or threaten resilience within complex adaptive systems.

Living systems across scales (from a cell to an organ, organism, community, and ecosystem) are complex adaptive systems (CAS) (Paina and Peters, 2012). CAS are made up of multiple distinct parts that are connected to one another in diverse and interactive relationships. The parts of a CAS are not inert like billiard balls that behave in linear and predictable ways. Instead, the parts themselves have agency and the interactions between them create emergent properties that are more than the sum of the parts. Human consciousness, for example, is an emergent property of human biology. It could not exist apart from the diverse relationships between neurons and other physical components of the brain, and yet it cannot be recreated simply by assembling these mechanical components. Another defining property of CAS is self-organization: the ability of a system to generate new layers of complexity (novel structures, behaviours, feedback loops) in response to changing conditions (Meadows, 2008; Rickles, Hawe, and Shiell, 2007). The principle of self-organization means that systemic behaviours are determined simultaneously by processes of bottom-up and top-down causation. The parts create the whole by making certain kinds of emergence possible, but in the same moment, the top as a systemic whole puts limits and boundaries on what the parts are able to do (Meadows, 2008).

Within CAS, health is a reflection of the richness and diversity of integrative and interactive relationships. Just as a human body relies on the interactions between a variety of cells that carry oxygen in the blood, mount immune responses, and metabolize nutrients, ecosystems rely on diverse relationships between predator and prey species, temperature, and levels of rainfall to maintain the characteristic properties of a particular ecology. Eliminating components (e.g. clear-cutting a patch of forest, extinction of a top predator, obliteration of good bacteria in the gut) or altering relationships between key variables within the system (e.g. preventing forest fires from periodically sweeping through a forest or failing to block the spread of cancer cells through a human body) can reduce the resilience of the system as a whole. Maintaining complexity is essential to the health of any CAS. This involves not only cultivating diversity in the components of the CAS, but also sustaining coherent, rich, and diverse relationships between significant components (Gell-Mann, 1994 and Holland, 1995 as cited in Levin, 1998). From a systemic perspective, health therefore resides in the relationships that promote resiliency, necessary redundancy, and robustness within a complex system (see Walker and Salt, 2006).

Acting across Scales

Cultivating complexity for health in the Anthropocene is also about acting across scales. We propose that a meta-medicine capable of responding to the health challenges that characterize the age of human impact must consider the interactions between three nested systems: the individual, the culture, and the ecology. Each of these levels has a significant degree of influence over the health of the CAS that make it possible for human life to flourish on this planet. Although the three "domains of health" are constantly interacting and are never functionally separate, it can be useful to perceive them as conceptually bounded systems in order to create a hierarchy of abstraction that can help us devise cross-cutting strategies for action.

As domains of health, the individual, the culture, and the ecology are nested within one another. They exist within a hierarchy that turns in on itself like a triple ouroboros. An individual organism is part of an ecosystem but is also itself a unique ecology of bacteria and other microorganisms (Foster et al., 2017). This internal ecology is vulnerable to the same systemic risks that face external ecosystems, including the destabilizing forces of invasive species and mass-extinction events. Recent research into the microbiome of hunter-gatherers illustrates the interplay between the three domains of health. The Hadza of the East African Rift Valley possess extremely diverse gut bacteria that act as a protective force against the specific environmental pressures encountered by the nomadic foragers in their immediate environment, pressures that include endemic diseases, parasites, and food shortages (Schnorr, 2015). In contrast, the microbiomes of people in urban industrialized areas are much less diverse. Cultural factors such as frequent exposure to antibiotics, availability of processed foods, and oversanitized living spaces have eroded microbial diversity, reducing the resilience and adaptability of the internal ecosystem. As a result, the microbiomes of industrialized populations are measurably less effective at digesting foods and combating disease than those of hunter-gatherers (Schnorr, 2015).

The treatments offered by modern medicine rarely address this reflexivity between the individual, the culture, and their environment. Instead, exploring the kinds of health practices that work at the intersection of the three domains of health often means venturing outside of formal health care systems. The care farming movement is a potent example of an approach that acts across the three domains of health. The practice involves engaging people experiencing mental health issues and social vulnerabilities (ranging from drug and alcohol addiction to learning disabilities, burnout, dementia, and long-term unemployment) in meaningful agricultural work (Elings, this volume). The tasks people perform on the farm are diverse and involve caring for plants and animals in a supportive social environment. At an individual level, participants experience a reduction in stress and improved physical health while building supportive social relationships. Culturally, care farming reestablishes linkages between urban and rural life while reinvigorating small farms that have been marginalized by industrial agriculture. At the ecosystem scale, the agricultural work itself is often directed towards ecological conservation and the preservation of rural landscapes (Hassink and van Dijk, 2006). Care farming does not require a lot of specialized equipment or extensive medical training, but instead makes use of existing infrastructure and local agricultural knowledge. The result is a successful way to address mental health issues from within communities by engaging with plants, animals, landscapes, and other people. The health benefits to individuals are not limited to this scale, but feed back into the culture and the ecology, generating multiple health benefits across scales.

Attending to History

The current state of an individual, a culture, or an ecosystem is also shaped by its history. In all living systems, the past informs the next possible. This is because small differences in starting conditions can lead to immense differences in the behaviour of the system over time, a principle of complex systems known as sensitive dependence on initial conditions or path dependence (Rickles, Hawe, and Shiell, 2007; Paina and Peters, 2012). At the individual level, history is the organism's ontogeny, its developmental pathway from the beginning of its life up to the present. An individual's ontogeny is shaped by factors such as nurturing during childhood, the presence or absence of environmental toxins, and behavioural patterns including level of exercise, cultivation of an artistic skill, or mastery of a trade. At the cultural level, history is the sum total of the events, experiences, material culture, and beliefs of a group of people through time as reflected in the system's current organization. Cultural histories are shaped by interactions of domination and oppression between groups, by language, by traditions of art, religion, and science, by migrations to new places, and by exposure to new ideas or ways of being. For ecosystems, the relevant historical scale is evolution, the trajectory of species-level adaptation to and interaction with the environment that has led to the current ecological mix. Histories at each of these scales are also intertwined. Cultural history shapes ontogeny through child rearing and body modification practices, diet, and social norms. Ontogeny in turn is a reflection of the evolutionary lineage within the individual, so that a developing infant first resembles a single-celled organism, then takes on the characteristics of an anatomically modern human as it grows.

If medicine is to effectively address health issues that intersect the levels of culture, ecology, and the individual, it must align its actions across each of these scales while at the same time respecting the historical trajectories that brought us to the present moment. It could be argued, for example, that many chronic diseases arise as a result of cultural departures from the evolutionary dictates of the human species (Price, 1945; Knobbe and Stojanoska, 2017). Chronic diseases like diabetes, heart disease, and cancers have been classified as "diseases of modernity" (Hidaka, 2012, p. 206). These modern diseases become more prevalent as our lifestyles depart further from the hunting and gathering patterns in which our species evolved. Highly sedentary daily routines combined with unhealthy diets that are low in essential micronutrients are primary culprits, as are less sleep, more social competition, and greater inequality and social isolation (Hidaka, 2012).

Modern medicine has been remarkably effective at improving population-level health. In the past sixty years the average global lifespan increased by over twenty years and under-five mortality fell dramatically (You et al., 2014 and Population Division of the Department of Economic and Social Affairs of the UN Secretariat, 2013 as cited in Whitmee et al., 2015). Despite these gains, the burden of chronic disease has grown steadily (Armelagos, Brown, and Turner, 2005), rates of depression and anxiety issues are rising (Hidaka, 2012), and diseases like dementia and Alzheimer's are afflicting aging populations around the world (WHO, 2015). These conditions arise not only because we are overstressing our physical bodies, but because the transition to modernity has moved us away from our evolutionary predispositions towards close social bonds, their cultural correlates, and adaptation to a particular ecology.

The modern diet is one of our most significant departures from the evolutionary dictates of the human species. Although human culture has evolved dramatically over the past 10,000 years since we began to settle in sedentary agricultural communities, the human genome evolves much more slowly and has not kept pace with changes in social arrangements and technologies. As a result, nutritional researchers have highlighted the discrepancy between the dietary patterns that contributed to shaping the human genome and those of modern, industrialized nations, and have proposed that returning to an ancestral human diet can be used to both prevent and treat chronic disease (O'Keefe and Cordain, 2004). Although the exact diets of hunter-gatherers differed substantially by ecological niche, hunter-gatherer diets were more similar to one another than to the diets of industrialized populations today (Eaton, 2006). Hunter-gatherers consumed diverse, locally available unprocessed foods foraged from their surrounding environments. While the specific foods varied by region and season, hunting and gathering invariably yields a diet that is high in fibre, micronutrients, lean protein, and antioxidants and low in saturated fat, sodium, and refined sugar and grains (O'Keefe and Cordain, 2004). Returning to a hunter-gatherer subsistence strategy is not feasible (or likely desirable) for contemporary urban populations. However, adopting the general principles of an ancestral human diet can reduce our susceptibility to chronic, diet-related diseases like cardiovascular disease, obesity, and diabetes (O'Keefe and Cordain, 2004; Eaton, 2006).

There is also evidence that intermittent fasting such as alternating one day of "feasting" with one day of "fasting" or limiting calorie intake during certain parts of the day can reduce risks for chronic metabolic diseases, neurodegenerative diseases, and cancers (Varady and Hellerstein, 2007; Choi et al., 2013; Rothschild, 2014). Fasting and feeding cycles were historically commonplace for all human populations that depended on local plant foods and wild game. The human metabolism evolved within a context of feeding, a time for building up muscles and tissues, and fasting, a time for breaking down, cleaning, and repairing. As studies of hunter-gatherer microbiomes demonstrate, the inner workings of our biology are not separate from the outer state of the surrounding ecology (Schnorr, 2015). Metabolism is an ecological process. As a result, dietary approaches to disease prevention and treatment offer ways to realign our individual biology (nutrition) and cultural practices (foodways) to evolutionary precedents. The influence of ecological evolution is embedded in our bodies (see Braakman and Smith, 2013). Humans share a substantial number of our metabolic pathways with bacteria (see Romero et al., 2004). As a result, our attempts to improve the health of CAS across scales cannot only take into account the present state of each of these systems, but must incorporate attention to their histories.

Creating Medicines That Are Contextually Whole

The examples above begin to illustrate what it looks like when healing affects the three domains of health simultaneously. We refer to medicines that act across scales as "contextually whole" medicines. By incorporating attention to individuals, the cultures in which they live, and the ecologies that encompass all human activity within a wider web of life, contextually whole medicines enhance the resilience of all three domains. As described in previous sections, they do so by actively building diversity, not only of components within each system, but of the types of relationships that bind components into complex networks capable of adapting to the shocks and disturbances that inevitably arise in CAS (see Levin, 1998; Walker and Salt, 2006).

Within the current medical paradigm, contextually whole approaches to healing are rare. Instead, interventions focused on the individual dominate the landscape of medicine (Harrison, 2004; Beck and Beck-Gernsheim, 2002; Foucault, 1994). Modern medicine (also called biomedicine) developed with our growing scientific knowledge of anatomy, sanitation, and disease transmission. In the nineteenth and twentieth centuries biomedicine became a central feature of modernization processes around the world and now provides the foundation for medical thinking and practice at a global scale (Harrison, 2004; Baer, Singer, and Susser, 2013). Closely tied to a mechanistic worldview and the rise of individualization in modern societies, the strengths of biomedicine lie in the development of interventions for individual bodies, and researchers and medical doctors have developed an impressive array of pharmaceutical and surgical innovations to treat disease. However, within modern health systems the myopic focus on curing individuals has created problems at higher scales (Zywert and Quilley, 2017; Quilley, this volume). The discovery of antibiotics revolutionized the treatment of infectious bacterial diseases and made it possible for patients to heal from major surgeries without the risk of dying from infection (Harrison, 2004). Over time, however, it has become clear that overuse and misuse of antibiotics breeds antibiotic-resistant pathogens that could undermine modern medicine's defining capabilities (Armelagos, Brown, and Turner, 2005; Søgaard Jørgensen et al., 2017). Through cultural misuse of antibiotics and by neglecting the evolutionary potentiality within bacteria to adapt to antibiotics, an intervention that works well at the level of the individual has created more virulent infectious diseases that threaten population health.

Critiques of modern medicine have targeted biomedicine's reductionism, proposing alternative "holistic" approaches that include integrative and functional medicines, selective appropriations of cultural medicines (Tibetan, Chinese medicine), and complementary or alternative medicines (Reiki, naturopathy, massage). The growth of holistic medicines illustrates the broad appeal of an approach to health that encompasses more than targeting individual pathology with the active ingredients of pharmaceutical treatments or the precision of a surgeon's knife. However, these medicines, while striving towards holism, are not necessarily contextually whole according to our understanding. Contextually whole medicines are not merely syncretic, pulling pieces from different traditions and assembling them into a (more or less) coherent approach. Instead, contextually whole medicines must be grounded in the unique developmental histories of individuals, their cultures, and the ecologies in which they coexist with other species.

Consider the Mediterranean diet. Beginning in the 1960s, health practitioners noticed that people in Mediterranean countries like Greece and Italy experienced comparatively low rates of NCDs like cardiovascular disease and cancer, and tended to live long, healthy lives (see Keys and Keys, 1975). In the attempt to replicate these results elsewhere, the central components of the Mediterranean diet were identified as low saturated fat intake, moderate consumption of wine, and a high proportion of complex carbohydrates and fibre through local grains, fruits, and vegetables (Ferro-Luzzi and Branca, 1997 as cited in Arnoni and Berry, 2015). Since then, studies of the Mediterranean diet have succumbed to biomedical reductionism, with researchers holding up one or another element of the diet (monounsaturated fatty acids, antioxidants, polyphenols) as the key to Mediterranean populations' longevity and good health. Yet while these micronutrients are important for individual health, the Mediterranean diet is about more than antioxidants or olive oil. It is a place-based, contextually whole way of living. The people who participated in the original research conducted on the Mediterranean diet in Crete and Southern Italy (see Keys and Keys, 1975) were born at the turn of the century. They were from largely agricultural regions, lived in the same place for most of their lives, and were immersed in local cultural traditions. The Mediterranean diet was a diet of farmers who got up with the light of day, picked their own food, made their own wine, and ate together at every meal. The daily lives of these farmers proceeded within the context of close extended family relationships, a stable and comfortable climate, gentle exercise through walking, and adequate levels of sleep (Trichopoulou and Lagiou, 1997 and Bach-Faig et al., 2011 as cited in Arnoni and Berry, 2015). The diet is an entire cultural experience in which food is enmeshed within patterns of social relationships that are in turn tied to ecosystem characteristics. Pursued within this broader context of health, the Mediterranean diet is a contextually whole medicine shaped by biological, cultural, and ecological history.

Although we insist that contextually whole medicines are best suited to addressing the health challenges facing CAS in the Anthropocene, it would be unrealistic and dangerous to imply that medicine does not sometimes need to respond to one scale more immediately than the others. For example, if someone is shot, emergency medicine may be the only approach that can save the person's life. The healing intervention that will take place in the case of a gunshot wound is appropriately aimed at the individual's body, even though in that moment their body may be an individual-level manifestation of a cultural pathology (e.g. if the person was shot in a war or during an altercation with the police, their wound likely has deep roots in a cultural history of intergroup hostility and inequality). In this case and many like it, the intervention at the individual scale takes priority, though actions at the level of the culture (e.g. establishing sociopolitical stability, redressing inequality) and ecology (e.g. addressing resource scarcity as a cause of conflict or climate change mitigation in a context where heat waves lead to a rise in violent crimes) could help to prevent someone else from being shot in the future. Similarly, no one should die of pneumonia when we have antibiotics that can cure the disease. When someone arrives in hospital presenting with pneumonia, doctors administer antibiotics in spite of the risks associated with microbial resistance at the ecological scale. In that moment, the individual intervention takes precedence. This is acceptable so long as healing is simultaneously occurring at the cultural level (e.g. reducing unnecessary prescriptions and enabling compliance with courses of treatment) and at the ecological scale (e.g. limiting the use of antibiotics in agricultural industries). From the perspective of a contextually whole medicine, an intervention aimed at a singular level should always be of last resort. Interventions targeting a single scale should also be limited to places where perturbations to the system can be assimilated, so as to avoid creating levels of stress that push the system across a threshold beyond which it is no longer resilient (see Walker and Salt, 2006).

Knowing When to Align and When to Intervene

In any medicine, we suggest that there are two overarching approaches for sustaining or restoring health: alignment and intervention. Alignment is a process of submitting to the rhythms and patterns that exist within a system and seeking to re-establish rich relationships between elements in a broader whole. For instance, changing one's diet or cultivating diversity within the microbiome to improve health and prevent disease both reflect the goals of alignment; they seek to strengthen existing patterns of feedback within the organism and between the individual and the ecosystem. Intervention, on the other hand, is a perturbative process that tries to change the basic structure and function of a system. The difficulty with interventionist approaches is that they have a high likelihood of generating unintended consequences because our knowledge of the whole will always be more limited than the whole itself. When treating illnesses with pharmaceuticals, for instance, beneficial outcomes are often accompanied by side effects of varying severity as well as unpredictable interactional effects that can lead to iatrogenic illness. Similarly, surgical interventions can save lives, but are also life-threatening. Although a person may not be able to survive without a surgery, their body will nonetheless need to heal post-operatively from the intervention itself.

Alignment and intervention create very different medicines, while a meta-medicine holds both within the realm of interactivity. Working in the space of interactivity means accepting that we are always acting within a system, one that encompasses other systems at different scales. Alignment and intervention both have healing potential as well as the potential to cause harm. When aligning, for instance, it is important to align across all three domains of health. If you align only to one domain, such as the individual, there is a greater likelihood of creating pathology at another scale. This is demonstrated in the case of antibiotic resistance, which accrues individual benefits but simultaneously alters microbial ecology, creating superbugs that pose a significant risk to health at a population level. It is also clear in the high and rising environmental footprint of health care services (Chung and Meltzer, 2009); by releasing greenhouse gasses into the atmosphere, the health care sector directly contributes to the environmental crises that undermine not only the health of people around the world, but the health of future generations. As a result, we must attempt to align to the right aspects of the system and to multiple levels at the same time, taking into account not only the current state of the system in question, but also the histories that led the system to its particular configuration in the present moment. As discussed in the previous section, interventions aimed at only one scale must be limited, and will ideally feed back to the individual, the culture, and the ecology. Yet addressing the interconnected health issues arising in CAS in the Anthropocene is not only about creating effective ecological medicines, cultural medicines, and individual medicines. It is also about finding ways for these to work together as a meta-medicine of interactivity that can both sustain and restore health across scales.

Cultivating Low-Energy States

Fortunately, the inherent properties of CAS can help us get there. In nature, the most resilient systemic configurations tend to be low-energy states. Consider, for example, how much energy it takes to maintain a pristine lawn with only one species of grass and no weeds. If you stopped putting energy into the system (water to feed the lawn, gas to power the lawnmower, pesticides to prevent the spread of weeds, hours of labour), the lawn would eventually become more biodiverse as trees or native plants took hold in the soil. Insects and animals would return, and over time the area that was once a lawn would come to resemble the surrounding ecosystem. This dynamic of complex systems can also be used to enhance health across scales. The Gardening for Health project in Totnes, for instance, uses gardening as a treatment for illnesses such as vascular disease and dementia. Local doctors can prescribe time in the "Lamb Garden" that is not only a low-energy alternative or complement to conventional pharmaceutical treatments, but has been shown to enhance overall well-being (Gardening for Health, 2015). People who spend time in the garden get healthy exercise while relaxing outside. The program reaches across the generations, with activities for toddlers and schoolchildren, adults, and elders. While treating an individual's illness, Gardening for Health simultaneously builds a stronger community and restores the local ecology (Gardening for Health, 2015). It acts across scales to realign the physical body through exercise and time outside, the community through reinvigorated social connections, and the ecosystem through sustainable cultivation of productive species. Compared to other biomedical or public health interventions aimed at preventing disease, fostering healthy social relationships, and promoting good nutrition and exercise, the Gardening for Health program requires low inputs of energy and resources. After start-up costs, it was estimated to cost only around £5,000 for its fourth year of operations (Gardening for Health, 2015).

Low-energy states can be cultivated by working with the inherent capacity of CAS to self-organize in ways that maximize energy and resources (see Odum, 2007). In the Gardening for Health program, for instance, the community self-organized to provide services that span the domains of childcare, mental health programming, nutritional education, social services, and physical exercise. If these services were instead offered separately by independent organizations, they would take more time and resources to deliver, and the synergies between multiple domains of health would be lost.

Contemporary health systems can be compared to a well-manicured lawn. The grass is a perfect shade of green, there are many comfortable lawn chairs, someone has strung up twinkly lights to turn on at night, and there is even a flock of pink flamingos poking into the grass. Many people with beautiful lawns are very proud of their lawns despite the fact that they take a lot of money and care to maintain, and are full of pesticides. The change that we propose in health systems is tantamount to letting go of this lawn and allowing the forest to re-emerge. Paradoxically, the high biological diversity of the forest takes less energy to maintain than the low biodiversity of the lawn. In a context where the ecological and economic resources available to health systems are diminishing, cultivating low-energy states that can generate high levels of health and well-being becomes increasingly crucial.

Conclusion

Responding to the unprecedented challenges to human health that have emerged in the Anthropocene will require us to reconceptualize the purpose and scope of medicine from its current focus on treating individual pathology to promoting health in complex adaptive systems across scales. These changes are not impossible, and in fact many of the most promising approaches involve minimal investments of resources and operate largely outside of formal health care systems. There is no single "medicine" that can ensure long-term human well-being in increasingly precarious times. Achieving health in complex adaptive systems will require a "meta-medicine" that encompasses diverse approaches to health among individuals, cultures, and ecosystems. In this paper, we propose the following six tenets of a meta-medicine for complex adaptive systems in the Anthropocene:

1. **Understand health as a function of complexity.** Health in complex adaptive systems depends on maintaining complexity. This involves cultivating diversity both of components in the system and of relationships between components.
2. **Act across scales.** The individual, the culture, and the ecology represent distinct but interconnected domains of health. Medicines that focus only on one domain risk creating pathology at another scale. Healing requires action across all three domains of health.
3. **Attend to history.** Ontogeny, cultural history, and evolution brought the complex adaptive systems that exist today to their present state. To effectively act across scales, healing must take into account these three histories.
4. **Create medicines that are contextually whole.** Contextually whole medicines use reductionism when necessary, but recognize the significance of personal behaviours, cultural patterns, and evolutionary dictates to maintaining health. They are grounded in place and use attention to context to heal across scales.
5. **Know when to align and when to intervene.** Alignment is a process of re-syncing a component to the rhythms and patterns of a well-functioning complex system, whereas intervention is a process of perturbation that seeks to change the system's behaviours or purpose. A meta-medicine will incorporate both intervention and alignment as appropriate to either maintain the resilience of an existing system or encourage the system to transform.
6. **Cultivate low-energy states.** The most resilient complex adaptive systems exist in low-energy states. Healing in the Anthropocene should cultivate health using low-energy approaches that work with the inherent principles and energies of complex adaptive systems to build resilience across scales.

REFERENCES

Armelagos, G., Brown, P., & Turner, B. (2005). Evolutionary, historical and political economic perspectives on health and disease. *Social Science & Medicine*, *61*(4), 755–65. https://doi.org/10.1016/j.socscimed.2004.08.066

Arnoni, Y., & Berry, E. M. (2015). On the origins and evolution of the Mediterranean diet. In V. R. Preedy & R. Ross Watson (Eds), *The Mediterranean diet: An evidence-based approach*. Elsevier: London.

Bach-Faig, A., Berry, E. M., Lairon, D., Reguant, J., Trichopoulou, A., Dermini, S. et al. (2011). Mediterranean diet pyramid today. *Public Health and Nutrition*, *14*(12A), 2274–84.

Baer, H., Singer, M., & Susser, I. (2013). *Medical anthropology and the world system: Second edition.* Westport, CT: Praeger.

Beck, U., & Beck-Gernsheim, E. (2002). *Individualization: Institutionalized individualism and its social and political consequences.* London: SAGE Publications.

Braakman, R., & Smith, E. (2013). The compositional and evolutionary logic of metabolism. *Physical Biology, 10*(1), 1–62. https://doi.org/10.1088/1478-3975/10/1/011001

Butler, C. (2016). Sounding the alarm: Health in the Anthropocene. *International Journal of Environmental Research and Public Health, 13*(7), 1–15. https://doi .org/10.3390/ijerph13070665

Choi, A. M. K., Ryter, S. W., & Levine, B. (2013). Autophagy in human health and disease. *The New England Journal of Medicine, 368*(7), 651–62. https://doi .org/10.1056/NEJMra1205406

Chung, J. W., & Meltzer, D. O. (2009). Estimate of the carbon footprint of the US health care sector. *JAMA, 302*(18), 1970–2. https://doi.org/10.1001/jama.2009.1610

Doherty, T., & Clayton, S. (2011). The psychological impacts of global climate change. *American Psychologist, 66*(4), 265–76. https://doi.org/10.1037/a0023141

Eaton, S. B. (2006). The ancestral human diet: What was it and should it be a paradigm for contemporary nutrition? *Proceedings of the Nutrition Society, 65*(1), 1–6. https:// doi.org/10.1079/PNS2005471

Ferro-Luzzi, A., Branca, F. (1995). Mediterranean diet, Italian style: Prototype of a healthy diet. *American Journal of Clinical Nutrition, 61*(Suppl.), 1338S–45S.

Foster, K. R. et al. (2007). The evolution of the host microbiome as an ecosystem on a leash. *Nature, 548*, 43–51. https://doi.org/10.1038/nature23292

Fouad, F. M. et al. (2017). Health workers and the weaponisation of health care in Syria: A preliminary inquiry for The Lancet American University of Beirut Commission on Syria. *The Lancet, 390*(10111), 2516–26. https://doi.org/10.1016 /S0140-6736(17)30741-9

Foucault, M. (1994). *The birth of the clinic.* New York: Vintage Books.

Gardening for Health. (2015). *Gardening for health five-year project report.* Retrieved from http://www.gardeningforhealth.org.uk/report2015(2).html

GBD 2013 Mortality and Causes of Death Collaborators. (2013). Global, regional, and national age-sex specific all-cause and cause-specific mortality for 240 causes of death, 1990–2013: A systematic analysis for the Global Burden of Disease Study 2013. *The Lancet, 385*(9963), 117–71. https://doi.org/10.1016/S0140-6736(14)61682-2

Gell-Mann, M. (1994). *The quark and the jaguar.* New York: W. H. Freeman.

Harrison, M. (2004). *Disease and the modern world: 1500 to the present day.* Cambridge: Polity Press.

Hassink, J., & van Dijk, M. (2006). *Farming for health: Green-care farming across Europe and the United States of America.* Netherlands: Springer.

Hidaka, Br. (2012). Depression as a disease of modernity: Explanations for increasing prevalence. *Journal of Affective Disorders, 140*, 205–14. https://doi.org/10.1016/j .jad.2011.12.036

Holland, J. (1995). *Hidden order: How adaptation builds complexity*. Reading, MA: Addison-Wesley.

Homer-Dixon, T. (2006). *The upside of down: Catastrophe, creativity and the renewal of civilization*. Toronto: Vintage Canada.

Honigsbaum, M. (2017). Between securitisation and neglect: Managing Ebola at the borders of global health. *Medical History, 61*(2), 270–94. https://doi.org/10.1017/mdh.2017.6

Keys, A., & Keys, M. (1975). *How to eat well and stay well the Mediterranean way*. New York: Doubleday.

Knobbe, C., & Stojanoska, M. (2017). The 'displacing foods of modern commerce' are the primary and proximate cause of age-related macular degeneration: A unifying singular hypothesis. *Medical Hypotheses, 109*, 184–98. https://doi.org/10.1016/j.mehy.2017.10.010

Levin, S. A. (1998). Ecosystems and the biosphere as complex adaptive systems. *Ecosystems, 1*, 431–6. https://doi.org/10.1007/s100219900037

Lovelock, J. (2014). *A rough ride to the future*. New York: The Overlook Press.

McMichael, A. (2014). Population health in the Anthropocene: Gains, losses and emerging trends. *The Anthropocene Review, 1*(1), 44–56. https://doi.org/10.1177/2053019613514035

Meadows, D. (2008). *Thinking in systems: A primer*. Stirling, VA: Earthscan.

Odum, H. T. (2007). *Environment, power, and society for the twenty-first century: The hierarchy of energy*. New York, NY: Columbia University Press.

O'Keefe, J., & Cordain, L. (2004). Cardiovascular disease resulting from a diet and lifestyle at odds with our Paleolithic genome: How to become a 21st century hunter-gatherer. *Mayo Clinic Proceedings, 79*(1), 101–8. https://doi.org/10.4065/79.1.101

Paina, L., & Peters, D. (2012). Understanding pathways for scaling up health services through the lens of complex adaptive systems. *Health Policy and Planning, 27*(5), 365–73. https://doi.org/10.1093/heapol/czr054

Population Division of the Department of Economic and Social Affairs of the UN Secretariat. (2013). *World population prospects: The 2012 revision*. New York, NY: United Nations.

Price, W. (1945). *Nutrition and physical degeneration*. San Diego, CA: Price-Pottenger Nutrition Foundation.

Rickles, D., Hawe, P., & Shiell, A. (2007). A simple guide to chaos and complexity. *Journal of Epidemiology and Community Health, 61*(11), 933–7. https://doi.org/10.1136/jech.2006.054254

Romero, P. et al. (2004). Computational prediction of human metabolic pathways from the complete human genome. *Genome Biology, 6*(1), R2.2–17. https://doi.org/10.1186/gb-2004-6-1-r2

Rothschild, J., Hoddy, K. K., Jambazian, P, & Varaday, K. A. (2014). Time-restricted feeding and risk of metabolic disease: A review of human and animal studies. *Nutrition Reviews, 72*(5), 308–18. https://doi.org/10.1111/nure.12104

Schnorr, S. (2015). The diverse microbiome of the hunter-gatherer. *Nature, 518*(7540), S14–15. https://doi.org/10.1038/518S14a

Shankar Balakrishnan, V. (2017). Cholera in Yemen. *The Lancet Infectious Diseases, 16*, 700–1. https://doi.org/10.1016/S1473-3099(17)30352-3

Singer, M. (2009). Ecosyndemics: Global warming and the coming plagues of the 21st century. In A. Swedlund and A. Herring (Eds), *Plagues and epidemics: Infected spaces past and present* (pp. 21–38). London: Berg.

Søgaard Jørgensen, P. et al. (2017). Changing antibiotic resistance: Sustainability transformation to a pro-microbial planet. *Current Opinion in Environmental Sustainability, 25*, 66–76. https://doi.org/10.1016/j.cosust.2017.07.008

Trichopoulou, A., & Lagiou, P. (1997). Healthy traditional Mediterranean diet: An expression of culture, history and lifestyle. *Nutritional Reviews, 55*, 383–9. https://doi.org/10.1093/ajcn/86.1.7

Varady, K., & Hellerstein, M. (2007). Alternate-day fasting and chronic disease prevention: A review of human and animal trials. *American Journal of Clinical Nutrition, 86*(1), 7–13. https://doi.org/10.1093/ajcn/86.1.7

Walker, B., & Salt, D. (2006). *Resilience thinking: Sustaining ecosystems and people in a changing world.* Washington, DC: Island Press.

Whitmee, S. et al. (2015). Safeguarding human health in the Anthropocene epoch: Report of The Rockefeller Foundation – Lancet Commission on planetary health. *The Lancet, 386*, 1973–2028. https://doi.org/10.1016/S0140-6736(15)60901-1

World Health Organization. (2015). *Health in 2015: From MDGs, Millennium Development Goals to SDGs, Sustainable Development Goals.* Geneva: World Health Organization.

You, D., Hug, L. Chen, Y., Wardlaw, T., & Newby, H. (2014). *Levels and trends in child mortality.* New York, NY: United Nations Inter-agency Group for Child Mortality Estimation.

Zwizwai, R. (2017). Infectious disease surveillance update. *The Lancet Infectious Diseases, 16*, 701. https://doi.org/10.1016/S1473-3099(17)30353-5

Zywert, K. & Quilley, S. (2017). Health systems in an era of biophysical limits: The wicked dilemmas of modernity. *Social Theory & Health*, Online First Article, 1–20. https://doi.org/10.1057/s41285-017-0051-4

PART III

Alternative Ontologies: Laying the Groundwork for Living Well within the Earth's Biophysical Limits

The chapters in part 3 turn their attention towards underlying ontologies of health, both those that currently exist and those that may emerge as societies adapt to deepening ecological constraints. Ontology considers the nature of reality, and as such ontologies of health concern one's underlying beliefs about health and disease: why one becomes ill, how one can be healed, what it means to live and die well. Such meaning frameworks shape how we conceptualize well-being and respond to illness, and how we perceive the role of the self, the social world, and the surrounding environment in processes of health and disease. Embedded within more encompassing cultural worldviews, ontologies of health both inform and reflect the social-ecological contexts in which they arise. This is evident in the marked differences that can be observed between pre-modern and modern ontologies of health. Although a great diversity of worldviews exist *within* societies, viewed through the lens of long-term processes of social and historical development, it is possible to identify distinctly pre-modern and modern orientations. Premodern cultures are generally more communal and more dependent on their local environment to provide shelter, sustenance, and meaning (Tönnies and Loomis, 1887). In this context, human bodies tend to be perceived as homologous to or connected to nature, existing within a series of "harmonious wholes" that include non-human beings, features of the landscape, and other natural phenomena (Schepper-Hughes and Lock, 1987, p. 12). For the Quollahuaya-Andean people in Bolivia, for example, diseases are conceptualized as damage to the mountain they call home, and are seen as analogous to rockslides and earthquakes (Schepper-Hughes and Lock, 1987). Pre-modern cultures generally understand disease to arise from disturbed social relations; healing is thus a communal process that engages the social world (often perceived broadly to include living relations, deceased ancestors, and other beings) in restoring health (Katz, 1982; Turner, 1977). The ceremonial healing dances of the Kalahari Kung, for example, seek to rebalance relationships between individuals, the community, and the environment through communal ritual (Katz, 1982). Modern ontologies of health, by contrast, were influenced by the rise of scientific worldviews, the discovery of germ theory, and rapid developments in medical technologies (Harrison, 2004; Lock and Nguyen, 2010). During processes of modernization, increasingly materialist, reductionist understandings of disease came to mirror mechanistic views of the body. Scientific medicine, a practice focused on curing individuals by targeting pathologies with active ingredients and surgical interventions, rose to prominence (Foucault, 1994; Harrison, 2004; Lock and Nguyen, 2010). In modern cultures, ontologies of health were further shaped by sociological trends towards rising individualization, which supported the medicalization of illness by focusing on individual behaviours and traits over attention to social dynamics or environmental factors (Beck and Beck-Gernsheim, 2002; Bauman, 1991, 2012; Zola, 1975).

Much of the shift between pre-modern and modern ontologies of health can be attributed to differences in what Norbert Elias describes as the process of psychogenesis (1978; Quilley and Loyal, 2004). Elias proposes that psychogenesis, the development of culturally specific mental states among members of a particular society, unfolds alongside processes of sociogenesis, or the developmental trajectory of the society as a whole (1978). Referring to a "triad of controls," he further argues that the development of such social and psychological architectures unfolds in tandem with ecological transformations and anthropogenic controls over nature (see Quilley, 2004). The ontological changes that occurred in dominant understandings of health and disease between pre-modern and modern periods illustrate the extent to which the key tenets of modernization – the embrace of progress (curing, self-improvement), a reductionist and economistic worldview (germ theory, patient as client) – have been internalized within modern personality structures. The coupled societal and psychological changes that established modern ontologies of health, however, do not follow a one-way trajectory, but respond to ongoing shifts in social-ecological systems. Over the last five centuries, the consistent direction of change has been from the *Gemeinschaft* (community) towards the *Gesellschaft* (society) (Tönnies and Loomis, 1887; Greenfield, 2009). Community-oriented ways of living are more place-based, with economic, health, and social care systems that are embedded in patterns of social relationships and extended kin group obligations. Conversely, "society" is displaced from local ecologies. It is urbanized and professionalized, with a political economy that operates within disembedded markets and health and social care systems that rely on state infrastructure (Tönnies and Loomis, 1887; Polanyi, 1944).

Were our societies to shed layers of social complexity in response to tightening ecological constraints, however, social arrangements would likely shift back towards the pole of *Gemeinschaft*. This is one possible outcome of the social-ecological pressures of the Anthropocene, specifically due to declining resource and energy availability and the resulting end of economic growth (Butler, 2017; Frumkin, Hess, and Vindigni, 2009; Zywert, 2017). In a context of more limited resources, greater reliance on the local environment to meet immediate needs, and renewed dependence on social networks for health and care functions that can no longer be supported by the state, world views and social structures would transition in tandem, becoming more community-centric, place-based, and relational (Zywert and Quilley, 2017; Greenfield, 2009). As has occurred in every major societal transition from the time when all humans were hunters and gatherers through the development of agricultural communities, early states, the industrial revolution, and the globally networked digital age, the Anthropocene will augur in distinct ontologies of health.

The papers in this section will consider what the content of these ontologies might be, how they could come into being, and how they may be experienced by those who inhabit the Anthropocene. Contributors present diverse views on possible directions forward, from the ontological implications of a degrowth transition to potential shifts in ecological consciousness, embodiment, public health research and practice, and the ways in which we perceive death and dying.

In "Our Affluence Is Killing Us," Jean-Louis Aillon draws on the work of Ivan Illich as well as a growing body of degrowth scholarship to consider how degrowth offers a new ontological framework for organizing health systems. He argues that health and degrowth form a virtuous cycle and demonstrates how new conceptualizations of health are essential for achieving broader social transformations. Mark Hathaway, Donald Cole, and Blake Poland then consider the role of ecological consciousness in the transition towards more sustainable lifestyles, presenting a range of transformational learning techniques they have used in ecological public health and community resilience courses to nurture ecological consciousness in practice. They propose that existing modes of consciousness are connected through complex feedback patterns to exploitative political and economic systems, and that practices that cultivate affective connections to the more-than-human world can act as a leverage point for broader systemic change. Moving from ecological consciousness to the embodiment of ontologies suited to enabling health in the Anthropocene, Alexander Foster discusses posthumanism and transhumanism as alternative future understandings of the human body. Building on studies of the cyborg, the human microbiome, and rhythmanalysis, Foster concludes that a posthumanist embodiment offers greater potential for health on a finite planet by promoting ontological connectedness to the environment alongside a conception of health as an active negotiation with one's surroundings.

The chapters in part 3 then focus on both the external and internal manifestations of emerging ontologies of health. Ann Del Bianco and colleagues explore the rise of socioecological approaches to health that reframe public health work and environmental health research. They examine both the underlying paradigmatic shifts reflected in fields such as ecohealth, one health, geohealth, and planetary health, as well as the development of indicators that connect environmental conditions to human health and well-being. Next, Blake Poland advocates for greater care and attention to be paid to processes of inner transition. Focusing on the attempt to bring about systemic shifts towards sustainable ways of living, Poland argues that inner work is a necessary and often overlooked component of meaningful change, creating the space for new ways of thinking, being, and doing to emerge. Specifically, inner work can act as a driver of change by cultivating a greater sense of connectedness to one another and to the natural world, improving our capacity to listen, enabling greater recognition of the sacredness of all life, and remedying the constant oscillation between distraction and addiction that currently stymies mainstream approaches to social change.

The section concludes with two papers that consider how alternative ontologies of death can play a crucial role in securing health and well-being on a finite planet. Sheldon Solomon describes how the human fear of death, and our attempts to manage this terror, affect the long-term prospects for human survival in the Anthropocene. Presenting insights from his extensive theoretical and empirical work in terror management theory, Solomon suggests that in the Anthropocene, the ramifications of death denial are likely to agitate political tensions and inter-group conflicts, exacerbate consumption and resource depletion, and solidify human disconnection from nature. As such, recognizing the effects of death anxiety on human behaviour will be crucial for long-term human well-being. Next, Barbara Jane Davy argues that becoming embedded in a gift economy through practices of ancestor veneration offers a promising pathway for mitigating the most negative implications of the human fear of death. By reconceptualizing death as part of the process of becoming a living ancestor, symbolic immortality is granted within a relational ontology. To demonstrate how this process unfolds in practice, Davy discusses ancestor veneration within contemporary Heathen revitalizations of pre-Christian European traditions.

Together, the papers in part 3 present an interdisciplinary overview (drawing on fields such as degrowth economics, public health, anthropology, ecohealth, social psychology, and religious studies) of the role of ontology in the transition to a more ecologically sustainable society that can support human health amid the social-ecological upheavals of the Anthropocene.

REFERENCES

Bauman, Z. (1991). *Modernity and ambivalence*. Cambridge: Polity Press.
Bauman, Z. (2012). *Liquid modernity*. Cambridge: Polity.
Beck, U. & Beck-Gernsheim, E. (2002). *Individualization: Institutionalized individualism and its social and political consequences*. London: SAGE Publications.

Butler, C. (2017). Limits to growth, planetary boundaries, and planetary health. *Current Opinion in Environmental Sustainability, 25,* 59–65. https://doi.org/10.1016/j.cosust.2017.08.002

Elias, N. (1978). *The civilizing process: Sociogenetic and psychogenetic investigations.* Oxford: Wiley-Blackwell.

Foucault, M. (1994). *The birth of the clinic.* New York: Vintage Books.

Frumkin, H., Hess, J., & Vindigni, S. (2009). Energy and public health: The challenge of peak petroleum. *Public Health Reports, 124*(1), 5–19. https://doi.org/10.1177/003335490912400103

Greenfield, P. M. (2009). Linking social change and developmental change: Shifting pathways of human development. *Developmental Psychology, 45*(2), 401–18. https://doi.org/10.1037/a0014726

Harrison, M. (2004). *Disease and the modern world: 1500 to the present day.* Cambridge: Polity Press.

Katz, R. (1982). *Boiling energy: Community healing among the Kalahari Kung.* Cambridge, MA: Harvard University Press.

Lock, M., & Nguyen, V.-K. (2010). *An anthropology of biomedicine.* Chichester: Wiley-Blackwell.

Polanyi, K. (1944). *The Great Transformation: The political and economic origins of our time.* Boston: Beacon Press.

Quilley, S. (2004). Ecology, 'human nature' and civilising processes: Biology and sociology in the work of Norbert Elias. In S. Loyal, & S. Quilley (Eds). *The sociology of Norbert Elias* (pp. 42–58). Cambridge: Cambridge University Press.

Quilley, S., & Loyal, S.. (2004). Towards a central theory: The scope and relevance of Norbert Elias. In S. Loyal, & S. Quilley (Eds). *The sociology of Norbert Elias* (pp. 1–22). Cambridge: Cambridge University Press.

Schepper-Hughes, N., & Lock, M. (1987). The mindful body: A prolegomenon to future work in medical anthropology. *Medical Anthropology Quarterly, 1*(1), 6–41. https://doi.org/10.1525/maq.1987.1.1.02a00020

Tönnies, F., & Loomis, C. P. (1887). *Community and society = Gemeinschaft und gesellschaft.* Mineola, NY: Dover Publications.

Turner, V. (1977). *The ritual process: Structure and anti-structure.* New York: Cornell University Press.

Zola, I. (1975). In the name of health and illness: On some socio-political consequences of medical influence. *Social Science & Medicine, 9*(2), 83–7. https://doi.org/10.1016/0037-7856(75)90098-0

Zywert, K. (2017). Human health and social-ecological systems change: Rethinking health in the Anthropocene. *The Anthropocene Review, 4*(3), 216–38. https://doi.org/10.1177/2053019617739640

Zywert, K., & Quilley, S. (2017). Health systems in an era of biophysical limits: The wicked dilemmas of modernity. *Social Theory & Health, 16*(2), 188–207. https://doi.org/10.1057/s41285-017-0051-4

15 Our Affluence Is Killing Us: What Degrowth Offers Health and Well-Being

JEAN-LOUIS AILLON AND GIACOMO D'ALISA

Limits of Growth

Continuous and indiscriminate economic growth is a particular characteristic of the Anthropocene that has been deeply analysed by degrowth scholars. Growth is based on the unlimited exploitation of natural and human capital in order to maximize profit. This type of growth is particularly exacerbated within the frame of capitalism and neoliberalism, in a globalized and consumerist world, but it also was (and can be) present in many socialist countries. The process does not respect the limits and the cyclic nature of the biosphere and, after a certain threshold, results in decreasing marginal returns, hence becoming "counterproductive": it produces more damages than benefits (Illich, 1973; Bonaiuti, 2014).

Growth produces an increase in inequalities, both in north-south world dynamics as well as within specific countries. It is ecologically unsustainable because it leads to irreparable damages to nature, such as climate change, loss of biodiversity, and pollution of the land, water, and air. Furthermore, the cultural paradigm that characterizes a growth-based society (consumerism, competition, individualism, work-alcoholism, no limits) does not produce more happiness (Easterlin paradox) and often can promote unhealthy lifestyles, because it generates high levels of stress and anxiety, fast rhythms, and reduced time and space to cultivate authentic relationships and creativity. Finally, growth is uneconomic because in the long term its costs are higher than the benefits and, in developed economies, might be coming to an end, mainly because of natural resource exhaustion and diminishing marginal returns (D'Alisa, Demaria, and Kallis, 2015; Latouche, 2006; Picketty, 2014; Eckerseley, 2006; Easterlin, 1974).

Degrowth

Degrowth offers an alternative ontological and epistemological approach for understanding the limits of growth and critically reframing the actual socioeconomic system. As D'Alisa, Demaria, and Kallis (2015, p. 3) explain, "Degrowth signifies, first and foremost, a critique of growth. It calls for the decolonization of public debate from the idiom of economism and for the abolishment of economic growth as a social objective. Beyond that, degrowth signifies also a desired direction, one in which societies will use fewer natural resources and will organize and live differently than today". From an ecological economics perspective, degrowth "calls for a democratically led redistributive downscaling of production and consumption in industrialized countries as a means to achieve environmental sustainability, social justice and well-being" (Demaria et al., 2013, p. 209). Degrowth means to break with capitalist and neoliberal ideologies in order to create another socioeconomic system, not only aimed at stopping the "growthist fever" but also and mainly for making possible human and non-human flourishing. However, it is not just an economic concept, but rather "a frame constituted by a large array of concerns, goals, strategies and actions [...] a confluence point where streams of critical ideas and political action converge" (Demaria et al., 2013, p. 193–4). Furthermore, degrowth aspires, in line with radical ecofeminism, to put at the centre of its concern the vulnerability of life (D'Alisa et al., 2015; Orozco, 2015).

In this line of thought the French economist Serge Latouche says that "degrowth is not the alternative, but a matrix of alternatives which re-opens a space for creativity by raising the heavy blanket of economic totalitarianism" (Latouche, 2010, p. 520).

Health Needs Degrowth

The principal determinants of health for populations are the general socioeconomic, environmental, and cultural conditions in which people live (WHO, 2008). Within these factors, inequalities (class, income, employment, education, gender, and ethnicity), environment and lifestyles are the principal determinants of health. Together they account for more than 50 per cent of population health, while non-modifiable factors (age, gender, and hereditary factors) and health care services account respectively for 15 per cent and 25 per cent of population health (Mikkonen and Raphael, 2010). As an example, the medical journal *The Lancet* defined climate change as "the biggest global health threat of the 21st century" (Costello et al., 2009, p. 1693), which could cause (directly and indirectly) 250,000 additional deaths per year between 2030 and 2050 (WHO, 2017).

If we combine these considerations with the effects of growth, we can argue, as quoted in the *Bologna Manifesto for Sustainability and Health* (INSH, 2014, p. 1), that "the present prevailing paradigm based on unlimited growth, indiscriminate pursuit and accumulation of capital without fair redistribution of wealth or upholding of human rights" is not sustainable from a health point of view because "it is unable to safeguard the health of present and future generations." Vice versa, a degrowth transition to a more sustainable, fair, and happy society could be one of the best ways to protect, promote, and safeguard the health of future generations; sustainable development is a weak and insufficient paradigm for achieving these goals, because it does not challenge growth. As a matter of fact, several principles and policies proposed by degrowth scholars could have huge benefits for population health: to reduce socioeconomic inequality through redistribution (maximum and basic income); to mitigate climate change; "to translate increased productivity to fewer working hours and more free time" and diminish unemployment; to relocalize economic life; to acknowledge and expand non-commercial forms of work (including care) and product exchange; to reduce waste and material consumption; to promote different forms of sociality such as urban gardening, cohousing, and eco-communities; etc. (Borowy and Aillon, 2017, p. 355; D'Alisa, Demaria, and Kallis, 2015). From this point of view, some studies have observed that periods of economic crises, accompanied by "policy regimes favouring a more egalitarian distribution of income and stronger social protections" (coherent with a degrowth scenario), can produce positive health outcomes (Borowy, 2013; De Vogli and Owusu, 2015, p. 15).

Degrowth Needs a Different Approach to Health

While degrowth is good for health, we argue that a revolution in the field of health is an essential step in order to achieve a degrowth transition to a more sustainable, fair, and happy society. More than forty years ago, Ivan Illich, one of the main pioneers of degrowth, deeply analysed the relationship between medicine and industrial expansion. He affirmed that "only a political program aimed at the limitation of professional management of health will enable people to recover their powers for health care, and that such a program is integral to a societywide criticism and restraint of the industrial mode of production," thus it is produced ("-genesis") by the healer/doctor ("iatròs") (Illich, 1976, p. 10). Illich described how the medicalization process carried out by the health system, after a certain threshold, produces more damages than benefits ("counterproductivity"): "Increasing and irreparable damage accompanies present industrial expansion in all sectors. In medicine, this damage appears as iatrogenesis" (Illich, 1976, p. 270–1). Iatrogenesis is clinical when "pain, illness and death result from medical care" (Illich, 1976, p. 270–1), but it could be also a social and cultural or symbolic process. Social iatrogenesis consists of "health policies that reinforce an industrial organization that generates ill health," while cultural iatrogenesis takes place "when medically sponsored behaviour and delusions restrict the vital autonomy of people by undermining their competence in growing up, caring for each other, and aging, or when medical intervention cripples personal responses to pain, disability, impairment, anguish and death" (Illich, 1976, p. 270–1).

The myth of growth pervades every aspect of our society and imaginary. Obviously, the concept of health is not immune from the influence of this totalitarian paradigm. The "cultural colonization" driven by medical techniques and apparatuses has expropriated citizens of control over their health. This occurred by transforming health into a commodity that could be managed only by professional workers, and by legitimizing as "natural" and "biological" diseases that were instead caused by social determinants and, in particular, linked to negative externalities of a society based on growth (pathologies related, for example, to pollution and inequalities).

Illich's intuitions have been further elaborated by several authors in the field of critical medical anthropology. This discipline, which started from the study of non-industrialized societies, has shown how medical systems, including the western ones, are "cultural systems," and how conceptions of health, illness, body, or care are not objective realities, but rather social and cultural constructs. From this point of view, medicine constitutes a tool for social control, and its privileged objects (illness and forms of suffering) can be seen both as the product of (historical and social forces and particular power relations are embodied as biological events) and forms of resistance to ("embodied critique") dominant ideologies (Quaranta, 2006; Scheper-Hughes and Lock, 1987). According to Taussig (1980), the biomedical system operates "reification" processes that reframe socioeconomic factors, human relationships, people, and their experiences as things, objects, and true facts of nature. This contributes to the construction of a social reality that aims to preserve a particular political order, reintegrating suffering people in a shared order of meanings and thus cancelling out the social, economic, and political dimensions of disease (Quaranta, 2006).

"Health and Degrowth:" A New Model in the Field of Sustainability

Serge Latouche describes degrowth as a political slogan with theoretical implications aimed at strongly underlining the need to abandon the dogmatic goal of exponential growth. Degrowth is not negative growth. It could be defined as "a-growth" (like atheism), in the sense of abandoning the absolute faith in economy, growth, progress, and development (Latouche, 2006, 2009). The myth of growth pervades every aspect of our economy, society, and imaginary. Health and the health system are not an exception. Hence, we think that it is possible and necessary to use the lens of degrowth theory to scrutinize health with the objective of proposing a different approach that might be called "Health and Degrowth."

What does it mean to abandon the faith in growth in the field of health? This process envisages an overturn of the mechanism of growth and its effects, both material and cultural, on health, thus modifying the concept of health, the health system, and health care. Human beings (and the environment) are nowadays only gears of a machine whose aim is uniquely to produce more and more, in order to increase gross domestic product (GDP). Degrowth, in this context, attempts to invert this mechanism and put human needs at the centre of the system, while reducing the economy to a means to achieve full realization of human beings (on a qualitative level and not just on a quantitative one), compatible with biosphere limits (Aillon, 2013).

A similar dynamic could be applied to patients and, generally speaking, to human beings, concerning health. Patients are often gears in an economic system focused more on GDP growth and satisfaction of stakeholders' interests (measured with objective and quantitative methods) than on their health. Implementing the "Health and Degrowth" approach involves rupturing the chains of economic pressure on health (health concept, health system, and health care) and putting the patient and his or her needs at the centre of the system. In this framework, the "health machine" and the underlining economic system would strive for real and full physical, mental, and social health, in dynamic harmony with the environment and would thus be sustainable in the long term, as foreseen by bioeconomy theory in a context of bioeconomic evolution (Georgescu-Roegen, 1971).

From the Eight Rs to the Four Steps

Latouche (2006), in order to put degrowth into practice, proposes eight interdependent changes, called the virtuous circle of eight Rs: re-evaluate (the vision of the world, decolonizing our imaginary from growth ideology); reconceptualize (adopt new values); re-structure (the productive apparatus); redistribute (money, land, and work); re-localize (economy and politics); reduce (overconsumption, wastefulness, mass tourism, displacements and work time), reuse, and recycle. In this work we will present four steps, derived from the application of the eight Rs to the health field:

1. Re-evaluation and reconceptualization of the ideas of health, illness, and care
2. Restructuring health services following the new conceptualization of health
3. Health promotion acting on socioeconomic, environmental, and cultural determinants of health
4. Involvement of citizens in health management (autonomy).

Re-evaluation and Reconceptualization of the Ideas of Health, Illness, and Care

Applying the degrowth frame to the health field would mean first to decolonize its imaginary (Latouche, 2006) from growth. This should imply, besides

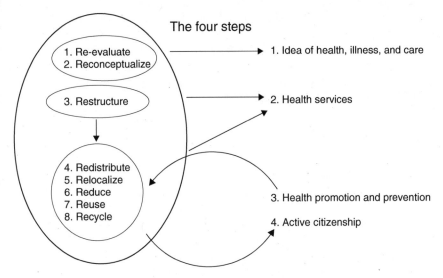

Figure 15.1 The four steps of "Health and Degrowth" building upon the eight Rs (Latouche, 2006)

a change in medical practice, a re-evaluation of certain values and episte-mological principles, which are still nowadays the basis of scientific medical knowledge.

It means to go beyond a certain vision of science and progress (materialis-tic, mechanistic, reductionist) that considers the human being as an "object of study," splitting emotion from reason and neglecting different essential (non-material) dimensions, including uniqueness and complexity. Reconcep-tualization of health calls for abandoning the arrogance ("hybris") of being able to reach objective knowledge, and avoiding reducing complexity to its basic components (cells, atoms, etc.) in order to propose the appropriate pharmaco-logical treatment. A "Health and Degrowth" process proposes instead to redi-rect the vision of health in a qualitative direction, to bring again the uniqueness of the person to the centre of the clinical process, and to promote all those prac-tices that aim at the real psycho-physical and social well-being of the person, understood in its entirety. Moreover, in opposition with the scientific/positiv-istic approach, a "Health and Degrowth" approach does not oppose mankind to nature through a logic of absolute domination and control (without limits), but sees human beings as part of nature itself, in harmony with it. It promotes a reconceptualization of health that takes into account care and respect for the environment and all beings (Pallante and Aillon, 2017).

Following this vision there is the need to develop a new model of health, illness, and care, that:

- Sees health not as the mere absence of disease caused by medical intervention but as a dynamic equilibrium resulting from several external (e.g. socioeconomic, environmental, and cultural factors) and internal determinants (e.g. psychological factors such as "resilience" and "sense of coherence;" Antonovsky, 1987). Health could be seen also as the "degree of lived freedom" that people have in order to manage the above-mentioned factors: "the range of autonomy within which a person exercises control over his own biological states and over the conditions of his immediate environment" (Illich, 1976, p. 91).
- Moves the focus of interest from pathogenesis (searching for causes of diseases and treating them) to salutogenesis. Salutogenesis is aimed at searching for factors that cause healthiness and promoting them both collectively and individually (Antonovsky, 1987). Moreover, it considers health and disease as two poles of a single process, where illness does not become an enemy to eliminate and destroy, but provides also a great opportunity for development, where overcoming illness becomes the foundation for better future health (Alivia, Guadagni, and Roberti di Sarsina, 2011).
- Considers the person in a holistic and systemic perspective, as a bio-psycho-socio-cultural and spiritual subject in continuous relationship with the surrounding physical and relational environment (Engel, 1977; Brody, 1999; George et al., 2000; Suls and Rothman, 2004; Roberti di Sarsina, 2010).
- Puts in the middle of the therapeutics/care process the relationship between health workers and patient, going beyond the neutrality of the "scientific approach," promoting the possibility of an empathic, authentic, and affective relationship (Roberti di Sarsina, 2010). In this approach the health professional shares his or her knowledge and promotes patient autonomy, in a process of relational co-construction of the treatment that goes beyond a paternalistic model of medicine.
- Tries to use the necessary reductionism without renouncing the complexity (and thus subjectivity) of the whole phenomenon (Albrecht, Freeman, and Higginbotham, 1998; Plsek and Greenhalgh, 2001; Miles, 2009).

Restructuring Health Services Following the New Conceptualization of Health

The second step consists of restructuring health services to align with the new health paradigm. In particular, besides the cultural changes proposed above, it will be fundamental to *redistribute* the resources of the health system, *re-localize* health care, *reduce* overconsumption of drugs, procedures, and wastefulness, and *reuse or recuperate* alternative medical knowledge.

a) *To redistribute* the resources of the health system

Health is a fundamental right (art. 25 of the Universal Declaration of Human Rights) and health systems should be considered as a common good from which every person can benefit. That calls for a national public health system, where there should be equity in access to and allocation of resources.

b) *To re-localize* health care

Re-localizing economic processes, strengthening local networks, cultivating local knowledge and invigorating local responsibilities through active local citizenship is recommended by several degrowth authors (Illich, 1973; Castoriadis, 1987; Latouche, 2006). Doctors should "hand back power to patients, encourage self care and autonomy," said Richard Smith, editor of the British Medical Journal, taking up the words used by Ivan Illich (Illich, 1976; Moynihan and Smith, 2002, p. 860). Such a structure of participatory and local management should include a re-localization of health care so that it is actively managed by citizens as a common good. It resembles a change of perspective from a hospital-based to a community-medicine approach, implementing the primary health care model advocated by the World Health Organization since Alma-Ata (WHO, 2008). That would be facilitated by the promotion of a community welfare model, where care, relationships, and reciprocity become central focuses of the community. From this perspective, care work is not only transferred to the economy or state sphere but is carried out autonomously by people, fairly distributed between gender, class, and ethnicity (D'Alisa, Deriu, and Demaria, 2015).

c) *To reduce* medicalization and overconsumption of drugs, procedures, wastefulness

As for general goods, there is nowadays a sort of "medical consumerism" driven by the media and big pharma companies. People are pushed to feel sick even if they are not and to use more and more pills, to undertake more and more exams and medical procedures, a form of medicalization now described as "disease mongering," namely "extending the boundaries of treatable illnesses to expand markets for new products. Alliances of pharmaceutical manufacturers, doctors, and patients groups use the media to frame conditions as being widespread and severe. Disease mongering can include turning ordinary ailments into medical problems, seeing mild symptoms as serious, treating personal problems as medical, seeing risks as diseases, and framing prevalence estimates to maximize potential markets" (Moynihan, Heath, and Henry, 2002, p. 886). Over-prescription of some medicines (e.g. antibiotics or painkillers or antidepressants) is very common, even though in most cases prescribed drugs turn out to be useless and sometimes harmful. In particular, over-prescription of antibiotics is evident in the community as well as in hospitals, in veterinary practice and in agriculture, with a prevalence that ranges from 20 to 50 per cent

(Wise, 1998). The campaign "Choosing Wisely," carried out by several medical specialty societies in the United States (Cassel and Guest, 2012), advocates for a reduction in unnecessary tests, procedures, and treatments, instead promoting appropriate ones.

Some estimates suggest that as much as 20 per cent of all health care expenses are wasted (Berwick and Hackbarth, 2012). Often an appropriate and higher-quality treatment is also a less expensive one (Ovretveit, 2009). In this context, as Maurizio Pallante theorized, less could be better (Pallante, 2011). If we no longer produce and consume a commodity (an object or service that we buy with money) that is not a good (an object or service that fulfils a need or a desire), gross domestic product and material/energy consumption decrease while our well-being as well as that of the planet increases (Pallante, 2009). Hence, a selective demedicalization could be seen as a degrowth practice.

In order to achieve the above-mentioned objectives, it is necessary to promote more independence of health workers and the health system overall from the market of drugs and medical devices ("big pharma"), and freedom from conflict of interest and corruption.

d) *To reuse/recuperate* alternative medical knowledge

Nowadays, the scientific paradigm of evidence-based Western medicine is dominating the health field, giving little space and often discrediting complementary and alternative medicine. The decolonization of our imaginary from this "culture of science" would contribute to the reuse of other medical knowledge, both concerning old traditional practices as well as other complementary and alternative medicines. Over 100 million Europeans are currently traditional and complementary medicine (T&CM) users, with one-fifth regularly using T&CM and the same number preferring health care that includes T&CM. There is also a significant demand for T&CM practices and practitioners worldwide (WHO, 2014). Some evidence demonstrates the clinical efficacy of several T&CM practices as cures for certain diseases. Moreover, there is emerging evidence of the cost effectiveness and possible cost savings in at least some clinical populations. A cure that, as an example, has lower costs and better health outcomes than usual care alone is acupuncture for low-back pain (Herman et al., 2012). Hence, a degrowth approach would aim to promote synergies between T&CM and conventional Western medicine and, as WHO advocates, to move towards the integration of T&CM into health systems (WHO, 2014). The holistic approach, typical of T&CM, is also very useful for individualized care and health promotion, as shown by the person-centred medicine paradigm (Roberti di Sarsina, 2007).

Finally, it will be important also to reuse or recuperate our capacity for self-care, both with conventional and unconventional medicine (Illich, 1976) as well as to learn to be "patient" and confident with our bodies simply waiting for healing.

e) *To reduce, reuse, recycle, and rethink*
Hospitals are a significant source of waste. The National Health Service in England, for instance, "produced 408,218 tonnes of waste in 2005–6, 29% of which was clinical waste [...] equivalent to 5.5 kg of waste per patient per day" (Hutchins and Stuart, 2009, p. 746). Consequently, both for ordinary and clinical waste, particular attention should be given to reducing the number of single-use devices, limiting the amount of packaging, and recycling objects and materials whenever possible. Furthermore, we should "rethink" the entire waste system, changing rules, culture, and practices in order to better manage waste by, for example, redesigning equipment and packaging or investigating new sterilization techniques and their environmental impacts (Hutchins and Stuart, 2009).

Health Promotion Acting on Socioeconomic, Environmental, and Cultural Determinants of Health

This step consists of the promotion of health, acting on social determinants of health, as a strategy for restructuring society following the "Health and Degrowth" approach together with the general degrowth transition (8 Rs). Health promotion, as defined by the Ottawa Charter, "is the process of enabling people to increase control over, and to improve, their health. To reach [...] physical, mental and social well-being, an individual or group must be able to identify and to realize aspirations, to satisfy needs, and to change or cope with the environment [...]. Therefore, health promotion is not just the responsibility of the health sector, but goes beyond healthy life-styles to well-being" (WHO, 1986, p. 1). It continues, "The fundamental conditions and resources for health", the prerequisites for health, "are peace, shelter, education, food, income, a stable eco-system, sustainable resources, social justice, and equity. Improvement in health requires a secure foundation in these basic prerequisites" (WHO, 1986, p. 1). In order to achieve these goals, it is fundamental to act both individually and collectively on the "determinants of health," restructuring society as defined in the first part of the chapter.

In order to promote health, better health care services are not sufficient: above all, we need more equity and solidarity in society, better living and working conditions, stronger and autonomous social and community networks, healthier lifestyles, and environmental protection. To achieve these objectives, it is necessary to build an alternative cultural paradigm and to restructure all of society, adopting individual changes combined with global politics actions. In fact, "the prerequisites and prospects for health cannot be ensured by the health sector alone. More importantly, health promotion demands coordinated action by all concerned: by governments, by health and other social and economic sectors, by nongovernmental and voluntary organizations, by local authorities, by industry and by the media" (WHO, 1986, p. 1). It "involves, in addition to the health sector, all related sectors [...], in particular agriculture, animal husbandry, food, industry, education, housing, public works, communications and other sectors; and demands the coordinated efforts of all those sectors" (WHO, 1978, n.p.).

Involvement of Citizens in Health Management (Autonomy)

In the degrowth movement, "degrowth is not an adaptation to inevitable limits, but a desirable project to be pursued for its own sake in the search for autonomy. For Castoriadis (1987), autonomy means the ability of a collective to decide its future in common, freed from external (heteronomous) imperatives and givens, such as the law of God (religion), or the laws of the economy (economics)" (D'Alisa, Demaria, and Kallis, 2015, p. 8). We could add to this list also the "law of medicine" and call for more autonomy in the health field. In fact, for Illich, "the recovery from society-wide iatrogenic disease is a political task, not a professional one" and thus citizens, and not health professionals, are the principal protagonists for this change (Illich, 1976, p. 6).

Degrowth scholars emphasize the need for participatory and local management of the commons, in other words, "processes of shared stewardship about things that a community (a network or all of humankind) possesses and manages in common," a process also defined as "commoning" (Helfrich and Bollier, 2014). Here we advocate for an involvement of citizens and patients in health management, at the clinical level as well as at the political one concerning all fields related to health, embracing a vision that considers health systems as a commons. Degrowth pushes for commoning health: "People have the right and duty to participate individually and collectively in the planning and implementation of their health care [...]. Primary health care requires and promotes maximum community and individual self-reliance and participation in the planning, organization, operation and control of primary health care, making fullest use of local, national and other available resources; and to this end develops through appropriate education the ability of communities to participate" (WHO, 1978, n.p.). This goal was theorized forty years ago but is still far from being achieved; we maintain that commoning health is the only sustainable way to achieve it.

An interesting example of action in this field is the Italian Network for Health and Sustainability (INHS) that emerged in 2014 with the *Bologna Manifesto for Sustainability and Health* (INHS, 2014). This network is composed of twenty-seven associations that work not only in health but also in environmental, cultural, and degrowth fields. The network includes, among many others, Doctors for the Environment, People's Health Movement, Slow Medicine, Democratic Psychiatry, and Italian medical students' and junior doctors' associations (SISM and Federspecializzandi) as well as Slow Food, Salutogenesis Foundation (Fondazione per la Salutogenesi Onlus), journalists (Italia che Cambia, Vivere Sostenibile), and degrowth associations (Movimento per la Decrescita Felice and L'Associazione per la Decrescita). INHS is spreading awareness concerning social and cultural change towards citizens and health professionals and doing advocacy towards politics and health institutions. IN-HS's vision is that health promotion means reconstructing a more sustainable and equitable society. To achieve this goal, it is necessary to build more and more alliances between the health sector and civil society.

Degrowth, Health, and the South

Some proposals presented above could be valid worldwide. However, these recommendations are conceived primarily for Western countries where the particular implementation of medicine we criticize has been developed. An ad hoc discourse is needed concerning degrowth and health in non-Westernized territories and the Global South.

Serge Latouche theorizes degrowth starting from the critique of development in the south, especially in Africa, highlighting how this concept has been used as a tool for imposing subliminally neoliberal policies to the rest of the world, colonizing their imaginary with growth and a consumerist culture. The pursuit of development, rhetorically implemented to aid those underdeveloped countries to catch up to those already developed and enjoy their level of well-being, has created and legitimized inequalities and subjugated the underdeveloped world to the colonial matrix of power (Quijano, 2000). Of course it has also had a role in delegitimizing the traditional local knowledge about health and disease in those territories, imposing a particular idea of what health is and what it is not (Connolly et al., 2017). Furthermore, trade liberalization affects health negatively "through a variety of mechanisms, such as changes in lifestyles; environmental degradation; reduced human security; sequestration of public wealth; privatization, and commercialization of health care" (Missoni, 2015, p. 441).

Consequently, Latouche describes a different path for the South, adding different Rs to his theoretical framework:

> Rompre [break], Renew, Rediscover, Reintroduce and Recuperate. Break away from economic and cultural dependency on the North. Renew contact with the thread of a history that was interrupted by colonization, development and globalization. Rediscover and reappropriate the cultural identity of the South. Reintroduce specific products that have been forgotten or abandoned, and 'anti-economic' values that are bound up with the past of these countries. Recuperate traditional technologies and skills. (Latouche, 2009, p. 58)

In this line D'Alisa et al. (2015, p. 3) also clarify: "Degrowth should be pursued in the North, not in order to allow the South to follow the same path, but first and foremost in order to liberate conceptual space for countries there to find their own trajectories to what they define as the good life."

From the health point of view, a global degrowth transition will create a fair distribution of wealth, resources, and ecological footprint between the Global North and South, acting on both the social and environmental determinants of health (in particular equity and climate change) as well as improving health services (quality and access). But above all, it is able to undo the growth-centric idea of what health is about and allow different conceptions of health and disease to emerge. Such a process is different from a sustainable development path and, consequently, extreme caution should be adopted concerning ideas such as "global health" or "health for all." Who decides what health is and what an appropriate cure is? The answer to this question, indeed, is a matter of power. In that sense, "global health is a product of nations whose histories are characterized by the struggle for power, wealth, and influence" and the spread of western health services and health visions around the world can be seen as a sort of neocolonial process (Horton, 2013, p. 1690), with the risk of pathologizing the Global South rather than globalizing health (Fernando, 2014). Therefore a "Health and Degrowth" approach (commoning health) for the south should not be guided by the mere adoption of a well-financed heteronomous western health care model, but, in order to break with cultural dependency on the north, it should renew contact with history and rediscover and reappropriate different health systems and visions of health and care to recuperate and re-evaluate traditional and resilient medical practices. It does not mean abandoning modern medical knowledge and apparatus, but having a more paritetic dialogue and exchange where biomedicine and other medical systems could be fruitfully integrated and autonomously developed in different contexts (WHO, 2014).

Conclusions

In a long-term perspective and on a global scale, a growth-based economy is unsustainable from a health standpoint because it progressively undermines the principal determinants of health (inequalities, climate change, pollution and lack of resources, unhealthy lifestyles related to consumerism). From this point of view, a wide socioeconomic and cultural change is required in order to protect and promote the health of future generations, and degrowth offers an interesting framework for this transition.

On the other hand, in order to achieve the required transformation of society, a revolution in conceptions of health is required. The "Health and Degrowth" model gives a theoretical frame for this transformation, combining Ivan Illich's intuitions and the eight Rs model of Serge Latouche. It requires us to "decolonize the health imaginary" from growth colonization, promoting a re-evaluation and reconceptualization of the ideas of health, illness, and care in a more systemic and holistic way. It will also be necessary to restructure health services following the new conceptualization of health by redistributing resources, re-localizing health care, reducing medicalization and overconsumption of drugs and procedures, curtailing wastefulness, and recuperating alternative medical knowledge and our capacity for self-care (a commoning health transformation). Furthermore, degrowthers have to promote health by fostering a broader socioeconomic, environmental, and cultural change, acting deeply on the principal determinants of health. Autonomous citizens will be the protagonists of this political task that "must be based on a grassroots consensus about the balance between the civil liberty to heal and the civil right to equitable health care" (Illich, 1976, p. 6).

ACKNOWLEDGMENTS

Giacomo D'Alisa participated in the development of this publication thanks to the support of the Portuguese Foundation for Science and Technology (FCT) and its strategic project (UID/SOC/50012/2013).

REFERENCES

Aillon, J.-L. (2013). *La decrescita, i giovani e l'utopia, comprendere le origini del disagio per riappropriarci del nostro futuro.* Rome, Italy: Edizioni per la Decrescita Felice.

Albrecht, G., Freeman, S., & Higginbotham, N. (1998).Complexity and human health: The case for a transdisciplinary paradigm. *Culture, medicine and psychiatry, 22*(1), 55–92. https://doi.org/10.1023/a:1005328821675

Alivia, M., Guadagni, P., & Di Sarsina, P. R. (2011). Towards salutogenesis in the development of a personalised and preventative healthcare. *EPMA Journal, 2*(4), 381–4. https://doi.org/10.1007/s13167-011-0131-9

Antonovsky, A. (1987). *Unravelling the mystery of health: How people manage stress and stay well.* San Francisco: Jossey-Bass.

Berwick, D. M., & Hackbarth, A. D. (2012). Eliminating waste in US health care. *JAMA, 307*(14), 1513–16. https://doi.org/10.1001/jama.2012.362

Bonaiuti, M. (2014). *The great transition.* Oxon and New York: Routledge.

Borowy, I. (2013). Degrowth and public health in Cuba: Lessons from the past? *Journal of Cleaner Production, 38,* 17–26. https://doi.org/10.1016/j.jclepro.2011.11.057

Borowy, I., & Aillon, J.-L. (2017). Sustainable health and degrowth: Health, health care and society beyond the growth paradigm. *Social Theory & Health, 15*(3), 346–68. https://doi.org/10.1057/s41285-017-0032-7

Brody, H. (1999). The biopsychosocial model, patient-centered care, and culturally sensitive practice. *Journal of Family Practice, 48*(8), 585–7.

Cassel, C. K., & Guest, J. A. (2012). Choosing wisely: Helping physicians and patients make smart decisions about their care. *JAMA, 307*(17), 1801–2. https://doi.org/10.1001/jama.2012.476

Castoriadis, C. (1987). *The imaginary institution of society.* Cambridge: Polity Press.

Connolly, C., Kotsila, P., & D'Alisa, G. (2017). Tracing narratives and perceptions in the political ecologies of health and disease. *Journal of Political Ecology, 24*(1), 1–10. https://doi.org/10.2458/v24i1.20778

Costello, A., Abbas, M., Allen, A., Ball, S., Bell, S., Bellamy, R., Friel, S. et al. (2009). Managing the health effects of climate change. *The Lancet, 373*(9676), 1693–733. https://doi.org/10.1016/s0140-6736(09)60935-1

D'Alisa, G., Deriu, M., & Demaria, F. (2015). Care. In G. D'Alisa, D. Federico, & G.Kallis (Eds), *Degrowth: A vocabulary for a new era* (pp. 90–3). London: Routledge.

D'Alisa, G., Federico, D., & Kallis, G. (2015). *Degrowth: A vocabulary for a new era.* London: Routledge.

Demaria, F., Schneider, F., Sekulova, F., & Martinez-Alier, J. (2013). What is degrowth? From an activist slogan to a social movement. *Environmental Values, 22*(2), 191–215. https://doi.org/10.3197/096327113x13581561725194

De Vogli, R., & Owusu, J. .. (2015). The causes and health effects of the Great Recession: From neoliberalism to 'healthy de-growth.' *Critical Public Health, 25*(1), 15–31. https://doi.org/10.1080/09581596.2014.957164

Easterlin, R. A. (1974). Does economic growth improve the human lot? In P. A. David and M. W. Readers (Eds), *Nations and households in economic growth: Essays in honour of Moses Abramovitz.* New York: Academic Press.

Eckersley, R. (2006). Is modern Western culture a health hazard? *International Journal of Epidemiology, 35*(2), 252–8. https://doi.org/10.1093/ije/dyi235

Engel, L. G. (1977). The need for a new medical model: A challenge for biomedicine. *Science, 196*(4286), 129–36. https://doi.org/10.1126/science.847460

Fernando, S. (2014). Globalising mental health or pathologising the Global South? Mapping the ethics, theory and practice of global mental health. *Disability and the Global South, 1*(2), 188–202.

George, L. K., Larson, D. B., Koenig, H. G., McCullough, M. E. (2000). Spirituality and health: What we know, what we need to know. *Journal of Social and Clinical Psychology, 19*(1), 102–16. https://doi.org/10.1521/jscp.2000.19.1.102

Georgescu-Roegen, N. (1971). *The entropy law and the economic process.* Cambridge: Harvard University Press.

Herman, M. P., Poindexter, L. B., Witt, M. C., Eisenberg, M. D. (2012). Are complementary therapies and integrative care cost-effective? A systematic review of economic evaluations. *British Medical Journal Open, 2*(5), e001046. https://doi.org/10.1136/bmjopen-2012-001046

Helfrich, S., & Bollierm D. (2014). Commons. In G. D'Alisa, D. Federico, & G. Kallis (Eds), *Degrowth: A vocabulary for a new era* (pp. 90–3). London: Routledge.

Horton, Richard. (2013). Offline: Is global health neocolonialist? *The Lancet, 382*(9906), 1690. https://doi.org/10.1016/s0140-6736(13)62379-x

Hutchins, C. J. D. & Stuart, M. W. (2009). Coming round to recycling. *BMJ, 338*, b609. https://doi.org/10.1136/bmj.b609

Illich, I. (1973). *Tools for conviviality*. London: Calder and Boyars.

Illich, I. (1976). *Medical nemesis: The expropriation of health*. New York: Pantheon Books.

Italian Network for Health and Sustainability. (2014). Bologna manifesto for sustainability health. Retrieved from http://www.sostenibilitaesalute.org /the-bologna-manifesto-for-sustainability-and-health/

Latouche, S. (2006). *Le pari de la décroissance*. Paris: Libraire Arthème Fayard.

Latouche, S. (2009). *Farewell to growth*. Cambridge: Polity Press.

Latouche, S. (2010). Degrowth. *Journal of Cleaner Production, 18*(6), 519–22. https://doi.org/10.1016/j.jclepro.2010.02.003

Mikkonen, J., & Raphael, D. (2010). *Social determinants of health: The Canadian facts*. Toronto: York University School of Health Policy and Management.

Miles, A. (2009). On a medicine of the whole person: Away from scientist reductionism and towards the embrace of the complex in clinical practice. *Journal of Evaluation in Clinical Practice, 15*(6), 941–9. https://doi.org/10.1111/j.1365-2753 .2009.01354.x

Missoni, E. (2015). Degrowth and health: Local action should be linked to global policies and governance for health. *Sustainability Science, 10*(3), 439–50. https://doi .org/10.1007/s11625-015-0300-1

Moynihan, R., Heath, I., & Henry, D. (2002). Selling sickness: The pharmaceutical industry and disease mongering. *British Medical Journal, 324*(7342), 886–91. https:// doi.org/10.1136/bmj.324.7342.886

Moynihan, R., & Smith, R. (2002). Too much medicine? Almost certainly. *British Medical Journal, 324*(7342), 859–60. https://doi.org/10.1136/bmj.324.7342.859

Orozco A. (2015). Palabras viva antes un sistema biocida. Prologo. In G. D'Alisa, D. Federico, & G. Kallis (Eds), *Decrecimiento: un vocabulario por una nueva era*. Barcelona: Icaria Editorial.

Ovretveit, J. (2009). Does improving quality save money? A review of evidence of which improvements to quality reduce costs to health service providers. London: The Health Foundation. Retrieved from https://www.health.org.uk/publications /does-improving-quality-save-money

Pallante, M. (2009). *La decrescita felice: La qualità della vita non dipende dal pil*. Rome, Italy: Edizioni per la Decrescita Felice.

Pallante, M. (2011). *Meno e meglio: Decrescere per progredire*. Milan: Bruno Mondadori.

Pallante, M., & Aillon, J.-L. (2017). Decrescita felice e costruzione della salute: un circolo virtuoso. *Riflessioni Sistemiche, 16*, 71–86. Retrieved from http://www.aiems .eu/files/pallanteaillon.pdf

Piketty, T. (2014). *Capital in the 21st century*. Cambridge: Harvard University Press.

Plsek, E. P., & Greenhalgh, T. (2001). The challenge of complexity in health care. *British Medical Journal, 323*(7313), 625–8. https://doi.org/10.1136/bmj.323.7313.625

Quaranta, I. (2006). *Antropologia medica: i testi fondamentali.* Milan: Raffaello Cortina Editore.

Quijano, A. (2000). Colonialidad del poder, eurocentrismo y América Latina. Retrieved from http://www.decolonialtranslation.com/espanol/quijano -colonialidad-del-poder.pdf

Roberti di Sarsina, P. (2007). The social demand for a medicine focused on the person: The contribution of CAM to healthcare and healthgenesis. *Evidence-Based Complementary and Alternative Medicine, 4*(S1), 45–51. https://doi.org/10.1093 /ecam/nem094

Roberti di Sarsina, P., & Iseppato, I. (2010). Person-centred medicine: Towards a definition. *Forsch Komplementärmedizin/Complementary Medicine Research, 17*(5), 277–8. https://doi.org/10.1159/000320603

Scheper-Hughes, N., & Lock, M. M. (1987). The mindful body: A prolegomenon to future work in medical anthropology. *Medical anthropology quarterly, 1*(1), 6–41. https://doi.org/10.1525/maq.1987.1.1.02a00020

Suls, J., & Rothman, A. (2004). Evolution of the biopsychosocial model: Prospects and challenges for health psychology. *Health Psychology, 23*(2), 119–25. https://doi .org/10.1037/0278-6133.23.2.119

Taussig, T. M. (1980). Reification and the consciousness of the patient. *Social Science & Medicine. Part B: Medical Anthropology, 14*(1), 3–13. https://doi .org/10.1016/0160-7987(80)90035-6

Wise, R., Hart, T., Cars, O., Streulens, M., Helmuth, R., Huovinen, P. et al. (1998). Antimicrobial resistance is a major threat to public health, *BMJ, 317*(7159), 609–10. https://doi.org/10.1136/bmj.317.7159.609

World Health Organization. (1978). Declaration of Alma-Ata. Retrieved from http:// www.who.int/publications/almaata_declaration_en.pdf?ua=1&ua=1

World Health Organization. (1986). The Ottawa charter for health promotion. Retrieved from http://www.who.int/healthpromotion/conferences/previous/ottawa/en/

World Health Organization. (2008a). The World Health report 2008: Primary health care (now more than ever). Retrieved from http://www.who.int/whr/2008/en/index .html

World Health Organization. (2008b). Commission on the social determinants of health, closing the gap in a generation: Health equity through action on the social determinants of health. Retrieved from http://www.who.int/social_determinants /thecommission/finalreport/en/

World Health Organization. (2014). WHO traditional medicine strategy: 2014–2023. Retrieved from http://apps.who.int/iris/bitstream/10665/92455/1/9789241506090 _eng.pdf

World Health Organization. (2017). Climate change and health. Retrieved from http:// www.who.int/mediacentre/factsheets/fs266/en/

16 Nurturing Ecological Consciousness

MARK HATHAWAY, DONALD COLE, AND BLAKE POLAND

We're in a race between consciousness and catastrophe. So my focus ... is on the inner work that can enable us to do the outer work of navigating this time of transition in the best ways possible.

—Terry Patten (2018, p. 1)

Humanity is facing a dire ecological crisis (Rockström et al., 2009) that threatens the future of civilization (Ehrlich and Ehrlich, 2013) and countless species with collapse, unless we undertake thoughtful, sensitive, and concerted action to address the interconnected problems threatening the health of the entire Earth community. The visible manifestations of this crisis could be seen as the "tips of icebergs...the visible portion of a much larger entity" that largely "lies beneath the surface, beyond our daily inspection" (Evernden, 1993, p. xii). It is this "submerged mass" – characterized by a separative, domineering, and exploitative form of consciousness – that may form our subtler, and perhaps deeper, challenge. Roszak (1992) asserts that we need an "altered sensibility ... a radically new standard of sanity that...uproots the fundamental assumptions of industrial life" (p. 232). In this chapter, we argue that a profound transformation towards a more encompassing, relational, intersubjective, and life-affirming modality of consciousness is an essential dimension of regenerative transformation. This consciousness is essentially *ecological* insofar as it is relational in nature and because it situates "the human within the horizon of emergent, interdependent life rather than viewing humanity as the vanguard of evolution...or a species apart from nature" (Tucker and Grim, 2001, p. 15).

Of course, addressing the ecological crisis is not *only* a question of changing consciousness. Radical social transformation is essentially a "wicked problem" because "every problem interacts with other problems and is therefore part of a system of interrelated problems" (Ackoff, 1974, p. 21). It is futile, then, to deal with each challenge as though it was separate from the others.

Because of this, Esbjörn-Hargens and Zimmerman (2009) propose that the ecological crisis must be understood as a complex set of experiential, cultural, behavioural, and systemic phenomena – including "fractured consciousness, unsustainable behaviours, dysfunctional cultures, and broken systems" (p. 299–300) – that interact with one another and must be addressed holistically. Transformations in consciousness therefore require corresponding shifts in embodied, habitual behaviours as well as cultural, social, and ecological systems. Moving towards a more just, regenerative, and fulfilling world means working for transformation "from the inside and from the outside, all in one" (Naess and Rothenberg, 1989, p. 89)

While keeping this in mind, this chapter focuses primarily on inner change – how ecological consciousness may be nurtured in practice. To do so, it begins by examining the nature of consciousness as an embodied reality connected to both perception and action. Then it outlines some key characteristics of the kinds of consciousness that might facilitate a transition from the Anthropocene (Crutzen, 2002) – an epoch characterized by a dominating, instrumental form of consciousness that has accompanied the growing exploitation and destruction of life – to an ecologically regenerative epoch. The latter – sometimes called the Symbiocene (Albrecht, 2014), Ecocene (Hathaway, 2015), or Ecozoic (Berry, 1991) – aims to reintegrate humans "psychologically and technologically, into nature and natural systems" (Albrecht, 2014, p. 58) and "establish a mutually enhancing mode of human-Earth relations" (Berry, 2006, p. 22) along with "a niche that is beneficial both for [humans] and the larger community" (Berry, 1999, p. 105). Next, theoretical insights from integral transformative learning theory and ecopsychology will be considered to better understand how ecological consciousness may be nurtured. Finally, examples from our teaching experiences will be examined to illuminate these processes in practice.

Understanding Ecological Consciousness

Ethics follows from how we experience the world.

—Arne Naess (Fox, 1995, p. 219)

When speaking of consciousness, we are not referring merely to intellectual conceptualization – what we think *about* reality – nor even our identity (the *persona* we present to the world). Rather, consciousness "is fluid, utterly insubstantial, and not so easily subject to rational control. It is the experience of existence" (Newman, 2012, p. 42). Consciousness is relational insofar as it continually evolves in our encounters with other beings and entities; it is the ever-emerging "context in which all...experiences, perceptions, thoughts, or feelings converge" (Schlitz, Vieten, and Amorok, 2008, p. 16). Shifts in consciousness affect the way we relate to ourselves and to other beings and are always "both visceral and intellectual" (Newman, 2012, p. 43). Expansive shifts enable us to feel, think, and act with greater intensity, clarity, and insight.

Several large-scale quantitative studies illuminate how ecological consciousness is entwined, not only with thinking, but with feeling and action. Studies by Mayer and Frantz (2004) and Nisbet, Zelenski, and Murphy (2009) found that persons who experience strong feelings of embeddedness, kinship, or belonging to nature tend to resist consumerism, become involved in environmental organizations, and experience a sense of well-being rooted in their experience of being connected with nature. Hedlund-de Witt, de Boer, and Boersema (2014) discovered that those who feel a strong interconnection to the more-than-human world tend to adopt sustainable food consumption, use bicycles and public transportation, and support pro-ecological political action. In all three studies, the correlations discovered were much stronger than those found in research that only measured participants' beliefs *about* ecological issues (Stern, Dietz, and Guagnano, 1995); indeed, an affectively experienced sense of being connected to the more-than-human world appears to be particularly important in motivating pro-ecological action. As Damasio (1994a, 1999) has demonstrated, emotions are essential to our decision-making processes. Consciousness, then, is understood here to involve both emotion and reason. Indeed, while many people "still believe that emotion disrupts reason," in actual fact "reason and emotion go hand in hand, with reason possible only if emotion is present" (Lakoff and Johnson, 1999, p. 414).

Lakoff and Johnson (1999) also affirm that the mind itself – including functions like memory – is embodied because "the very mechanisms responsible for perception, movements, and object manipulation" are also "responsible for conceptualization and reasoning" (p. 38). The embodied mind can be understood as the interwoven "matrix within which reasoning, memory, emotion, language, and all other aspects of mental life are embedded" (Kennedy-Reid, 2012, p. 15) which at the same time penetrates "both the body and its environment" (Ingold, 2000, p. 165), stretching out to encompass what it perceives beyond the boundaries of the skull. Consciousness, then, is understood here to function as an embodied integration (or living system) of disposition, habits, feelings, and assumptions that orient the way we perceive, understand, and live in the world.

Based on his experience with the Apsaalooke Indigenous culture, Grim (2009) speaks of a somatic process of sensing, minding, and creating that illuminates this understanding of consciousness. *Sensing* connects "us to the world prior to any self-reflexive awareness" (p. 208). Sensing awakens attention in a process of *minding* that seeks – discursively, intuitively, or sensually – meaning and significance: what we could see as the central dimension of consciousness. Finally, minding "gives rise to creating" or, perhaps more broadly, to *enacting*, engaging with the world as it "changes, waxes, and wanes" (Grim, 2009, p. 208). This ecological understanding of consciousness is "directly relevant to action" and "intimates acquaintance and understanding rather than impersonal or abstract results" (Naess and Rothenberg, 1989, p. 37).

One of the hallmarks of ecological consciousness is that it perceives reality as an interconnected, relational community as opposed to an atomistic, separative world of mere "things." This sense is captured in Berry's (1999) affirmation that "the universe is a communion of subjects, not a collection of objects" (p. 82). Naess (1993) believed that an experiential sense of connection and identification with the more-than-human world was fundamental to a deeply ecological consciousness. This broadened sense of an ecological self extends beyond the skin-encapsulated ego, continually deepening the potentialities of life. Ecopsychologists speak of the related idea of an "ecological unconscious," the "compacted ecological intelligence of our species, the source from which culture unfolds as the self-conscious reflection of nature's own steadily emerging mindlikeness" (Roszak, 1992, p. 304). From this perspective – similar to Wilson's (1984) biophilia, the tendency to affiliate with life – humans have an innate capacity for this ecological orientation that flows out of our long evolution in intimate contact with the more-than-human world. The repression of this "ecological unconscious is the deepest root of collusive madness in industrial society," leading to a perception that humans are separate from nature and providing a licence to instrumentally exploit other beings, while "open access to the ecological unconscious is the path to sanity" (Roszak, 1992, p. 320). Reawakening to an ecological consciousness rooted in experiencing biophilia – our psychic connection to all life – can be understood as a key dimension to healing both ourselves and the Earth community.

Out of this sense of deep interconnection with the more-than-human world comes an epistemological orientation based on an intersubjective, participatory knowing where the "experiential knower shapes perceptually what is there" and where "the very process of perceiving is also a meeting, a transaction, with what there is.... To experience anything is to participate in it, and to participate is both to mould and to encounter" (Heron and Reason, 1997, p. 278). Such knowing is rooted in an empathic form of perception that opens oneself to "the wisdom of Earth herself...which discloses unto us once we are open to understand it [and] stand under the spell of what she is revealing to us" (Panikkar, 1995, p. 2). The fruit of such perception, in the words of Merleau-Ponty (1968), is that "the world seen is not 'in' my body, and my body is not 'in' the visible world.... There is reciprocal insertion and intertwining of one in the other" (p. 138) experienced as a participatory kinship. Indeed, Panikkar (1995) affirms that *scientia* traditionally required an act of loving identification, or liberating communion, with what we desire to know – something that Sewall (1999) refers to as "sympathetic perception." This intersubjective knowing may enable humans to work humbly *with* and *as part of* the greater Earth community – where all beings are our teachers – rather than seeking to manipulate, dominate, exploit, or control others.

Simultaneously, this intersubjective, participatory, and relational consciousness may lead to a spontaneous ethic rooted in care and compassion that does not flow out of duty or external rules, but rather one's perception of communion-with. Drawing on Kant's affirmation that ethical actions may be motivated either out of duty or a spontaneous inclination, Naess (1987) suggests that we should stress inclination and "beautiful" actions: "The requisite care flows naturally if the 'self' is widened and deepened so that protection of free Nature is felt" (p. 40).

Living in deeper communion with the more-than-human world may also lead to a deeper sense of purpose, meaning, and satisfaction – as indicated by Mayer and Frantz (2004) – enabling one to move away from consumerism as a life orientation and instead seek to simply "live well." In Indigenous Andean cultures, this idea of *buen vivir* (or *sumak kawsay* in Quechua) speaks of the ideal of human fulfilment within a communitarian vision focusing on the quality of life and relationships rather than on acquisition, accumulation, or consumption – living in a reality in which "human beings are part of a more harmonious whole which includes both nature and other humans, with the alterity (or otherness) that enriches us daily" (de la Cuadra, 2015, p. 5).

Transformative Learning and Ecological Consciousness

What sets the idea of transformation apart from other forms of change is that it is "a change of" not just "a change in...." Trans-form means to move across forms, to change the very form of ... The fundamental deep structure of the organism is changed, not just the surface appearance.

—Elizabeth Lange (2012, p. 202)

How can shifts towards ecological consciousness be nurtured and facilitated? One perspective is provided by O'Sullivan's (2002) integral transformative learning, which seeks "a deep, structural shift in the basic premises of thought, feelings, and actions" that "dramatically and irreversibly alters our way of being in the world" (p. 11). Learning may occur via many modalities, including critical reflection, but also non-verbally (through the body or emotions); it is conceived as being simultaneously an "inner" and "outer" process involving personal, social, and even ecological change. Transformative learning also seeks to move "toward an ecological consciousness" that enables persons to overcome "the despair of our current condition;" "create an expansive, life-giving vision" engaging the human spirit; and "foster ecological values such as connection, generosity, partnership, and celebration" (Morrell and O'Connor, 2002, p. 11). Drawing on ecopsychology, this transformation can be understood as both the discovery and *recovery* of an expansive ecological self, marked by a vital awareness of relationships and process.

In contrast to Mezirow's (1978, 1994) more linear understanding of transformative learning as a process of moving from a disorienting dilemma to critical reflection and then to perceptual and behavioural shifts, O'Sullivan's integral transformative learning draws primarily on systems theory to understand change in terms of self-organization or *autopoiesis*. In this perspective, there are many potential triggers, processes, and practices that may – under the right conditions – lead to a radical transformation of consciousness, but there are no simple recipes for change. Indeed, while Meadows (2008) notes there are "leverage points" in living systems, these are not always easily accessible, even if one knows how to use them. While reflective, critical thinking may play a useful role in transformative learning, it also has limits; ultimately one must accept "the humility of not-knowing" which involves "strategically, profoundly, madly, letting go and dancing with the system" (Meadows, 2008, p. 165).

At the same time, since the mind is embodied and involves the action of neural networks – which themselves may be understood as a complex relational system – insights from neurophysiology may illuminate how transformations in consciousness occur. While the ability to form new neural connections – neuroplasticity – is strongest in children, researchers have discovered that the adult brain is also capable of forming new pathways (Ratey, 2001) – as happens when stroke victims recover over time.

Two key factors seem to promote the formation of the new neural pathways that facilitate new forms of perception, action, and consciousness. The first is that of *attention* or mindfulness. By choosing to pay attention, we also shape our experience: "Moment by moment we choose and sculpt how our ever-changing minds will work ... and these choices are left embossed in physical form on our material selves" (Mezenich and deCharms, 1996, p. 76). Sewall (1999) explains that "our habitual focus of attention, determines the structure of our neuronal ensembles," which in turn condition what we perceive depending on "whatever resonates in the mix between inner and outer landscapes" (p. 110). The more a neural network is used, the greater the resonance, creating the conditions for perceiving "more of the same." This in turn forms habits of mind – or an embodied worldview – that sculpts the flow of consciousness. Empathy may further extend the transformative potential of attention via the action of mirror neurons that fire in both the visual and motor areas of the brain in sympathetic response to the emotions of others (Hall, 2010).

Secondly, new neural pathways are cemented and broadened via *practice*. "Repetitive behaviors – whether functional or dysfunctional – actually change the way our brains work" (Schlitz, Vieten, and Amorok, 2008, p. 106), reinforcing certain neural connections. Ongoing practice – regularly playing a musical instrument, walking in nature, doing t'ai chi, or weaving – is necessary to shift neuronal pathways, modes of perception, and behaviours. In the continually evolving process of sensing-minding-enacting, transformative learning towards an ecological consciousness may be facilitated by both attention (redirecting, extending, and transforming perception) and action (engaging physically with the land, practicing new habits and techniques, or creating a work of art or story). On the perceptual side, Sewall (1995) proposes that we need to learn the "skill of ecological perception" envisioned as a kind of devotional practice based on learning to be mindful (paying attention, attending to beauty, and feeling with aesthetic appreciation); perceiving relationships (focusing on interactions and interfaces rather than discrete objects); developing perceptual flexibility (spanning temporal and spatial scales); perceiving depth (seeking meaning, learning from other beings); and intentionally using imagination to extend perception, empathize with other beings, and conceive new possibilities. While the skill of ecological perception is envisioned as a sensorial practice, activating the full potential of transformative learning may entail other, more physical practices, including those found in working in community, being involved in social movements for change, working with the land, and interacting directly with a variety of living beings and ecosystems.

Nurturing Ecological Consciousness in Practice

How, though, may ecological consciousness be evoked, midwifed, and nurtured in practice? As previously noted, there are no simple recipes to stimulate shifts towards an ecological consciousness. Yet there are ways to create learning environments and processes that may facilitate transformation by providing opportunities to develop new perceptual skills, engage in novel practices, listen to and share stories, or experiment with different perspectives via the imagination or critical reflection. In this section, we will explore several examples from our own teaching practice – in particular, Donald Cole's teaching on ecological public health, Blake Poland's courses on building community resilience, and Mark Hathaway's teaching on ecological worldviews.

Ecological Public Health

Donald Cole, together with several other public health professors at the University of Toronto, noted increasing preoccupation among health studies, masters' in public health, and doctoral students around global changes, particularly climate and health; however, the dominant "environment as harm" approach needed to give way to eco-health and other emerging approaches grappling with multispecies, global interactions linking ecosystems and health (Buse et al., 2018).

Building upon others' resources (Parkes et al., 2017, McCullagh et al., 2012), they developed an Ecological Public Health (EPH) course. In fall 2014, they began with a group of dedicated graduate students from a variety of fields, combining theoretical and applied readings with intensive group discussions.

While it was challenging to grapple with the complexity of EPH problems and adequate responses to them, students found that experiential sessions, such as the talking circle, deepened their feelings and sense of relationship. In a visit to an urban farm located on Conservation Authority land, sensing the earth, hearing the wind in the hedgerows, talking with the growers from multiple cultures, and seeing the abundance of food grown within the city was a revelation of different possibilities.

The spring 2016 version, with a focus on watersheds, involved a field trip walking up the lower portion of the Don River in Toronto. In so doing, students affectively experienced the river, originally meandering through fertile wetlands, but then polluted by sewage and industrial effluents, and violently constrained within cement walls. The contested views of the Don and its regeneration exemplified the intermeshing of the social and ecological. In the winter 2017 undergraduate version, students noted artefacts of the history of the now-buried Taddle Creek through different theoretical lenses. A walk up University Avenue and the University of Toronto campus connecting Toronto-based mining interests with health and education infrastructure was a jarring revelation of dominant practice, summed up by the comment, "I had no idea." In the fall 2017 offering, community health centre staff shared concrete examples of slowly transformational work – a discussion of what constraints students experience in growing food, how these were shared with other urban residents, and the role of community gardens (including the rooftop garden they visited) in responding.

Based on these experiences, the combinations of theory and practice, problematizing and responding, outdoor engagement and interior work, all seemed to be important in fostering students' slowly emerging ecological consciousness during the course.

Building Community Resilience

Building Community Resilience began as a reading course in 2009 when Blake Poland invited students to join him as co-learners in an exploration of what was then and still is a relatively new topic – inspired in part by Blake's experience with Transition Towns as well as a run for the Green Party in the 2008 federal election in Oakville, Ontario. The course evolved over time into both a graduate (CHL5126, School of Public Health) and undergraduate offering (GGR434, Department of Geography). Over the years, the emphasis shifted significantly from reviewing the evidence of emerging threats (climate change, peak oil, ecological destruction) to emerging "solutions" and the role of social movements in (re)inventing the future. This reflected a shift in emphasis in Blake himself, but also the reality that students were increasingly aware of the challenges ahead, demoralized by relentlessly having their "noses rubbed in it" without accompanying attention to viable responses, and eager to learn more about what was being done and how to respond proactively.

The course incorporates transformative learning to nurture ecological consciousness, firstly, by engaging the whole person in the learning process. Students are invited to notice how they respond emotionally to reading material and class discussion, and how what is covered resonates (or not) with their own lived experience. To do this, a series of "resonant texts" form a component of the course assignments, whereby students are encouraged to experiment with different modalities of expression (painting, poetry, collage, sculpture, etc.), accompanied by a short explanatory text, to share what resonated from that week's reading material and in-class discussion. Engaging the whole person has led to a more fulsome engagement with the course material, several self-reported epiphanies, and a better inclusion of students for whom articulate academic writing is more of a challenge (but who may excel when other options are provided).

Second, partway through the course, an optional "empathy circle" is offered focusing on learners' feelings around emerging threats and opportunities. Following a "lead-in" guided meditation, participants are invited to speak into the circle what they are feeling, to keep it short, and to listen to others without commenting or offering advice. Often this is done with eyes closed and with many periods of silence. Inevitably, some report discomfort with sitting still and concern about inability to quiet the mind. Nevertheless, the shift in energy and empathy in the group is palpable as they hear each other share from the heart and notice how what is shared resonates for them.

Third, the course emphasizes how social movements and other groups are responding with creativity, passion, and innovation to the challenges and opportunities at hand. Indeed, following an initial focus on emerging challenges and resilience as the capacity to "bounce back" from adversity (including disaster-resilient cities and climate adaptation), the second half of the course is devoted to the wide range of initiatives that operationalize the notion of resilience as the capacity to embrace change and "bounce forward" into new ways of being and doing. Guest speakers from local social movements are featured, including Transition Towns, sustainability transitions work (Alberta Energy Futures Lab, TransformTO), ecovillages, cohousing and intentional communities, the minimalist and tiny house movements, homesteading, relocalization, degrowth, Indigenous, and Global South perspectives.

Finally, each year a different local group is engaged in greater depth, leading one or more sessions and fashioning a final assignment option around that group's work in a way that supports both student learning and the group's goals. In 2017, that group was the Conscious Minds Collective, youth engaged in critical consciousness-raising around social and environmental justice issues in Toronto. In 2018, the focus was on CREW (Community Resilience for Extreme

Weather), a group engaging neighbourhood residents in asset mapping and planning for extreme weather events.

Transformative Learning and Ecological Worldviews

Mark Hathaway's teaching has centred on transformative learning and ecological worldviews, particularly in an undergraduate course at the University of Toronto (ENV333) and the Earth Charter Initiative based in Costa Rica. To help undergraduates studying a course on ecological worldviews experience a deeper form of ecological consciousness, an assignment was developed that invited them to engage in a series of ecological practices[1] and to journal about their experiences. After an initial orientation session, students were encouraged to engage in these meditative exercises on five separate occasions in an outdoor space such as a park, ravine, yard, or forest.

The practices include an "elemental breaths" meditation that seeks to build a sense of connection with earth, water, fire, and air – and through these – with all living beings so as to open participants to a more expansive, ecological self. Students also engage in an "intersubjective meditation" – based on ecophenomenology (Abram, 1997, 2005; Brown and Toadvine, 2003) and Sewall's (1995, 1999) skill of ecological perception – in which they were asked to focus on an other-than-human entity (a leaf, an insect, a squirrel, or even running water) and attempt to perceive it without preconceptions. In so doing, they are to ask, "What is this entity communicating to me or teaching me?" After the exercises, participants journal about their experiences, incorporating writing, drawings, photos, or even leaves or twigs.

Based on an analysis of student journals and reflection papers, many appear to experience shifts in perception and consciousness. One wrote of sitting in a familiar tree at night gazing at the stars, sensing "the core *soul*" of the tree and its long lifetime along with an embrace of friendship. Another spoke of sitting very still in a forest and feeling that she had become invisible as squirrels and birds began to approach her, "beings who I considered to be highly perceptive." Another began to notice "patterns and connections...such as the reciprocal calls among birds, and the freezing response of squirrels to sudden noises."

While many initially found it difficult to engage in meditation – disconnected from electronic devices – over time most noted an improvement in their ability to focus and be attentive. Among the benefits of the experience, one spoke of moving from being a mere observer to being "part of the landscape," which enabled her to see the "animate qualities and contributions to the reciprocal dialogue" she had sought. Another found that she "really started to fall in love with the Earth as [Aldo] Leopold suggests simply by just actively interacting with it and increasing my awareness." Many became more aware of beauty and encountered a sense of peace along with connection to the more-than-human world. Many also found artistic ways of expressing their experiences, indicating that both their imaginations and creativity were stimulated in the process. While attention and practice played a large role in their transformative learning, it is also clear that reflection and art played a significant role.

Based on experiences both in formal academic (an optional workshop in a UT undergraduate course) and in less formal contexts (with the Earth Charter), Hathaway has also found that the Work that Reconnects (WTR) (Macy and Brown, 1998) provides helpful insights, processes, and exercises that can be used to nurture the formation of ecological consciousness, particularly in persons with some level of commitment to work for sustainability and social justice. The WTR assumes that understanding and working with our emotional response to pressing problems is essential to empowering transformative action. While it has been noted that feelings – particularly those of connection with the more-than-human world – can provide a powerful motivation for pro-ecological action, it is also true that emotions such as shame, fear, and despair may actually *impede* effective action (Damasio, 1994b, Hathaway, 2017b): "The very danger signals that should rivet our attention, summon up the blood, and bond us in collective action" instead "make us want to pull down the blinds and busy ourselves with other things" (Macy and Brown, 1998, p. 26). While blocked or repressed emotions impede our ability to respond, experiencing and reframing emotions may serve as a source of energy to bring about change (Johnstone, 2002). Using a variety of interactive and meditative exercises along with insights from systems theory, the WTR begins by seeking to root participants in self-transcendent emotions (Stellar et al., 2017) such as gratitude, awe, and compassion that tend to widen one's sense of self; then it moves to experience feelings of pain, anger, and grief – not to stimulate guilt – but rather to recognize that the source of our pain lies in connection, the same connection that is also the foundation of our collective power to act. Then, using systems perspectives and experiences of deep time (imaginatively connecting to past and future beings), it works to form a more ecological consciousness and, ultimately, motivate learners to become transformative agents working to bring forth a just and ecologically regenerative epoch.

For example, in an online course offered by the Earth Charter, participants write letters to their imaginary descendants in the distant future explaining how they began working to bring about a sustainable, regenerative, and fulfilling human future. In turn, they receive letters of encouragement from others playing the role of their descendants. The use of imagination seems particularly effective in helping facilitate these kinds of shifts in perception as well as to extend one's sense of empathy and compassion to other-than-human and future beings.

In reflecting on the WTR process, one undergraduate student noted that worldviews cannot be changed via facts and debate alone; rather, transformation involves "the body, mind, imagination and a supportive community." Another spoke of moving beyond a more limited sense of self and overcoming "divisions between mind and body, spirit and breath, and human and environment" (Hathaway, 2017a).

Conclusion

Considering these examples of working to nurture ecological consciousness, several insights may be discerned. In all our work, we are aware that different participants engaged in the same activities may have very different experiences of learning, some more transformational than others. As well, different approaches engage some learners more than others, so providing a variety of entry points and processes may be helpful.

In addition to seeking to overcome a sense of separation from the more-than-human world via meditations and exercises that refocus and reframe attention, it is clear that resonant reflection, dialogue, engagement with the land, emotional work, artistic and creative expression, community support, and interactions with social movements may all play important roles in facilitating transformative learning towards ecological consciousness. Together, these experiences may also help learners to reframe their experience from a narrative of "The Great Unravelling" – the story of a self-reinforcing spiral of death and destruction facilitated by the systems, technologies, and exploitative consciousness of the Anthropocene – to that of "The Great Turning" – marked by social movements seeking to reinvent the future by building community, opening to Earth's wisdom, experimenting with ecologically regenerative technologies, and deepening ecological consciousness to bring forth the Ecocene.

To continue this exploration into how ecological consciousness and regenerative social movements may be nurtured in practice, our research is taking several approaches. Cole is working with Indigenous and peasant organizations in Ecuador who are adopting agro-ecological approaches to farming. Cole and Poland are engaged in a project on land-based learning for eco-social transformation in the Anthropocene, while Hathaway is investigating transformative ecological learning in permaculture. Poland, together with Hathaway and others, has applied for funding to explore transformational engagement strategies by using a series of generative dialogues to create intentional communities of practice where ecological consciousness may be experienced and translated into action, drawing on Indigenous and Global South ways of knowing. In all these undertakings, we are aware that ecological consciousness is just one – albeit arguably a very important – element in a wider matrix of change encompassing political action, building creative communities as seeds of ecological and social regeneration, and reshaping cultures and habitual behaviours.

NOTE

1 See http://markhathaway.org/files/ecopractices.pdf.

REFERENCES

Abram, D. (1997). *The spell of the sensuous: Perception and language in a more-than-human world* (1st Vintage Books ed). New York, NY: Vintage Books.

Abram, D. (2005). Between the body and the breathing Earth: A reply to Ted Toadvine. *Environmental Ethics, 27*(2), 171–90. https://doi.org/10.5840/enviroethics200527229

Ackoff, R. L. (1974). *Redesigning the future: A systems approach to societal problems.* New York, NY: Wiley.

Albrecht, G. (2014). Ecopsychology in the Symbiocene. *Ecopsychology, 6*(1), 58–9. https://doi.org/10.1089/eco.2013.0091

Berry, T. (1991). *The ecozoic era.* Great Barrington, MA: Schumacher Society for a New Economics.

Berry, T. (1999). *The great work: Our way into the future* (1st ed.). New York, NY: Bell Tower.

Berry, T. (2006). *Evening thoughts: Reflecting on Earth as sacred community.* M. E. Tucker (Ed.). San Francisco, CA: Sierra Club Books.

Brown, C. S., & Toadvine, T. (2003). *Eco-phenomenology: Back to the Earth itself, SUNY series in environmental philosophy and ethics.* Albany, NY: SUNY Press.

Buse, C. G., Oestreicher, J. S., Ellis, N. R., Patrick, R., Brisbois, B., Jenkins, A. P., McKellar, K., Kingsley, J., Gislason, M., & Galway, L. (2018). Public health guide to field developments linking ecosystems, environments and health in the Anthropocene. *Journal of Epidemiology & Community Health, 36*(5), 1–6. https://doi.org/10.1136/jech-2017-210082

Crutzen, P. J. (2002). Geology of mankind. *Nature, 415*(6867), 23. https://doi.org/10.1038/415023a

Damasio, A. R. (1994a). Descartes' error and the future of human life. *Scientific American, 271*(4), 144. https://doi.org/10.1038/scientificamerican1094-144

Damasio, A. R. (1994b). *Descartes' error: Emotion, reason, and the human brain.* New York, NY: Avon Books.

Damasio, A. R. (1999). *The feeling of what happens: Body and emotion in the making of consciousness* (1st ed.). New York, NY: Harcourt Brace & Company.

de la Cuadra, F. (2015). Buen vivir: ¿Una auténtica alternative post-capitalista? *Polis: Revista Latinoamericana, 40.* Retrieved from: http://polis.revues.org/10893.

Ehrlich, P. R, & Ehrlich, A. H. (2013). Can a collapse of global civilization be avoided? *Proceedings of the Royal Society B: Biological Sciences, 280*(1754), 1–9. https://doi.org/10.1098/rspb.2012.2845

Esbjörn-Hargens, S., & Zimmerman, M. E. (2009). *Integral ecology: Uniting multiple perspectives on the natural world* (1st ed.). Boston, MA: Integral Books.

Evernden, N. (1993). *The natural alien: Humankind and environment* (2nd ed.). Toronto, ON: University of Toronto Press.

Fox, W. (1995). *Toward a transpersonal ecology: Developing new foundations for environmentalism.* Albany, NY: State University of New York Press.

Grim, J. A. (2009). Indigenous embodied knowing: A study in Crow/Apsaalooke. In S. Bergmann, P. M. Scott, M. J. Samuelsson, & H. Bedford-Strohm (Eds), *Nature, space and the sacred: Transdisciplinary perspectives* (pp. 203–22). Farnham, UK: Ashgate.

Hall, S. (2010). *Wisdom: From philosophy to neuroscience* (1st ed.). New York, NY: Alfred A. Knopf.

Hathaway, M. (2015). The practical wisdom of permaculture: An anthropoharmonic phronesis for an ecological epoch. *Environmental Ethics, 37*(4), 445–63. https://doi .org/10.5840/enviroethics201537442

Hathaway, M. (2017a). Activating hope in the midst of crisis: Emotions, transformative learning, and 'the work that reconnects.' *Journal of Transformative Education.* Online Advance Publication. https://doi.org/10.1177/1541344616680350.

Hathaway, M. (2017b). Overcoming fear, denial, myopia, and paralysis: Scientific and spiritual perspectives on addressing the emotional factors affecting our response to the ecological crisis. *Worldviews: Global Religions, Culture, and Ecology, 21*(2), 175–93. https://doi.org/10.1163/15685357-02002100.

Hedlund-de Witt, A., de Boer, J., & Boersema, J. J. (2014). Exploring inner and outer worlds: A quantitative study of worldviews, environmental attitudes, and sustainable lifestyles. *Journal of Environmental Psychology, 37*, 40–54. https://doi.org/10.1016 /j.jenvp.2013.11.005

Heron, J., & Reason, P. (1997). A participatory inquiry paradigm. *Qualitative inquiry, 3*(3), 274–94. https://doi.org/10.1177/107780049700300302

Ingold, T. (2000). *The perception of the environment: Essays on livelihood, dwelling and skill.* London, UK: Routledge.

Johnstone, C. (2002). Reconnecting with our world. In A. Chesner and H. Hahn (Eds), *Creative advances in group work* (pp. 186–216). London, UK: Jessica Kingsley Publishers Ltd.

Kennedy-Reid, S. K. (2012). Exploring the habitus: A phenomenological study of transformative learning processes. (Doctoral dissertation). The Graduate School of Education and Human Development, The George Washington University.

Lakoff, G., & Johnson, M. (1999). *Philosophy in the flesh: The embodied mind and its challenge to Western thought.* New York, NY: Basic Books.

Lange, E. A. (2012). Transforming transformative learning through sustainability and new science. In E. W. Taylor, & P. Cranton (Eds), *The handbook of transformative learning: Theory, research, and practice* (pp. 195–211). San Francisco, CA: Jossey-Bass.

Macy, J., & Brown, M. (1998). *Coming back to life: Practices to reconnect our lives, our world.* Gabriola Island, BC: New Society Publishers.

Mayer, F. S., & Frantz, C. M. (2004). The connectedness to nature scale: A measure of individuals' feeling in community with nature. *Journal of Environmental Psychology, 24*(4), 503–15. https://doi.org/10.1016/j.jenvp.2004.10.001

McCullagh, S., Hunter, B., Houle, K., Massey, C., Waltner-Toews, D., Lemire, M., Saint-Charles, J., Surette, C., Webb, J., Beck L., Parkes, M., Woollard, R., Berbés-Blázquez, M., Feagan, M., Halpenny, C., Harper, S., Oestreicher, S., & Morrison, K. (Eds) (2012). *Ecosystem approaches to health teaching manual.* Montreal, QC: Canadian Community of Practice in Ecosystem Approaches to Health. Retrieved from http://www.copeh-canada.org/upload/files/teaching_manual_ecohealth.pdf.

Meadows, D. H. (2008). *Thinking in systems: A primer.* D. Wright (ed.). White River Junction, VT: Chelsea Green Publishing.

Merleau-Ponty, M. (1968). *The visible and the invisible: Followed by working notes.* Evanston, IL: Northwestern University Press.

Mezenich, M. M., & deCharms, R. C. (1996). Neural representations, experience, and change. In P. S. Churchland, & R. R. Llinás (Eds), *The mind-brain continuum: Sensory processes* (pp. xi, 315). Cambridge, MA: MIT Press.

Mezirow, J. (1978). Perspective transformation. *Adult Education Quarterly, 28*(2), 100–10. https://doi.org/10.1177/074171367802800202

Mezirow, J. (1994). Understanding transformation theory. *Adult Education Quarterly, 44*(4), 222–44. https://doi.org/10.1177/074171369404400403

Morrell, A., & O'Connor, M. A. (2002). Introduction. In E. O'Sullivan, A. Morrell, & M. A. O'Connor (Eds), *Expanding the boundaries of transformative learning: Essays on theory and praxis* (pp. xv–xx). New York, NY: Palgrave.

Naess, A. (1993). Simple in means, rich in ends: An interview with Arne Naess by Stephan Bodian. In M. E. Zimmerman (Ed.). *Environmental philosophy: From animal rights to radical ecology* (pp. 182–92). Englewood Cliffs, NJ: Prentice-Hall.

Naess, A., & Rothenberg, D. (1989). *Ecology, community, and lifestyle: Outline of an ecosophy.* Cambridge, UK: Cambridge University Press.

Naess, A. (1987). Self-realization: An ecological approach to being in the world. *The Trumpeter, 4*(3), 34–41.

Newman, M. (2012). Calling transformative learning into question: Some mutinous thoughts. *Adult Education Quarterly, 62*(1), 36–55. https://doi.org/10.1177/0741713610392768

Nisbet, E. K., Zelenski J. M., & Murphy, S. A. (2009). The nature relatedness scale: Linking individuals' connection with nature to environmental concern and behavior. *Environment and Behavior, 41*(5), 715–40. https://doi.org/10.1177/0013916508318748

O'Sullivan, E. V. (2002). The project and vision of transformative learning. In E. V. O'Sullivan, A. Morrell, & M. A. O'Connor (Eds), *Expanding the boundaries of transformative learning: Essays on theory and praxis* (pp. 1–12). New York, NY: Palgrave Macmillan.

Panikkar, R. (1995). Ecosophy. *The New Gaia, 4*(1), 2–7.

Parkes, M. W., Saint-Charles, J., Cole, D. C., Gislason, M., Hicks, E., Bourdais, C. L., McKellar, K. A., & Bouchard, M. S.-C. (2017). Strengthening collaborative capacity: Experiences from a short, intensive field course on ecosystems, health and society. *Higher Education Research & Development, 36*(5), 1031–46. https://doi.org/10.1080 /07294360.2016.1263937

Patten, T. (2018). *A new republic of the heart: An ethos for revolutionaries – A guide to inner work for holistic change.* Berkeley, CA: North Atlantic Books.

Ratey, J. J. (2001). *A user's guide to the brain: Perception, attention, and the four theatres of the brain.* New York, NY: Vintage Books.

Rockström, J., Steffen, W. L., Noone, K., Persson, Å., Chapin III, F. S., Lambin, E., Lenton, T. M., Scheffer, M., Folke, C., & Schellnhuber, H. J. (2009). Planetary boundaries: Exploring the safe operating space for humanity. *Ecology and society, 14*(2), 32. https://doi.org/10.5751/es-03180-140232

Roszak, T. (1992). *The voice of the Earth.* New York, NY: Simon & Schuster.

Schlitz, M., Vieten, C., & Amorok, T. (2008). *Living deeply: The art & science of transformation in everyday life.* Oakland, CA: New Harbinger Publications.

Sewall, L. (1995). The skill of ecological perception. In M. Gomes, A. Kanner, & T. Roszak (Eds), *Ecopsychology: Restoring the earth, healing the mind* (pp. 201–15). San Francisco, CA: Sierra Club Books.

Sewall, L. (1999). *Sight and sensibility: The ecopsychology of perception.* New York, NY: J.P. Tarcher/Putnam.

Stellar, J. E., Gordon, A. M., Piff, P. K., Cordaro, D., Anderson, C. L., Bai, Y., Maruskin, L. A., & Keltner, D. (2017). Self-transcendent emotions and their social functions: Compassion, gratitude, and awe bind us to others through prosociality. *Emotion Review, 9*(3), 200–7. https://doi.org/10.1177/1754073916684557

Stern, P. C., Dietz, T., & Guagnano, G. A. (1995). The new ecological paradigm in social-psychological context. *Environment and Behavior, 27*(6), 723–43. https://doi .org/10.1177/0013916595276001

Tucker, M. E., & Grim, J. A. (2001). Introduction: The emerging alliance of world religions and ecology. *Daedalus, 130*(4), 1–22. https://doi.org/10.2307/20027715

Wilson, E. O. (1984). *Biophilia: The human bond with other species.* Cambridge, MA: Harvard University Press.

17 Bodies of the Anthropocene: Health, Ontology, Ecology

ALEXANDER FOSTER

Introduction

From this field of difference, replete with promises and terrors of cyborg embodiment and situated knowledge, there is no exit. *Anthropologists of possible selves, we are technicians of realizable futures.*

—Haraway, 1991, p. 230, emphasis added

The announcement of the Anthropocene brings with it a choice. Either we reflect on the ways in which we currently live, as individuals, groups, nations, and as a species, or we keep on going as usual, perhaps attempting to change energy sources and keep our current ways of life viable, but without truly challenging them and asking whether there are better means to go about the act of living. As Bruno Latour (2015) pugilistically puts it, this choice is one of choosing between being humans in the Holocene, or being earthbound in the Anthropocene. To choose to be earthbound, Latour (2014) argues, is to seek to understand the critical systems amid which we live, and so attempt to live *with* them, rather than merely on them. Realizing that this is a choice – whether we choose to live roughly as we have done, or whether we choose to explore new possibilities for human society – is to engage with the notion that we must not talk about what the future is, but rather what prospects there might be (Latour, 2010).

This chapter aligns itself with the desire to be earthbound in the Anthropocene, focusing on what this might mean for health. Taking the human body as its subject, it aims to enquire as to how we might build prospective health possibilities that are more aligned with the natural history of the human body than the socially created body. To develop this enquiry is to question Rose's (1994, p. 67) statement that "[o]ur present is suffused with the ethic of the humanist, the ethic of the normal social person, which is intrinsically the ethic of the healthy body." To what extent is the ethic of the normal social person *intrinsically* the ethic of the healthy body? Do normal social ways of being interfere with the healthy body? If so, what tools do we have to create new ways of looking at the body and develop ways of critiquing contemporary modes of existence in service of the human body and its health? Over the course of this chapter, one prospective future is argued for, in line with the Anthropocene and the desire to live well.

Turning first to the human microbiome as a means to illustrate the interconnections between humans and ecological systems, Castree's (2014) recommendation of "engaged analysis" is used as the basis for social scientists engaging with findings in the natural sciences in the Anthropocene. Noting that the microbiome provides a mass of evidence of the human body's ecological entanglements,[1] this section goes on to introduce the ways in which the microbiome has the potential to affect health through alterations to it and the ways of life it permits. In addition, this section allows for the opening of an enquiry into contemporary ways of life and what they mean for the microbial health of the self. This sets up the first of three argumentative pillars that will later be used in order to develop a novel approach to health, and ways of living, in the Anthropocene. Following this, the chapter turns to examine what futures are being put forward for the human body, namely transhumanism and posthumanism. Whilst the former refers to the belief that investment in technology will save humanity from itself, even going to the extent of granting freedom from death, the latter refers to the belief that humanity should be mindful of the cosmic and ecological forces with which it is entangled, and thus should seek to live with – rather than attempt to conquer – them. Ultimately, this section raises concern for the ecological soundness of the transhumanist position, and thus promotes posthumanism as a starting point. This section, therefore, serves as the ontological second pillar of the argument delivered in this chapter. The following section, the third pillar of the argument, ties in the political aspect of the argument, or: How can we produce an affirmative critique of contemporary modes of existence that can allow us to live posthuman lives? This section promotes Henri Lefebvre's work on rhythmanalysis as a useful tool. By emphasizing Lefebvre's concern for the human body, this section demonstrates how a deep reading of rhythmanalysis opens the possibility of affirmative criticism based on rhythmic relations and their effects on human health. This allows for crucial links to be made between the health of the body, everyday life, and capitalism. Finally, this chapter reflects on what a posthumanist, rhythmanalytic shift might mean, not only for health but for human ways of life as a whole. What is therefore argued is the need to face up to the challenge of how we might best live, if the human body was placed at the forefront of our concerns.

The Human Microbiome

[T]he human is an integrated colony of amoebid beings, just as those amoebid beings (protocists) are integrated colonies of bacteria. *Like it or not, our origins are in slime.*
—Ansell Pearson, 1997, p. 124

As a recent spate of popular science books seeks to remind us (see Yong, 2016; McAuliffe, 2016; DeSalle and Perkins, 2016; Blaser, 2015; Knight, 2015), we humans are inescapably microbial. Often, the figure that we are only 10 per cent human comes up in conversation (Savage, 1977; Collen, 2015), not to mention the 99 per cent of those genes in the human body that comes from microbial bodies (Xu and Gordon, 2003). Whilst the exact human:microbe ratio is contested (see Sender et al., 2016), we cannot ignore these microbes, entangled as they are not just within the life of a human, but within the development of these human bodies.

Dupré (2012) argues that these microbes are necessary for "normal" phys-iological development. Tamper with them and the fallout is immense. The microbiome has been observed to affect the development of allergies (Arrieta and Finlay, 2014; Stefka et al., 2014), the methods by which the body is able to gain nutrients from food (Smith et al., 2013; Trehan et al., 2013), the matur-ing of the immune system (Umesaki and Setoyama, 2000), metabolic function (Berg, 1996) and, potentially, mental health (Cryan and Dinan, 2012; Machos et al., 2013; Ohland et al., 2013). What is more, the 5–8 per cent of the human genome that has been found to be retroviral – coming from ancient viruses that have, at some point in time, merged with the human genome (Zimmer, 2015) – is thought to play a critical role in assisting the immune system (Chuong et al, 2016). Without these microbial symbionts, Dupré notes, "the whole [human] would be seriously dysfunctional and non-viable" (2012, p. 125). The microbi-ome, therefore, provides a significant challenge to the idea that "there are no 'good' Germs or 'bad' Germs. All Germs are bad" (Helman, 1978, p. 119).

This drive for *Homo microbis* (Sagan, 2013; Helmreich, 2016) first resonates with Donna Haraway's (1991) promotion of the cyborg as an approach that runs contrary to notions of contagion and penetration of an otherwise healthy, purely human, body. Second, it echoes (and provides further fuel for) Emily Martin's (1998) argument against a modernist mode of thought that would envision the body as a machine, with clear definite boundaries, machine-like solidarity, and with self defending against non-self.

What the microbiome represents, therefore, is an indication of our envi-ronmental intra-connections. As Hird (2010, p. 60) notes, what this sym-biosis reveals is "a much more intimate relationship between organism and environment: in the case of symbiogenesis, the environment literally becomes the organism." The microbiome provides a concrete link between, and even through, beings by means of ecological entanglements. Nowhere is this more evident than in the psychological effects of the parasite *Toxoplasma gondii*, which, once picked up from another being, such as a domestic cat, is able to alter how one experiences and encounters the world (see Coccaro et al., 2016). Deleuze and Guattari perhaps best summarized these inter- and intra-linkages among species when they noted that "[w]e form a rhizome with our viruses, or rather our viruses cause us to form a rhizome with other animals" (1987, p. 10).

How we live in the time of the Anthropocene must, therefore, account for our microbial symbionts. Julia Scott (2014) – and latterly James Hamblin (2016) – demonstrated in an experiment with her own skin hygiene that modern approaches to cleanliness decimated her native skin microbiome. Such actions can leave the skin at risk of blooms of bacteria, such as *Staphylococcus aureus*, that in turn has been causally linked to cases of eczema (Gong et al., 2006). As well, a recent study by Nakatsuji et al. (2017) illustrated that balancing out the skin microbiome, through the application of native strains to the infected area, successfully eliminates the majority of the *S. aureus* bloom.

For the matter of health in the Anthropocene, the microbiome offers definitive evidence of those intimate relations between humans and ecologies on which humans depend. When taking the stance of the engaged analyst, such findings, particularly in relation to how modern life affects the microbiome, cause a question to arise about how well the microbial health of the self is being cared for, or not, through modern ways of life. As Martin noted above, the modern conception of the body is not appropriate to the realities of the body. For the sake of thinking about human health, new ways of thinking about the human body will be required.

Ontologies of the Body

When speaking of ontologies of the body in modern society, and of hopes for the future, the figure of the cyborg – mentioned above – arises almost without effort. Though for some this is an embodiment of techno-humanism, it is perhaps best articulated in the work of Donna Haraway. In *Simians, Cyborgs and Women* (Haraway, 1991), her perspective is not only that it signifies the blurring of the machine-organism divide (as techno-humanism would suggest), but also of human-animal and physical-nonphysical boundaries. This cyborg emphasizes responsibility in its construction, without a final determination of the body at a historical juncture.

Transhuman Approaches

Though finding its influences in the science fiction work of H.G. Wells and Aldous Huxley, and its first articulation by Julian Huxley (1968), transhumanism's contemporary force comes through Max More, Anders Sandberg, and Nick Bostrom, among others (O'Connell, 2018). In seeking to define what this transhumanist movement concerns itself with, More (1990) writes:

Transhumanism is a class of philosophies of life that seek the continuation and acceleration of the evolution of intelligent life *beyond* its currently human form and limitations by means of science and technology, guided by life-promoting principles and values.

This drive for "beyond" is one that seeks to transcend human bodies through the use of science and technology, such that biological limits, such as intelligence, physicality, and even death, can be overcome. Nick Bostrom (2005) is more specific about what science and technology should be employed, citing genetic engineering and information technology, as well as molecular nanotechnology and artificial intelligence.

However, transhumanism is not a singular thing. As Ferrando (2013) notes, this vision for the human body has been promoted in libertarian (free market as a regulator of human enhancement), democratic (equal access to technological enhancement), and extropian (emphasis on practical optimism about self-direction and a rational, open society) ways. What remains constant across these forms, nonetheless, is an emphasis on technologically driven human enhancement.

Whilst this movement is one that has gained significant traction, with multiple books having been written (see Tegmark, 2017; Harari, 2016; Kurzweil, 2006; Hayles, 1999) and institutions such as the Future of Life Institute in Oxford having been set up, surprisingly little attention has been paid to what ontology of the body transhumanism employs. Ferrando (2014) concludes that the body comes off as neutral, lacking attention on the multitude of bodies that make up the human species, as well as their ecological entanglements. Advocates of transhumanism note that the movement does not think of there being a dichotomy between nature and culture, but it nevertheless pushes the position that humanity is the pinnacle of nature.[2] Furthermore, in support of Ferrando's argument, though transhumanism declares itself in support of "essential human values," there has been a lack of considering the positionality of these values. Perhaps this naivety of transhumanism is best summarized by Mark O'Connell, who, having spoken with multiple advocates of the transhumanist movement, saw that:

[F]or all that transhumanism presented itself as ... oriented forwards toward a vision of a world to come, it felt ... almost nostalgically evocative of a human past in which radical optimism seemed a viable position to take with respect to the future. (2018, p. 7)

It is this same radical optimism that guides projects like geo-engineering, already lambasted by Anthropocene scholars (see Clark and Yusoff, 2017). It is this same radical optimism that believes that human life will be able to go on just as it has been doing: that technology will prevail. Such a position, as Ansell Pearson (1997) damningly argues, is ill thought. There is, he notes, no escape from the human condition and from the biological foundations of humanity. To adopt the transhumanist position risks alienation from this biological self, from one's ecological entanglements, and from the Earth on which one lives. Such a position can only be deemed unsustainable for the time of the Anthropocene.

Posthuman Approaches

Posthumanism offers radically different prospects to those presented by transhumanism. The term, however, is not without significant confusion. As Castree et al. (2004) note, the term has been used to refer to:

- That which comes after the human (see Fukuyama, 2002), as the point at which the transhuman becomes almost god-like
- Scepticism about claims made in the human, employing a deconstructive approach to those texts that seek to designate what is and is not human (see Derrida, 2008)
- The ontological thesis that we have never been human

Lorimer (2009) has, in turn, referred to these as hyperbolic, deconstructive, and vitalist forms. For him, the first of these terms is not only technocentric but politically naive regarding capitalism. The second of these terms is deemed to be textual to such an extent that the possibility of action in the world becomes difficult at best. As such, it is the vitalist form of posthumanism to which it is best to turn.

This mode of thought draws attention to the creative role of the human body in making space, emphasizing contingencies and emergence whilst making room for an expanded ethics towards the nonhuman and a greater openness to experimental and folk practices. This allows for an expansion of what constitutes politics, firmly located and interested in the micro-political and minoritarian aspects of everyday life (Braidotti, 2013). What this vitalist form crucially allows for is an elaboration of the body as a system, furthering Emily Martin's (1998) claims contra the modern body in favour of fluidity. As Grosz (2004) emphasizes, there is a need to understand the body as a series of open-ended systems through which it can access and acquire its abilities and capabilities. Saldanha (2006) has taken this a step further in his machinic geography of bodies seeking to account for how certain bodies "stick" to places. This takes us towards a need to examine the spatiotemporality of the posthuman body, an enterprise that will be examined in the discussion, in combination with Henri Lefebvre's rhythmanalysis.

The human body, therefore, is not corporeal in a traditional sense. Rather, it is trans-corporeal. This term requires us to think not only through theories of corporeality but also of environmental theories and science studies (Alaimo, 2010). What, however, does this mean for thinking through the human body in the Anthropocene?

Primarily, given the ecological and technological connection the posthumanist perspective makes us confront, "[w]e (but not only 'we humans') are always already responsible to the other with whom or which we are entangled ...through the various ontological entanglements that materiality entails" (Barad, 2007, p. 393). Returning to the microbiome, we can see this ethic expressed in Heather Paxson's (2008) work on the relations between humans and the microbiological, which function as an "expression [for] a people's connection to a piece of land" (p. 26). Consequently, the posthuman position offers the possibility of an ecological form of "care of the self", in which one cares for oneself through caring for one's environment, navigating the micropolitics of everyday life with an ethics of trans-corporeality.[3] As the previous section on the human microbiome demonstrated, an ecological approach to the self can lead not only to healthier beings but reduced resource use through the reduction in those diseases that would occur due to purist ideas of the human. However, as can be shown by the rise of microbiome-friendly products, a posthuman positionality does not grant one resistance to the lures of capitalism. For this, rhythmanalysis is required.

Rhythmanalysis and the Body

Engagement with Henri Lefebvre in the medical humanities has been limited. Of those writings that seriously contend with his work, the focus has been on his 1974 text, *The Production of Space* (e.g. Morton, 2011; McDonald et al., 2017; Gutierrez and DasGupta, 2015). Engagement with rhythmanalysis has been nonexistent. Nonetheless, outside of the medical humanities, rhythmanalysis has been increasingly used for identifying social rhythms (see O'Conner, 2017; Osman and Mulíček, 2017; Marcu, 2017), the interplay of natural rhythms with particular activities (see Rickly, 2017; Edensor and Larsen, in press), and rhythms as involved in the creation of particular subjects (see Jones and Warren, 2016; Wozniak, 2017). Only Meadows et al.'s (2017) work on sleep gets at what this chapter understands to be the core focus of rhythmanalysis. This focus is, as Elden (in Lefebvre, 2015) notes, the human body – particularly the body under capitalism. Here, the body is the first point of analysis and a tool for subsequent investigations. To engage with rhythmanalysis is, therefore, to attempt to investigate contemporary modes of existence from the perspective of the body. From this, it becomes possible to develop critiques of these modes of existence. Such an approach is not merely material but attempts to account for the production of those multiple bodies that "we have, we do, and we are" (see Mol and Law, 2004; Mol, 2002). Indeed:

> There is neither separation nor an abyss between so-called material bodies, living bodies, social bodies and representations, ideologies, traditions, projects and utopias. They are all composed of (reciprocally influential) rhythms in interaction. These rhythms are analysed, *but the analyses in thought are never brought to term.* (Lefebvre, 2015, p. 51, emphasis added)

If this is the task of rhythmanalysis, how is it to be done? Lefebvre suggests that rhythm has three forms, the latter two of which are statements of health about the first. First, there is polyrhythmia, the presence of a multitude of overlapping, interacting rhythms. Second, there is eurhythmia, the uniting of rhythms such that a normal state of health emerges. Third, there is arrhythmia, the discordance of rhythms such that suffering is the outcome. These types of rhythm are able to be fitted to a framework, which concerns linear rhythms (the repetition of the same, linked to capitalist ways of life – i.e. the timetabling of a subway system or of shift work) and cyclical rhythms (the repetition where what returns is not quite the same, linked to cosmic and ecological rhythms – i.e. breathing), where each rhythm is subject to birth, growth, peaks, declines, and, ultimately, death. All things are noted to have their own multitude of rhythms, both innate and those imposed upon it, with various speeds and slownesses. As Lefebvre and Regulier (in Lefebvre, 2015, p. 86) note, "each one of us *is* this unity of diverse relations." Furthermore, it is not only that each organ in the human body has its own rhythms, but that:

> The living body must consider itself as an intervention of organs situated inside it, where each organ has its own rhythm but is subject to a spatio-temporal whole. Furthermore, this human body is the site and place of interaction between the biological, the physiological (nature) and the social (often called the cultural), where each of these levels, each of these dimensions, has its own specificity, therefore its spatio-time: its rhythm. (Lefebvre, 2015, p. 89–90)

Thus, this emphasis on the interaction of multiple rhythms provides a crucial link between the body and the society in which it exists, through rhythm.

In protest against capitalism's attempts to negate the human body, rhythmanalysis offers an analytic tool to push back against this negation. Indeed, one of the areas that Lefebvre sees as being of particular concern is the trinity of activity-repose-entertainment, through which bodies are disciplined by means of "educated" rhythms such as, similar to Foucault (1991), the timetable. For Lefebvre, these "educated" rhythms are linear, produced through, and for the sake of, the relations of capital. They are therefore to be critiqued in relation to how they may colonize more cyclical rhythms and produce arrhythmia.

Two points of clarification are due before moving to consider what a post-humanistic rhythmanalytic framework might mean for health in the Anthropocene. First, whilst the emphasis here has been on a reading of rhythmanalysis as centred on the human body, rhythmanalysis is also an analysis of space over time. This is important to keep in mind because, as Rose (1994) notes, public space is organized as a field of possibilities, with (im)probabilities established, in which individuals are able to conduct themselves freely. Thus, the organization of space makes certain rhythms more or less likely, in turn affecting the rhythms of the bodies that move through this space. Second, whilst Lefebvre speaks of bodies-in-the-world, we, in keeping with the posthumanist approach, should speak of bodies-*of*-the-world (Barad, 2007) that are deeply ecological (as noted with regards to the microbiome) and geological. This sense of the geological[4] is well elaborated by Nigel Clark's (2017) reading of Cormac McCarthy's *The Road* and Anne Michaels's *Fugitive Pieces*, both of which Clark views as representative of "the struggle to sustain life under catastrophic conditions" (p. 156). From this, bodies are argued to be redistributed from individuated selves out into the Earth and Cosmos, beyond lines of "biological filiation." Clark argues that "the historical unfolding of *human* bodies is fully implicated in the *inhuman* productive and destructive forces of the planet itself" (2017, p. 169). The direction of this argument is not to devalue human life, but to raise the value of each individual life in its ability to shape the world through the "connective tissue of bodies and forces" (Clark, 2017, p. 176). This position is one in which, for Barad (2007, p. 172) bodies do not have "inherent boundaries and properties," but are "phenomena that acquire specific boundaries and properties through open-ended dynamics of intra-activity."

In the section that follows, the implications of the posthuman, rhythmanalytic body, both for health and more broadly in society, are considered.

Discussion

We now have three interrelated themes and the task of comparing these in a manner that relates to health in the Anthropocene (figure 17.1). Each of these different parts is required in order to make this perspective on the body function.

From the microbiome, we have irrefutable evidence, not only that we (and not only "we humans") are entangled within our environments, which are in turn entangled within us, but that there is a mutually beneficial relationship that exists between humans and microbes. Geographical studies of microbiomes have shown that gut microbiota are less diversified in developed nations than in Indigenous communities (Clemente et al., 2015). Similarly, as was shown

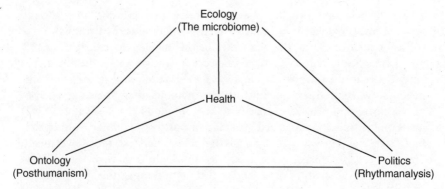

Figure 17.1 Posthuman rhythmanalysis

above with the example of *Staphylococcus aureus*, we know that there are a host of illnesses that are caused by disruptions to the microbiome, and others that can be treated successfully through microbial-based interventions. It is possible, therefore, to speculate that it is our ways of life that are causing damage to, or maldevelopment of, our own bodies. As such, any novel approach to health in the Anthropocene must account for these ways of life. It must, in the pursuit of health, speak not of the individual, but of the community as the smallest unit of examination (O'Malley and Dupré, 2007). Doing so requires an engagement with an affirmative biopolitics (see Lorimer, 2017), in which people productively engage with other species in an effort to promote particular kinds of life through engagement with the powers of life itself, rather than simply attempting to eliminate particular kinds of life.

From posthumanism, we have an approach that allows for the ecological insights from the microbiome to be developed into an ontology upon which a new, anthropocenic form of health can be based. In turning to posthumanism, we have an alternative to the "highly anthropocentric" time of technology, delivered by transhumanism, that would blind us to future prospects (Ansell Pearson, 1997). As such, we are able to create non-anthropocentric modes of becoming. In turning to posthumanism, we have the ontological foundations, such as the emphasis on emergence and contingency, from which we can begin to speak of phenomena, such as sickness, that are manifestations of environmental flows and complex interactions at a molecular level (Helmreich, 2016).

From rhythmanalysis, we have a critical tool that allows for contemporary modes of existence to be examined through the body, with the body as the measure of the health of a society. Health is therefore required to be focused on the maintenance of eurhythmia and the elimination of arrhythmia. Posthuman rhythmanalysis becomes a means of wrestling our multiple human becomings away from the composition of docile bodies through educated rhythms, and towards individuation through an ecologically engaged approach to the self at the micro-political level. Without this rhythmanalysis, the fluid, posthuman approaches to the self could potentially feed into capitalist enterprise (compare Martin, 1998). Engaging with this kind of thought allows for resistance to attempts to develop profits off of treatment endeavours, for there is no escape from the human condition, nor the embodied truths of the self (compare Lorde, 1980).

When rhythmanalysis is spoken of as a counter to capitalist rhythms, what is meant is that rhythmanalysis allows for different rhythms to be detected and assessed according to the body doing the assessing. Those rhythms that conspire to produce arrhythmia can thus be rejected, whilst those that produce eurhythmia can be promoted. What emerges is the opportunity of rejecting hegemonic statements about monolithic capitalism, and instead choosing to examine practices of modernity linked to specific rhythms of capital. What is in turn permitted is the possibility of enfolding capital within rhythms of the body, rather than surrendering the body to be enfolded within rhythms of capital. Through this shift in degree, it may latterly be possible to develop novel ways of being-with-the-world, outside of capitalist modernities.

Such novel ways of being-with-the-world in the time of the Anthropocene are, as other chapters of this text have pointed both implicitly and explicitly, urgently needed for the sake of human health. If we want our food systems to stop making us sick, using posthuman rhythmanalysis opens up opportunities for considering how bodily rhythms change with regards to both the food taken in, those processes that have helped generate that food, and how those factors link to health. If we wish to encourage degrowth, posthuman rhythmanalysis asks that we look not for what can be made and commodified, but that through learned practice we can understand how the processes of the body can be used for the sake of health (see, for example, recent work on autophagy generated through fasting). If we hope, in the time of the Anthropocene, to build communities that are resilient in an ecological sense, posthuman rhythmanalysis offers a suggestion on how to take care of such communities in line with ecological networks, and thus a way in which improving the health of individuals can also contribute to returning the Earth to the climatic conditions of the Holocone.

Atul Gawande (2015), in an article for the New Yorker, noted that the proliferation of low-value care – due to overdiagnosis and overtesting – cost the US around $750 billion (figure from the Institute of Medicine, 2010). Whilst for him, the key issues were that people will have some issue or another as, in part, their bodies do not match up to the ideal body of modern medicine, as well as the possibility that people may not be affected by their affliction within their lifetime, there is a greater issue beyond this. How much, on top of this $750 billion, is wasted in health care because our ways of life do not match up to the human body in all its diversity? Though this approach in itself is not novel,[5] it draws greater attention to how we compose our bodies, how we embody this composition, and whether this embodied composition maps onto the truth of the self. As Seiler (2007, p. 43) notes, "[h]ow we construct the human biological self has consequences for understanding our health, how we reproduce, and what we are." Thus, the body can become its own counter-memory (see Foucault, 2004) to societal attempts to implicitly define boundaries that are not in keeping with the biological self. Through practices such as meditation, natural movement, breathing exercises such as the Wim Hof method, and the no-shampoo movement, people are finding that, with practice, the human body is much more resilient than we might otherwise believe. The challenge then is how we develop these experiences into ways of life fit for the Anthropocene. Through posthuman rhythmanalysis, we have an answer to this challenge.[6]

NOTES

1   The term "entanglement" is one that deserves definition, given its frequent use in this chapter. As Ingold (2008) notes – though he prefers the term *meshwork* – rather than simply referring to a static set of connected points, this term should evoke the sense of interwoven lines, each with their own characters of growth and movement. Extending this further, Ingold continues, observing that "every organism – indeed, every thing – is itself an entanglement, a tissue of knots whose constituent strands, as they become tied up with other strands, in other bundles, make up the [entanglement]" (2008, p. 1806). Similar in character to Gilles Deleuze and Felix Guattari's concept of the rhizome, and therefore linked to the concepts of assemblage and *agencement*, entanglement should be seen as the knotting together of the multiple processual lines of potential becomings and pasts of multitudinous entities. Each of these processes can additionally be said to influence those other processes with which it is mixed, through the means of actions, intentions, and perceptions. Furthermore, processes are able to enter, exit, and re-enter (and so on) the entanglement, without necessarily affecting the character of the entanglement.
2   "Nature has, in humanity, become conscious and self-reflective" (What is Transhumanism? 2018)
3   This ethics of trans-corporeality "calls us to ... find ways of navigating through the simultaneously material, economic, and cultural systems that are so harmful to the living world and yet so difficult to contest or transform" (Alaimo, 2010, p. 18).
4   Kathryn Yusoff (2013, p. 781) provides a relatively early definition of geological bodies, in which she urges that we view ourselves as "geologic subjects, not only capable of geomorphic acts, but as beings who have something *in common* with the geologic forces that are mobilised and incorporated."

5 Gilbert Welch (2015) advocates a healthier approach to medicine with less testing and a greater interest in life fulfilment rather than longevity.

6 One of the greatest fallouts that could come from this would be the effect on biomedical industries. Here, where ill bodies are required to keep the industry going, the potential proliferation of healthy bodies could mean this industry would resist such a move. However, would such an alleviation not also mean that more intellectual space is available for diseases that occur independently of societal modes of existence (i.e. genetic illnesses)? Such a move could allow for biomedical industries to participate in changing current approaches to pharmaceuticals, for example, allowing for the development of individuated subjects, rather than people who are subject to biomedical approaches built on an understanding of the human body that fails to match up to the realities of that body.

REFERENCES

Alaimo, S. (2010). *Bodily natures: Science, environment, and the material self.* Bloomington: Indiana University Press.

Ansell-Pearson, K. (1997). *The transhuman condition: A report on machines, technics and evolution.* United Kingdom: Taylor & Francis.

Arrieta, M.-C., & Finlay, B. (2014). The intestinal microbiota and allergic asthma. *Journal of Infection, 69*, S53–5. https://doi.org/10.1016/j.jinf.2014.07.015.

Barad, K. (2007). *Meeting the universe halfway: Quantum physics and the entanglement of matter and meaning* (2nd ed.). Durham: Duke University Press.

Berg, R. (1996). The indigenous gastrointestinal microflora. *Trends in Microbiology, 4*(11), 430–5. https://doi.org/10.1016/0966-842x(96)10057-3.

Blaser, M. (2015). *Missing microbes: How killing bacteria creates modern plagues.* United Kingdom: Oneworld Publications.

Bostrom, N. (2005). Transhumanist values. *Journal of Philosophical Research, 30*(Supplement), 3–14. https://doi.org/10.5840/jpr_2005_26

Braidotti, R. (2013). *The posthuman.* Cambridge: Polity Press.

Castree, N. (2014). The Anthropocene and the environmental humanities: Extending the conversation. *Environmental Humanities, 5*(1), 233–60. https://doi.org/10.1215/22011919-3615496

Castree, N., Nash, C., Badmington, N., Braun, B., Murdoch, J., & Whatmore, S. (2004). Mapping posthumanism: An exchange. *Environment and Planning A, 36*(8), 1341–63. https://doi.org/10.1068/a37127

Chuong, E. B., Elde, N. C., & Feschotte, C. (2016). Regulatory evolution of innate immunity through co-option of endogenous retroviruses. *Science, 351*(6277), 1083–7. https://doi.org/10.1126/ science.aad5497.

Clark, N. (2017). Anthropocene bodies, geological time and the crisis of natality. *Body & Society, 23*(3), 156–80. https://doi.org/10.1177/1357034x17716520

Clark, N., & Yusoff, K. (2017). Geosocial formations and the Anthropocene. *Theory, Culture & Society, 34*(2–3), 3–23. https://doi.org/10.1177/0263276416688946

Clemente, J. C. et al. (2015). The microbiome of uncontacted Amerindians. *Science Advances, 1*(3), e1500183. https://doi.org/10.1126/sciadv.1500183.

Coccaro, E. F. et al. (2016). Toxoplasma gondii infection: Relationship with aggression in psychiatric subjects. *The Journal of Clinical Psychiatry*, 334–41. https://doi.org/10.4088/jcp.14m09621.

Collen, A. (2015). *10% human: How your body's microbes hold the key to health and happiness*. United Kingdom: William Collins.

Cryan, J. F., & Dinan, T. G. (2012). Mind-altering microorganisms: The impact of the gut microbiota on brain and behaviour. *Nature Reviews Neuroscience, 13*(10), 701–12. https://doi.org/10.1038/nrn3346.

Deleuze, G., & Guattari, F. (1987). *A thousand plateaus: Capitalism and schizophrenia*. B. Massumi (Trans.). Minneapolis: University of Minnesota Press.

Derrida, J. (2008). *The animal that therefore I am*. New York: Fordham University Press.

DeSalle, R., & Perkins, S. L. (2016). *Welcome to the microbiome: Getting to know the trillions of bacteria and other microbes in, on, and around you*. United States: Yale University Press.

Dupré, J. (2012). *Processes of life: Essays in the philosophy of biology*. Oxford: Oxford University Press.

Edensor, T., & Larsen, J. Rhythmanalysing marathon running: 'A drama of rhythms.' *Environment and Planning A, 50*(3), 730–46. https://doi.org/10.1177/0308518x17746407

Ferrando, F. (2013). Posthumanism, transhumanism, antihumanism, metahumanism, and new materialisms: Differences and relations. *Existenz, 8*(2), 26–32. Retrieved from https://existenz.us/volumes/Vol.8-2Ferrando.html

Ferrando, F. (2014). Is the post-human a post-woman? Cyborgs, robots, artificial intelligence and the futures of gender: A case study. *European Journal of Futures Research, 2*(1). https://doi.org/10.1007/s40309-014-0043-8

Foucault, M. (1991). *Discipline and punish*. London: Penguin Books.

Foucault, M. (2004). *Society must be defended: Lectures at the Collège De France, 1975–76*. London: Penguin.

Fukuyama, F. (2002). *Our posthuman future: Consequences of the biotechnology revolution*. New York: Farrar, Straus and Giroux.

Gawande, A. (2015). Overkill. *The New Yorker*. Retrieved from https://www.newyorker.com/magazine/2015/05/11/overkill-atul-gawande.

Gong, J. Q. et al. (2006). Skin colonization by Staphylococcus aureus in patients with eczema and atopic dermatitis and relevant combined topical therapy: A double-blind multicentre randomized controlled trial. *British Journal of Dermatology, 155*(4), 680–7. https://doi.org/10.1111/j.1365-2133.2006.07410.x

Grosz, E. (2004). *The nick of time: Politics, evolution, and the untimely*. Durham: Duke University Press.

Gutierrez, K. J., & DasGupta, S. (2015). The space that difference makes: On marginality, social justice and the future of the health humanities. *Journal of Medical Humanities, 37*(4), 435–48. https://doi.org/10.1007/s10912-015-9347-3

Hamblin, J. (2016). I quit showering, and life continued. *The Atlantic.* Retrieved from https://www.theatlantic.com/health/archive/2016/06/i-stopped-showering-and -life-continued/486314/

Harari, Y. N. (2016). *Homo deus: A brief history of tomorrow.* London: Harvill Secker.

Haraway, D. (1991). *Simians, cyborgs, and women: The reinvention of nature.* New York: Routledge.

Hayles, N. K. (1999). *How we became posthuman: Virtual bodies in cybernetics, literature, and informatics.* Chicago: University of Chicago Press.

Helman, C. G. (1978). 'Feed a cold, starve a fever' – Folk models of infection in an english suburban community, and their relation to medical treatment. *Culture, Medicine and Psychiatry, 2*(2), 107–37. https://doi.org/10.1007/bf00054580.

Helmreich, S. (2016). *Sounding the limits of life: Essays in the anthropology of biology and beyond.* United States: Princeton University Press.

Hird, M. (2010). Indifferent globality: Gaia, symbiosis and 'other worldliness.' *Theory, Culture & Society, 27*(2–3), 54–72. https://doi.org/10.1177/0263276409355998.

Huxley, J. (1968). Transhumanism. *Journal of Humanistic Psychology, 8*(1), 73–6. https://doi.org/10.1177/002216786800800107

Ingold, T. (2008). Bindings against boundaries: Entanglements of life in an open world. *Environment and Planning A, 40*(8), 1796–810. https://doi.org/10.1068/a40156

Jones, P., & Saskia, W. (2016). Time, rhythm and the creative economy. *Transactions of the Institute of British Geographers, 41*(3), 286–96. https://doi.org/10.1111/tran.12122

Knight, R. (2015). *Follow your gut: How the bacteria in your stomach steer your health, mood and more.* United Kingdom: Simon & Schuster.

Kurzweil, R. (2006). *The singularity is near: When humans transcend biology.* New York: Penguin Books.

Latour, B. (2010). An attempt at a 'compositionist manifesto.' *New Literary History, 41,* 471–90. http://doi.org/10.1353/nlh.2010.0022

Latour, B. (2014). War and peace in an age of ecological conflicts. *Revue Juridique De L'Environnement, 39*(1), 51–63. https://doi.org/10.3406/rjenv.2014.6228

Latour, B. (2015). Telling friends from foes in the time of the Anthropocene. In *The Anthropocene and the global environment crisis – Rethinking modernity in a new epoch* (pp. 145–55). London: Routledge.

Lefebvre, H. (2015). *Rhythmanalysis.* London: Bloomsbury Academic.

Lorde, A. (1980). *The cancer journals.* San Francisco: Aunt Lute Books.

Lorimer, J. (2009). Posthumanism/posthumanistic geographies. In *International encyclopedia of human geography* (pp. 344–54). Oxford: Elsevier.

Lorimer, J. (2017). Probiotic environmentalities: Rewilding with wolves and worms. *Theory, Culture & Society, 34*(4), 27–48. https://doi.org/10.1177/0263276417695866

Machos, A. R. et al. (2013). Probiotic lactobacillus reuteri attenuates the stressor-enhanced severity of Citrobacter rodentium infection. *Infection and Immunity*, *81*(9), 3253–63. https://doi.org/10.1128/iai.00278-13

Marcu, S. (2017). Tears of time: A Lefebvrian rhythmanalysis approach to explore the mobility experiences of young Eastern Europeans in Spain. *Transactions of the Institute of British Geographers, 42*(3), 405–16. https://doi.org/10.1111/tran.12174

Martin, E. (1998). Fluid bodies, managed nature. In *Remaking reality: Nature at the millenium* (pp. 63–82). London: Routledge.

McAuliffe, K. (2016). *This is your brain on parasites: How tiny parasites manipulate our behavior and shape society*. Boston: Houghton Mifflin Harcourt.

McDonald, R., Furtado, V., & Völlm, B. (2017). Medicine, madness and murderers: The context of English forensic psychiatric hospitals. *Journal of Health Organization and Management, 31*(5), 598–611. https://doi.org/10.1108/jhom-10-2016-0202

Meadows, R., Nettleton, S., & Neale, J. (2017). Sleep waves and recovery from drug and alcohol dependence: Towards a rhythm analysis of sleep in residential treatment. *Social Science & Medicine, 184*, 124–33. https://doi.org/10.1016/j.socscimed.2017.05.016

Mol, A. (2002). *The body multiple: Ontology in medical practice*. Durham: Duke University Press.

Mol, A., & Law, J. (2004). Embodied action, enacted bodies: The example of hypoglycaemia. *Body & Society, 10*(2–3), 43–62. https://doi.org/10.1177/1357034x04042932

More, M. (1990). Transhumanism: Toward a futurist philosophy. *Extropy, 6*(Summer), 6–12.

Morton, C. (2011). When bare breasts are a 'threat': The production of bodies/spaces in law. *Canadian Journal of Women and the Law, 23*(2), 600–26. https://doi.org/10.3138/cjwl.23.2.600

Nakatsuji, T., et al. (2017). Antimicrobials from human skin commensal bacteria protect against Staphylococcus aureus and are deficient in atopic dermatitis. *Science Translational Medicine, 9*(378), eaah4680. https://doi.org/10.1126/scitranslmed.aah4680

O'Connell, M. (2018). *To be a machine: Adventures among cyborgs, utopians, hackers, and the futurists solving the modest problem of death*. London, UK: Granta.

O'Connor, P. (2017). Rhythmanalysis as a tool in social analysis on ethnicity in Hong Kong. *Asian Ethnicity, 19*(1), 1–15. https://doi.org/10.1080/14631369.2017.1292118

O'Malley, M., & Dupré, J. (2007). Towards a philosophy of microbiology. *Studies in History and Philosophy of Science Part C: Studies in History and Philosophy of Biological and Biomedical Sciences, 38*(4), 775–9. https://doi.org/10.1016/j.shpsc.2007.09.002

Ohland, C. L. et al. (2013). Effects of Lactobacillus helveticus on murine behavior are dependent on diet and genotype and correlate with alterations in the gut microbiome. *Psychoneuroendocrinology, 38*(9), 1738–47. https://doi.org/10.1016/j.psyneuen.2013.02.008

Osman, R., & Mulíček, O. (2017). Urban chronopolis: Ensemble of rhythmized dislocated places. *Geoforum, 85*, 46–57. https://doi.org/10.1016/j.geoforum.2017.07.013

Paxson, H. (2008). Post-pasteurian cultures: The microbiopolitics of raw-milk cheese in the United States. *Cultural Anthropology, 23*(1), 15–47. https://doi.org/10.1111/j.1548-1360.2008.00002.x

Rickly, J. (2017). 'They all have a different vibe': A rhythmanalysis of climbing mobilities and the Red River Gorge as place. *Tourist Studies, 17*(3), 223–44. https://doi.org/10.1177/1468797617717637

Rose, N. (1994). Medicine, history and the present. In *Reassessing Foucault* (pp. 48–72). London: Routledge.

Sagan, D. (2013). *Cosmic apprentice: Dispatches from the edges of science.* United States: University of Minnesota Press.

Saldanha, A. (2006). Reontologising race: The machinic geography of phenotype. *Environment and Planning D: Society and Space, 24*(1), 9–24. https://doi.org/10.1068/d61j

Savage, D. C. (1977). Microbial ecology of the gastrointestinal tract. *Annual Review of Microbiology, 31*(1), 107–33. https://doi.org/10.1146/annurev.mi.31.100177.000543.

Scott, J. (2014, May 25). My no-soap, no-shampoo, bacteria-rich hygiene experiment. *The New York Times.* Retrieved from https://www.nytimes.com/2014/05/25/magazine/my-no-soap-no-shampoo-bacteria-rich-hygiene-experiment.html

Seiler, L. H. (2007). What are we? The social construction of the human biological self. *Journal for the Theory of Social Behaviour, 37*(3), 243–77. https://doi.org/10.1111/j.1468-5914.2007.00341.x.

Sender, R., Fuchs, S., & Milo, R. (2016). Revised estimates for the number of human and bacteria cells in the body. *PLOS Biology, 14*(8), e1002533. https://doi.org/10.1371/journal.pbio.1002533

Smith, M. I. et al. (2013). Gut microbiomes of Malawian twin pairs discordant for kwashiorkor. *Science, 339*(6119), 548–54. https://doi.org/10.1126/science.1229000

Stefka, A. T. et al. (2014). Commensal bacteria protect against food allergen sensitization. *Proceedings of the National Academy of Sciences, 111*(36), 13145–50. https://doi.org/10.1073/pnas.1412008111.

Tegmark, M. (2017). *Life 3.0: Being human in the age of artificial intelligence.* New York: Knopf.

Trehan, I. et al. (2013). Antibiotics as part of the management of severe acute malnutrition. *New England Journal of Medicine, 368*(5), 425–35. https://doi.org/10.1056/nejmoa1202851

Umesaki, Y., & Setoyama, H. (2000). Structure of the intestinal flora responsible for development of the gut immune systemin a rodent model. *Microbes and Infection, 2*(11), 1343–51. https://doi.org/10.1016/s1286-4579(00)01288-0

Welch, H. G. (2015). *Less medicine, more health.* Boston, MA: Beacon Press.

What is Transhumanism? (2018). *What is transhumanism?* Retrieved from http://whatistranshumanism.org

Wozniak, J. T. (2017). Towards a rhythmanalysis of debt dressage: Education as rhythmic resistance in everyday indebted life. *Policy Futures in Education, 15*(4), 495–508. https://doi.org/10.1177/1478210317715798

Xu, J., & Gordon, J. I. (2003). Honor thy symbionts. *Proceedings of the National Academy of Sciences, 100*(18), 10452–9. https://doi.org/10.1073/pnas.1734063100

Yong, E. (2016). *I contain multitudes: The microbes within us and a grander view of life.* London: Vintage.

Yusoff, K. (2013). Geologic life: Prehistory, climate, futures in the Anthropocene. *Environment and Planning D: Society and Space, 31*(5), 779–95. https://doi.org/10.1068/d11512

Zimmer, C. (2015). *Our inner viruses: Forty million years in the making.* Retrieved from http://phenomena.nationalgeographic.com/2015/02/01/our-inner-viruses-forty-million-years-in-the-making/

18 The Exploration of Socioecological Approaches and Indicators in the Anthropocene

ANN DEL BIANCO,[1] DAVID MALLERY, KAMAL PAUDEL, AND MARTIN J. BUNCH

Introduction

A variety of socioecological frameworks and indicators provide useful cognitive and applied tools that can illuminate the coupling of human and natural systems. Such tools help elucidate characteristics inherent to the Anthropocene such as societal influences and interactions with natural processes, feedbacks and system dynamics, and thresholds (Verburg et al., 2016). An overview of the origins, theoretical background, and fundamental concepts is provided and applications of each approach and indicator are used to demonstrate different ways in which to understand the impact of human systems on underlying natural systems, and the interconnectedness of human health and well-being in relation to ecological, social, cultural, and economic dimensions. Some of the challenges associated with their use are also highlighted. A review of the main elements of each approach is summarized in table 18.1, followed by some challenges and recommendations.

Socioecological Approaches

Ecohealth

Ecohealth (ecosystem approaches to human health and well-being) has historical roots in the writings of James Hutton, who developed the concept of Earth as an integrated system, and Aldo Leopold, whose idea of community included "the land" defined as both human and non-human elements (e.g. water, plants, animals) (Rapport et al., 1999, p. 83). Its development can be followed through paradigm shifts associated with five key Canadian public health documents and related human health models (VanLeeuwen et al., 1999; Forget and Lebel, 2001). Its theoretical backdrop draws from environmental resource management, systems sciences, geography, ecology, public health, health promotion, epidemiology, anthropology, philosophy, participatory action research, management methodology, and complexity theory (Waltner-Toews, 2001; Butler and Friel, 2006; Bunch et al., 2011; Leung, Middleton, and Morrison, 2012).

Ecohealth aims to promote human and ecosystem health in the context of social, cultural, economic, and ecological interactions implemented by participatory and collaborative processes to intervene in conditions of complexity and uncertainty (Charron, 2012; Bunch and Waltner-Toews, 2015; Buse et al., 2018). It is informed by systems thinking, specifically critical and interpretive systems thinking, and ideas about self-organizing, holarchic, open-systems (SOHO) (Kay et al., 1999). Frameworks utilized for intervention are subsumed in an ongoing cycle of adaptive management, and since every situation is different, methods, tools, and techniques vary (Bunch, 2016, p. 618).

Ecohealth is applied at a community level and defined within an ecological space, such as in the context of mining, agriculture, environmental, and human health management of vector-borne and zoonotic diseases, usually in the Global South (Lebel, 2003; Parkes, Panelli, and Weinstein, 2003; Bunch et al., 2006; Boischio et al., 2009; Charron, 2012). The knowledge produced can be immediately applied and is often generalizable (Forget and Lebel, 2001; Charron, 2012, p. 6, 8–9). Six principles inform Ecohealth research, with the first three focusing on *process* and the latter three on *intrinsic goals*: (i) systems thinking, (ii) transdisciplinary research, (iii) participation, (iv) sustainability, (v) gender and social equity, (vi) knowledge to action (Charron, 2012, p. 9–18). Ecohealth research consists of four overlapping and multidirectional phases: (i) participatory design, (ii) knowledge development, (iii) intervention strategy and testing, and (iv) systematization of knowledge, whereby several iterations and adaptations of these phases occur (Charron, 2012, p. 20–3).

Ecohealth is more encompassing than earlier paradigms of health as its fundamental understanding is that humans are part of a larger intricate system. For example, in Northern Malawi, Kerr et al. (2012) sought to improve soil fertility, food security, and human health and nutrition by implementing new legume options for farmers as an alternative to commercial fertilizers. Also, Okello-Onen, Mboera, and Mugisha (2012) demonstrate sustained malaria control in Uganda and Tanzania through the implementation of agro-ecosystem interventions like the management of water bodies and improvement in the design and structure of houses to reduce the number of mosquitoes, and a change in cultural practices and enhanced community capacity (p. 148–9). These case studies exemplify how social and technological innovations have been applied as solutions for living well within ecological limits.

Ecohealth research can be difficult to navigate given challenges of interdisciplinary teamwork and problem context, such as language barriers (including jargon), inclusiveness, and feasibility impacted by time, skills, and available resources (Lebel, 2003; Charron, 2012, p. 10–11). Involvement of community members throughout all phases is essential as stakeholders are more likely to accept responsibility and facilitate change when empowered within a process – an approach not often implemented in traditional health research. Some other issues faced by Ecohealth researchers include: balancing the needs of the community with goals of decision-makers and scientists, the lack of links in communication of information and education, the influence of political agendas, and cultural resistance to change (Okello-Onen, Mboera, and Mugisha, 2012; Riojas-Rodriguez and Rodriguez-Dozal, 2012; Monroy et al., 2012).

One Health

One Health is defined as "any added value in terms of human and animal health, financial savings or social and environmental benefits from closer cooperation of professionals in the health, animal and environment sectors at all levels of organization" (Zinsstag et al., 2012, p. 63). Its historical underpinnings are "one medicine" – the general science of all human and animal health and disease – whose development can be traced back to the ancient priests and healers, but whose acceptance did not occur until the nineteenth century (Zinsstag et al., 2005, p. 2142). Rudolf Virchow, Calvin W. Schwabe, William Osler, Karl F. Meyer, Robert Koch, John McFadyean, and James Steele have been instrumental in its development (Zinsstag et al., 2015). Concepts used interchangeably with One Health despite differences include: one medicine, comparative medicine, translational medicine, zoobiquity, and evolutionary medicine (Lerner and Berg, 2015, p. 2). "One Health has emerged out of a complex and shifting coalition of international health bodies, veterinary associations, environmental organizations, academic advocates and pharmaceutical companies" (Bresalier, Cassidy, and Woods, 2015, p. 10).

In 2009, experts worldwide devised the "Manhattan principles" at the "One World – One Health" symposium. These are known as the "twelve recommendations for establishing a more holistic approach to preventing epidemic/epizootic disease and for maintaining ecosystem integrity for the benefit of humans, their domesticated animals and the foundational biodiversity that supports us" (Cook, Karesh, and Osofsky, 2009, n.p.). The "One Health umbrella" developed by the networks One Health Sweden and One Health Initiative (figure 18.1) depicts the scope of One Health (Lerner and Berg, 2015, p. 2). It illustrates the theoretical affinity with fields such as environmental health, ecology, veterinary medicine, public health, human medicine, molecular and microbiology, and health economics in the context of individual, population, and ecosystem health.

Although data may originate from different studies or sources (given it is comparable by location, time, level of aggregation, details, and quality), a One Health approach requires that data analysis and interpretation is conducted in tandem. This approach generates insights impossible without such intersectoral

Figure 18.1 The "One Health umbrella" (Lerner and Berg, 2015)

collaboration. Applications typically explore the relationship between multi-host infections on humans, animal and ecosystem health, and economics (Schelling and Hattendorf, 2015, p. 107–8).

One Health takes into account multiple scales, whether for surveillance or to monitor, assess, or manage complex issues. To date there are very few One Health studies; "the most difficult step is the initiation of a process that leads to change and health improvement" (Schelling and Hattendorf, 2015, p. 109; 108). One example includes the emergence of Nipah virus in Bangladesh, Malaysia, and Singapore as well as Hendra virus in Australia. Multiple interdependent factors and scales were examined ranging from anthropogenic changes in the environment and natural events, to the role of flying foxes and horses as sources of infection, to public perception and political agendas threatening the implementation of management strategies, and the influence of health care policy and financing affecting the quality of health services in infection control (Whittaker, 2015, p. 66–9).

An animal-human connection may not always be relevant, as was demonstrated in Ethiopia, where bovine tuberculosis, an important animal disease, was not a threat to humans, who reported few cases (Zinsstag, Mahamat, and Schelling, 2015, p. 54). One Health challenges are similar to those of epidemiological studies (e.g. sampling error, bias, confounding, and chance) (Schelling and Hattendorf, 2015). For studies including surveillance, underreporting is often a challenge, as are other issues surrounding existing and joint surveillance systems (Schelling and Hattendorf, 2015, p. 112; 119). Disease control programmes are not always transferrable to other contexts and cannot be successfully implemented without the cooperation of neighbouring communities, especially for most zoonoses (Schelling and Hattendorf, 2015, p. 108).

GeoHealth

The origins of GeoHealth can be attributed to Dr John Snow and his use of spatial analysis to address the public health panics in relation to the spread of cholera in England in the 1850s (Hempel, 2007). It is an emerging field with "location" at the forefront, examining how "place" impacts one's health. In 2014, this approach was integrated in the first GeoHealth Master's program, led by Dr Shubha Kumar of the University of Southern California – Keck School of Medicine.

GeoHealth is a location-based public health framework using geospatial technology to identify how location matters to human health and well-being. It is used to identify and analyse social, environmental, and ecological determinants by mapping the complex phenomena at local, regional, or national levels where multiple health inequalities, access to health care services, and influences of health care policies coexist. The modern GeoHealth approach is closely linked to geomedicine, "a new type of medical intelligence that will leverage national spatial data infrastructures to benefit personal human health" (Davenhall, 2012, p. 3). Davenhall (2012) discusses how future research on diseases such as cancer, diabetes, and hypertension should focus on the intersections of geographic location and socioecological determinants.

The GeoHealth Laboratory in New Zealand was created to collaborate with academia and public policymakers in thirteen priority projects identified by the Ministry of Health, such as health inequalities, contextualizing understandings of suicide, and neighbourhood determinants of health (Pearce, 2007). Since the late 1980s, the "spatial polarization in health" has prompted researchers to find policy-based resolutions by monitoring health inequalities (Pearce, 2007, p. 151). For instance, the laboratory found a strong locational effect on suicide with female rates higher in urban areas and male rates higher in rural areas. Except for two regions, young males' suicide rates quickly increased in the 1980s and 1990s and remained high. These studies provided a framework for the 2006–16 suicide prevention strategy. The potential of using such geomatic methods has been demonstrated by many applications. For example, Przybysz and Bunch (2017) explore spatial patterns of sudden cardiac arrests in the city of Toronto using "Poisson kriging" and hot-spot analyses; Jerrett et al. (2005) demonstrate health impacts of proximity to expressways due to traffic pollution, employing standard and spatial multilevel Cox regression models; and Crouse et al. (2017) associate rates of mortality in large Canadian cities with "greenness" using a normalized vegetation difference index derived from remote sensing imagery.

GeoHealth approaches have also focused on mobile-based solutions to provide more efficient health care services. Sa et al. (2016) discuss how the Primary Care Information System in Brazil was used to create a mobile solution in six primary care units in the city of São Paulo, highlighting that current primary data collection and analysis could be more efficient. Kjeldskov et al. (2010, p. 3) designed a mobile location-based prototype for home health care workers to support information sharing and outlined the benefits and drawbacks of the system.

Although geospatial technology holds a lot of promise, its underlying empirical data and the technology on which it depends has limitations. There are various complex systems at play when it comes to human health and well-being. It is important that the evolution of GeoHealth takes place with theoretical advancement and practical discovery in the field.

Planetary Health

Originating from global health, with roots in tropical medicine, Planetary Health encompasses concepts from socioecological approaches such as GeoHealth, One Health, and Ecohealth. Howard Frumkin is the founding father in the field, whereas Richard Horton put forth its definition. Planetary Health is a systems approach to human health and well-being that cannot be understood without viewing ecosystem health at a global scale. It is guided by principles similar to Commoner's (1971) four laws of ecology: (i) everything is connected to everything else, (ii) everything must go somewhere, (iii) nature knows best, and (iv) there is no such thing as a free lunch. *The Planetary Health Alliance* identified two primary categories (ecosystem transformations and health impacts) which comprise fifteen thematic areas – Planetary Health explores the links and relationships between these themes (Frumkin, 2017).

Human exploitation of the environment impacts population health. Planetary Health is designed to mitigate those challenges so that human health and well-being can be protected and sustained. "Planetary Health is the health of human civilization and the state of the natural systems on which it depends; including the wise stewardship of those natural systems" (Whitmee et al. 2015, p. 1978; p. 1974). It targets two dimensions: (i) "human health within the human systems" including threats to our species such as pandemics, and (ii) "natural systems within which our species evolve" including the health and diversity of the biosphere (Schütte et al., 2018, p. e58). "Planetary Health draws together a critique of overconsumption with a perception of health that extends the relevant timescale from the life of an individual to the survival of the human species and the planetary systems that support all life on Earth" (Zywert, 2017, p. 231).

From the sudden disappearance of the American chestnut to coverage of red maple in Eastern United States (Shackleton, Larson, and Biggs, 2018), and a pandemic Ebola outbreak potentially originating from a fruit bat linked to habitat loss in Africa (Leroy et al., 2009), there is enough evidence to suggest that future environmental threats to our health will be unexpected and uncertain. "Uncertainty is the rule, rather than the exception, when thinking about Planetary Health" (Whitmee et al., 2015, p. 2013). From a food systems perspective, if continued, recent dietary trends will lead to an 80 per cent increase in global agricultural greenhouse gas emissions due to the growing demand for animal products (Whitmee et al., 2015, p. 2000). Humans in the Holocene live within the safe zones of planetary boundaries. If the boundaries of those zones are compromised, our conditions for survival diminish (Horton and Lo, 2015). This highlights the importance of Planetary Health policies, which employ precautionary principles where conventional approaches fail or are too slow to be implemented due to a lack of sufficient information.

The non-linearity of complex systems follows the thinking that the whole is greater than the sum of its parts. To achieve the whole, it is important that academia and researchers embrace transdisciplinary approaches. Also, "improved governance is necessary to aid in the integration of social, economic, and environmental policies and for the creation, synthesis, and application of interdisciplinary knowledge to strengthen Planetary Health" (Whitmee et al., 2015, p. 1974). Strong storytelling may be an effective strategy to communicate complex ideas such as Planetary Health to the public.

Health, Well-Being, and the Millennium Ecosystem Assessment (MEA)

Coordinated by the United Nations Development Program and overseen by an international multi-stakeholder board, the Millennium Ecosystem Assessment (Millennium Ecosystem Assessment, 2005) was undertaken in the early 2000s. It "assess[ed] the consequences of ecosystem change for human well-being and established the scientific basis for actions needed to enhance the conservation and sustainable use of ecosystems and their contributions to human well-being" (Reid et al., 2005, p. v), including research into the impact of ecosystem change on human health. This call to the health sector was published as the *Ecosystems and Well-Being: Health Synthesis* (Corvalan, Hales, and McMichael, 2005).

Using the idea of ecosystem services, which Reid et al. (2005, p. v) define as "the benefits people obtain from ecosystems," the report presents a framework for understanding relationships between the environment and human health and well-being. Covalan et al. (2005) identify a causal pathway from human pressure on the environment to environmental impacts (e.g. ozone depletion, desertification, freshwater contamination) to health impacts (see figure 18.2).

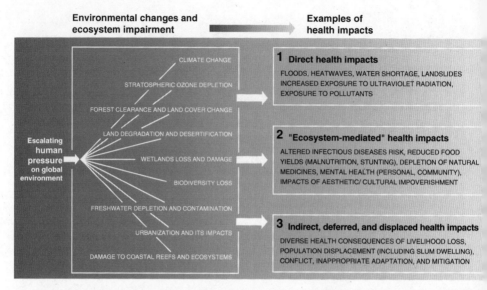

Figure 18.2 Harmful effects of ecosystem change on human health (Corvalan, Hales, and McMichael, 2005, 1 – Figure SDM1)

They identify direct health impacts (e.g. exposure to ultraviolet radiation and water shortage), "ecosystem-mediated" health impacts (e.g. reduced food yields and mental health impacts), and indirect, deferred, and displaced health impacts (e.g. the consequences of livelihood loss and population displacement). This causal pathway is reminiscent of the classic pressure-state-response model in environmental management, and the WHO's extension of that to health – the DPSEEA (driving forces, pressure, state, exposure, effect, and action) model (Corvalan, Briggs, and Kjellstrom, 1996).

The MEA health synthesis report made a profound contribution to understanding and communicating the message that individual, familial, and community health depend on ecosystem health in multiple, sometimes diffuse and interacting ways. Corvalan et al. (2005) and Reid et al. (2005) presented a conceptual framework (figure 18.3) that characterizes linkages between four categories of ecosystem services: (i) supporting, (ii) provisioning, (iii) regulating, and (iv) cultural; and five domains of health and well-being: (i) security, (ii) basic materials for a good life, (iii) physical health, (iv) good social relations, and (v) freedom of choice and action. These relationships can be more or less direct, intense, and vulnerable to human influence or amenable to mediation by human action.

Figure 18.3 depicts a linear direction moving from ecosystems to human health and well-being. This linearity can undermine our understanding that

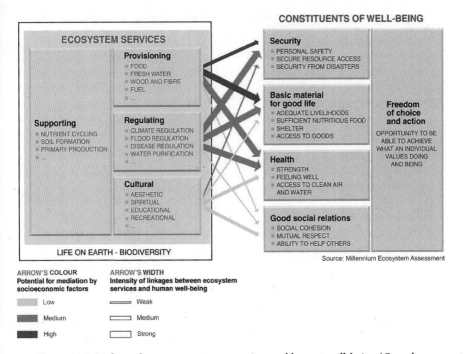

Figure 18.3   Linkages between ecosystem services and human well-being (Corvalan, Hales, and McMichael, 2005, 15 – Figure 1.3; Reid et al., 2005, vi – Figure A)

both ecosystem health and human health are emergent properties of interconnected and co-evolving human and natural systems, and thus require more holistic approaches to manage such coupled systems. Figure 18.3 is useful for communication about the importance of ecosystem services and ecosystem change on human health and well-being, but less useful at informing specific interventions. For studies adopting MEA conceptual frameworks such as these, the integration of measures and tools such as photovoice (Berbés-Blázquez, 2012) and household surveys (Sherrouse, Clement, and Semmens, 2011; Yang et al., 2013) are necessary to better understand the link between ecosystem services and human elements, social values, and the local context.

Socioecological Indicators

Planetary Boundaries

The Planetary Boundaries (PB) framework was developed in 2009 by a group of environmental scientists, led by Johan Rockström and Will Steffen, who identified and quantified critical threshold values associated with a set of Earth system control variables, "the crossing of which may trigger nonlinear changes in the functioning of the Earth System, thereby challenging social-ecological resilience at regional to global scales" (Rockström et al., 2009, n.p.). It builds on previous boundary concepts such as maximum sustainable yield, limits to growth (Meadows et al., 1972), carrying capacity (Arrow et al., 1995), and tipping elements (Lenton et al., 2008), as well as theoretical contributions from systems ecology, complex adaptive systems, and resilience thinking (Holling, 1973; Gunderson and Holling, 2002; Folke et al., 2004; Folke, 2006). PBs emphasize "threshold values" as "intrinsic features" of complex adaptive systems that are "defined by a position along one or more control variables" and are characterized by "abrupt non-linear change, reflected in critical transitions from one stability domain to another" (Rockström et al., 2009, n.p.). PB researchers argue that the Holocene represents one such stability domain that risks destabilization in the transition to the Anthropocene (Rockström et al., 2009).

The PB framework identifies nine PBs or critical processes that regulate Earth system functioning and quantifies their associated threshold values (Steffen et al., 2015, p. 736). PBs are not analogous to biophysical thresholds; rather, boundary values are set "upstream" of tipping points within "zones of uncertainty" to allow "society time to react to early warning signs that it may be approaching a threshold and consequent abrupt or risky change" (Steffen et al., 2015, 1259855-2). The nine PBs include: (i) climate change (core boundary – "increasing risk"), (ii) stratospheric ozone depletion, (iii) ocean acidification, (iv) biochemical flows ("high risk"), (v) freshwater use, (vi) land-system change ("increasing risk"), (vii) novel entities, (viii) atmospheric aerosol loading, and (ix) biosphere integrity (core boundary – "high risk") (Rockström et al., 2009; Steffen et al., 2015). Of the nine boundaries, PB researchers estimate that four have already transgressed, two of which are core boundaries because of their critical importance to the Earth system. These have been categorized as either "high risk," being well beyond the zone of uncertainty, or as "increasing risk," because of their high uncertainty. Three boundaries: (i) novel entities, (ii) aerosol loading, and (iii) functional diversity (as a component of biosphere integrity) have yet to be quantified (Steffen et al., 2015).

Amid criticisms regarding the usefulness of defining set quantitative threshold values associated with Earth system processes (Montoya, Donohue, and Pimm, 2018), a series of operational challenges, such as the uncertainty due to interacting boundaries, have been identified. The Earth system represents a complex organizational pattern characterized by interdependent processes across multiple spatial and temporal scales. While the framework identifies nine PBs that "operate as an interdependent set," "systematic quantitative analysis of iterations among all of the processes for which boundaries are proposed remains beyond the scope of current modelling" (Steffen et al., 2015, p. 1259855-8-9). The PB framework currently examines the global scale and "is not designed to be 'down-scaled' or 'disaggregated' to smaller levels, such as nations or local communities" (Steffen et al., 2015, p. 1259855-8). As such, its implementation within specific socioeconomic contexts presents challenges. Thus, PB researchers have called for further development of the framework in tandem with a "truly global evidence base, with much greater integration among issues" (Steffen et al., 2015, p. 1259855-8-9). Although the framework "does not dictate how societies should develop" (Steffen et al., 2015, p. 736), "transgressions of boundaries that have already occurred, are unevenly caused by different human societies and different social [and economic] groups" (Steffen et al., 2015, p. 1259855-8), suggesting a strong relationship between equity and threshold risk (Steffen and Stafford Smith, 2013).

The Ecological, Water, and Carbon Footprint

Sustainability in the Anthropocene requires reducing the reliance on non-renewable *stocks* along with an increasing reliance on renewable *funds* of goods and services provided by the Earth's natural processes (Georgescu-Roegen, 1975). Within closed systems, Daly (1990, p. 2) notes that "harvest rates should equal regeneration rates ... [and] waste emission rates should equal the natural assimilative capacities of the ecosystems into which the wastes are emitted." Currently, consumption patterns of highly urbanized countries have already exceeded the planet's natural productive capacity. Ecological Footprint Accounting attempts to quantify this discrepancy. The Ecological Footprint Framework (EFF) was conceptualized by William Rees (Rees, 1992), and Mathis Wackernagel (Wackernagel, 1994; Wackernagel and Rees, 1996) as a measure that compares the global bioproductive capacity to the economic demand imposed by human consumption (Wackernagel et al., 2002). Ecological Footprint (EF) analysis operationalizes the concept of biocapacity, whereby "the ecological impact of humanity is measured as the area of biologically productive land and water required to produce the resources consumed and to assimilate the wastes generated by humanity, under the predominant management and production practices in any given year" (Wackernagel et al., 2002, p. 9266). Footprint analysis accounts for six "impact components" or "human activities that require biologically productive space," including:

(i) growing crops for food, animal feed, fibre, oil, and rubber; (ii) grazing animals for meat, hides, wool, and milk; (iii) harvesting timber for wood, fibre, and fuel; (iv) marine and freshwater fishing; (v) accommodating infrastructure for housing, transportation, industrial production, and hydroelectric power; and (vi) burning fossil fuel. (Wackernagel et al., 2002 p. 9266-7)

Footprint analysis and biocapacity can be applied at individual, regional, national, and global scales. The Water and Carbon Footprint have been developed to account for indicators not captured by EFF.

The "footprint family of indicators" is a concept that includes the ecological, water, and carbon footprint (Galli et al., 2012). All three footprint indicators follow a similar logic, whereby values are seen as "embedded" biophysical values in products being produced and consumed. The Water Footprint measures the volume of water required for the production of "water-intensive commodities" by separately accounting for the appropriation of "blue water" (e.g. irrigation water), "green water" (e.g. rainwater), and "grey water" (e.g. water for assimilating pollution) (Hoekstra, 2015, p. 36). The Carbon Footprint "measures the total mass of greenhouse gas emissions that are caused by an activity or are accumulated over the life stages of a product" (Galli et al., 2012, p. 102).

Although underestimating human impacts, the EFF is effective in elucidating the general pattern of unsustainable human activity. The utility of the EFF as an indicator for informing decision making processes is the subject of ongoing criticism (van den Bergh and Verbruggen, 1999; Fiala, 2008; Ponthiere, 2009; Bastianoni et al., 2012; Giampietro and Saltelli, 2014a) and debate (Blomqvist et al., 2013a; Blomqvist et al., 2013b; Rees and Wackernagel, 2013; Galli et al., 2016). Despite lacking "globally consistent datasets," the Global Footprint Network's system of accounts represents "the most comprehensive assessments of ecological status of nations available" (Rees and Wackernagel, 2013, p. 1–2) and therefore embodies "a necessary, but not sufficient, condition for sustainability" (Galli et al., 2016, p. 225). The footprint has been adopted by numerous countries and cities as an official indicator and National Footprint Reviews have been conducted worldwide (e.g. Boev et al., 2016; WWF-Korea, 2016; Global Footprint Network, 2013–18).

Critics argue that the EFF provides conclusions that may result in harmful policies due to widespread media coverage and overenthusiastic adoption. For example, Giampietro and Saltelli (2014a, 2014b) note the EF protocol could be used to justify "replacing natural ecosystems with more productive human-managed vegetation," however this would result in ecological degradation despite the perceived increase in biocapacity (Galli et al., 2016, p. 226). Tabi and Csutora (2011) suggest the addition of a parameter for "naturalness" to improve the accuracy of EFF accounting. Although the EFF has made inroads into mainstream discourses where other approaches have failed, it requires further development to improve its efficacy for decision support. As such, the National Ecological Footprint (EF) accounts database alongside the advancement of science around the EF and production of its figures are moving from the Global Footprint Foundation to an international academic network led by researchers at York University in Canada.

Multi-scale Integrated Analysis of Societal and Ecosystem Metabolism

Multi-scale integrated analysis of societal and ecosystem metabolism (MuSIASEM) is a framework for resource accounting and sustainability assessment that "organizes quantitative information in reference to different dimensions of analysis" and "different hierarchical scales of analysis referring to both socioeconomic and ecological narratives" (González-López and Giampietro, 2017, p. 2). Conceptualized by Mario Giampietro and Kozo Mayumi (Giampietro and Mayumi, 2000a, 2000b), MuSIASEM is continually redeveloped by the LIPHE4 research team of the Institute for Environmental Science and Technology at the Autonomous University of Barcelona. MuSIASEM draws from various epistemological traditions including bioeconomics (Georgescu-Roegen, 1971, 1975), cybernetics (Maturana and Humberto, 1980; Ashby, 1991), non-equilibrium thermodynamics (Prigogine and Stengers, 1984), theoretical ecology (Ulanowicz, 1986, 1997), complex adaptive systems (Gunderson and Holling, 2002), hierarchy theory (Pattee, 1973; Allen and Hoekstra, 1992; Allen and Ahl, 1996), and relational biology (Rosen, 1985, 1991; Louie, 2008). It attempts to operationalize these theories to address challenges associated with quantitative analyses for the nexus between land, energy, food, and water at multiple scales (Giampietro et al., 2012). Through a synthesis of systems-based theories and concepts, Giampietro et al. (2012) argue that both ecosystems and human societies are self-organizing, far from equilibrium, autopoetic (i.e. "self-making"), holarchic (systems embedded within systems), complex systems that exhibit "metabolic patterns" of energy, materials, and information. The future of human and ecosystem health will depend heavily on whether these patterns are maintained in feasible, viable, and desirable conditions (Giampietro, Mayumi, and Sorman, 2012).

MuSIASEM characterizes a societal metabolic pattern by identifying "the expected patterns of relations" in the organization of societal systems in terms of structural and functional components (e.g. agriculture, households, energy sector). It then analyses the inputs, in terms of necessary flows (e.g. electricity, fuel, freshwater, or food) and funds (e.g. hectares of managed land, kilowatts of technical capacity, or available hours of human activity). Since each functional component relies on outputs from other components, MuSIASEM is able to generate a consistent mapping of feedbacks that characterize the system at different scales, assessing the *viability* of scenarios to determine whether internal components will be able to support one another. Internal requirements are then compared against the external biophysical source-sink capacity of the environmental context to determine scenario *feasibility*. Ecological impact is assessed through an array of indicators, such as ecosystem integrity (Kay, 1991; Andreasen et al., 2001), nature index (Certain et al., 2011), and ecosystem ascendancy (Ulanowicz, 1997). MuSIASEM is then able to compare societal and ecological feedback to anticipate scenarios where the exigencies of certain societal metabolic patterns will result in crossing ecological thresholds. Finally, scenario *desirability* is determined as "whether the characteristics of the metabolic pattern are acceptable to those living inside the system" (González-López and Giampietro, 2017, p. 2).

MuSIASEM responds to traditional, reductionist approaches to environmental management that are limited in their capacity to analyse complex problems (Rosen, 1991). Different dimensions and scales of analysis relevant to sustainability science (e.g. societal, biophysical, economic, ecological) must be formalized separately within "non-equivalent descriptive domains." Separate analyses corresponding to different types of biophysical flows are represented as non-equivalent "grammars" (e.g. water, food, or energy) that are integrated through relational analysis.

Unlike PBs, MuSIASEM can be applied to issues at various scales while integrating perspectives on many different environmental issues (Gomiero and Giampietro, 2001; Giampietro et al., 2013; The Energy Team of the Climate, NRC and FAO, 2013; Silva-Macher and Farrell, 2014; Cabello et al., 2015; Madrid-López and Giampietro, 2015; Aragão and Giampietro, 2016; González-López and Giampietro, 2017). Unlike EF, MuSIASEM can be aggregated or disaggregated without losing descriptive power, occasionally revealing serious flaws in proposed sustainability interventions (Giampietro and Mayumi, 2009). The comprehensive nature of MuSIASEM entails new and different challenges than those associated with other methodologies. Its assessments are highly demanding in time and data.

Summary

This chapter identified four socioecological approaches, one assessment (providing conceptual frameworks), and three indicators (table 18.1). Ecohealth, One Health, and GeoHealth are approaches utilized by researchers in complex and uncertain situations and are embedded in systems thinking and adaptive management; the former two include the use of a transdisciplinary, collaborative team in their efforts. The focus of Ecohealth is on the interconnectedness of human and ecosystem health, whereas One Health also emphasizes animal health. GeoHealth is a geographical-epidemiological approach concerned with location in relation to human health. Planetary Health focuses on mitigating human exploitation of the environment for human health and well-being through the application of governance and stewardship. The MEA was an extensive assessment undertaken to assess the consequences that changes in ecosystem services have on human health and well-being. It highlighted a number of conceptual frameworks utilized in Ecohealth, One Health, and GeoHealth research.

Table 18.1 Synoptic summary of socioecological approaches and indicators

Socioecological approaches and indicators		Application	Focus	Scale	Amenable to intervention strategies?
Ecohealth	Approach	Transdisciplinary collaborative research, assessment, management, and intervention	Human and ecosystem health	Local to regional	Yes
One Health	Approach	Transdisciplinary collaborative research, assessment, management, and intervention	Animal, human, and ecosystem health	Multi	Yes
GeoHealth	Approach	Geographic-epidemiological research, assessment, management, and intervention	Location and human health and preventative technological solutions	Local to regional/ national	Yes
Planetary Health	Approach	Governance and stewardship	Mitigating human exploitation of environment for human health and well-being	Global	Yes
Millennium Ecosystem Assessment (MEA)	Conceptual frameworks	Major assessment	Ecosystem services, human health and well-being	Multi	No
Planetary Boundaries	Framework and indicators	Identification, quantification, and setting threshold values of Earth's system processes	Integrity of planetary processes essential to human health	Global – aggregated processes from local	No
Footprint Family of Indicators	Indicators	Accounting system measuring demand and supply of nature Ecological footprint: biocapacity Water footprint: appropriated green, blue, and grey water Carbon footprint: mass of carbon emissions	Impact of human demand on nature	Multi	Yes

(continued)

Table 18.1 Synoptic summary of socioecological approaches and indicators (continued)

Socioecological approaches and indicators	Application	Focus	Scale	Amenable to intervention strategies?
Multi-scale integrated analysis of societal and ecosystem metabolism (MuSIASEM)	Framework and indicators	Resource accounting for sustainability assessment	Energy, food, land, and water use relative to societal and/ or economic factors	Multi	Yes

The socioecological indicators Planetary Boundaries; the Ecological, Water, and Carbon Footprint; and MuSIASEM are oriented towards quantitative analysis for charting sustainable pathways through the Anthropocene. They can be categorized according to which problems they attempt to address. The PB framework and its indicators address the complexity of the Earth system and the potential for human activity to destabilize the feedback loops that maintain the natural systems humanity relies upon. The Ecological Footprint addresses the biophysical scale of human societies in relation to the provisioning capacity of the environment. The Water Footprint and Carbon Footprint address the impact of human demand on nature relative to water for the former and carbon emissions for the latter. MuSIASEM attempts to address both issues simultaneously by comparing internal feedbacks within human societies to external feedbacks that support ecological processes, determining when the biophysical requirements for each are at odds. These indicators act as quantitative filters meant to constrain the option space for future development; each implies through analysis that dramatic systematic change is necessary.

The Path Forward

In recent years, the changing intellectual climate has led to transdisciplinary efforts allowing for the adoption of more holistic ways of thinking and acting such as those adopted by Ecohealth and One Health. The emergence of GeoHealth and Planetary Health calls for an extension of these efforts, maintaining that the Earth's natural systems have reached levels threatening to drive the majority of the global burden of disease (Almada et al., 2017, p. 77). The path forward then is to generate rigorous scientific evidence (including that informed by systems and complexity thinking), more robust policy and resource management decisions (which take into account ecosystem, environmental, and human health, as well as animal health as applicable) and collective behavioural change that will minimize our demands on environmental resources such that a genuine societal epiphany ensues (Almada et al., 2017, p. 77).

However, Zywert (2017) suggests this is not an easy feat since instilling fear and despair through public communication, about, for example, the devastating effects of climate change, may result in opposite unintended effects (p. 231–2). Thus, reframing messages to emphasize the interconnectedness of human health and social-ecological resilience may make it easier for people to perceive the environment as part of the self (Zywert, 2017, p. 232). This, alongside the integration of more systemic ontologies is necessary if we are to live well within ecological limits (Zywert, 2017, p. 231–2).

Some commonalities exist between theoretical models of resilience thinking applied to complex social-ecological systems and the socioecological approaches presented here. However, both can be further developed through closer collaboration between fields (Berbés-Blázquez et al., 2014; Cumming and Cumming, 2015). Resilience (as persistence), adaptability, and transformability are central to resilience thinking (Folke et al., 2010). Folke et al. (2010, n.p.) suggest that "society must begin to consider ways to foster more flexible socio-ecological systems that *contribute* to Earth system resilience, and explore options for deliberate transformation of socio-ecological systems that *threaten* Earth System resilience."

Since the Anthropocene is characterized by rapid global change, the challenge also rests on how adaptive governance can be operationalized (Berkes, 2017). Berkes (2017) reiterates the importance of: (i) fostering collaborative approaches to improve social and institutional learning, with an emphasis on collaborative learning at all levels – from local to international, (ii) considering resilience in addressing uncertainty and adaptation to unforeseen future changes, and (iii) the recognition that people and the environment need to be considered together as social and ecological subsystems. It is only once these changes are implemented that we will begin to see real progress in addressing some of the challenges that we face in the Anthropocene.

NOTE

1 This author has previously published under the name Ann Novogradec.

REFERENCES

Allen, T. F. H., & Ahl, V. (1996). *Hierarchy theory: A vision, vocabulary and epistemology*. New York: Columbia University Press.

Allen, T. F. H., & Hoekstra, T. W. (1992). *Toward a unified ecology.* New York: Columbia University Press.

Almada, A. A., Golden, C. D., Osofsky, S. A., & Myers, S. S. (2017). A case for planetary health/geohealth. *GeoHealth, 1*(2), 75–8. https://doi.org/10.1002/2017GH000084

Andreasen, J. K., O'Neill, R. V., Noss, R., & Slosser, N. C. (2001). Considerations for the development of a terrestrial index of ecological integrity. *Ecological Indicators, 1*(1), 21–35. https://doi.org/10.1016/S1470-160X(01)00007-3

Aragão, A., & Giampietro, M. (2016). An integrated multi-scale approach to assess the performance of energy systems illustrated with data from the Brazilian oil and natural gas sector. *Energy, 115,* 1412–23. https://doi.org/10.1016/j.energy.2016.06.058

Arrow, K., Bolin, B., Costanza, R., Dasgupta, P., Folke, C., Holling, C. S., Jansson, B.-O., Levin, S., Mäler, K.-G., Perrings, C., & Pimentel, D. (1995). Economic growth, carrying capacity, and the environment. *Science, 268*(5210), 520–1. https://doi.org/10.1126/science.268.5210.520

Ashby, W. R. (1991). Principles of the self-organizing system. In G. J. Klir (Ed.), *Facets of systems science* (pp. 521–36). Boston: Springer.

Bastianoni, S., Niccolucci, V., Pulselli, R. M., & Marchettini, N. (2012). Indicator and indicandum: 'Sustainable way' vs 'prevailing conditions' in the ecological footprint. *Ecological Indicators, 16,* 47–50. https://doi.org/10.1016/j.ecolind.2011.10.001

Berbés-Blázquez, M. (2012). A participatory assessment of ecosystem services and human wellbeing in rural Costa Rica using photo-voice. *Environmental Management, 49*(4), 862–75. https://doi.org/10.1007/s00267-012-9822-9

Berbés-Blázquez, M., Oestreicher, J. S., Mertens, F., & Saint-Charles, J. (2014). Ecohealth and resilience thinking: A dialog from experiences in research and practice. *Ecology and Society, 19*(2). https://doi.org/10.5751/es-06264-190224

Berkes, F. (2017). Environmental governance for the Anthropocene? Social-ecological systems, resilience, and collaborative learning. *Sustainability, 9*(7), 1232. https://doi.org/10.3390/su9071232

Blomqvist, L., Brook, B. W., Ellis, E. C., Kareiva, P. M., Nordhaus, T., & Shellenberger, M. (2013a). Does the shoe fit? Real versus imagined ecological footprints. *PLOS Biology, 11*(11), e1001700. https://doi.org/10.1371/journal.pbio.1001700

Blomqvist, L., Brook, B. W., Ellis, E. C., Kareiva, P. M., Nordhaus, T., & Shellenberger, M. (2013b). The ecological footprint remains a misleading metric of global sustainability. *PLOS Biology, 11*(11), e1001702. https://doi.org/10.1371/journal.pbio.1001702

Boev, P. A., Burenko, D. L., Shvarts, E., Diep, A., Hanscom, L., Iha, K., Kelly, R., Martindill, J., Wackernagel, M., & Zokai, G. (2016). In P. A. Boev, & D. Burenko (Eds), *Ecological footprint of the Russian regions.* Moscow: WWF-Russia.

Boischio, A., Sanchez A., Orosz Z., & Charron, D. (2009). Health and sustainable development: Challenges and opportunities of ecosystem approaches in the prevention and control of Dengue and Chagas disease. *Cad Saude Publica, 25*(1), S149–54. https://doi.org/10.1590/s0102-311x2009001300014

Bresalier, M., Cassidy, A., & Woods, A. (2015). One Health in history. In J. Zinsstag, E. Schelling, D. Waltner-Toews, M. Whittaker, & M. Tanner (Eds), *One Health: The theory and practice of integrated health approaches* (pp. 1–15). United Kingdom: CABI.

Bunch, M. J. (2016). Ecosystem approaches to health and well-being: Navigating complexity, promoting health in social-ecological systems. *Systems Research and Behavioral Science, 33*(5), 614–32. https://doi.org/10.1002/sres.2429

Bunch, M. J., Morrison, K. E., Parkes, M. W., & Venema, H. D. (2011). Promoting health and well-being by managing for social-ecological resilience: The potential of integrating ecohealth and water resources management approaches. *Ecology and Society, 16*(1). https://doi.org/10.5751/es-03803-160106

Bunch, M. J., Suresh, M. V., Finnis, B., Wilson, D., Kumaran, V. T., Murthy, R., Jerrett, M. J., & Eyles, J. (2006). Environment and health in Chennai, India: An ecosystem approach to managing the urban environment for human health. *Indian Geographical Journal, 81*(1), 5–22.

Bunch, M. J., and Waltner-Toews, D. (2015). Grappling with complexity: The context for One Health and the ecohealth approach. In J. Zinsstag, E. Schelling, D. Waltner-Toews, M. Whittaker, & M. Tanner (Eds), *One Health: The theory and practice of integrated health approaches* (pp. 415–26). United Kingdom: CABI.

Buse, C. G., Oestreicher, J. S., Ellis, N. R., Patrick, R., Brisbois, B., Jenkins, A. P., McKellar, K., Kingsley, J., Gislason, M., Galway, L., McFarlane, R. A., Walker, J., Frumkin, H., and Parkes, M. W. (2018). Public health guide to field developments linking ecosystems, environments and health in the Anthropocene. *Journal of Epidemiology and Community Health, 72*(5), 420–5. https://doi.org/10.1136/jech-2017-210082

Butler, C. D., & Friel, S. (2006). Time to regenerate: Ecosystems and health promotion. *PLOS Medicine, 3*(10), 1692–5. https://doi.org/10.1371/journal.pmed.0030394

Cabello, V., Willaarts, B. A., Aguilar, M., & del Moral Ituarte, L. (2015). River basins as social-ecological systems: Linking levels of societal and ecosystem water metabolism in a semiarid watershed. *Ecology and Society, 20*(3). https://doi.org/10.5751/es-07778-200320

Certain, G., Skarpaas, O., Bjerke, J.-W., Framstad, E., Lindholm, M., Nilsen, J.-E., Norderhaug, A., Oug, E., Pedersen, H.-C., Schartau, A.-K., van der Meeren, G. I., Aslaksen, I., Engen, S., Garnåsjordet, P.-A., Kvaløy, P., Lillegård, M., Yoccoz, N. G., & Nybø, S. (2011). The nature index: A general framework for synthesizing knowledge on the state of biodiversity. *PLOS One, 6*(4), e18930. https://doi.org/10.1371/journal.pone.0018930

Charron, D. F. (2012). Ecohealth: Origins and approach. In D. F. Charron (Ed.), *Ecohealth research in practice: Innovative applications of an ecosystem approach to health* (pp. 1–30). New York: Springer.

Commoner, B. (1971). *The closing circle: Nature, man, and technology.* New York: Random House.

Cook, R. A., Karesh, W. B., & Osofsky, S. A. (2009). *One World – One Health: Brazil, October 22 2009 Symposium*. Wildlife Conservation Society. Retrieved from http://www.oneworldonehealth.org/

Corvalan, C., Briggs, D., & Kjellstrom, T. (1996). Development of environmental health indicators. In C. Briggs, C. Corvalan, & M. Nurminen (Eds), *Linkage methods for environment and health analysis: General guidelines* (pp. 19–53). Geneva: UNEP, USEPA, WHO.

Corvalan, C., Hales, S., & McMichael, A. (2005). *Ecosystems and human well-being: Health synthesis – A report of the Millennium Ecosystem Assessment*. Geneva: WHO.

Crouse, D. L., Pinault, L., Balram, A., Hystad, P., Peters, P. A., Chen, H., van Donkelaar, A., Martin, R. V., Ménard, R., Robichaud, A., & Villeneuve, P. J. (2017). Urban greenness and mortality in Canada's largest cities: A national cohort study. *The Lancet Planetary Health, 1*(7), e289–97. https://doi.org/10.1016/S2542-5196(17)30118-3

Cumming, D. H. M., & Cumming, G. S. (2015). One Health: An ecological and conservation perspective. In J. Zinsstag, E. Schelling, D. Waltner-Toews, M. Whittaker, & M. Tanner (Eds), *One Health: The theory and practice of integrated health approaches* (pp. 38–52). United Kingdom: CABI.

Daly, H. E. (1990). Toward some operational principles of sustainable development. *Ecological Economics, 2*(1), 1–6. https://doi.org/10.1016/0921-8009(90)90010-R

Davenhall, B. (2008). *Geomedicine: Geography and personal health*. ESRI 2012. Retrieved from https://www.esri.com/library/ebooks/geomedicine.pdf

The Energy Team of the Climate, Energy and Tenure Division (NRC) of the UN Food and Agriculture Organisation (FAO). (2013). The Nexus Assessment Project. Retrieved from http://www.nexus-assessment.info/

Fiala, N. (2008). Measuring sustainability: Why the ecological footprint is bad economics and bad environmental science. *Ecological Economics, 67*(4), 519–25. https://doi.org/10.1016/j.ecolecon.2008.07.023

Folke, C. (2006). Resilience: The emergence of a perspective for social-ecological systems analyses. *Global Environmental Change, 16*(3), 253–67. https://doi.org/10.1016/j.gloenvcha.2006.04.002

Folke, C., Carpenter, S. R., Walker, B., Scheffer, M., Chapin, T., & Rockström, J. (2010). Resilience thinking: Integrating resilience, adaptability and transformability. *Ecology and Society, 15*(4), 20. https://doi.org/10.5751/es-03610-150420

Folke, C., Carpenter, S. R., Walker, B., Scheffer, M., Elmqvist, T., Gunderson, L., & Holling, C. S. (2004). Regime shifts, resilience, and biodiversity in ecosystem management. *Annual Review of Ecology, Evolution, and Systematics, 35*(1), 557–81. https://doi.org/10.1146/annurev.ecolsys.35.021103.105711

Forget, G., & Lebel, J. (2001). An ecosystem approach to human health. *International Journal of Occupational and Environmental Health, 7*(2), S1–S37.

Frumkin, H. (2017). *Planetary health education*. Planetary Health Alliance 2017. Retrieved from https://planetaryhealthalliance.org/education

Galli, A., Giampietro, M., Goldfinger, S., Lazarus, E., Lin, D., Saltelli, A., Wackernagel, M., & Müller, F. (2016). Questioning the ecological footprint. *Ecological Indicators, 69*, 224–32. https://doi.org/10.1016/j.ecolind.2016.04.014

Galli, A., Wiedmann, T., Ercin, E., Knoblauch, D., Ewing, B., & Giljum, S. (2012). Integrating ecological, carbon and water footprint into a 'footprint family' of indicators: Definition and role in tracking human pressure on the planet. *Ecological Indicators, 16*, 100–12. https://doi.org/10.1016/j.ecolind.2011.06.017

Georgescu-Roegen, N. (1971). *The entropy law and the economic process.* Cambridge: Harvard University Press.

Georgescu-Roegen, N. (1975). Energy and economic myths. *Southern Economic Journal, 41*(3), 347–81. https://doi.org/10.2307/1056148

Giampietro, M., Aspinall, R. J., Bukkens, S. G. F., Benalcazar, J. C., Diaz-Maurin, F., Gomiero, T., Kovacic, Z., Madrid, C., Ramos-Martin, J., & Serrano-Tovar, T. (2013). *An innovative accounting framework for the food-energy-water nexus: Application of the MuSIASEM.* Rome: Food and Agriculture Organization of the United Nations (Energy Team of Climate).

Giampietro, M., & Mayumi, K. (2000a). Multiple-scale integrated assessment of societal metabolism: Introducing the approach. *Population and Environment, 22*(2), 109–53. https://doi.org/10.1023/a:1026691623300

Giampietro, M., & Mayumi, K. (2000b). Multiple-scale integrated assessments of societal metabolism: Integrating biophysical and economic representations across scales. *Population and Environment, 22*(2), 155–210. https://doi.org/10.1023/a:1026643707370

Giampietro, M., & Mayumi, K. (2009). *The biofuel delusion: The fallacy of large-scale biofuel production.* London: Earthscan.

Giampietro, M., & Mayumi, K. & Sorman, A. (2012). *The metabolic pattern of societies.* New York: Routledge.

Giampietro, M., & Saltelli, A. (2014a). Footprints to nowhere. *Ecological Indicators, 46*, 610–21. https://doi.org/10.1016/j.ecolind.2014.01.030

Giampietro, M., & Saltelli, A. (2014b). Footworking in circles: Reply to Goldfinger et al. (2014) 'Footprint facts and fallacies: A response to Giampietro and Saltelli (2014) Footprints to nowhere.' *Ecological Indicators, 46*, 260–3. https://doi.org/10.1016/j.ecolind.2014.06.019

Global Footprint Network: Advancing the science of sustainability. (2013–18). Retrieved from https://www.footprintnetwork.org/resources/publications/

Gomiero, T., & Giampietro, M. (2001). Multiple-scale integrated analysis of farming systems: The Thuong Lo commune (Vietnamese Uplands) case study. *Population and Environment, 22*(3), 315–52. https://doi.org/10.1023/a:1026624630569

González-López, R., & Giampietro, M. (2017). Multi-scale integrated analysis of charcoal production in complex social-ecological systems. *Frontiers in Environmental Science, 5*(54), 1–11. https://doi.org/10.3389/fenvs.2017.00054

Gunderson, L. H, & Holling, C. S. (2002). *Panarchy: Understanding transformations in human and natural systems.* Washington DC: Island Press.

Hempel, S. (2007). *The strange case of the Broad Street pump: John Snow and the mystery of cholera*. Berkeley: University of California Press.

Hoekstra, A. Y. (2015). The water footprint: The relation between human consumption and water use. In M. Antonelli, & F. Greco (Eds), *The water we eat* (pp. 35–48). Switzerland: Springer International Publishing.

Holling, C. S. (1973). Resilience and stability of ecological systems. *Annual Review of Ecology and Systematics, 4*(1), 1–23. https://doi.org/10.1146/annurev .es.04.110173.000245

Horton, R., & Lo, S. (2015). Planetary health: A new science for exceptional action. *The Lancet, 386*(10007), 1921–2. https://doi.org/10.1016/s0140-6736(15)61038-8

Jerrett, M., Burnett, R. T., Ma, R., Arden P. C., Krewski, D., Newbold, B. K., Thurston, G., Shi, Y., Finkelstein, N., Calle, E. E., & Thun, M. J. (2005). Spatial analysis of air pollution and mortality in Los Angeles. *Epidemiology* (Cambridge, MA), *16*(6), 727–36. https://doi.org/10.1097/01.ede.0000181630.15826.7d

Kay, J. J. (1991). A nonequilibrium thermodynamic framework for discussing ecosystem integrity. *Environmental Management, 15*(4), 483–95. https://doi.org /10.1007/bf02394739

Kay, J. J., Regier, H. A., Boyle, M., & Francis, G. (1999). An ecosystem approach for sustainability: Addressing the challenge of complexity. *Futures, 31*(7), 721–42. https://doi.org/10.1016/S0016-3287(99)00029-4

Kerr, R. B., Msachi, R., Dakishoni, L., Shumba, L., Nkhonya, Z., Berti, P., Bonatsos, C., Chione, E., Mithi, M., Chitaya, A., Maona, E., & Pachanya, S. (2012). Growing healthy communities: Farmer participatory research to improve child nutrition, food security, and soils in Ekwendeni, Malawi. In D. F. Charron (Ed.), *Ecohealth research in practice: Innovative applications of an ecosystem approach to health* (pp. 37–46). New York: Springer.

Kjeldskov, J., Christensen, C. M., & Rasmussen, K. K. (2010). GeoHealth: A location-based service for home healthcare workers. *Journal of Location Based Services, 4*(1), 3–27. https://doi.org/10.1080/17489721003742819

Lebel, J. (2003). *Health: An ecosystem approach*. Ottawa: International Development Research Centre.

Lenton, T. M., Held, H., Kriegler, E., Hall, J. W., Lucht, W., Rahmstorf, S., & Schellnhuber, H. J. (2008). Tipping elements in the Earth's climate system. *Proceedings of the National Academy of Sciences, 105*(6), 1786–93. https://doi.org /10.1073/pnas.0705414105.

Lerner, H., & Berg, C. (2015). The concept of health in One Health and some practical implications for research and education: What is One Health? *Infection Ecology & Epidemiology, 5*(1), 25300. https://doi.org/10.3402/iee.v5.25300

Leroy, E. M., Epelboin, A., Mondonge, V., Pourrut, X., Gonzalez, J.-P., Muyembe-Tamfum, J.-J., & Formenty, P. (2009). Human Ebola outbreak resulting from direct exposure to fruit bats in Luebo, Democratic Republic of Congo, 2007. *Vector-Borne and Zoonotic Diseases, 9*(6), 723–8. https://doi.org/10.1089/vbz.2008.0167

Leung, Z., Middleton, D., & Morrison, K. (2012). One Health and EcoHealth in Ontario: A qualitative study exploring how holistic and integrative approaches are shaping public health practice in Ontario. *BMC Public Health, 12*(1), 1–15. https://doi.org/10.1186/1471-2458-12-358

Louie, A. H. (2008). Functional entailment and immanent causation in relational biology. *Axiomathes, 18*(3), 289–302. https://doi.org/10.1007/s10516-008-9047-y

Madrid-López, C., & Giampietro, M. (2015). The water metabolism of socio-ecological systems: Reflections and a conceptual framework. *Journal of Industrial Ecology, 19*(5), 853–65. https://doi.org/doi:10.1111/jiec.12340

Maturana, H. R., & Humberto, R. (1980). *Autopoiesis and cognition: The realization of the living.* Dordrecht: D. Reidel Publishing Company.

Meadows, D. H., Meadows, D. L., Randers, J., & Behrens, W. W. (1972). *The limits to growth.* New York: Universe Books.

Millennium Ecosystem Assessment. (2005). *Overview of the Millennium Ecosystem Assessment.* Retrieved from https://www.millenniumassessment.org/en/About.html#

Monroy, C., Castro, X., Bustamante, D. M., Pineda, S. S., Rodas, A., Moguel, B., Ayala, V., & Quinonez, J. (2012). An ecosystem approach for the prevention of Chagas disease in rural Guatemala. In D. F. Charron (Ed.), *Ecohealth research: Innovative applications of an ecosystem approach to health* (pp. 153–62). New York: Springer.

Montoya, J. M., Donohue, I., & Pimm, S. L. (2018). Planetary boundaries for biodiversity: Implausible science, pernicious policies. *Trends in Ecology & Evolution, 33*(2), 71–3. https://doi.org/10.1016/j.tree.2017.10.004

Okello-Onen, J., Mboera, L. E. G., & Mugisha, S. (2012). Malaria research and management need rethinking: Uganda and Tanzania case studies. In D. F. Charron (Ed.), *Ecohealth research in practice: Innovative applications of an ecosystem approach to health* (pp. 139–51). New York: Springer.

Parkes, M., Panelli, R., & Weinstein, P. (2003). Converging paradigms for environmental health theory and practice. *Environmental Health Perspectives, 111*(5), 669–75. https://doi.org/10.1289/ehp.5332

Pattee, H. H. (1973). The physical basis and origin of hierarchical control. In H. H. Pattee (Ed.), *Hierarchy theory* (pp. 71–108). New York: George Braziller.

Pearce, J. (2007). Incorporating geographies of health into public policy debates: The GeoHealth laboratory. *New Zealand Geographer, 63*(2), 149–53. https://doi.org/10.1111/j.1745-7939.2007.00102.x

Ponthiere, G. (2009). The ecological footprint: An exhibit at an intergenerational trial? *Environment, Development and Sustainability, 11*(4), 677–94. https://doi.org/10.1007/s10668-007-9136-x

Prigogine, I., & Stengers, I. (1984). *Order out of chaos: Man's new dialogue with nature.* New York: Bantam Books.

Przybysz, R., & Bunch, M. (2017). Exploring spatial patterns of sudden cardiac arrests in the city of Toronto using Poisson kriging and Hot Spot analyses. *PLOS One, 12*(7), e0180721. https://doi.org/10.1371/journal.pone.0180721

Rapport, D. J., Böhm, G., Buckingham, D., Cairns, J., Costanza, R., Karr, J. R., De Kruijf, H. A. M., Levins, R., McMichael, A. J., Nielsen, N. O., & Whitford, W. G. (1999). Ecosystem health: The concept, the ISEH, and the important tasks ahead. *Ecosystem Health, 5*(2), 82–90. https://doi.org/10.1046/j.1526-0992.1999.09913.x.

Rees, W. E. (1992). Ecological footprints and appropriated carrying capacity: What urban economics leaves out. *Environment and Urbanization, 4*(2), 121–30. https://doi.org/10.1177/095624789200400212

Rees, W. E., & Wackernagel, M. (2013). The shoe fits, but the footprint is larger than Earth. *PLOS Biology, 11*(11), e1001701. https://doi.org/10.1371/journal.pbio.1001701

Reid, W. V., Mooney, H. A., Cropper, A., Capistrano, D., Carpenter, S. R., Chopra, K., Dasgupta, P. et al. (2005). Ecosystems and human well-being: Synthesis – A report of the Millennium Ecosystem Assessment. Washington DC.

Riojas-Rodriguez, H., & Rodriguez-Dozal, S. (2012). An ecosystem study of manganese mining in Molango, Mexico. In D. Charron (Ed.), *Ecohealth in practice: Innovative applications of an ecosystem approach to health* (pp. 87–97). New York: Springer.

Rockström, J., Steffen, W., Noone, K., Persson, A., Chapin III, F. S., Lambin, E., Lenton, T. M. et al. (2009). Planetary boundaries: Exploring the safe operating space for humanity. *Ecology and Society, 14*(2). https://doi.org/10.5751/es-03180-140232

Rosen, R. (1985). *Anticipatory systems: Philosophical, mathematical, and methodological foundations*. Oxford: Pergamon Press.

Rosen, R. (1991). *Life itself: A comprehensive inquiry into the nature, origin, and fabrication of life*. New York: Columbia University Press.

Sa, J. H. G., Rebelo, M. S., Brentani, A., Grisi, S. J. F. E., Iwaya, L. H., Simplicio, M. A., Carvalho, T. C. M. B., & Gutierrez, M. A. (2016). Georeferenced and secure mobile health system for large scale data collection in primary care. *International Journal of Medical Informatics, 94*, 91–9. https://doi.org/10.1016/j.ijmedinf.2016.06.013

Schelling, E., & Hattendorf, J. (2015). One Health study designs. In J. Zinsstag, E. Schelling, D. Waltner-Toews, M. Whittaker, & M. Tanner (Eds), *One Health: The theory and practice of integrated health approaches* (pp. 107–21). United Kingdom: CABI.

Schütte, S., Gemenne, F., Zaman, M., Flahault, A., & Depoux, A. (2018). Connecting planetary health, climate change, and migration. *The Lancet Planetary Health, 2*(2), e58–9. https://doi.org/10.1016/S2542-5196(18)30004-4

Shackleton, R., Larson, B., & Biggs, R. (O.). (2018). *American chestnut dominant forests to red maple dominant forests*. Retrieved from http://www.regimeshifts.org/item/617-american-chestnut-dominant-forests-to-red-maple-dominant-forests

Sherrouse, B. C., Clement, J. M., & Semmens, D. J. (2011). A GIS application for assessing, mapping, and quantifying the social values of ecosystem services. *Applied Geography, 31*(2), 748–60. https://doi.org/10.1016/j.apgeog.2010.08.002

Silva-Macher, J. C., & Farrell, K. N. (2014). The flow/fund model of Conga: Exploring the anatomy of environmental conflicts at the Andes-Amazon commodity frontier. *Environment, Development and Sustainability, 16*(3), 747–68. https://doi.org/10.1007/s10668-013-9488-3

Steffen, W., Richardson, K., Rockström, J., Cornell, S. E., Fetzer, I., Bennett, E. M., Biggs, R., Carpenter, S. R., de Vries, W., de Wit, C. A., Folke, C., Gerten, D., Heinke, J., Mace, G. M., Persson, L. M., Ramanathan, V., Reyers, B., & Sörlin, S. (2015). Planetary boundaries: Guiding human development on a changing planet. *Science, 347*(6223), 736; 1259855-1-10. https://doi.org/10.1126/science.1259855

Steffen, W., and Smith, M. S. (2013). Planetary boundaries, equity and global sustainability: Why wealthy countries could benefit from more equity. *Current Opinion in Environmental Sustainability, 5*(3), 403–8. https://doi.org/10.1016/j.cosust.2013.04.007

Tabi, A., & Csutora, M. (2011). Representing the forest management dilemmas in the ecological footprint indicator. *Applied Ecology and Environmental Research, 10*(1), 65–73. https://doi.org/10.15666/aeer/1001_065073

Ulanowicz, R. E. (1986). *Growth and development: Ecosystems phenomenology*. San Jose: toExcel Press.

Ulanowicz, R. E. (1997). *Ecology, the ascendant perspective*. New York: Columbia University Press.

van den Bergh, J. C. J. M., & Verbruggen, H. (1999). Spatial sustainability, trade and indicators: An evaluation of the 'ecological footprint.' *Ecological Economics, 29*(1), 61–72. https://doi.org/10.1016/s0921-8009(99)00032-4

VanLeeuwen, J. A., Waltner-Toews, D., Abernathy, T., & Smit, B. (1999). Evolving models of human health toward an ecosystem context. *Ecosystem Health, 5*(3), 204–19. https://doi.org/10.1046/j.1526-0992.1999.09931.x

Verburg, P. H., Dearing, J. A., Dyke, J. G., van der Leeuw, S., Seitzinger, S., Steffen, W., & Syvitski, J. (2016). Methods and approaches to modelling the Anthropocene. *Global Environmental Change, 39*, 328–40. https://doi.org/10.1016/j.gloenvcha.2015.08.007

Wackernagel, M. (1994). *Ecological footprint and appropriated carrying capacity: A tool for planning toward sustainability.* (Doctoral dissertation). University of British Columbia.

Wackernagel, M., & Rees, W. (1996). *Our ecological footprint: Reducing human impact on the earth*. Philadelphia: New Society Publishers.

Wackernagel, M., Schulz, N. B., Deumling, D., Linares, A. C., Jenkins, M., Kapos, V., Monfreda, C. et al. (2002). Tracking the ecological overshoot of the human economy. *Proceedings of the National Academy of Sciences, 99*(14), 9266–71. https://doi.org/10.1073/pnas.142033699

Waltner-Toews, D. (2001). An ecosystem approach to health and its applications to tropical emerging diseases. *Cad. Saude Publica, Suppl. 17*, 7–36. https://doi.org/10.1590/s0102-311x2001000700002

Whitmee, S., Haines, A., Beyrer, C., Boltz, F., Capon, A. G., de Souza Dias, B. F., Ezeh, A., Frumkin, H., Gong, P., Head, P., Horton, R., Mace, G. M., Marten, R., Myers, S. S., Nishtar, S., Osofsky, S. A., Pattanayak, S. K., Pongsiri, M. J., Romanelli, C., Soucat, A., Vega, J., & Yach, D. (2015). Safeguarding human health in the

Anthropocene epoch: Report of The Rockefeller Foundation – Lancet Commission on planetary health. *The Lancet*, *386*(10007), 1973–2028. https://doi.org/10.1016/s0140-6736(15)60901-1

Whittaker, M. (2015). The role of social sciences in One Health – Reciprocal benefits. In J. Zinsstag, E. Schelling, D. Waltner-Toews, M. Whitaker, & M. Tanner (Eds), *One Health: The theory and practice of integrated health approaches* (pp. 60–72). United Kingdom: CABI.

WWF – Korea. (2016). Korea ecological footprint report 2016: Measuring Korea's impact on nature. Seoul: Simon Yoon, CEO, WWF – Korea.

Yang, W., Dietz, T., Liu, W., Luo, J., & Liu, J. (2013). Going beyond the millennium ecosystem assessment: An index system of human dependence on ecosystem services. *PLOS One*, *8*(5), e64581. https://doi.org/10.1371/journal.pone.0064581

Zinsstag, J., Schelling, E., Wyss, K., & Mahamat, M. B. (2005). Potential of cooperation between human and animal health to strengthen health systems. *The Lancet*, *366*(9503), 2142–5. https://doi.org/10.1016/s0140-6736(05)67731-8

Zinsstag, J., Schelling, E., Waltner-Toews, D., Whittaker, M., & Tanner, M. (2015). *One Health: The theory and practice of integrated health and approaches.* United Kingdom: CABI.

Zinsstag, J., Mahamat, M. B., & Schelling, E.. (2015). Measuring added value from integrated methods. In J. Zinsstag, E. Schelling, D. Waltner-Toews, M. Whitaker, & M. Tanner (Eds), *One Health: The theory and practice of integrated health approaches* (pp. 53–9). United Kingdom: CABI.

Zinsstag, J., Meisser, A., Schelling, E., Bonfoh, B., & Tanner, M. (2012). From 'two medicines' to 'One Health' and beyond. *Onderstepoort Journal of Veterinary Research*, *79*(2), 62–6. https://doi.org/10.4102/ojvr.v79i2.492

Zywert, K. (2017). Human health and social-ecological systems change: Rethinking health in the Anthropocene. *The Anthropocene Review*, *4*(3), 216–38. https://doi.org/10.1177/2053019617739640

19 Coming Back to Our True Nature: What Is the Inner Work That Supports Transition?

BLAKE POLAND

All of humanity's problems stem from man's inability to sit quietly in a room alone.
—Blaise Pascal, *Pensées*

If humans clear inner pollution, then they will cease to create outer pollution
—Eckhart Tolle, *A New Earth*

Every day, priests minutely examine the Law
and endlessly chant complicated sutras.
Before doing that, though, they should learn
how to read the love letters sent by the wind
and rain, the snow and moon.
—Ikkyu (in *Spiritual Ecology*, Vaughan-Lee, 2013, p. 23)

Each one of us on earth at this time is being called to rebuild the sacred circle in ourselves.
—Dhyani Ywahoo, Cherokee (in Gray, 2010, *Returning to Sacred World*)

Climate change. Toxic contamination. Soil loss. Deforestation. Fisheries collapse. Species extinction. Resource depletion. Energy insecurity. Peak oil. Hunger. Poverty. Economic instability. Rising inequality. Forced migration. The signs of ecological and social disintegration are being felt more keenly than ever, even as those with the luxury to do so find ever more enticing ways of distracting, numbing, and entertaining themselves. Our responses to mounting crisis can seem alarmingly ineffective: ongoing global negotiations (e.g. about climate change) seem to produce more friction than substance, national governments drag their feet, beholden to vested interests, watered down and mired in lengthy phase-in periods. Local efforts seem more promising and proliferate, but also prone to being overwhelmed by broader systems and trends. Social movements ramp up protests and social experiments in the creation of vibrant enticing alternatives to mainstream economics in the form of community gardens, the sharing economy, and much else. These mostly proliferate along the margins of the dominant order, largely ignored by the mainstream media, awaiting more fruitful conditions to scale up that will be engendered, it is imagined, by anticipated crises, breakdowns, and awakenings. When we're not too busy distracting ourselves from what we sense to be the "awful truth" lurking at our door, we redouble our efforts to do what we can in our personal lives, continually bumping our heads against the challenge of living environmentally in a fundamentally unsustainable society, embedded as we are in systems of convenience that ensnare those of us in the relatively privileged Global North. Meanwhile, scientists and leading scholars become more vocal about approaching climatic and ecological tipping points that they believe will send us headlong into catastrophe. Some write openly about the possibility of civilization collapse (Ehrlich and Ehrlich, 2013; Lovelock, 2006; Steffen et al., 2011) and now even an approximate date has been put on it: in an article in the prestigious journal *Nature*, Anthony Barnosky and environmental researchers from around the world conclude that without significant shifts in current trajectory, we will face cascading global ecological systems collapse by 2045, well within the lifetimes of most of you reading this chapter (Barnosky et al., 2012).

In this context, building resilience is increasingly proffered as our best hope of riding out the coming storms (Carpenter et al., 2012; Folke, 2006; Poland et al., 2011; Rees, 2010; Zolli and Healy, 2012), although this has yet to register in mainstream politics. Politicians have thus far been steadfastly committed to restarting or preserving economic growth at all costs. Nevertheless, a growing number have embraced resilience as a collective project of preparing ourselves to bounce back from anticipated storms and adversity, hoping against hope to preserve some of the comforts to which we've become accustomed, to buy ourselves some security in an increasingly turbulent and unpredictable world. Just as we start to get the hang of that, we are told that nothing less than transformative whole systems change is required. Resilience as the capacity to bounce back from adversity, we are told, is still playing small, and nothing less than embracing change and bouncing *forward* (Manyena et al., 2011; URP, 2015) into entirely new ways of thinking and doing (and some "old" ones too, given the salience of Indigenous knowledge) will do (Olssen et al., 2014; Westley et al., 2011). With the exception of a few intriguing road maps, however (Holman, 2010; Jaworski, 2012; Scharmer & Kaufer, 2013), *how* to actually catalyse whole-system transformative change remains hotly debated, leaving many so-called "ordinary" citizens overwhelmed. Furthermore, previously inspiring social change writers like Margaret Wheatley (2012) come out with books like *So Far from Home*, suggesting that the battle for social justice and sustainability has likely been lost and it's time to give up the fight and turn inwards and to each other, and Carolyn Baker (2009, 2011, 2013) comes out with yet another book announcing that collapse is unavoidable and asks what we are doing to prepare ourselves emotionally and psychologically. A person could be forgiven for not knowing which end is up, freaking out, and reaching for another glass of wine or a Netflix film.

There is a tendency in western culture to approach the whole issue of transformative change as a matter of considerable urgency, as a kind of race of the tipping points: climatic and ecological on the one hand, and social tipping points and evolutionary leaps in human consciousness on the other, with the future of humanity and the planet hanging in the balance. We glimpse for the first time the awesome power we have as a species to determine the fate of the planet – what is now referred to as the birth of the Anthropocene (Steffen et al., 2011). Yet paradoxically we are also paralysed with a sense of powerlessness to decisively redirect the broadly entrenched institutional, cultural, and economic forces that threaten our survival and that of the planet. Consumerism, economic growth, political systems, meritocracy, dominant narratives about human nature – it all seems way beyond the control of mere ordinary citizens, and even most "world leaders."

To be sure, there are many inspiring efforts to respond effectively to these challenges, although we rarely hear about them, the dominant media being oriented to other things ("the economy," sensationalism, cynicism, celebrity, sports, to name a few). A decade ago already, in his book *Blessed Unrest*, Paul Hawken (2007) estimated that groups working on social justice and environmental issues numbered in the hundreds of thousands worldwide, a trend that has continued in response to worsening conditions. There is a small alternative news culture that focuses on these inspiring efforts that includes *Yes!* magazine (http://www.yesmagazine.org), *The Daily Good* (http://www.dailygood.org), *Kosmos Journal* (http://www.kosmosjournal.org) and *Uplift* (http://upliftconnect.com), as well as a growing number of books such as *Walk Out Walk On* (Wheatley and Frieze, 2011), *Nowtopia* (Carlsson, 2008), *The Geography of Hope* (Turner, 2007), *Active Hope* (Macy and Johnstone, 2012), and *Hope Beneath Our Feet* (Keogh, 2010), to name but a few. Inspiring reading for sure, but most days transformative whole systems change still seems frustratingly elusive.

As I see it, some of the frustration that we feel as activists arises from a belief that we need to *make* change happen. When you feel that you have to *make* change, it can be discouraging that there seems to be still so few of us deeply committed to this, that we don't have much time, that the scale of the problem seems overwhelming, and that change on the scale required will take a lot of time and a whole lot of effort against significant odds and multiple barriers and sources of resistance.

But what if not all of these assumptions are true? What if social change is non-linear and sudden (just like the fall of the Berlin Wall)? As with ecosystem change, the tipping points might be closer than we think. Haven't evolutionary leaps always worked this way (Hubbard, 1998, 2001)? What if a groundswell of readiness for paradigm change has gone unreported and hides behind what many activists fear is public "apathy" but what might be, from a practice theory perspective (Haluza-Delay, 2008; Shove et al., 2012; Shove and Walker, 2010), a reflection of how dominant systems govern everyday practice until it starts unravelling and they jump ship? What if scale doesn't matter, or matters very differently than we think, where we can't know, in complex adaptive systems, what is a "small" action and what is a "big" one (the proverbial "butterfly effect" in chaos theory) (Eisenstein, 2013)? What if our frantic efforts to make change happen is part of the problem rather than part of the solution?

Transformation Is Not Something We *Make* Happen.
It Is Something We Make Ourselves Available *for*

Where are we coming from when we try to *make* change happen? From what quality of being are we sourcing our doing? Are we agitated, animated with fear, desperate to avoid looming calamities, angry at the forces of injustice and perceived apathy, disillusioned and despairing of what we take to be "human nature?" Of course we are, and with apparent good reason! But what if, as a growing number of prominent thinkers now propose, we are indeed in transition from a dominant paradigm based on fear, desire to predict and control, exploitation (of people and nature), and imposing our will (on nature and on others – power over), to something more life-centred (reconnected with nature, ourselves, and each other, in harmony, reciprocity, sufficiency – power with)? What would that suggest about our propensity to fuel our work in the world from anger, fear, and desperation to make change happen? Are we bringing more of the same into the world? And what does it mean to find ourselves in that bizarre liminal space between paradigms, with one foot in the old and one in the as-yet-emerging new? In *Active Hope*, Johanna Macy and Chris Johnstone (2012) suggest that "a shift in consciousness" is one of the three dimensions of "The Great Turning," a profound paradigm shift that is already underway.

The challenge of being "in transition," with one foot in the old and one foot in the new, is not easy. No matter how well grounded we think we are in "being the change we want to see in the world," we don't have to wait long to see how we have internalized the dominant culture in so many subtle and not-so-subtle ways. What in us wants to predict and control the future? What in us wants to play it safe? What in us is propelled to *make* the world conform to what we want to get or to avoid? What in us acts out of fear, anger, or revenge, imagining that these will bring about a different and better world? We know the wisdom in Einstein's words that it is folly to try to "fix problems with the same level of thinking that created them," but we remain so often stuck in old conditioned ways of being, thinking, and doing.

No wonder. Our culture gives us excellent specialized training in how to make ourselves miserable. From a young age we practice the fine art of taking everything personally. Everything becomes an opportunity to notice how we're never good enough to earn the love we long for. We learn to avoid discomfort by distracting or numbing ourselves with a dizzying array of activities and substances, only to have the malaise pop up more insistently in some other area of our lives. In other words, we are conditioned to consume and distract in response to discomfort, with significant ecological, psychological, and societal consequences. And to believe that the circumstances that are to blame for our malaise can be "improved" upon to "make" us happier, and that we should have the ability (and right) to do so (and that failing to do so makes us lazy or incompetent or lacking in ingenuity).

What does it mean to shift from *making* change happen to making ourselves available for transformative change? Peter Senge and colleagues in their book *Presence: An Exploration of Profound Change in People, Organizations and Society* (2004), Otto Scharmer in *Theory U* (2009) and *Leading from the Emerging Future* (Scharmer and Kaufer, 2013), Joseph Jaworski's extension of this work and that of David Bohm in *Source: The Inner Path of Knowledge Creation* (2012), and Peggy Holman in her pathbreaking work on *Engaging Emergence* (2010), give us some key pointers to doing effective change work in complex adaptive systems from a new paradigm. They point to the power of intention, the capacity to hold space for transformative dialogue, the emergent quality of collective work wherein the whole is more than the sum of the parts, the capacity to tap into collective wisdom, the importance of suspending judgement and seeing with new eyes, letting go and letting come, sensing into and aligning with the future that already wants to emerge, following the energy, and developing the capacity to listen deeply (to our inner landscape, to each other, to the land), intuition, and tapping in to subtle but increasingly well-documented realms of interconnection (what Jaworski calls "Source," Nobel physicist David Bohm called the "Implicate Order," Adyashakti calls "Reality," Richard Moss and Miki Kashtan both refer to as "Radical Aliveness," etc.). This is not the space or time to describe that work in greater detail – readers who are intrigued can track down the original works that lay out the foundations much better than I can summarize here. Nor is this the place to repeat existing work on the psychology of transition by Johanna Macy (2009), Carolyn Baker (2009, 2011, 2013, 2015), Raymond de Young (2013, 2014), Hillary Prentice (2012) and others.

What intrigues me most is the emphasis that many of these authors put on the essential contribution that inner work makes to the effectiveness of outer change work. Jaworski in particular describes how efforts to extend David Bohm's original work on transformative dialogue (Bohm, 2004) initially produced outstanding results in terms of organizational change but eventually bumped up against the limits of participants' capacities to go deeper. His conclusion, based on research at MIT and around the world, is that transformative change requires engaged participants who have done and are committed to continued deepening of their own inner work so that they are less triggered and more open and available to each other and to the work of the group (Jaworski,

2012). Since much of this work relies on a capacity to be radically present and hold space for what is emerging, this should come as no surprise.

My own explorations, which include three years of schooling with Krishnamurti at Brockwood Park (including some time with David Bohm himself); mindfulness meditation; extensive reading and engagement with the work of Buddhist teachers such as Pema Chodron (2005, 2012), Tara Brach (2003), Thich Nhat Han (1992, 2006, 2007), and the work of Almaas (2008) and Adyashanti (2013); Inner Relationship Focusing (Cornell, 1996); Non-Violent Communication (Rosenberg, 2003a, 2003b, 2004; Kashtan, 2014); The Presence Process (Brown, 2010); and the transformative healing work of Gina Cenciose (www.EmbodyingEmpathy.ca), have caused me to fundamentally reconsider my assumptions about what inner change work is and the role it plays in "The Great Turning." A common thread in this work is the cultivation of Presence, the capacity to be with reality as it is. Does that mean we just accept how things are and don't try to change things? Not necessarily. But we start with clear-eyed realism about how things are. "Not arguing with reality," as Byron Katie puts (an argument you're sure to always lose, she adds) (Katie, 2002), doesn't mean not acting to reduce unnecessary suffering. "Yes, this is how things are, and what is right action in the face of this reality?" is a different starting point than "I can't believe this is happening, this is so horrible, we have to act now to stop this." Being the calm at the centre of the storm, rather than part of the chaos and confusion, allows us to discern a right next step from a space of presence and alignment with life, rather than striking out in reactivity or projection. Interestingly, and somewhat ironically, it also enables us to hold a clear vision of the future we want that helps to call it into being without having to know exactly how that will be co-created.

Attending to the inner landscape doesn't mean abandoning the outer world and the real suffering of human and non-human species. On the contrary: it is to dive into deeper relationship with it. And shift where we're coming from so that we consciously respond from a space of stillness that enables us to behold the bigger picture and tap into intuition and other ways and sources of knowing for a more fully informed conscious response, rather than reacting to what is happening around us from a space of contraction, projection, and desire to control.

Going Deeper: The Wisdom of No Escape

Wendell Berry writes in a recent article in *Yes!* magazine that in his observation we are so busy running around trying to fix the future that no-one is *here now* (Berry, 2015). For Berry, our fixation on the future distracts us from living now in alignment with what we know to be important, regardless of what the future holds in store.

How have we come to this? Much of our inner life and our actions in the world (including consumption) is a consequence of a pervasive sense of lack. According to Michael Brown,

> Our wanting ... leads us to believe that what we seek in order to feel satisfied is something solid and tangible – money, a car, a new house, a position in the workplace. But it isn't. It's never the "thing" that we are really after, but the resonance associated with possessing the thing... Instead of attempting to get whatever we feel is missing in our experience...if we first give it to ourselves unconditionally by feeling the resonance associated with it, our sense of lack noticeably decreases. Lack is a resonance that arises from not having the capacity to feed ourselves emotionally. (Brown, 2010, pp. 218–19)

> In our angst, we are turning over every piece of this planet in a desperate search for an awareness of peace, yet nothing we do brings the awareness of peace into our state of frantic "doing." The behaviour we generate in order to feel safe and accepted in the world is a substitute for real peace ... In this upside down state, we mistakenly spend our experience trying to get something instead of simply receiving that which is already and eternally given. (ibid., pp. 7–8)

The good news, he adds, is that this bundle of avoidance strategies seeking desperately to find fulfilment in the outside world isn't an accurate reflection of who we really are.

In a similar vein, we can see that much of how we are with others and how we treat nature is a reflection of our inner struggles. Pema Chodron writes persuasively about the unbearableness of being human as the perpetual search for security in a fundamentally unpredictable world:

> As human beings we share a tendency to scramble for certainty whenever we realize that everything around us is in flux. In difficult times the stress of trying to find solid ground – something predictable and safe to stand on – seems to intensify ... We think that if only we did this or didn't do that, somehow we could achieve a secure, dependable, controllable life. How disappointed we are when things don't work out quite the way we planned ... What a predicament! ... Our attempts to find lasting pleasure, lasting security, are at odds with the fact that we're part of a dynamic system in which everything and everyone is in process. (Chodron, 2012, pp. 3–4)

She continues: "it's not impermanence per se, or even knowing we're going to die, that is the cause of our suffering... Rather, it's our resistance to the fundamental uncertainty of our situation. Our discomfort arises from all of our efforts to put ground under our feet, to realize our dream of constant okayness. When we resist change, it's called suffering" (ibid., p. 6).

In response to this fundamental discomfort of the human condition, Chodron suggests turning towards, rather than away from, discomfort. Our attachment to having things a certain way, the way we think they "should" be:

arises involuntarily – our habitual response to feeling insecure ... we turn to anything to relieve the discomfort – food, alcohol, sex, shopping, being critical or unkind. But there's something more fruitful we can do when that edgy feeling arises ... Instead of trying to avoid the discomfort, you open yourself completely to it. You become receptive to the painful sensation without dwelling on the story your mind has concocted: "It's bad; I shouldn't feel this way; maybe it will never go away." (ibid., p. 10)

She continues:

Most of us want to avoid emotions that make us feel vulnerable, so we'll do almost anything to get away from them. But if, instead of thinking of these feelings as bad, we could think of them as road signs or barometers that tell us we're in touch with groundlessness, then we would see the feelings for what they really are: the gateway to liberation, an open doorway to freedom from suffering, the path to our deepest well-being and joy. We have a choice. We can spend our whole life suffering because we can't relax with how things really are, or we can relax and embrace the open-endedness of the human situation, which is fresh, unfixated, unbiased. So the challenge is to notice the emotional tug of *shenpa* [grasping or pushing away, contraction response to discomfort] when it arises and to stay with it for one and a half minutes [the time most emotions last without grasping or aversion] without the story line. Can you do this once a day, or many times throughout the day, as the feeling arises? This is the challenge. This is the process of unmasking, letting go, opening the mind and heart. (ibid., p. 14)

I quote Pema Chodron at length here because as I see it this kind of "hardwiring" of the western mind to avoid discomfort and to look to the outside (shopping, addictions, distractions) for "solutions"/relief is at the root of many of our ecological and social problems, and that trying to address these challenges from a similar space of reaction to discomfort (in this case about an imagined dooms-day future) fails to take us to the root of the problem. Chodron is not alone in pointing to how our experience of difficult emotions transforms when we turn towards and allow, being with it while simultaneously dropping our identification with the storyline. Charged emotions that previously had us in their grip are experienced as a passage of energy, no more intrinsically pleasant or unpleasant than any other. As Chodron and others tell us, "the only way through is through."

Returning to the world situation, could this all be an invitation to go inside, to see that beneath the struggle to avoid catastrophe is a deeper calling to heal the soul, reconnect to our true nature, our interdependence, and rekindle an appreciation for the sacredness of all life on animate Earth (to borrow the title from Stephen Harding's book *Animate Earth*, 2006)? I think so. And I'm also well aware that this could be easily misinterpreted as an invitation to just "accept" the inevitable, a new-age reinterpretation of the law of karma, or a kind of privileged-class fascination with "personal growth" and "conscious evolution"[1] that allows us to conveniently sidestep inconvenient truths about the extensiveness of human (and non-human) suffering, and the complicit nature of our own privilege.

For me there are two fundamental reasons to connect inner and outer transition, attending more fully to the former and to the link between the two than we have in the past. First, freed from the reactivity of powerful emotions of fear, desire, and the need for security, we can more readily listen and sense into what is needed and respond to what is, more freely and creatively, and in ways that are more effortlessly in alignment with the flow of life, tapping into a deeper collective wisdom (of the sort described by Brown, Senge, Scharmer, Bohm, Jaworski, Carl Rogers, and others), "seeing with new eyes" (Macy and Johnstone, 2012) and working to manifest "what already wants to emerge" (Scharmer and Kaufer, 2013). Second, deep inner work holds the potential for transformative change in the here and now. It is not conditional on world leaders, corporate executives, our family and friends, coworkers, or anyone else "getting it" or changing. More importantly, it brings the lasting inner peace that is arguably the deeper longing behind our social change strategies, and in ways that are not conditional on what happens on the outside, and which then allows us to manifest and radiate that in all our relations and in our outer work (which may ironically turn out to be much more transformative in impact).

Inner and outer change are joined at the hip. For Michael Brown and others, training ourselves to recognize and follow insight and intuition, through a deepened capacity to listen (to our inner life, to each other, to nature, to source) with our heart, brings a relaxation of the need to plan, figure out, and preemptively control.

Trusting our insight is the greatest of accomplishments because to accomplish this is to open a line directly from source's mouth into our inner ear. Then we require no intermediaries – no priests, fortune tellers, or even weather forecasters. We mainline source. Then, where is fear? Where is anxiety? These disperse and we walk directly and intimately in the vision source has for us. We live in awe at the miracle called life. Learning to live is learning to listen ... When we are able to listen, we realize we always receive all we require. (Brown, 2010, p. 270)

Then we can relax into abundance, trusting life, showing up in the world without a fixed agenda but deeply committed to be of service: "We serve our planet by standing at the centre of our experience and allowing source to be as present as possible within each breath" (ibid., p. 271) Free from the desire to manipulate the world to provide what our egos think we need in order to be happy, we can engage fully, in the moment, from a deep sense of rightness, unencumbered by the need to predict and control or the need to know the outcome, and with a focus on authentically embodying our deepest intentions rather than micromanaging for predetermined results.

What could this look like as a practical strategy for meaningful social change? I turn to that now, in the section that follows.

Bringing It All Together: A Few Ingredients for Deep Change Work

Far be it for me to offer a nicely packaged "recipe" for transformative social change, were that even possible (or desirable). No, catalysing transformative social change will be a necessarily messy and emergent affair, resistant to facile recipes and so-called "best practices." Still, there are a few key ingredients that are sufficiently noteworthy to be included here. What follows is a necessarily personal list of what I find most inspiring.

Nurturing New Stories

The stories we tell ourselves and each other about who we are and where we're going matter (Baldwin, 2005). These are as much collective stories as they are familial and individual. The contours of the dominant narrative are familiar to most: the pre-eminence of the economy, the value of the market, meritocracy, efficiency and innovation as keys to future prosperity, and the dubious nature of human nature that is to be kept in check with a plethora of formal systems and legal frameworks. Alternative framings abound, including that of the Transition movement (building community resilience through reskilling, community-building, and relocalization – see Hopkins, 2008 and www .TransitionNetwork.org), and Indigenous prophesies about this time of crisis and opportunity for awakening (e.g. Hill, 2009). Held lightly, stories can be sources of inspiration, collective action, and invitations to think outside the box. Held tightly as gospel they can become dogmatic, restrictive tools for manipulation and social control. For me it's less about "which story is more true", and more about "which story do I feel called to devote my life to." Investigating our own stories and those of our culture and choosing consciously the stories that bring out the best in us and in others is integral to transformative change work. In most cases this will require a deep questioning of many of our assumptions and current dominant narratives about "progress," the linearity of change, meritocracy, human nature, and how change happens. Put differently, we are called into a deep commitment to decolonize ourselves from the dominant western paradigm/story inculcated in us.[2]

Naomi Klein (2014, n.p.) puts it well:

> A great deal of the work of deep social change involves having debates during which new stories can be told to replace the ones that have failed us. Because if we are to have any hope of making the kind of civilizational leap required of this fateful decade, we will need to start believing, once again, that humanity is not hopelessly selfish and greedy: the image ceaselessly sold to us by everything from reality shows to neoclassical economics. Fundamentally, the task is to articulate not just an alternative set of policy proposals, but an alternative worldview to rival the one at the heart of the ecological crisis – embedded in interdependence rather than hyperindividualism, reciprocity rather than dominance, and cooperation rather than hierarchy.

As Joanna Macy notes in her recent book *Active Hope*, "When we find a good story and fully give ourselves to it, that story can act through us, breathing new life into everything that we do" (Macy & Johnstone, 2012, p. 33).

Decolonization

The exploration of alternative stories to live by necessarily calls us into a process of decolonization from the dominant western paradigm inculcated in us through the formal education system and the dominant culture. In her *Briarpatch* article "Decolonizing Together," Harsha Walia (2012) cites Toronto-based activist Syed Hussan in stating: "Decolonization is a dramatic reimagining of relationships with land, people and the state. Much of this requires study. It requires conversation. It is a practice; it is an unlearning,"

Decolonization is of course not just an "inside job:" it calls us into allyship with Indigenous peoples in their struggles for self-determination and a mutual commitment to reconciliation (Davis, 2010; Max, 2005; O'Connell, 2017; Wallace, 2013). It also calls for a rethinking of the role of Indigenous knowledges in the academy (Broadhead and Howard, 2011; Dei, 2000) and its contested and contestable role in (western attempts at) environmental stewardship (Dove, 2006; Reo et al., 2017), as well as a call to take (environmental) education outside the classroom and to learn on and from the land (Datta, 2016; Davidson-Hunt and O'Flaherty, 2007; Tuck et al., 2014; Riggs, 2005; Simpson, 2014; Styres et al., 2013). Heather Davis and Zoe Todd go further still, arguing for the decolonization of the Anthropocene itself (Davis and Todd, 2017).

Engaging Emergence

Drawing on the work of Peggy Holman on engaging emergence (2010), Otto Scharmer's *Theory U* (Scharmer, 2009; Scharmer and Kaufer, 2013; Senge et al.,

2004), Jaworski's (2012) related work on the ingredients of transformative group process building on the work of Nobel Prize–winning physicist David Bohm (Bohm, 2004), chaos theory (Merry, 1995) and complexity science perspectives on the social/ecological nature of complex adaptive systems (Berkes, Colding, and Folke, 2003; Fisher, 2011; Gunderson & Holling, 2001; Morin, 2000; Norberg and Cumming, 2006; Resnicow and Page, 2008), Carl Rogers's work on encounter groups (Rogers, 1978, 1980; Cornelius-White, 2006), accumulated experience from a variety of circle methods (Baldwin and Linnea, 2010; Cavalcante, 1999; Holman et al., 2007) and dialogical processes (Bohm, 2004; Born, 2012; Brady, 2003; Brown and Isaacs, 2005; Isaacs, 1999; O'Hara and Wood, 2005), and Byham's work on empowerment (Byham, 1993; Byham and Cox, 1988), we can outline the contours of an organic emergent collaborative process that is very different from the current mainstream preoccupation with regulation, hierarchy, and predict-and-control risk management. Processes that engage emergence harness the collective wisdom of groups in ways that demonstrate how the whole is more than the sum of the parts, tap into multiple layers and ways of knowing (implicit and explicit), and illustrate the power of intentions and the importance of how facilitators create and hold space for transformative dialogue.

Personal Direct Experience

We are called to tap into our own direct experience of how things really are, inside and out, rather than deferring to authority or simplistic recipes for how to "make" change happen. People no longer want to be lectured or preached to: they want to be inspired. They can be encouraged to learn how to trust their own authority, intuition (Einstein, 1997; Harding, 2006), sensing what feels right, and discovery of the deepest longings of the soul and the power of intention when it is aligned with the wisdom of life.

Trusting Life

We have lost trust in life itself, and so we live in fear, in a supposedly dog-eat-dog world where we believe that things happen *to* us unless we manage to "get the upper hand." We act from a space of perpetual lack that engenders competition under conditions of manufactured scarcity. This is used to justify repression, exploitation and injustice, in resonance with a dominant cultural narrative of "human nature" as untrustworthy, selfish, competitive, and unruly. At this juncture in human history, transformative change implies a shift from an industrial growth paradigm characterized by fear, lack, and exploitation to a "trusting life" paradigm characterized by harmony, collaboration, appreciation, interdependence, and a recovery of a sense of the sacredness of all life.

Recovering a Sense of the Sacred

Sufi writer Llewelyn Vaughan-Lee opens his edited book *Spiritual Ecology* with the following: "The world is not a problem to be solved; it is a living being to which we belong. The world is part of our own self and we are part of its suffering wholeness. Until we go to the root of our image of separateness, there can be no healing. And the deepest part of our separateness from creation lies in our forgetfulness of its sacred nature, which is also our own sacred nature" (Vaughan-Lee, 2013, p. i). Recovering a sense of the sacred is an inevitable consequence of coming into full relationship with the living world, not as "resources" for our exploitation, but as wondrous living beings and manifestations of spirit, recognizing the divine in "all our relations" that is foundational to most, if not all, Indigenous cultures.

Practices That Connect

In *We Are the Ones We Have Been Waiting For: Inner Light in a Time of Darkness* (2006, p. 109–10), Alice Walker states:

> This is not a time to live without a practice. It is a time when all of us will need the most faithful, self-generated enthusiasm ... in order to survive in human fashion. Whether we reach this inner state of recognized divinity through prayer, meditation, dancing, swimming, walking, feeding the hungry, or enriching the impoverished is immaterial. We will be doubly bereft without some form of practice that connects us, in a caring way, to what begins to feel like a dissolving world... [So] ... we must also ask: What is my practice? What is steering this boat that is my fragile human life?

There are many practical tools for self-connection, learning to be with, turning towards, and listening deeply (inside, to our inner landscape, to others, to animals, to the land, to what wants to emerge, to the wisdom of life). Carolyn Baker describes and offers several in the context of developing emotional resiliency in the face of challenging times ahead (Baker, 2009, 2011, 2013). Stephen Gray covers many others in his book *Returning to Sacred World: A Spiritual Toolkit for the Emerging Reality* (O-Books, 2010). Any listing here is necessarily partial and subjective.

Nature contact, increasingly established as foundational to health and health equity (Frumkin, 2001, 2003; Mitchell and Popham, 2008) is also essential for developing self-connection, an expanded relationality, capacity to listen, reverence for the sacredness of all life. David Abram (*The Spell of the Sensuous*, 1996), Bill Plotkin (*SoulCraft*, 2003), Starhawk (*The Earth Path*, 2004), Stephen

Harding (*Animate Earth*, 2006), Catriona MacGregor (*Partnering with Nature*, 2010), and Bill Pfeiffer (*Wild Earth, Wild Soul*, 2013) among others, offer deeper understanding of the power of nature, and a variety of practices for (re)connection with nature.

Making Joy Our Yardstick

What if joy was our yardstick? Not an effervescent manufactured entertainment-induced "bubbly happiness," but the kind of deep joy that comes from living in alignment with what we know inside to be true, right for us, in alignment with the greater good and in reverence for the sacredness of all life, where clarity of intention is matched with a letting go of the need to micro-manage for specific "results," and where, to paraphrase Brian Murphy (1999), how we are in the world is not the outcome of a strategic calculus of effort versus impact but rather a natural outgrowth of our deepest authenticity, wherein doing anything else is unthinkable. Where action is motivated not by fear or anger or the projection of unresolved childhood wounds, not as an act of desperation, revenge, or even hope, but as an act of love?

In *Soul Stories* (2000, n.p.), Gary Zukav offers the following illustrative analogue to help understand the importance of where we're coming from when we do what we do, and the critical difference between fear and love as a motivator for change work:

Billions of tiny organisms called microbes live on your body. Imagine that they organize themselves into groups and build cities. They don't know that you're alive. They take whatever they need, without asking you, or thinking about you. Eventually, you're covered with microbes like these, and all of them take whatever they want, whenever they want to. Eventually you get sick. The microbes notice this because their air gets dirty, their water gets polluted, and their forests start to die. "We are in trouble," they say to each other. They get so frightened that they organize into environmental movements. What would you feel like having billions of frightened microbes on you, each taking what it needs for itself? Does the idea make you feel good? Or does it make you itch all over? Now suppose that the microbes that are living on you know that you are alive. They're very grateful for you because everything that they have and everything that they need comes from you. They love you, and they are thinking of good things to do for you all the time. Which kind of microbes would you want to have growing on you? The first kind thinks about itself. Even when it tries to take care of you, it is really only taking care of you in order to take care of itself. The second kind loves you. It takes care of you because it is grateful for you, and happy that you are its home. People who call the Earth a "resource" are like the first kind of microbe. They want clean air because they want to continue to breathe. People who see the Earth like a wonderful living

Mother, are like the second kind. They want the Earth to be healthy because they love her. Which group are you in?

What if our actions were expressions of love, interdependence, celebration, and co-creativity aimed at unleashing collective wisdom and mutual empowerment? Not preaching, fixing, or even healing, but integrating, allowing, unblocking, enabling?

And what if we saw that everything and everyone has its own intelligence and capacity for movement towards fuller flourishing, in their own rhythm, timing, and style? That rather than having to *make* change happen, and working to "convince" and "coordinate," we could support each other to let go of what's blocking the change that wants to manifest in the world (and inside us)? To let go of our resistance? What if we could trust the innate intelligence of nature and what Bohm called the "implicate order?"

This is a future worth working towards, not because of what it avoids, but because of what it calls forth in us. It calls us into deep resonance and alignment with our greatest potential, in realization of our deepest longings, to flourish in harmony with nature and with life itself. As proponents of the Transition movement put it, "we want to be known for what we stand *for*, not what we stand *against*." May it be so.

ACKNOWLEDGMENTS

I owe a debt of gratitude to so many people who have influenced me deeply in my path and supported my work that I scarcely know where to begin, and risk leaving someone out who really should be included. I'd specifically like to mention Ed O'Sullivan and Eimear O'Neill for their warm welcome into the fold of the Transformative Learning Centre at OISE/UT and their pioneering work in transformative learning; my partner, Alexandra Poggi, for willingness to walk wholeheartedly the path of awakening together; Gina Cenciose and the Fireflies group for holding our feet to the fire with love; the many authors who've influenced me and who are cited in this text; and the countless colleagues and students with whom I've had the pleasure of working and who have walked this journey with me and each contributed in their own way.

NOTES

1 See Barbara Hubbard (1998, 2001) for a compelling alternative framing of "conscious evolution."
2 See also Heather Davis and Zoe Todd on decolonizing the Anthropocene (Davis and Todd, 2017).

REFERENCES

Abram, D. (1996). *The spell of the sensuous.* New York, NY: Vintage Books.

Adyashanti. (2013). *Falling into grace: Reflections on the end of suffering.* Sounds True.

Almaas, A. H. (2008). *The unfolding now: Realizing your true nature through the practice of presence.* Boston: Shambhala.

Baker, C. (2009). *Sacred demise: Walking the spiritual path of industrial civilization's collapse.* Bloomington, IN: iUniverse.com.

Baker, C. (2011). *Navigating the coming chaos: A handbook for inner transition.* Bloomington, IN: iUniverse.com.

Baker, C. (2013). *Collapsing consciously: Transformative truths for turbulent times.* Berkeley, CA: North Atlantic Books.

Baldwin, C. (2005). *Storycatcher: Making sense of our lives through the power and practice of story.* Novato, CA: New World Library.

Baldwin, C., & Linnea, A. (2010). *The circle way: A leader in every chair.* San Francisco, CA: Berrett-Koehler.

Barnosky, A. D., Hadley, E. A., Bascompte, J., Berlow, E. L., Brown, J. H., Fortelius, M. et al. (2012). Approaching a state shift in Earth's biosphere. *Nature, 486*(7401), 52–8. https://doi.org/10.1038/nature11018

Berkes, F., Colding, J., & Folke, C. (Eds) (2003). *Navigating social-ecological systems: Building resilience for complexity and change.* Cambridge, UK: Cambridge University Press.

Berry, W. (2015). Revolution starts small and close to home. *Yes!* magazine, Spring, 45–7.

Bohm, D. (2004). *On dialogue* (2nd ed.). London, UK: Routledge.

Born, P. (2012). *Community conversations: Mobilizing the ideas, skills, and passion of community organizations, governments, businesses, and people* (2nd ed.). Toronto, ON: BPS Books.

Brach, T. (2003). *Radical acceptance: Embracing your life with the heart of a Buddha.* New York, NY: Bantam.

Brady, M. (ed.). (2003). *The wisdom of listening.* Boston: Wisdom Publications.

Broadhead, L. A., & Howard, S. (2011). Deepening the debate over 'sustainable science': Indigenous perspectives as a guide on the journey. *Sustainable Development, 19*(5), 301–11. https://doi.org/10.1002/sd.421

Brown, M. (2010). *The presence process.* Vancouver, BC: Namaste Publishing.

Brown, J., & Isaacs, D. (2005). *The world cafe: Shaping our futures through conversations that matter.* San Francisco, CA: Berrett-Koehler.

Byham, W. C. (1993). *Zapp! Empowerment in health care.* New York, NY: Fawcett Columbine.

Byham, W. C., & Cox, J. (1988). *Zapp! The lightening of empowerment.* New York: Fawcett Columbine.

Carlsson, C. (2008). *Nowtopia: How pirate programmers, outlaw bicyclists, and vacant-lot gardeners are inventing the future today!* Oakland, CA: AK Press.

Carpenter, S. R., Arrow, K. J., Barrett, S., Biggs, R., Brock, W. A., Crépin, A.S. et al. (2012). General resilience to cope with extreme events. *Sustainability, 4*(12), 3248–59. https://doi.org/10.3390/su4123248

Cavalcante Jr, F. S. (1999). Circles of literacies: A practice in cultural therapy. *Revista de Psicologia, 17/18*(1/2), 14–22.

Chodron, P. (2005). *When things fall apart: Heart advice for difficult times*. Boston, MA: Shambhala Press.

Chodron, P. (2012). *Living beautifully with uncertainty and change*. Boulder, CO: Shambhala Press.

Cornelius-White, J. (2006). Environmental responsibility, the formative tendency and well-being. *Person-Centred Quarterly, 11–12*.

Cornell, A. W. (1996). *The power of focusing: A practical guide to emotional self-healing*. Oakland, CA: New Harbinger Publications.

Datta, R. K. (2016). Rethinking environmental science education from Indigenous knowledge perspectives: An experience with a Dene First Nation community. *Environmental Education Research, 1416–5871*. https://doi.org/10.1080/13504622 .2016.1219980

Davidson-Hunt I. J., & O'Flaherty, R. M. (2007). Researchers, Indigenous peoples, and place-based learning communities. *Society & Natural Resources, 20*(4), 291–305. https://doi.org/10.1080/08941920601161312

Davis, H., & Todd, Z. (2017). On the importance of a date, or decolonizing the Anthropocene. *ACME: An International Journal for Critical Geographies, 16*(4), 761–80.

Davis, L. (2010). *Alliances: Re/Envisioning Indigenous-non-Indigenous relationships*. Toronto, ON: University of Toronto Press.

Dei, G. J. S. (2000). Rethinking the role of Indigenous knowledges in the academy. *International Journal of Inclusive Education, 4*(2), 111–32. https://doi.org /10.1080/136031100284849

de Young, R. (2013). Transitioning to a new normal: How ecopsychology can help society prepare for the harder times ahead. *Ecopsychology, 5*(4), 237–9. https://doi .org/10.1089/eco.2013.0065

de Young, R. (2014). Some behavioral aspects of energy descent: How a biophysical psychology might help people transition through the lean times ahead. *Frontiers in Psychology, 5*(1255), 1–16. https://doi.org/10.3389/fpsyg.2014.01255

Dove, M. R. (2006). Indigenous people and environmental politics. *Annual Review of Anthropology, 35*(1), 191–208. https://doi.org/10.1146/annurev.anthro.35.081705.123235

Ehrlich, P. R., & Ehrlich, A. H. (2013). Can a collapse of global civilization be avoided? *Proceedings of the Royal Society Biological Sciences, 280*(1754). https://doi .org/10.1098/rspb.2012.2845

Einstein, P. (1997). *Intuition: The path to inner wisdom (A guide to discovering and using your greatest natural resource)*. Boston: Element.

Eisenstein, C. (2013). *The more beautiful world our hearts know is possible*. Berkeley, CA: North Atlantic Books.

Fisher, L. (2011). *The perfect swarm: The science of complexity in everyday life.* New York, NY: Basic Books.

Folke, C. (2006). Resilience: The emergence of a perspective for social-ecological systems analyses. *Global Environmental Change, 16*(3), 253–67. https://doi.org /10.1016/j.gloenvcha.2006.04.002

Frumkin, H. (2001). Beyond toxicity: Human health and the natural environment. *American Journal of Preventative Medicine, 20*, 234–40.

Frumkin, H. (2003). Healthy places: Exploring the evidence. *American Journal of Public Health, 93*(9), 1451–6. https://doi.org/10.2105/ajph.93.9.1451

Gray, S. (2010). *Returning to sacred world: A spiritual toolkit for the emerging reality.* Winchester, UK: O-Books.

Gunderson, L. H., & Holling, C. S. (Eds) (2001). *Panarchy: Understanding transformations in human and natural systems.* Washington, DC: Island Press.

Haluza-DeLay, R. (2008). A theory of practice for social movements: Environmentalism and ecological habitus. *Mobilization: The International Quarterly, 13*(2), 205–18.

Harding, S. (2006). *Animate earth: Science, intuition and Gaia.* White River Junction, VT: Chelsea Green.

Hawken, P. (2007). *Blessed unrest: How the largest movement in the world came into being, and why no one saw it coming.* New York, NY: Viking/Penguin.

Hill, W. (2009). *Understanding life: What my ancestors taught me through my dreams.* Pittsburgh, PA: Red Lead Press.

Holman, P. (2010). *Engaging emergence: Turning upheaval into opportunity.* San Francisco, CA: Berret-Koehler.

Holman, P., Devane, T., & Cady, S. (2007). *The change handbook: The definitive resource on today's best methods for engaging whole systems* (2nd ed.). San Francisco, CA: Berret-Koehler.

Hopkins, R. (2008). *The transition handbook: From oil dependency to local resilience.* Devon, UK: Green Books.

Hubbard, B. M. (1998). *Conscious evolution: Awakening the power of our social potential.* Novato, CA: New World Publishers.

Hubbard, B. M. (2001). *Emergence: The shift from ego to essence.* Charlottesville, VA: Hampton Roads.

Isaacs, W. (1999). *Dialogue and the art of thinking together.* New York, NY: Doubleday/ Currency.

Jaworski, J. (2012). *Source: The inner path of knowledge creation.* San Francisco: Berrett-Koehler.

Kashtan, M. (2014). *Reweaving our human fabric: Working together to create a nonviolent future.* Oakland, CA: Fearless Heart Publications.

Kashtan, M. (2014). *Spinning threads of radical aliveness: Transcending the legacy of separation in our individual lives.* Oakland, CA: Fearless Heart Publications.

Katie, B. (2002). *Loving what is.* New York, NY: Harmony Books.

Keogh, M. (Ed.). (2010). *Hope beneath our feet: Restoring our place in the natural world.* Berkeley, CA: North Atlantic Books.

Klein, N. (2014). Climate change is a people's shock. *The Nation.* October 6. Retrieved from http://www.thenation.com/article/climate-change-peoples-shock/

Lovelock, J. (2006). *The revenge of Gaia.* New York, NY: Penguin.

MacGregor, C. (2010). *Partnering with nature: The wild path to reconnecting with the earth.* New York, NY: Atria/Beyond Words.

Macy, J. (2009). The greening of the self. In L. Buzzell & C. Chalquist (Eds), *Ecotherapy: Healing with nature in mind* (pp. 238–45). San Francisco: Sierra Club Books.

Macy, J., & Johnstone, C. (2012). *Active hope: How to face the mess we're in without going crazy.* Novato, CA: New World.

Manyena, S. B., O'Brian, G., O'Keefe, P., & Rose, J. (2011). Disaster resilience: A bounce back or bounce forward ability? *Local Environment, 16*(5), 417–24. https://doi.org/10.1080/13549839.2011.583049

Max, K. (2005). Anti-colonial research: Working as an ally with Aboriginal peoples. *Counterpoints, 252,* 79–94.

Merry, U. (1995). *Coping with uncertainty: Insights from the new sciences of chaos, self-organization, and complexity.* Westport, CT: Praeger.

Mitchell, R., & Popham, F. (2008). Effect of exposure to natural environment on health inequalities: An observational population study. *The Lancet, 372*(9650), 1655–60. https://doi.org/10.1016/s0140-6736(08)61689-x

Morin, E., & LeMoigne, J. L. (2000). The intelligence of complexity. *World Pumps, 8*(1), 87. https://doi.org/10.1016/s1240-1307(00)88825-1

Murphy, B. (1999). *Transforming ourselves, transforming the world: An open conspiracy for social change.* Black Point, NS: Zed Books.

Norberg, J., & Cumming, G. S. (Eds) (2006). *Complexity theory for a sustainable future.* New York, NY: Columbia University Press.

O'Connell, C. (2017). Becoming an ally to Indigenous people. In S. Voogd-Cochrane, M. Chhabra, M. A. Jones, & D. Spragg (Eds), *Culturally responsive teaching and reflection in higher education: Promising practices from the cultural literacy curriculum project* (pp. 53–62). London, UK: Routledge.

O'Hara, M., & Wood, J. K. (2005). Building a conscious group through deep dialogue. In B. H. Banathy & P. M. Jenlink (Eds), *Dialogue as a means of collective communication.* New York, NY: Kluwer Academic/Plenum.

Olsson, P., Galaz, V., & Boonstra, W. J. (2014). Sustainability transformations: A resilience perspective. *Ecology and Society, 19*(4), 1. https://doi.org/10.5751/es-06799-190401

Pfeiffer, B. (2013). *Wild Earth, wild soul.* Alresford, UK: Moon Books

Plotkin, B. (2003). *Soulcraft: Crossing into the mysteries of nature and psyche.* Novato, CA: New World Library.

Poland, B., Dooris, M., & Haluza-DeLay, R. (2011). Securing 'supportive environments' for health in the face of ecosystem collapse: Meeting the triple threat with a sociology of creative transformation. *Health Promotion International, 26*(S2), ii202–15. https://doi.org/10.1093/heapro/dar073

Prentice, H. (2012). 'Heart and soul': Inner and outer within the Transition movement. In M.J. Rust, & N. Totten (Eds), *Vital signs – Psychological responses to ecological crisis*. London, UK: Karnac Books. Retrieved from http://www .hilaryprenticepsychotherapy.net/article%206%20inner%20and%20outer.htm

Rees, W. E. (2010). Thinking resilience. In R. Heinberg & D. Lerch (Eds), *The post carbon reader: Managing the 21st century's sustainability crises* (pp. 25–42). Healdsburg, CA: Watershed Media.

Reo, N. J., Whyte, K. P., McGregor, D., Smith, P., & Jenkins, J. F. (2017). Factors that support Indigenous involvement in multi-actor environmental stewardship. *AlterNative: An International Journal of Indigenous Peoples, 13*(2), 58–68. https://doi .org/10.1177/1177180117701028

Resnicow, K., & Page, S. E. (2008). Embracing chaos and complexity: A quantum change for public health. *American Journal of Public Health, 98*(8), 1382–9. https:// doi.org/10.2105/ajph.2007.129460

Riggs, E. M. (2005). Field-based education and Indigenous knowledge: Essential components of geoscience education for Native American communities. *Science Education, 89*(2), 296–313. https://doi.org/10.1002/sce.20032

Rogers, C. (1978). The formative tendency. *Journal of Humanistic Psychology, 18*(1), 23–6. https://doi.org/10.1177/002216787801800103

Rogers, C. (1980). *A way of being*. New York, NY: Houghton Mifflin.

Rosenberg, M. B. (2003a). Liberating ourselves through nonviolent communication. In M. Brady (Ed.), *The wisdom of listening* (pp. 225–36). Boston, MA: Wisdom Publishers.

Rosenberg, M. B. (2003b). *Nonviolent communication: A language of life* (2nd Ed.). Encinitas, CA: PuddleDancer Press.

Rosenberg, M. B. (2004). *The heart of social change: How you can make a difference in your world*. Encinitas, CA: Puddle Dancer Press.

Scharmer, C. O. (2009). *Theory U: Leading from the future as it emerges*. San Francisco, CA: Berrett-Koehler.

Scharmer, C. O., & Kaufer, K. (2013). *Leading from the emerging future: From ego-system to eco-system economies*. San Francisco, CA: Berrett-Koehler.

Senge, P., Scharmer, C. O., Jaworski, J., & Flowers, B. S. (2004). *Presence: An exploration of profound change in people, organizations, and society*. New York, NY: Currency/ Doubleday/Random House.

Shove, E., Pantzar, M., & Watson, M. (2012). *The dynamics of social practice: Everyday life and how it changes*. Thousand Oaks, CA: Sage.

Shove, E., & Walker, G. (2010). Governing transitions in the sustainability of everyday life. *Research Policy, 39*(4), 471–6. https://doi.org/10.1016/j.respol.2010.01.019

Simpson, L. B. (2014). Land as pedagogy: Nishnaabeg intelligence and rebellious transformation. *Decolonization: Indigeneity, Education & Society, 3*(3), 1–25. https:// doi.org/10.1007/978-3-319-46328-5_1

Starhawk. (2004). *The Earth path: Grounding your spirit in the rhythms of nature*. New York, NY: Harper Collins.

Steffen, W., Persson, A., Deutsch, L., Zalasiewicz, J., Williams, M., Richardson, K. et al. (2011). The Anthropocene: From global change to planetary stewardship. *Ambio: A Journal of the Human Environment, 40*(7), 739–61. https://doi.org/10.1007 /s13280-011-0185-x

Styres, S., Haig-Brown, C., & Blimkie, M. (2013). Towards a pedagogy of land: The urban context. *Canadian Journal of Education, 36*(2), 34–67.

Tolle, E. (2005). *A new Earth.* New York, NY: Dutton/Penguin.

Tuck, E., McKenzie, M., & McCoy, K. (2014). Land education: Indigenous, post-colonial, and decolonizing perspectives on place and environmental education research. *Environmental Education Research, 20*(1), 1–23. https://doi.org/10.1080 /13504622.2013.877708

Turner, C. (2007). *The geography of hope: A tour of the world we need.* Toronto, ON: Random House Canada.

Urban Resilience Project. (2015). Bounce forward: Urban resilience in the era of climate change. Island Press & The Kresge Foundation. Retrieved from http://kresge .org/sites/default/files/Bounce-Forward-Urban-Resilience-in-Era-of- Climate -Change-2015.pdf

Vaughan-Lee, L. (2013) *Spiritual ecology: The cry of the Earth.* Point Reyes, CA: The Golden Sufi Center.

Walia, H. (2012). Decolonizing together: Moving beyond a politics of solidarity toward a practice of decolonization. *Briarpatch,* Jan./Feb., 27–30.

Walker, A. (2006). *We are the ones we have been waiting for: Inner light in a time of darkness.* New York, NY: The New Press.

Wallace, R. (2013). *Merging fires: Grassroots peacebuilding between Indigenous and non-Indigenous peoples.* Halifax, NS: Fernwood.

Westley, F., Olsson, P., Folke, C., Homer-Dixon, T., Vredenburg, H., Loorback, D. et al. (2011). Tipping toward sustainability: Emerging pathways of transformation. *Ambio: A Journal of the Human Environment, 40*(7), 762–80. https://doi.org/10.1007 /s13280-011-0186-9

Wheatley, M. J. (2012). *So far from home: Lost and found in our brave new world.* San Francisco, CA: Berrett-Koehler.

Wheatley, M. J., & Frieze, D. (2011). *Walk out walk on: A learning journey into communities daring to live the future now.* San Francisco, CA: Berret-Koehler.

Zolli, A., & Healy, A. M. (2012). *Resilience: Why things bounce back.* New York, NY: Free Press/Simon & Schuster.

Zukav, G. (2000). *Soul stories.* Chagrin Falls, OH: Fireside Books.

20 Death Denial in the Anthropocene

SHELDON SOLOMON

> Humanity today is like a waking dreamer, caught between the fantasies of sleep and the chaos of the real world. The mind seeks but cannot find the precise place and hour. We have created a Star Wars civilization, with Stone Age emotions, medieval institutions, and godlike technology. We thrash about. We are terribly confused by the mere fact of our existence, and a danger to ourselves and to the rest of life
> —E.O. Wilson, *The Social Conquest of Earth* (2012, p. 7)

History is replete with examples of societies reduced to rubble by wars, toxic demagoguery, environmental degradation, and seemingly insatiable material consumption; moreover, social collapses can occur abruptly in the midst of seemingly auspicious conditions (Diamond, 2005). The Anthropocene, however, is unprecedented in that human-induced climate instability, rampant population growth and associated resource depletion, sophisticated weapons of mass destruction, political instability amplified by the rapid proliferation of information (and misinformation) technology, and the obligatory interdependence of a globalized economy are such that it is entirely possible that we will have the ignominious distinction of being the first form of life to be directly responsible for our own extinction by rendering the planet unfit for human habitation.

In the 1970s, cultural anthropologist Ernest Becker argued that humankind's most unsavoury and dysfunctional affectations are malignant manifestations of repressed death anxiety. At the outset of the twenty-first century, political philosopher John Gray proposed that Enlightenment-based faith in the power of rationality and technological progress inexorably leading to unlimited growth and prosperity is a widespread death-denying delusion that undermines our capacity to respond effectively to the challenges of the Anthropocene.

The purpose of this chapter is to provide an overview of Becker's and Gray's views of the role of death anxiety and belief in the inevitability of progress in human affairs, present empirical evidence in support of their claims, and consider the long-term viability of humanity in the Anthropocene in light of them.

The Denial of Death

You have all the fears of mortals and all the desires of immortals.
—Seneca (AD 49/195, p. 295)

Ernest Becker's effort to address the question "What makes people act the way they do?" (Becker, 1971, p. vii) starts with the relatively non-controversial Darwinian assumption that human beings share with all forms of life a basic biological predisposition towards self-preservation in the service of survival and reproduction. We are, however, unique in our facility for abstract symbolic thought (including, but not confined to, language), mental "time-travel" (reflecting on the past and pondering the future), mental simulations (prospective imagination), self-awareness, and theory of mind (the realization that others have internal mental states). This mental agility has surely enabled us to proliferate in diverse and rapidly changing physical environments. Moreover, explicit self-awareness can be emotionally uplifting; in our finest moments we are sublimely appreciative of being alive and knowing that we are alive. However, explicit self-awareness also gives rise to the unsettling realization that life is of finite duration, that death can occur at any time for reasons that often cannot be anticipated or controlled, and that we are embodied creatures who are ultimately no more significant or enduring than apricots or armadillos.

Becker (1973, 1975) posited that the unvarnished awareness of death, tragedy, and corporeality engenders potentially debilitating existential terror that would undermine our capacity for effective instrumental behaviour, reducing reproductive fitness and compromising the viability of consciousness as a uniquely human form of mental organization. Consequently, in order to assuage existential terror, humans embrace *cultural worldviews*: beliefs about reality that infuse life with meaning and purpose by providing an account of the origin of the universe, and prescriptions for appropriate conduct for the social roles individuals inhabit in the context of their culture.[1] Meeting or exceeding the standards for appropriate conduct yields *self-esteem*: the perception that one is a person of *value* in a world of *meaning*. Self-esteem fosters psychological equanimity by buffering anxiety (in general and of death in particular) in the present, and increasing the prospect for immortality in the future. Immortality can be literal, through the heavens, afterlives, reincarnations, resurrections and indestructible souls central to most religions; or symbolic, by having children, amassing great fortunes, producing great works of art or science, or being a member of a great and enduring tribe or nation. People are therefore highly motivated to maintain faith in their cultural worldviews and self-esteem as a psychological bulwark against existential dread.

Three lines of empirical enquiry provide convergent support for Becker's argument that cultural worldviews and self-esteem serve to manage existential terror (see Solomon, Greenberg, and Pyszczynski, 1991; Greenberg, Solomon, and Pyszczynski, 1997; Pyszczynski, Solomon, and Greenberg, 2015; and Solomon, Greenberg, and Pyszczynski, 2015, for reviews of this research). First, temporarily elevated or dispositionally high self-esteem reduces anxiety and autonomic arousal in response to threat. For example, Greenberg et al. (1992) gave participants false positive feedback on an intelligence test to momentarily increase their self-esteem (control participants did not receive any feedback); thereafter, participants either expected to watch some coloured lights or to receive some painful electrical shocks while their physiological responses were assessed. Results indicated that increased self-esteem reduced self-reported anxiety and autonomic arousal (skin conductance).

A second line of research is based on the hypothesis that if cultural world-views serve to manage existential terror, then making people aware of their own mortality (*mortality salience*) should magnify the need for the protection afforded by their beliefs, resulting in efforts to bolster faith in their cultural worldviews. Mortality salience is typically induced by having people write about their own death, specifically by responding to two open-ended questions: "Please describe the emotions that the thought of your own death arouses in you" and "Write down as specifically as you can, what you think will happen to you physically as you die and once you are dead." Control participants respond to parallel questions about neutral activities such as eating or watching television, or aversive but not fatal experiences such as an upcoming exam or being in extreme pain (other mortality salience inductions include viewing graphic depictions of death, being interviewed in front of a funeral parlour, or subliminal exposure to the word "dead" or "death"). For example, Rosenblatt, Greenberg, Solomon, Pyszczynski, and Lyon (1989) predicted and found that reminded of their mortality, municipal court judges set substantially higher bonds for an alleged prostitute than judges in the control condition. An additional study found that, in response to a death reminder, participants recommended a higher monetary reward for a citizen who reputedly behaved in a heroic fashion by thwarting a bank robbery.

The third line of research is based on the hypothesis that when cherished aspects of cultural worldviews or self-esteem are threatened, implicit (i.e. non-conscious) death thoughts come more readily to mind. Implicit death thoughts are typically assessed by the number of incomplete word stems completed in death-related ways (e.g. C O F F _ _ could be COFFEE or COFFIN; G R _ V E could be GROVE or GRAVE). For example, implicit death thoughts increased when Christian fundamentalists were confronted with logical inconsistencies in the bible (Friedman & Rholes, 2007); or after participants received negative feedback about their intelligence, or were told their personality is incompatible with their career aspirations (Hayes, Schimel, Faucher, and Williams, 2008).

Sacred and Secular: Providence and Progress

For many, the promises of religion lack credibility; but the fear that inspires them has not gone away ... Secular societies believe they have left religion behind, when all they have done is substitute one set of myths for another.
—John Gray, *Heresies: Against Progress and Other Illusions* (2004, p. 23, 47)

There is a kind of existential terror associated with the concept of "limits to growth" for the Western person ... The reason for the terror is evident enough. The type of growth associated with the expansion in population and economic productivity has somehow come to be synonymous with growth in personhood and growth in the body social. This produces the equation in people's minds: limits to growth equals death.
—Elise Boulding, *Education for Inventing the Future* (1977, p. 297)

For most of human history, and to this day, humans managed existential terror primarily by embracing religious worldviews that provide pathways to transcend death via literal immortality in the form of the heavens, reincarnations, resurrections, afterlives, and souls.[2] In the Christian tradition, humans were created in God's image and given command and control over the earth and its inhabitants: "And God said, Let us make man in our image, after our likeness: and let them have dominion over the fish of the sea, and over the fowl of the air, and over the cattle, and over all the earth, and over every creeping thing that creepeth upon the earth." (*Genesis* 1:26, King James Bible). Humans are, from this perspective, qualitatively different than, superior to, and ultimately detached from all other life forms and their planetary abode.

Although secular worldviews, by contrast, have no explicit religious or spiritual basis, they are nevertheless, according to Becker (1973, p. 5), "mythical hero-system(s) in which people serve in order to earn a feeling of primary value, of cosmic specialness, of ultimate usefulness to creation, of unshakable meaning." Moreover, John Gray (2004) argues, secular belief systems are derived from, and retain thinly veiled remnants of, religious belief systems. The Enlightenment, also known as the Age of Reason, originated in Europe in the eighteenth century. Reason and science were viewed as vastly superior to orthodox religious beliefs for improving the human condition, and Enlightenment thinkers were confident that the stunning advances of knowledge produced by the Scientific Revolution and resultant technological innovations of the Industrial Revolution would inevitably persist on an inexorable path of progress culminating in conditions on earth comparable to those purported to exist in heaven. At the end of the eighteenth century, Ben Franklin regretted that he had been born too soon to witness extraordinary progress in agricultural production, levitation as a means of transportation, and the cure or prevention of all diseases, including old age. "For noble deeds grant scope abounding," Goethe wrote in his 1790 version of *Faust*, "I sense accomplishments astounding," and his last word prior to his death in 1832 was reputedly "progress" (May, 1991, p. 248, 255).

Unbridled faith in the inevitability of progress through reason and science continued in the twentieth century, either in the form of Marx's revolutionary socialism promising to eliminate poverty by disposing of private property and class conflicts, or global capitalism's mission to parlay the "invisible hand" of the marketplace into a rising tide of shared prosperity culminating in "The End of History" (Fukuyama, 1992) with western democracy as the ultimate and final form of government for all nations.

The Enlightenment belief in progress has certainly increased scientific knowledge, and this in turn has undoubtedly benefited a large proportion of humanity. However, Gray argues, the belief that progress is inevitable and that advances in scientific knowledge are always advantageous (see e.g. Pinker, 2018) is based on wishful thinking to ward off death anxiety: "Late modern cultures are haunted by the dream that new technologies will conjure away the immemorial evils of human life. But no new technology can abolish scarcity, do away with the necessity of choice or alter the fact of human mortality" (Gray, 2004, p. 22). Belief in progress is a secular worldview derived from Christianity in that, like Christianity, it views humans as fundamentally different than, superior to, and with dominion over, nature and all other forms of life, and promises salvation as the end of history, albeit on earth in a globalized free-market economy.

To demonstrate that belief or faith in progress serves to manage existential terror, Rutjens, van der Pligt, and van Harreveld (2009) found that, in response to a death reminder, participants reported great disagreement with an essay proposing that human progress is illusory (including statements such as "I think progress is definitely an illusion. We always seem to focus on progress in science and technology, but meanwhile there still exist wars and conflicts in the world. There's plenty of evidence that we haven't witnessed any real progress since the Middle Ages"). A second study found that reading the same essay declaring that progress is illusory increased the accessibility of implicit death thoughts.

Death Denial in the Anthropocene

The charm of history and its enigmatic lesson consist in the fact that, from age to age, nothing changes and yet everything is completely different.

—Aldous Huxley, *The Devils of Loudun* (1952, p. 259)

Humans have been ardently devoted to transcending death in pursuit of immortality since antiquity. Such efforts have often had deleterious personal and interpersonal consequences that are particularly problematic in the Anthropocene.

Destroying the World to Save It

Perhaps the whole root of our trouble, the human trouble, is that we will sacrifice all the beauty of our lives, will imprison ourselves in totems, taboos, crosses, blood sacrifices, steeples, mosques, races, armies, flags, nations, in order to deny the fact of death.
                        —James Baldwin, *The Fire Next Time* (1962/1993, p. 91)

To the extent that cultural worldviews mitigate death anxiety, humans are prone to react with hostility and disdain to others who do not subscribe to their beliefs, for two reasons. First, the mere existence of people who harbour different beliefs is problematic to the extent that acknowledging the validity of alternative cultural worldviews undermines confidence in the veracity of one's own beliefs. If, for example, the Fulani in Africa are correct in their view that the earth originated from a giant drop of milk, then the Judeo-Christian view that God created the earth and all of its inhabitants in six days (sans dairy products) is implicitly or explicitly challenged. This in turn elicits the existential anxieties that cultural worldviews generally serve to buffer. Second, although cultural worldviews serve as potent bulwarks against death anxiety, they are nonetheless ultimately symbolic efforts to manage anxiety engendered by death, a profoundly physical event. It is therefore impossible for cultural worldviews (religious or secular) to eliminate death anxiety. Residual death anxiety is in turn repressed and projected onto groups or individuals inside or outside of the culture designated as all-encompassing repositories of evil (i.e. scapegoats), who are subsequently denigrated and dehumanized, coerced into relinquishing their cherished beliefs and adopting those of the dominant group, or physically annihilated. Consequently, and ironically, Becker (1975) concluded that most of the evil in the world results from self-righteous efforts to rid the world of evil.

A substantial body of research confirms that arousing existential anxieties stokes prejudice and intolerance. For example, in response to mortality salience Christians had more favourable reactions to fellow Christians and less favourable reactions to Jews (Greenberg et al., 1990); Germans sat closer to a fellow German and farther away from someone who appeared to be a Turkish immigrant (Ochsmann and Mathy, 1994); Americans were more physically aggressive towards others who did not share their political views (McGregor et al., 1998); Iranians were more supportive of suicide bombers and more willing to become suicide bombers themselves; and conservative Americans were more supportive of the pre-emptive use of nuclear, chemical, and biological weapons of mass destruction against countries who pose no direct threat to the US. (Pyszczynski et al., 2006). George Bernard Shaw (1919/1996, p. 12) was literally correct then in his observation that "When the angel of death sounds his trumpet, the pretences of civilization are blown from men's heads into the mud like hats in a gust of wind."

Fatal Attraction

Helpless and fearful people are drawn to magical figures, mythic figures, epic men who intimidate and darkly loom.

—Don DeLillo, *White Noise* (1985/1986, p. 287)

Sociologist Max Weber (1925/1968) proposed that followers' attachment to, and enthusiasm for, seemingly larger-than-life leaders intensifies in times of historical upheaval. Similarly, Eric Hoffer (1951), reflecting on the rise of charismatic leaders in the twentieth century, including Hitler, Stalin, and Mussolini, argued that the primary impetus for all populist movements is a critical mass of frustrated and disaffected citizens subject to grave economic or psychological insecurity "in desperate need of something ... to live for" (p. 15). This results in unwavering dedication and loyalty to leaders who confidently espouse a cause that infuses their lives with a sense of "worth and meaning" (p. 15) and faith in the future via "identification; the process by which the individual ceases to be himself and becomes part of something eternal" (p. 63).

Hoffer observed that charismatic leaders are rarely exceptionally intelligent, noble, or original. Rather, the primary qualifications "seem to be: audacity and a joy in defiance; an iron will; a fanatical conviction that he is in possession of the one and only truth; faith in his destiny and luck; a capacity for passionate hatred; contempt for the present; a cunning estimate of human nature; a delight in symbols (spectacles and ceremonials) ... the arrogant gesture, the complete disregard of the opinion of others, the singlehanded defiance of the world ...[and] some deliberate misrepresentation of facts" (p. 114). Finally, Hoffer (as well as Becker, 1975) noted that mass movements require an external enemy to enable the charismatic leader to transform the fears of their frustrated and disaffected followers into unrelenting rage directed towards tangible scapegoats.

President George W. Bush's popularity skyrocketed when he declared that he believed God had chosen him to rid the world of "evil-doers" in the aftermath of the 11 September 2001 terrorist attacks on the World Trade Center and the Pentagon. In studies conducted prior to the 2004 presidential election, Landau et al. (2004) found that whereas American control participants rated Senator John Kerry more favourably than President Bush, President Bush was rated more favourably than Senator Kerry in response to mortality salience. Additionally, Cohen, Ogilvie, Solomon, Greenberg, and Pyszczynski

(2005) found that while registered voters in a control condition intended to vote for Senator Kerry by a 4:1 margin, other registered voters randomly assigned to think about their mortality subsequently reported intending to vote for President Bush by a more than 2:1 margin. Similarly, Donald Trump was elected president in 2016 by claiming that the United States was under siege by terrorists, Muslims, and immigrants, and that only he could keep US citizens safe by "Making America Great Again." Cohen, Solomon, and Kaplin (2017) found that while American participants in a control condition rated Hillary Clinton more positively than Donald Trump, Trump's ratings increased significantly in response to a death reminder.

I Am Not an Animal!

The body is the closest that we come to touching any kind of reality. And yet we have the desire to flee the body: many religions are based entirely on disembodiment, because the body brings with it mortality, fear of death. If you accept the body as reality, then you have to accept mortality and people are very afraid to do that.
—David Cronenberg, in Simon (2001, p. 45–6)

Although people often disparagingly allude to others as animals, we go to extraordinary lengths to deny our own animality. This fosters hostility towards animals, alienation from nature, and contempt for the environment. The awareness of death gives rise to paralyzing terror. To dampen the dread, humans subscribe to cultural worldviews that infuse the world with meaning, and provide opportunities to acquire self-esteem and literal or symbolic immortality to transcend death. But animals are a stark reminder that death cannot be banished so easily. Animals die. If humans are animals, then we too are respiring bits of finite flesh, and this is a disquieting realization for those whose psychological equanimity depends on denying their mortality. Animals are a problem because they remind us of death; nature is a problem because that's where animals live.

Consequently, humans are prone to distancing themselves from animals and nature, especially when existential anxieties are aroused. After being reminded of their mortality, people take vigorous exception to the claim that humans are animals (Goldenberg et al., 2001), have more negative attitudes towards animals (Beatson and Halloran, 2007), and report higher support for killing animals in general (Lifshin, Greenberg, Zestcott, and Sullivan, 2017). Death reminders also reduced Dutch participants' perceived beauty of wilderness, and viewing pictures of wilderness inspired more thoughts about death than either cultivated nature or urban environments (Koole and Van den Berg, 2005).

Moreover, consumption of scarce natural resources increases when death is on one's mind. After thinking about dying or listening to music, Kasser and Sheldon (2000) had participants engage in a forest-management simulation in which they were asked to imagine themselves as owners of a logging company bidding against three other companies to harvest trees in a national forest. "Owners" were informed that harvesting large amounts of timber would produce short-term profit, but ultimately deplete the forest to the point where there would be no trees and bankrupt all four companies. They were then asked how many of 100 acres of available forest they intended to harvest in their first year, how much they expected the other companies to harvest, and how much they wanted to profit more than the other companies. The researchers interpreted responses to the last two questions as reflecting fear and greed respectively. They reasoned that if owners thought other companies were going to cut lots of timber, they might also do so, fearing there would be none left otherwise. However, if owners thought other companies would exercise restraint in the service of long-term preservation of forest, harvesting a great deal themselves would amount to greedy exploitation for immediate short-term profit. Results were striking. Those who pondered their own mortality intended to harvest considerably more acres of forest (62 acres) than those who thought about music (49 acres), and reported a greater desire for profit than the other companies although they did not expect those companies to harvest more wood. Reminders of death did not make people needier. It made them greedier.

Lethal Consumption

The human animal is a beast that dies and if he's got money he buys and buys and buys and I think the reason he buys everything he can buy is that in the back of his mind he has the crazy hope that one of his purchases will be life ever-lasting.
—Tennessee Williams, *Cat on a Hot Tin Roof* (1940/2004, p. 91)

Plundering the environment is also the inevitable result of humankind's seemingly insatiable desire for money and stuff. Classical economists (see e.g. G. Becker, 1978) typically view money as a symbol that people rationally employ to exchange goods and services. They also assume that people amass material possessions in the service of addressing satiable needs and desires. Ernest Becker argued, however, that money and material possessions have always had, and still have, sacred connotations with intimations of immortality, and this is why people seem to have an insatiable desire for infinite amounts of both. Money originated in religious rituals. In ancient Greece, families held communal feasts to honour their heroic ancestors, who they believed had the power of immortal gods and could thus offer protection, advice, and direction. Coins bearing the images of ancestors that were used to gain admittance to the feasts were highly valued because they were believed to confer the same magical powers as the ancestors themselves. As anthropologist Géza Róheim (1934, p. 402) put it, "originally people do not desire money because you can buy things for it, but you can buy things for money because people desire it."

Money confers supernatural power. So do material possessions. For centuries, Native American tribes of the Pacific coast from Oregon to Alaska held potlatches on special occasions to display their wealth. After accumulating excess resources, wealthy families hosted celebrations that began with dancing, singing, speeches, and feasting. For several days, guests were showered with an immodest barrage of gifts. The guests were in turn obligated to hold their own potlatches to reciprocate and escalate the exchange. The primary objective of the potlatch "was to create an impression of an endless supply of wealth" (Kan, 1989, p. 232).

In contemporary western society, potlatch-like behaviour persists in the form of conspicuous consumption. More Americans shop on Black Friday (the day after Thanksgiving), than who vote in presidential elections. According to one account (reported in Solomon and Thompson, 2019, p. 292): "On the day after Thanksgiving 1999, the *San Antonio Express News* reported that thousands of shoppers began lining up outside of WalMarts, Best Buys, and Targets at 2 am for the new 'tradition' of after-Thanksgiving shopping. The newspaper reported that most shoppers said they had no idea what they wanted to buy. They were simply lured out by the promise of sales."

Research demonstrates that death anxiety underlies the insatiable desire for money and "stuff." High death anxiety is associated with materialism and consumption. Participants who viewed death most negatively reported being more materialistic than those who viewed death more positively as the natural end to life (Christopher, Drummond, Jones, Marek, and Therriault, 2006). Another study found a significant positive correlation between death anxiety and brand name consumption (i.e. endorsement of "I try to stick to well-known brand names" and "I prefer to buy products with designer names") and compulsive consumption (i.e. endorsement of "I frequently buy things even when I can't afford them" and "I am an impulse buyer") (Choi, Kwan, and Lee, 2007).

In response to a death reminder, people were more eager to buy expensive luxury items such as a Lexus and Rolex (Mandel and Heine, 1999) and reported higher estimates of their overall worth and greater intended future expenditures on clothing and entertainment (Kasser and Sheldon, 2000). In response to a death reminder, people ate more cookies (Mandel and Smeesters, 2008), smoked more cigarettes (Arndt et al., 2013), and purchased more alcohol (Ein-Dor et al., 2014). Additionally, participants reminded of their mortality reported higher monetary standards for what would define someone as wealthy and demanded greater compensation for deferring immediate payment of money; moreover, just counting a stack of money (relative to counting a stack of paper) reduced death anxiety (Zaleskiewicz, Gasiorowska, Kesebir, Luszczynska, and Pyszczynski, 2013).

The Future of Life in the Anthropocene

Come to terms with death; thereafter, anything is possible.
— Albert Camus, *Notebooks* (Melville, 1851/1986, p. 799)

Human survival in the Anthropocene will require coordinated efforts by cognitively nimble and emotionally intelligent individual and state actors willing to explore a variety of political, economic, technical, and religious approaches to fostering a sustainable future. This would be a tremendous challenge even under ideal conditions. However, as the environment deteriorates, conflicts over natural resources accelerate, economic inequality and instability escalates, political volatility and ideological demagoguery intensifies, and it becomes increasingly apparent that cultural worldviews dedicated to the inevitability of progress via continuous growth within a globalized multinational market economy are unsustainable – there will likely be a commensurate increase of death anxiety. Like a natural mortality salience induction, this will in turn make people (even more) hateful, warmongering, proto-fascists alienated from nature and plundering the environment in a drug, alcohol, shopping, television, Facebook, Twittering stupor ... which does not bode well for humankind's prospects in the Anthropocene.

Perhaps, however, Albert Camus was correct in his observation in *The Plague* (1947/1972, p. 278) that "we learn in time of pestilence ... that there are more things to admire in men than to despise." And while it may be far-fetched to claim that coming to terms with death will make anything possible, perhaps recognizing the pervasive and pernicious effects of death anxiety on human affairs will, as Ernest Becker (1975, p. 170) hoped, "introduce just that minute measure of reason to balance destruction."

NOTES

1 Becker's claim that cultural worldviews serve to diminish death anxiety does not preclude them having other functions; for example, that cultural belief systems foster social cohesion and social coordination (Sloan-Wilson, 2002), or that cultural belief systems contain highly adaptive information gleaned from generations of cumulative experience in specific environments (Henrich, 2016).
2 After a reminder of their mortality, religious believers report being more religious, a stronger belief in God, and greater confidence that God exists and that God answers prayers (Norenzayan and Hansen, 2006).

REFERENCES

Arndt, J., Vail, K. E., Cox, C. R., Goldenberg, J. L., Piasecki, T. M., & Gibbons, F. X. (2013). The interactive effect of mortality reminders and tobacco craving on smoking topography. *Health Psychology, 32*(5), 525–32. http://doi.org/10.1037/a0029201

Baldwin, J. (1962/1993). *The fire next time.* New York, NY: Vintage Books.

Beatson, R. M., & Halloran, M. J. (2007). Humans rule! The effects of creatureliness reminders, mortality salience and self-esteem on attitudes towards animals. *The British Journal of Social Psychology, 46*(3), 619–32. http://doi.org/10.1348/014466606X147753

Becker, E. (1975). *Escape from evil.* New York, NY: Free Press.

Becker, E. (1973). *The denial of death.* New York, NY: Free Press.

Becker, E. (1971). *The birth and death of meaning: an interdisciplinary perspective on the problem of man* (2nd ed.). New York, NY: Free Press.

Becker, G. S. (1978). *The economic approach to human behavior.* Chicago, IL: University of Chicago Press.

Boulding, E. (1977). Education for inventing the future In D. L. Meadows (Ed.), *Alternatives to Growth: A Search for Sustainable Futures.* Cambridge, MA: Ballinger.

Camus, A. (1947/1972). *The plague.* New York, NY: Vintage Books.

Choi, A. S. J., Kwon, K., & Lee, M. (2007). Understanding materialistic consumption: A terror management perspective. *Journal of Research for Consumers, 13,* 1–19.

Christopher, A. N., Drummond, K., Jones, J. R., Marek, P., & Therriault, K. M. (2006). Beliefs about one's own death, personal insecurity, and materialism. *Personality and Individual Differences, 40*(3), 441–51. http://doi.org/10.1016/j.paid.2005.09.017

Cohen, F., Ogilvie, D. M., Solomon, S., Greenberg, J., & Pyszczynski, T. (2005). American roulette: The effect of reminders of death on support for George W. Bush in the 2004 presidential election. *Analyses of Social Issues and Public Policy, 5*(1), 177–87. http://doi.org/10.1111/j.1530-2415.2005.00063.x

Cohen, F., Solomon, S., & Kaplin, D. (2017). You're hired! Mortality salience increases Americans' support for Donald Trump. *Analyses of Social Issues and Public Policy, 17*(1), 339–57. http://doi.org/10.1111/asap.12143

DeLillo, D. (1985/1986). *White noise.* New York, NY: Penguin Books.

Diamond, J. (2005). *Collapse: How societies choose to fail or succeed.* New York, NY: Viking.

Ein-Dor, T., Hirschberger, G., Perry, A., Levin, N., Cohen, R., Horesh, H., & Rothschild, E. (2014). Implicit death primes increase alcohol consumption. *Health Psychology, 33*(7), 748–51. http://doi.org/10.1037/a0033880

Friedman, M., & Rholes, S. W. (2007). Successfully challenging fundamentalist beliefs results in increased death awareness. *Journal of Experimental Social Psychology, 43*(5), 794–801. http://doi.org/10.1016/j.jesp.2006.07.008

Fukuyama, F. (1992). *The end of history and the last man.* New York, NY: Free Press.

Goldenberg, J. L., Pyszczynski, T., Greenberg, J., Solomon, S., Kluck, B., & Cornwell, R. (2001). I am not an animal: Mortality salience, disgust, and the denial of human creatureliness. *Journal of Experimental Psychology: General, 130*(3), 427–35. http:// doi.org/10.1037/0096-3445.130.3.427

Gray, J. (2004). *Heresies: Against progress and other illusions.* London, UK: Granta Books.

Greenberg, J., Solomon, S., Pyszczynski, T., Rosenblatt, A., Burling, J., Lyon, D., & ... Pinel, E. (1992). Why do people need self-esteem? Converging evidence that self-esteem serves an anxiety-buffering function. *Journal of Personality and Social Psychology, 63*(6), 913–22. http://doi.org/10.1037/0022-3514.63.6.913

Greenberg, J., Pyszczynski, T., Solomon, S., & Rosenblatt, A. (1990). Evidence for terror management theory II: The effects of mortality salience on reactions to those who threaten or bolster the cultural worldview. *Journal of Personality and Social Psychology, 58*(2), 308–18. http://doi.org/10.1037/0022-3514.58.2.308

Greenberg, J., Solomon, S., & Pyszczynski, T. (1997). Terror management theory of self-esteem and cultural worldviews: Empirical assessments and conceptual refinements. In M. P. Zanna (Ed.), *Advances in experimental social psychology.* (Vol. 29, pp. 61–139). San Diego, CA: Academic Press.

Hayes, J., Schimel, J., Faucher, E. H., & Williams, T. J. (2008). Evidence for the DTA hypothesis II: Threatening self-esteem increases death-thought accessibility. *Journal of Experimental Social Psychology, 44*(3), 600–13. http://doi.org/10.1016/j .jesp.2008.01.004

Henrich, J. (2016). *The secret of our success: How culture is driving human evolution, domesticating our species, and making us smarter.* Princeton, NJ: Princeton University Press.

Hoffer, E. (1951). *The true believer: Thoughts on the nature of mass movements.* New York, NY: Harper and Row.

Huxley, A. (1952). *The devils of Loudun.* New York, NY: Harper & Row.

Kan, S. (1989). *Symbolic immortality: The Tlingit potlatch of the nineteenth century.* Washington, DC: Smithsonian Institution Press.

Kasser, T., & Sheldon, K. M. (2000). Of wealth and death: Materialism, mortality salience, and consumption behavior. *Psychological Science, 11*(4), 348–51. http://doi .org/10.1111/1467-9280.00269

Koole, S. L., & Van den Berg, A. E. (2005). Lost in the wilderness: Terror management, action orientation, and nature evaluation. *Journal of Personality and Social Psychology, 88*(6), 1014–28. http://doi.org/10.1037/0022-3514.88.6.1014

Landau, M. J., Solomon, S., Greenberg, J., Cohen, F., Pyszczynski, T., Arndt, J., Miller, C. H., Ogilvie, D. M., & Cook, A. (2004). Deliver us from evil: The effects of mortality salience and reminders of 9/11 on support for President George W. Bush. *Personality and Social Psychology Bulletin, 30*(9), 1136–50. http://doi.org /10.1177/0146167204267988

Lifshin, U., Greenberg, J., Zestcott, C. A., & Sullivan, D. (2017). The evil animal: A terror management theory perspective on the human tendency to kill animals. *Personality and Social Psychology Bulletin, 43*(6), 743–57. http://doi.org /10.1177/0146167217697092

Mandel, N., & Heine, S. J. (1999). Terror management and marketing: He who dies with the most toys wins. *Advances in Consumer Research, 26,* 527–32.

Mandel, N., & Smeesters, D. (2008). The sweet escape: Effects of mortality salience on consumption quantities for high-and low-self-esteem consumers. *Journal of Consumer Research, 35*(2), 309–23. http://doi.org/10.1086/587626

May, R. (1991). *The cry for myth.* New York, NY: W.W. Norton & Company.

McGregor, H. A., Lieberman, J. D., Greenberg, J., Solomon, S., Arndt, J., Simon, L., & Pyszczynski, T. (1998). Terror management and aggression: Evidence that mortality salience motivates aggression against worldview-threatening others. *Journal of Personality and Social Psychology, 74*(3), 590–605. http://doi .org/10.1037/0022-3514.74.3.590

Melville, H. (1851/1986). *Moby-Dick.* H. Beaver (Ed.). New York, NY: Penguin Classics.

Norenzayan, A., & Hansen, I. G. (2006). Belief in supernatural agents in the face of death. *Personality and Social Psychology Bulletin, 32*(2), 174–87. http://doi .org/10.1177/0146167205528025

Ochsmann, R., & Mathy, M. (1994). *Depreciating of and distancing from foreigners: Effects of mortality salience.* Unpublished manuscript. Mainz, Germany: Universitat Mainz.

Pinker, S. (2018). *Enlightenment now.* New York, NY: Random House.

Pyszczynski, T., Abdollahi, A., Solomon, S., Greenberg, J., Cohen, F., & Weise, D. (2006). Mortality salience, martyrdom, and military might: The great Satan versus the axis of evil. *Personality and Social Psychology Bulletin, 32*(4), 525–37. http://doi .org/10.1177/0146167205282157

Pyszczynski, T., Solomon, S., & Greenberg, J. (2015). Thirty years of terror management theory: From Genesis to Revelation. In *Advances in experimental social psychology* (Vol. 52, pp. 1–70). Cambridge, MA: Academic Press Inc. http://doi.org/10.1016 /bs.aesp.2015.03.001

Róheim, G. (1934). The evolution of culture. *International Journal of Psycho-Analysis, 15,* 387–418.

Rosenblatt, A., Greenberg, J., Solomon, S., Pyszczynski, T., & Lyon, D. (1989). Evidence for terror management theory I: The effects of mortality salience on reactions to those who violate or uphold cultural values. *Journal of Personality and Social Psychology, 57*(4), 681–90. http://doi.org/10.1037/0022-3514.57.4.681

Rutjens, B. T., van der Pligt, J., & van Harreveld, F. (2009). Things will get better: The anxiety-buffering qualities of progressive hope. *Personality & Social Psychology Bulletin, 35*(5), 535–43. http://doi.org/10.1177/0146167208331252

Seneca. (AD 49/1951). On the shortness of life. In J. W. Basore (Trans.) *Moral essays* (Volume II). Cambridge, MA: Harvard University Press.

Shaw, G.B. (1919/1996). *Heartbreak house.* New York, NY: Dover Publications.

Simon, A. (2001). The existential deal: An interview with David Cronenberg. *Critical Quarterly, 43,* 34–56. https://doi.org/10.1111/1467-8705.00371

Sloan-Wilson, D. (2002). *Darwin's cathedral: Evolution, religion, and the nature of society.* Chicago, IL: University of Chicago Press.

Solomon, S., Greenberg, J., & Pyszczynski, T. (2015). *The worm at the core: On the role of death in life.* New York, NY: Random House.

Solomon, S., Greenberg, J., & Pyszczynski, T. (1991). A terror management theory of social behavior: The psychological functions of self-esteem and cultural worldviews. In M. P. Zanna (Ed.), *Advances in experimental social psychology* (pp. 91–159). Orlando: Academic Press.

Solomon, S., & Thompson, S. (2019). Secular cultural worldviews. In C. Rouledge, & M. Vess (Eds), *Handbook of terror management theory* (pp. 287–302). San Diego, CA: Elsevier.

Weber, M. (1925/1968). The types of legitimate domination. In G. Roth, & C. Wittich, (Eds), *Economy and society: An outline of interpretive sociology* (pp. 212–301). New York, NY: Bedminster Press.

Williams, T. (1940/2004). *Cat on a hot tin roof.* New York, NY: New Directions.

Wilson, E. O. (2012). *The social conquest of earth.* New York, NY: Liveright.

Zaleskiewicz, T., Gasiorowska, A., Kesebir, P., Luszczynska, A., & Pyszczynski, T. (2013). Money and the fear of death: The symbolic power of money as an existential anxiety buffer. *Journal of Economic Psychology, 36,* 55–67. http://doi.org/10.1016/j.joep.2013.02.008

21 To Become Ancestors of a Living Future

BARBARA JANE DAVY

When I die, I want to be eaten. I want to give my body to a bear, or crows, or failing the tolerance of my surviving kin for this, into the ground to be eaten by bugs, worms, and bacteria. I want to be a gift. I want to become part of other living things. This gives me a sense of meaningful participation in the life of the world.

This is not a common perspective on death in the modern world. Death is a necessary part of life – without it, evolutionary adaptation is not possible – but we shy away from thinking about it. Studies in the social psychology subfield known as Terror Management Theory (TMT) that empirically test Ernest Becker's theories (1962, 1973), find that when we are reminded of the fact that we are going to die, arousing mortality salience, we use identification with our worldviews as a shield against the perceived threat (Solomon, Greenberg, and Pyszczynski, 2015; Burke, Martens, and Faucher, 2010; Greenberg, Pyszczynski, and Solomon, 1986). In the industrialized world this prompts overconsumption because the dominant modern worldview is consumerism (Arndt et al., 2004). Modern individualized ontology, with a sense of self as separate and self-interested, is threatened by mortality salience, prompting the creation of heroic immortality projects or worldview defences. Consumerism, the most common worldview defence in modernity, is leading us to surpass the capacity of ecosystems to regenerate, surpassing the biophysical limits of the planet (Wackernagel et al., 2002; Meadows, Randers, and Meadows, 2004; Rockström et al., 2009; Turner, 2012). The denial of death has significant social-ecological costs.

One alternative is to pursue "green hero projects" (Dickinson, 2009) to uphold environmental values; for example, as eco-warriors who endeavour to be immortalized through self-sacrifice (see e.g. Pike, 2017). This approach opposes the existing system while remaining dependent upon it, rather than living adaptively embedded in the ecosystems that wilderness defenders want to preserve. Another alternative is to become ancestors of a living future by becoming embedded in a gift economy,[1] a network of relations maintained through the giving of gifts, living and dying within adaptive systems. Ancestor veneration, a widespread cross-cultural phenomenon (Reuter, 2014; Sheils, 1975) of ritually showing respect or reverence for one's ancestors, can provide a different shield against mortality salience than hero projects (e.g. consumption, or its antithesis of eco-warrior activism) by reframing death as part of the process of becoming an ancestor in the context of a relational ontology understood as a way of relating through giving and being given. Contemporary Heathen revitalization of pre-Christian European traditions provides an example of how this alternative ontology frames death in a way that promotes adaptive relations within social-ecological systems.

This alternative practice of giving death a seat at the table rather than denying it has the potential to promote a more sustainable way of life and approach to health in the Anthropocene. Heathenism treats the sickness of individualization rather than shoring up the efficacy of worldview defence. Individualized ontology is inherently insecure, questing after an unachievable immortality. Reframing death in a relational ontology has positive psychological and social-ecological effects, evident in an examination of the consequences of Heathen rituals of ancestor veneration in ethnographic study of Heathens in Canada, and supported further by a survey of international Heathens and other contemporary Pagans (n=643) in comparison with the general Canadian population (n=241).[2]

Heroic Measures

Family members all too often want to pursue heroic measures when faced with the imminent death of loved ones, increasing health care costs at the expense of quality of life. Consider also the environmental impact of preserving existing lives at the expense of future generations, and at the lost potential of ongoing adaptive evolution through biological reproduction rather than technical means. What if we succeed in curing cancer, or in egregious medical pursuits such as the body transplant research of surgeons Sergio Canavero and Xiaoping Ren? Taken to this extreme heroic measure, at an estimated cost of US$13 million for a single such surgery (Kirkey, 2017), the absurdities of the pursuit of physical immortality become clear.

Pursuit of symbolic immortality through hero projects raising the defence of worldviews is common in modern society, and also has social-ecological costs. More than 500 studies in Terror Management Theory have empirically demonstrated the psychological effects of mortality salience (Solomon, Greenberg, and Pyszczynski, 2015, p. 211). When we are reminded of the fact that we are going to die, we typically unconsciously respond by trying to use identification with our worldview as a shield against the perceived threat. In the context of the industrialized world this generally leads people to want to buy things, because the dominant modern worldview is consumerism (Arndt et al., 2004). TMT is based on modern individualized ontology with an egoic sense of self as separate and self-interested, threatened by awareness of one's own impending death. This fragile self requires shielding from mortality salience through the creation of heroic immortality projects or worldview defences.

Janis Dickinson, who has demonstrated how climate change discourse unwittingly increases consumption by raising mortality salience (2009), recommends the creation of "green hero projects" as an alternative to using consumption as a shield defending against mortality salience. Some environmental activists do pursue green hero projects to uphold environmental values, such as the eco-warriors Sarah Pike studies (2017), who endeavour to be immortalized through self-sacrifice in the service of environmental protection. This is a familiar religious trajectory, and ultimately preserves its oppositional status to the dominant system without changing the structures that produce it. Although some eco-warriors develop an expanded sense of self that includes the environment, or a more relational sense of self (Pike, 2017, p. 76), eco-warriors present themselves in opposition to the existing system while remaining dependent upon it for supplies, rather than living adaptively embedded in the ecosystems they want to preserve from human impact. Pike notes, for example, that activists on tree-sits require "food supply runs" (Pike, 2017, p. 124).

While eco-warriors may be commended for their willingness to substitute the suffering and potential death of their own bodily selves for those of non-human others, unless they eat and die within the ecosystems they aim to protect they are not living adaptively within the system but trying to preserve "wilderness" apart from humanity. Pike notes a conflict that developed when such activists were offered meat to eat by local Indigenous peoples, who were offended when vegetarians refused the food (Pike, 2017, p. 183). Emulating Indigenous peoples' practices presents difficulties for non-Indigenous people, too often resulting in disregard for the embeddedness of those practices in cultural traditions. But settlers need a model for living that does not entail seeing humans as alien to a wilderness set aside to preserve, protected by warriors who cannot be sustained within it. We need to restore our connections with the adaptive cycles of the others with whom we share the land, water, and atmosphere – to eat and be eaten, to give and to receive. Ancestor veneration can facilitate this, potentially through any religious tradition, but perhaps most easily in the context of a relational ontology and gift economy.

Green hero projects retain an individualized ontological approach in contrast to practices of ancestor veneration embedded in gift economies. Relational ontology, a way of relating, builds esteem from developing a reputation for generosity, engaging in good guesting, hosting, and gifting relations with others. Ancestor veneration potentially offers a better shield against mortality salience than modern terror management hero projects (e.g. consumption, or its antithesis of eco-warrior activism) by reframing death as part of the process of becoming an ancestor, in the context of a relational ontology understood as a way of relating through giving and being given. Offerings to ancestors raise the value salience of generosity and gratitude in conjunction with mortality salience. Studies testing the effects of making different values salient in TMT indicate that when values alternative to consumption are made salient, provided those values are also part of the participant's worldview, they are expressed in attitude and behaviour (Jonas et al., 2002; Gailliot et al., 2008). Contemporary Heathen revitalization of pre-Christian European traditions provides an example of how this alternative ontological approach reframes death in a way that promotes adaptive relations within social-ecological systems.

Giving Death a Seat at the Table

Ritual practices of giving offerings to ancestors change the focus from individual success to community remembrance by shifting ontology from self and way of being to way of relating, and maintaining the quality of ongoing relations rather than the length of one's life. Rituals of making offerings and giving gifts to ancestors have social-ecological consequences. Seligman et al. (2008) describe ritual as specially framed actions that has social consequences. They focus on the power of ritual to negotiate social relations through the creation of a shared subjunctive, a collective sense of participating in a world "as if" presented in ritual. They frame this as the creation of a shared sense of order. Building on Seligman et al.'s understanding of ritual, I see Heathen rituals of making offerings to ancestors as an ongoing negotiation of ways of relating within the more-than-human world through the giving of gifts, the creation of shared stories, and shared meaning. Heathen rituals of giving gifts promote a relational ontology and gift economy. Making offerings to ancestors, which entails giving gifts and giving thanks for gifts received, puts Heathens in gifting relations with the ancestors. These ritual practices create a sense of gratitude for what the ancestors have given them, and a felt sense of obligation to "pay it forward," or, better, "give in turn." This creates a system of delayed, indirect reciprocity. While the ritual examples Seligman et al. provide focus on relations between humans, cross-culturally and over a longer time frame ritual has been a negotiation with the more-than-human world, including the full social-ecological system of relations mediated by gift economies in relational ontologies. The consequences of ritual offerings made to ancestors and landvaettir (other-than-human persons understood as nature "spirits" or land wights) by Heathens in Canada include an awareness of wyrd (relations of fate) shared not only with human kin and kindred, but with the broader ecosystem community, supporting what Aldo Leopold (1949) called a "land ethic."

Dísablót, as celebrated by Vindisir Kindred, provides an illustrative example of the psychological and social-ecological consequences of rituals of ancestor veneration. "Dísablót" refers to a feast of offerings to female ancestors,[3] based on historical practices of pre-Christian northwestern Europe, revived by contemporary Heathens such as members of *Vindisir*, a kindred (bonded group of Heathens) in southwestern Ontario that is made up primarily of women and femme-identified people, and includes a preponderance of second-generation Pagans. Hilda R. Ellis Davidson, in her analysis of Old Norse understanding of death (1968, p. 136–7), notes evidence of offerings made to the *dísir* at the beginning of winter, or later at different times depending on place and time, not based on calendar date but local practice.

Jade Pichette, one of the *gythias*[4] (religious leaders), of Vindisir, describes Dísablót as a "time to reconnect and honour the women who came before.... What it came down to was family coming together, having good food, honouring our ancestors, but especially the dísir in particular" (interview with Jade, Feb. 3, 2018). Usually this event, held annually by the group in January of each year, includes sharing stories about female ancestors (including "ancestors of affinity"[5] as well as blood relations), as well as sharing food and drink with ancestors and kindred members and other guests.

In 2018, because they had shared these stories in previous years, and some of them were suffering "burnout" from their contributions to the wider Heathen and other communities, the gythias decided to "the feed the ancestors in ourselves." The event, held in one of the gythia's homes, was quite informal apart from an opening statement from Jade and another one of the gythias welcoming everyone, and included a ritual passing of a shared horn of drink, and making offerings of all the food and drink brought to share at the feast to the dísir. This *blót*,[6] which I attended as a participant observer, included the giving of a number of gifts between participants, and an evening spent catching up over a potluck dinner and drinks in a familial atmosphere, in addition to the more formal opening of the event.

As can be seen in the picture from the blót (figure 21.1), death rather literally has a seat at the table, in the form of an actual human skeleton. Not included in the frame is the plate symbolically set for the ancestors, in which each of us gave a portion of what we brought to share in the potluck. Offerings given to the dísir at this event function as reminders of participants' mortality, while at the same time raising the salience of values such as gratitude, generosity, and sharing, which together make those values operational in the participants' lives.

While the majority of TMT studies indicate that raising mortality salience increases consumption in modern industrial society, some TMT studies have demonstrated that when values marginal to the dominant value system of consumerism are made salient with mortality salience, people express the alternative salient value if it is felt to be part of their worldview. For example, when diversity is discussed as an American value, Americans are more likely to express tolerance than when it is not brought up in conjunction with mortality

Figure 21.1 Giving death a seat at the table. Author's photo.

salience (Gailliot et al., 2008), and when helping is made salient, research participants become more helpful (Jonas et al., 2002).

Wyrd Relations

A consequence of rituals of ancestor veneration in Vindisir Kindred is a different social psychology from the mainstream. Members of Vindisir, in common with other contemporary Heathens, experience a more relational ontology than the dominant individualized ontology of modern society. The most obvious evidence of this among Heathens is their understanding of "wyrd," or relations of fate, as threads of intergenerational interdependence that connect all life. Auz Lawrence, gothi of Raven's Knoll, a private campground in eastern Ontario that hosts most of the region's Pagan festivals, indicates that each person is like a knot of threads gathered together within the ongoing fabric of reality that is wyrd: "In Norse tradition we're a weaving, a tapestry, and those threads, the threads that are bound together gather in the knot that is my life, my life and my consciousness, my period here, those threads already exist.... My knot is part of another thread, and that is going to be going on into the future, and those threads are bound up differently by different people" (interview with Auz, 2 May 2018). Gifting relations with ancestors and between kindred members are part of the larger gift economy of wyrd that supports interspecies reciprocity and generosity towards the non-human others, as well as a sense of being integral participants in the life of the world, conferring a sense of relational value and mutual recognition.

While some Heathens may pursue hero projects as part of a warrior ethos, those I have encountered are more interested in developing good relations and building community. The Havamal, part of *The Poetic Edda* from which many contemporary Heathens draw inspiration for their reconstructed traditions, instructs seeking "immortality" through building "reputation:"

> Cattle die, kinsmen die,
> the self must also die;
> but the glory of reputation never dies,
> for the man who can get himself a good one.

> Cattle die, kinsmen die,
> the self must also die;
> I know one thing which never dies:
> the reputation of each dead man.
> (Havamal, p. 76–7; Larrington, 2014, p. 22–3)

I would suggest that an appropriate contemporary rendering of this for the Heathens of Vindisir and Raven's Knoll is:

> Wealth dies, kinfolk die,
> the self must also die;
> but those who are remembered live on,
> in the community that keeps them.

Relational ontology does not raise self-esteem or worldview defence as a shield against the fear of death so much as satisfy a more basic need for what Avner Offer calls "regard" (1997). As members of a social species we have a psycho-social need to feel valued by others. This is an adaptive need that motivates us to help one another. We depend on one another, so to make us dependable for others we have adapted a psycho-social need to feel valued for being dependable. The development of individualized ontology leads people to try to satisfy this more basic need for regard with self-esteem. It is not that we need new hero projects, but that we need a meaningful sense of belonging and participation in the life of the world and community. We need to know that we are necessary, valued, and make a meaningful contribution to feel good about ourselves. Heathens with a more relational ontology satisfy this need through the process of becoming a venerated ancestor who will continue to be honoured and given gifts after death, a process that begins before death in participating in good gifting relations while alive.

When I interviewed members of Vindisir about the Dísablót and ancestor veneration, they said that making offerings to the dísir makes them feel grateful for what they have, and want to contribute to community building. Luna (interview, Feb. 12, 2018) emphasized that thinking about how her ancestors would have lived gave her a sense of appreciation for the ease and comfort of modern life. Jade similarly noted that they[7] "have gained more of an appreciation of the women in my family, even the ones I really struggled with, because of doing that honouring." Jade also noted that organizing and leading events like Dísablót are important and powerful in their life because it is a way "to give back to my ancestors. I owe it to them because I exist" (interview, Feb. 3, 2018).

When I asked Auz, gothi of Raven's Knoll, what the ancestors give him he made the connection between giving offerings and the creation of gratitude explicit:

> When you're thinking about receiving gifts, it's almost like you've already received them.... One of the amazing things about the way Heathen worship is done is that it focuses gratitude. Gratitude for other people, gratitude for ideas, for virtues, values, and for ancestors, and for what ancestors have given us. And so when we realize those gifts, we feel richer, and we become better people because we focus on those gifts, and then those are the things that we start to give as gifts more often. Those are threads we throw out more often in our daily existence. I don't own those things. Those are things that I've just noticed more, and now I start to give those gifts too. It's part of the Heathen metaphysics. (interview, May 2, 2018)

Some of the wider social-ecological consequences of rituals of ancestor veneration are visible in survey data comparing an international sample of Heathens and other Pagans with a random sampling of Canadians (see table 21.1).[8] Heathens and other Pagans surveyed strongly agree that giving thanks is important more than the random sample of Canadians do. Heathens and other Pagans were (self-reportedly) more than twice as likely to support ethical consumption, prioritizing humane production, environmental effects, and supporting local business over cost and quality than the random Canadian sample. Most Heathens and other Pagans said their sense of community includes plants, animals, the land, and water (an indication of espousing Leopold's "land ethic"), compared to two-thirds of random Canadians. Almost two-thirds of Heathen and other Pagans strongly agreed that environmental protection should be a high priority for government, while considerably less than half of random Canadians said so. The greatest difference between Heathen and Pagan respondents in comparison with the random sample was that ritual practice is much more important to them than the general population. This suggests that ritual practices can effectively operationalize environmental values for Heathen and other Pagan practitioners. While these values have not been operationalized in the dominant culture, the survey results indicate that they are present

Table 21.1 Value survey results

	Heathens and Pagans (%)	Random Canadians (%)
Giving thanks is important		
strongly agree:	44.5	36.1
Ethical consumption		
most important consideration:	44.0	20.7
Support for "land ethic"		
strongly agree or agree:	83.5	66.4
Prioritize environmental protection		
strongly agree:	64.1	34.9
Ritual practices are important		
agree or strongly agree:	65.1	24.5

within it. If made salient more effectively these environmental values could be operationalized to create a more sustainable society.

Ritual is an effective means of making values salient and operational. If everyone made offerings to their ancestors, this could trigger a systems-level change in society. If everyone were in gifting relationships with their ancestors, we would have a longer time awareness and sense of self embedded in past and future relations, which presumably would encourage a greater concern for the long-term effects of excessive consumption. Modernity scales us back to the nuclear family and individual selves, while relations with ancestors facilitate healthier understandings of parents as also sons and daughters, and of oneself as a descendant of family and a possible ancestor of the future (see Foor, 2017, p. 123–4). The effects of rituals of giving offerings to ancestors in Heathenry suggest that such practices amplify practitioners' feelings of gratitude and contentment and increase their prioritization of ethical considerations when consuming.

It is possible that if we all made offerings to our ancestors some negative consequences may follow. A focus on ancestry presents a "wicked dilemma" in that while it may be beneficial for social-ecological relations in terms of facilitating a land ethic, it can also foster the development of racialized consciousness. Some Heathens are notably racist, and overlap with white supremacy movements (see Snook, 2015; von Schnurbein, 2016). Practitioners I have interviewed indicate that they do think that ancestor veneration within Heathenry can promote the development of racialized consciousness and racism, and that there is an ongoing need for careful vetting of new people to keep racists out of Heathen groups. Heathens such as Jade Pichette have responded to this problem by initiating "The Canadian Pagan Declaration on Intolerance" in Canada, broadening the anti-racist "Declaration 127" by Huggin's Heathen Hof, an international Heathen website. "Declaration 127" cites verse 127 from the Havamal: "When you see misdeeds, speak out against them, and give your enemies no frið," in an explicit denunciation of racism perpetuated by the Heathen group Asatru Free Assembly in the United States. To give "no frið" to enemies means to give them no peace, or respect, and to exclude them from the community. This is an ongoing struggle within Heathenry that is actively resisted by many, but embraced by others.

Reviving ancestor veneration, relational ontology, and gifting economies may help us to transition society to a more sustainable social-ecological system, but this is a complex process, and there are likely to be a number of tradeoffs to consider. The fact that inclusion is non-negotiable for Vindisir members and other Heathens who frequent Raven's Knoll gives me hope that a more sustainable option is possible between the heroic projects of consumerism and the fetishization of a warrior ethos in fascist efforts to replace the current system, and even the more benign, if ineffectual route of eco-warrior martyrs pursuing "green hero projects." If we want a sustainable, diverse, and inclusive future, we need to become the ancestors who will be remembered for helping create it.

NOTES

1   There is a considerable literature on gift economies. My understanding of gift economies is derived primarily from Malinowski (1922) and Polanyi (1944). In common with Bird-David (1990), and Bird-David and Darr (2009), I do not regard competitive destruction of material goods in displays of prestige, such as in the late developments of Pacific Northwest potlatch rituals in response to colonial pressures, to represent the original forms of gift economies, or giving economies, in Bird-David's terms.

2   The survey was conducted in December 2017 via SurveyMonkey. The sample of the general Canadian population was randomly selected by SurveyMonkey, while the international sample of Heathens and other contemporary Pagans was purposively selected through contacting individuals and publicly identified groups. I intentionally contacted individuals and groups outside my political and religious orientation in an effort to obtain a diversified sample. The ethnographic study is part of ongoing participant observation research that began in January 2018, building on my longer experience as a practitioner. This research is generously supported by the Faculty of Environment at the University of Waterloo, and the Government of Ontario via Ontario Graduate Scholarships.

3   "Dísir" is the plural form of "dís," which is an Old Norse term variously interpreted as "goddess" (see e.g. Ellis Davidson, 1998, pp. 47, 146, 177, 185) and "supernatural female guardian" (Ellis, 1968, p. 134–8, 184), reflecting the historical evolution of the concept. In the contemporary Heathen context, "dísir" often refers to female ancestors, but can also refer to other female personnages. The name "Vindisir,"

meaning "friends of the dísir," for example, references the connection group members have with the goddesses Freya, Skadi, and Frigga.

4   Some Heathens (such as the Asatru Alliance, https://www.asatru.org/roleofgothar .php, accessed 3 May 2018) use the term "gothar" to refer collectively to a group of gythia or gothi (the corresponding masculine term to gythia), but I have not heard this term used in my interviews.

5   My use of this phrase comes from Daniel Foor (2017). He notes that some people also develop relationships with ancestors of place, meaning original peoples of the land to which one is not a blood relation. Heathens I have encountered typically use "ancestor" in this expanded sense to include blood relations as well as ancestors of affinity (such as those regarded as role models) and ancestors of place.

6   Blóts historically included a blood sacrifice, but the animals killed would be shared between ancestors and still-living participants in a communal feast. Some Heathens restrict the use of the word "blót" to events that feature blood sacrifice, but those I have interviewed use the term for any Heathen feast that involves sharing food and drink with ancestors, landvaettir, and/or deities. See Strmiska (2009) for further discussion of blót traditions and blood sacrifice.

7   Jade's preferred pronouns are they/them/their.

8   These figures are based on cross-tabulations conducted in SPSS, with chi-square and z-tests to check for statistical significance, on survey data collected by the author via SurveyMonkey in December 2017. All figures cited have p values of less than 0.05. The sample sizes for the international sample of Heathens and other Pagans (n=643) and the random sample of Canadians (n=241) are not large enough to give an error margin of less than 6 per cent, and strictly speaking are not directly comparable, but indicate larger future studies in this direction could be worthwhile.

REFERENCES

Arndt, J., Solomon, S., Kasser, T., & Sheldon, K. M. (2004). The urge to splurge: A terror management account of materialism and consumer behavior. *Journal of Consumer Psychology, 14*(3), 198–212.

Becker, E. (1962). *The birth and death of meaning: An interdisciplinary perspective on the problem of man.* New York, NY: Free Press.

Becker, E. (1973). *The denial of death.* New York, NY: Free Press.

Bird-David, N. (1990). The giving environment: Another perspective on the economic system of gatherer-hunters. *Current Anthropology, 31*(2), 189–96.

Bird-David, N., & Darr, A. (2009). Community, gift and mass-gift: On gift-commodity hybrids in advanced mass consumption cultures. *Economy and Society, 38*(2), 304–25.

Burke, B. L., Martens, A., & Faucher, E. H. (2010). Two decades of terror management theory: A meta-analysis of mortality salience research. *Personality and Social Psychology Review, 14,* 155–95.

Dickinson, J. L. (2009). The people paradox: Self-esteem striving, immortality ideologies, and human response to climate change. *Ecology and Society, 14*(1), 34. http://www. ecologyandsociety.org/vol14/iss1/art34.

Ellis, H. R. (1968). *The road to Hel: A study of the conception of the dead in old Norse literature.* New York, NY: Greenwood Press.

Ellis Davidson, H. (1998). *Roles of the northern goddess.* London: Routledge.

Foor, D. (2017). *Ancestral medicine: Rituals for personal and family healing.* Rochester, VT: Bear & Company.

Gailliot, M. T., Sillman, T. F., Schmeichel, B. J., Maner, J. K., & Plant, E. A. (2008). Mortality salience increases adherence to salient norms and values. *Personality and Social Psychology Bulletin, 34,* 993–1003.

Greenberg, J., Pyszczynski, T., & Solomon, S. (1986). The causes and consequences of a need for self-esteem: A terror management theory. In R. F. Baumeister (Ed.), *Public self and private self* (pp. 189–212). New York, NY: Springer-Verlag.

Jonas, E., Schimel. J., Greenberg J., & Pyszczynski, T. (2002). The Scrooge effect: Evidence that mortality salience increases prosocial attitudes and behavior. *Personality and Social Psychology Bulletin, 28,* 1342–53.

Kirkey, S. (2017). Head case: Meet Sergio Canavero, the brain behind the world's first head transplant, and, perhaps, the key to everlasting life. *National Post.* Retrieved from http://nationalpost.com/features/head-transplant.

Larrington, C. (Trans). (2014). *The poetic Edda.* Oxford: Oxford University Press.

Leopold, A. (1949). The land ethic. In *Sand County almanac and sketches here and there.* New York, NY: Oxford University Press.

Malinowski, B. (2015). *Argonauts of the Western Pacific: An account of native enterprise and adventure in the archipelagoes of Melanesian New Guinea* (11th ed). London: Forgotten Books.

Meadows, D., Randers, J., Meadows, D. (2004). *Limits to growth: The 30-year update* (3rd ed.). White River Junction, VT: Chelsea Green Publishing.

Offer, A. (1997). Between the gift and the market: The economy of regard. *Economic History Review, 50*(3), 450–76.

Pike, S. M. (2017). *For the wild: Ritual and commitment in radical eco-activism.* Oakland, CA: University of California Press.

Polanyi, Karl. (1944). *The Great Transformation: The political and economic origins of our time.* Boston, MA: Beacon Press.

Reuter, Thomas. (2014). Is ancestor veneration the most universal of all world religions? A critical of modernist cosmological bias. *Wacana, 15*(2), 223–53.

Rockström, J. et al. (2009). A safe operating space for humanity. *Nature, 461*(24), 472–5.

Seligman, A. B., Weller, R. P., Puett, M. J., & Bennett, S. (2008). *Ritual and its consequences: An essay on the limits of sincerity.* New York: Oxford University Press.

Sheils, D. (1975). Toward a unified theory of ancestor worship: A cross-cultural study. *Social Forces, 54*(2), 427–40.

Snook, J. (2015). *American heathens: The politics of identity in a Pagan religious movement.* Philadelphia, PA: Temple University Press.

Solomon, S., Greenberg, J., & Pysznczynski, T. (2015). *The worm at the core: On the role of death in life.* New York, NY: Random House.

Strmiska, M. (2007). Putting the blood back into the blót: The revival of animal sacrifice in modern Nordic Paganism. *The Pomegranate: The International Journal of Pagan Studies, 9*(2), 154–89. https://doi.org/10.1558/pome.v9i2.154

Turner, G. M. (2012). On the cusp of global collapse? Updated comparison of *The Limits to Growth* with historical data. *GAIA, 21*(2), 116–24.

von Schnurbein, S. (2016). *Norse revival: Transformations of Germanic Neopaganism.* Leiden: Brill.

Wackernagel, M., Schultz, N. B., Deuming, D., Callejas Linares, A. Jenkins, M., Kapos, V., Monfreda, C., Loh, J., Myers, N., Norgaard, R., & Randers, J. (2002). Tracking the ecological overshoot of the human economy. *Proceedings of the Academy of Science, 99*(1), 9266–71.

Conclusion – Pursuing Health in the Anthropocene: A Synthesis of Current and Future Research Priorities

KATHARINE ZYWERT AND STEPHEN QUILLEY

In the Anthropocene, social-ecological systems are changing at an unprecedented rate. Human activities are pushing the Earth's biophysical processes across thresholds into new patterns of feedback (Rockström et al., 2009), making the long-term prospects for human health on this planet increasingly uncertain. As researchers, health practitioners, activists, and members of diverse (human and more-than-human) communities, we are both witnesses to and participants in the unfolding of the geological epoch of human impact. From the earliest stages of human cultural evolution through to the present, each era has borne its own risks and burdens, its own understandings of health and well-being, and its own potential for continuity and change. Over the next century, finding ways to live well that do not erode the ecological foundations of human life on Earth is our most pressing challenge. In some ways, this task has always been intrinsic to the human condition. Whether organized as hunter-gatherer bands, horticultural and pastoral societies, complex urban-agrarian civilizations, and now globally connected industrial-consumer societies, human communities have always either flourished or languished according to the fit between collective activities and the capacities of the ecosystems on which survival depends. And because by virtue of culture, human beings have a propensity to innovate new technologies and patterns of social organization and so to change periodically their ecological niche, this relationship has always been dynamic and unstable. We have seen what can happen when the fit is not right. The fall of civilizations around the world, from the Lowland Maya to the Roman Empire, can be attributed to a structural overconsumption of resources that was necessary to support layers of social complexity which, over time, generated diminishing returns and could no longer be maintained (Tainter, 1988; 2014). Although ecological destruction and resource depletion have been perennial problems, in a globalized world, the scale of the issue has expanded (Homer-Dixon, 2007; Bardi, 2017). In the Anthropocene, human activities are influencing not only local ecologies, but the functioning of the Earth's highest-order biophysical systems (McNeil and Engelke, 2016; Steffen et al., 2015). Human influence over the biosphere has never been so great, and yet our ability to mitigate the negative and unintended effects of our actions and to adapt to the changes that are now evident across local and global scales have never been so thoroughly tested. At this particular moment of contingency for human health, there are multiple paths before us. Each one crosses difficult terrain, leading us not only figuratively but also quite literally through the fog and through the heat, through the extremes of water and earth, towards an uncertain future.

The chapters in this collection lay the groundwork for a process of multi-disciplinary research and reflection that will at least help sensitize both activists and policymakers as to likely trade-offs and possibly begin to identify viable ways forward. While they may not all represent steps along the same path, they all point towards potential futures in which human beings and the Earth's bio-physical systems support one another, reinforcing not only ongoing survival, but health and well-being over the long-term. In this concluding section, we aim to draw together the core themes that unite the work presented in this volume. As we have emphasized throughout, this collection departs quite significantly from mainstream approaches to health in the Anthropocene. Many contributions do not fall squarely into any recognized health-related field, whether public health, planetary health, or ecological health. Similarly, they are not bound together by any single discipline or school of thought. Instead, they mobilize the diverse backgrounds of contributors who have been trained variously in public health, ecological economics, political science, sociology, anthropology, religious studies, medicine, and philosophy. The result is not merely a multi- or trans-disciplinary collection, but a book that invites seemingly strange bedfellows to bring their own disciplinary and experiential backgrounds to bear on the question of how to live well in the Anthropocene. Having identified the commonalities that unite the various chapters, this conclusion will also consider the tensions and discontinuities that exist between chapters. Although contributors may not agree on how best to address these issues, it is clear to all that more work is needed to investigate (though not necessarily to resolve) these points of tension. The conclusion will also outline priorities for future research identified collectively by contributing authors. The list assembled here is based on conversations held among contributors at a meeting hosted by the School of Environment, Resources and Sustainability at the University of Waterloo and funded by the Canadian Institute of Health Research's Institute of Population and Public Health, and the Waterloo Institute for Social Innovation and Resilience. The goal of this event was to allow our authors to share their contributions, learn from the work of others, and begin to build a network of researchers investigating health in the Anthropocene from a range of disciplinary, interdisciplinary, and trans-disciplinary vantage points.

To say that the workshop was lively and sometimes even fractious underlines the difficulty of the subject matter and the extent to which our existing means of orientation politically, ethically, institutionally, and technologically are no longer adequate. Discussions between contributing authors were often contentious; nobody agreed. And nobody could agree, because the Anthropocene has us walking blind into a landscape that has never before been seen. Imagine being a person from the twelfth century trying to understand the ontology that underlies a modern health system. For instance, imagine how strange it would have been to countenance a world in which not everyone believed in God. It would have been very difficult to consider such things in a detached way, and it might have even seemed like the end of times to someone from the twelfth century. Today, it may be equally strange and difficult to imagine that our commitment to individualism or technological innovation might need to be constrained, or that species health might need to be privileged over individual health. We are conditioned to the Holocene, but these conditions are becoming destabilized. Nobody has a map of the new terrain, so disagreements and uncertainty are unavoidable. The mere fact that the authors who contributed to this collection gathered for a workshop and are publishing under one umbrella demonstrates that all bets are off. It is time to have contentious conversations about the future of health. These conversations are not only interdisciplinary, but inter-ontological. Because one often only becomes aware of one's ontological assumptions when they are challenged, this collection will at times make readers feel awkward or uncomfortable. In doing so, we hope the volume will inspire more difficult conversations and that through these discussions, the themes and tensions presented below will receive greater attention from researchers, health practitioners, and social innovators pursuing health in the age of human impact.

Themes for an Alternate Route

Increasingly, global and public health researchers, governments, foundations, and multilateral organizations are seeking to describe, quantify, and address the challenges facing health in the Anthropocene (see WHO, 2015; 2018; Whitmee et al., 2015; CPHA, 2015; Smith et al., 2014). These publications and initiatives have drawn significant attention to the troubling outcomes of climate change, pollution, loss of access to nature, and the degradation of landscapes and biodiversity for human health. They have also emphasized the potential of preventative health, new economic models, and climate change mitigation in generating mutual benefits for human well-being and ecological integrity. However, at their core, many of the strategies and approaches proposed in mainstream publications remain grounded in theories of change that emphasize sustainable development, formal governance, and the expansion of

Western-style biomedical health system infrastructures as primary pathways for change. Although we are not suggesting that these efforts will not improve quality of life, we remain sceptical of the ability of managerial approaches to meaningfully address the fundamental social-ecological dynamics that perpetuate ill health. In particular, such approaches fail to address biophysical limits to growth and the need to curtail the associated throughputs of both energy and materials. Instead, many chapters in this volume have argued for the inclusion of other mechanisms for securing both population health and ecological integrity into the long-term future. During this period of contingency, we must consider not only solutions that rely on the dynamics of the current system (e.g. growth economics, the welfare state, cosmopolitan liberal values), but also those that instantiate new ontological commitments, cultural meaning frameworks, and appropriate technologies that can be sustained in a dramatically different social-ecological regime that exerts increasing ecological constraints on social arrangements, psycho-spiritual orientations, and embodied practices (see Quilley, 2013; 2017). These approaches offer crucial yet often overlooked leverage points for change, tracing out an alternate route through the creative destruction of industrial modernity and the transition to a more ecologically viable, alternative modernity (see introduction to part 2, this volume). The chapters in this collection, united by four overarching themes, map out the touchstones of this alternate route.

Attending to Wicked Dilemmas

Many of the chapters in this volume are premised on the understanding that the challenges facing health in the Anthropocene are "wicked," paradoxical problems (Quilley, this volume; Kish, this volume; Cole, this volume; Hathaway, Cole and Poland, this volume). As discussed in the introduction to part 2, wicked problems are constantly negotiated rather than solved. In complex adaptive systems, interventions of any kind inevitably engender unintended consequences (Rittel and Webber, 1973; Meadows, 2008). Ways of reconciling the paradoxical aspects of such problems may emerge where we least expect them, including in practices and ideas that blend elements of typically disparate worldviews. Because of this, researchers and practitioners who attend to wicked dilemmas often develop approaches that are uncomfortable and perhaps unappealing (at least initially) to mainstream audiences (Kish, this volume; Quilley, this volume). Nonetheless, in an era of limits, humanity's long-term survival and well-being may well depend on large-scale social-ecological system change, and not least on the transition to a radically different kind of political economy. In this context, learning to live well on a finite planet will require us to train our attention on the wickedness of the problems we encounter, embracing their contradictions, paradoxes, and discomforts to unearth unanticipated solutions.

Working outside of Formal Health Care Systems

The literatures on public health, social determinants of health, and ecological determinants of health demonstrate that health is not only (or even mostly) a function of health care. Rather, health outcomes are bound to our positions within broader economic and political systems, to the living and non-living features of the environments that surround us, and to our interactions with our families and communities (Hancock, 2017). The chapters in this collection emphasize the importance of stepping outside of formal health care institutions to secure health and well-being in the Anthropocene. Domains as diverse as education, agriculture, work, domestic life, housing, the political economy, and culture can often affect our health and well-being more strongly than biomedical interventions (Mychajluk, this volume; Elings, this volume; Pershouse, this volume; Zywert, this volume). When considered from another angle, activities like growing food and gardening, spiritual practices and rituals, outdoor activities, artistic and creative pursuits, and participation in community-building social movements can all act as their own kind of preventative "medicines" (Poland, this volume; Poland et al., this volume; Zywert and Sutherland, this volume). By offering ways to live well, these informal "medicines" have the potential to improve physical, mental, social, and ecological health.

Embracing Complexity and Systems Thinking

Human health is a social-ecological process, determined as much by the state of the Earth's biophysical systems as by the social systems that reduce or perpetuate inequities and that privilege either short-term economic gains or long-term environmental sustainability (Butler, this volume; Del Bianco et al., this volume; Poland et al., this volume). When contemplating health in the Anthropocene, complexity science and systems thinking can therefore help us consider how seemingly disparate variables and patterns of feedback interact to generate positive health outcomes or to reduce well-being. For instance, embracing complexity and systems thinking makes it possible to perceive the growing mental health crisis as connected to broader ecological crises, not just externally (e.g. heat waves creating stress, destruction of nature causing anxiety), but also internally (e.g. anxiety induced by extinction of the microbiome with the rise of processed foods and antibiotics), opening up new opportunities for action and alignment. Effective engagement in the Anthropocene asks us to think across scales, taking into account past causes, current states, and future trajectories simultaneously (Zywert and Sutherland, this volume; Butler, this volume; Pershouse, this volume; Quilley, this volume).

Investigating Diverse Pathways to Ontological and Behavioural Change

Securing human health and ecological integrity into the future is not only about establishing functional infrastructures and governance systems that extend across the globe. It is also about achieving significant cultural shifts, changing our understandings of the nature of reality, and profoundly altering our relationships with one another and with the ecosystems in which we live (and that live within us). Initiating the kinds of cultural transformations that could anchor a sustainable society into the future, however, has proved to be exceedingly difficult. The chapters in this collection suggest that the changes we are pursuing will require a greater depth of understanding about the interactions between ontological change and behavioural change, thought and practice, and theory and embodiment (Poland, this volume; Foster, this volume; Solomon, this volume; Davy, this volume). It will require us to lower thresholds to action, reduce the transaction costs for behaviours that improve human and planetary health, and change the default options. It may also ask us to consider the possibilities for enforcing compulsory action and leveraging the human needs for acceptance and esteem by making these contingent on behaviours that enhance rather than detract from human and environmental well-being. This could suggest, for instance, taking seriously the dangerous territory of social engineering, as well as recognizing the power of ritual, spirituality, and shared meaning frameworks. Such avenues clearly conflict with liberal shibboleths of individual rationality and sovereignty.

Ongoing Tensions

While the above four themes run through much of the work assembled in this collection, it is also clear that a number of discontinuities and points of contention exist across its varied contributions. These divisions are not superficial; many involve disagreements over the primary assumptions that contributors take for granted when framing their research questions and interventions. The goal of this collection was never to resolve these tensions, but to bring them to light and spark deeper reflection by presenting divergent perspectives alongside one another. We encourage other researchers, practitioners, and activists pursuing health in the Anthropocene to also consider how the following tensions affect their work.

How Should We Address Limits to Growth?

Since the publication of the original "Limits to Growth" study in the early 1970s (Meadows et al., 1972), the warning that humanity will need to curtail its activities to avoid overexploiting resource and energy reserves has for the most part fallen on deaf ears. Mainstream economists and neoliberals have eschewed the issue, putting their faith in markets and the human capacity for technological innovation. Social democrats and many greens in the west have continued to rely on growth to sustain the social compact and consensus politics; and the Global South has of course insisted on growth as prerequisite for "catch up" development. The result has been a consensus at the level of governance and policy on the part of government, academia, corporations, and the third sector on some version of "sustainable" ("green," "smart") development and its technical corollary, "ecological modernization" (Butler, 2017; Dryzek, 2013; Quilley, 2017). The majority of the papers in this collection are aligned regarding the existence of limits and the health risks associated with crossing "planetary boundaries" (see Rockström et al., 2009). However, they present a range of potential pathways for addressing these limits, from embracing coercive social constraints (Quilley, this volume) to transitioning to a degrowth political economy (Aillon, this volume), to shifting ecological consciousness (Hathaway, Cole, and Poland, this volume). Each of these pathways for transition imply unique (and at times incompatible) theories of change. Although contributors agree that we must remain within the earth's biophysical limits to enable human health and well-being, the mechanisms through which these limits are to be enforced or encouraged is a subject of ongoing debate.

Who Is Best Positioned to Lead the Sustainability Transition?

The social-ecological transformations unfolding in the Anthropocene are exceedingly complex. Their course and outcome cannot be attributed to any one problem domain, sector, or population. The complexity of the issues facing health in the Anthropocene makes them difficult to comprehend; it is even more difficult to determine causation or to assign accountability (see Meadows, 2008 for a discussion of agency within complex systems). In this context, the chapters in this collection present unsurprisingly divergent views regarding who (or what) is best positioned to lead the transition towards a more sustainable society. For instance, Poland et al. sees a substantial role for public health, while Poland and the Transition Emerging Study research team and Mychajluk highlight the contributions that can be made by social movements. Zywert and Sutherland perceive medicine as an agent of change, Foster suggests that posthuman embodiment can improve health on a finite planet, and chapters by Solomon and Davy both elaborate the effects of alternative approaches to coping with death anxiety. These perspectives are not necessarily mutually exclusive. However, they do leave several questions without a definite answer. For instance: Does change begin internally, at the level of consciousness? Are individuals responsible for changing their own behaviour? What role can social norms play, and who will enforce more sustainable behaviours (e.g. governments, the school system, religious leaders, social movements)? Are academics scientific observers, activists, allies, or a combination of all three? And what is the role of systemic crisis or even collapse? In considering the sustainability transition, the most appropriate agents of change and the strategies perceived to have the greatest impact remain topics of scholarly and practical concern.

What Is the Most Effective Way to Communicate about Health in the Anthropocene?

In the course of in-person conversations among contributors to this collection, the language with which we communicate about the challenges and opportunities facing health in the Anthropocene came under scrutiny. Studies in terror management theory demonstrate that scaring people with the threat of climate change and social collapse can make them cling more strongly to mainstream materialistic, consumerist worldviews (see Solomon, this volume; Davy, this volume). If this is the case, should researchers focus on sharing positive messages about climate change and sustainability transitions? Contributors who are highly engaged in activism suggest that it is valuable to reframe challenges and difficulties as opportunities and possibilities. Is it useful and relevant to talk about "ecological constraints," as many authors in this collection have done, or should we focus our attention elsewhere, for instance, on the "conditions that enable life?" Will we be more effective change-makers if we use different tactics to communicate with different audiences? Academic researchers have some influence over how the problem of "health in the Anthropocene" emerges as a discourse in the public sphere, and can contribute to informing the ways in which scientific insights are incorporated into policies, health practices, and social movements. As such, it is important to continue to hone effective strategies for communicating about the connections between health and social-ecological systems.

How Can We Account for Deep Time When Considering the Impact of Social-Ecological Change on Human Health?

For most of us, health is a highly personal concern. While even the most profound ecological issues can feel abstract and distant, health rarely does. It permeates our everyday lives and the lives of those we love. When it comes down to it, even those of us who support a more restrained and limited use of medical interventions in theory may unexpectedly find ourselves accepting life-saving surgeries, agreeing to high-energy treatments, or counselling doctors to extend the lives of our aging relations at any cost. In this context, another ongoing tension among contributors to this volume concerns how we as researchers and inhabitants of the Anthropocene account for deep time in our research, writing, and activism. The transition to the Anthropocene implies a long time scale for thought and action. It asks us to look at the trajectory of humanity from the earliest days of our evolution into the present and even the distant future (Zywert, this volume). When stepping back to perceive the world from the perspective of deep time, it may be conscionable to consider things like population die-backs as a "natural" part of our species' continued evolution. These are much more difficult to countenance when they occur in the present (see Butler, this volume). The implications of perceiving health from the perspective of deep time therefore continue to be negotiated, and must be considered carefully by researchers and practitioners working in fields related to health in the Anthropocene.

Priorities for Future Research

When the authors of this collection gathered in Waterloo in the spring of 2018, one of our central goals was to develop a series of priorities for future research. Our aim was not to reach consensus in such a diverse and emergent field, but to work together to develop a stronger sense of the landscape of health in the Anthropocene; to find a place where we could see our own research agendas reflected and discover opportunities for collaboration. The priorities identified below represent significant points of connection within the work of the diverse researchers and practitioners included in this collection.

Investigating the Core Requirements for the Health
of Humans and the Biosphere

We know that the social-ecological trajectories of the Great Acceleration are limiting the prospects for human health and damaging the environments on which we depend for survival (Whitmee et al., 2015). We have not, however, collected sufficient data about the basic requirements for maintaining health and well-being alongside ecological integrity over the coming decades. Work by O'Neill and colleagues (2018) to quantify the resource use associated with various social goods begins to answer this question, as does the work of several contributors and their colleagues about the ecological determinants of health (CPHA, 2015). Yet there remain important areas of research to develop further. For instance, what are the low-hanging fruit for health in the Anthropocene? Are there simple changes we could make to our food systems, energy systems, patterns of work and education, health care infrastructures, and informal care practices that would reduce consumption of resources and energy while significantly improving human health? Developing models for the optimal health of populations and gathering data could help us to answer questions like: What are the healthiest environments for human beings? How can these be scaled to support the current global population without exceeding planetary boundaries? What is the optimal level of population health that we should we be striving for in the Anthropocene? Gathering more data regarding the foundational requirements for the health of humans and the biosphere will enable the development of more effective strategies as we transition into an alternative social-ecological regime.

Preparing Public Health Systems for a New, Expanded Mandate

Public health systems will be key players in the adaptation to life in the Anthropocene (see Hancock, 2017). As environmental constraints become more pronounced, we are likely to lose layers of complexity in Western-style biomedical health systems (Zywert, 2017; Zywert, this volume). This could mean, for instance, more limited access to the kinds of high-technology hospital facilities to which most people in affluent countries have become accustomed, especially as we age. Governments and health practitioners will need to make difficult decisions about the care that is offered at different stages of life (see Cole, this volume). In a context of much more limited resources, for instance, how will we balance the needs of an aging population with the goal of giving every child the best start in life? In the transition to a post-growth economy, public health will be increasingly essential in creating preventative health measures and ensuring population health (Aillon, this volume; Missoni, 2015). More research is needed to prepare public health systems for the future and to design public health institutions that can be resilient over the long-term.

Developing and Studying Low-Energy Medicines

Biomedical health systems are extremely high consumers of energy and resources. To cope in a resource-constrained future, it is important to research low-energy alternatives now so that we can develop social and institutional momentum around them before ecological and economic crises deepen (see the introduction to part 2, this volume). Potential low-energy medicines to investigate include non-medicalized responses to rising rates of stress, anxiety, and mental illness. For instance, care farming (Elings, this volume), horticultural therapies, incorporating mindfulness and meditation into the classroom (Hathaway, Cole, and Poland, this volume), social or green prescriptions (in which doctors "prescribe" time in nature or social activities such as volunteering or participating in a walking group to improve mental and physical health as well as social integration), and lifestyle interventions such as changes to one's diet, more physical activity, or periods of separation from social media. Many of these practices have clear mutual co-benefits for ecology. For instance, care farming and other horticultural practices restore local environments while building social connections and greater engagement in place. They can also encourage lower consumption of processed foods and pharmaceuticals, as well as greater use of active transportation, reducing GHG emissions. When studying low-energy medicines, it is important to investigate the effect of the choice architecture on their uptake and success. For instance, is meditation in the classroom or participation in a community garden at school more successful at improving mental health if it is compulsory? How do we shift from an opt-in approach to an opt-out system for some of these interventions? These and other questions will need to be considered as we move towards greater adoption of low-energy medicines to replace certain biomedical interventions that may no longer be justifiable in a context of rising resource constraints.

Rethinking the Political Economy to Support Human and Environmental Health

From a systems perspective, the current configuration of the global economy, which is dependent on growth to support expanding medical infrastructures and formalized, professional health and welfare systems through fiscal transfers, cannot be decoupled from substantial ecological impacts (see Hensher, this volume; Kish, this volume). As a result, it will be necessary over the coming decades to rethink our macro-economic models, invigorate local economies, and transition to a post-growth economy that can provide for social goods without undermining their ecological foundations (Kish, this volume; Hensher, this volume; Aillon, this volume). Most health economists, however, receive very little training in ecological economics, and so are unaware of the extent to which the growth economy is compromising biophysical integrity (Hensher, personal communication). The economic dilemmas facing health systems are exacerbated by our growing awareness that we are either rapidly approaching or have already surpassed the limits to growth. In this context, it will be essential to cross-pollinate insights from ecological economics among health economists and administrators who are responsible for making decisions about how to allocate resources within health systems. It will also be necessary to investigate alternative models of transformative economics, such as those enacted on ecovillages (communal ownership and support) (Mychajluk, this volume) and in social movements like the Transition movement (local currencies, barter systems, etc.) (Poland et al., this volume) to support promising innovations.

Identifying Leverage Points for Public Action and Behaviour Change

As noted above, the ways in which academic researchers and activists have communicated about the dangers posed by climate change and other ecological crises have not always translated into meaningful action for sustainability (Davy, this volume). As a result, there are opportunities now to leverage the issues that community members already care about in order to promote public action and sustainable behaviour change to improve human and environmental health. While the issue of climate change may be experienced as abstract and distant for many people in affluent countries who are sheltered from its effects, other connected domains may gain more traction. For instance, attention to food security, loss of green spaces, and child mental health could become entry points into a discussion about the effects of social-ecological systems change on health. Research must also be undertaken to determine what kinds of actions and changes in behaviour could serve as meta-activities to generate mutual benefits for both people and the planet. For example, can ecological restoration work bring people living in the same place together to enhance their local environment while building social connections? Can time in nature reduce anxiety and depression while building ecological consciousness? It is important to devote research attention to identifying and exploring these potential points of intervention to begin building broader movements that can support health in the Anthropocene.

Conclusion

The purpose of this collection was to bring together a series of chapters that both address the core challenges facing health in the Anthropocene and offer novel frameworks for living well on a finite planet. Our approach has been decidedly alternative in that we have not focused so much on the need to develop more sustainable ways to provision health care services or structure health systems, but to navigate the transition towards social-ecological systems that can support long-term human and environmental health. This requires broad shifts in thought and action, not only in formal health-related fields, but in our economic models, food systems, ontologies, politics, and practices of daily living.

As editors, our research embraces the themes and tensions presented above, often taking them in more radical directions. Our lab at the University of Waterloo, Navigators of the Anthropocene, is pursuing questions related to ritual and ontological meaning, enchantment and disenchantment, and the social implications of living in a world that has exceeded planetary boundaries. For instance, can we reconcile scientific rationality with the possible need for reenchanted worldviews and communitarian ways of being in a context of ecological constraints on human action? Which ontologies, technologies, and practices can reframe individual and collective species relationships between human beings and the biosphere? Fundamentally, we are concerned with whether modernity was just a passing phase, or whether an alternative, ecologically sound modernity is possible. The Anthropocene destabilizes everything about the future, including how human communities might live their lives, what their commitments might be, what units of analysis may be most relevant for various aspects of health, and what these changes mean for progressive political positions in areas ranging from feminism to economics, development work, health care, and social justice. The extent of the epoch's destabilizing effects is the direct subject of several chapters in this collection, while in others it is implicit in the author's approach to research or activism. Recognition of the truly disruptive effect of the Anthropocene is often imminent if not explicit in initiatives like the Transition movement, care farming, ecovillages, and the degrowth movement, though the more radical positions associated with such potentials are not necessarily shared by all. For a number of authors, such questions are beyond the horizons of their work. Several contributors remain committed to sustainable development and see ways to make an enlightenment vision rooted in individualism, rationality, and democratic politics compatible with a green modernity. Others, including the editors and members of our research lab, are expecting more paradigmatic change: a transition akin to the break-up of Pangea. It is for this reason that we have assembled such a diverse group of researchers whose work broadly addresses the future of health in the Anthropocene. We did not bring these authors together to entreat them to agree on first principles for this work, or on research methodologies or tactics for action. Rather, we wanted them to come without a map. It is from this starting place that the diverse papers in this collection begin to suggest alternative pathways for sustaining human well-being and ecological integrity through the precarity of a new geological epoch.

REFERENCES

Bardi, U. (2017). *The Seneca effect: Why growth is slow but collapse is rapid.* Basel, Switzerland: Springer.

Butler, C. (2017). Limits to growth, planetary boundaries, and planetary health. *Current Opinion in Environmental Sustainability, 25*, 59–65. https://doi.org/10.1016/j.cosust.2017.08.002

Canadian Public Health Association. (2015). *CPHA (2015) global change and public health: Addressing the ecological determinants of health.* Ottawa: Canadian Public Health Association.

Dryzek, J. (2013). *The politics of the Earth: Environmental discourses.* Oxford, UK: Oxford University Press.

Hancock, T. (2017). Beyond health care: The other determinants of health. *CMAJ, 189*(50), E1571. https://doi.org/10.1503/cmaj.171419

Homer-Dixon, T. (2007). *The upside of down: Catastrophe, creativity and the renewal of civilization.* Toronto: Vintage Canada.

McNeill, J. R., & Engelke, P. (2016). *The Great Acceleration.* Boston, MA: Harvard University Press.

Meadows, D. (2008). *Thinking in systems: A primer.* Vermont: Chelsea Green Publishing.

Meadows, D. H., Meadows, D. L., Randers, J. J., & Behrens, W. W. (1972). *The limits to growth (Report to the Club of Rome).* New York, NY: University Books.

Missoni, E. (2015). Degrowth and health: Local action should be linked to global policies and governance for health. *Sustainability Science, 10*(3), 439–50. https://doi.org/10.1007/s11625-015-0300-1

O'Neill, D. et al. (2018). A good life for all within planetary boundaries. *Nature Sustainability, 1*, 88–95. https://doi.org/10.1038/s41893-018-0021-4

Quilley, S. (2013). De-growth is not a liberal agenda: Relocalisation and the limits to low energy cosmopolitanism. *Environmental Values, 22*(2), 261–85. https://doi.org/10.3197/096327113X13581561725310

Quilley, S. (2017). Navigating the Anthropocene: Environmental politics and complexity in an era of limits. In B. Dolter and P. Victor (Eds), *Handbook on growth and sustainability* (pp. 439–70). Cheltanham: Edward Elgar.

Rittel, H., & Webber, M. (1973). Dilemmas in a general theory of planning. *Policy Sciences, 4*(2), 155–69. https://doi.org/10.1007/BF01405730

Rockström, J. et al. (2009). A safe operating space for humanity. *Nature, 461*, 472–5. https://doi.org/10.1038/461472a

Smith, K. R., Woodward, A. et al. (2014). Human health: Impacts, adaptation, and co-benefits. In *Climate change 2014: Impacts, adaptation, and vulnerability. Part A: Global and sectoral aspects. Contribution of working group II to the fifth assessment report of the intergovernmental panel on climate change* (pp. 709–54). Cambridge University Press, Cambridge, United Kingdom and New York, NY, USA,.

Steffen, W. et al. (2015). The trajectory of the Anthropocene: The Great Acceleration. *The Anthropocene Review, 2*(1), 81–98. https://doi.org/10.1177/2053019614564785

Tainter, J. A. (1988). *The collapse of complex societies.* Cambridge: Cambridge University Press.

Tainter, J. A. (2014). Collapse and sustainability: Rome, the Maya, and the modern world. *Archeological Papers of the American Anthropological Association, 24*(1), 201–14. https://doi.org/10.1111/apaa.12038

Whitmee, S. et al. (2015). Safeguarding human health in the Anthropocene epoch: Report of The Rockefeller Foundation – Lancet Commission on planetary health. *The Lancet, 386*, 1973–2028. https://doi.org/10.1016/S0140-6736(15)60901-1

World Health Organization. (2015). *Health in 2015: From MDGs, Millennium Development Goals to SDGs, Sustainable Development Goals.* Geneva: World Health Organization.

World Health Organization. (2018). *World health statistics 2018: Monitoring health for the SDGs.* Geneva: World Health Organization.

Zywert, K. (2017). Human health and social-ecological systems change: Rethinking health in the Anthropocene. *The Anthropocene Review, 4*(3), 216–38. https://doi.org/10.1177/2053019617739640

Contributors

Jean-Louis Aillon, Medical doctor; Psychotherapist at the Frantz Fanon Center; PhD student in Psychology, Anthropology, and Cognitive Sciences at the University of Genoa; Spokesperson for the Italian Network for Health and Sustainability

Martin J. Bunch, Professor and Associate Dean, Faculty of Environmental Studies, York University

Chris Buse, CIHR postdoctoral fellow, Centre for Environmental Assessment Research, University of British Columbia

Colin Butler, Principal research fellow, College of Arts, Humanities and Social Sciences, Flinders University, Australia; Campus Visitor, National Centre for Epidemiology and Population Health, Australian National University, Australia; Adjunct Professor, Health Research Institute, University of Canberra, Australia

Dan Carruthers Den Hoed, Senior fellow and manager, Canadian Parks Collective for Innovation and Leadership, Mount Royal University

Andrea Chircop, Assistant Professor, School of Nursing, Dalhousie University

Donald Cole, Professor Emeritus, Dalla Lana School of Public Health, University of Toronto

Jennifer Cole, Research fellow, AMR, Department of Geography, Royal Holloway, University of London

Giacomo D'Alisa, FCT postdoc in Political Ecology at the Center for Social Studies at the University of Coimbra, Portugal; Founding member of the Research and Degrowth (RnD) Barcelona, Spain

Barbara Jane Davy, PhD candidate, School of Environment, Resources and Sustainability, University of Waterloo

Ann Del Bianco, Adjunct Professor, Faculty of Environmental Studies, York University

Marjolein Elings, Scientist, Green Care, Agrosystems Research, Wageningen University and Research

Alexander Foster, MPhil. candidate, School of Anthropology and Museum Ethnography, University of Oxford

Randolph Haluza-DeLay, Associate Professor, Sociology, The King's University

Trevor Hancock, Retired Professor and senior scholar, School of Public Health and Social Policy, University of Victoria

Rebecca Hasdell, Food Policy postdoctoral fellow, School of Health Administration, Dalhousie University

Mark Hathaway, SSHRC postdoctoral fellow, School of Environment, Resources and Sustainability, University of Waterloo

Katie Hayes, PhD candidate, Dalla Lana School of Public Health, University of Toronto

Martin Hensher, Associate Professor of Health Systems Financing and Organization, Institute for Health Transformation, Deakin University; Adjunct Associate Professor and PhD candidate, Menzies Institute for Medical Research, University of Tasmania

Sonya L. Jakubec, Professor, School of Nursing and Midwifery, Mount Royal University

Kaitlin Kish, Postdoctoral researcher, Department of Natural Resource Sciences, McGill University

Ashok Krishnamurthy, Associate Professor, Department of Mathematics and Computing, Mount Royal University

Chris Ling, Associate Professor, Royal Roads University

David Mallery, PhD student, Faculty of Environmental Studies, York University

George McKibbon, Adjunct faculty, University of Guelph; McKibbon Wakefield Inc.

Lisa Mychajluk, PhD candidate, Ontario Institute for Studies in Education, University of Toronto

Lenore Newman, Associate Professor, Department of Geography, University of the Fraser Valley

André-Anne Parent, Assistant Professor, Social Work, Université de Montréal

Margot W. Parkes, Canada Research Chair in Health, Ecosystems and Society; Associate Professor, School of Health Sciences, University of Northern British Columbia and Northern Medical Program, University of British Columbia

Kamal Paudel, PhD student, Faculty of Environmental Studies, York University

Didi Pershouse, Founder of the Centre for Sustainable Medicine and the Land and Leadership Initiative; Author; Systems-based ecological medicine practitioner

Blake Poland, Associate Professor, Dalla Lana School of Public Health, University of Toronto

Stephen Quilley, Associate Professor, School of Environment, Resources and Sustainability, University of Waterloo

Heather Ray, Associate Professor, Department of Health and Physical Education, Mount Royal University

Sheldon Solomon, Professor, Skidmore College

William Sutherland, Medical doctor; Founder and director of the Institute of Complexity and Connection Medicine; Adjunct Faculty, School of Environment, Resources and Sustainability, University of Waterloo

Cheryl Teelucksingh, Professor, Sociology, Ryerson University

Mary Jane Yates, Health promotion facilitator and certified nature therapy guide; Founder and director of Marigold Enterprises Nature Therapy Services in Edmonton, Alberta

Katharine Zywert, PhD candidate, School of Environment, Resources and Sustainability, University of Waterloo